D0547475

ODESSA

Written and illustrated by JONATHAN HILL
Art assistance by XAN DRAKE

Edited by ROBIN HERRERA
Designed by SONJA SYNAK

PUBLISHED BY ONI-LION FORGE PUBLISHING GROUP, LLC

JAMES LUCAS JONES, **president & publisher**
SARAH GAYDOS, **editor in chief**
CHARLIE CHU, **e.v.p. of creative & business development**
BRAD ROOKS, **director of operations**
AMBER O'NEILL, **special projects manager**
HARRIS FISH, **events manager**
MARGOT WOOD, **director of marketing & sales**
DEVIN FUNCHES, **sales & marketing manager**
KATIE SAINZ, **marketing manager**
TARA LEHMANN, **publicist**
TROY LOOK, **director of design & production**
KATE Z. STONE, **senior graphic designer**
SONJA SYNAK, **graphic designer**
HILARY THOMPSON, **graphic designer**
SARAH ROCKWELL, **junior graphic designer**
ANGIE KNOWLES, **digital prepress lead**
VINCENT KUKUA, **digital prepress technician**
JASMINE AMIRI, **senior editor**
SHAWNA GORE, **senior editor**
AMANDA MEADOWS, **senior editor**
ROBERT MEYERS, **senior editor, licensing**
GRACE BORNHOFT, **editor**
ZACK SOTO, **editor**
CHRIS CERASI, **editorial coordinator**
STEVE ELLIS, **vice president of games**
BEN EISNER, **game developer**
MICHELLE NGUYEN, **executive assistant**
JUNG LEE, **logistics coordinator**

JOE NOZEMACK, **publisher emeritus**

onipress.com 🅕 🅨 🅘 lionforge.com

First Edition: November 2020

ISBN 978-1-62010-789-8
eISBN 978-1-62010-810-9

Printed in China.
Library of Congress Control Number: 2020934315

3 5 7 9 10 8 6 4 2

For Jeremiah and Justin.

And for anyone else who's ever
been left behind and gone searching for answers.

———————————————————

CHAPTER 1

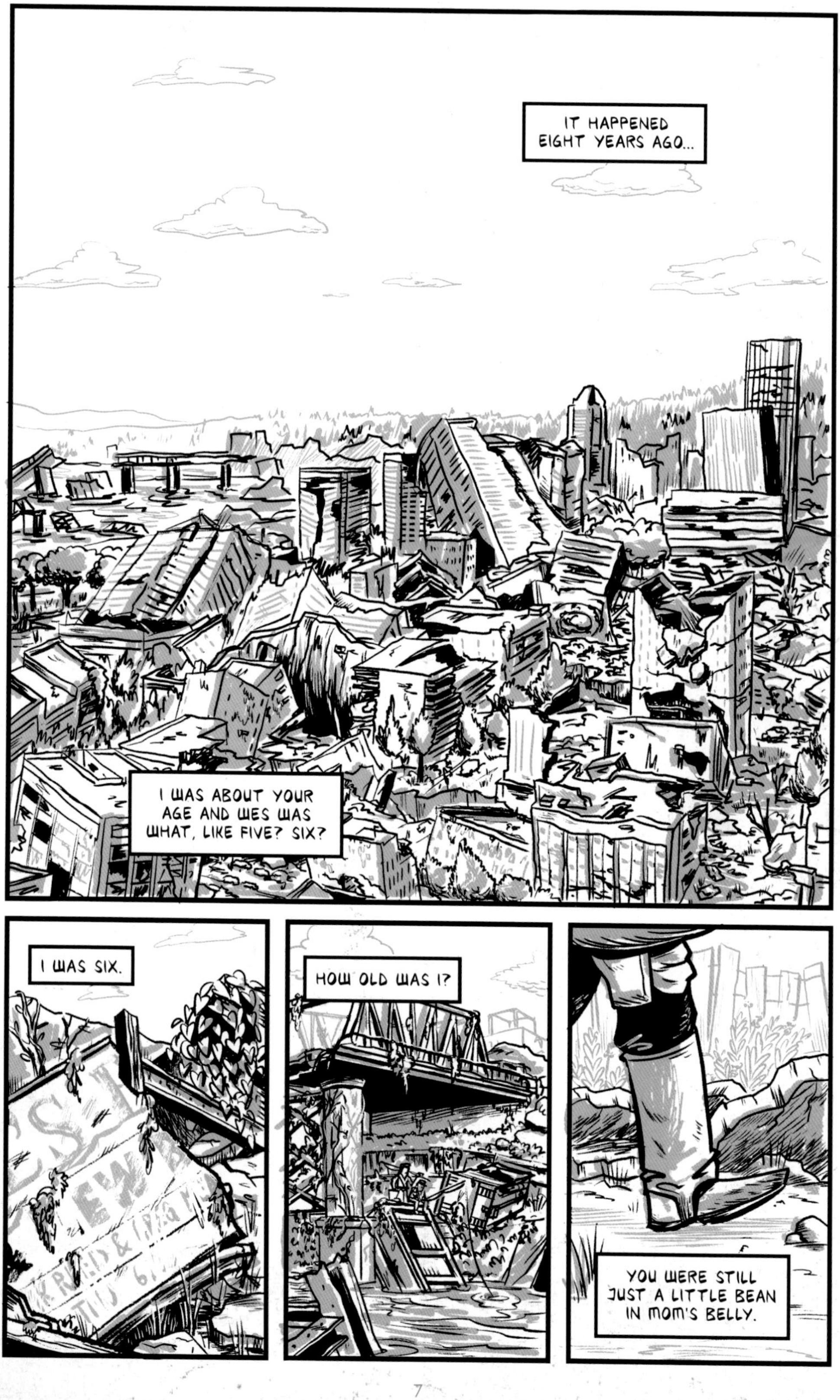
IT HAPPENED EIGHT YEARS AGO...
I WAS ABOUT YOUR AGE AND WES WAS WHAT, LIKE FIVE? SIX?
I WAS SIX.
HOW OLD WAS I?
YOU WERE STILL JUST A LITTLE BEAN IN MOM'S BELLY.

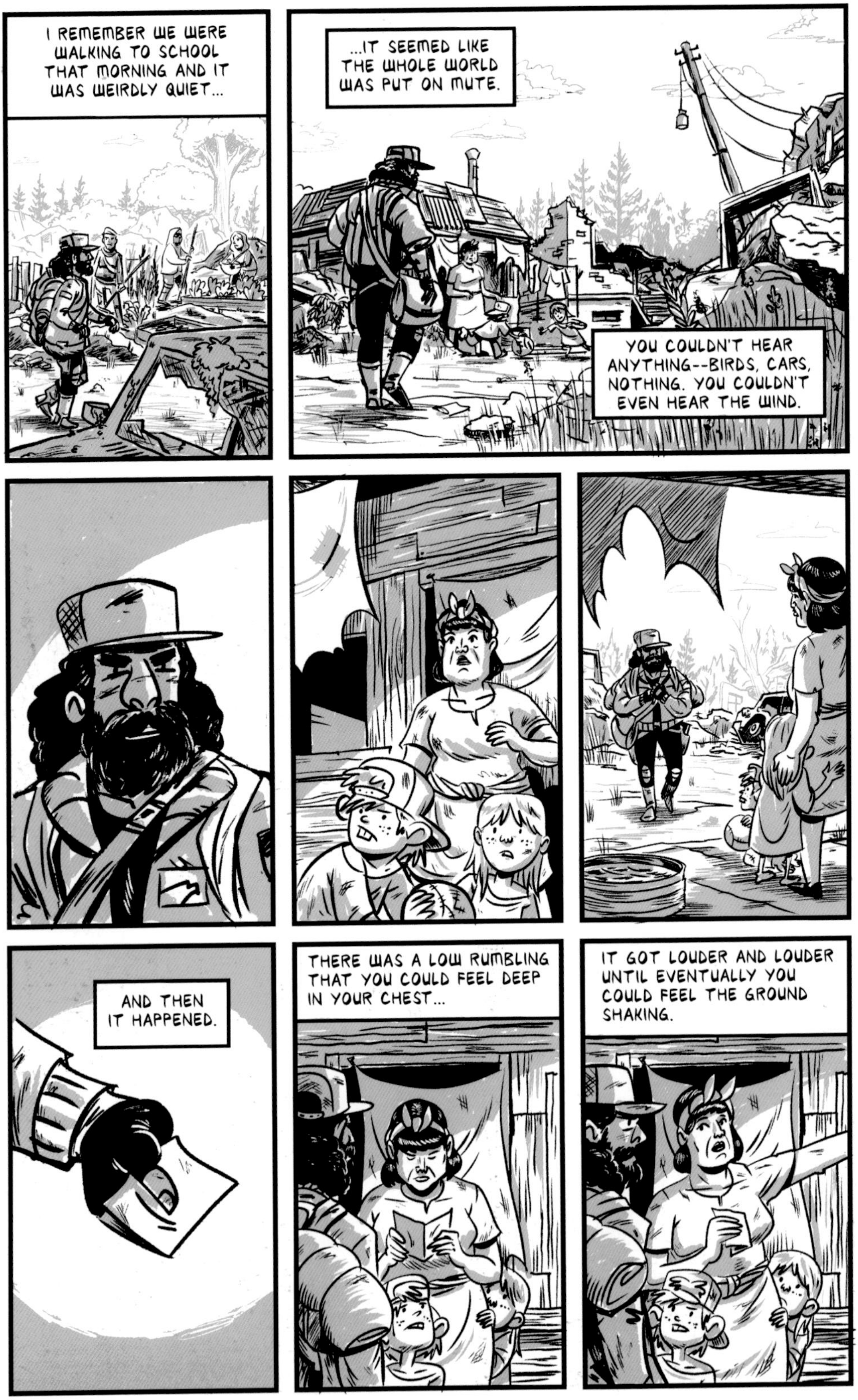
I REMEMBER WE WERE WALKING TO SCHOOL THAT MORNING AND IT WAS WEIRDLY QUIET...
...IT SEEMED LIKE THE WHOLE WORLD WAS PUT ON MUTE.
YOU COULDN'T HEAR ANYTHING--BIRDS, CARS, NOTHING. YOU COULDN'T EVEN HEAR THE WIND.
AND THEN IT HAPPENED.
THERE WAS A LOW RUMBLING THAT YOU COULD FEEL DEEP IN YOUR CHEST...
IT GOT LOUDER AND LOUDER UNTIL EVENTUALLY YOU COULD FEEL THE GROUND SHAKING.

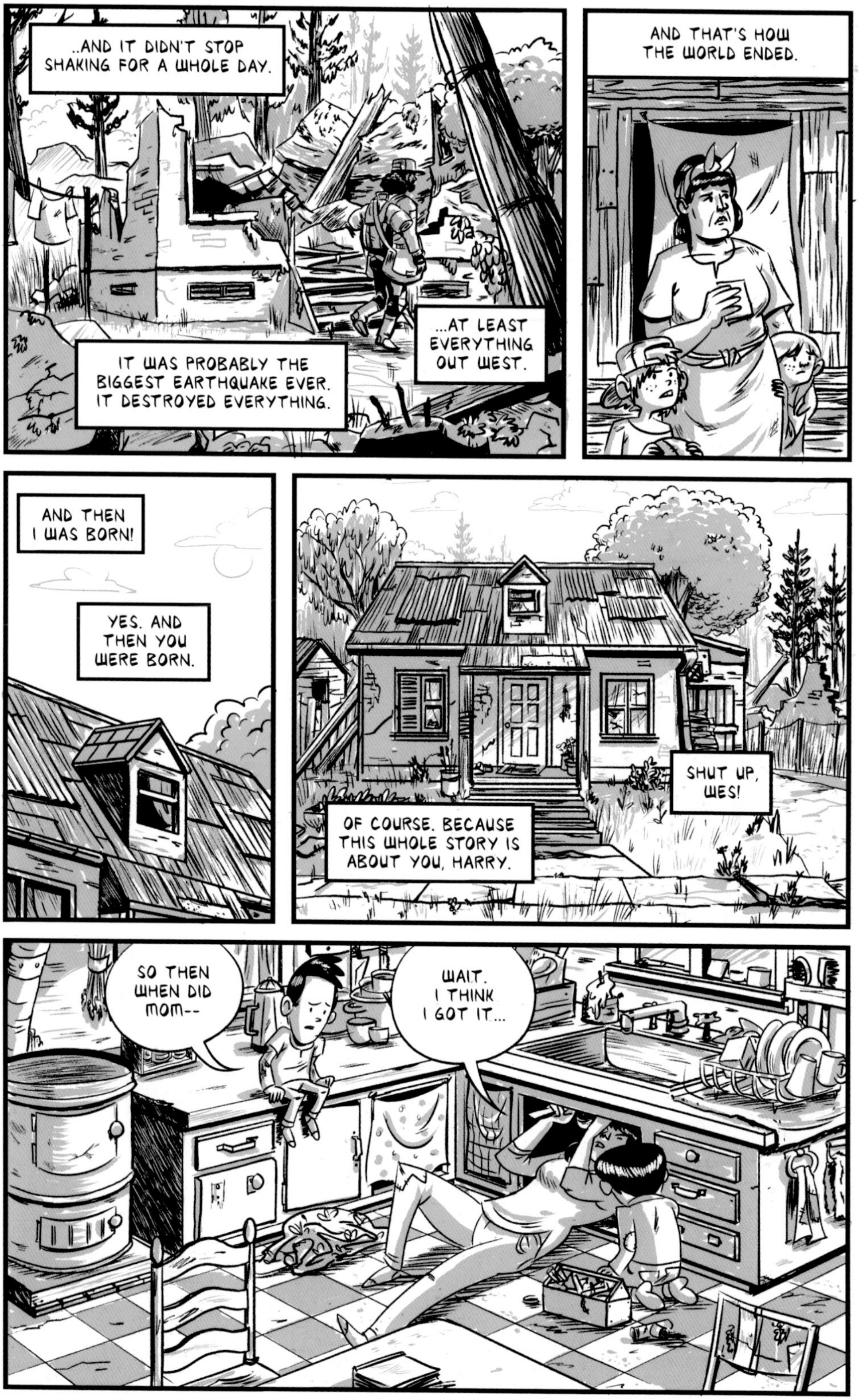
..AND IT DIDN'T STOP SHAKING FOR A WHOLE DAY.
IT WAS PROBABLY THE BIGGEST EARTHQUAKE EVER. IT DESTROYED EVERYTHING.
...AT LEAST EVERYTHING OUT WEST.
AND THAT'S HOW THE WORLD ENDED.
AND THEN I WAS BORN!
YES. AND THEN YOU WERE BORN.
OF COURSE. BECAUSE THIS WHOLE STORY IS ABOUT YOU, HARRY.
SHUT UP, WES!
SO THEN WHEN DID MOM--
WAIT. I THINK I GOT IT...

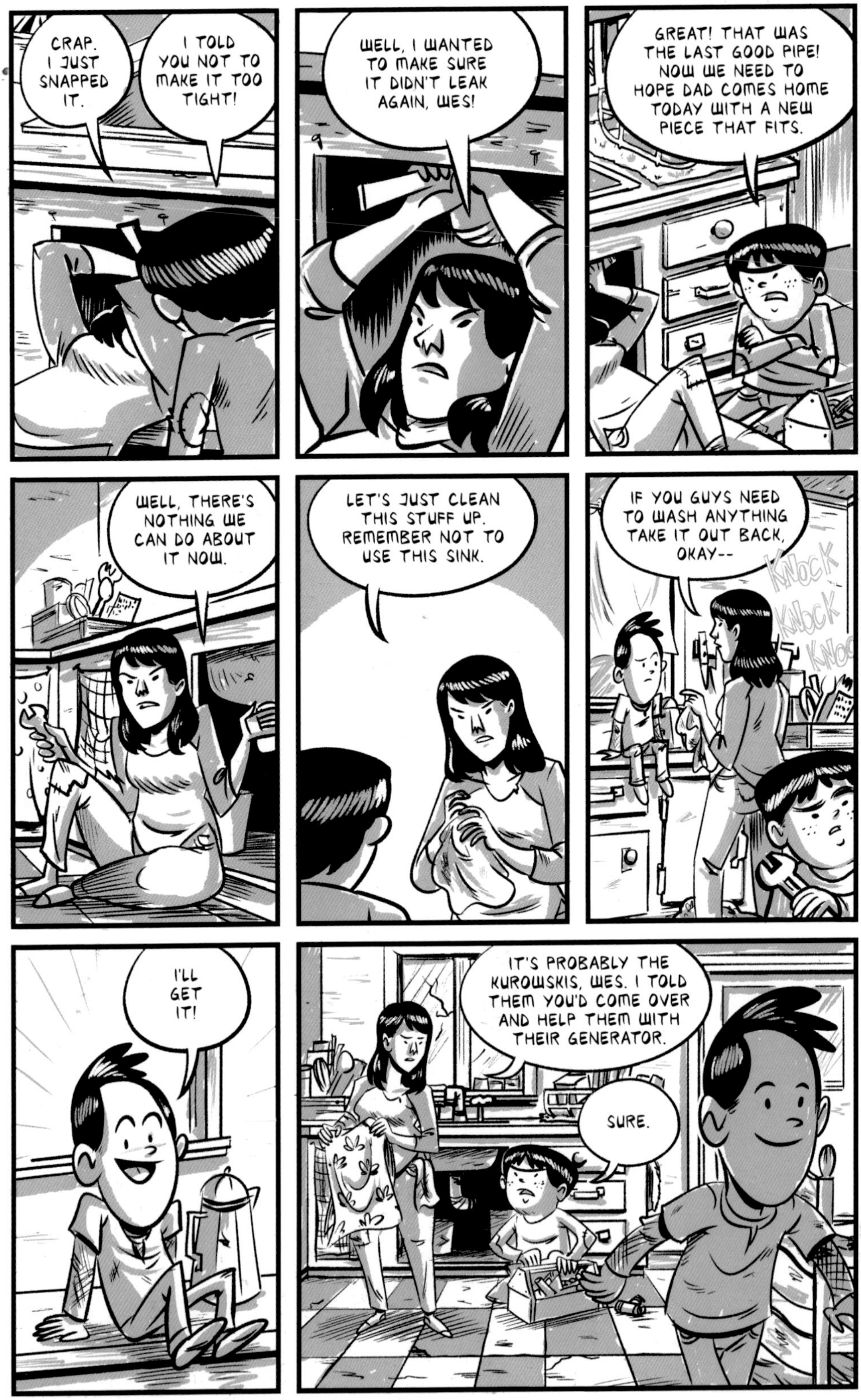
CRAP. I JUST SNAPPED IT.
I TOLD YOU NOT TO MAKE IT TOO TIGHT!
WELL, I WANTED TO MAKE SURE IT DIDN'T LEAK AGAIN, WES!
GREAT! THAT WAS THE LAST GOOD PIPE! NOW WE NEED TO HOPE DAD COMES HOME TODAY WITH A NEW PIECE THAT FITS.
WELL, THERE'S NOTHING WE CAN DO ABOUT IT NOW.
LET'S JUST CLEAN THIS STUFF UP. REMEMBER NOT TO USE THIS SINK.
IF YOU GUYS NEED TO WASH ANYTHING TAKE IT OUT BACK, OKAY--
KNOCK
KNOCK
I'LL GET IT!
IT'S PROBABLY THE KUROWSKIS, WES. I TOLD THEM YOU'D COME OVER AND HELP THEM WITH THEIR GENERATOR.
SURE.

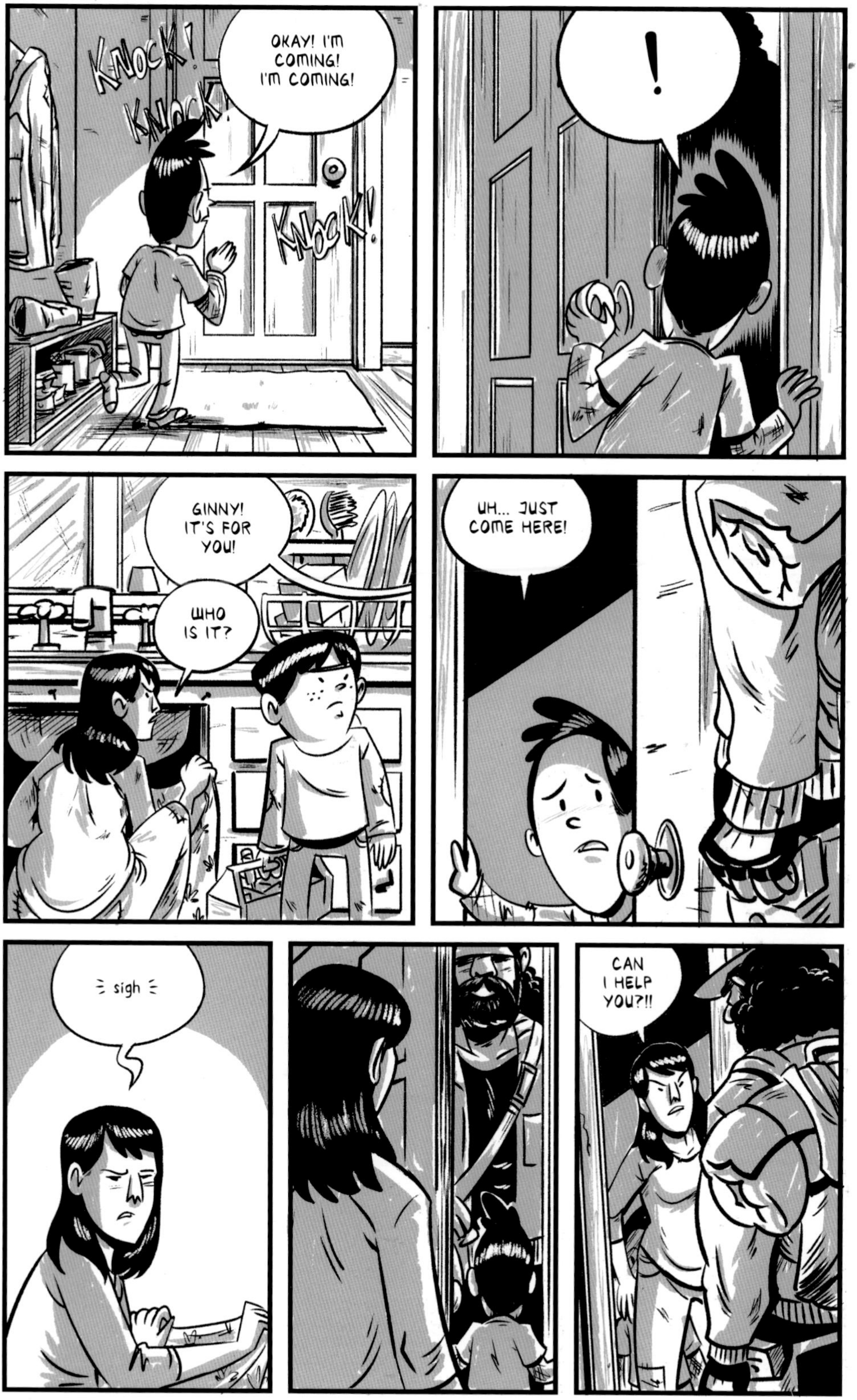
KNOCK!
KNOCK!
OKAY! I'M COMING! I'M COMING!
KNOCK!
!
GINNY! IT'S FOR YOU!
WHO IS IT?
UH... JUST COME HERE!
sigh
CAN I HELP YOU?!!

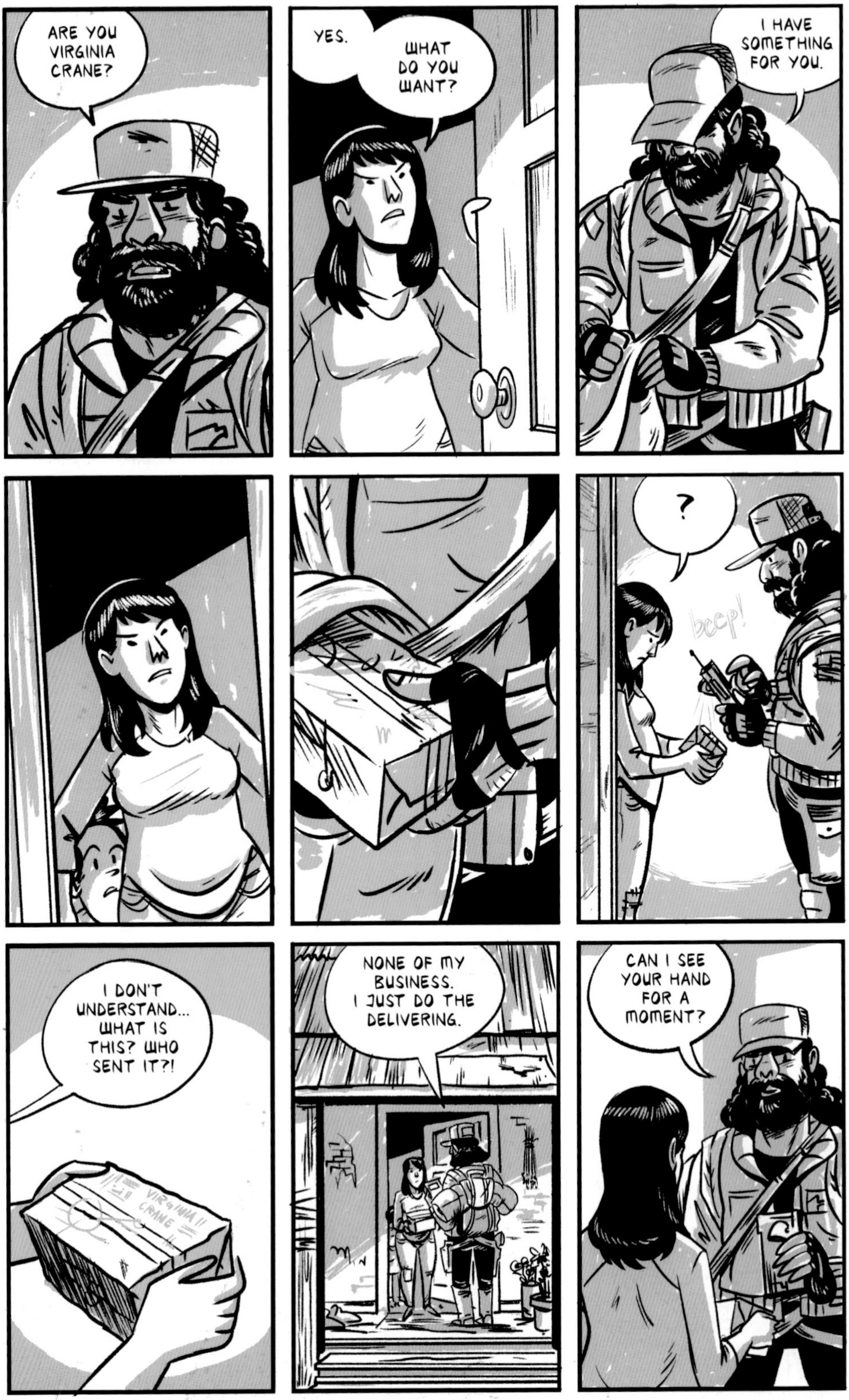
ARE YOU VIRGINIA CRANE?
YES.
WHAT DO YOU WANT?
I HAVE SOMETHING FOR YOU.
?
beep!
I DON'T UNDERSTAND... WHAT IS THIS? WHO SENT IT?!
VIRGINIA CRANE
NONE OF MY BUSINESS. I JUST DO THE DELIVERING.
CAN I SEE YOUR HAND FOR A MOMENT?

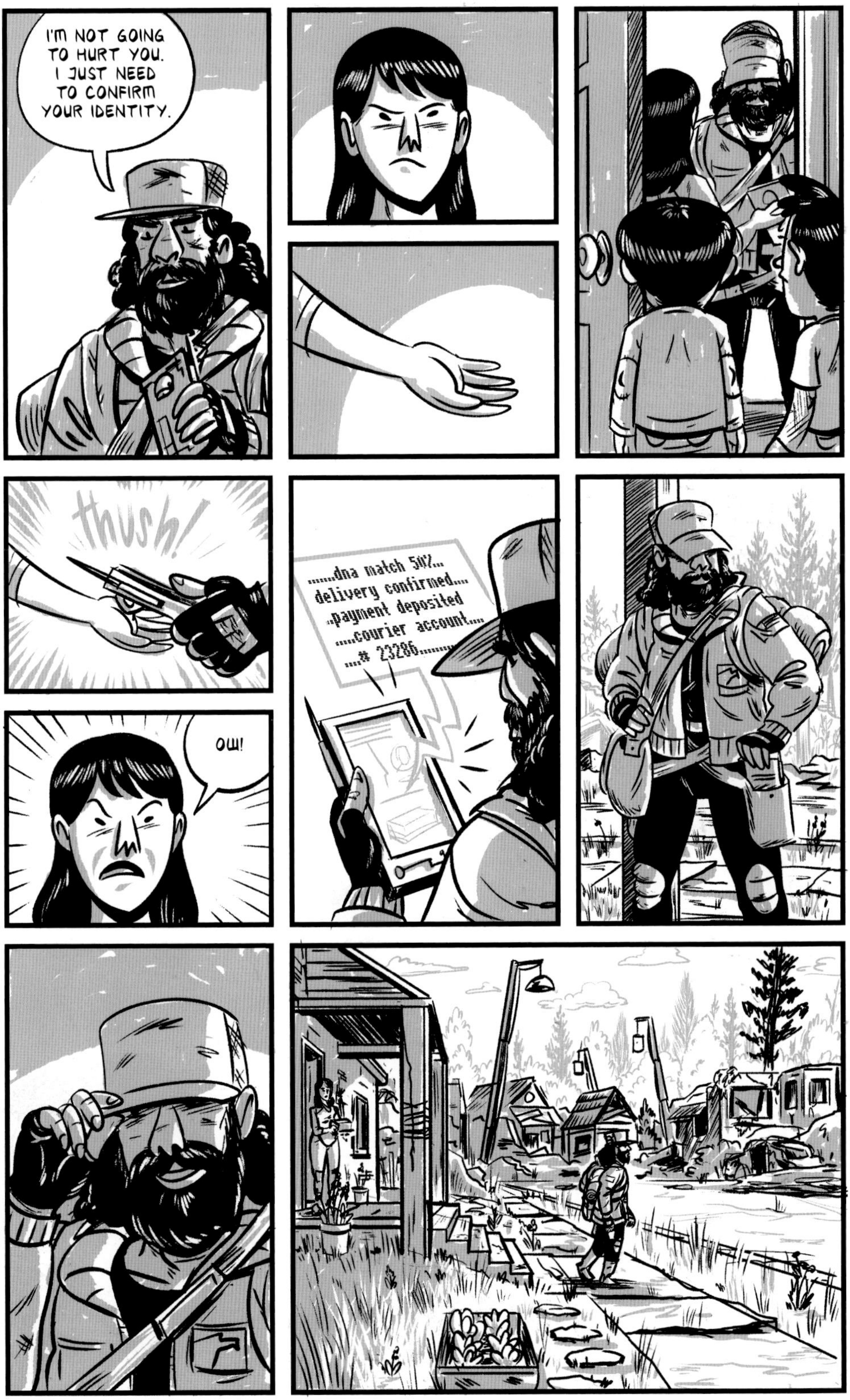
I'M NOT GOING TO HURT YOU. I JUST NEED TO CONFIRM YOUR IDENTITY.
thush!
OW!
......dna match 50%...
delivery confirmed....
..payment deposited
.....courier account....
....# 23286..........

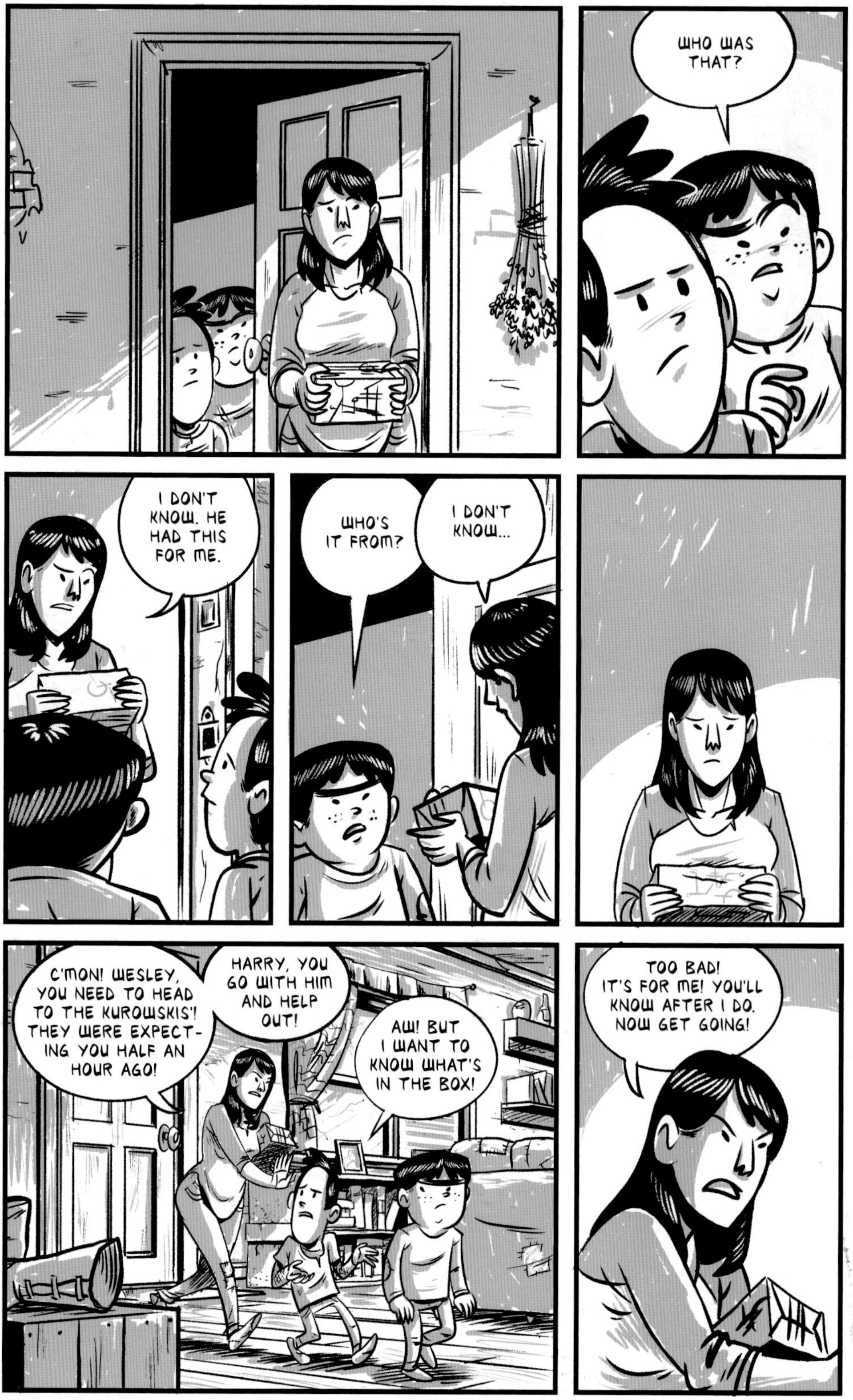
WHO WAS THAT?
I DON'T KNOW. HE HAD THIS FOR ME.
WHO'S IT FROM?
I DON'T KNOW...
C'MON! WESLEY, YOU NEED TO HEAD TO THE KUROWSKIS'! THEY WERE EXPECTING YOU HALF AN HOUR AGO!
HARRY, YOU GO WITH HIM AND HELP OUT!
AW! BUT I WANT TO KNOW WHAT'S IN THE BOX!
TOO BAD! IT'S FOR ME! YOU'LL KNOW AFTER I DO. NOW GET GOING!

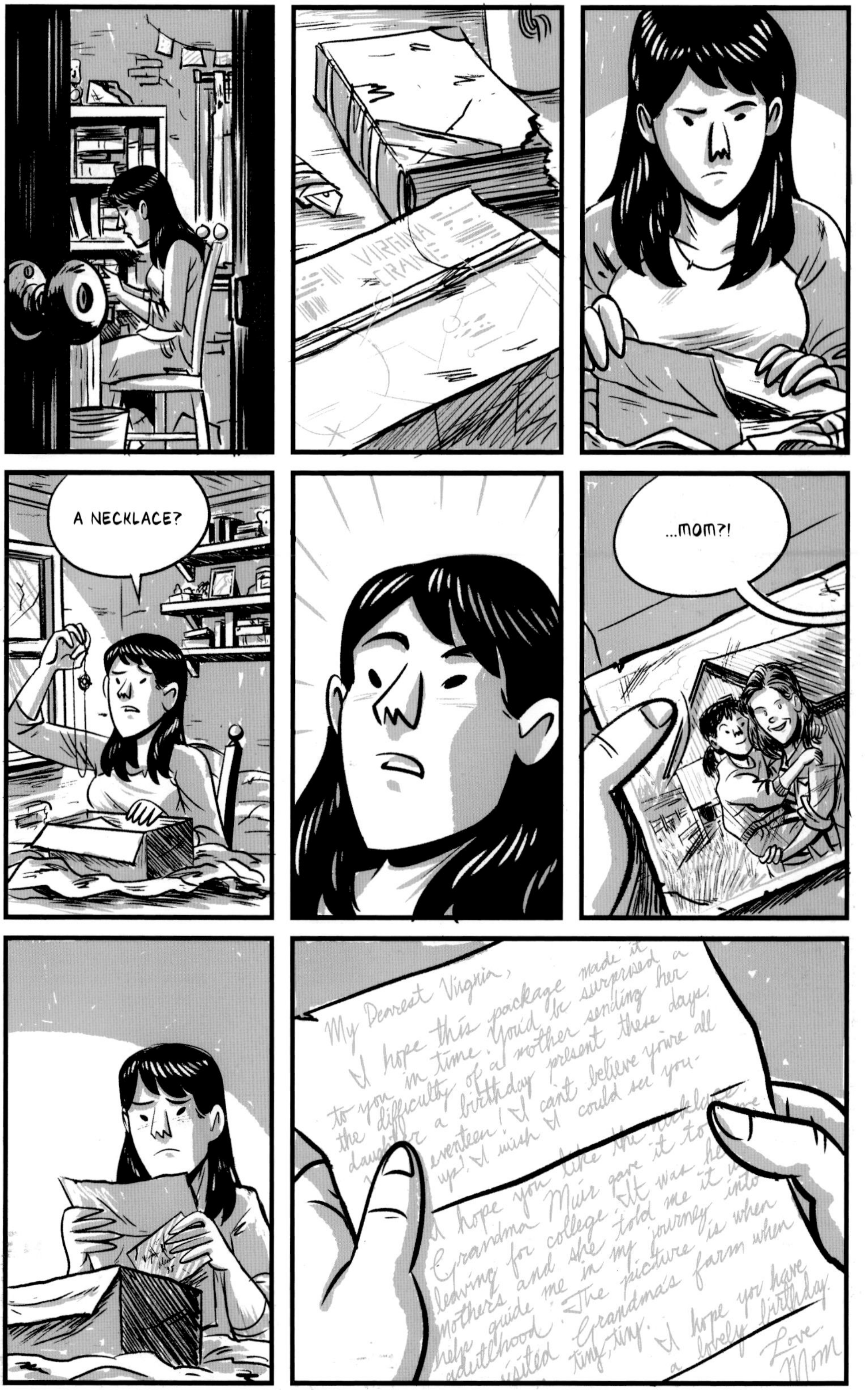
VIRGINIA CRANE
A NECKLACE?
...mom?!
My Dearest Virginia,
I hope this package made it to you in time. You'd be surprised a the difficulty of a mother sending her daughter a birthday present these days.
eventeen! I can't believe you're all up! I wish I could see you.
I hope you like the necklace.
Grandma Muir gave it to
leaving for college. It was he
mothers and she told me it
help guide me in my journey into adulthood. The picture is when
Grandma's farm when
tiny, tiny.
I hope you have a lovely birthday.
Love Mom

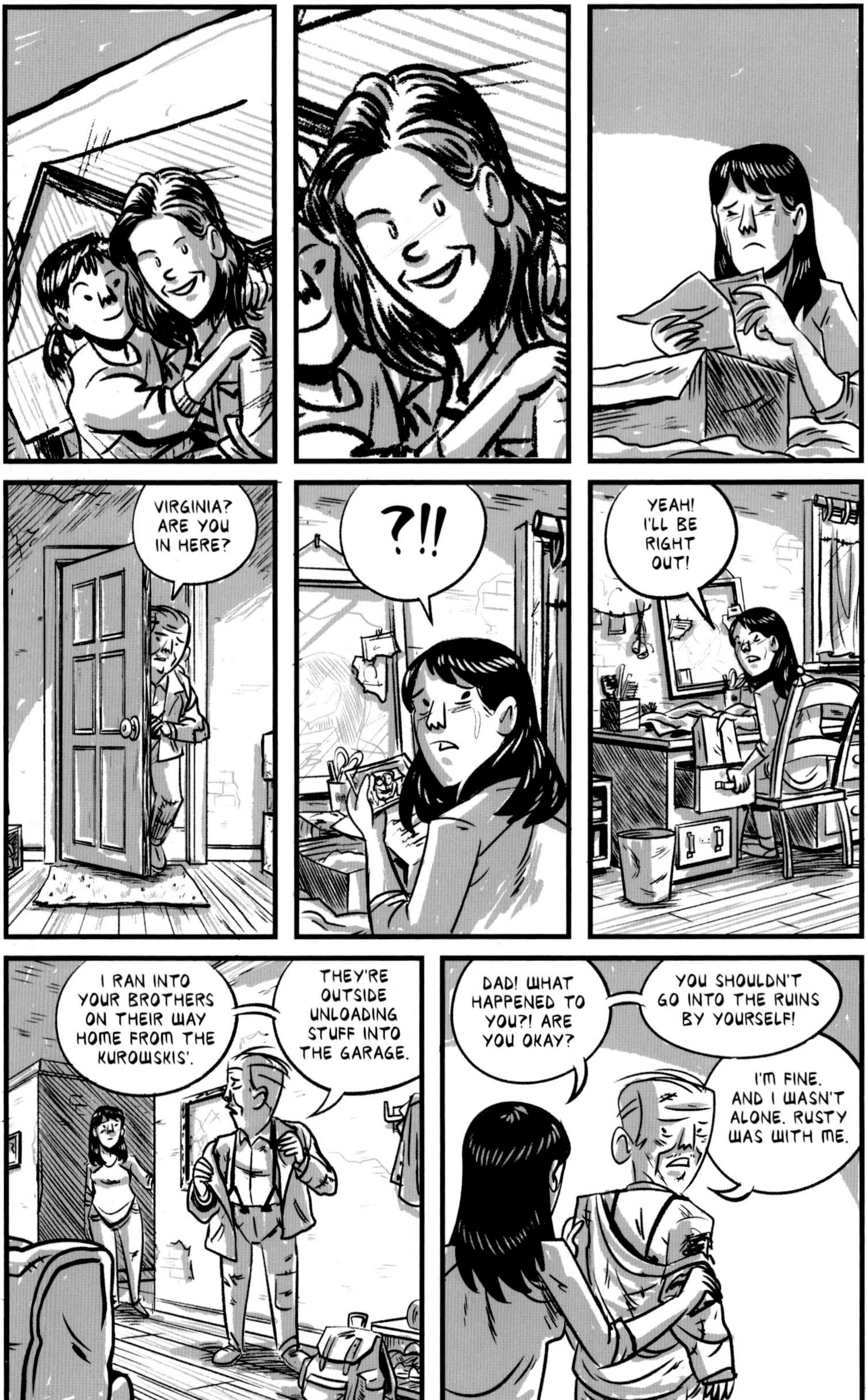
VIRGINIA? ARE YOU IN HERE?
?!!
YEAH! I'LL BE RIGHT OUT!
I RAN INTO YOUR BROTHERS ON THEIR WAY HOME FROM THE KUROWSKIS'.
THEY'RE OUTSIDE UNLOADING STUFF INTO THE GARAGE.
DAD! WHAT HAPPENED TO YOU?! ARE YOU OKAY?
YOU SHOULDN'T GO INTO THE RUINS BY YOURSELF!
I'M FINE. AND I WASN'T ALONE. RUSTY WAS WITH ME.

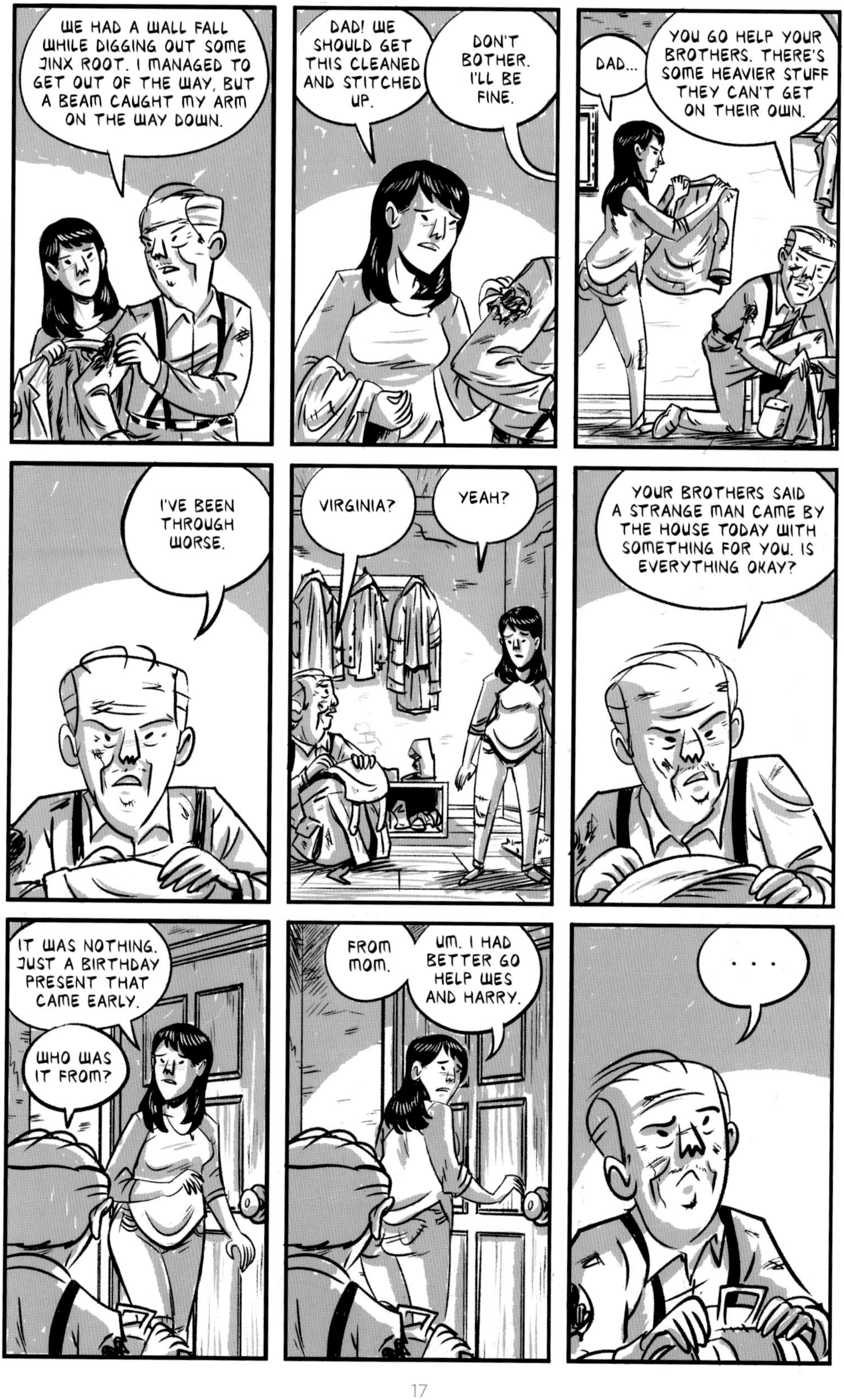
WE HAD A WALL FALL WHILE DIGGING OUT SOME JINX ROOT. I MANAGED TO GET OUT OF THE WAY, BUT A BEAM CAUGHT MY ARM ON THE WAY DOWN.
DAD! WE SHOULD GET THIS CLEANED AND STITCHED UP.
DON'T BOTHER. I'LL BE FINE.
DAD...
YOU GO HELP YOUR BROTHERS. THERE'S SOME HEAVIER STUFF THEY CAN'T GET ON THEIR OWN.
I'VE BEEN THROUGH WORSE.
VIRGINIA?
YEAH?
YOUR BROTHERS SAID A STRANGE MAN CAME BY THE HOUSE TODAY WITH SOMETHING FOR YOU. IS EVERYTHING OKAY?
IT WAS NOTHING. JUST A BIRTHDAY PRESENT THAT CAME EARLY.
WHO WAS IT FROM?
FROM MOM.
UM. I HAD BETTER GO HELP WES AND HARRY.
. . .

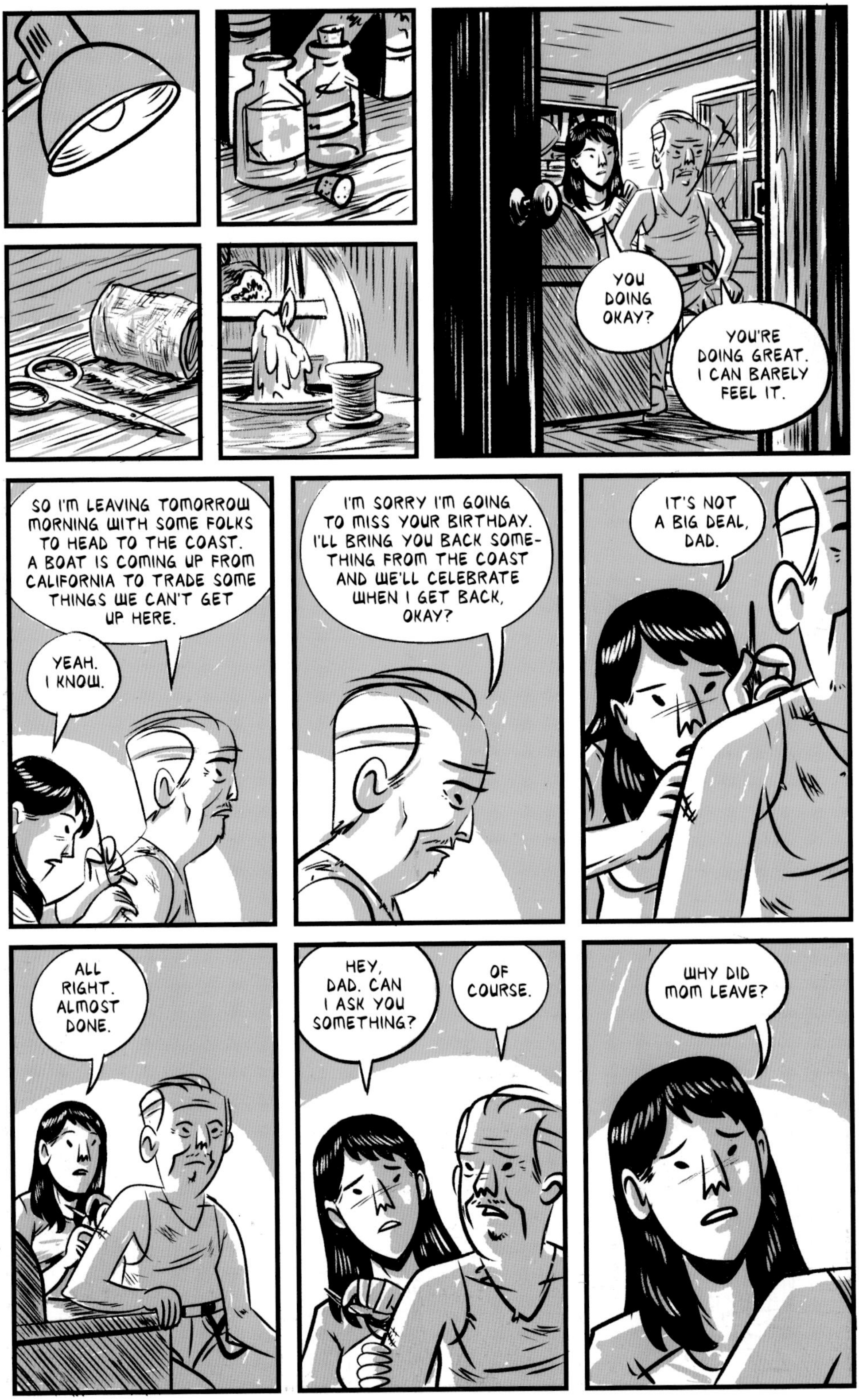

YOU DOING OKAY?
YOU'RE DOING GREAT. I CAN BARELY FEEL IT.
SO I'M LEAVING TOMORROW MORNING WITH SOME FOLKS TO HEAD TO THE COAST. A BOAT IS COMING UP FROM CALIFORNIA TO TRADE SOME THINGS WE CAN'T GET UP HERE.
YEAH. I KNOW.
I'M SORRY I'M GOING TO MISS YOUR BIRTHDAY. I'LL BRING YOU BACK SOMETHING FROM THE COAST AND WE'LL CELEBRATE WHEN I GET BACK, OKAY?
IT'S NOT A BIG DEAL, DAD.
ALL RIGHT. ALMOST DONE.
HEY, DAD. CAN I ASK YOU SOMETHING?
OF COURSE.
WHY DID MOM LEAVE?

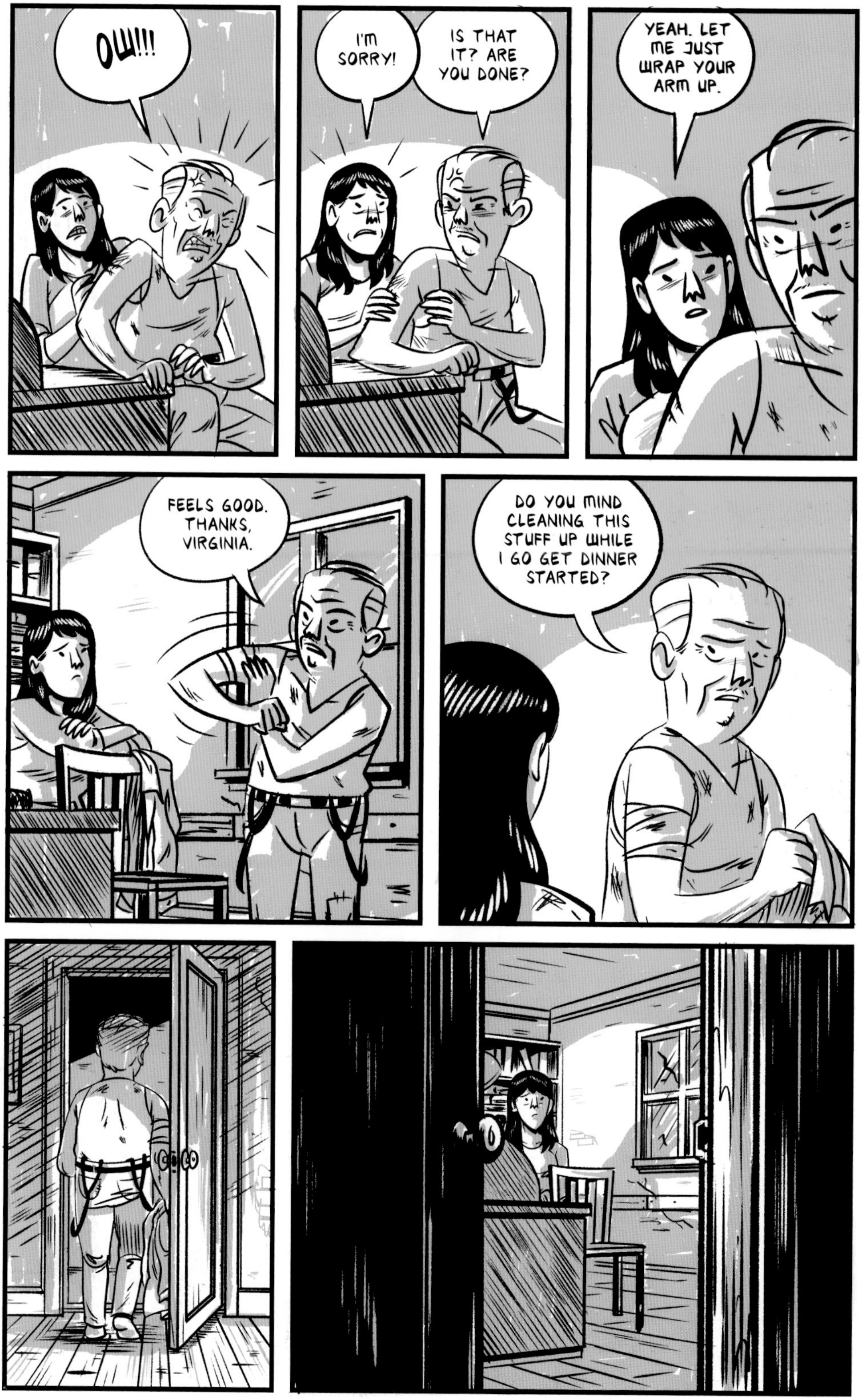
OW!!!
I'M SORRY!
IS THAT IT? ARE YOU DONE?
YEAH. LET ME JUST WRAP YOUR ARM UP.
FEELS GOOD. THANKS, VIRGINIA.
DO YOU MIND CLEANING THIS STUFF UP WHILE I GO GET DINNER STARTED?

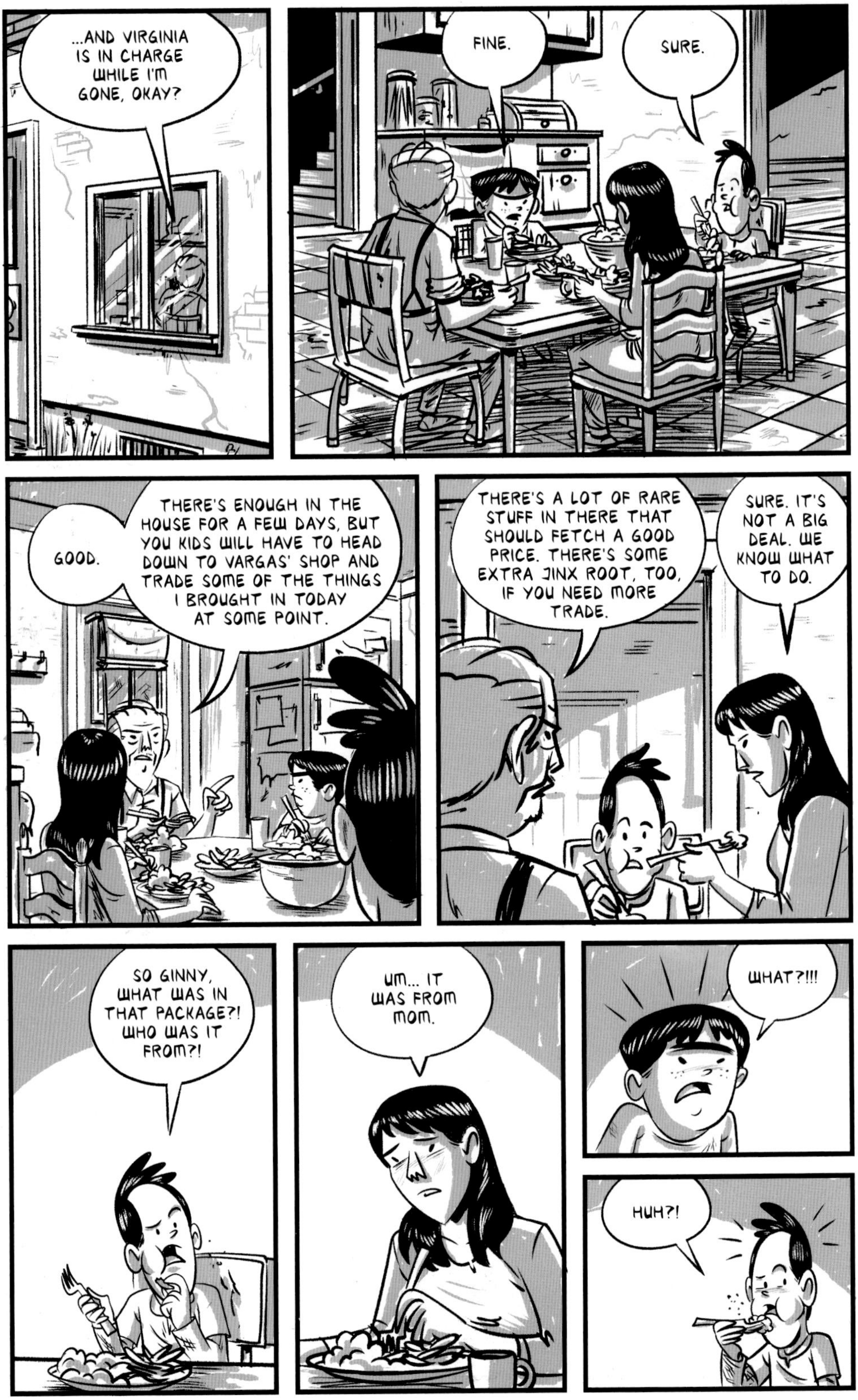
...AND VIRGINIA IS IN CHARGE WHILE I'M GONE, OKAY?
FINE.
SURE.
GOOD.
THERE'S ENOUGH IN THE HOUSE FOR A FEW DAYS, BUT YOU KIDS WILL HAVE TO HEAD DOWN TO VARGAS' SHOP AND TRADE SOME OF THE THINGS I BROUGHT IN TODAY AT SOME POINT.
THERE'S A LOT OF RARE STUFF IN THERE THAT SHOULD FETCH A GOOD PRICE. THERE'S SOME EXTRA JINX ROOT, TOO, IF YOU NEED MORE TRADE.
SURE. IT'S NOT A BIG DEAL. WE KNOW WHAT TO DO.
SO GINNY, WHAT WAS IN THAT PACKAGE?! WHO WAS IT FROM?!
UM... IT WAS FROM MOM.
WHAT?!!!
HUH?!

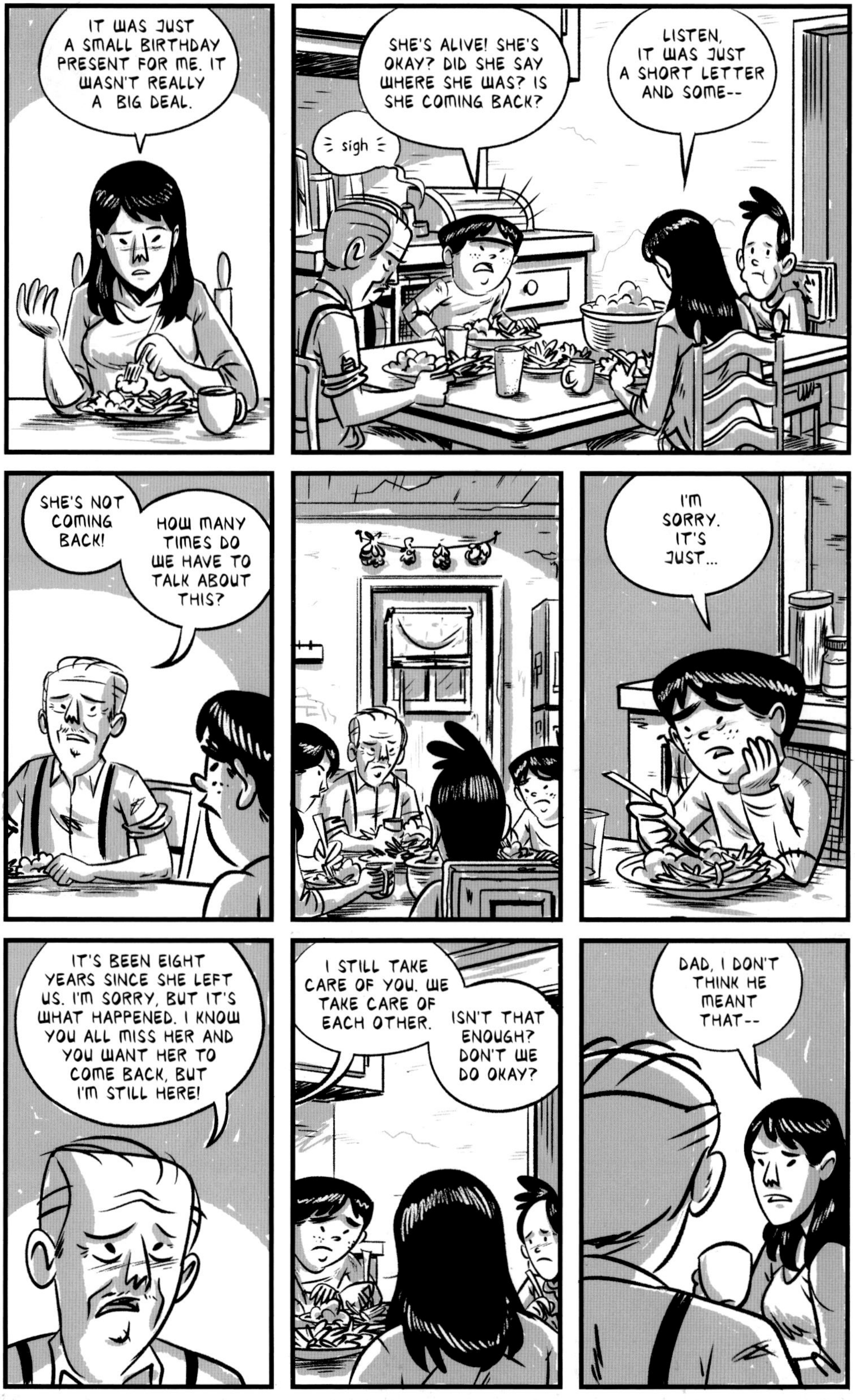
IT WAS JUST A SMALL BIRTHDAY PRESENT FOR ME. IT WASN'T REALLY A BIG DEAL.
sigh
SHE'S ALIVE! SHE'S OKAY? DID SHE SAY WHERE SHE WAS? IS SHE COMING BACK?
LISTEN, IT WAS JUST A SHORT LETTER AND SOME--
SHE'S NOT COMING BACK!
HOW MANY TIMES DO WE HAVE TO TALK ABOUT THIS?
I'M SORRY. IT'S JUST...
IT'S BEEN EIGHT YEARS SINCE SHE LEFT US. I'M SORRY, BUT IT'S WHAT HAPPENED. I KNOW YOU ALL MISS HER AND YOU WANT HER TO COME BACK, BUT I'M STILL HERE!
I STILL TAKE CARE OF YOU. WE TAKE CARE OF EACH OTHER.
ISN'T THAT ENOUGH? DON'T WE DO OKAY?
DAD, I DON'T THINK HE MEANT THAT--

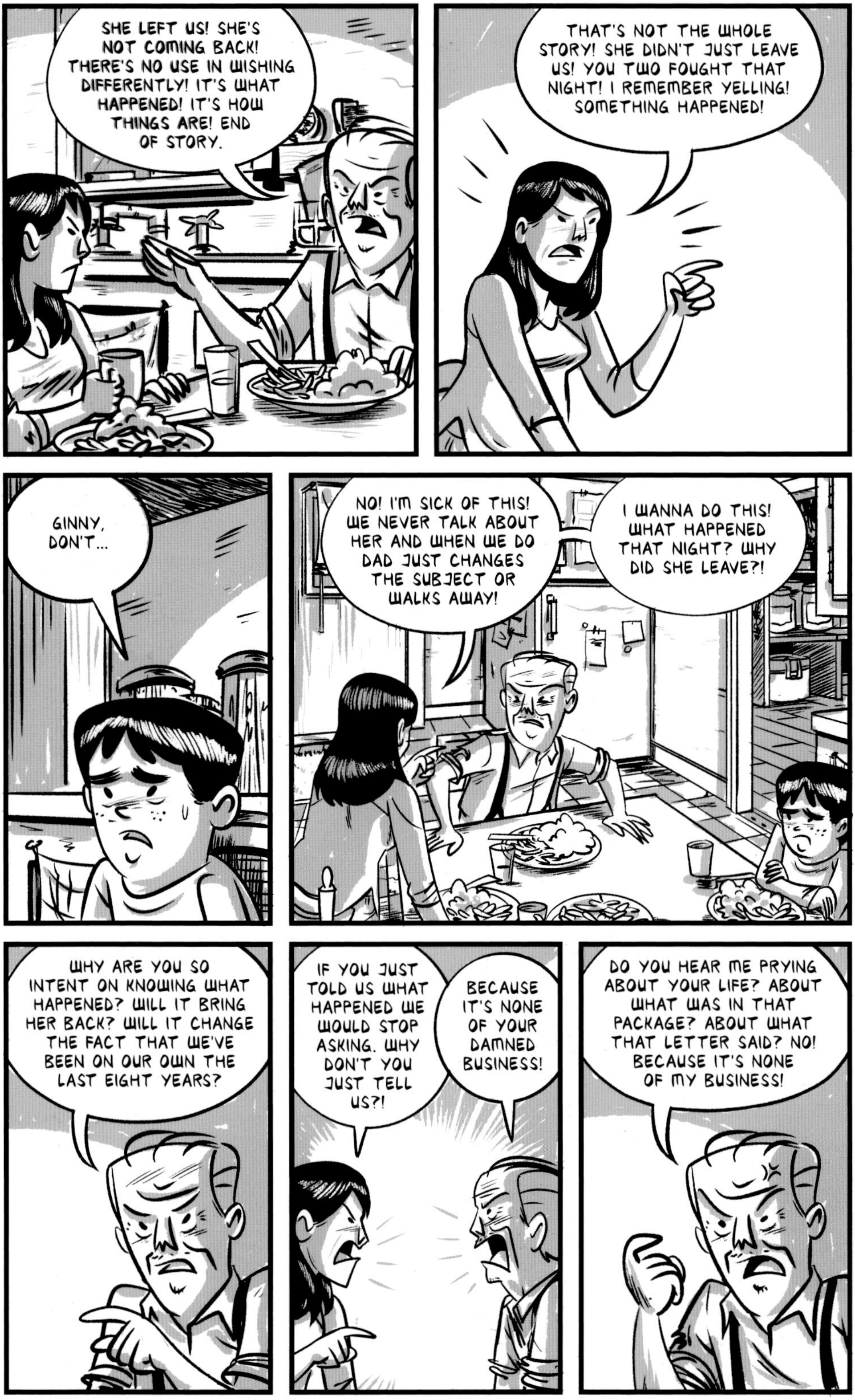
SHE LEFT US! SHE'S NOT COMING BACK! THERE'S NO USE IN WISHING DIFFERENTLY! IT'S WHAT HAPPENED! IT'S HOW THINGS ARE! END OF STORY.
THAT'S NOT THE WHOLE STORY! SHE DIDN'T JUST LEAVE US! YOU TWO FOUGHT THAT NIGHT! I REMEMBER YELLING! SOMETHING HAPPENED!
GINNY, DON'T...
NO! I'M SICK OF THIS! WE NEVER TALK ABOUT HER AND WHEN WE DO DAD JUST CHANGES THE SUBJECT OR WALKS AWAY!
I WANNA DO THIS! WHAT HAPPENED THAT NIGHT? WHY DID SHE LEAVE?!
WHY ARE YOU SO INTENT ON KNOWING WHAT HAPPENED? WILL IT BRING HER BACK? WILL IT CHANGE THE FACT THAT WE'VE BEEN ON OUR OWN THE LAST EIGHT YEARS?
IF YOU JUST TOLD US WHAT HAPPENED WE WOULD STOP ASKING. WHY DON'T YOU JUST TELL US?!
BECAUSE IT'S NONE OF YOUR DAMNED BUSINESS!
DO YOU HEAR ME PRYING ABOUT YOUR LIFE? ABOUT WHAT WAS IN THAT PACKAGE? ABOUT WHAT THAT LETTER SAID? NO! BECAUSE IT'S NONE OF MY BUSINESS!

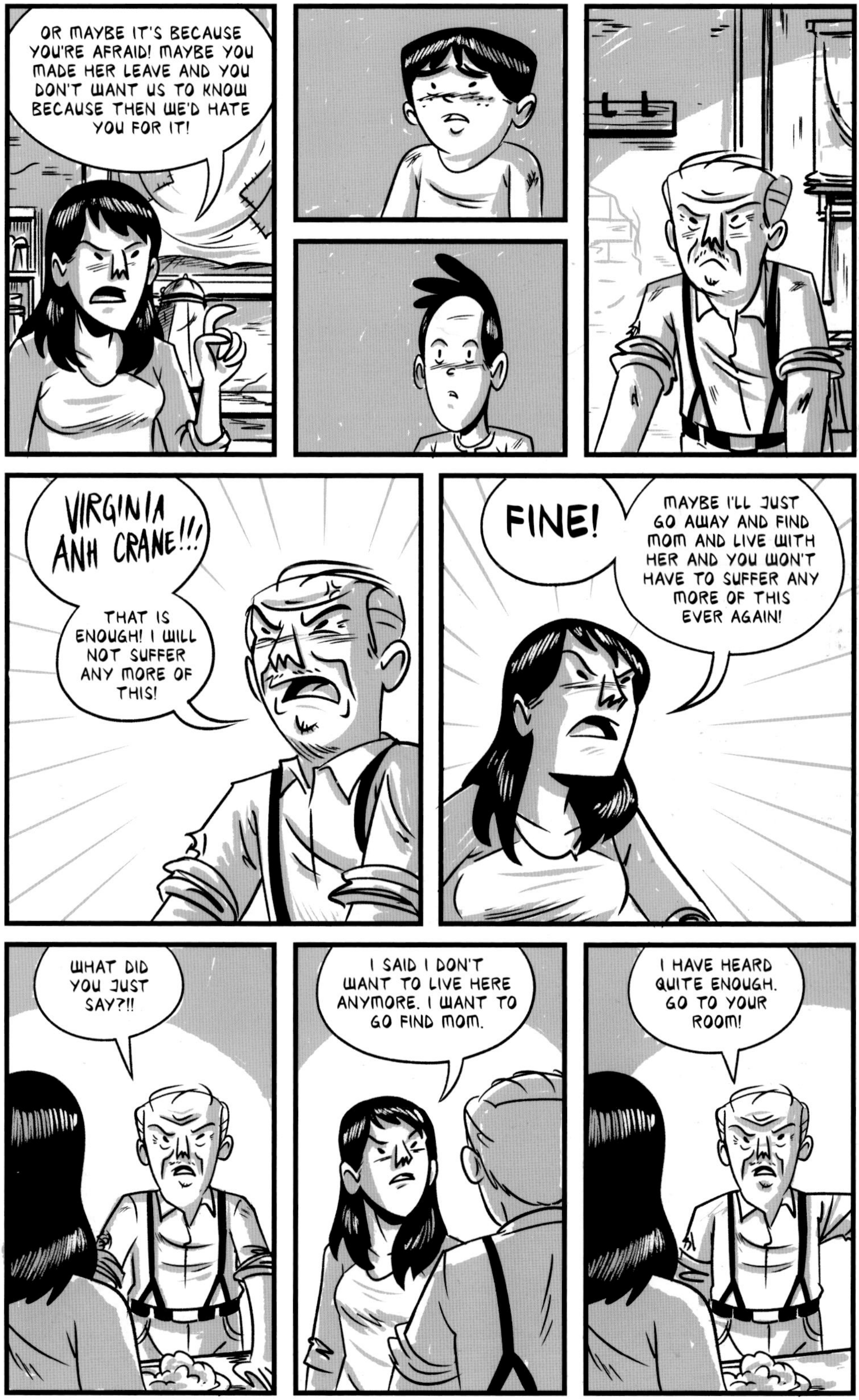
OR MAYBE IT'S BECAUSE YOU'RE AFRAID! MAYBE YOU MADE HER LEAVE AND YOU DON'T WANT US TO KNOW BECAUSE THEN WE'D HATE YOU FOR IT!
VIRGINIA ANH CRANE!!!
THAT IS ENOUGH! I WILL NOT SUFFER ANY MORE OF THIS!
FINE!
MAYBE I'LL JUST GO AWAY AND FIND MOM AND LIVE WITH HER AND YOU WON'T HAVE TO SUFFER ANY MORE OF THIS EVER AGAIN!
WHAT DID YOU JUST SAY?!!
I SAID I DON'T WANT TO LIVE HERE ANYMORE. I WANT TO GO FIND MOM.
I HAVE HEARD QUITE ENOUGH. GO TO YOUR ROOM!

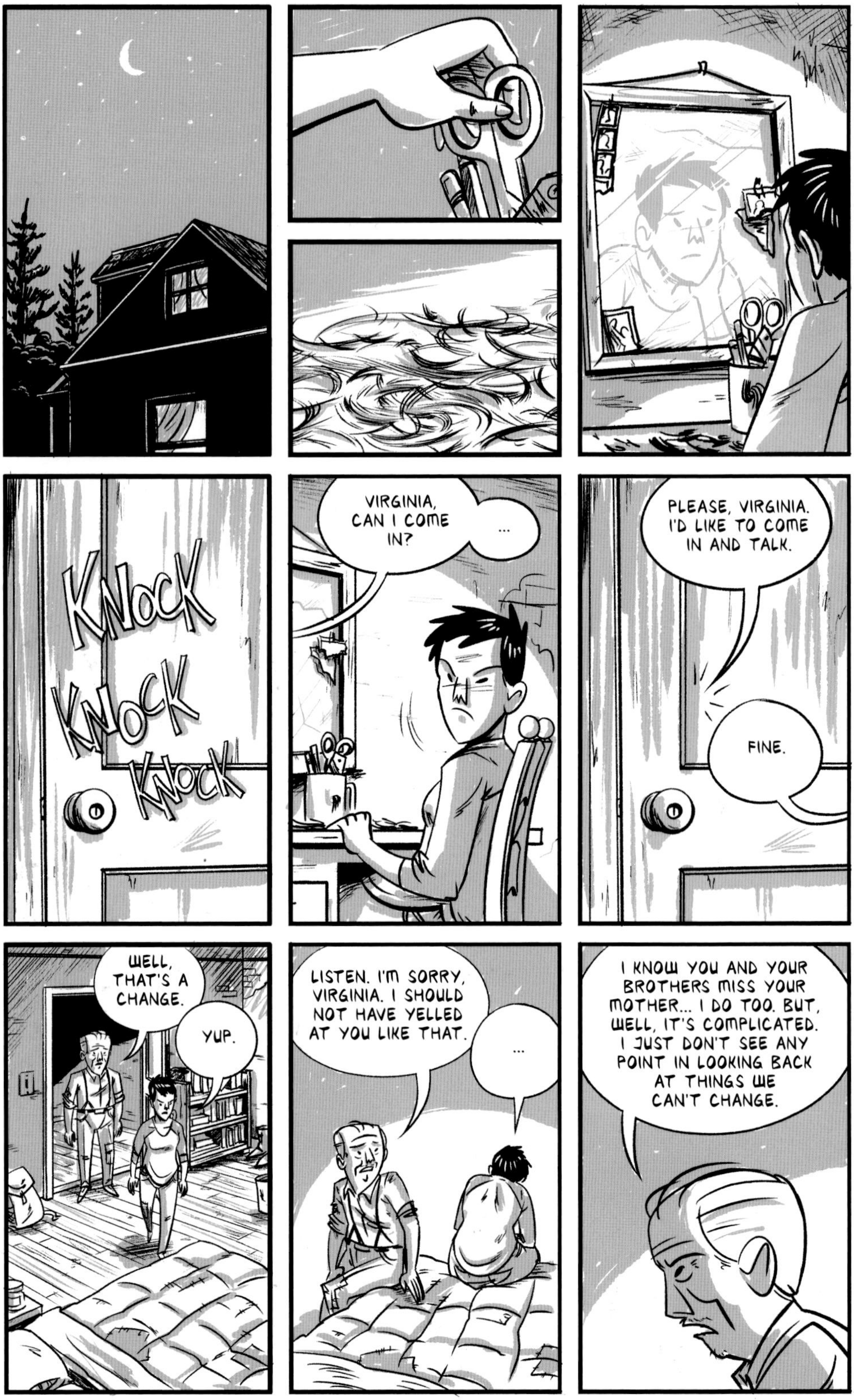

KNOCK
KNOCK
KNOCK
VIRGINIA, CAN I COME IN?
...
PLEASE, VIRGINIA. I'D LIKE TO COME IN AND TALK.
FINE.
WELL, THAT'S A CHANGE.
YUP.
LISTEN. I'M SORRY, VIRGINIA. I SHOULD NOT HAVE YELLED AT YOU LIKE THAT.
...
I KNOW YOU AND YOUR BROTHERS MISS YOUR MOTHER... I DO TOO. BUT, WELL, IT'S COMPLICATED. I JUST DON'T SEE ANY POINT IN LOOKING BACK AT THINGS WE CAN'T CHANGE.

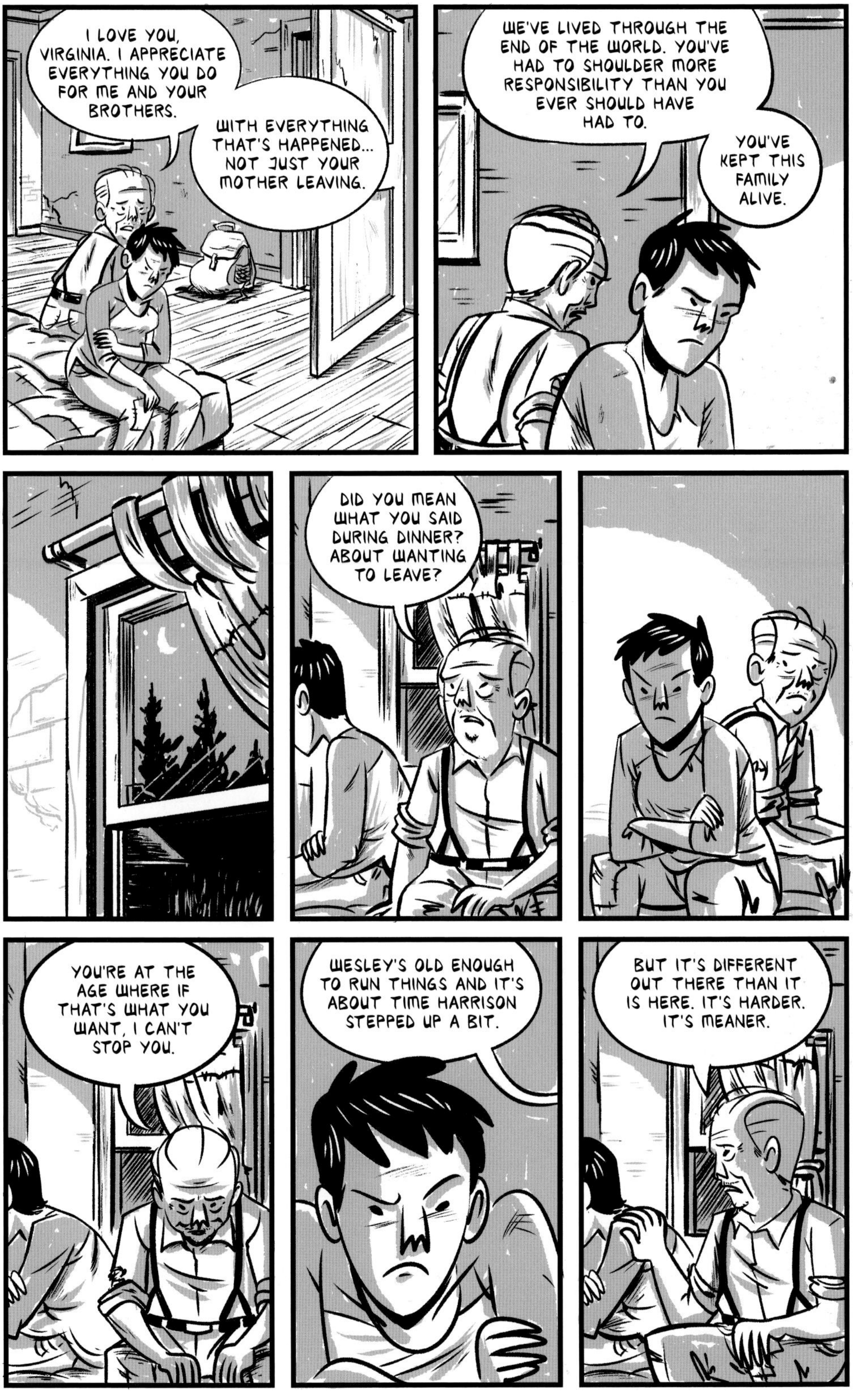
I LOVE YOU, VIRGINIA. I APPRECIATE EVERYTHING YOU DO FOR ME AND YOUR BROTHERS.
WITH EVERYTHING THAT'S HAPPENED... NOT JUST YOUR MOTHER LEAVING.
WE'VE LIVED THROUGH THE END OF THE WORLD. YOU'VE HAD TO SHOULDER MORE RESPONSIBILITY THAN YOU EVER SHOULD HAVE HAD TO.
YOU'VE KEPT THIS FAMILY ALIVE.
DID YOU MEAN WHAT YOU SAID DURING DINNER? ABOUT WANTING TO LEAVE?
YOU'RE AT THE AGE WHERE IF THAT'S WHAT YOU WANT, I CAN'T STOP YOU.
WESLEY'S OLD ENOUGH TO RUN THINGS AND IT'S ABOUT TIME HARRISON STEPPED UP A BIT.
BUT IT'S DIFFERENT OUT THERE THAN IT IS HERE. IT'S HARDER. IT'S MEANER.

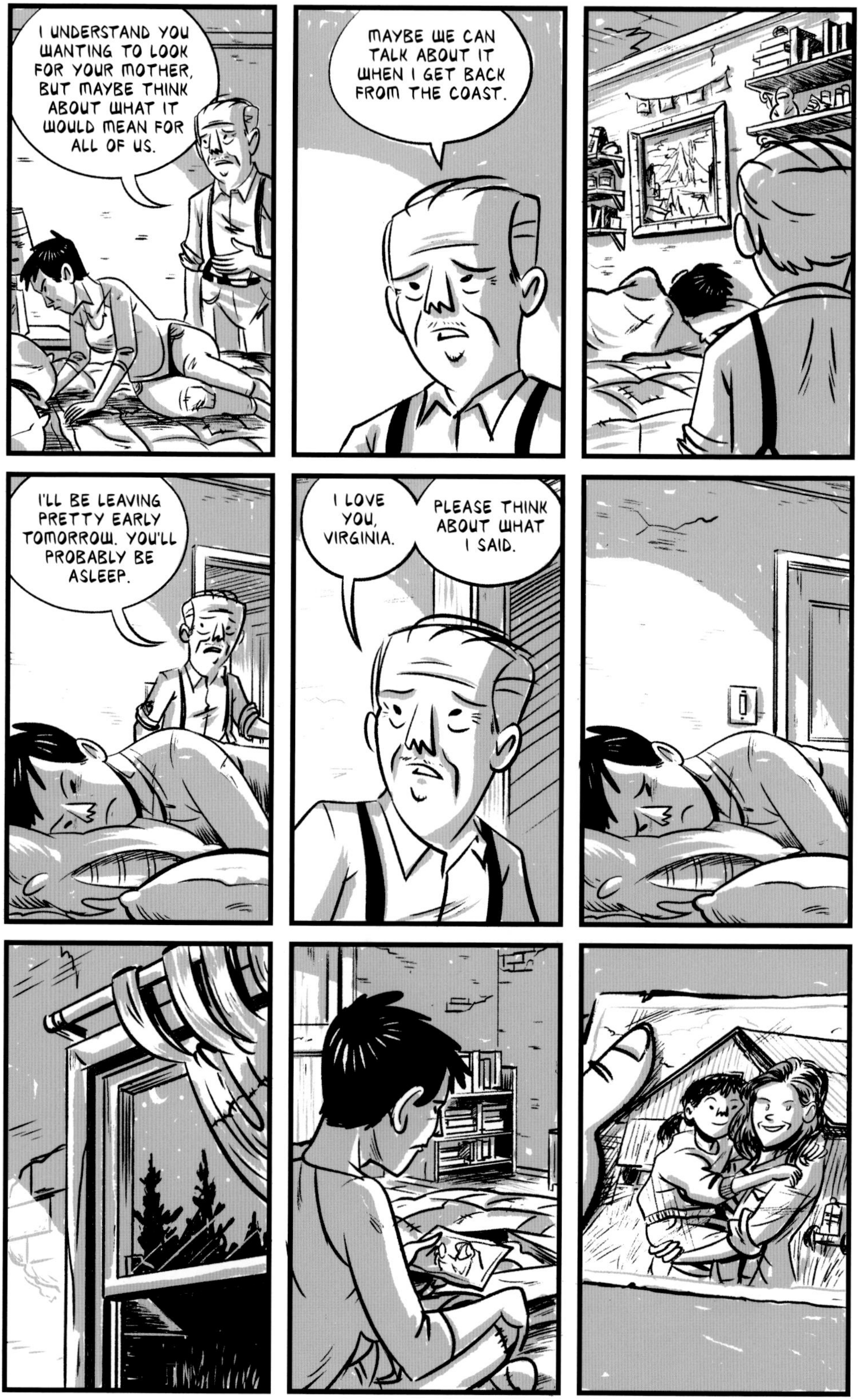
I UNDERSTAND YOU WANTING TO LOOK FOR YOUR MOTHER, BUT MAYBE THINK ABOUT WHAT IT WOULD MEAN FOR ALL OF US.
MAYBE WE CAN TALK ABOUT IT WHEN I GET BACK FROM THE COAST.
I'LL BE LEAVING PRETTY EARLY TOMORROW. YOU'LL PROBABLY BE ASLEEP.
I LOVE YOU, VIRGINIA.
PLEASE THINK ABOUT WHAT I SAID.

CHAPTER 2

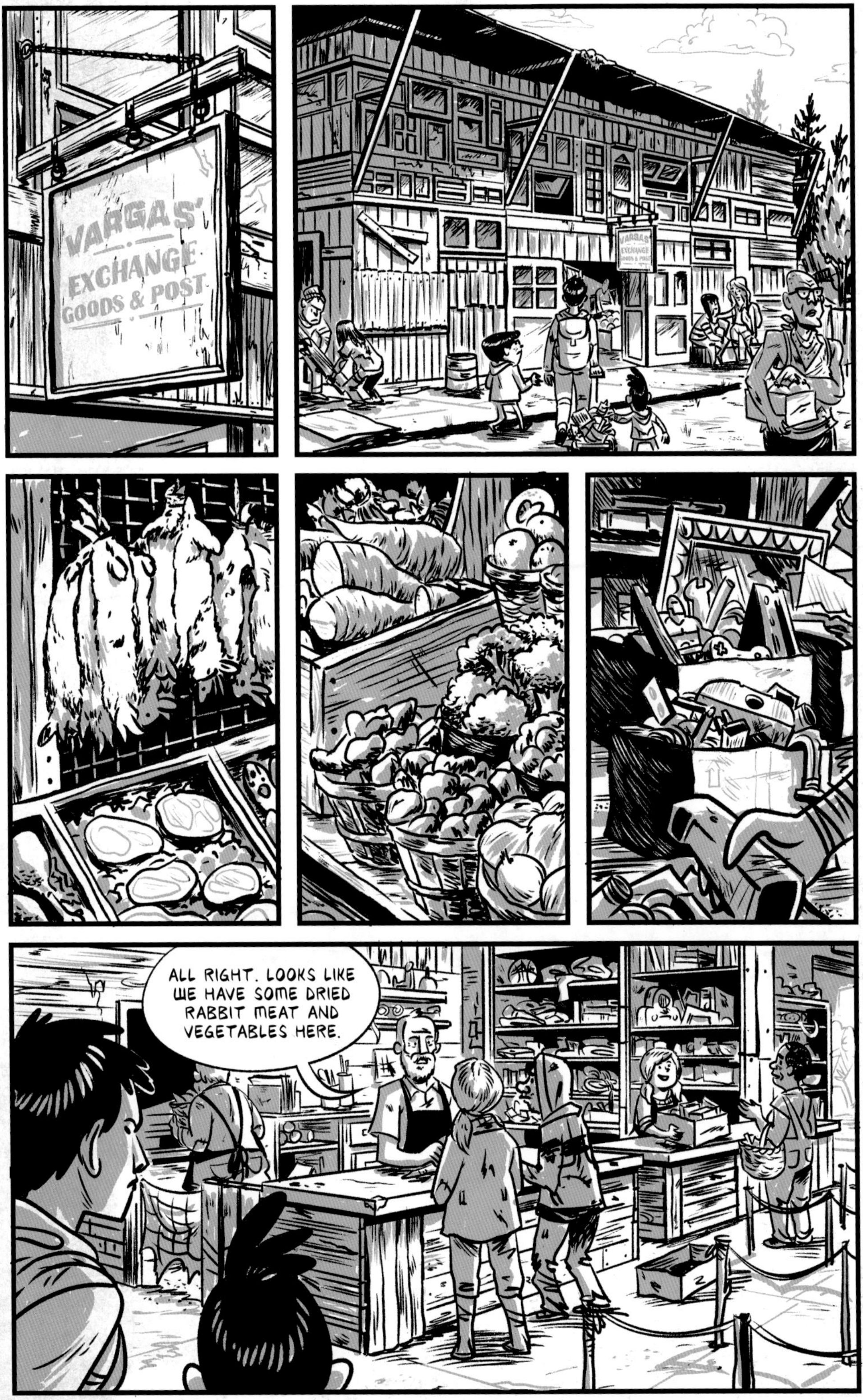
VARGAS'
EXCHANGE
GOODS & POST
ALL RIGHT. LOOKS LIKE WE HAVE SOME DRIED RABBIT MEAT AND VEGETABLES HERE.

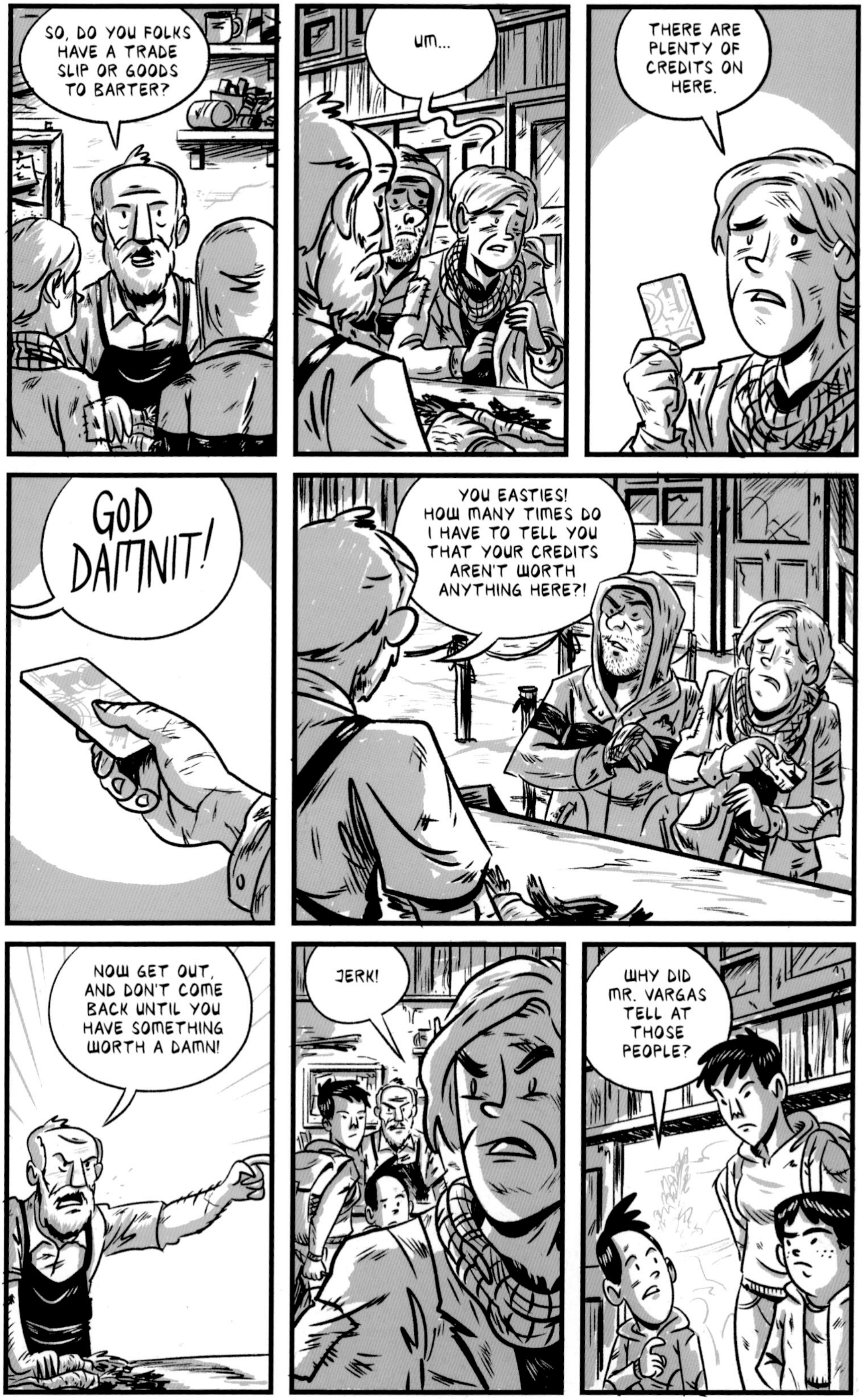
SO, DO YOU FOLKS HAVE A TRADE SLIP OR GOODS TO BARTER?
UM...
THERE ARE PLENTY OF CREDITS ON HERE.
GOD DAMNIT!
YOU EASTIES! HOW MANY TIMES DO I HAVE TO TELL YOU THAT YOUR CREDITS AREN'T WORTH ANYTHING HERE?!
NOW GET OUT, AND DON'T COME BACK UNTIL YOU HAVE SOMETHING WORTH A DAMN!
JERK!
WHY DID MR. VARGAS TELL AT THOSE PEOPLE?

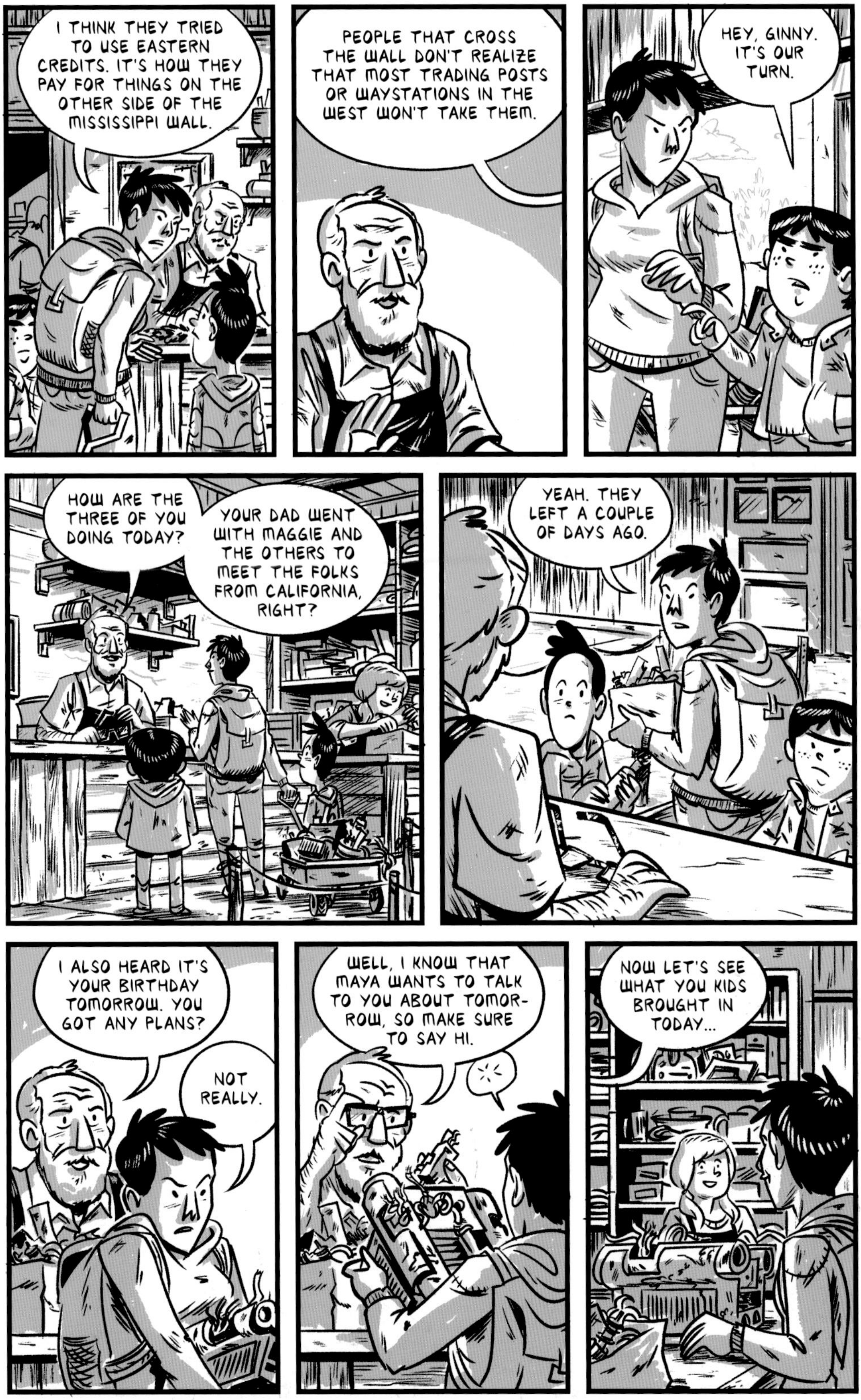
I THINK THEY TRIED TO USE EASTERN CREDITS. IT'S HOW THEY PAY FOR THINGS ON THE OTHER SIDE OF THE MISSISSIPPI WALL.
PEOPLE THAT CROSS THE WALL DON'T REALIZE THAT MOST TRADING POSTS OR WAYSTATIONS IN THE WEST WON'T TAKE THEM.
HEY, GINNY. IT'S OUR TURN.
HOW ARE THE THREE OF YOU DOING TODAY?
YOUR DAD WENT WITH MAGGIE AND THE OTHERS TO MEET THE FOLKS FROM CALIFORNIA, RIGHT?
YEAH. THEY LEFT A COUPLE OF DAYS AGO.
I ALSO HEARD IT'S YOUR BIRTHDAY TOMORROW. YOU GOT ANY PLANS?
NOT REALLY.
WELL, I KNOW THAT MAYA WANTS TO TALK TO YOU ABOUT TOMORROW, SO MAKE SURE TO SAY HI.
NOW LET'S SEE WHAT YOU KIDS BROUGHT IN TODAY...

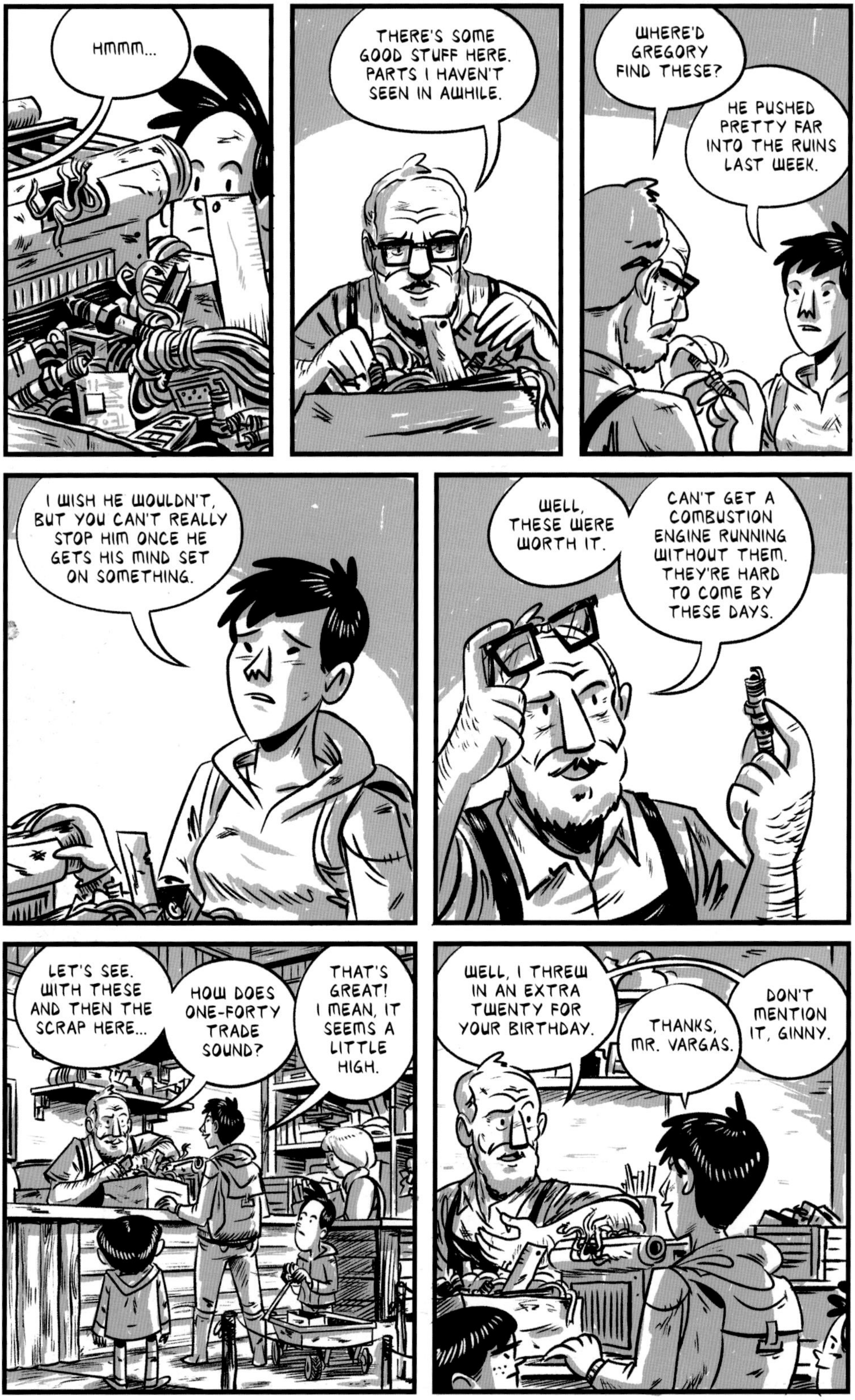
HMMM...
THERE'S SOME GOOD STUFF HERE. PARTS I HAVEN'T SEEN IN AWHILE.
WHERE'D GREGORY FIND THESE?
HE PUSHED PRETTY FAR INTO THE RUINS LAST WEEK.
I WISH HE WOULDN'T, BUT YOU CAN'T REALLY STOP HIM ONCE HE GETS HIS MIND SET ON SOMETHING.
WELL, THESE WERE WORTH IT.
CAN'T GET A COMBUSTION ENGINE RUNNING WITHOUT THEM. THEY'RE HARD TO COME BY THESE DAYS.
LET'S SEE. WITH THESE AND THEN THE SCRAP HERE...
HOW DOES ONE-FORTY TRADE SOUND?
THAT'S GREAT! I MEAN, IT SEEMS A LITTLE HIGH.
WELL, I THREW IN AN EXTRA TWENTY FOR YOUR BIRTHDAY.
THANKS, MR. VARGAS.
DON'T MENTION IT, GINNY.

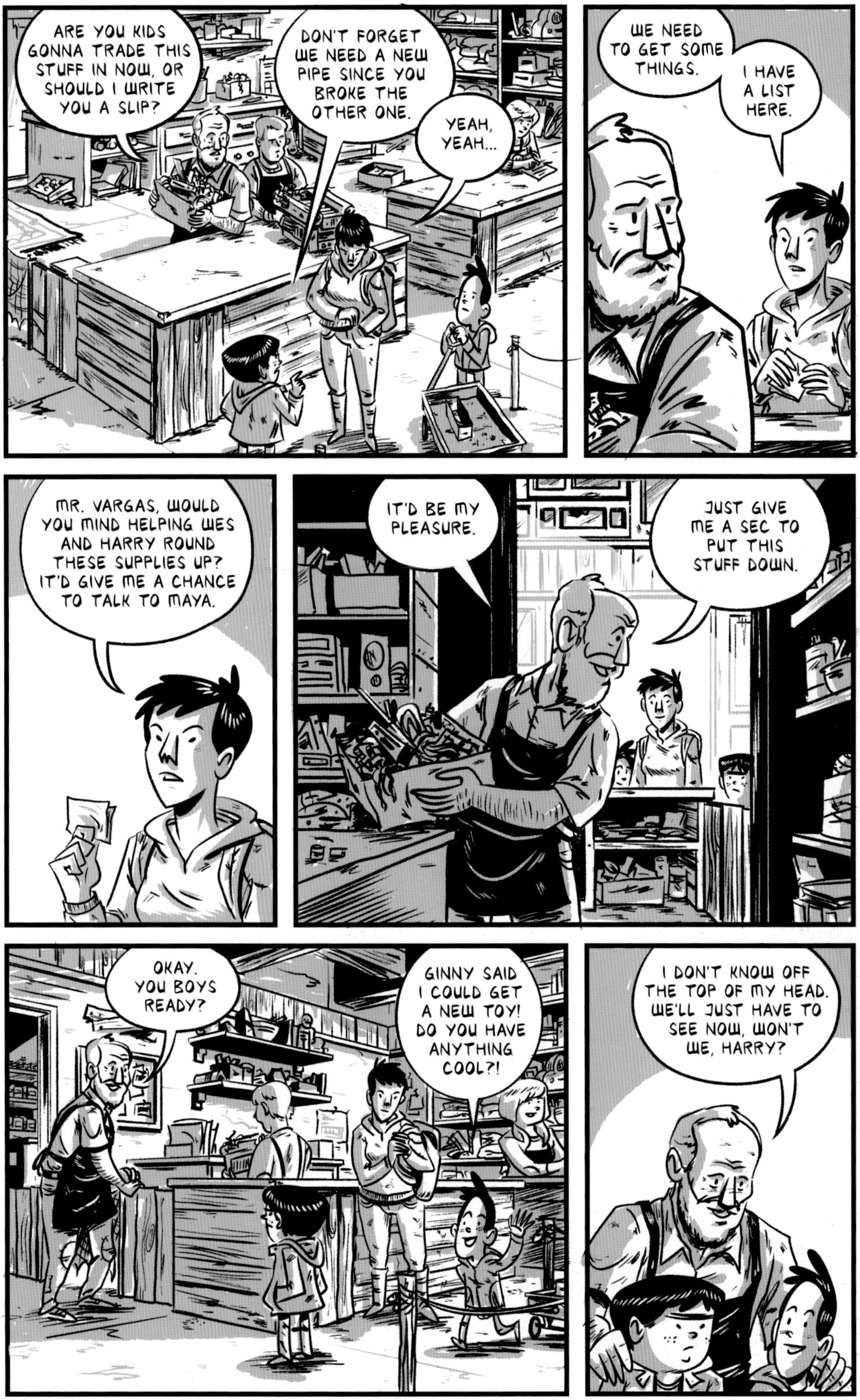
ARE YOU KIDS GONNA TRADE THIS STUFF IN NOW, OR SHOULD I WRITE YOU A SLIP?
DON'T FORGET WE NEED A NEW PIPE SINCE YOU BROKE THE OTHER ONE.
YEAH, YEAH...
WE NEED TO GET SOME THINGS.
I HAVE A LIST HERE.
MR. VARGAS, WOULD YOU MIND HELPING WES AND HARRY ROUND THESE SUPPLIES UP? IT'D GIVE ME A CHANCE TO TALK TO MAYA.
IT'D BE MY PLEASURE.
JUST GIVE ME A SEC TO PUT THIS STUFF DOWN.
OKAY. YOU BOYS READY?
GINNY SAID I COULD GET A NEW TOY! DO YOU HAVE ANYTHING COOL?!
I DON'T KNOW OFF THE TOP OF MY HEAD. WE'LL JUST HAVE TO SEE NOW, WON'T WE, HARRY?

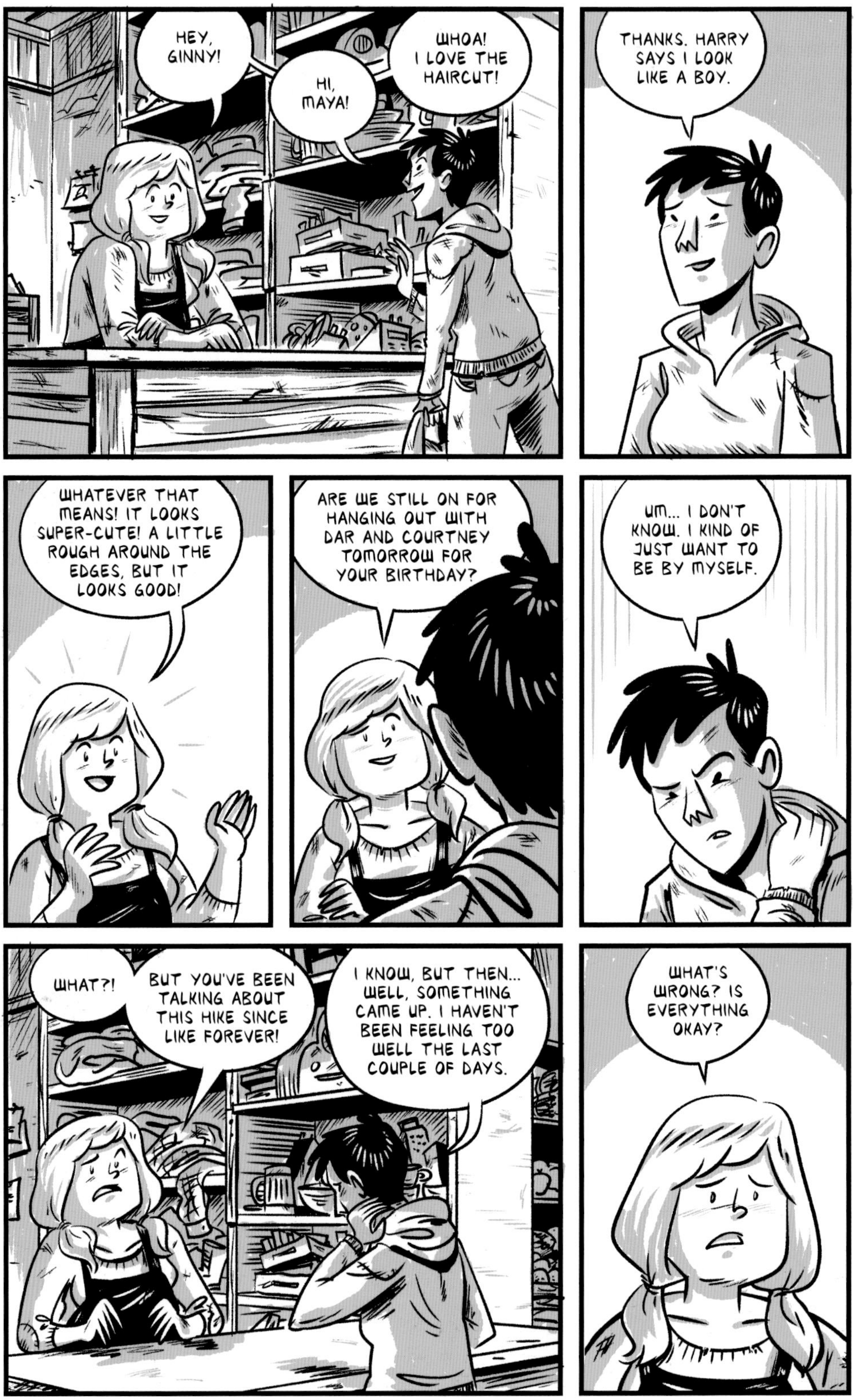
HEY, GINNY!
HI, MAYA!
WHOA! I LOVE THE HAIRCUT!
THANKS. HARRY SAYS I LOOK LIKE A BOY.
WHATEVER THAT MEANS! IT LOOKS SUPER-CUTE! A LITTLE ROUGH AROUND THE EDGES, BUT IT LOOKS GOOD!
ARE WE STILL ON FOR HANGING OUT WITH DAR AND COURTNEY TOMORROW FOR YOUR BIRTHDAY?
UM... I DON'T KNOW. I KIND OF JUST WANT TO BE BY MYSELF.
WHAT?!
BUT YOU'VE BEEN TALKING ABOUT THIS HIKE SINCE LIKE FOREVER!
I KNOW, BUT THEN... WELL, SOMETHING CAME UP. I HAVEN'T BEEN FEELING TOO WELL THE LAST COUPLE OF DAYS.
WHAT'S WRONG? IS EVERYTHING OKAY?

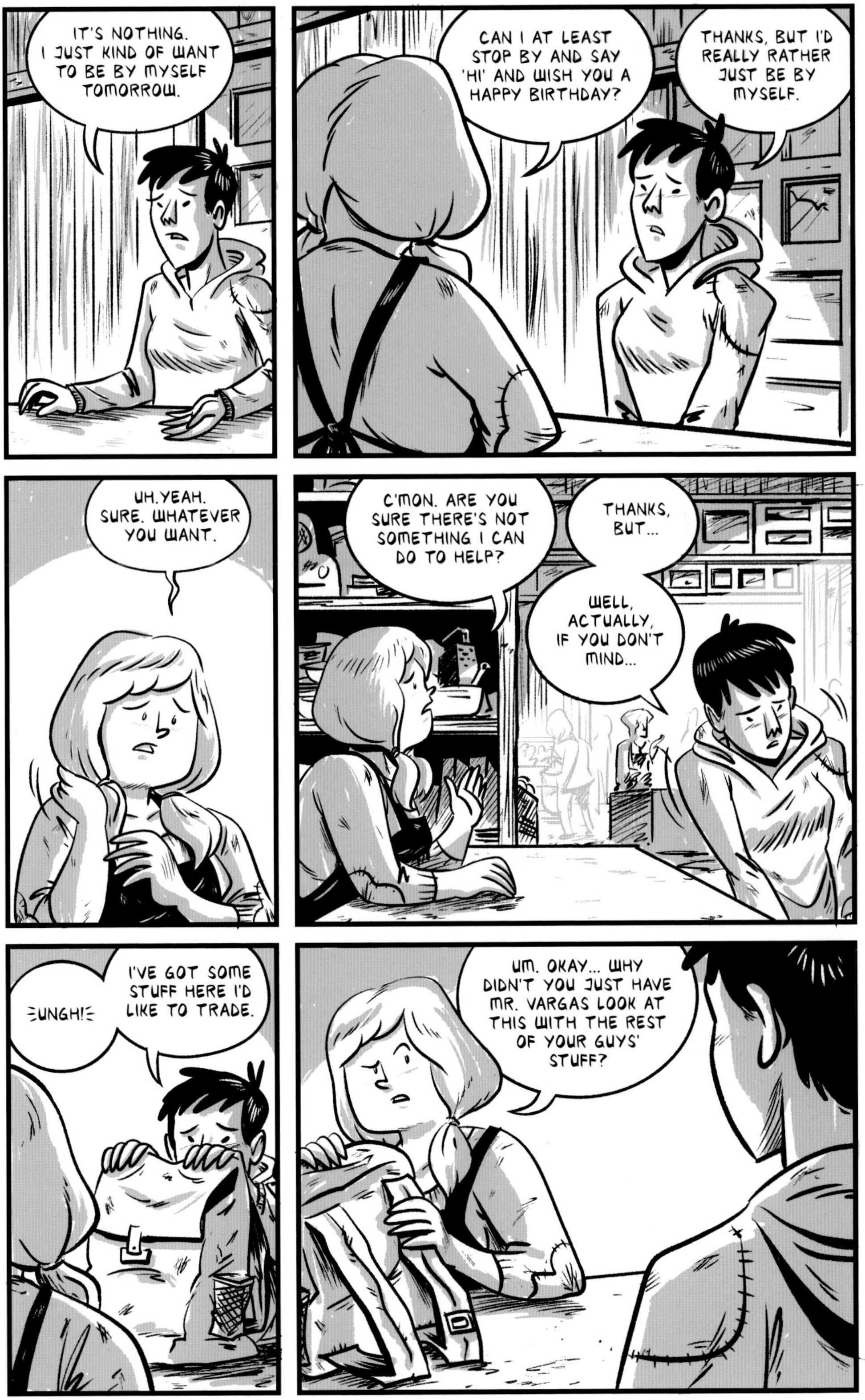
IT'S NOTHING. I JUST KIND OF WANT TO BE BY MYSELF TOMORROW.
CAN I AT LEAST STOP BY AND SAY 'HI' AND WISH YOU A HAPPY BIRTHDAY?
THANKS, BUT I'D REALLY RATHER JUST BE BY MYSELF.
UH.YEAH. SURE. WHATEVER YOU WANT.
C'MON. ARE YOU SURE THERE'S NOT SOMETHING I CAN DO TO HELP?
THANKS, BUT...
WELL, ACTUALLY, IF YOU DON'T MIND...
UNGH!
I'VE GOT SOME STUFF HERE I'D LIKE TO TRADE.
UM. OKAY... WHY DIDN'T YOU JUST HAVE MR. VARGAS LOOK AT THIS WITH THE REST OF YOUR GUYS' STUFF?

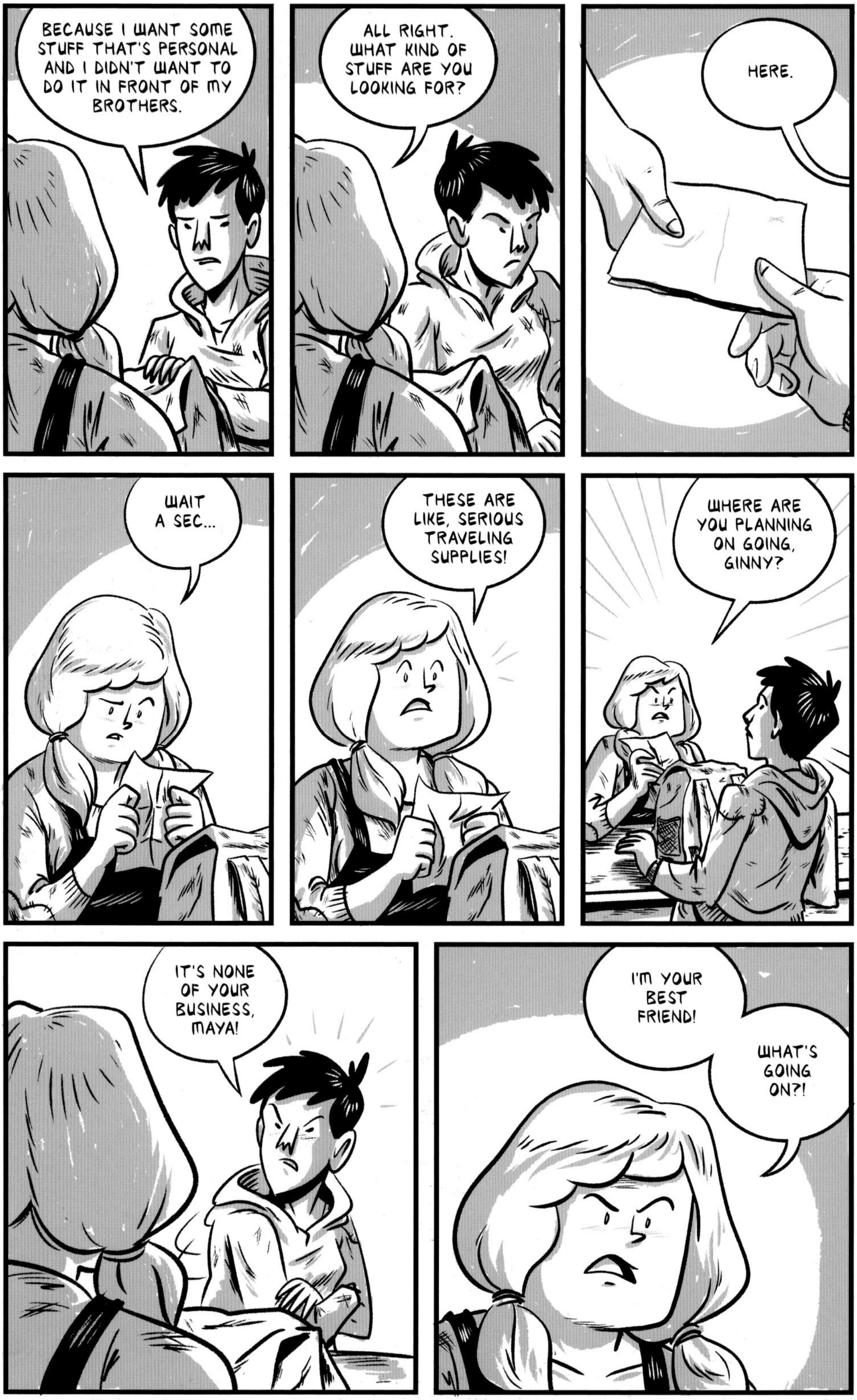
BECAUSE I WANT SOME STUFF THAT'S PERSONAL AND I DIDN'T WANT TO DO IT IN FRONT OF MY BROTHERS.
ALL RIGHT. WHAT KIND OF STUFF ARE YOU LOOKING FOR?
HERE.
WAIT A SEC...
THESE ARE LIKE, SERIOUS TRAVELING SUPPLIES!
WHERE ARE YOU PLANNING ON GOING, GINNY?
IT'S NONE OF YOUR BUSINESS, MAYA!
I'M YOUR BEST FRIEND!
WHAT'S GOING ON?!

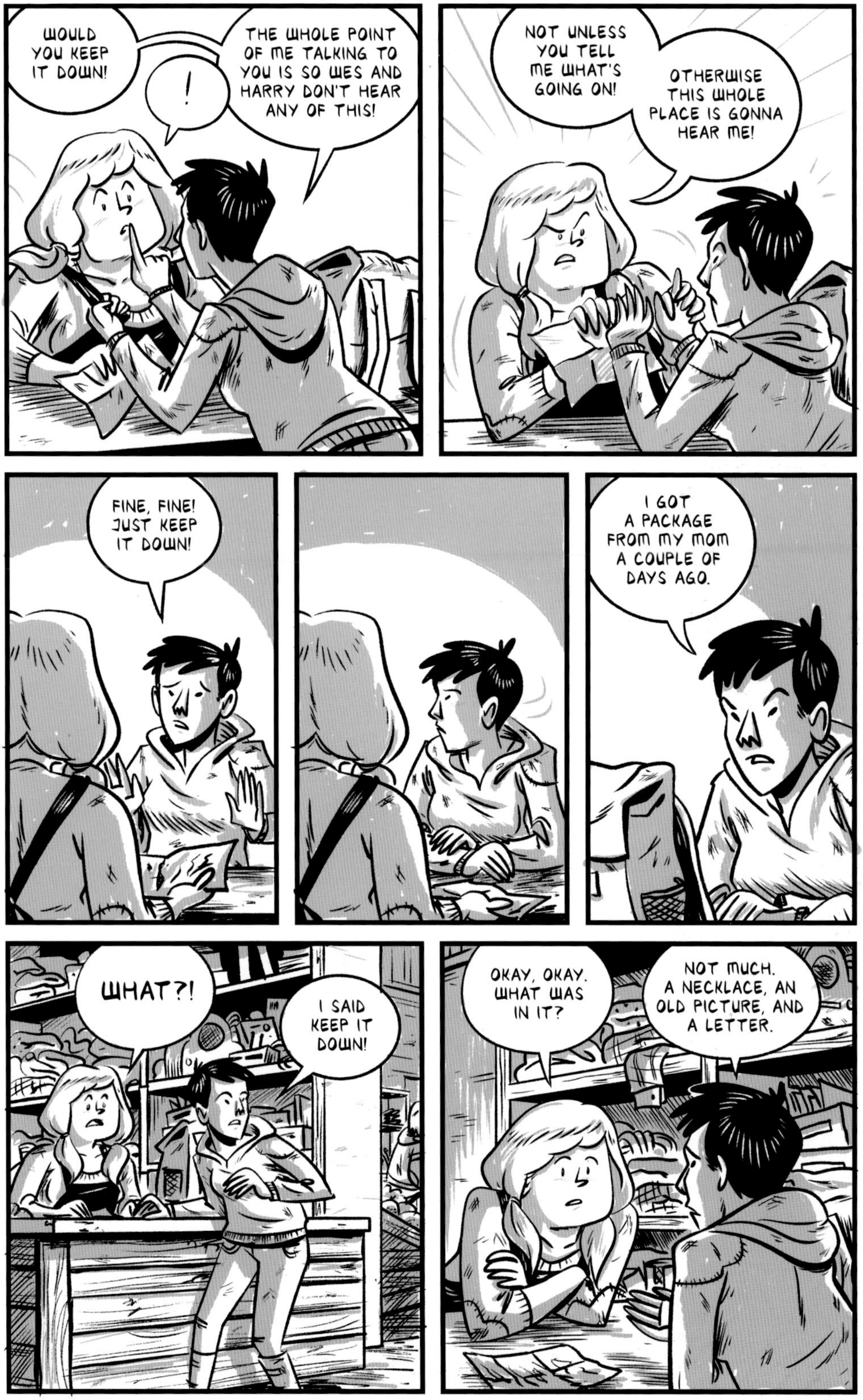
WOULD YOU KEEP IT DOWN!
THE WHOLE POINT OF ME TALKING TO YOU IS SO WES AND HARRY DON'T HEAR ANY OF THIS!
!
NOT UNLESS YOU TELL ME WHAT'S GOING ON!
OTHERWISE THIS WHOLE PLACE IS GONNA HEAR ME!
FINE, FINE! JUST KEEP IT DOWN!
I GOT A PACKAGE FROM MY MOM A COUPLE OF DAYS AGO.
WHAT?!
I SAID KEEP IT DOWN!
OKAY, OKAY. WHAT WAS IN IT?
NOT MUCH. A NECKLACE, AN OLD PICTURE, AND A LETTER.

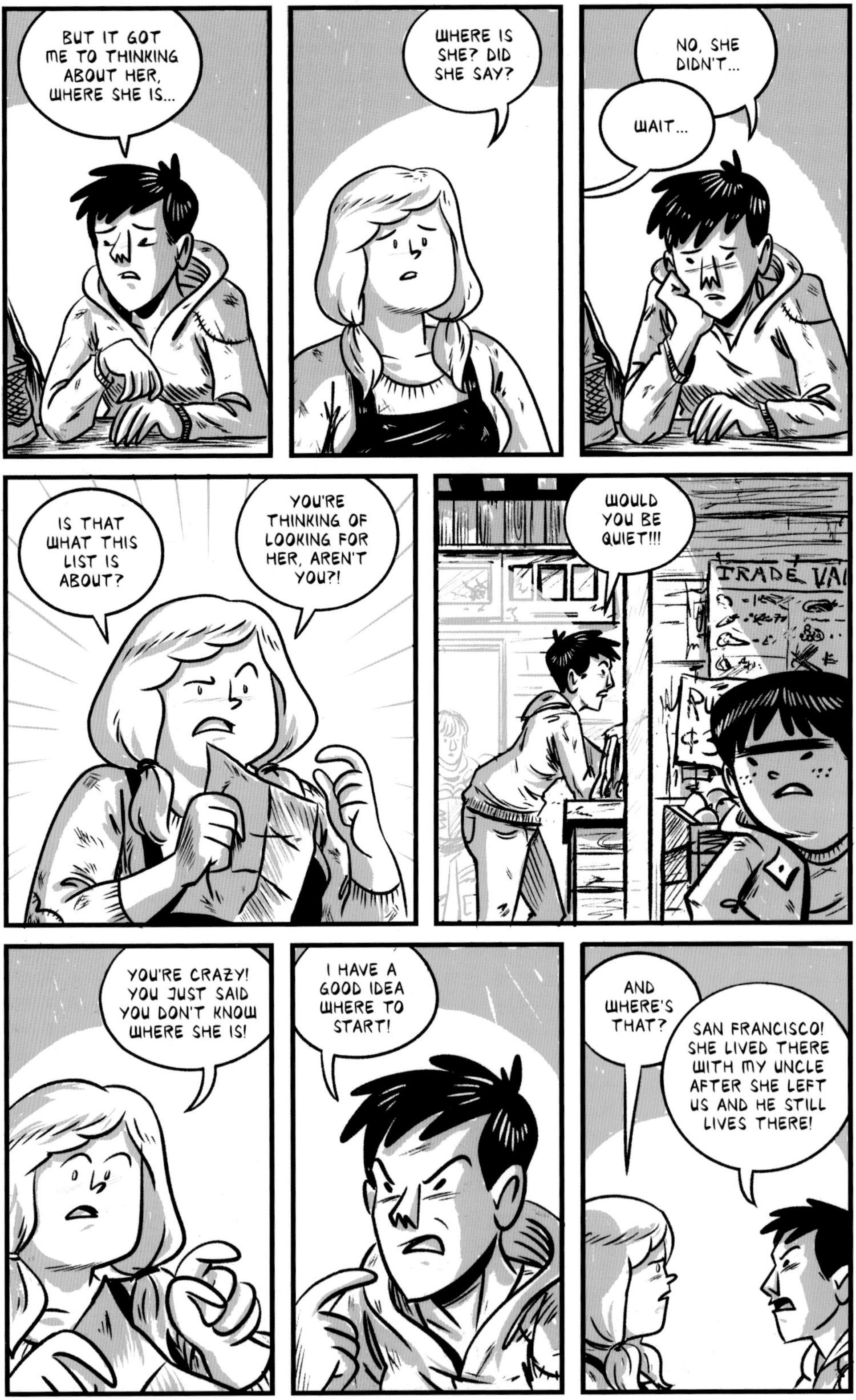
BUT IT GOT ME TO THINKING ABOUT HER, WHERE SHE IS...
WHERE IS SHE? DID SHE SAY?
NO, SHE DIDN'T...
WAIT...
IS THAT WHAT THIS LIST IS ABOUT?
YOU'RE THINKING OF LOOKING FOR HER, AREN'T YOU?!
WOULD YOU BE QUIET!!!
TRADE VA
YOU'RE CRAZY! YOU JUST SAID YOU DON'T KNOW WHERE SHE IS!
I HAVE A GOOD IDEA WHERE TO START!
AND WHERE'S THAT?
SAN FRANCISCO! SHE LIVED THERE WITH MY UNCLE AFTER SHE LEFT US AND HE STILL LIVES THERE!

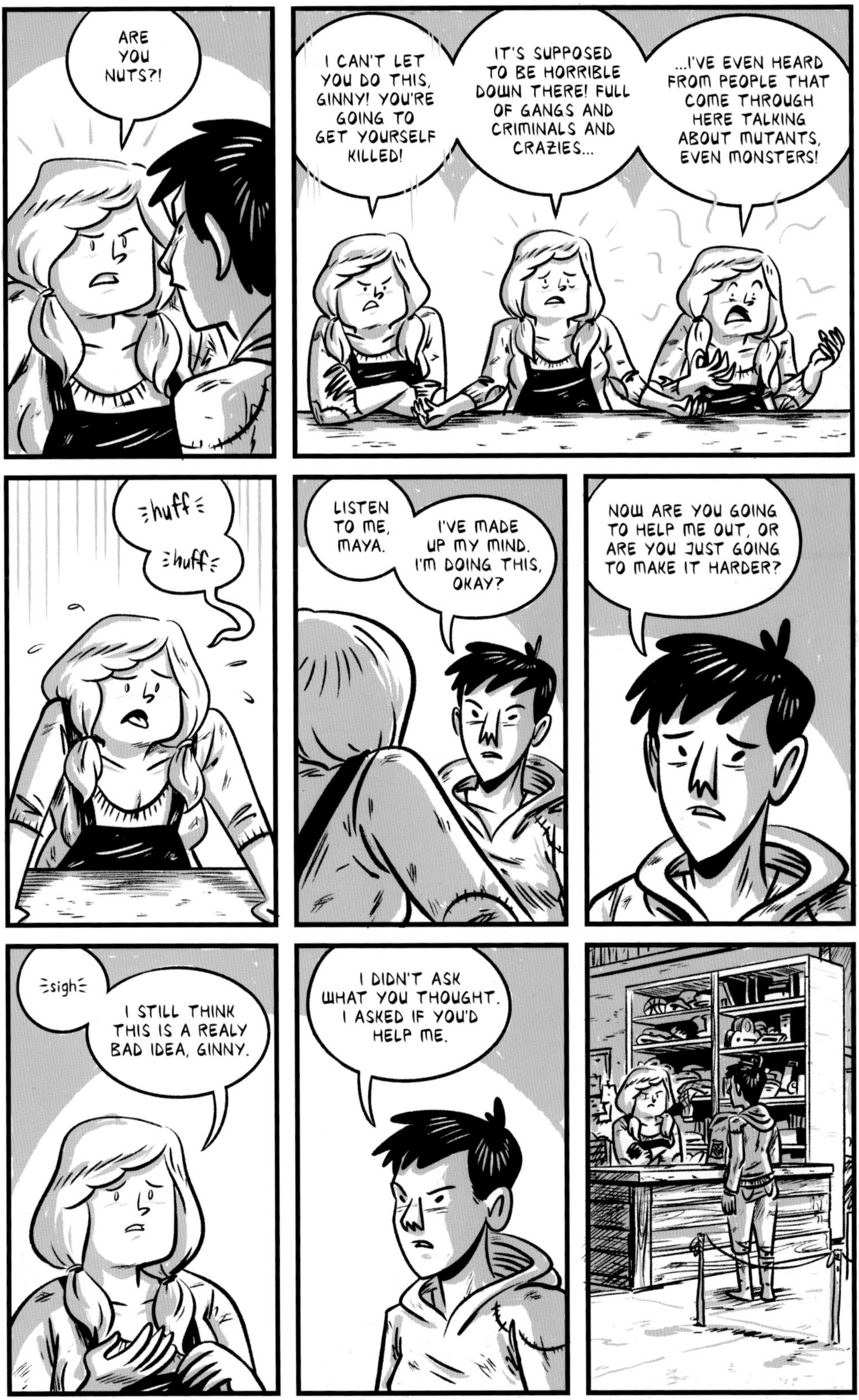
ARE YOU NUTS?!
I CAN'T LET YOU DO THIS, GINNY! YOU'RE GOING TO GET YOURSELF KILLED!
IT'S SUPPOSED TO BE HORRIBLE DOWN THERE! FULL OF GANGS AND CRIMINALS AND CRAZIES...
...I'VE EVEN HEARD FROM PEOPLE THAT COME THROUGH HERE TALKING ABOUT MUTANTS, EVEN MONSTERS!
huff
huff
LISTEN TO ME, MAYA.
I'VE MADE UP MY MIND. I'M DOING THIS, OKAY?
NOW ARE YOU GOING TO HELP ME OUT, OR ARE YOU JUST GOING TO MAKE IT HARDER?
sigh
I STILL THINK THIS IS A REALY BAD IDEA, GINNY.
I DIDN'T ASK WHAT YOU THOUGHT. I ASKED IF YOU'D HELP ME.

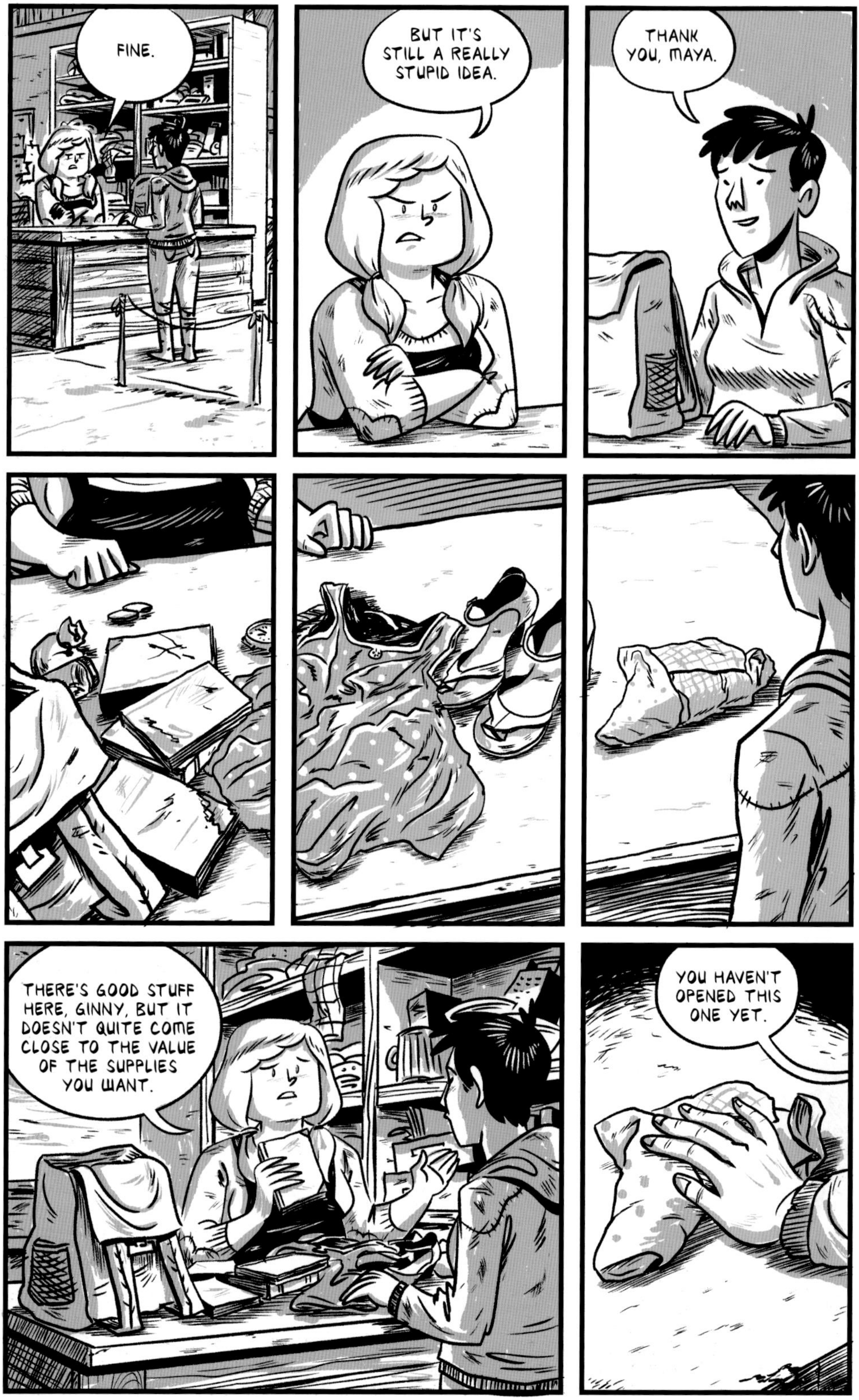
FINE.
BUT IT'S STILL A REALLY STUPID IDEA.
THANK YOU, MAYA.
THERE'S GOOD STUFF HERE, GINNY, BUT IT DOESN'T QUITE COME CLOSE TO THE VALUE OF THE SUPPLIES YOU WANT.
YOU HAVEN'T OPENED THIS ONE YET.

WHAT'S IN HERE?

JUST OPEN IT. I THINK IT WILL COVER WHAT I NEED.

!

GINNY, WHERE DID YOU GET THIS?

MY DAD AND I FOUND TWO GUNS IN AN OLD TRUCK RIGHT AFTER IT HAPPENED...

HE HAS ALWAYS HATED GUNS, BUT PEOPLE WERE SO CRAZY AND HORRIBLE RIGHT AFTER THE GREAT DISASTER...

HE DID A LOT OF DESPERATE THINGS TO KEEP US SAFE IN THOSE EARLY DAYS. THINGS I KNOW STILL HAUNT HIM.

...I DON'T KNOW WHAT HE DID WITH HIS GUN. I NEVER USED MINE. I KEPT IT HIDDEN AWAY ALL THESE YEARS, NEVER REALLY THINKING ABOUT IT.

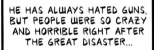

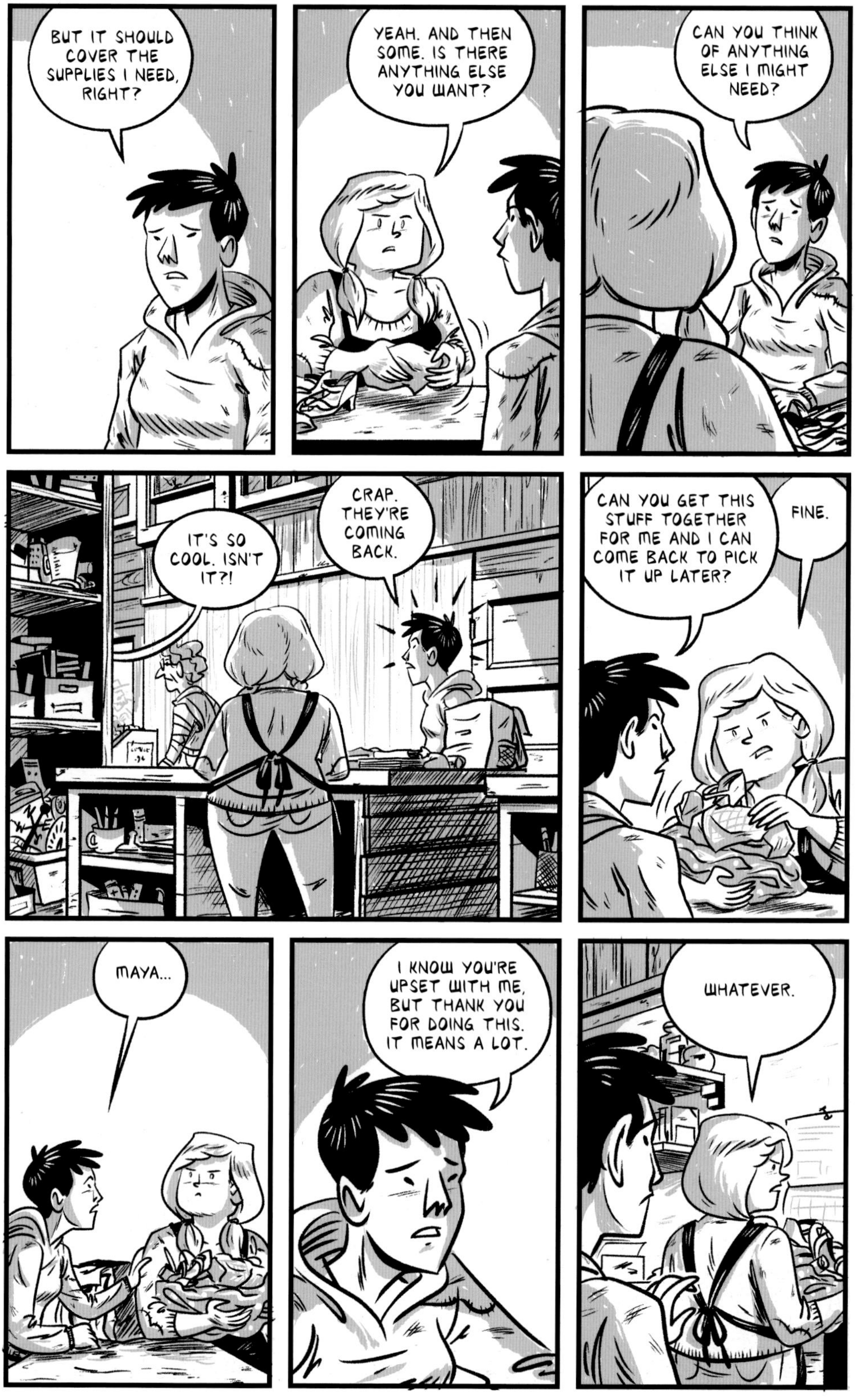
BUT IT SHOULD COVER THE SUPPLIES I NEED, RIGHT?
YEAH. AND THEN SOME. IS THERE ANYTHING ELSE YOU WANT?
CAN YOU THINK OF ANYTHING ELSE I MIGHT NEED?
IT'S SO COOL. ISN'T IT?!
CRAP. THEY'RE COMING BACK.
CAN YOU GET THIS STUFF TOGETHER FOR ME AND I CAN COME BACK TO PICK IT UP LATER?
FINE.
MAYA...
I KNOW YOU'RE UPSET WITH ME, BUT THANK YOU FOR DOING THIS. IT MEANS A LOT.
WHATEVER.

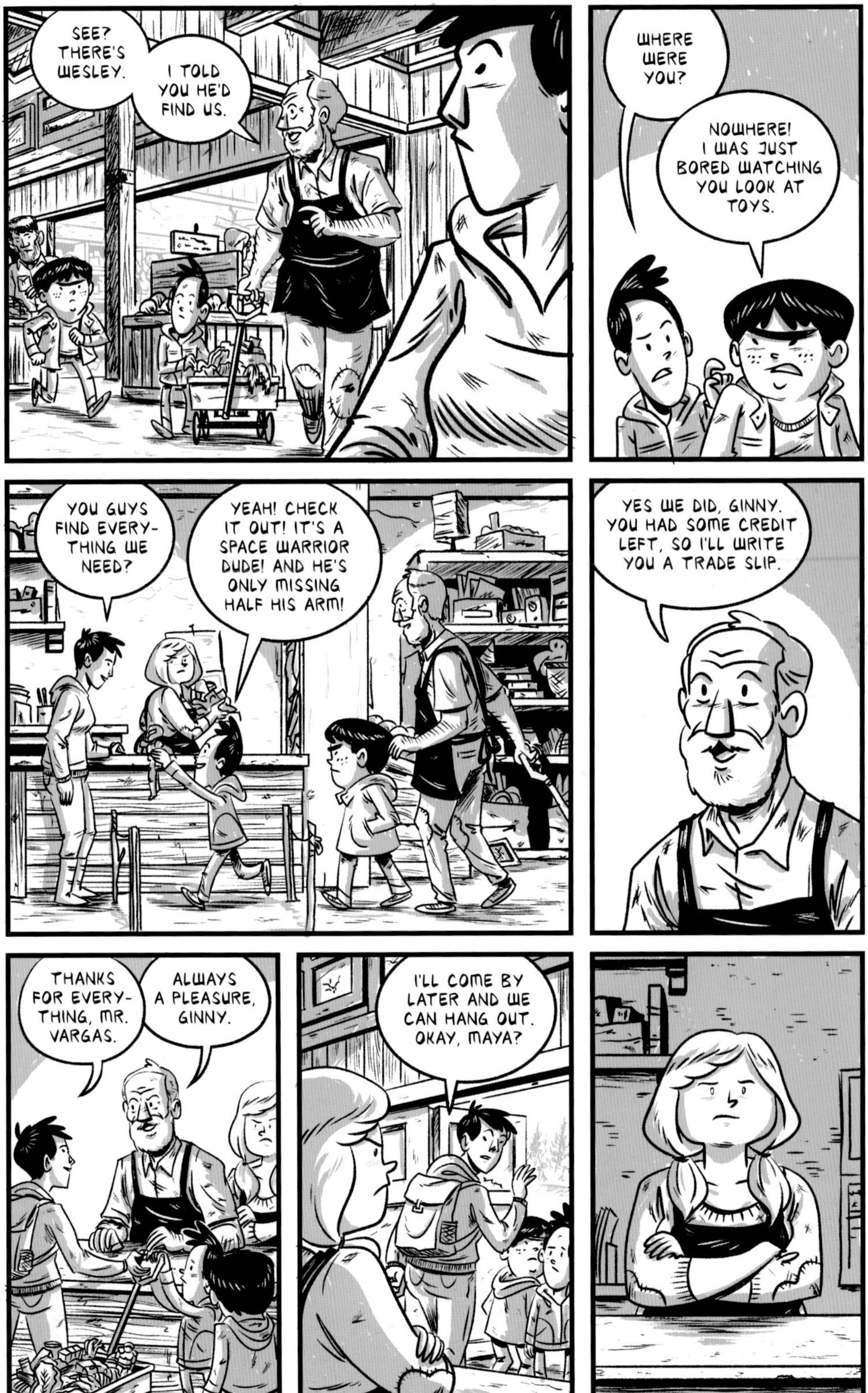
SEE? THERE'S WESLEY.
I TOLD YOU HE'D FIND US.
WHERE WERE YOU?
NOWHERE! I WAS JUST BORED WATCHING YOU LOOK AT TOYS.
YOU GUYS FIND EVERY-THING WE NEED?
YEAH! CHECK IT OUT! IT'S A SPACE WARRIOR DUDE! AND HE'S ONLY MISSING HALF HIS ARM!
YES WE DID, GINNY. YOU HAD SOME CREDIT LEFT, SO I'LL WRITE YOU A TRADE SLIP.
THANKS FOR EVERY-THING, MR. VARGAS.
ALWAYS A PLEASURE, GINNY.
I'LL COME BY LATER AND WE CAN HANG OUT. OKAY, MAYA?

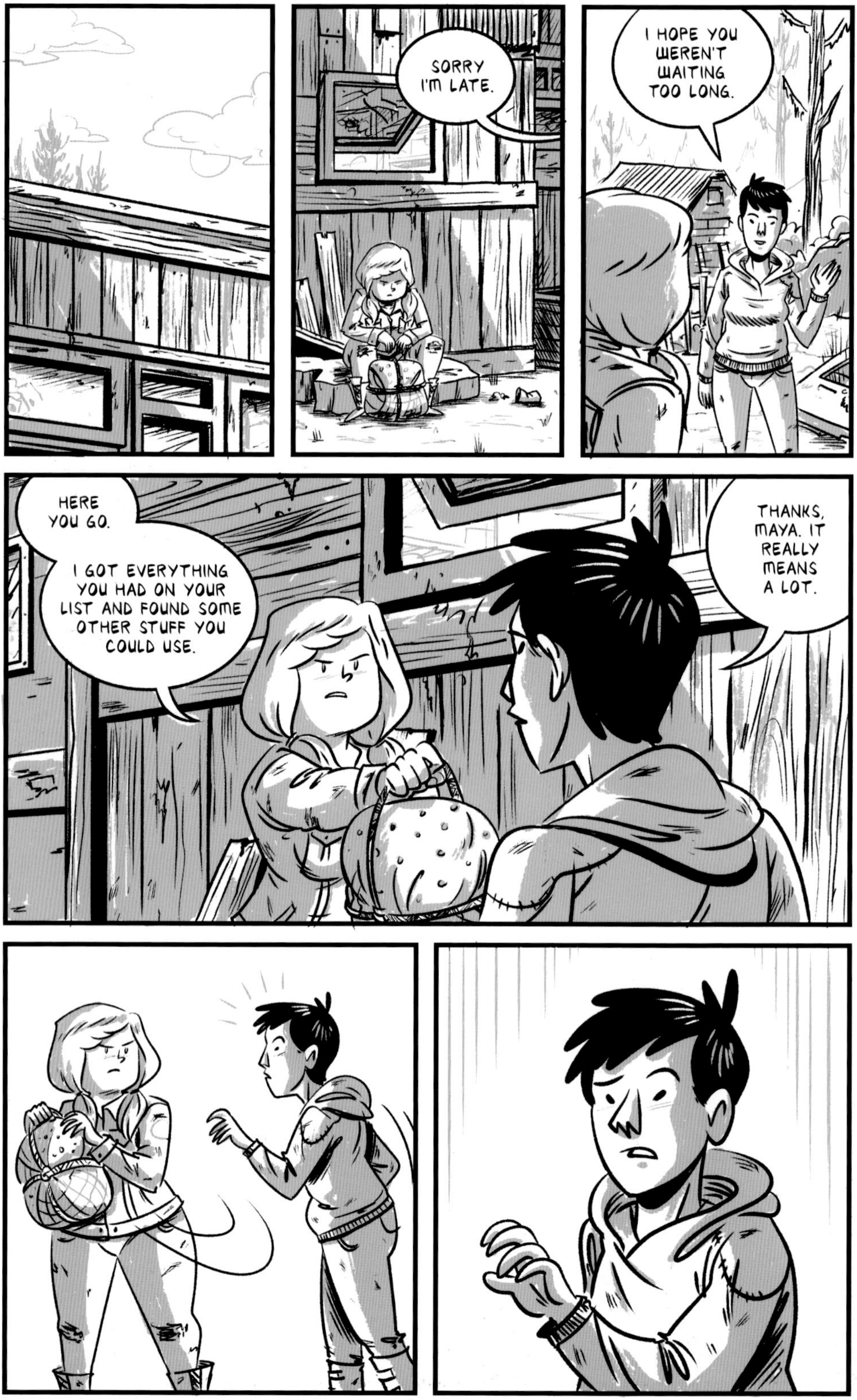
SORRY I'M LATE.
I HOPE YOU WEREN'T WAITING TOO LONG.
HERE YOU GO.
I GOT EVERYTHING YOU HAD ON YOUR LIST AND FOUND SOME OTHER STUFF YOU COULD USE.
THANKS, MAYA. IT REALLY MEANS A LOT.

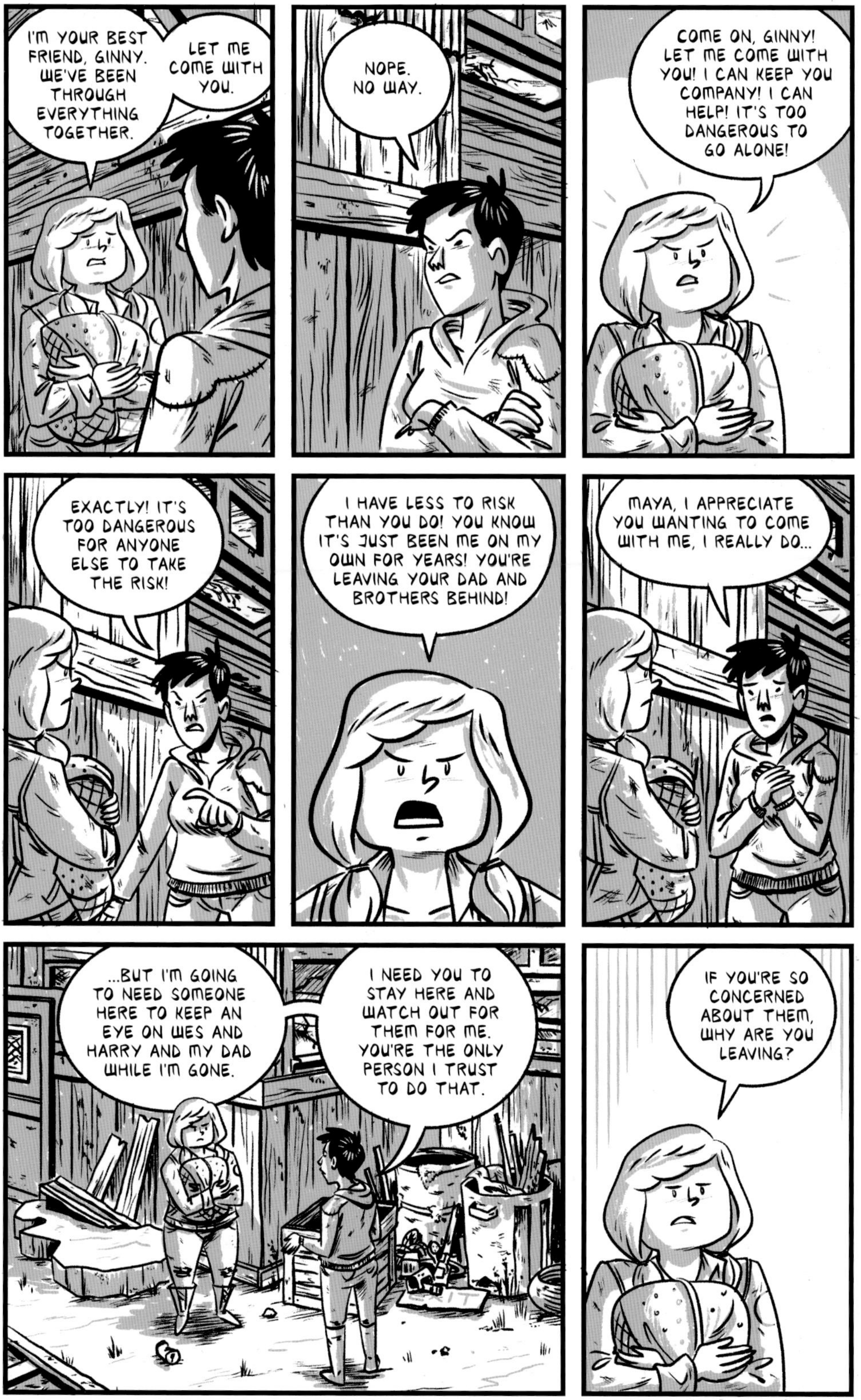
I'M YOUR BEST FRIEND, GINNY. WE'VE BEEN THROUGH EVERYTHING TOGETHER.
LET ME COME WITH YOU.
NOPE. NO WAY.
COME ON, GINNY! LET ME COME WITH YOU! I CAN KEEP YOU COMPANY! I CAN HELP! IT'S TOO DANGEROUS TO GO ALONE!
EXACTLY! IT'S TOO DANGEROUS FOR ANYONE ELSE TO TAKE THE RISK!
I HAVE LESS TO RISK THAN YOU DO! YOU KNOW IT'S JUST BEEN ME ON MY OWN FOR YEARS! YOU'RE LEAVING YOUR DAD AND BROTHERS BEHIND!
MAYA, I APPRECIATE YOU WANTING TO COME WITH ME, I REALLY DO...
...BUT I'M GOING TO NEED SOMEONE HERE TO KEEP AN EYE ON WES AND HARRY AND MY DAD WHILE I'M GONE.
I NEED YOU TO STAY HERE AND WATCH OUT FOR THEM FOR ME. YOU'RE THE ONLY PERSON I TRUST TO DO THAT.
IF YOU'RE SO CONCERNED ABOUT THEM, WHY ARE YOU LEAVING?

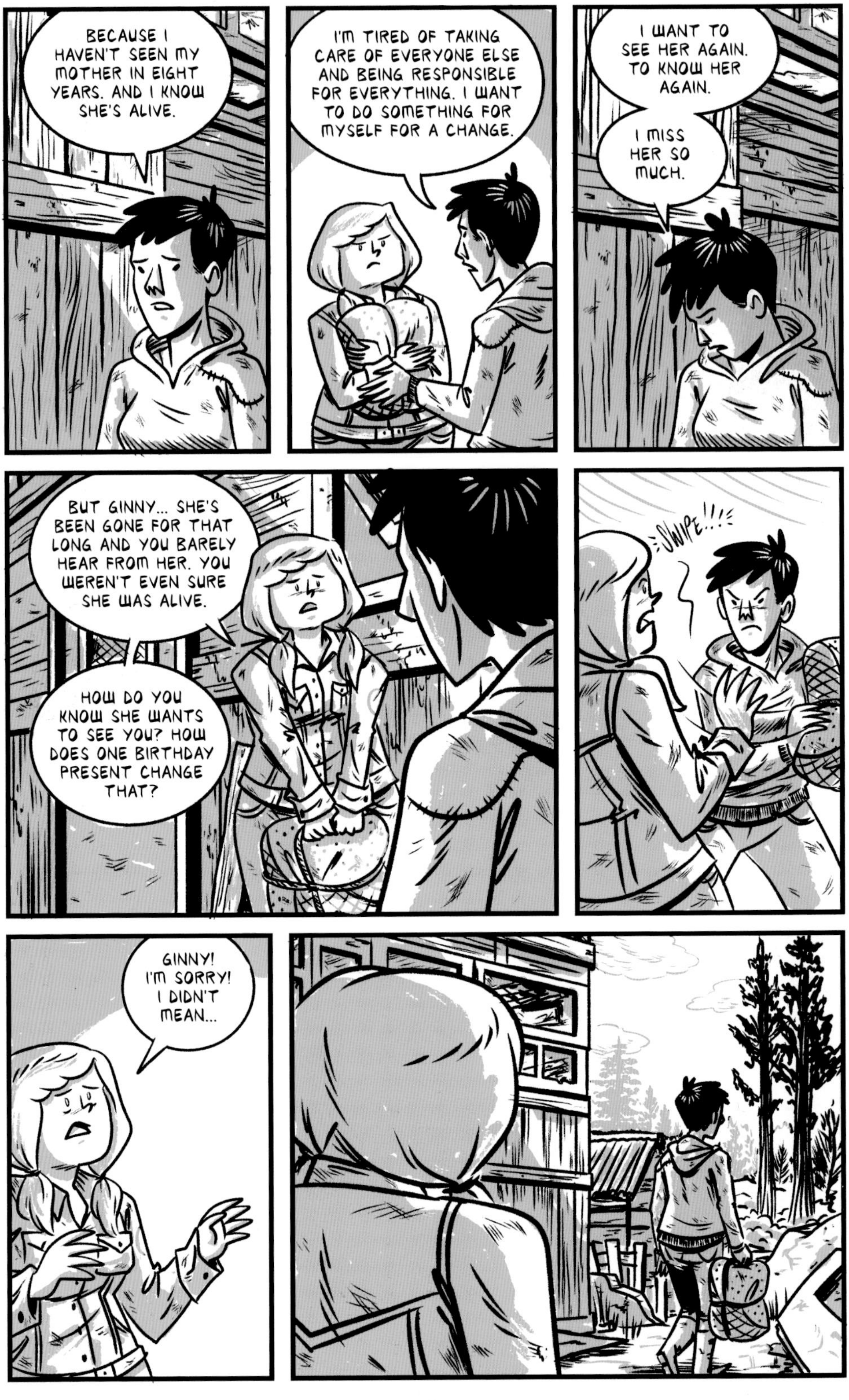
BECAUSE I HAVEN'T SEEN MY MOTHER IN EIGHT YEARS. AND I KNOW SHE'S ALIVE.
I'M TIRED OF TAKING CARE OF EVERYONE ELSE AND BEING RESPONSIBLE FOR EVERYTHING. I WANT TO DO SOMETHING FOR MYSELF FOR A CHANGE.
I WANT TO SEE HER AGAIN. TO KNOW HER AGAIN.
I MISS HER SO MUCH.
BUT GINNY... SHE'S BEEN GONE FOR THAT LONG AND YOU BARELY HEAR FROM HER. YOU WEREN'T EVEN SURE SHE WAS ALIVE.
HOW DO YOU KNOW SHE WANTS TO SEE YOU? HOW DOES ONE BIRTHDAY PRESENT CHANGE THAT?
SWIPE!!!
GINNY! I'M SORRY! I DIDN'T MEAN...

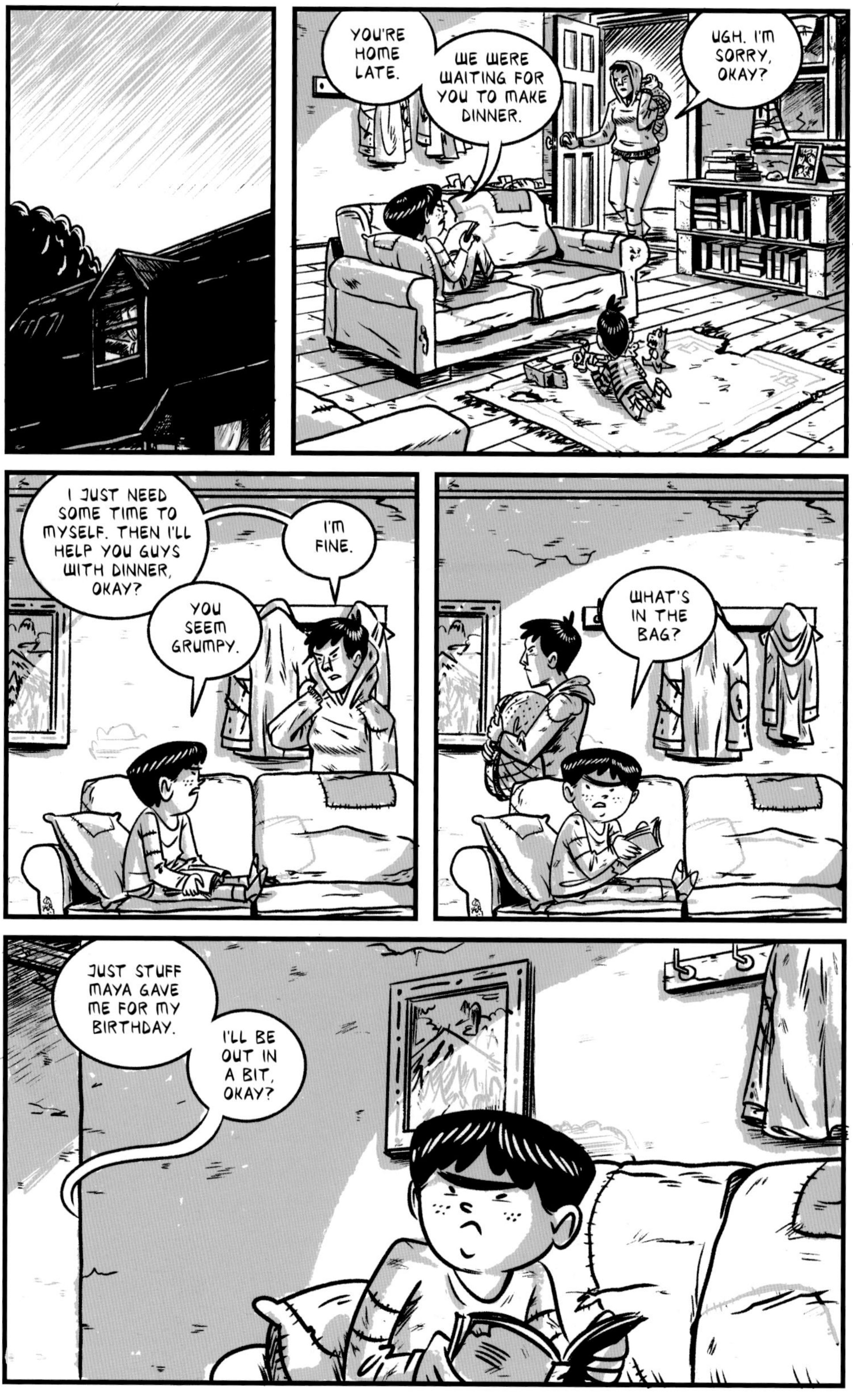
YOU'RE HOME LATE.
WE WERE WAITING FOR YOU TO MAKE DINNER.
UGH. I'M SORRY, OKAY?
I'M FINE.
I JUST NEED SOME TIME TO MYSELF. THEN I'LL HELP YOU GUYS WITH DINNER, OKAY?
YOU SEEM GRUMPY.
WHAT'S IN THE BAG?
JUST STUFF MAYA GAVE ME FOR MY BIRTHDAY.
I'LL BE OUT IN A BIT, OKAY?

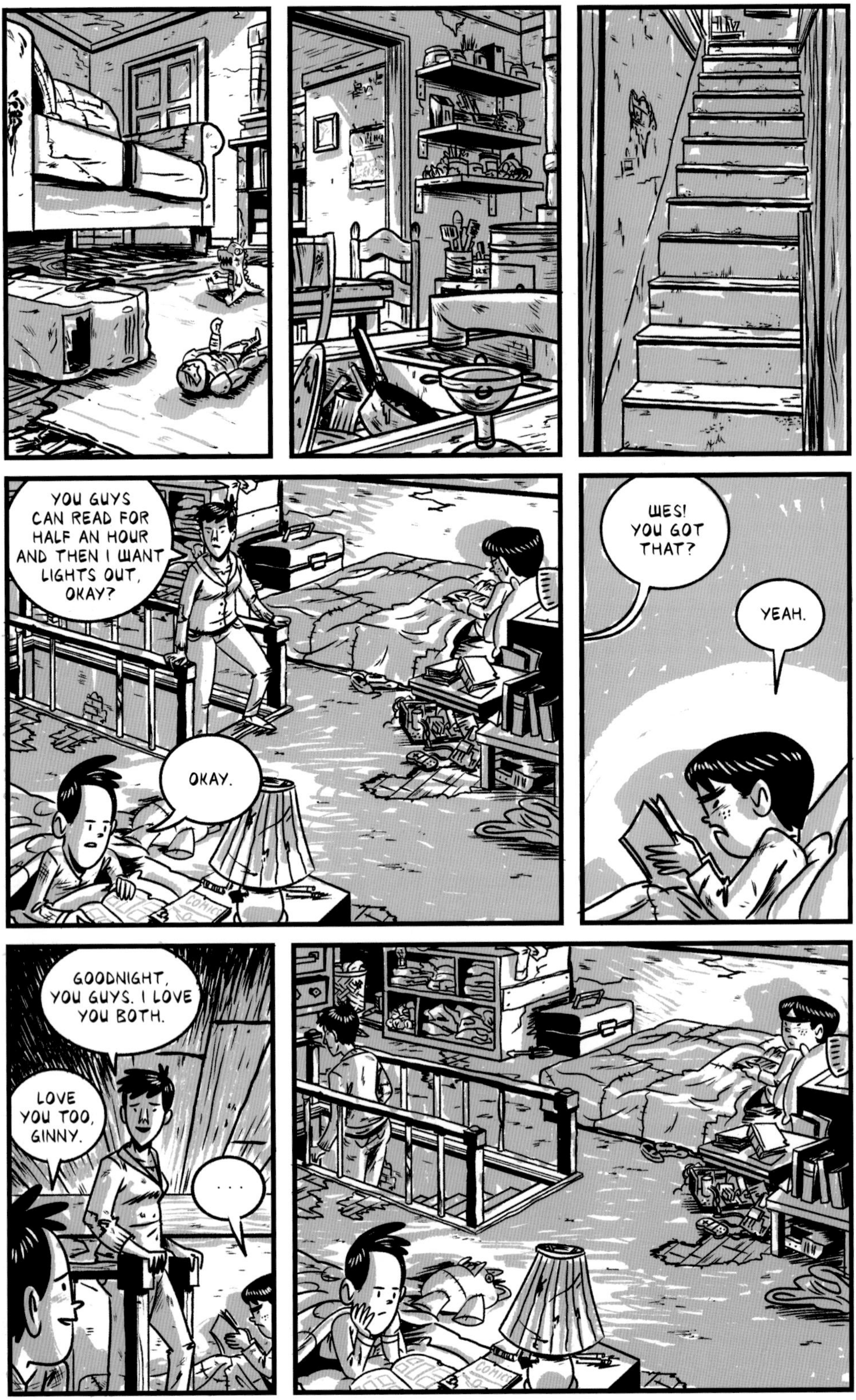
YOU GUYS CAN READ FOR HALF AN HOUR AND THEN I WANT LIGHTS OUT, OKAY?
OKAY.
WES! YOU GOT THAT?
YEAH.
GOODNIGHT, YOU GUYS. I LOVE YOU BOTH.
LOVE YOU TOO, GINNY.
. . .

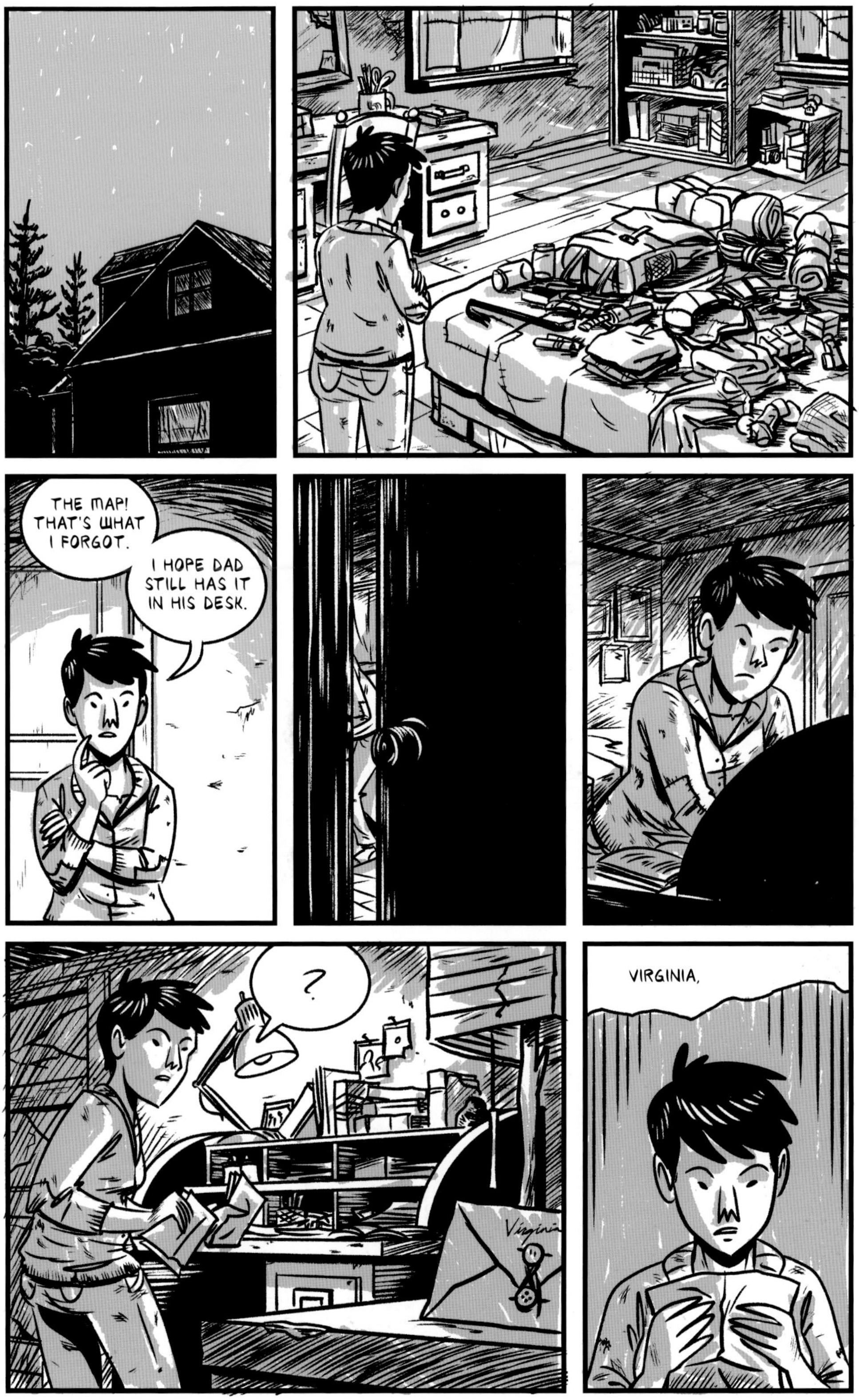
THE MAP! THAT'S WHAT I FORGOT.
I HOPE DAD STILL HAS IT IN HIS DESK.
?
Virginia
VIRGINIA,

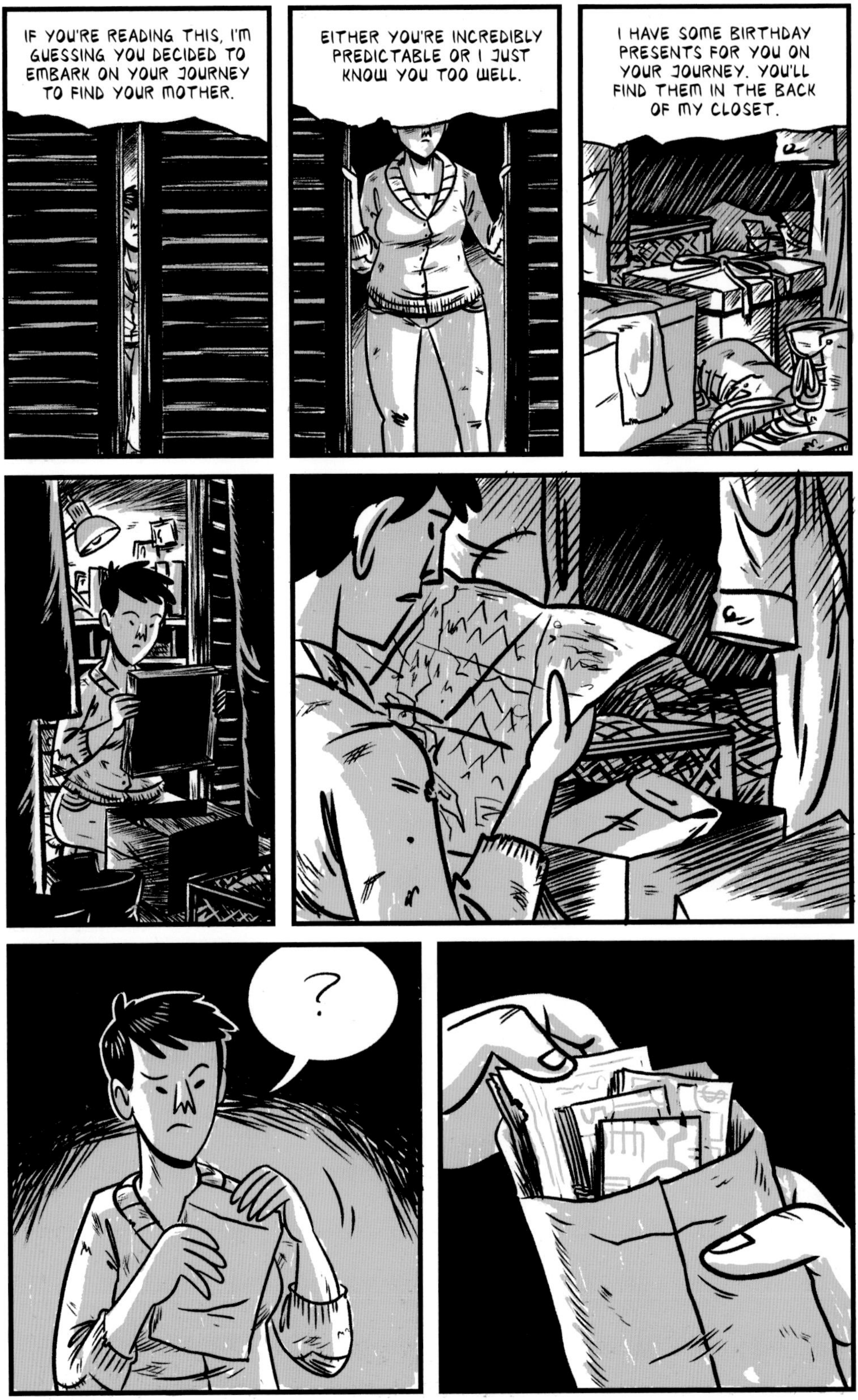
IF YOU'RE READING THIS, I'M GUESSING YOU DECIDED TO EMBARK ON YOUR JOURNEY TO FIND YOUR MOTHER.
EITHER YOU'RE INCREDIBLY PREDICTABLE OR I JUST KNOW YOU TOO WELL.
I HAVE SOME BIRTHDAY PRESENTS FOR YOU ON YOUR JOURNEY. YOU'LL FIND THEM IN THE BACK OF MY CLOSET.
?

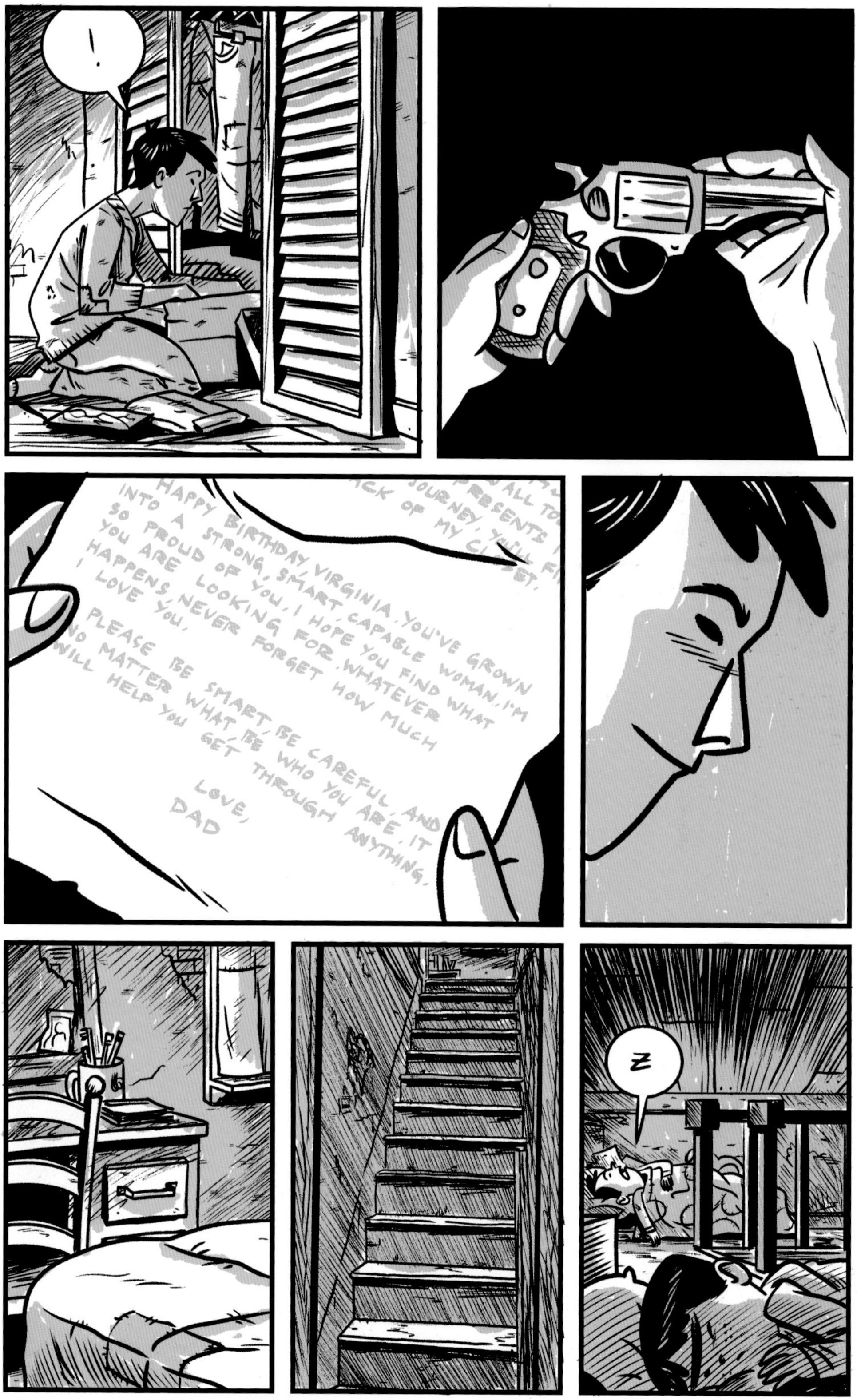

!
HAPPY BIRTHDAY, VIRGINIA. YOU'VE GROWN INTO A STRONG, SMART, CAPABLE WOMAN. I'M SO PROUD OF YOU. I HOPE YOU FIND WHAT YOU ARE LOOKING FOR. WHATEVER HAPPENS, NEVER FORGET HOW MUCH I LOVE YOU.
PLEASE BE SMART, BE CAREFUL, AND NO MATTER WHAT, BE WHO YOU ARE. IT WILL HELP YOU GET THROUGH ANYTHING.
LOVE,
DAD
Z

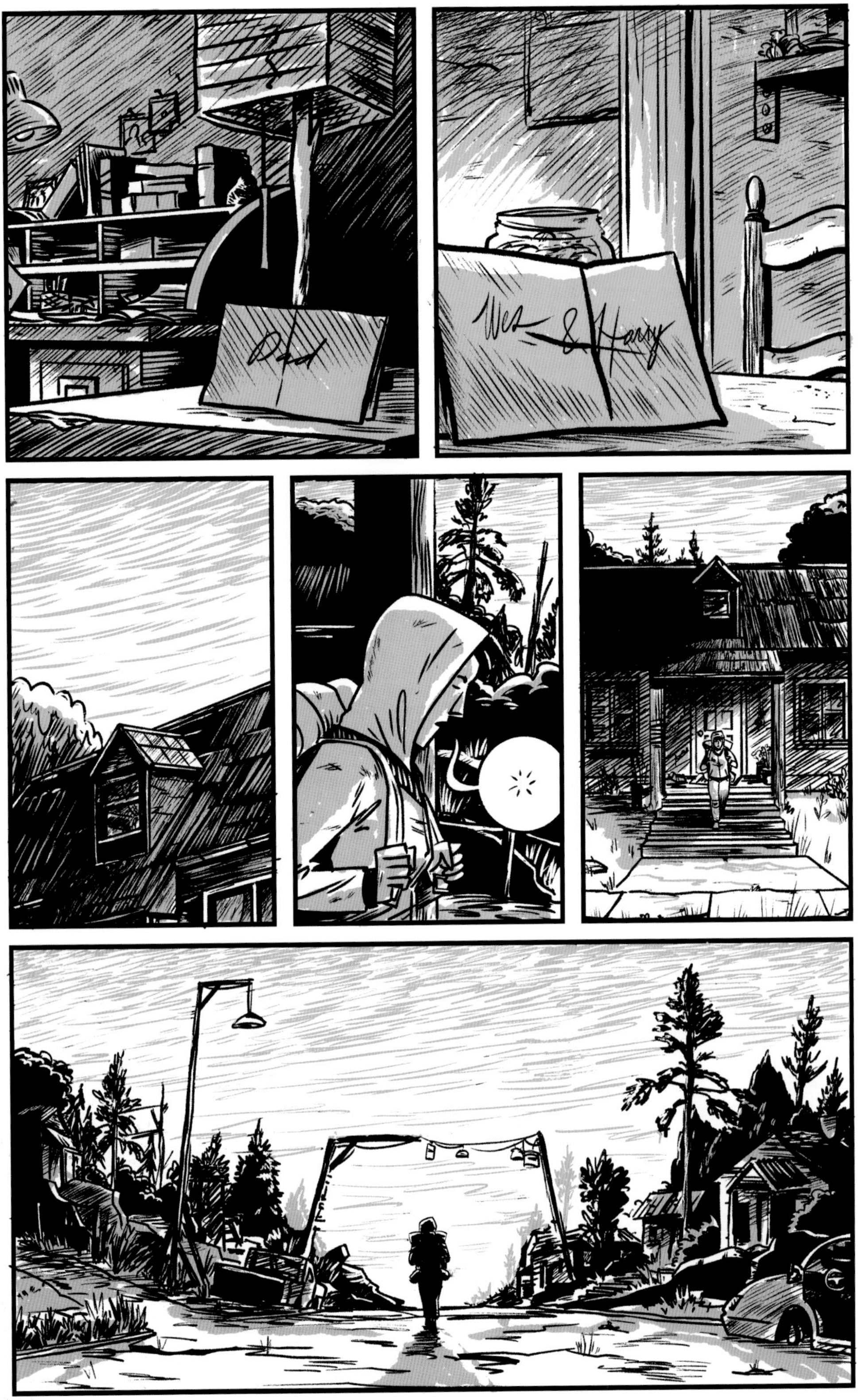
Dad
Wes & Harry

CHAPTER 3

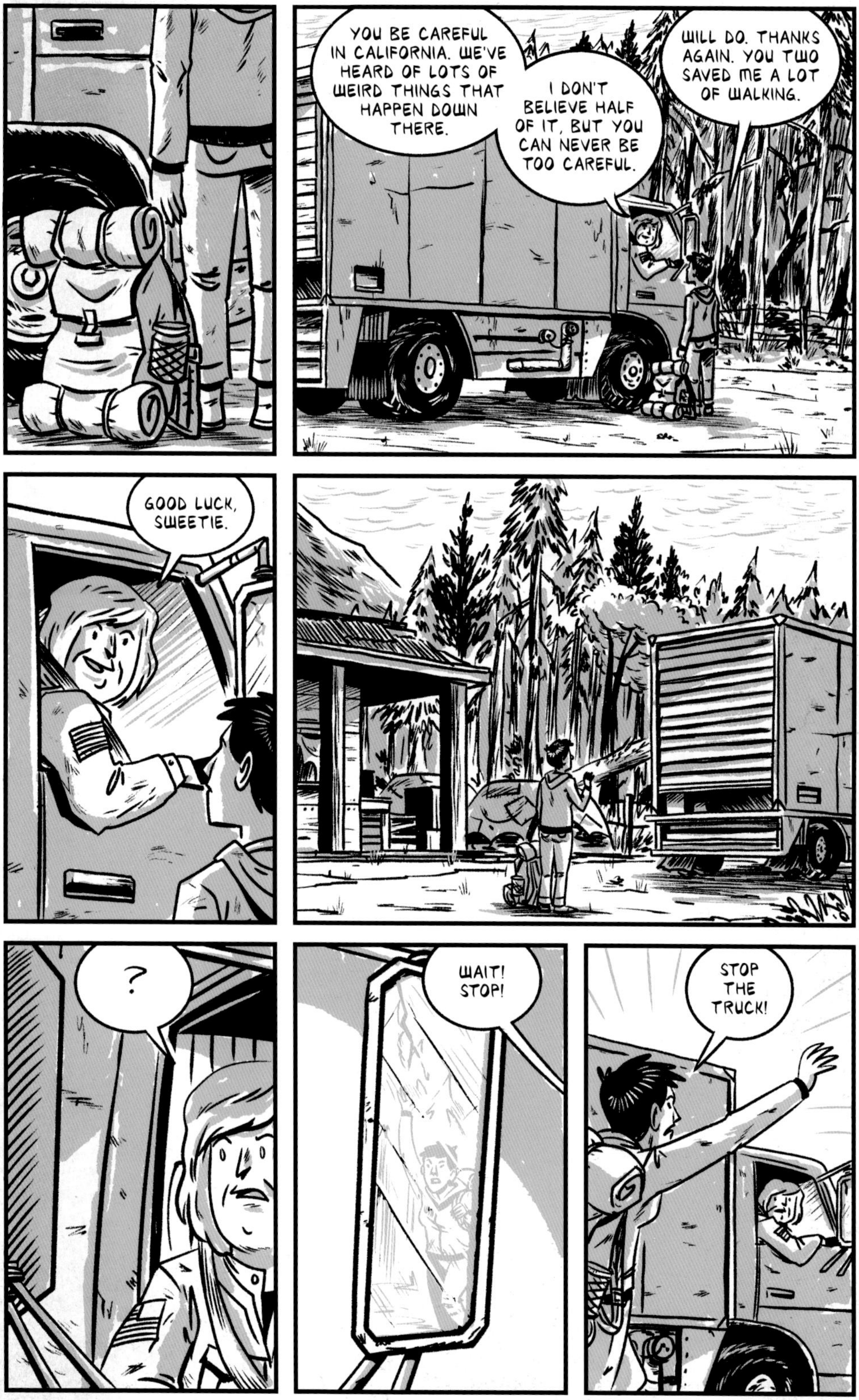
YOU BE CAREFUL IN CALIFORNIA. WE'VE HEARD OF LOTS OF WEIRD THINGS THAT HAPPEN DOWN THERE.
I DON'T BELIEVE HALF OF IT, BUT YOU CAN NEVER BE TOO CAREFUL.
WILL DO. THANKS AGAIN. YOU TWO SAVED ME A LOT OF WALKING.
GOOD LUCK, SWEETIE.
?
WAIT! STOP!
STOP THE TRUCK!

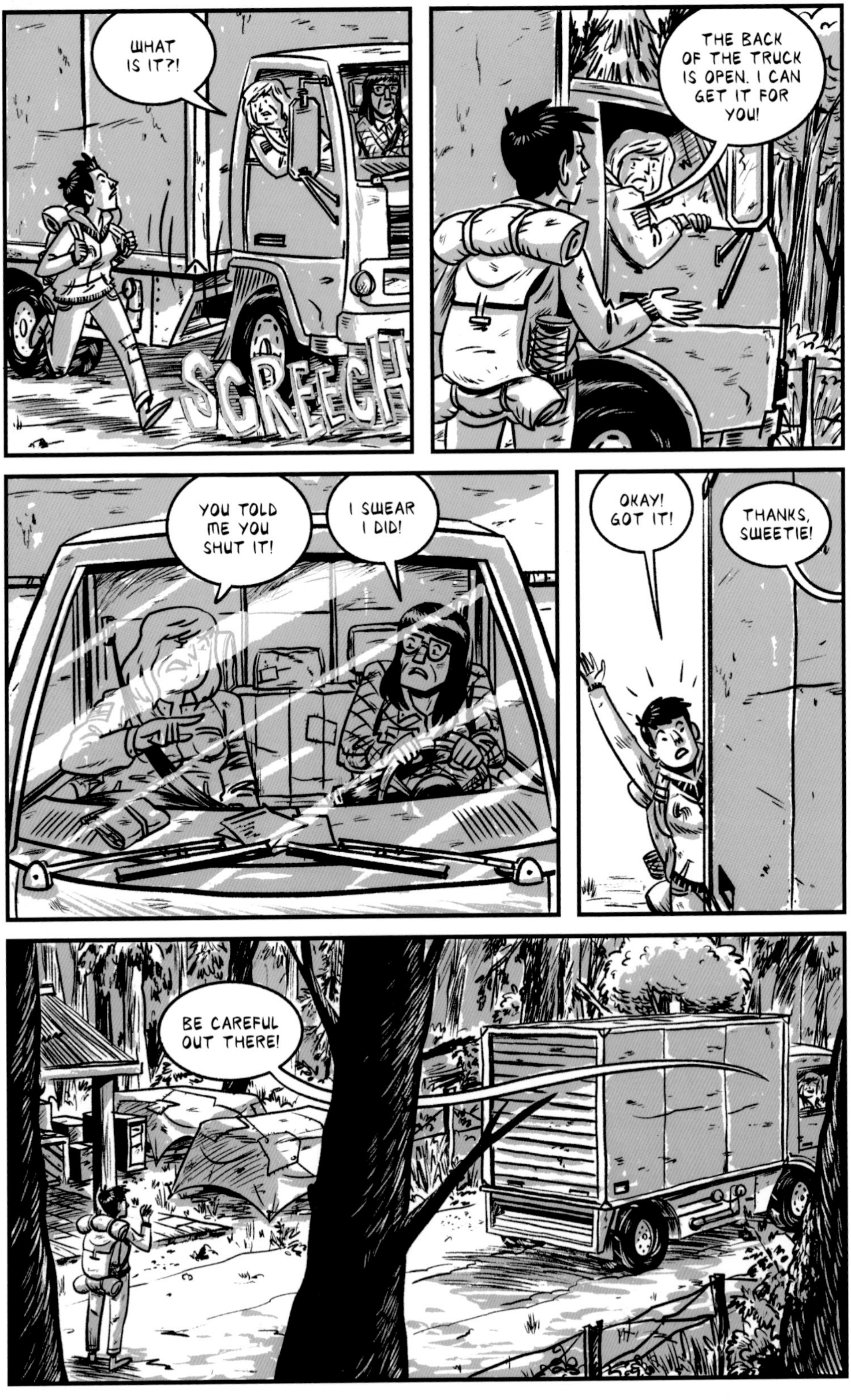
WHAT IS IT?!
SCREECH
THE BACK OF THE TRUCK IS OPEN. I CAN GET IT FOR YOU!
YOU TOLD ME YOU SHUT IT!
I SWEAR I DID!
OKAY! GOT IT!
THANKS, SWEETIE!
BE CAREFUL OUT THERE!

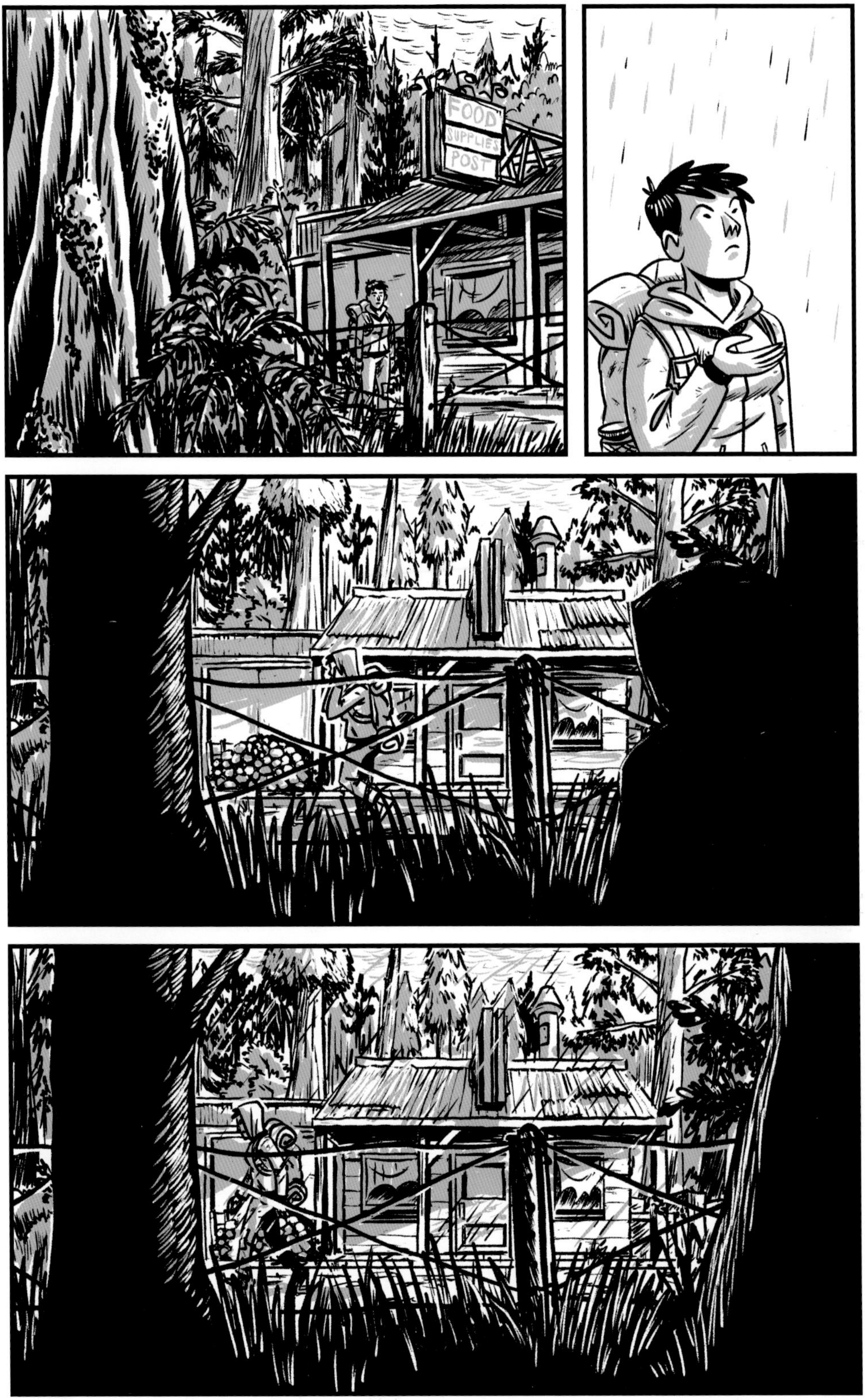
FOOD
SUPPLIES
POST

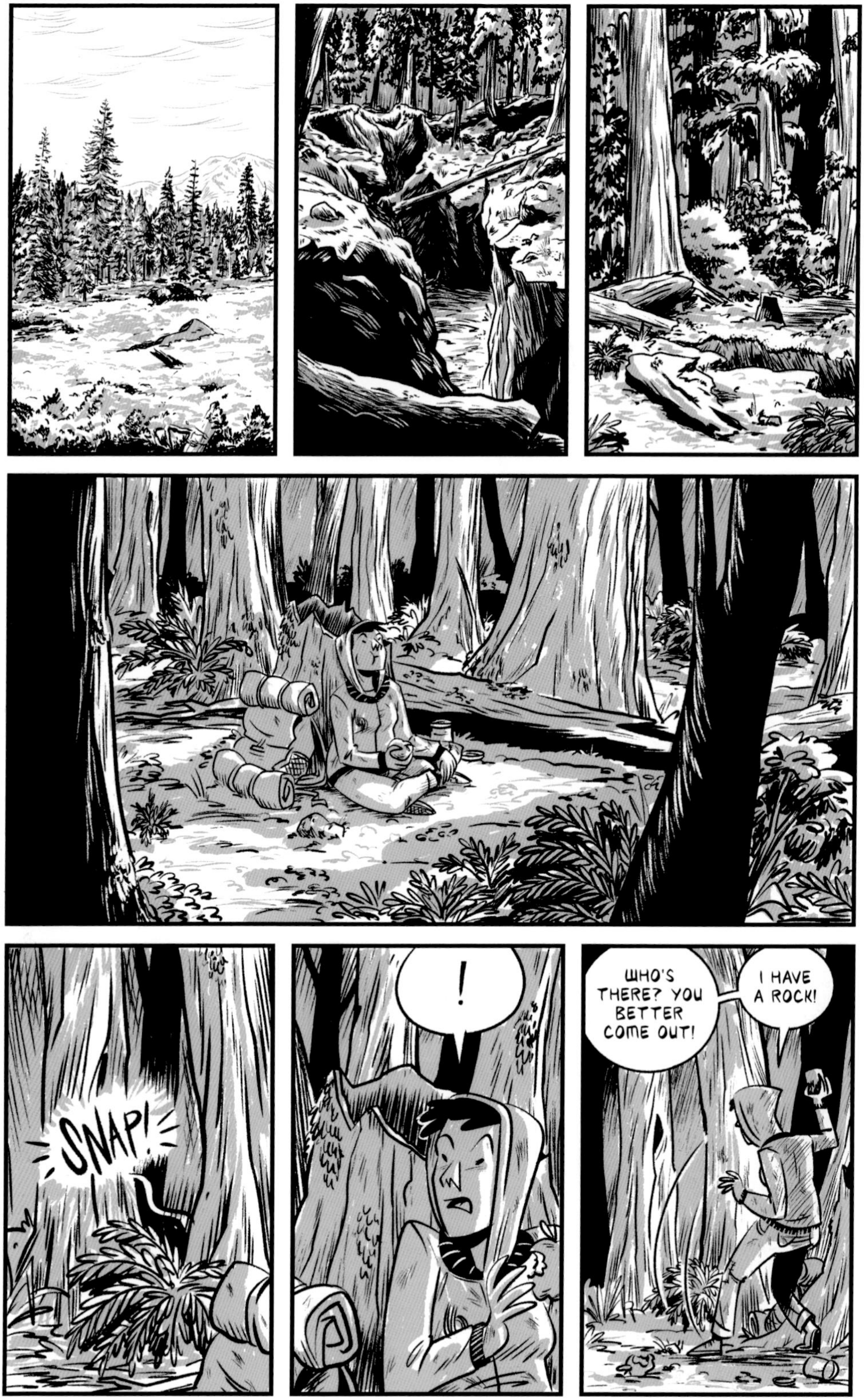
SNAP!
!
WHO'S THERE? YOU BETTER COME OUT!
I HAVE A ROCK!

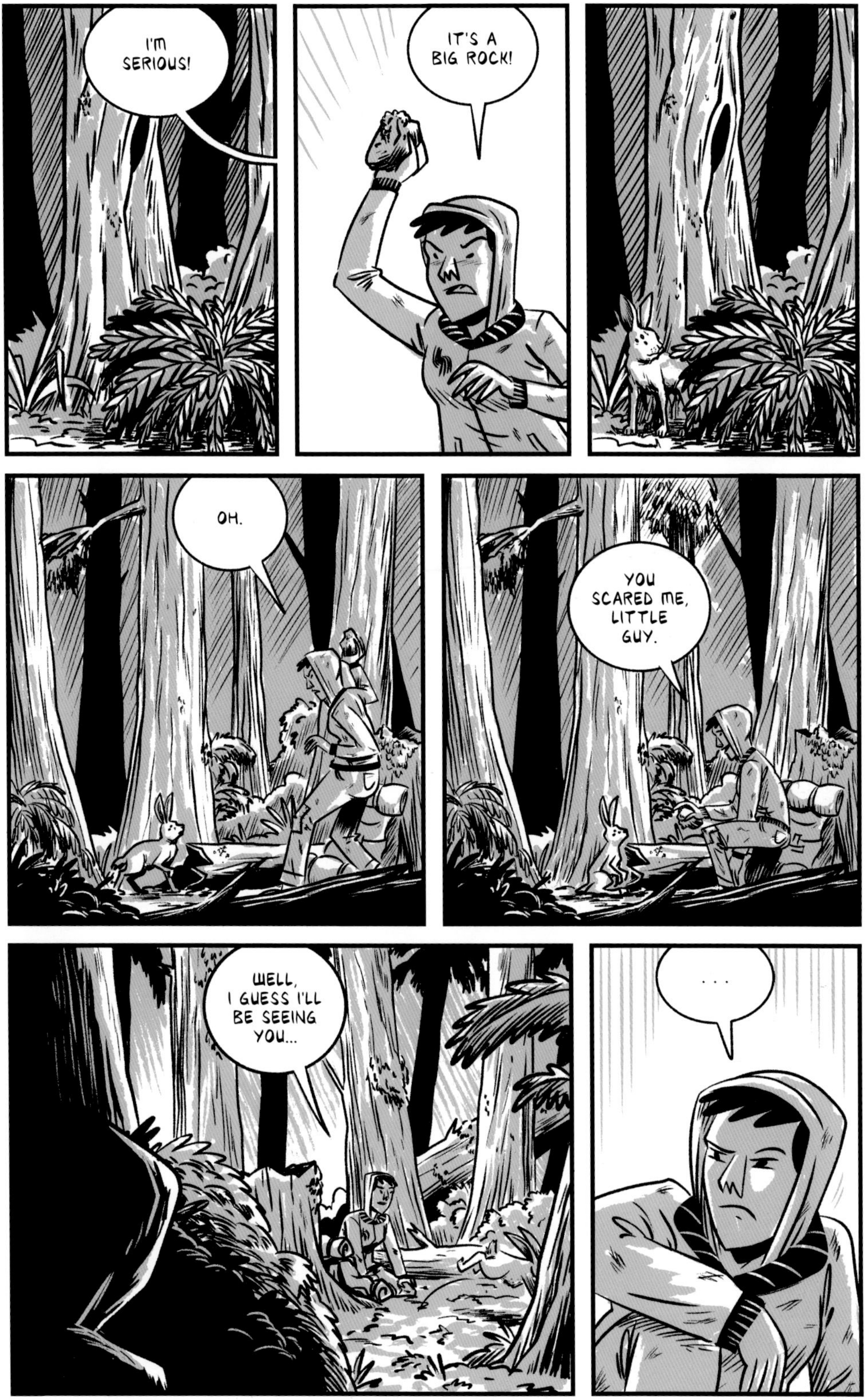
I'M SERIOUS!
IT'S A BIG ROCK!
OH.
YOU SCARED ME, LITTLE GUY.
WELL, I GUESS I'LL BE SEEING YOU...
. . .

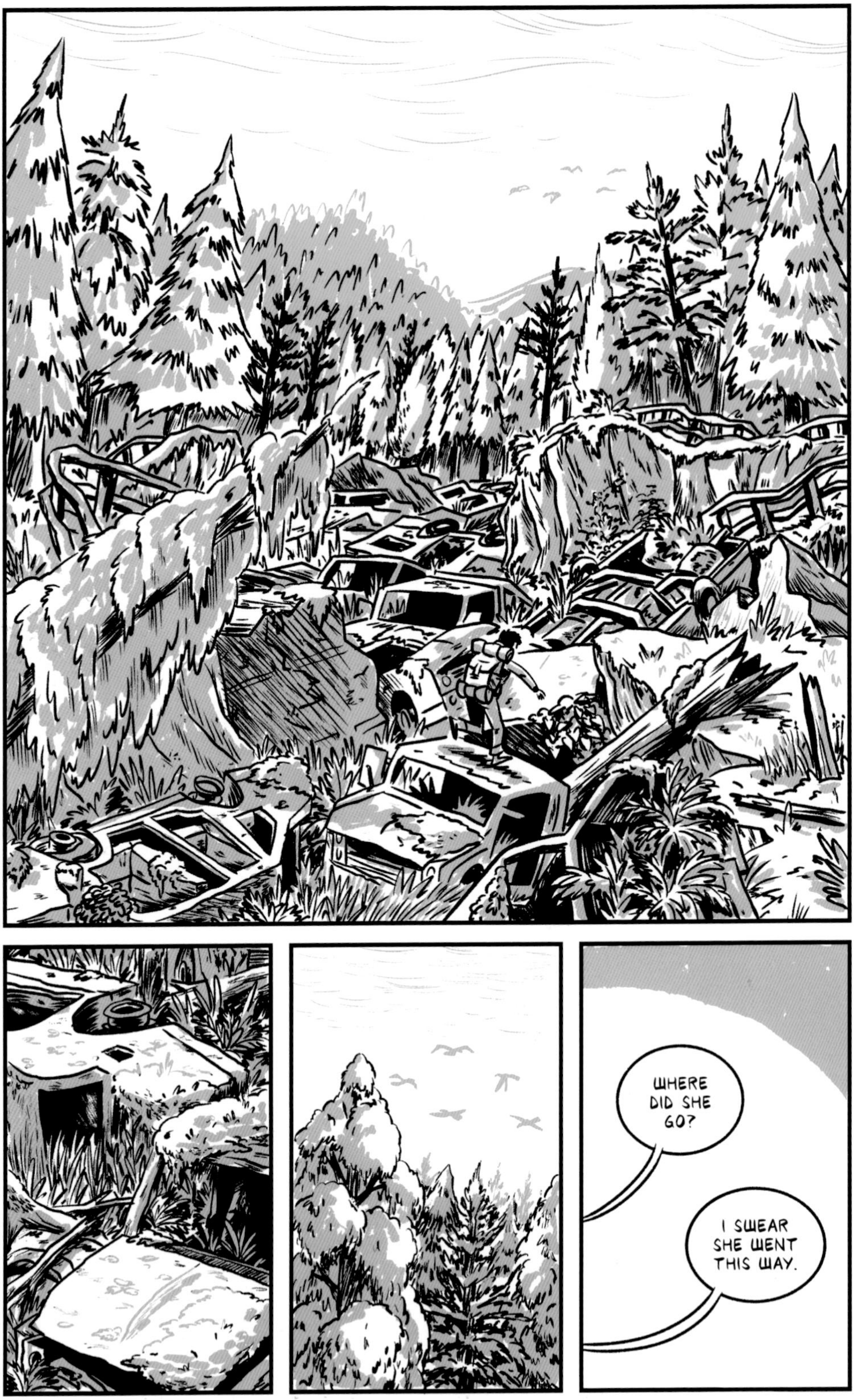
WHERE DID SHE GO?
I SWEAR SHE WENT THIS WAY.

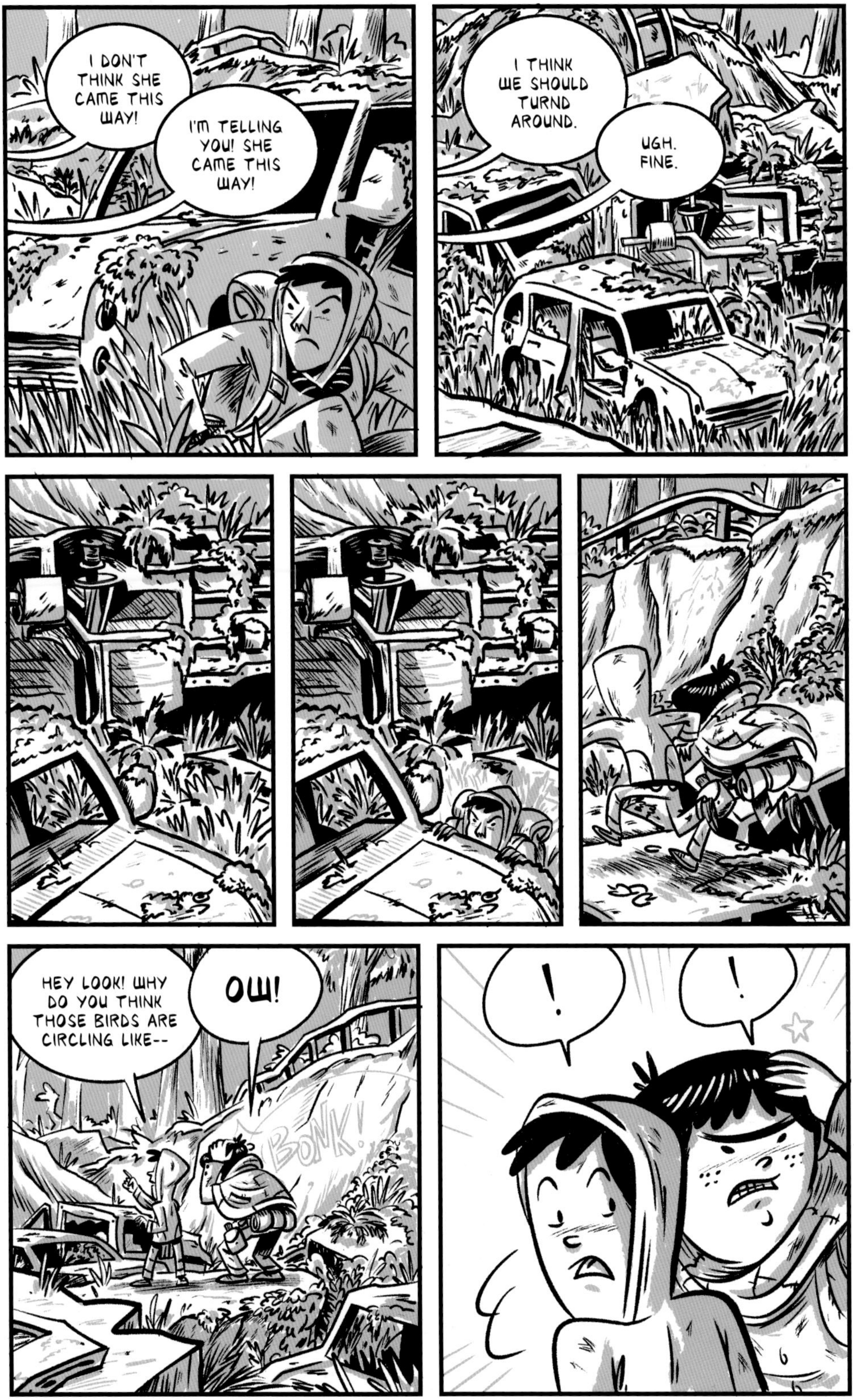
I DON'T THINK SHE CAME THIS WAY!
I'M TELLING YOU! SHE CAME THIS WAY!
I THINK WE SHOULD TURND AROUND.
UGH. FINE.
HEY LOOK! WHY DO YOU THINK THOSE BIRDS ARE CIRCLING LIKE--
OW!
BONK!
!
!

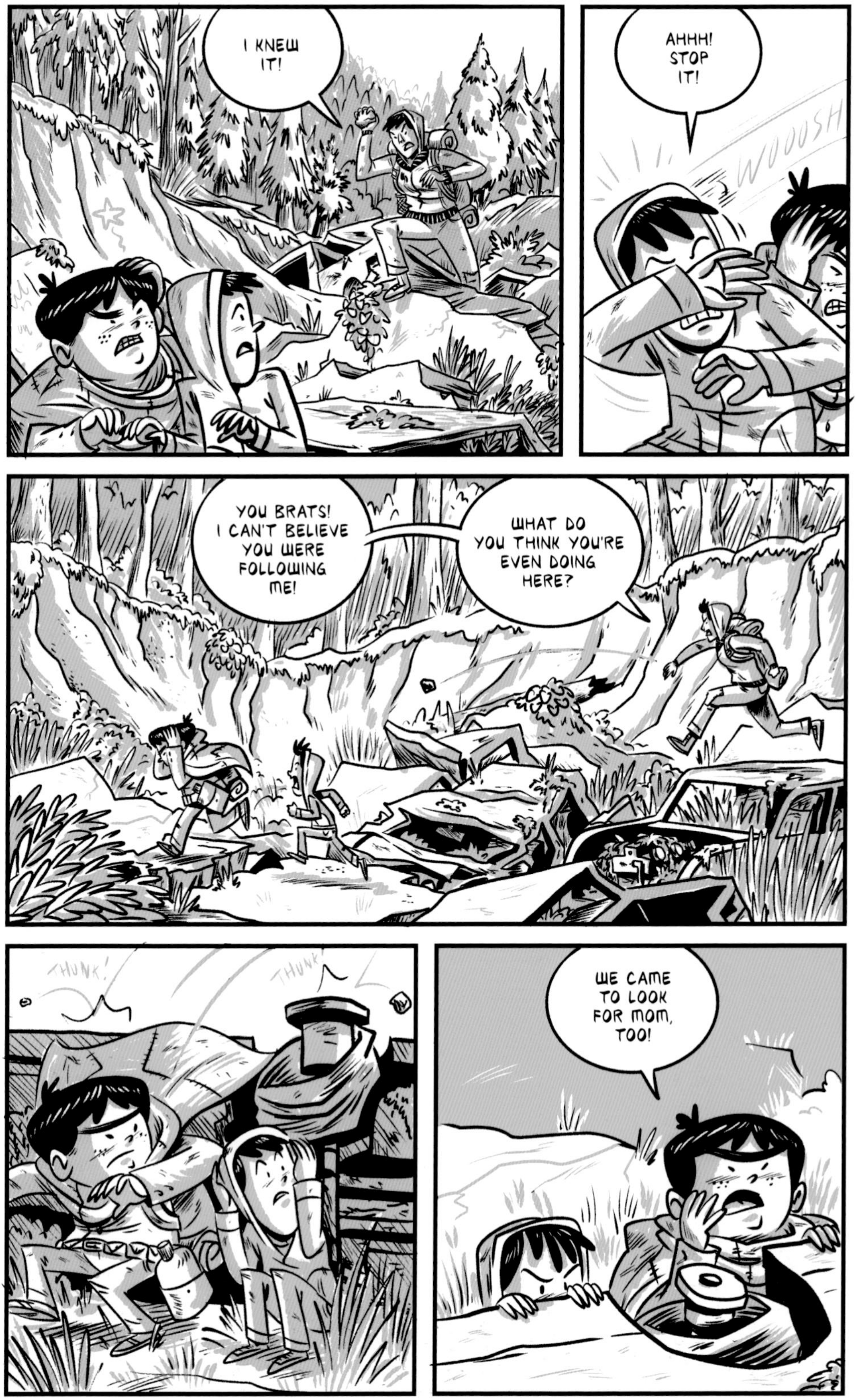
I KNEW IT!
AHHH! STOP IT!
WOOOSH
YOU BRATS! I CAN'T BELIEVE YOU WERE FOLLOWING ME!
WHAT DO YOU THINK YOU'RE EVEN DOING HERE?
THUNK!
THUNK!
WE CAME TO LOOK FOR MOM, TOO!

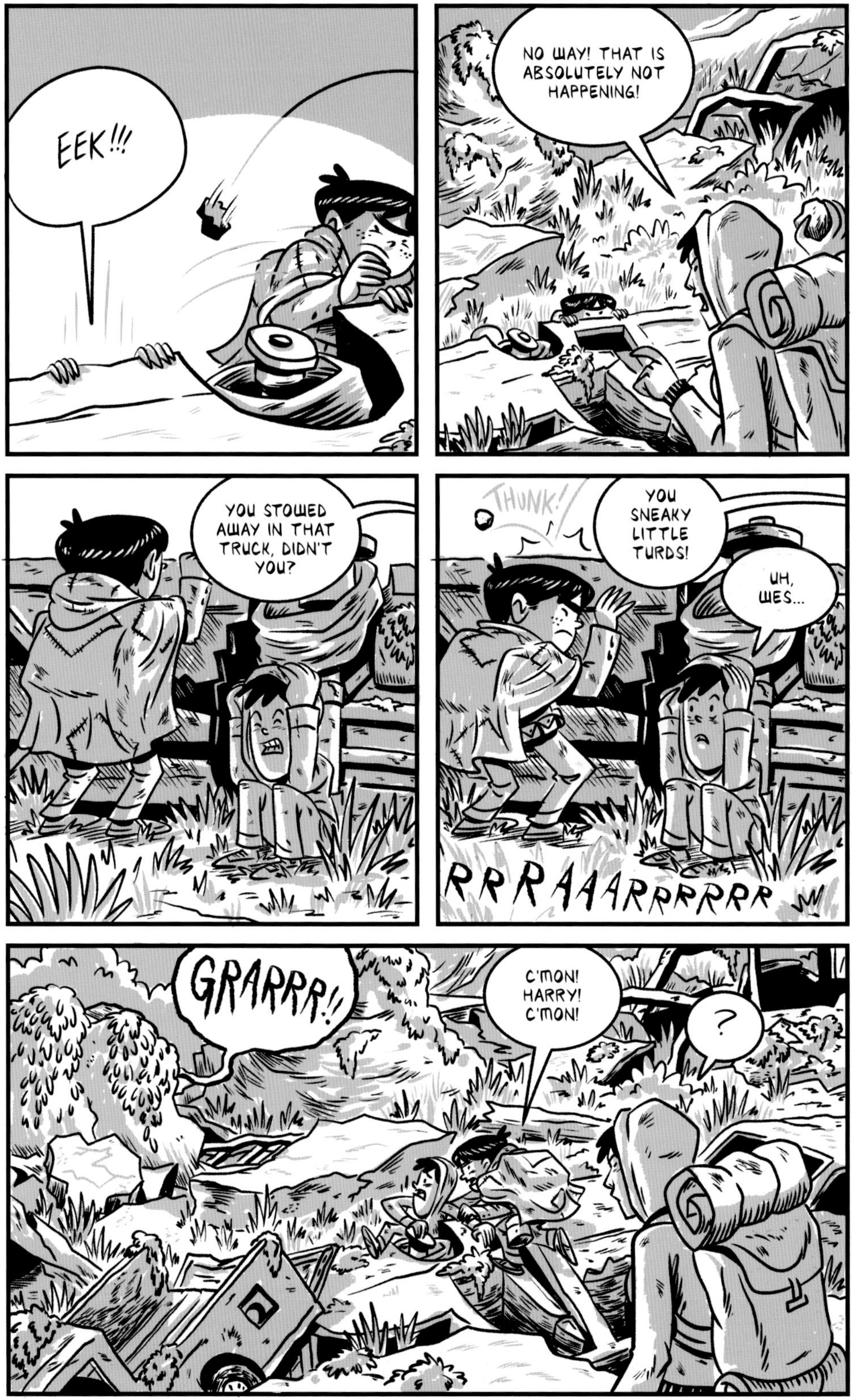
EEK!!!
NO WAY! THAT IS ABSOLUTELY NOT HAPPENING!
YOU STOWED AWAY IN THAT TRUCK, DIDN'T YOU?
THUNK!
YOU SNEAKY LITTLE TURDS!
UH, WES...
RRRAAARRRRRR
GRARRR!!
C'MON! HARRY! C'MON!
?

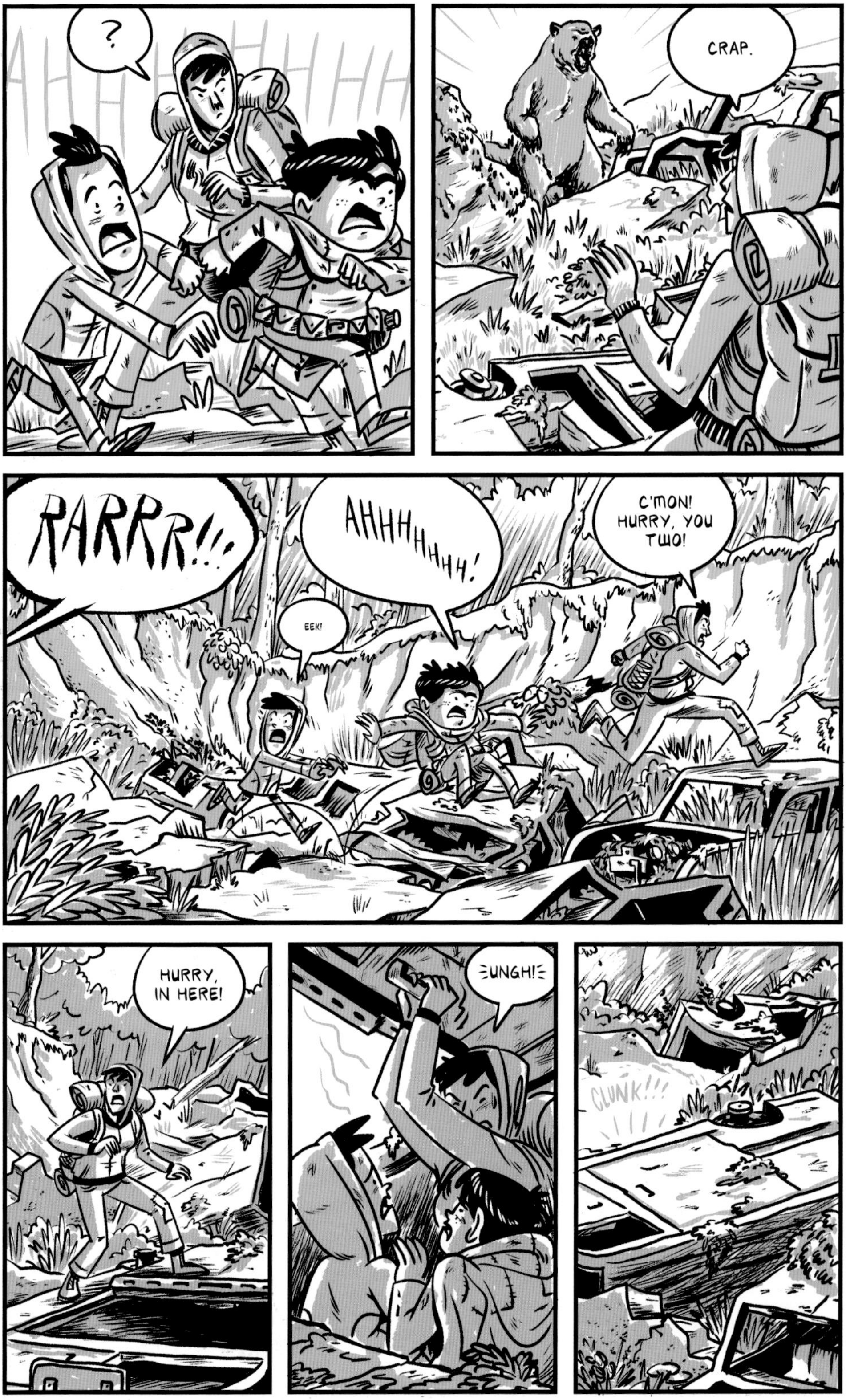
?
CRAP.
RARRR!!!
EEK!
AHHHHHHH!
C'MON! HURRY, YOU TWO!
HURRY, IN HERE!
UNGH!
CLUNK!!!

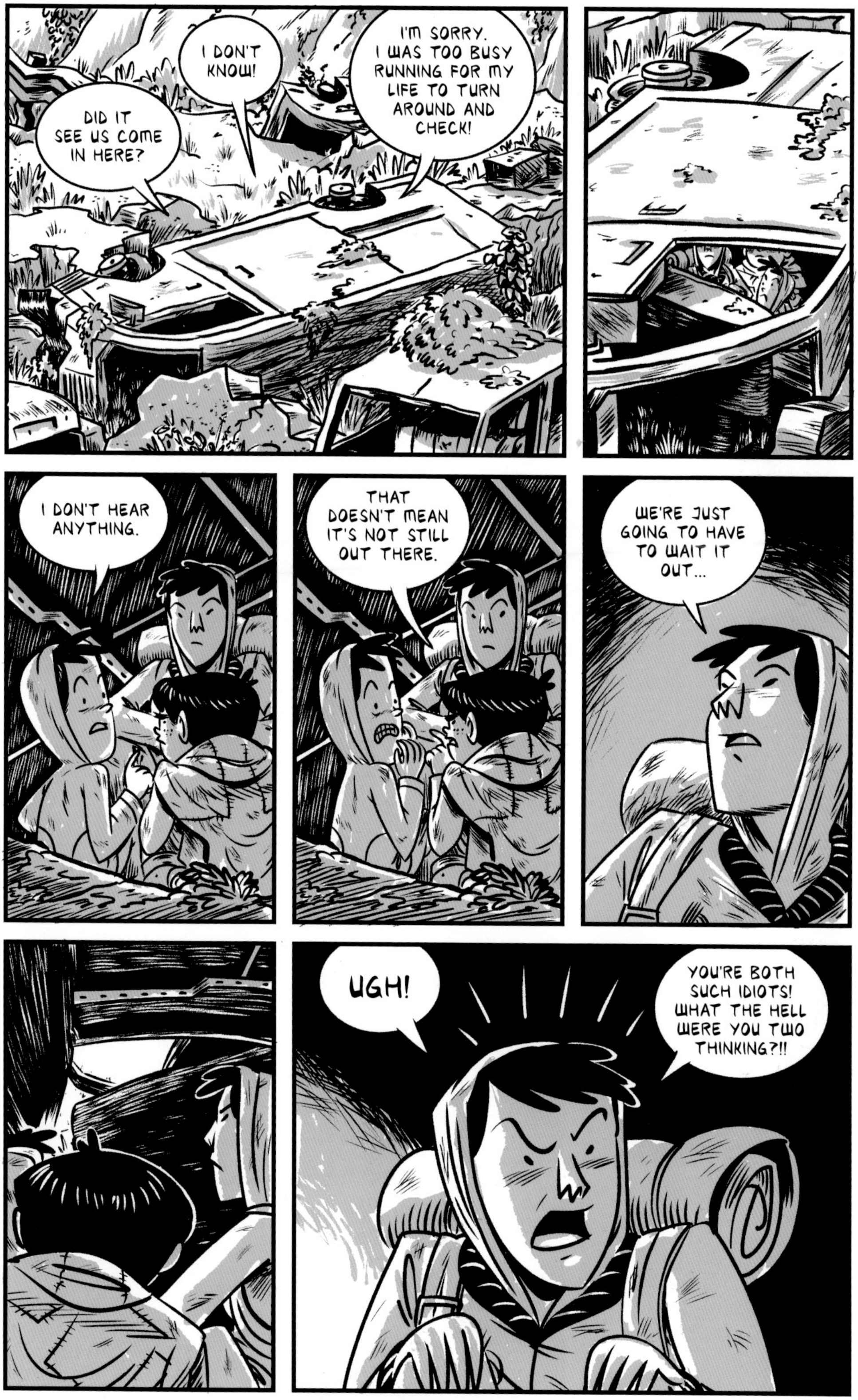
DID IT SEE US COME IN HERE?
I DON'T KNOW!
I'M SORRY. I WAS TOO BUSY RUNNING FOR MY LIFE TO TURN AROUND AND CHECK!
I DON'T HEAR ANYTHING.
THAT DOESN'T MEAN IT'S NOT STILL OUT THERE.
WE'RE JUST GOING TO HAVE TO WAIT IT OUT...
UGH!
YOU'RE BOTH SUCH IDIOTS! WHAT THE HELL WERE YOU TWO THINKING?!!

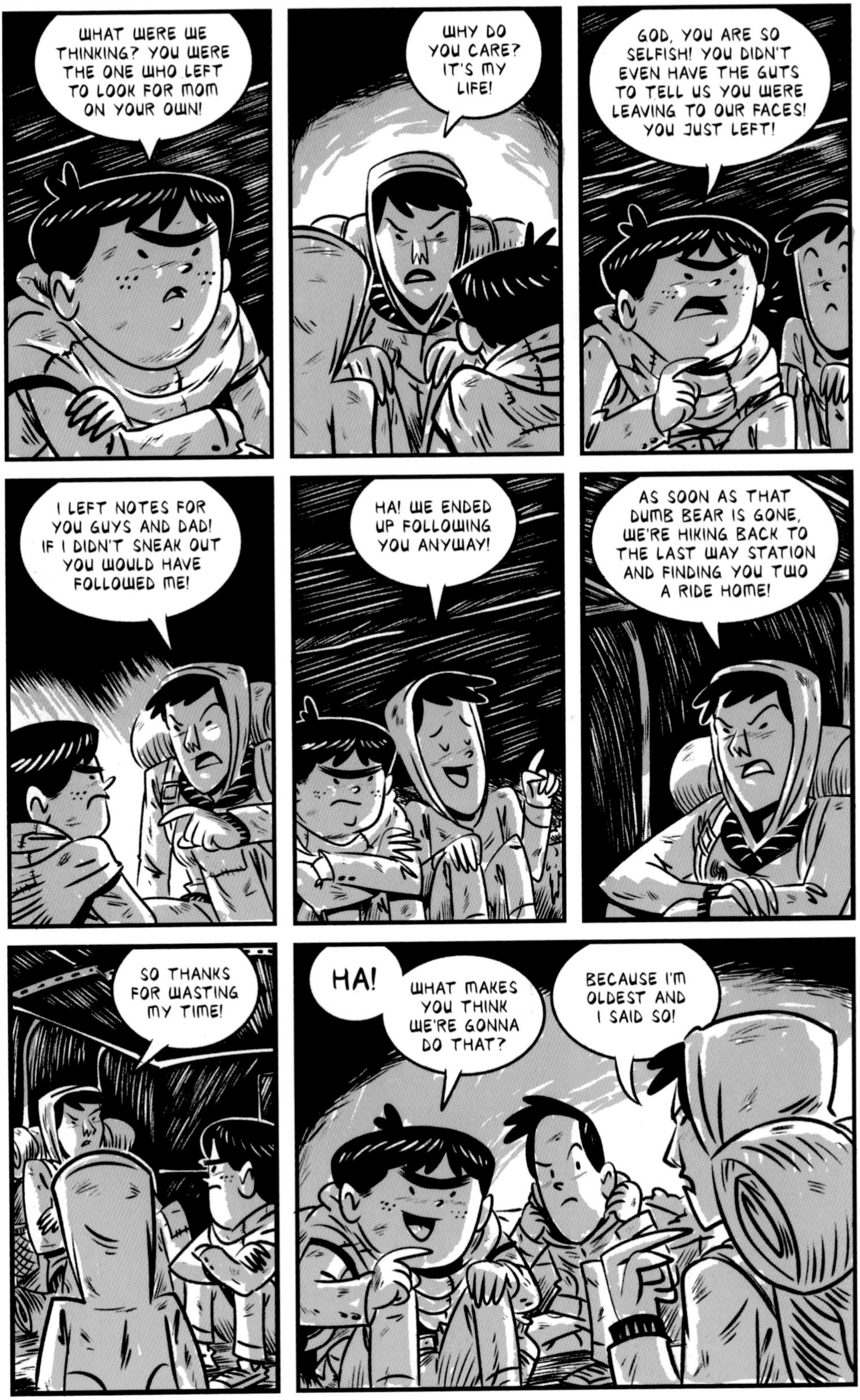
WHAT WERE WE THINKING? YOU WERE THE ONE WHO LEFT TO LOOK FOR MOM ON YOUR OWN!
WHY DO YOU CARE? IT'S MY LIFE!
GOD, YOU ARE SO SELFISH! YOU DIDN'T EVEN HAVE THE GUTS TO TELL US YOU WERE LEAVING TO OUR FACES! YOU JUST LEFT!
I LEFT NOTES FOR YOU GUYS AND DAD! IF I DIDN'T SNEAK OUT YOU WOULD HAVE FOLLOWED ME!
HA! WE ENDED UP FOLLOWING YOU ANYWAY!
AS SOON AS THAT DUMB BEAR IS GONE, WE'RE HIKING BACK TO THE LAST WAY STATION AND FINDING YOU TWO A RIDE HOME!
SO THANKS FOR WASTING MY TIME!
HA!
WHAT MAKES YOU THINK WE'RE GONNA DO THAT?
BECAUSE I'M OLDEST AND I SAID SO!

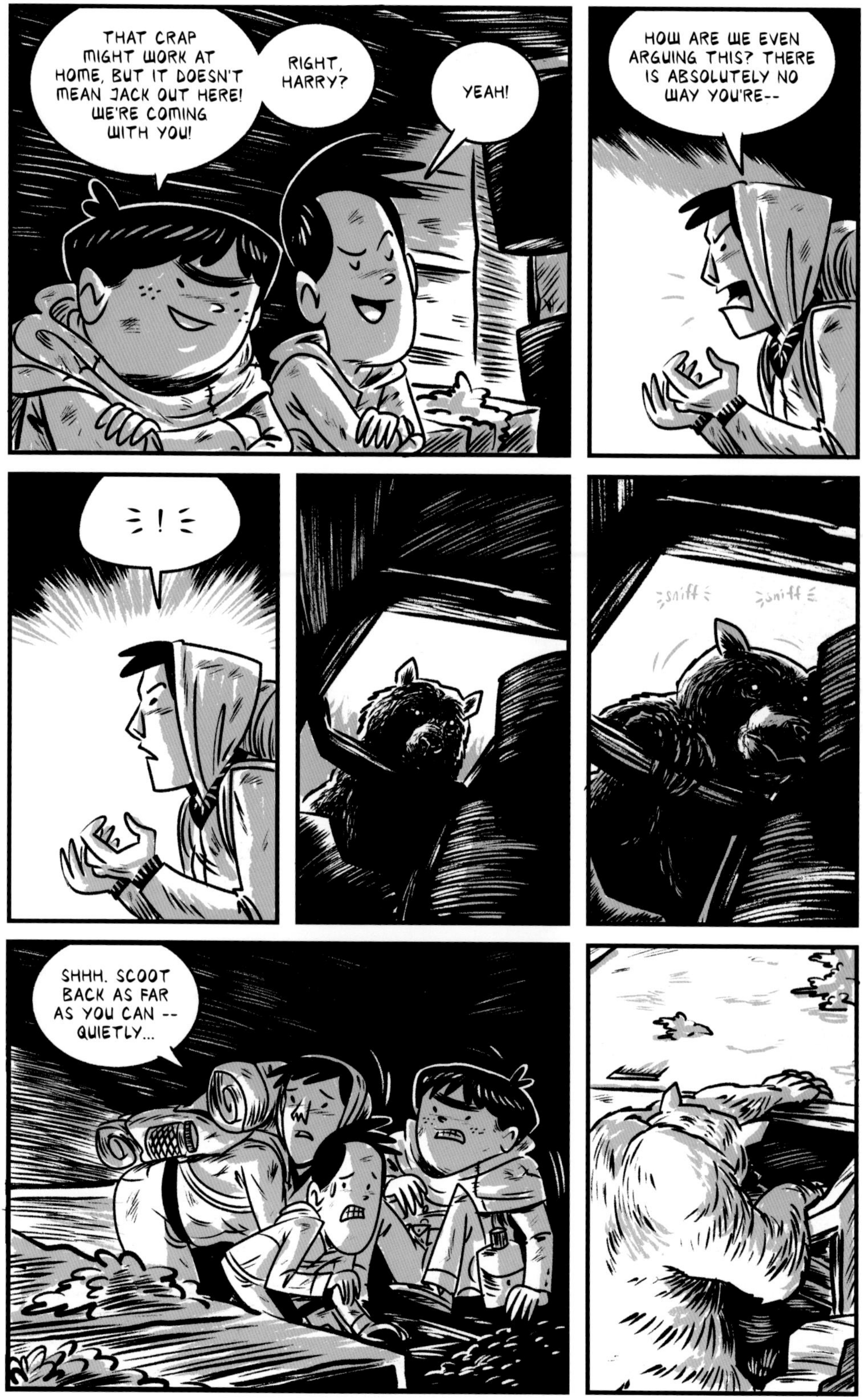
THAT CRAP MIGHT WORK AT HOME, BUT IT DOESN'T MEAN JACK OUT HERE! WE'RE COMING WITH YOU!
RIGHT, HARRY?
YEAH!
HOW ARE WE EVEN ARGUING THIS? THERE IS ABSOLUTELY NO WAY YOU'RE--
!
sniff
sniff
SHHH. SCOOT BACK AS FAR AS YOU CAN -- QUIETLY...

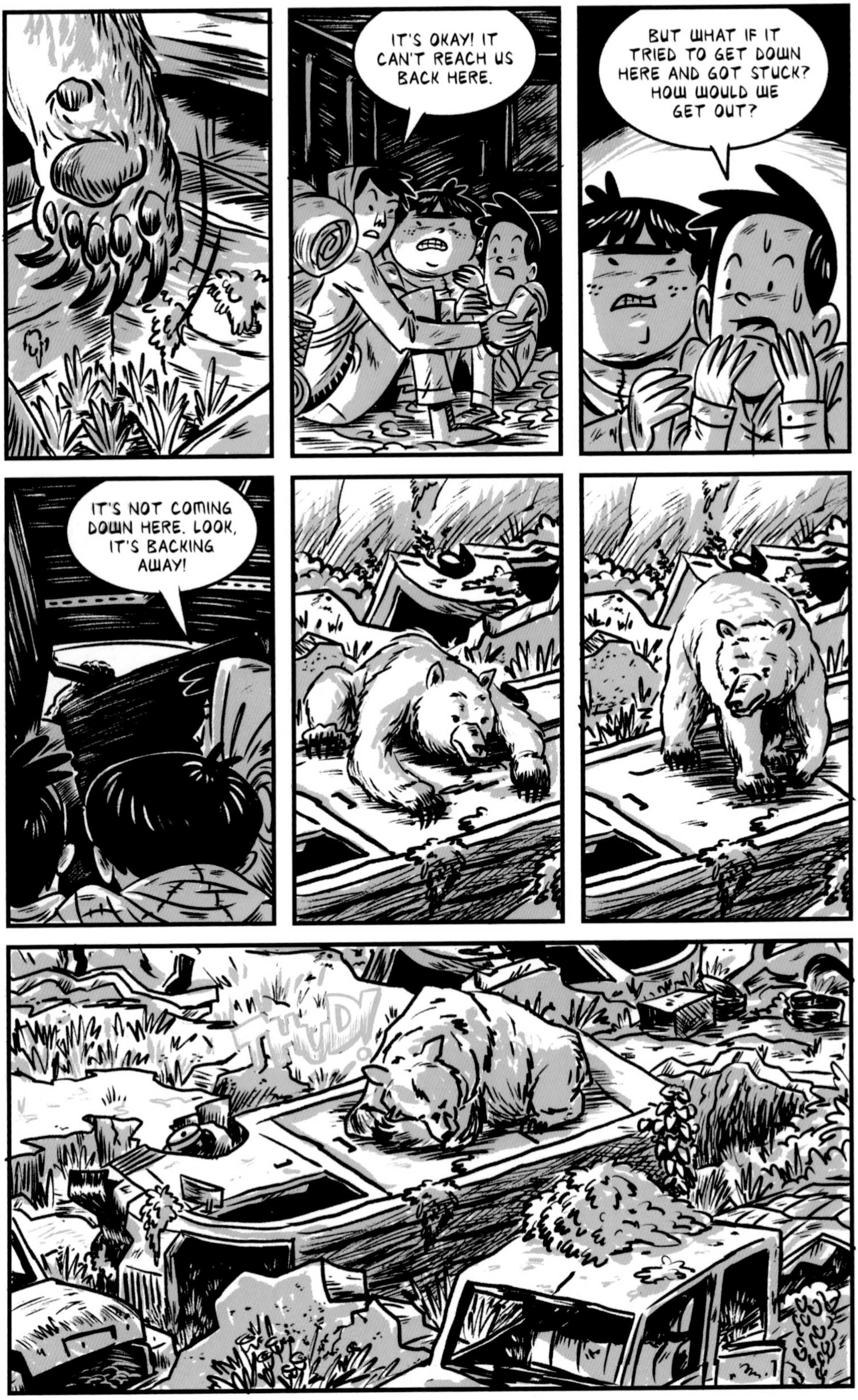
IT'S OKAY! IT CAN'T REACH US BACK HERE.
BUT WHAT IF IT TRIED TO GET DOWN HERE AND GOT STUCK? HOW WOULD WE GET OUT?
IT'S NOT COMING DOWN HERE. LOOK, IT'S BACKING AWAY!
THUD!

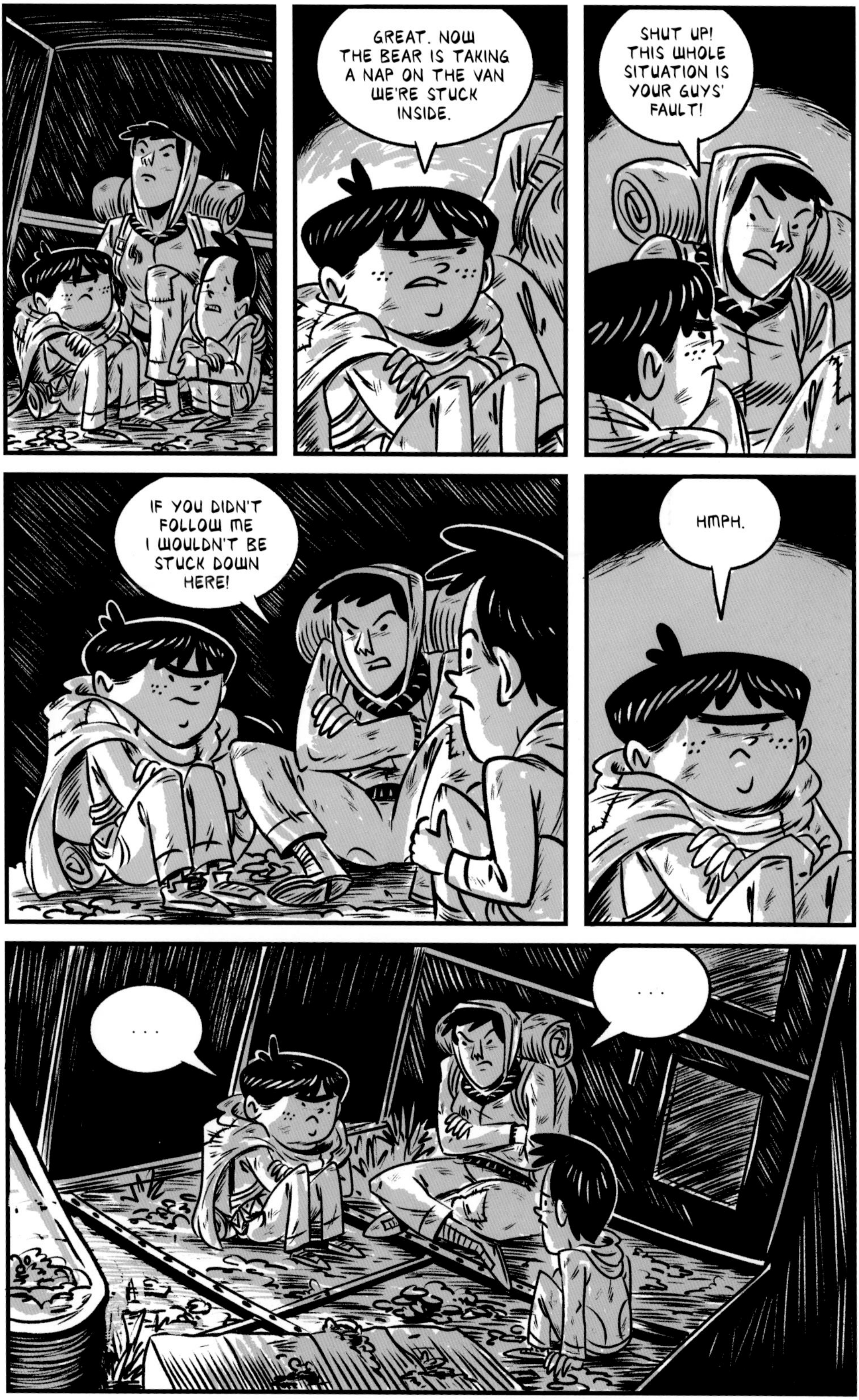
GREAT. NOW THE BEAR IS TAKING A NAP ON THE VAN WE'RE STUCK INSIDE.
SHUT UP! THIS WHOLE SITUATION IS YOUR GUYS' FAULT!
IF YOU DIDN'T FOLLOW ME I WOULDN'T BE STUCK DOWN HERE!
HMPH.
. . .
. . .

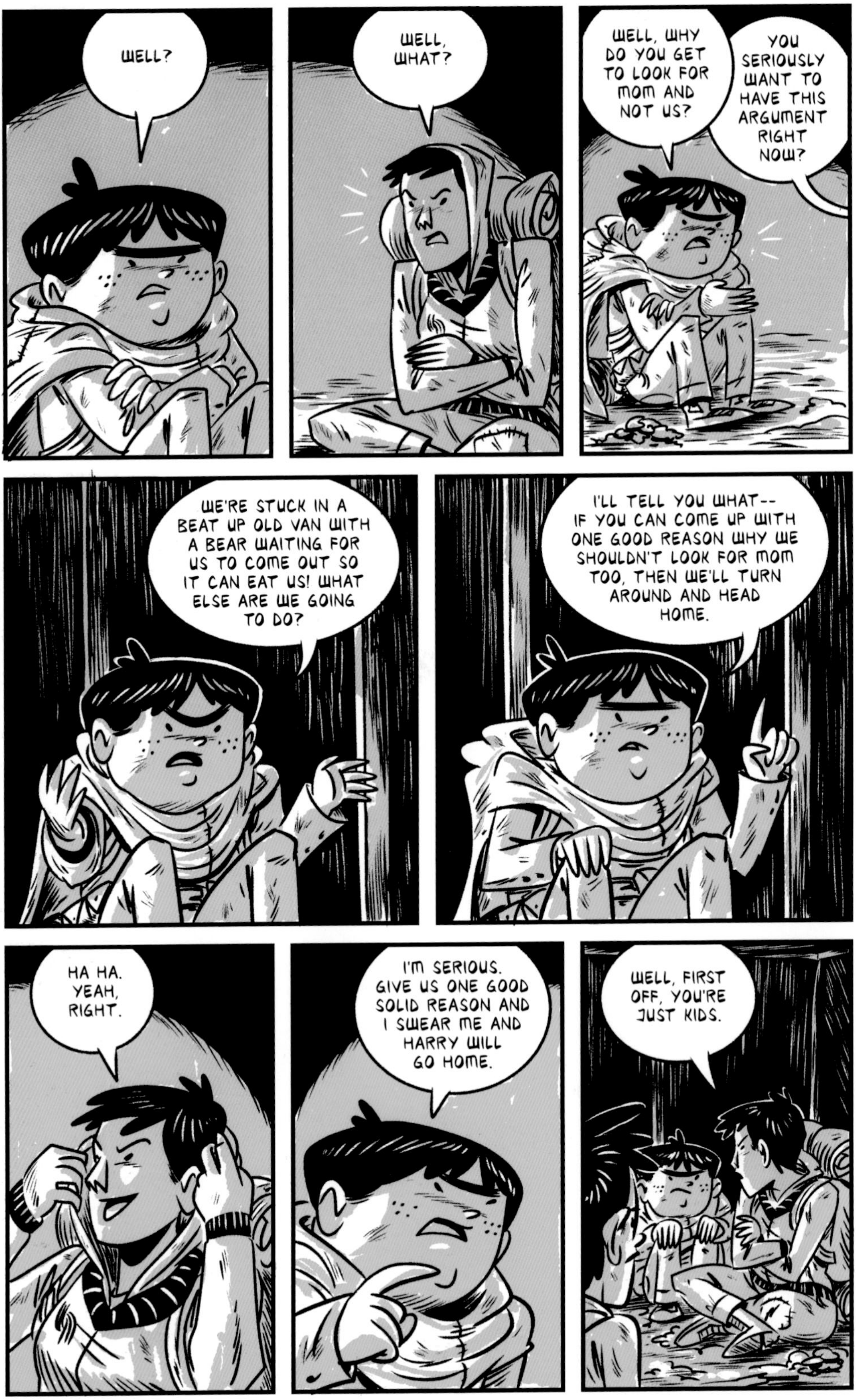
WELL?
WELL, WHAT?
WELL, WHY DO YOU GET TO LOOK FOR MOM AND NOT US?
YOU SERIOUSLY WANT TO HAVE THIS ARGUMENT RIGHT NOW?
WE'RE STUCK IN A BEAT UP OLD VAN WITH A BEAR WAITING FOR US TO COME OUT SO IT CAN EAT US! WHAT ELSE ARE WE GOING TO DO?
I'LL TELL YOU WHAT-- IF YOU CAN COME UP WITH ONE GOOD REASON WHY WE SHOULDN'T LOOK FOR MOM TOO, THEN WE'LL TURN AROUND AND HEAD HOME.
HA HA. YEAH, RIGHT.
I'M SERIOUS. GIVE US ONE GOOD SOLID REASON AND I SWEAR ME AND HARRY WILL GO HOME.
WELL, FIRST OFF, YOU'RE JUST KIDS.

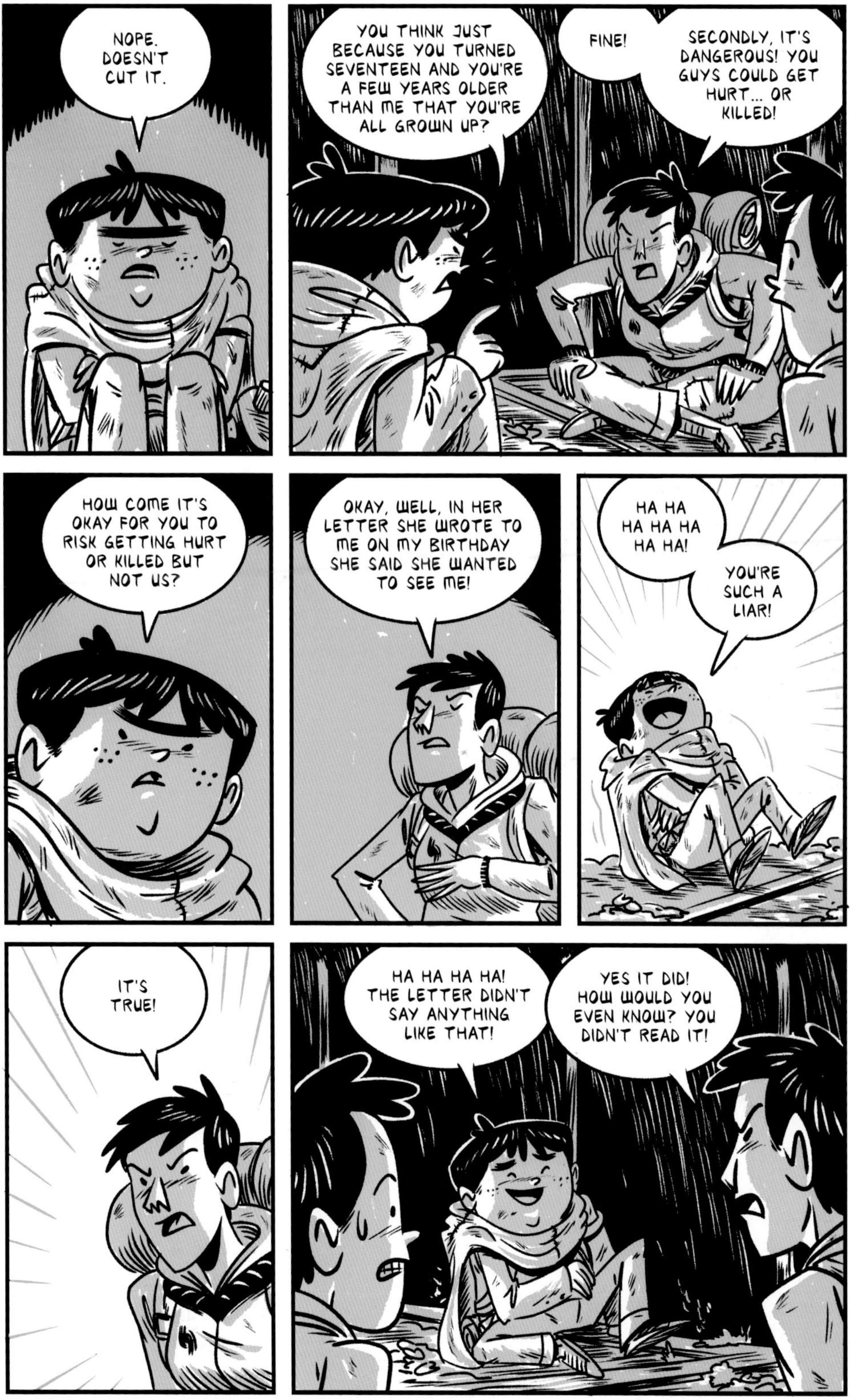
NOPE. DOESN'T CUT IT.
YOU THINK JUST BECAUSE YOU TURNED SEVENTEEN AND YOU'RE A FEW YEARS OLDER THAN ME THAT YOU'RE ALL GROWN UP?
FINE!
SECONDLY, IT'S DANGEROUS! YOU GUYS COULD GET HURT... OR KILLED!
HOW COME IT'S OKAY FOR YOU TO RISK GETTING HURT OR KILLED BUT NOT US?
OKAY, WELL, IN HER LETTER SHE WROTE TO ME ON MY BIRTHDAY SHE SAID SHE WANTED TO SEE ME!
HA HA HA HA HA HA HA!
YOU'RE SUCH A LIAR!
IT'S TRUE!
HA HA HA HA! THE LETTER DIDN'T SAY ANYTHING LIKE THAT!
YES IT DID! HOW WOULD YOU EVEN KNOW? YOU DIDN'T READ IT!

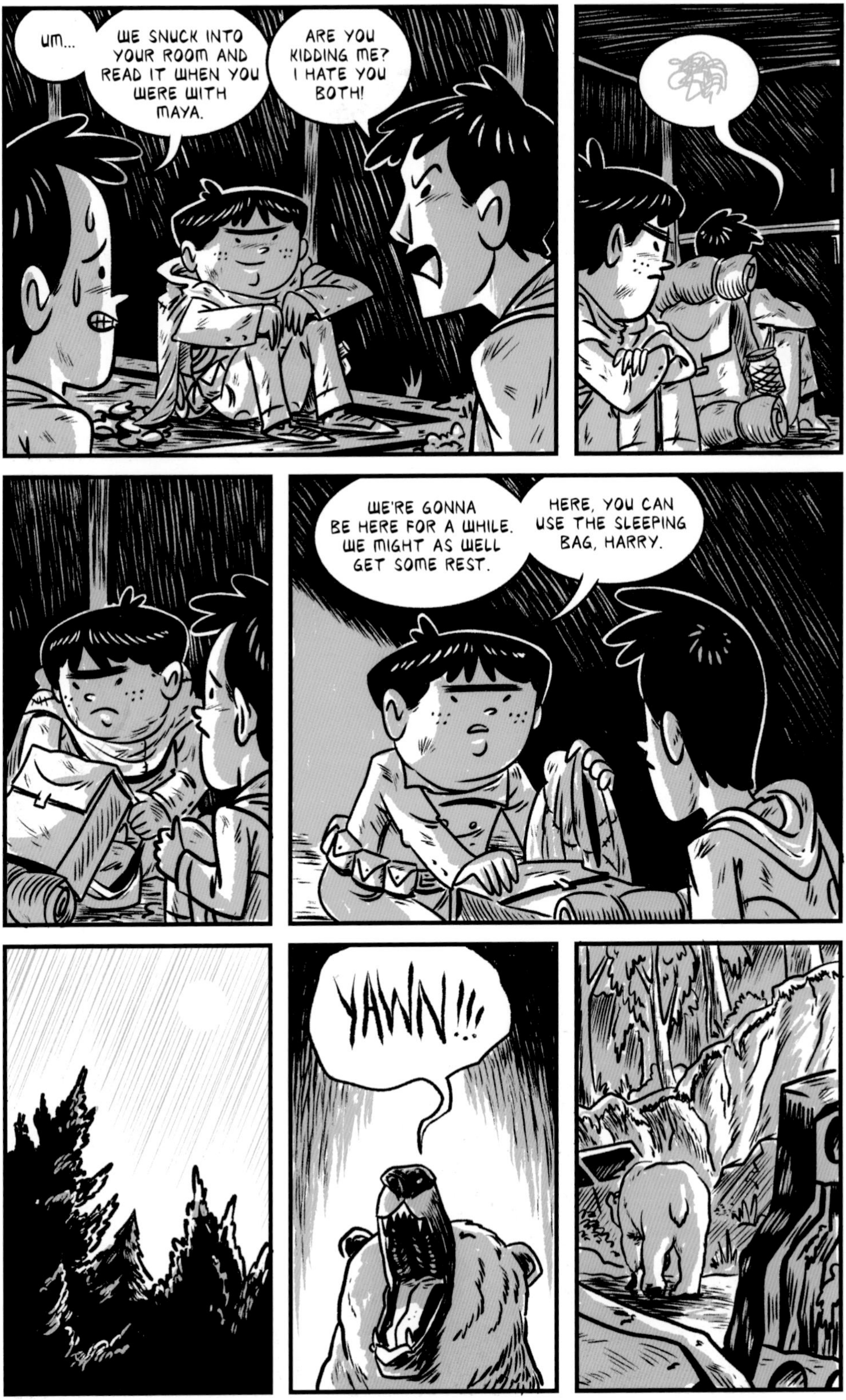
UM...
WE SNUCK INTO YOUR ROOM AND READ IT WHEN YOU WERE WITH MAYA.
ARE YOU KIDDING ME? I HATE YOU BOTH!
WE'RE GONNA BE HERE FOR A WHILE. WE MIGHT AS WELL GET SOME REST.
HERE, YOU CAN USE THE SLEEPING BAG, HARRY.
YAWN!!!

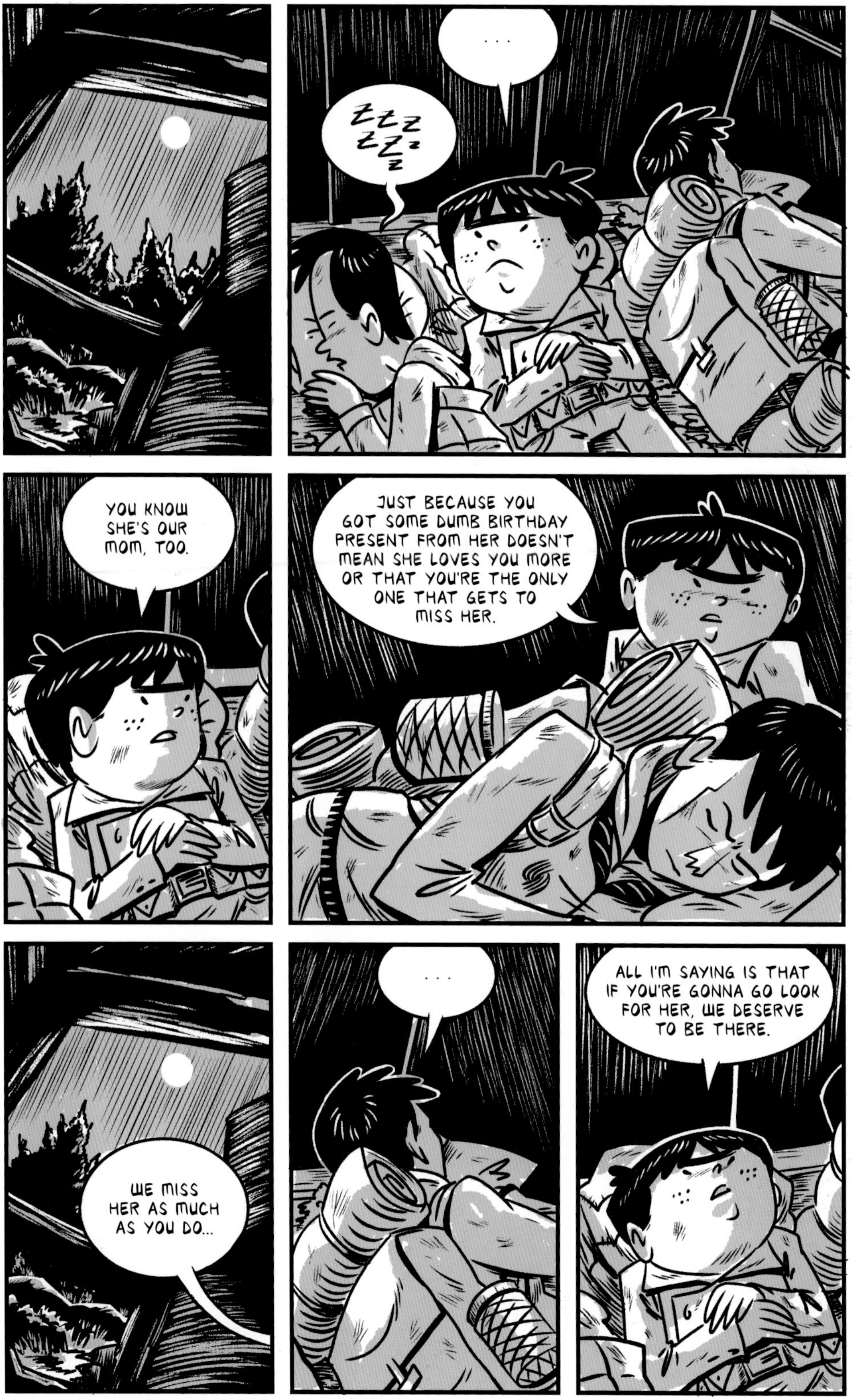
. . .
ZZZ
ZZZ
Z
YOU KNOW SHE'S OUR MOM, TOO.
JUST BECAUSE YOU GOT SOME DUMB BIRTHDAY PRESENT FROM HER DOESN'T MEAN SHE LOVES YOU MORE OR THAT YOU'RE THE ONLY ONE THAT GETS TO MISS HER.
WE MISS HER AS MUCH AS YOU DO...
. . .
ALL I'M SAYING IS THAT IF YOU'RE GONNA GO LOOK FOR HER, WE DESERVE TO BE THERE.

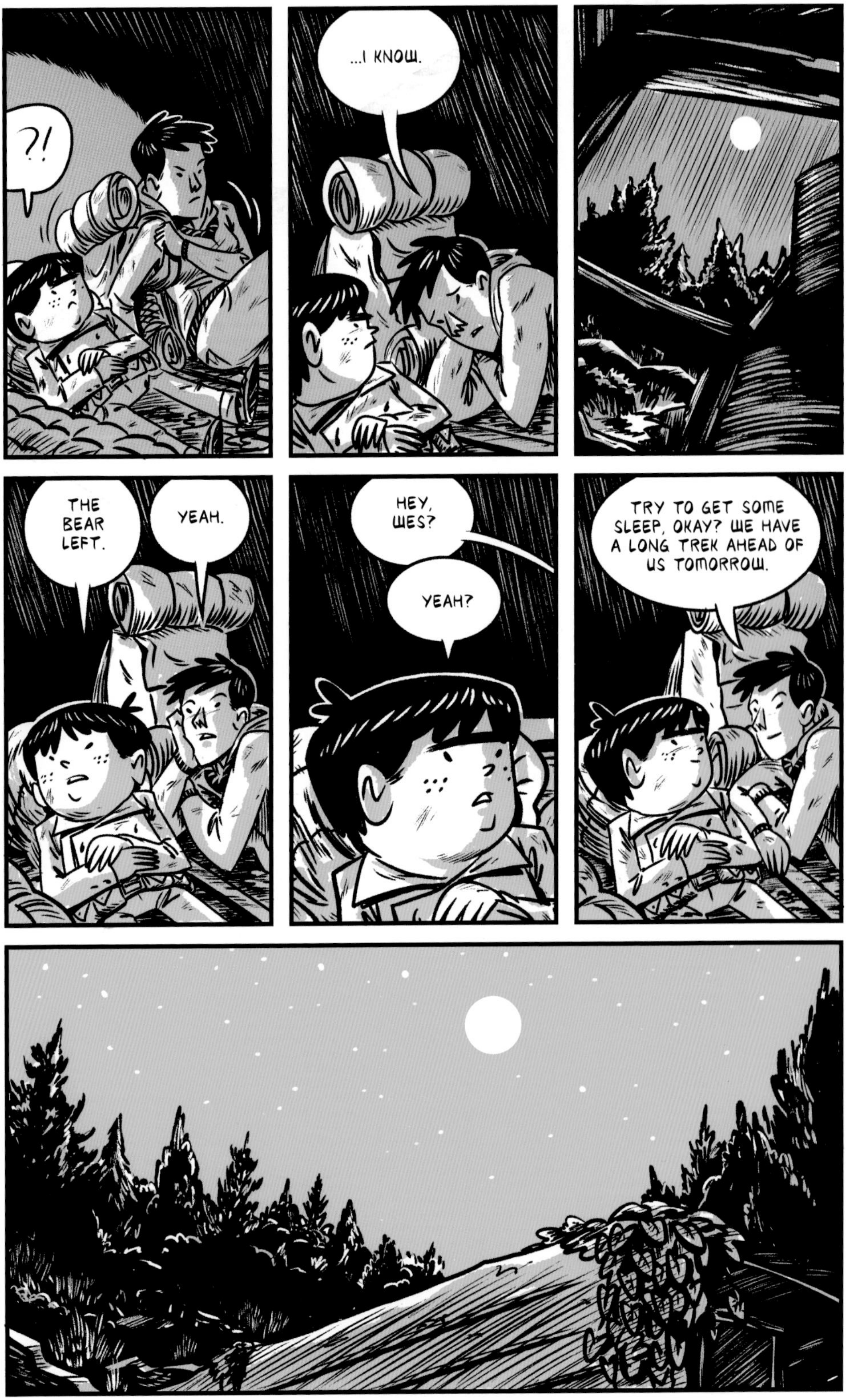
?!
...I KNOW.
THE BEAR LEFT.
YEAH.
HEY, WES?
YEAH?
TRY TO GET SOME SLEEP, OKAY? WE HAVE A LONG TREK AHEAD OF US TOMORROW.

CHAPTER 4

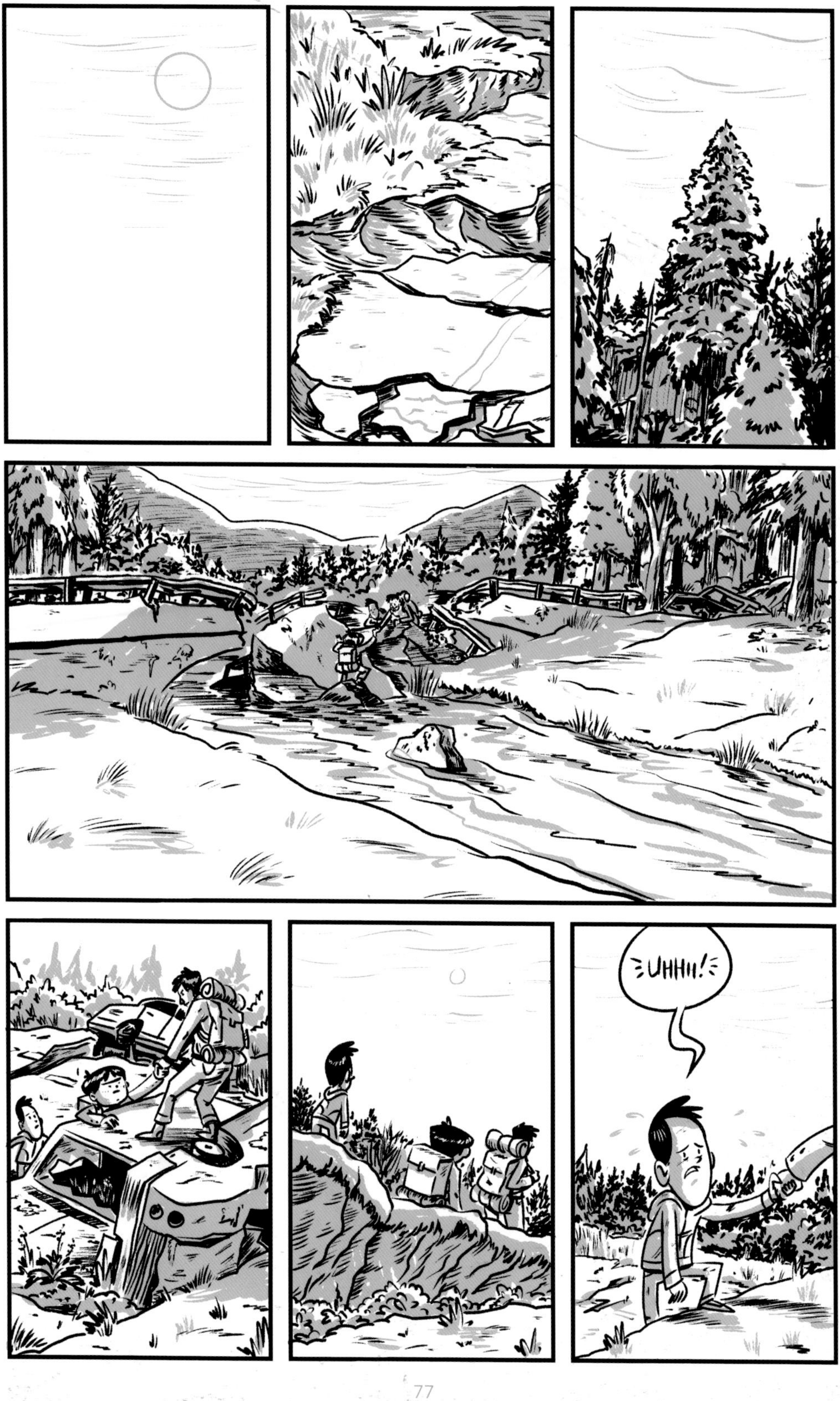
UHHH!

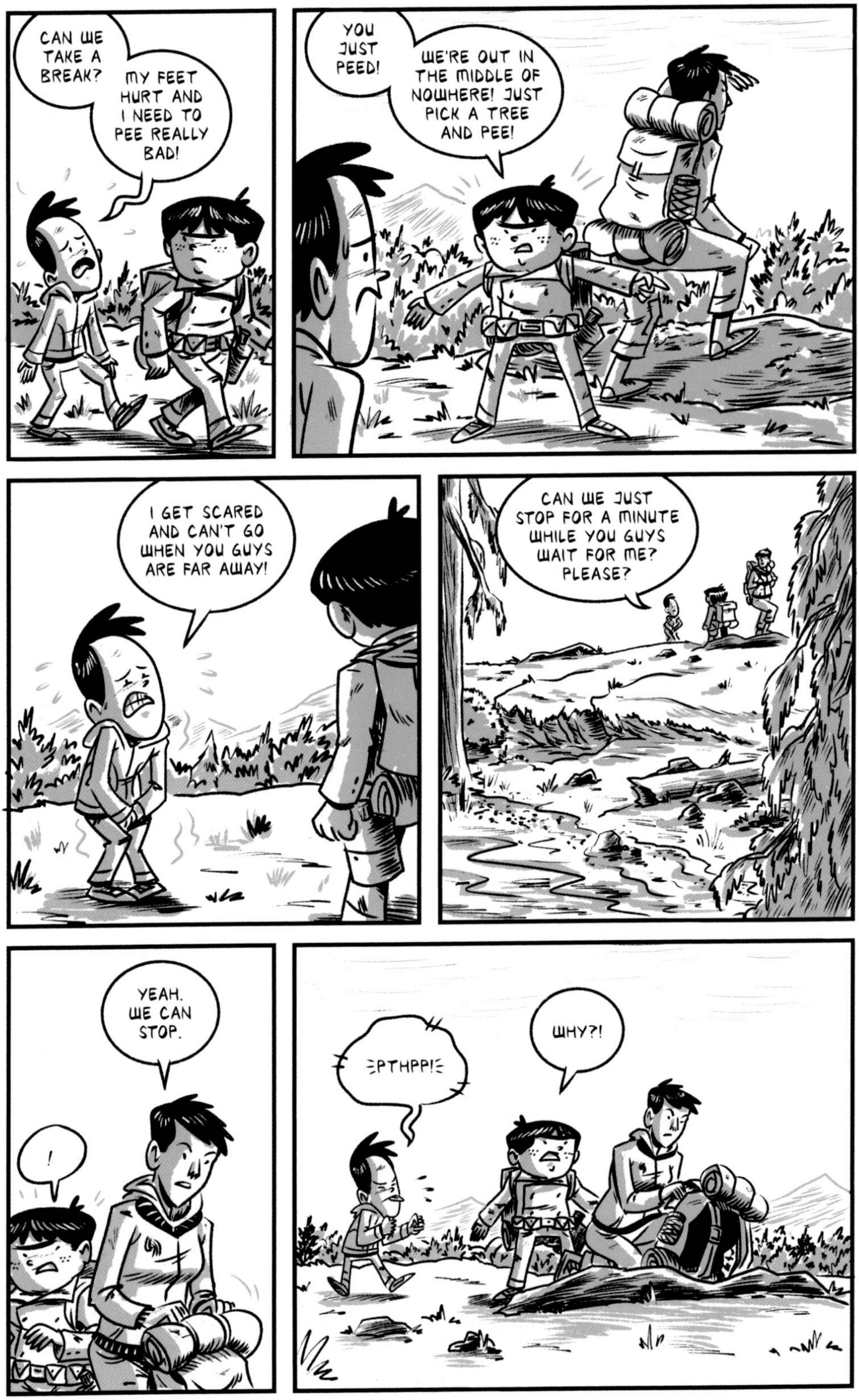
CAN WE TAKE A BREAK?
MY FEET HURT AND I NEED TO PEE REALLY BAD!
YOU JUST PEED!
WE'RE OUT IN THE MIDDLE OF NOWHERE! JUST PICK A TREE AND PEE!
I GET SCARED AND CAN'T GO WHEN YOU GUYS ARE FAR AWAY!
CAN WE JUST STOP FOR A MINUTE WHILE YOU GUYS WAIT FOR ME? PLEASE?
YEAH. WE CAN STOP.
!
PTHPP!
WHY?!

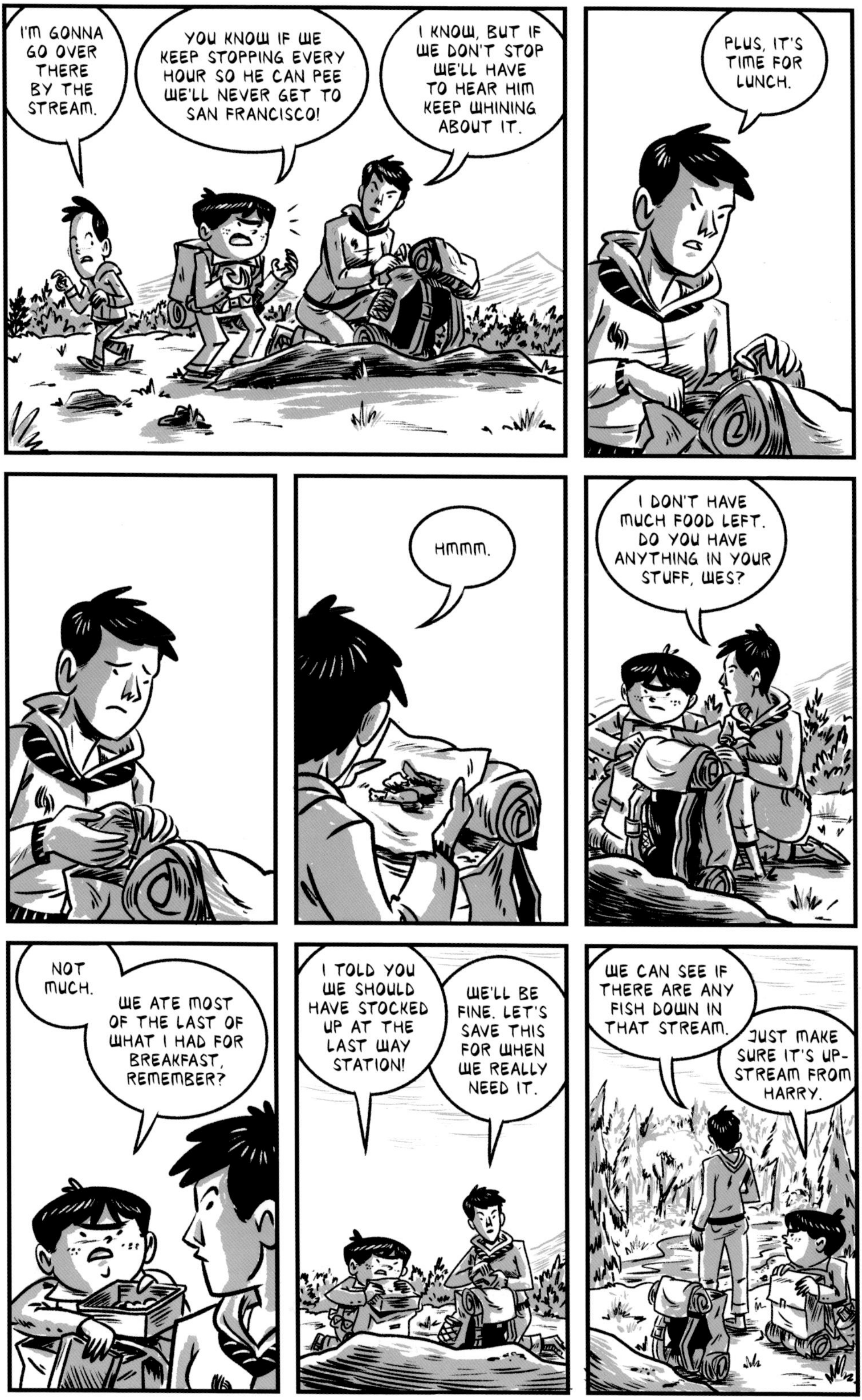
I'M GONNA GO OVER THERE BY THE STREAM.
YOU KNOW IF WE KEEP STOPPING EVERY HOUR SO HE CAN PEE WE'LL NEVER GET TO SAN FRANCISCO!
I KNOW, BUT IF WE DON'T STOP WE'LL HAVE TO HEAR HIM KEEP WHINING ABOUT IT.
PLUS, IT'S TIME FOR LUNCH.
HMMM.
I DON'T HAVE MUCH FOOD LEFT. DO YOU HAVE ANYTHING IN YOUR STUFF, WES?
NOT MUCH.
WE ATE MOST OF THE LAST OF WHAT I HAD FOR BREAKFAST, REMEMBER?
I TOLD YOU WE SHOULD HAVE STOCKED UP AT THE LAST WAY STATION!
WE'LL BE FINE. LET'S SAVE THIS FOR WHEN WE REALLY NEED IT.
WE CAN SEE IF THERE ARE ANY FISH DOWN IN THAT STREAM.
JUST MAKE SURE IT'S UP-STREAM FROM HARRY.

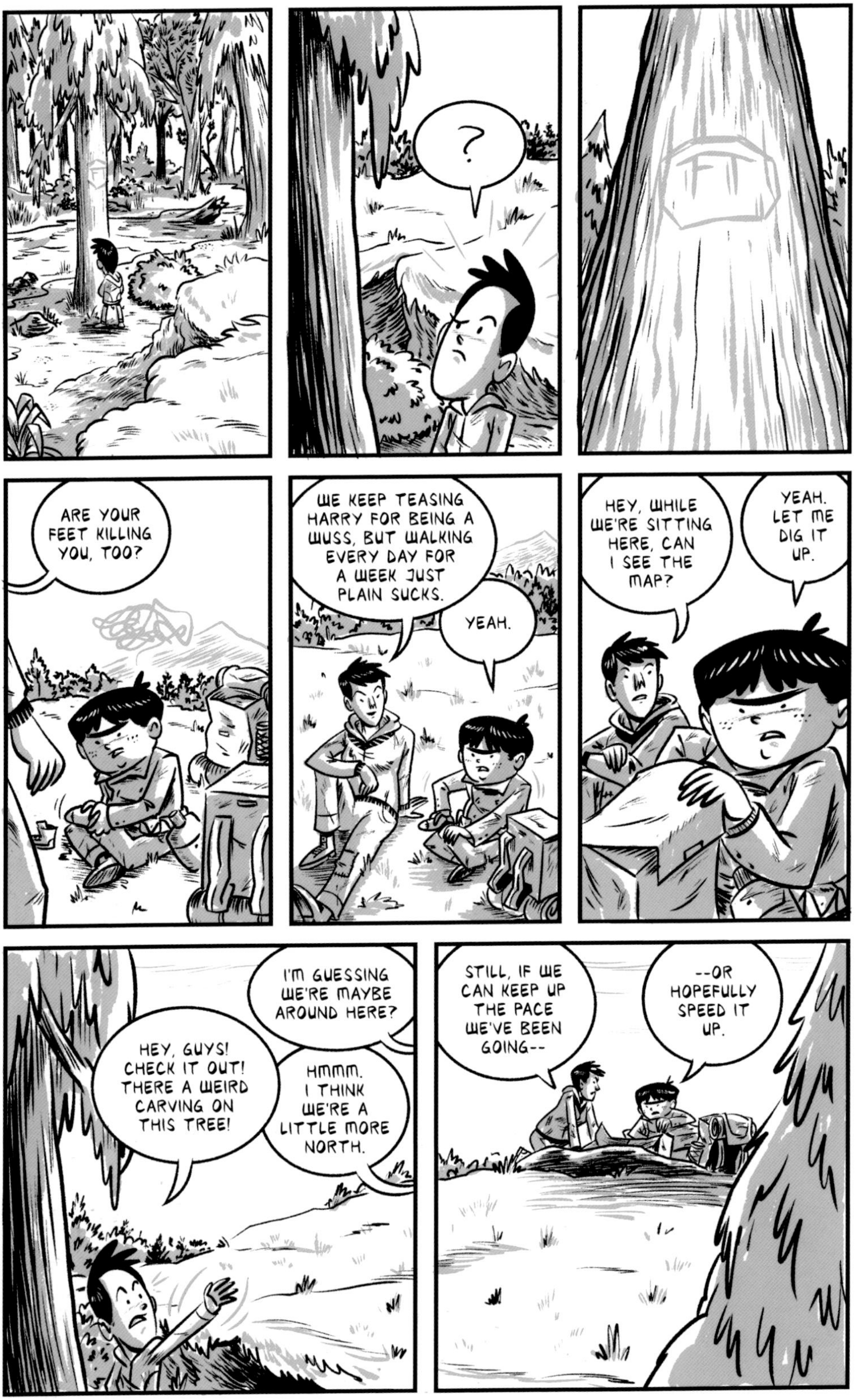
?
ARE YOUR FEET KILLING YOU, TOO?
WE KEEP TEASING HARRY FOR BEING A WUSS, BUT WALKING EVERY DAY FOR A WEEK JUST PLAIN SUCKS.
YEAH.
HEY, WHILE WE'RE SITTING HERE, CAN I SEE THE MAP?
YEAH. LET ME DIG IT UP.
I'M GUESSING WE'RE MAYBE AROUND HERE?
HEY, GUYS! CHECK IT OUT! THERE A WEIRD CARVING ON THIS TREE!
HMMM. I THINK WE'RE A LITTLE MORE NORTH.
STILL, IF WE CAN KEEP UP THE PACE WE'VE BEEN GOING--
--OR HOPEFULLY SPEED IT UP.

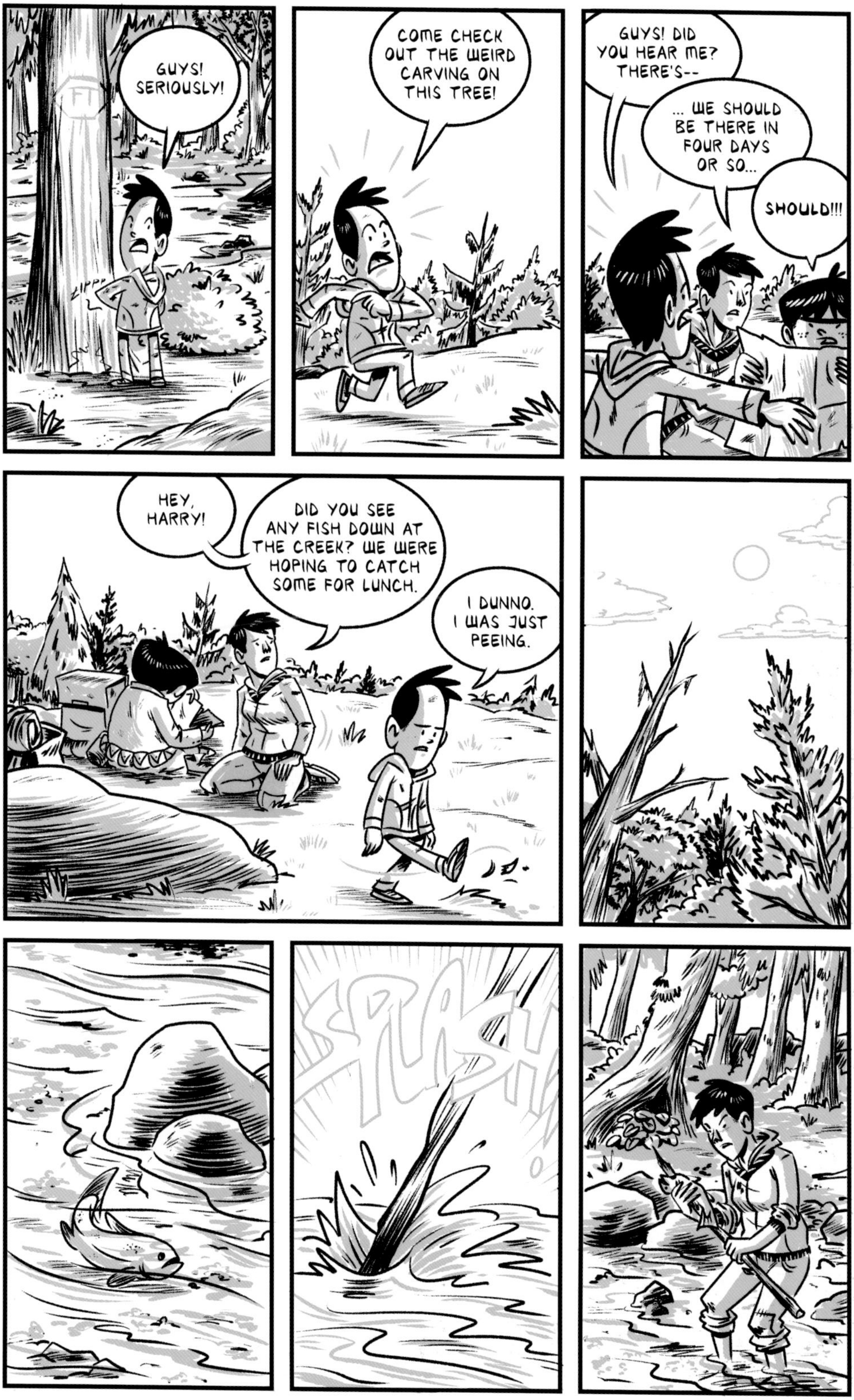
GUYS! SERIOUSLY!
COME CHECK OUT THE WEIRD CARVING ON THIS TREE!
GUYS! DID YOU HEAR ME? THERE'S--
... WE SHOULD BE THERE IN FOUR DAYS OR SO...
SHOULD!!!
HEY, HARRY!
DID YOU SEE ANY FISH DOWN AT THE CREEK? WE WERE HOPING TO CATCH SOME FOR LUNCH.
I DUNNO. I WAS JUST PEEING.
SPLASH

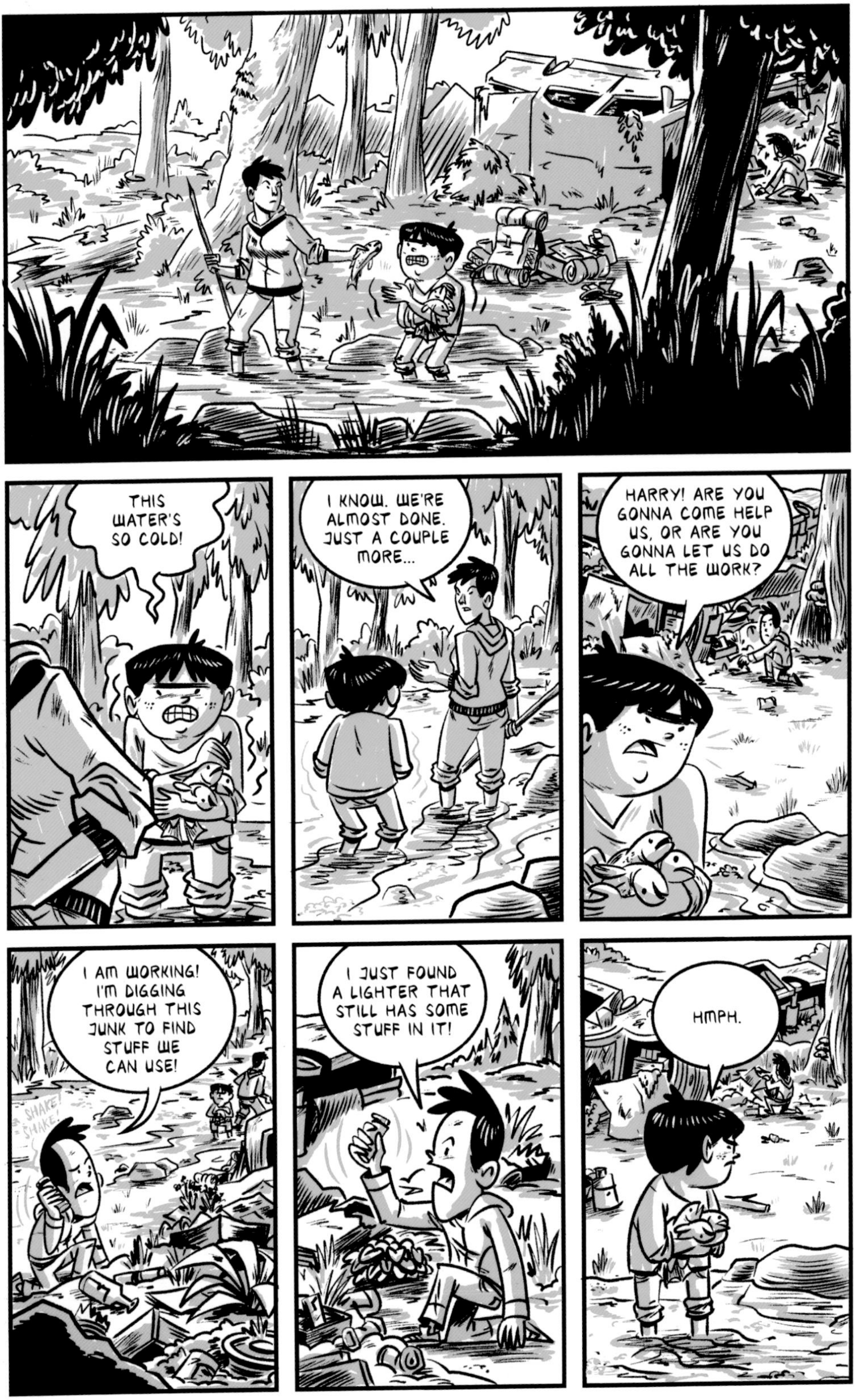
THIS WATER'S SO COLD!
I KNOW. WE'RE ALMOST DONE. JUST A COUPLE MORE...
HARRY! ARE YOU GONNA COME HELP US, OR ARE YOU GONNA LET US DO ALL THE WORK?
I AM WORKING! I'M DIGGING THROUGH THIS JUNK TO FIND STUFF WE CAN USE!
SHAKE! SHAKE!
I JUST FOUND A LIGHTER THAT STILL HAS SOME STUFF IN IT!
HMPH.

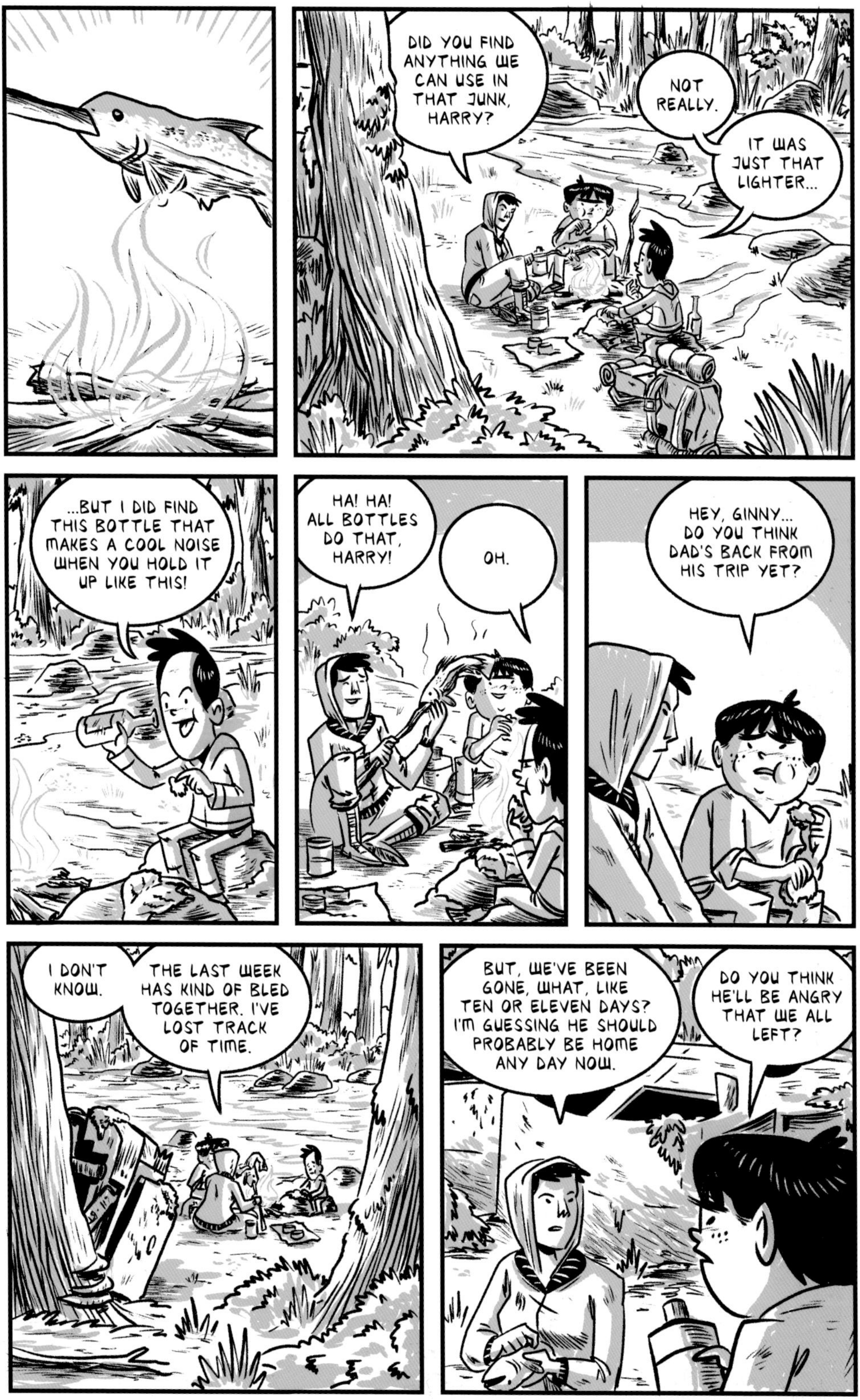

DID YOU FIND ANYTHING WE CAN USE IN THAT JUNK, HARRY?
NOT REALLY.
IT WAS JUST THAT LIGHTER...
...BUT I DID FIND THIS BOTTLE THAT MAKES A COOL NOISE WHEN YOU HOLD IT UP LIKE THIS!
HA! HA! ALL BOTTLES DO THAT, HARRY!
OH.
HEY, GINNY... DO YOU THINK DAD'S BACK FROM HIS TRIP YET?
I DON'T KNOW.
THE LAST WEEK HAS KIND OF BLED TOGETHER. I'VE LOST TRACK OF TIME.
BUT, WE'VE BEEN GONE, WHAT, LIKE TEN OR ELEVEN DAYS? I'M GUESSING HE SHOULD PROBABLY BE HOME ANY DAY NOW.
DO YOU THINK HE'LL BE ANGRY THAT WE ALL LEFT?

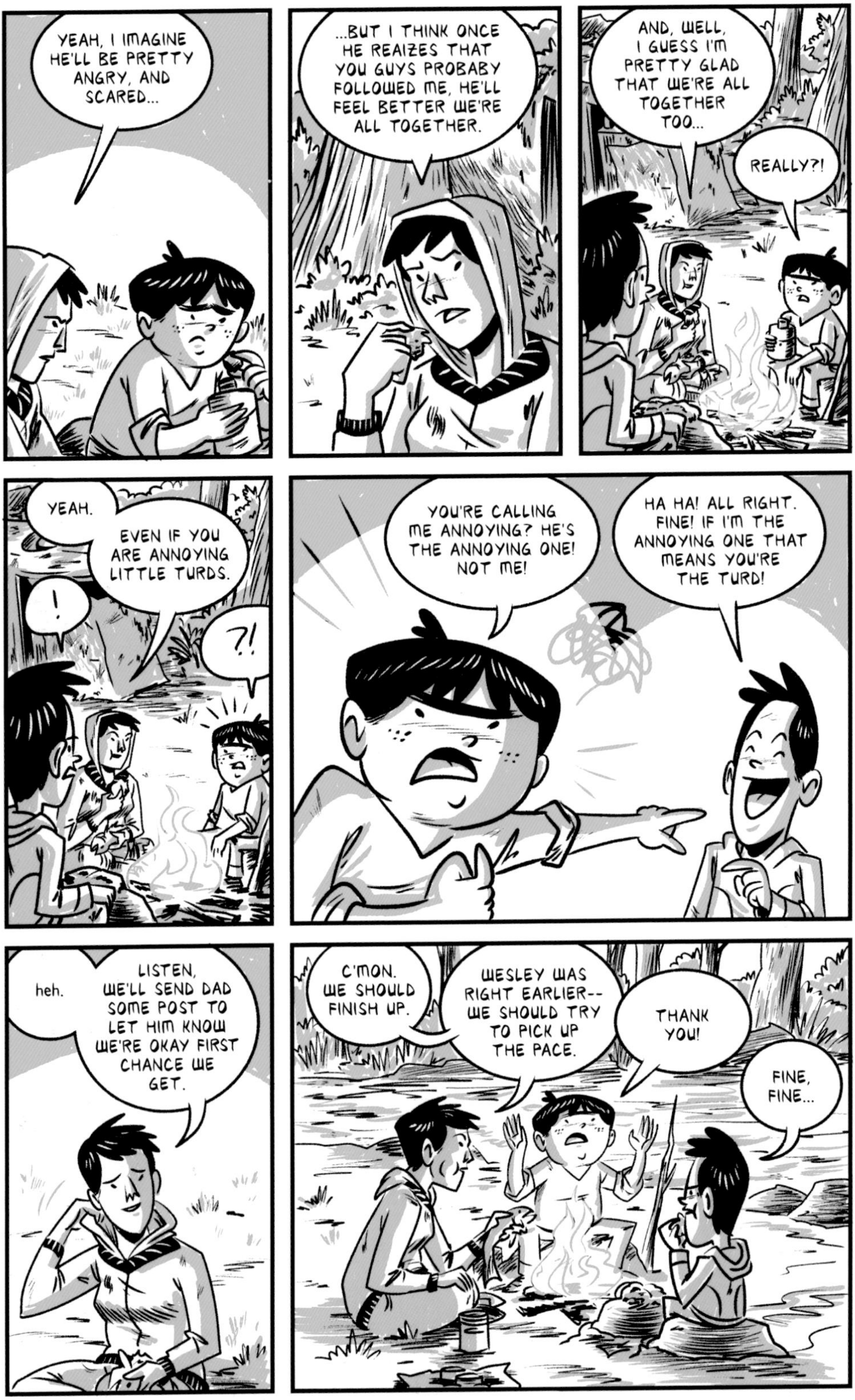
YEAH, I IMAGINE HE'LL BE PRETTY ANGRY, AND SCARED...
...BUT I THINK ONCE HE REAIZES THAT YOU GUYS PROBABY FOLLOWED ME, HE'LL FEEL BETTER WE'RE ALL TOGETHER.
AND, WELL, I GUESS I'M PRETTY GLAD THAT WE'RE ALL TOGETHER TOO...
REALLY?!
YEAH.
EVEN IF YOU ARE ANNOYING LITTLE TURDS.
!
?!
YOU'RE CALLING ME ANNOYING? HE'S THE ANNOYING ONE! NOT ME!
HA HA! ALL RIGHT. FINE! IF I'M THE ANNOYING ONE THAT MEANS YOU'RE THE TURD!
heh.
LISTEN, WE'LL SEND DAD SOME POST TO LET HIM KNOW WE'RE OKAY FIRST CHANCE WE GET.
C'MON. WE SHOULD FINISH UP.
WESLEY WAS RIGHT EARLIER-- WE SHOULD TRY TO PICK UP THE PACE.
THANK YOU!
FINE, FINE...

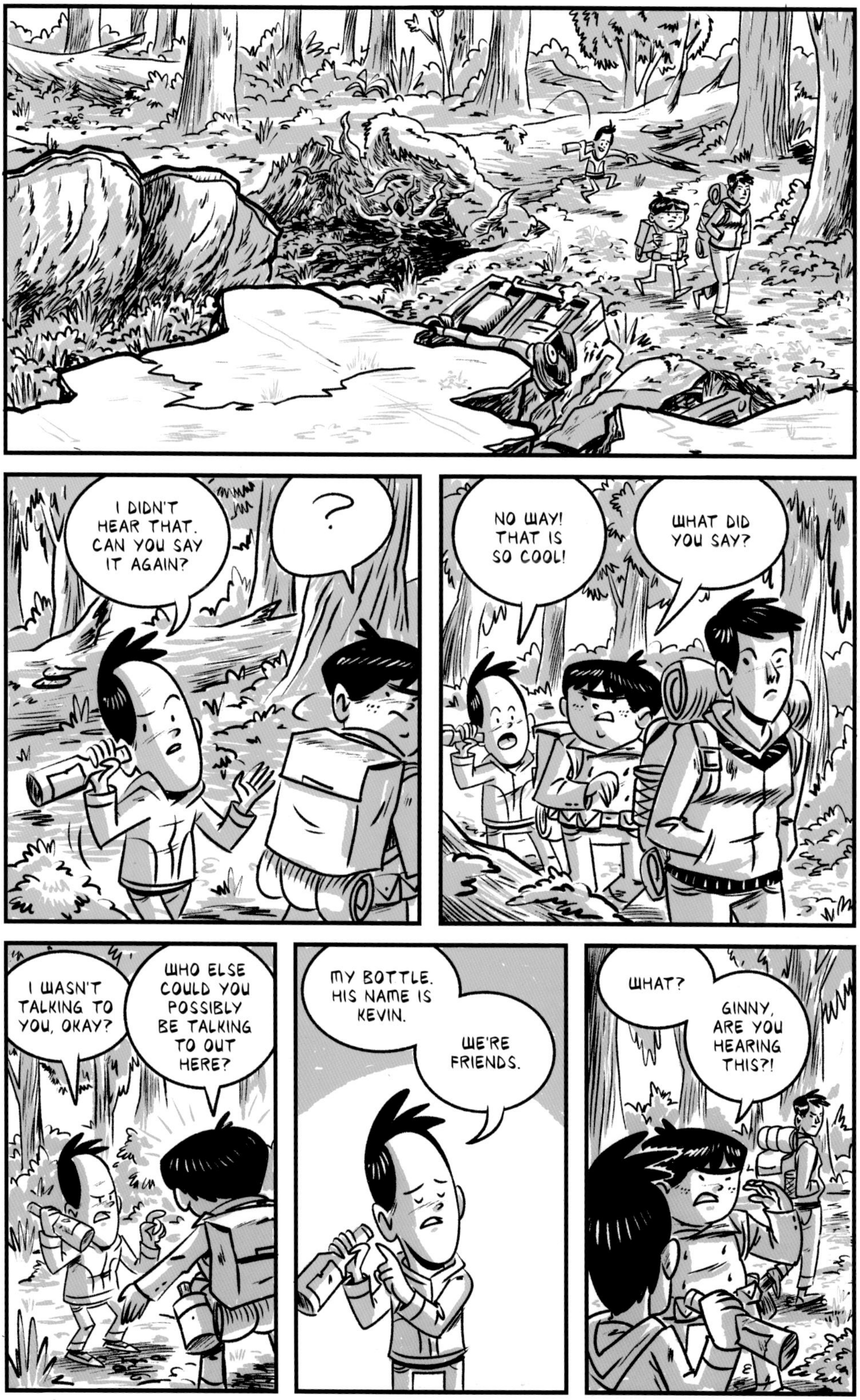
I DIDN'T HEAR THAT. CAN YOU SAY IT AGAIN?
?
NO WAY! THAT IS SO COOL!
WHAT DID YOU SAY?
I WASN'T TALKING TO YOU, OKAY?
WHO ELSE COULD YOU POSSIBLY BE TALKING TO OUT HERE?
MY BOTTLE. HIS NAME IS KEVIN.
WE'RE FRIENDS.
WHAT?
GINNY, ARE YOU HEARING THIS?!

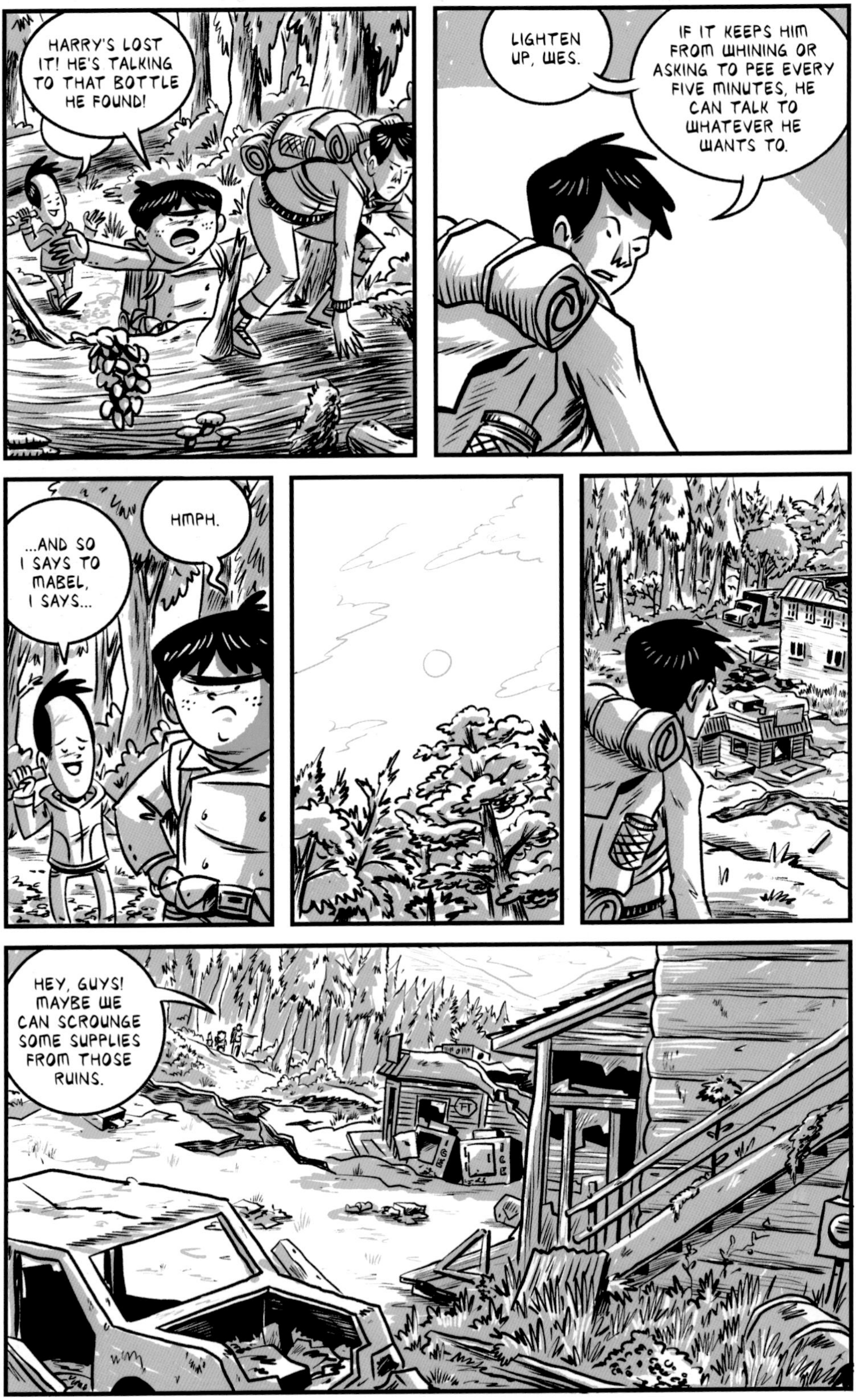
HARRY'S LOST IT! HE'S TALKING TO THAT BOTTLE HE FOUND!
LIGHTEN UP, WES.
IF IT KEEPS HIM FROM WHINING OR ASKING TO PEE EVERY FIVE MINUTES, HE CAN TALK TO WHATEVER HE WANTS TO.
...AND SO I SAYS TO MABEL, I SAYS...
HMPH.
HEY, GUYS! MAYBE WE CAN SCROUNGE SOME SUPPLIES FROM THOSE RUINS.

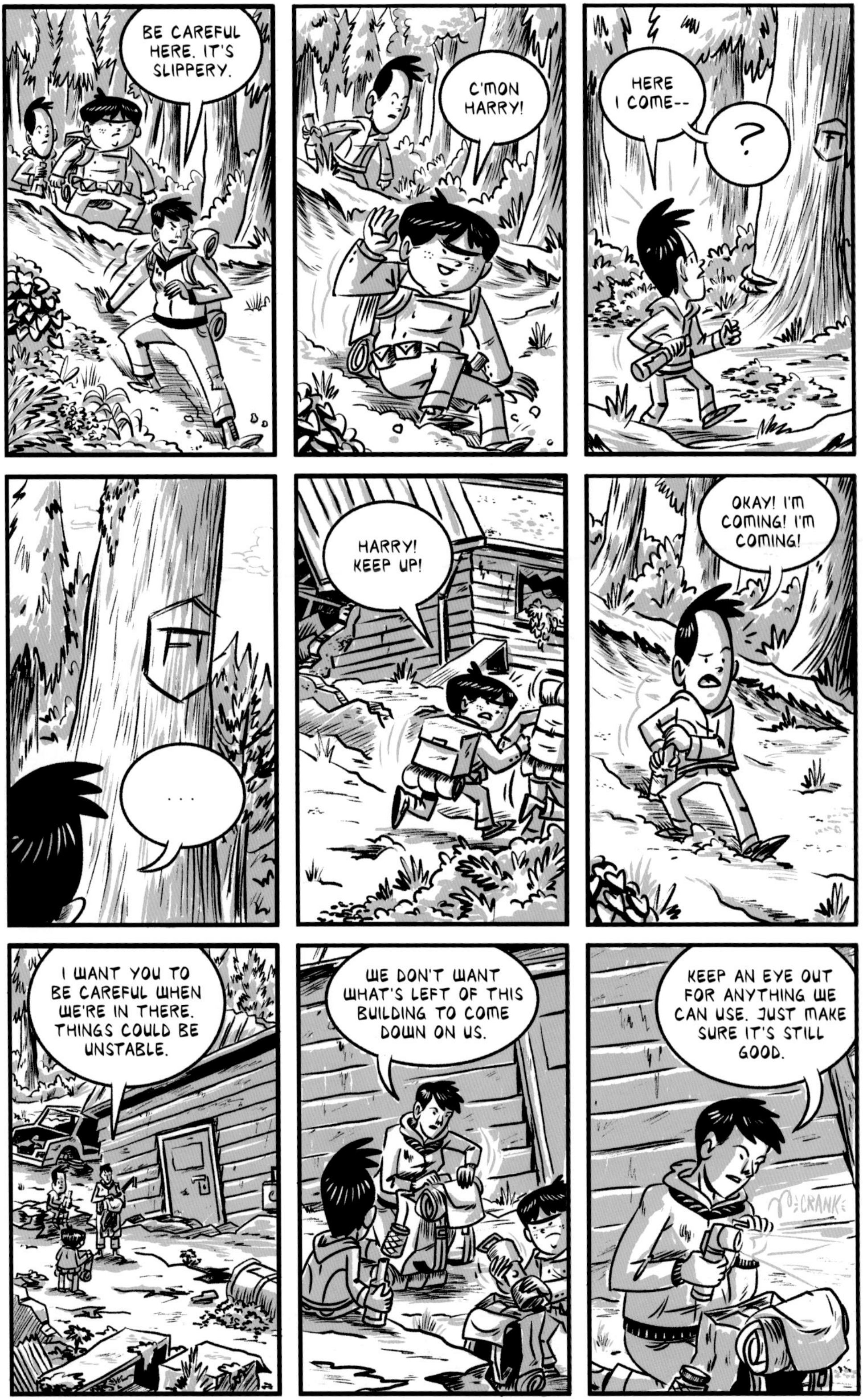
BE CAREFUL HERE. IT'S SLIPPERY.
C'MON HARRY!
HERE I COME--
?
. . .
HARRY! KEEP UP!
OKAY! I'M COMING! I'M COMING!
I WANT YOU TO BE CAREFUL WHEN WE'RE IN THERE. THINGS COULD BE UNSTABLE.
WE DON'T WANT WHAT'S LEFT OF THIS BUILDING TO COME DOWN ON US.
KEEP AN EYE OUT FOR ANYTHING WE CAN USE. JUST MAKE SURE IT'S STILL GOOD.
CRANK

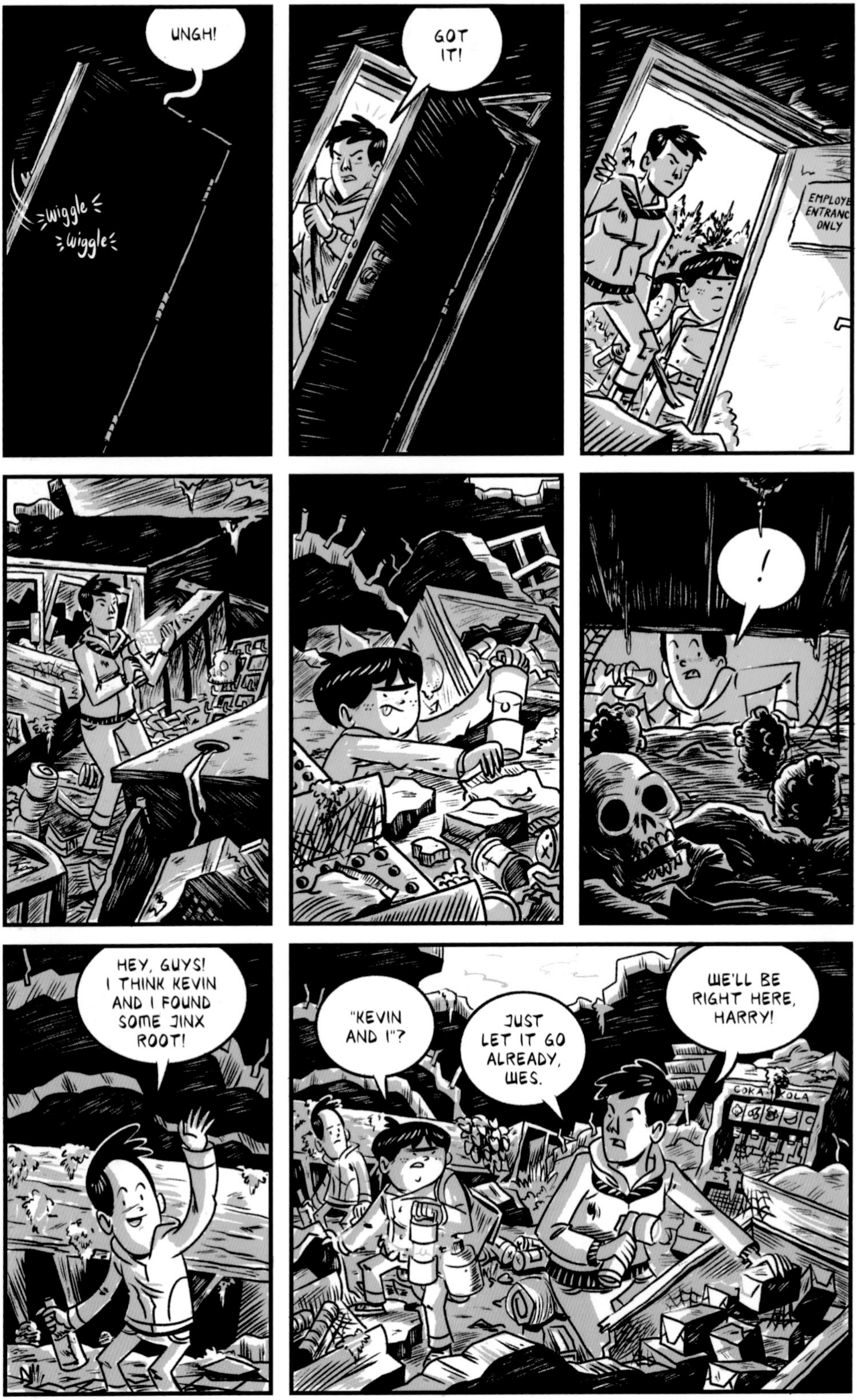
UNGH!
wiggle
wiggle
GOT IT!
EMPLOYE
ENTRANC
ONLY
!
HEY, GUYS! I THINK KEVIN AND I FOUND SOME JINX ROOT!
"KEVIN AND I"?
JUST LET IT GO ALREADY, WES.
WE'LL BE RIGHT HERE, HARRY!
COKA KOLA

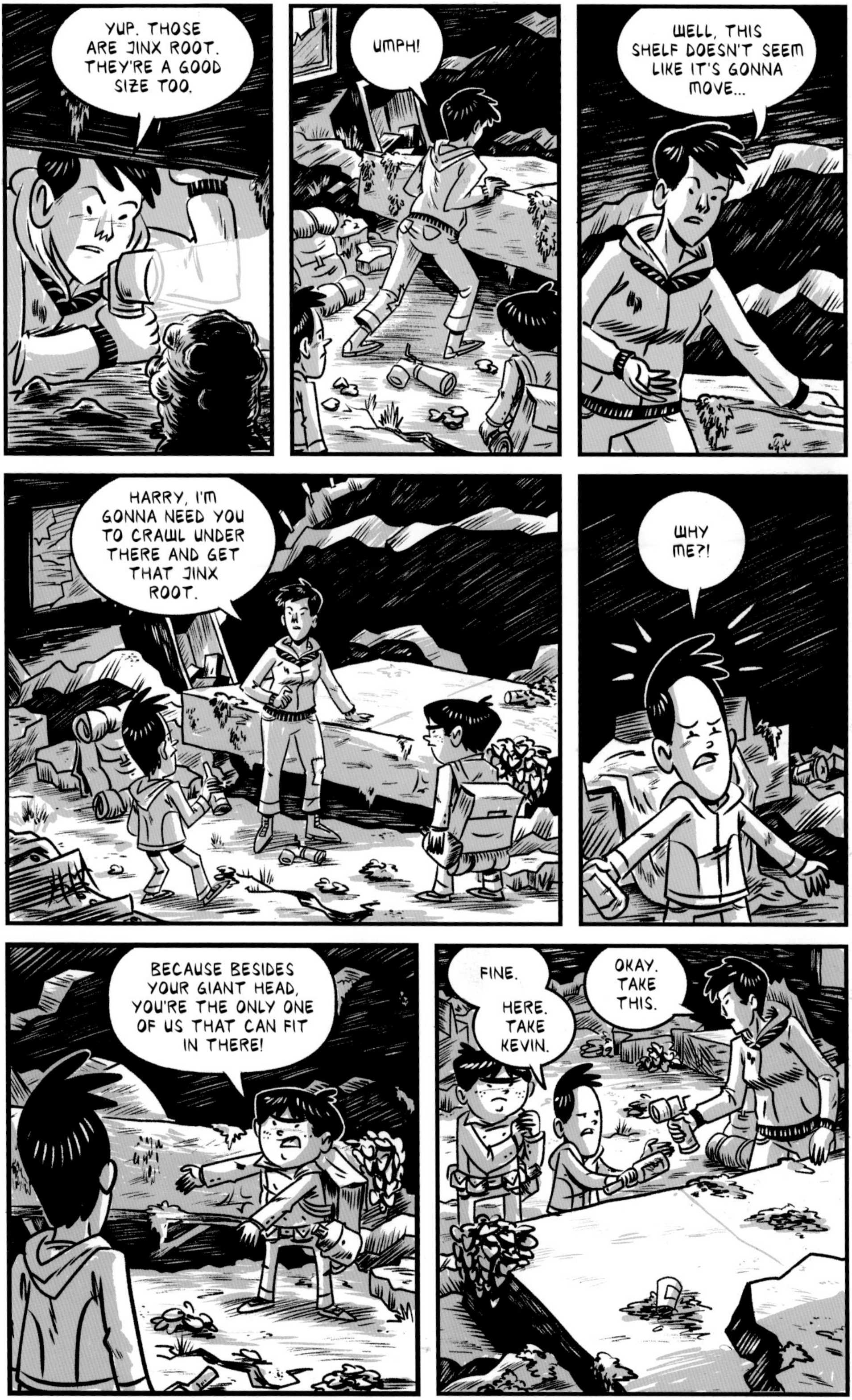
YUP. THOSE ARE JINX ROOT. THEY'RE A GOOD SIZE TOO.
UMPH!
WELL, THIS SHELF DOESN'T SEEM LIKE IT'S GONNA MOVE...
HARRY, I'M GONNA NEED YOU TO CRAWL UNDER THERE AND GET THAT JINX ROOT.
WHY ME?!
BECAUSE BESIDES YOUR GIANT HEAD, YOU'RE THE ONLY ONE OF US THAT CAN FIT IN THERE!
FINE.
HERE. TAKE KEVIN.
OKAY. TAKE THIS.

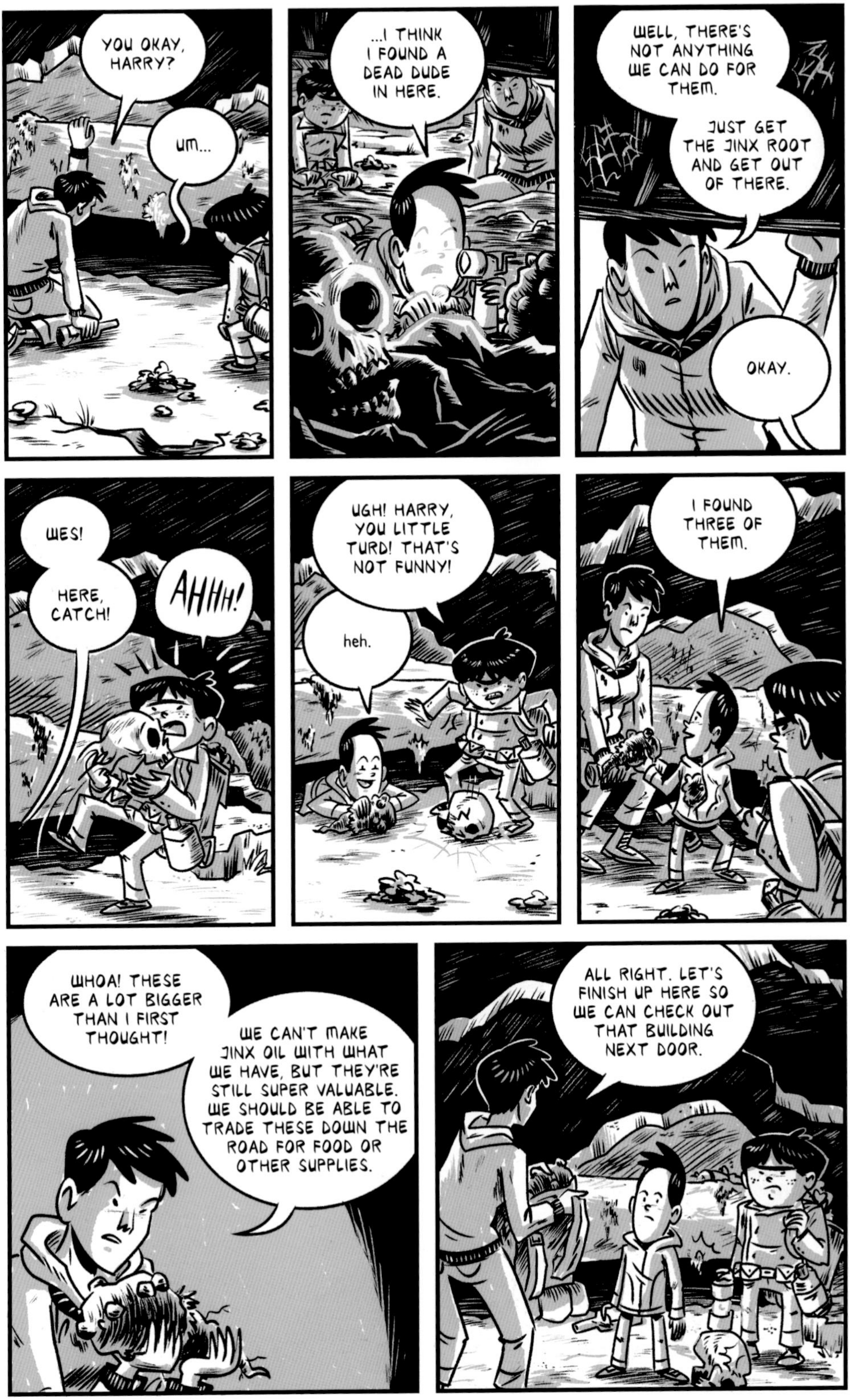

YOU OKAY, HARRY?
um...
...I THINK I FOUND A DEAD DUDE IN HERE.
WELL, THERE'S NOT ANYTHING WE CAN DO FOR THEM.
JUST GET THE JINX ROOT AND GET OUT OF THERE.
OKAY.
WES!
HERE, CATCH!
AHHH!
UGH! HARRY, YOU LITTLE TURD! THAT'S NOT FUNNY!
heh.
I FOUND THREE OF THEM.
WHOA! THESE ARE A LOT BIGGER THAN I FIRST THOUGHT!
WE CAN'T MAKE JINX OIL WITH WHAT WE HAVE, BUT THEY'RE STILL SUPER VALUABLE. WE SHOULD BE ABLE TO TRADE THESE DOWN THE ROAD FOR FOOD OR OTHER SUPPLIES.
ALL RIGHT. LET'S FINISH UP HERE SO WE CAN CHECK OUT THAT BUILDING NEXT DOOR.

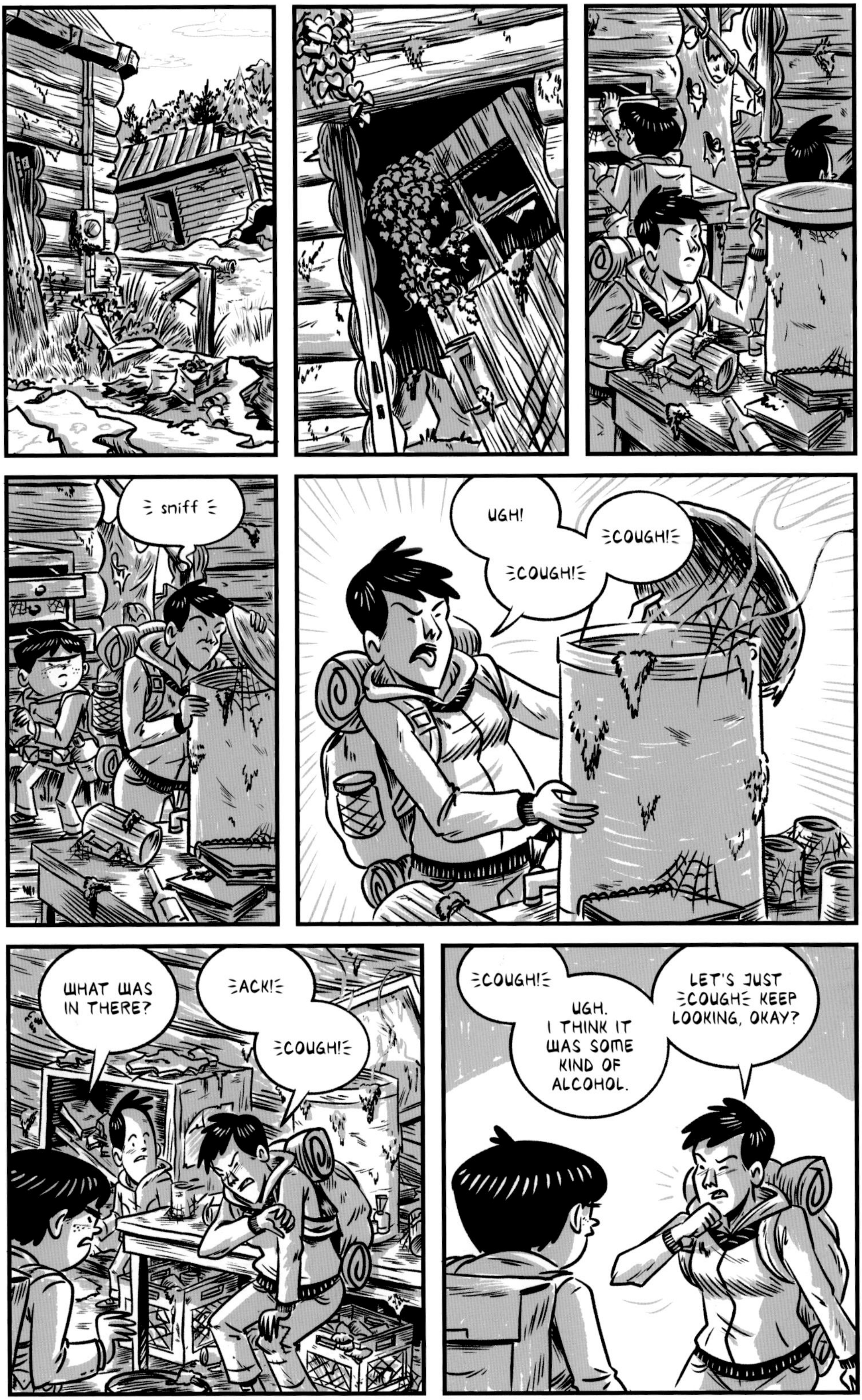
sniff
UGH!
COUGH!
COUGH!
WHAT WAS IN THERE?
ACK!
COUGH!
COUGH!
UGH. I THINK IT WAS SOME KIND OF ALCOHOL.
LET'S JUST COUGH KEEP LOOKING, OKAY?

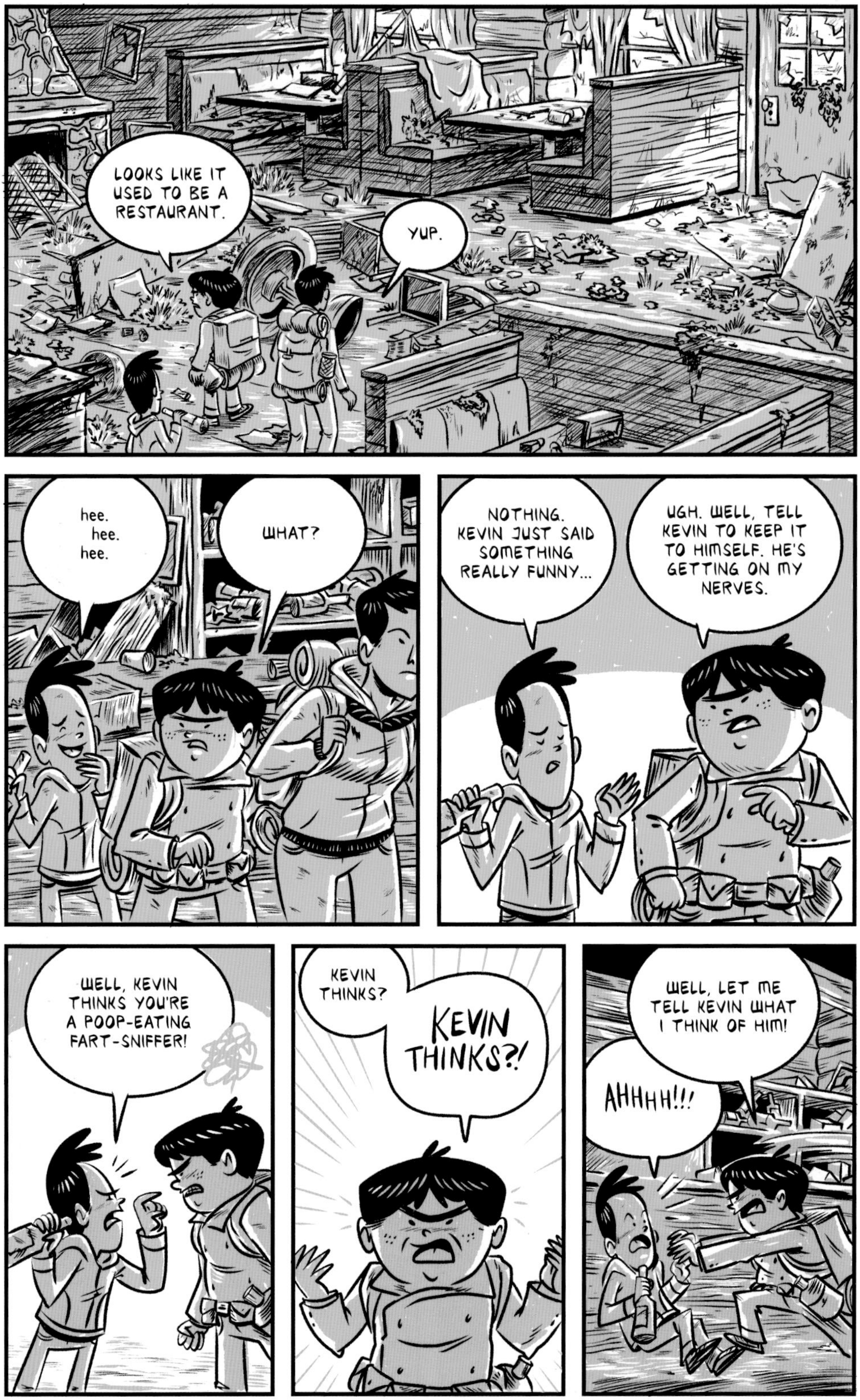

LOOKS LIKE IT USED TO BE A RESTAURANT.
YUP.
hee. hee. hee.
WHAT?
NOTHING. KEVIN JUST SAID SOMETHING REALLY FUNNY...
UGH. WELL, TELL KEVIN TO KEEP IT TO HIMSELF. HE'S GETTING ON MY NERVES.
WELL, KEVIN THINKS YOU'RE A POOP-EATING FART-SNIFFER!
KEVIN THINKS?
KEVIN THINKS?!
WELL, LET ME TELL KEVIN WHAT I THINK OF HIM!
AHHHH!!!

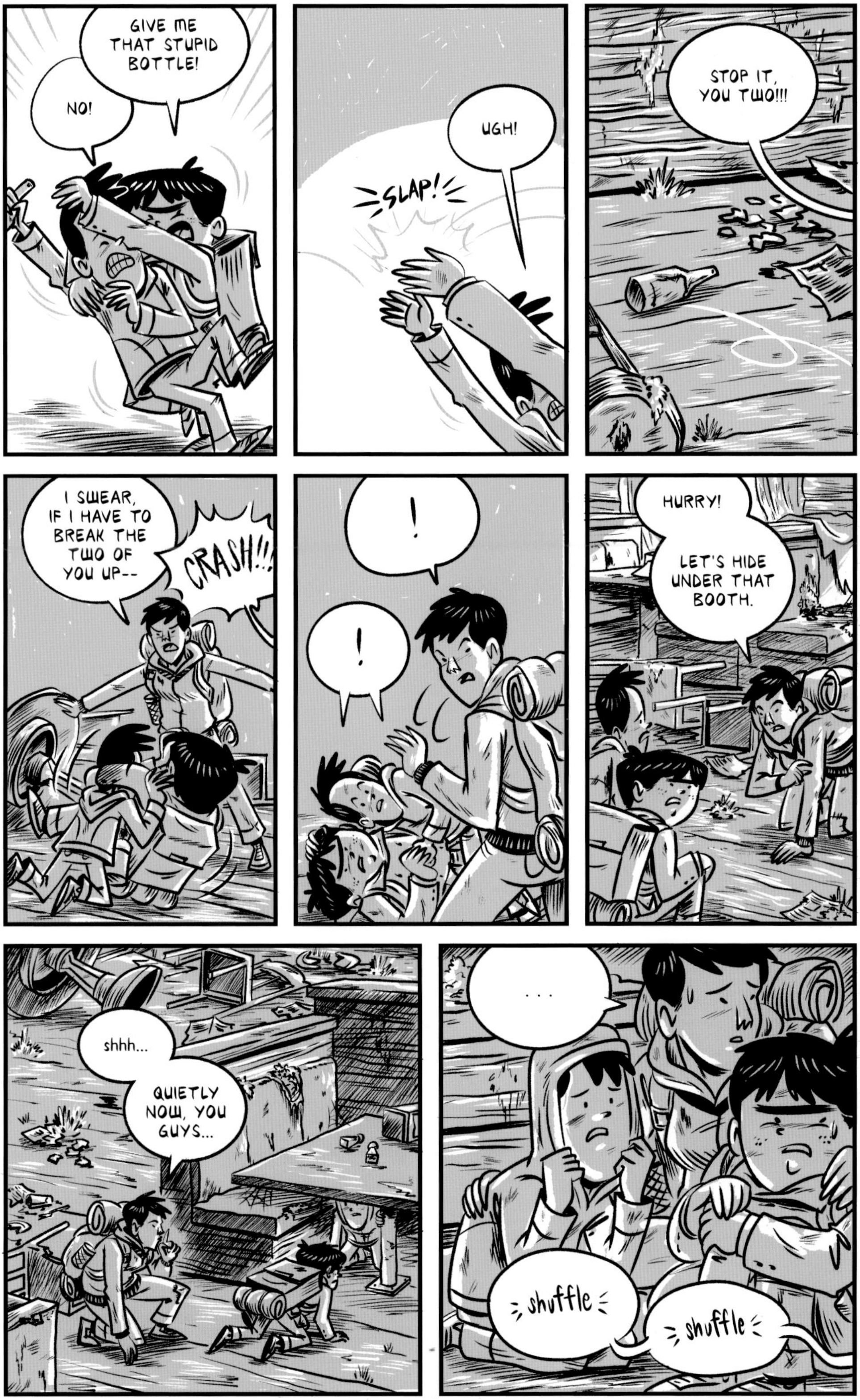
GIVE ME THAT STUPID BOTTLE!
NO!
UGH!
SLAP!
STOP IT, YOU TWO!!!
I SWEAR, IF I HAVE TO BREAK THE TWO OF YOU UP--
CRASH!!!
!
!
HURRY!
LET'S HIDE UNDER THAT BOOTH.
shhh...
QUIETLY NOW, YOU GUYS...
. . .
shuffle
shuffle

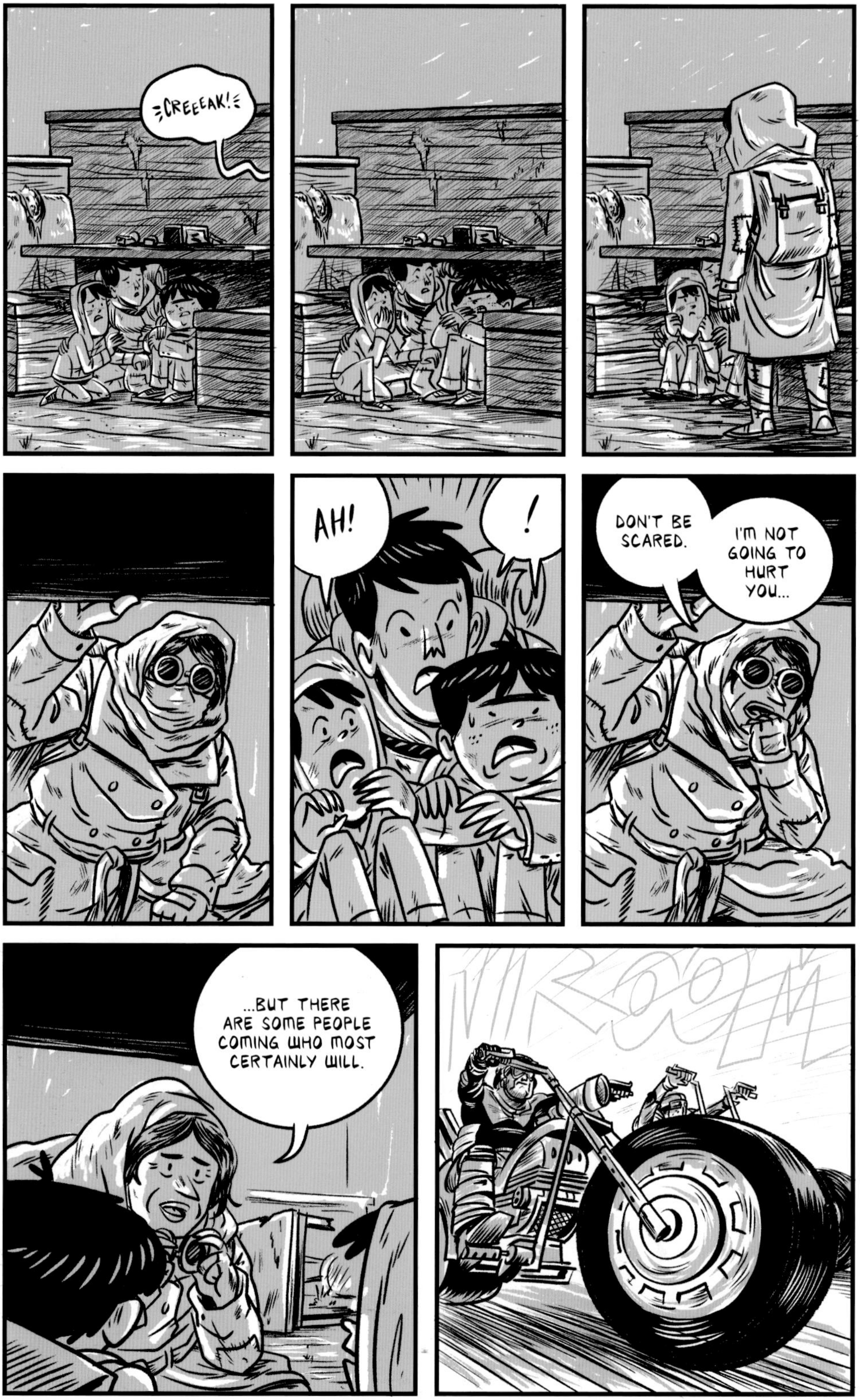
CREEEAK!
AH!
!
DON'T BE SCARED.
I'M NOT GOING TO HURT YOU...
...BUT THERE ARE SOME PEOPLE COMING WHO MOST CERTAINLY WILL.
VROOM

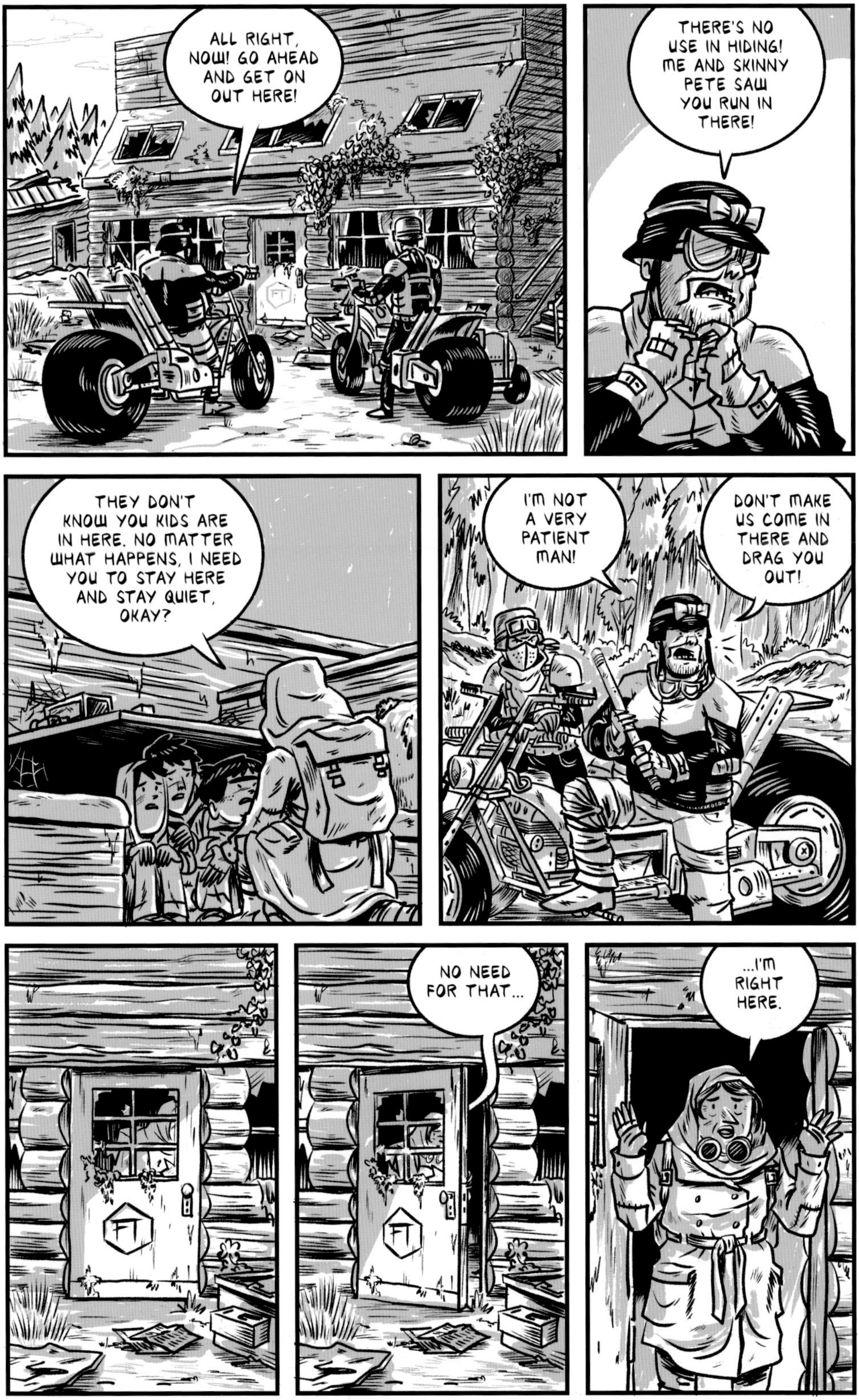
ALL RIGHT, NOW! GO AHEAD AND GET ON OUT HERE!
THERE'S NO USE IN HIDING! ME AND SKINNY PETE SAW YOU RUN IN THERE!
THEY DON'T KNOW YOU KIDS ARE IN HERE. NO MATTER WHAT HAPPENS, I NEED YOU TO STAY HERE AND STAY QUIET, OKAY?
I'M NOT A VERY PATIENT MAN!
DON'T MAKE US COME IN THERE AND DRAG YOU OUT!
NO NEED FOR THAT...
...I'M RIGHT HERE.

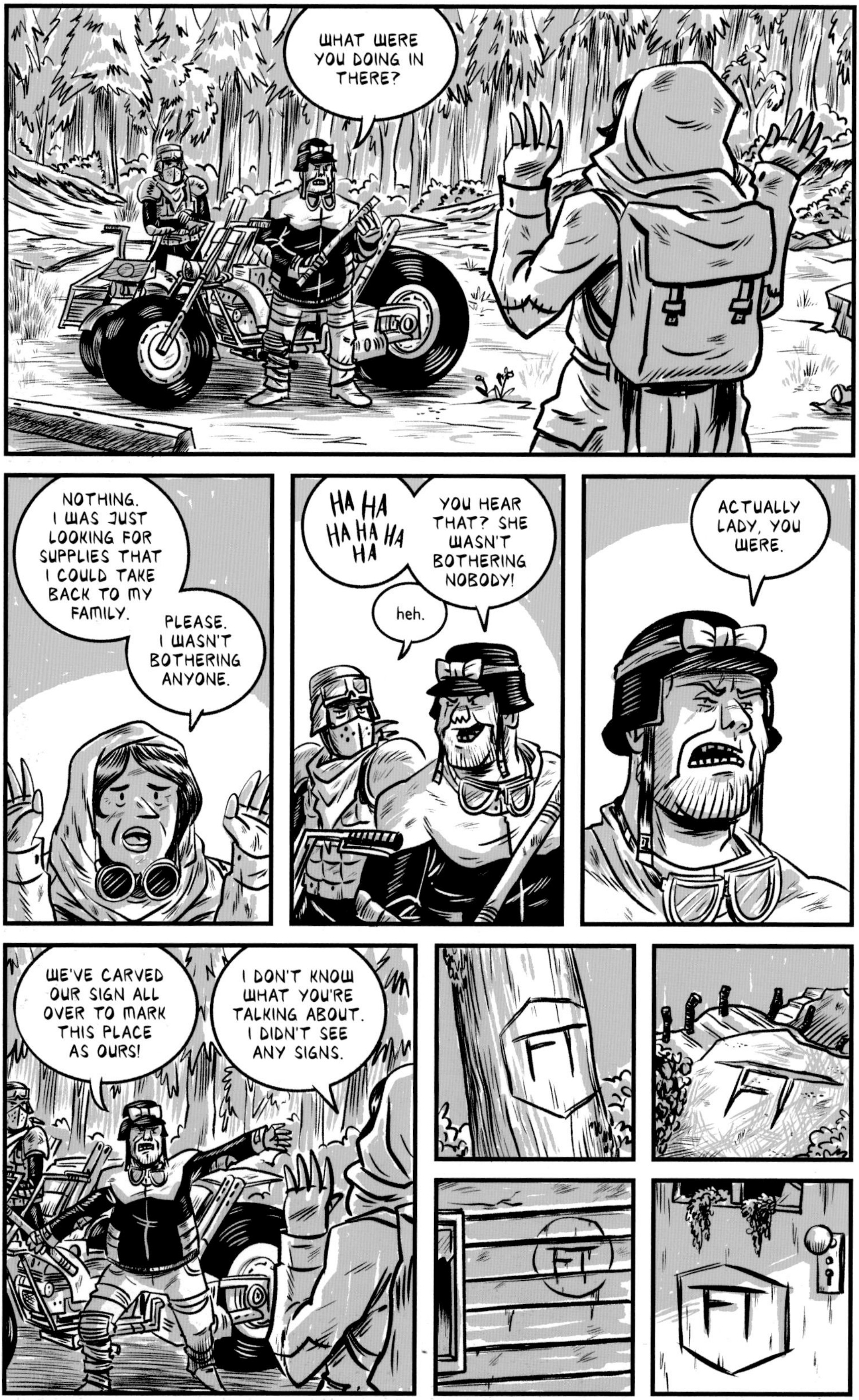
WHAT WERE YOU DOING IN THERE?
NOTHING. I WAS JUST LOOKING FOR SUPPLIES THAT I COULD TAKE BACK TO MY FAMILY.
PLEASE. I WASN'T BOTHERING ANYONE.
HA HA HA HA HA HA
YOU HEAR THAT? SHE WASN'T BOTHERING NOBODY!
heh.
ACTUALLY LADY, YOU WERE.
WE'VE CARVED OUR SIGN ALL OVER TO MARK THIS PLACE AS OURS!
I DON'T KNOW WHAT YOU'RE TALKING ABOUT. I DIDN'T SEE ANY SIGNS.
FT
FT
FT
FT

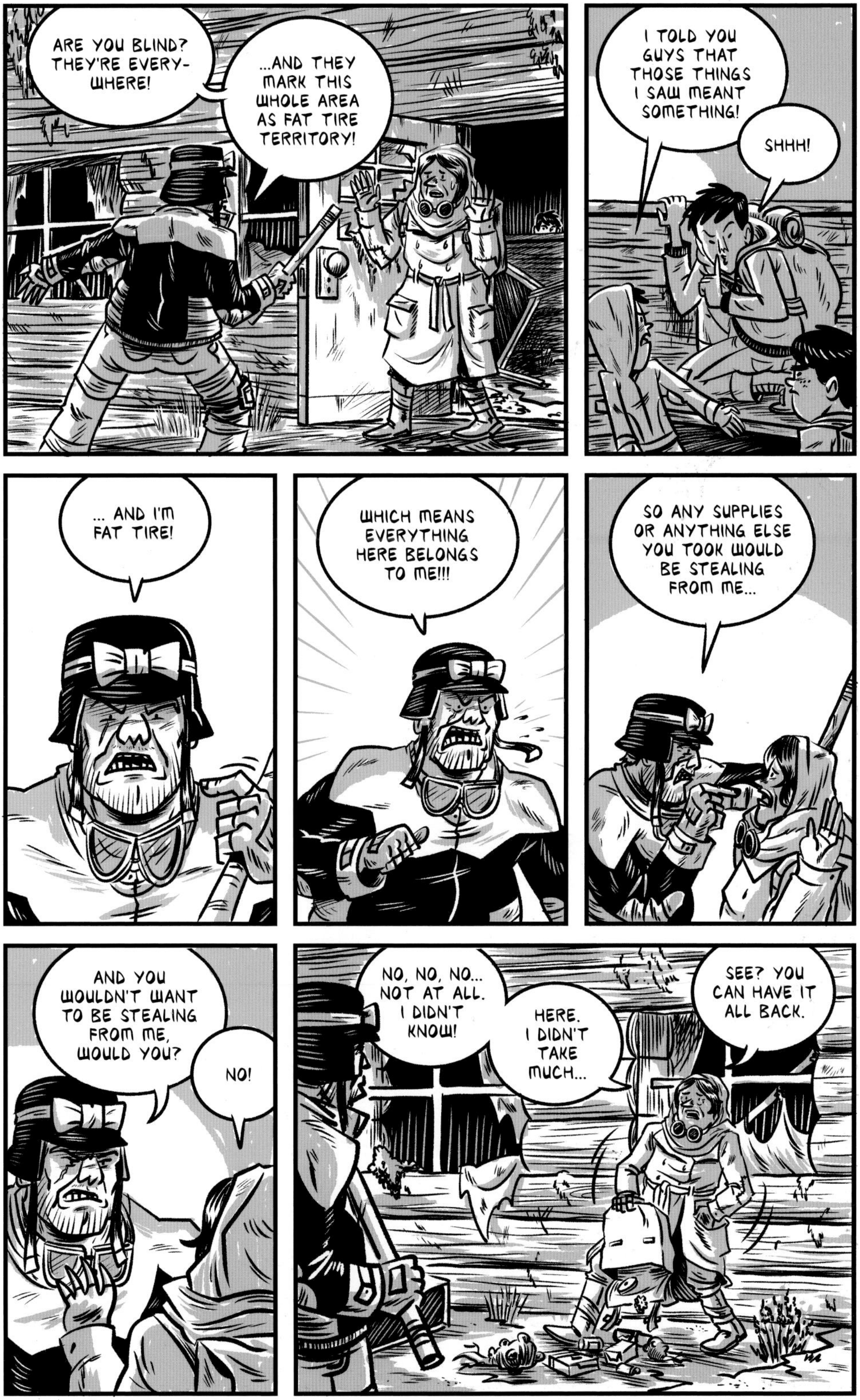

ARE YOU BLIND? THEY'RE EVERY-WHERE!
...AND THEY MARK THIS WHOLE AREA AS FAT TIRE TERRITORY!
I TOLD YOU GUYS THAT THOSE THINGS I SAW MEANT SOMETHING!
SHHH!
... AND I'M FAT TIRE!
WHICH MEANS EVERYTHING HERE BELONGS TO ME!!!
SO ANY SUPPLIES OR ANYTHING ELSE YOU TOOK WOULD BE STEALING FROM ME...
AND YOU WOULDN'T WANT TO BE STEALING FROM ME, WOULD YOU?
NO!
NO, NO, NO... NOT AT ALL. I DIDN'T KNOW!
HERE. I DIDN'T TAKE MUCH...
SEE? YOU CAN HAVE IT ALL BACK.

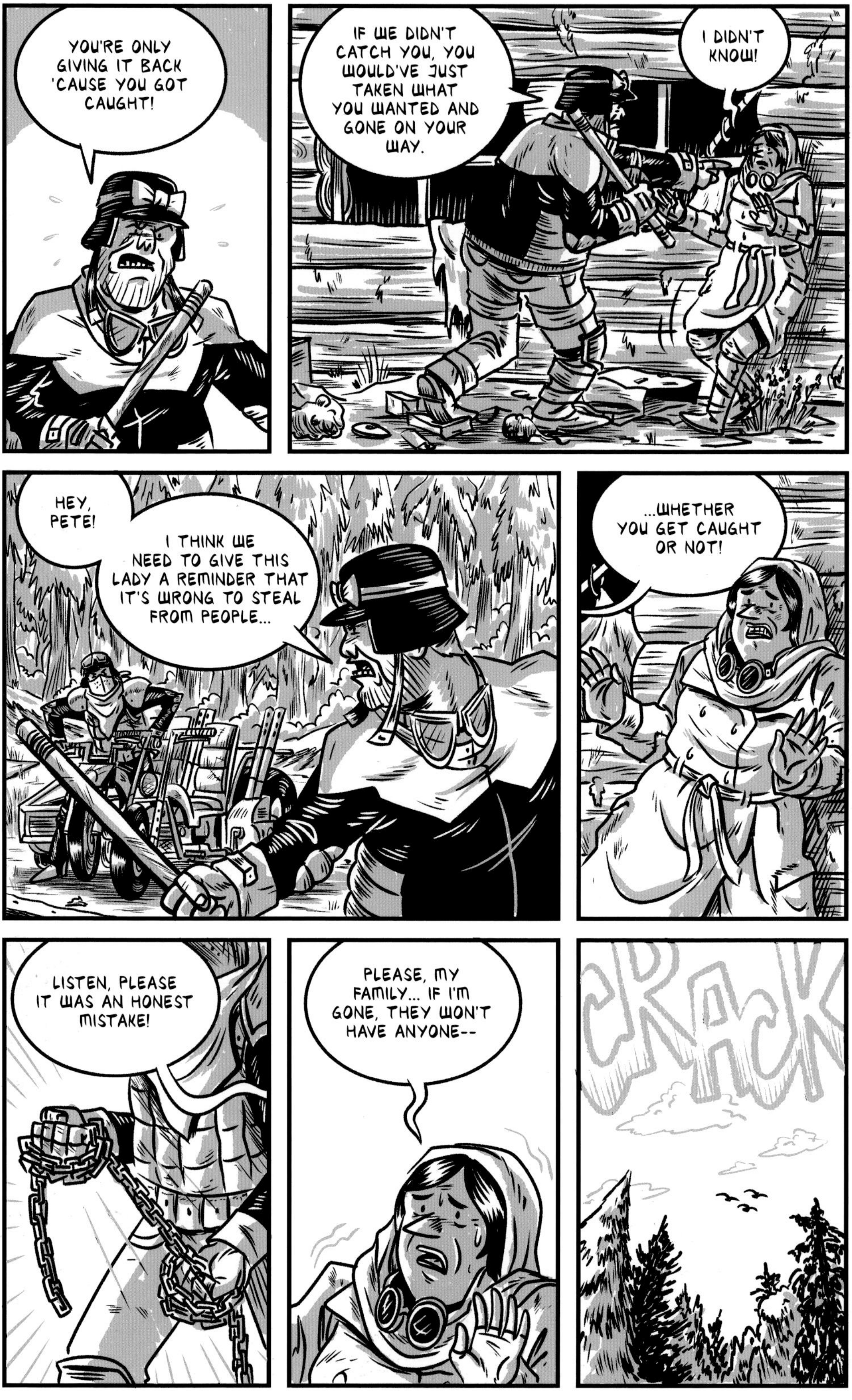
YOU'RE ONLY GIVING IT BACK 'CAUSE YOU GOT CAUGHT!
IF WE DIDN'T CATCH YOU, YOU WOULD'VE JUST TAKEN WHAT YOU WANTED AND GONE ON YOUR WAY.
I DIDN'T KNOW!
HEY, PETE!
I THINK WE NEED TO GIVE THIS LADY A REMINDER THAT IT'S WRONG TO STEAL FROM PEOPLE...
...WHETHER YOU GET CAUGHT OR NOT!
LISTEN, PLEASE IT WAS AN HONEST MISTAKE!
PLEASE, MY FAMILY... IF I'M GONE, THEY WON'T HAVE ANYONE--
CRACK

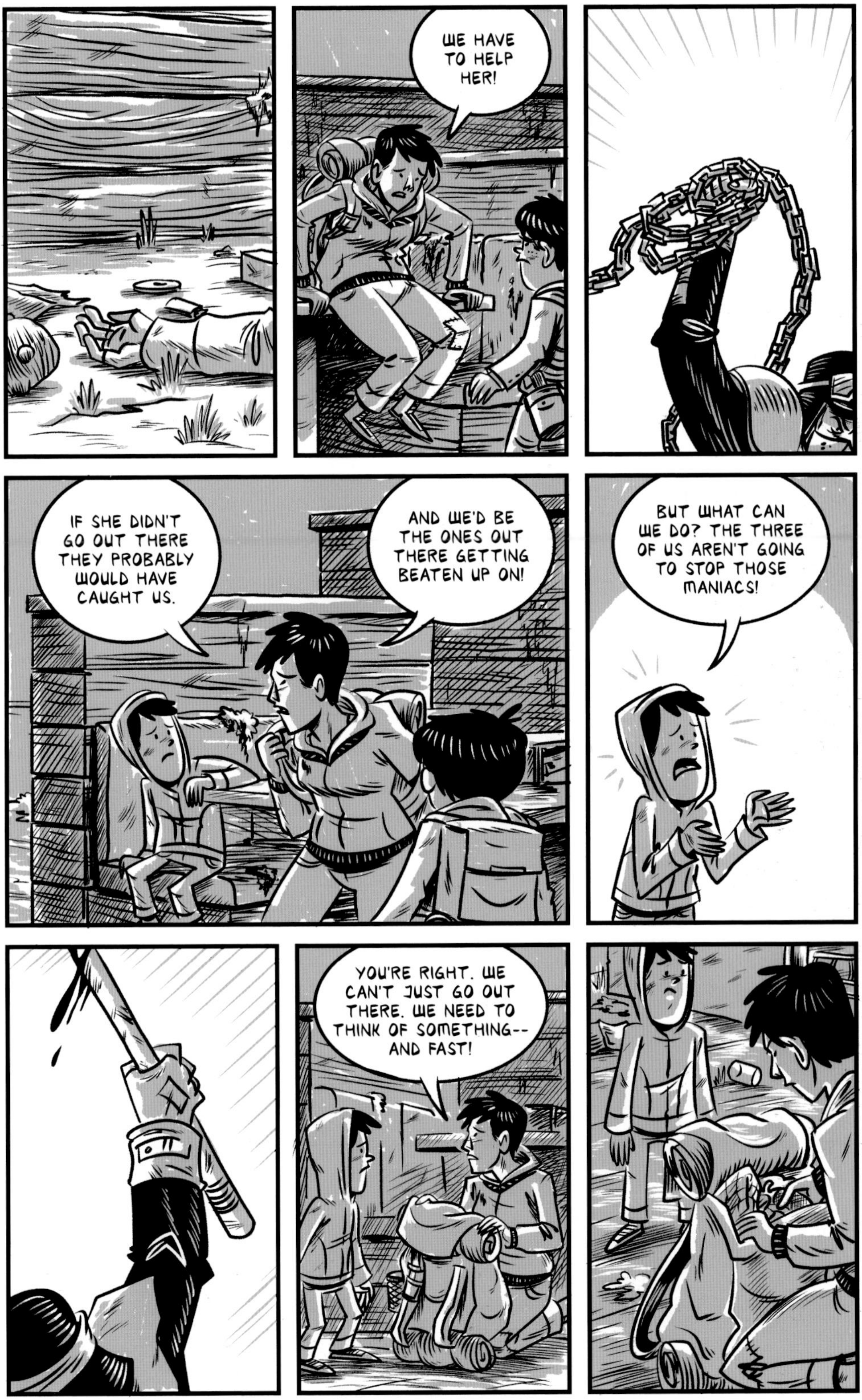

WE HAVE TO HELP HER!
IF SHE DIDN'T GO OUT THERE THEY PROBABLY WOULD HAVE CAUGHT US.
AND WE'D BE THE ONES OUT THERE GETTING BEATEN UP ON!
BUT WHAT CAN WE DO? THE THREE OF US AREN'T GOING TO STOP THOSE MANIACS!
YOU'RE RIGHT. WE CAN'T JUST GO OUT THERE. WE NEED TO THINK OF SOMETHING-- AND FAST!

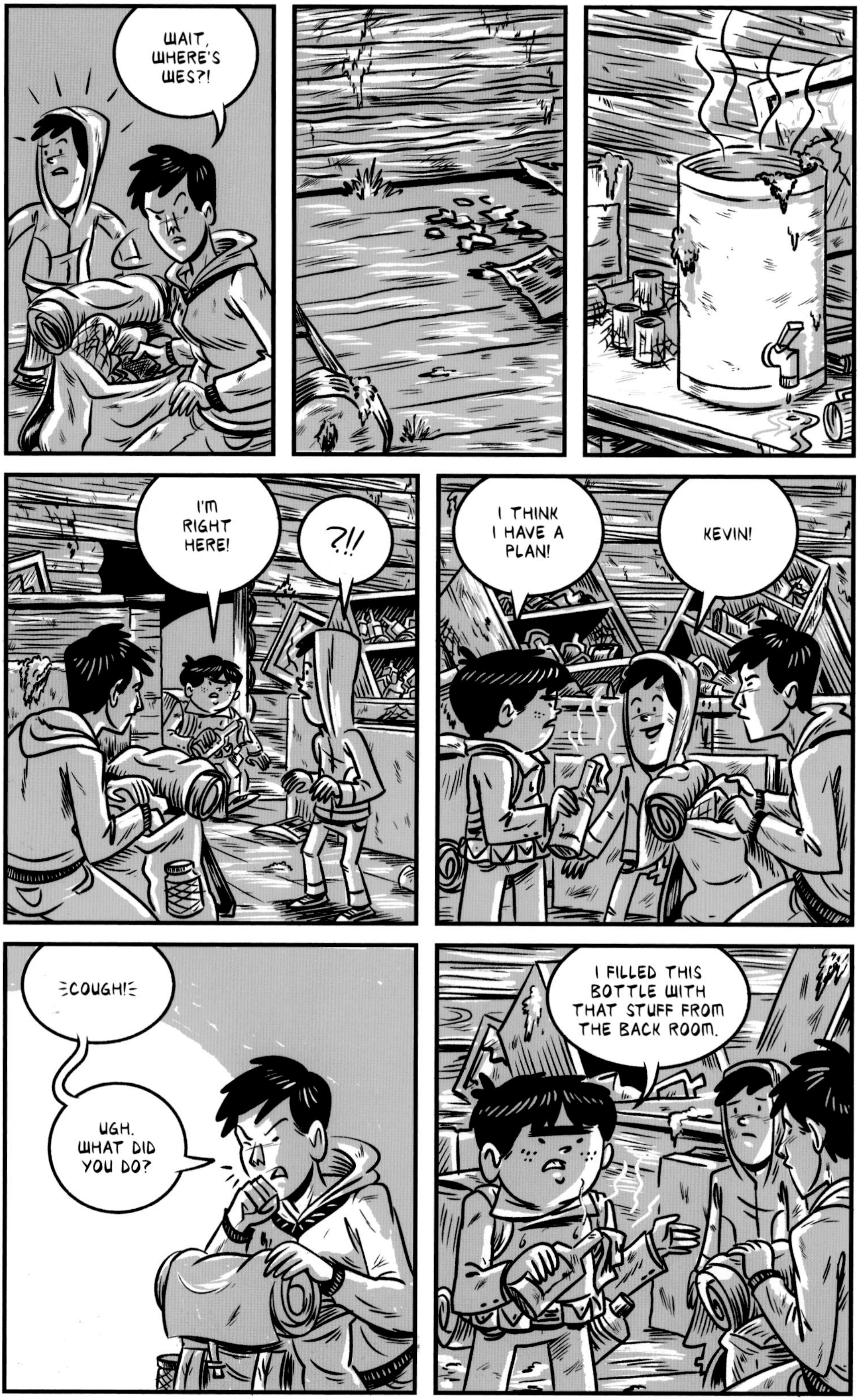
WAIT, WHERE'S WES?!
I'M RIGHT HERE!
?!!
I THINK I HAVE A PLAN!
KEVIN!
COUGH!
UGH. WHAT DID YOU DO?
I FILLED THIS BOTTLE WITH THAT STUFF FROM THE BACK ROOM.

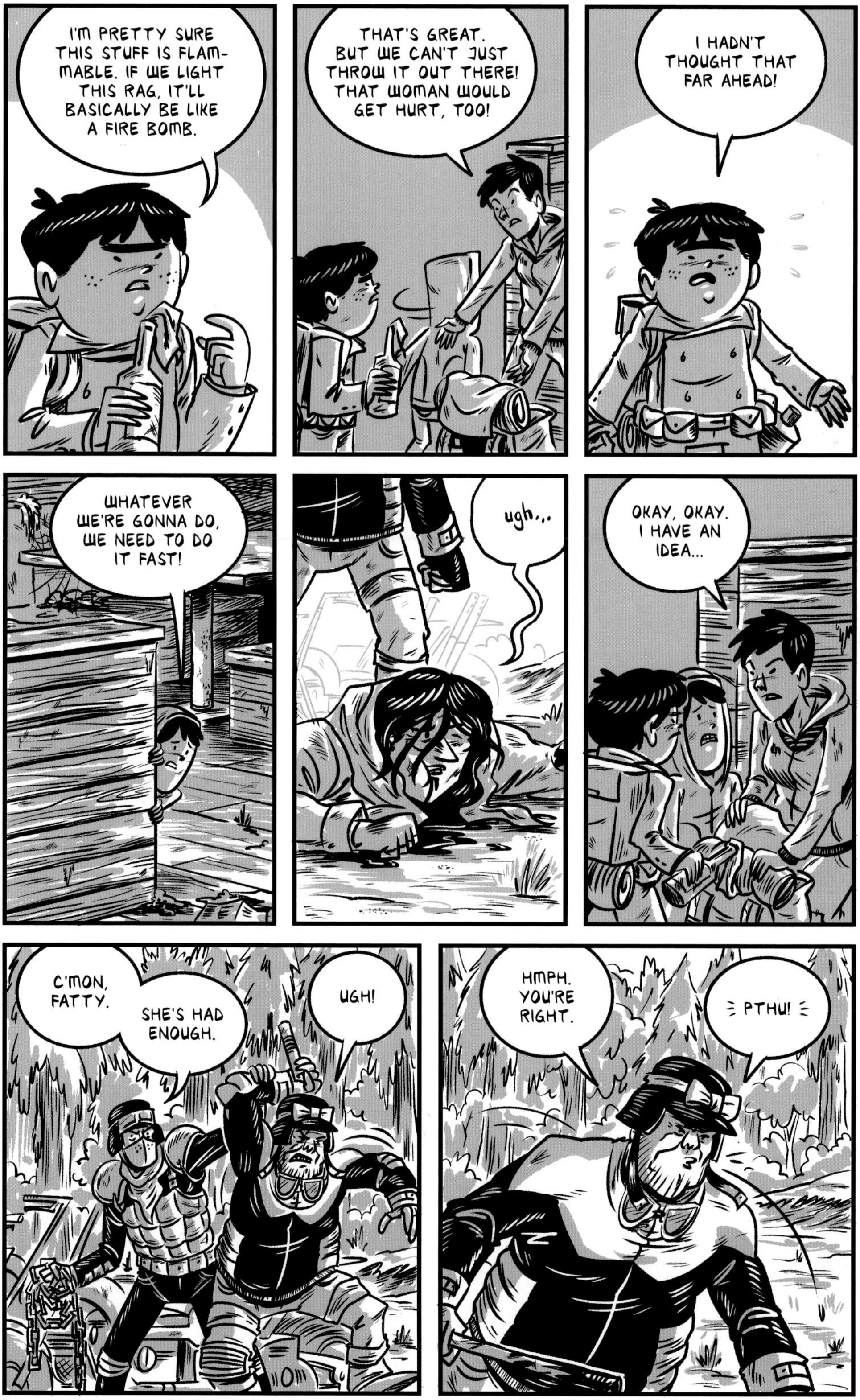
I'M PRETTY SURE THIS STUFF IS FLAM-MABLE. IF WE LIGHT THIS RAG, IT'LL BASICALLY BE LIKE A FIRE BOMB.
THAT'S GREAT. BUT WE CAN'T JUST THROW IT OUT THERE! THAT WOMAN WOULD GET HURT, TOO!
I HADN'T THOUGHT THAT FAR AHEAD!
WHATEVER WE'RE GONNA DO, WE NEED TO DO IT FAST!
ugh...
OKAY, OKAY. I HAVE AN IDEA...
C'MON, FATTY.
SHE'S HAD ENOUGH.
UGH!
HMPH. YOU'RE RIGHT.
PTHU!

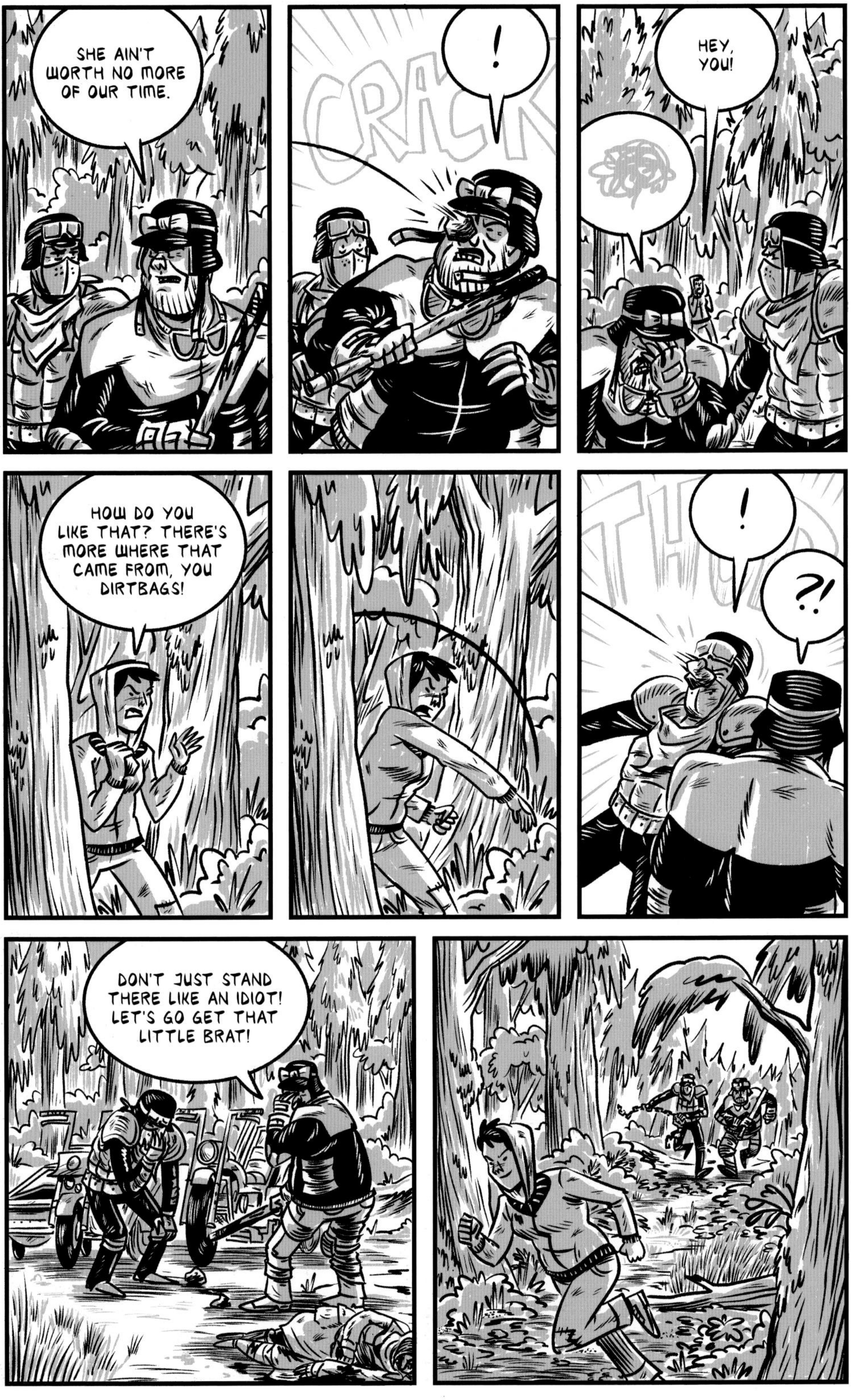
SHE AIN'T WORTH NO MORE OF OUR TIME.
CRACK
!
HEY, YOU!
HOW DO YOU LIKE THAT? THERE'S MORE WHERE THAT CAME FROM, YOU DIRTBAGS!
!
?!
DON'T JUST STAND THERE LIKE AN IDIOT! LET'S GO GET THAT LITTLE BRAT!

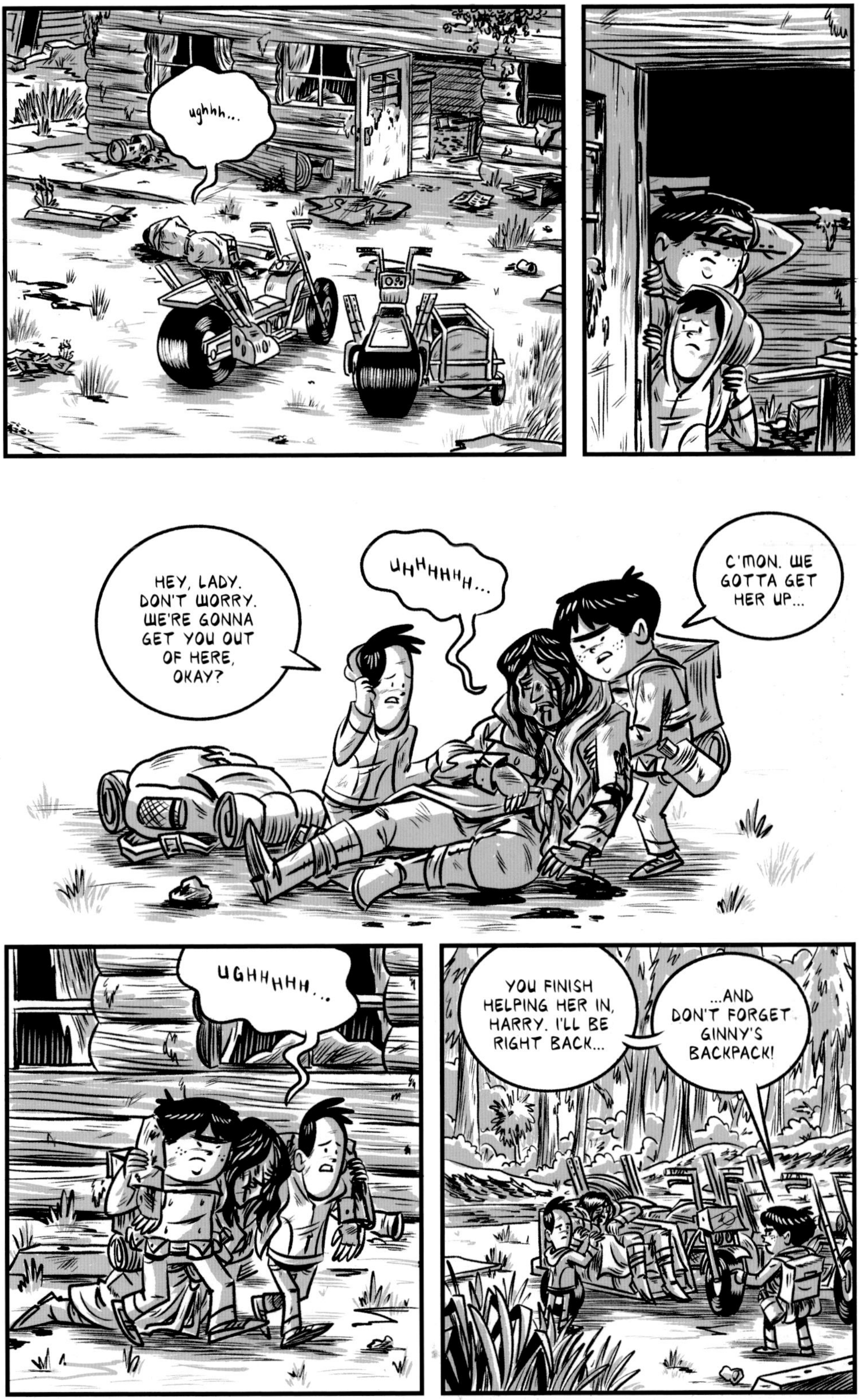
ughhh...
HEY, LADY. DON'T WORRY. WE'RE GONNA GET YOU OUT OF HERE, OKAY?
UHHHHHH...
C'MON. WE GOTTA GET HER UP...
UGHHHHH...
YOU FINISH HELPING HER IN, HARRY. I'LL BE RIGHT BACK...
...AND DON'T FORGET GINNY'S BACKPACK!

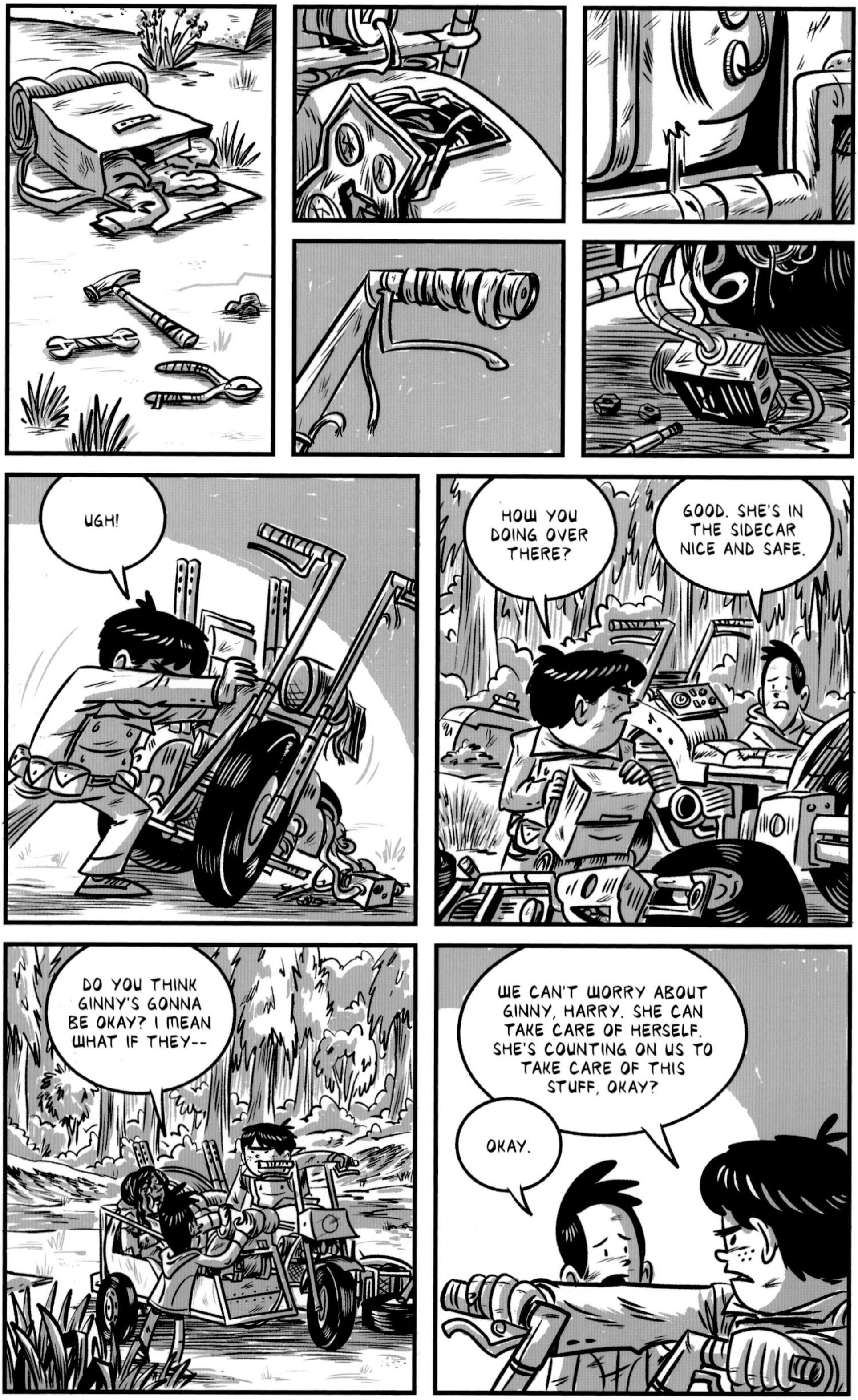
UGH!
HOW YOU DOING OVER THERE?
GOOD. SHE'S IN THE SIDECAR NICE AND SAFE.
DO YOU THINK GINNY'S GONNA BE OKAY? I MEAN WHAT IF THEY--
WE CAN'T WORRY ABOUT GINNY, HARRY. SHE CAN TAKE CARE OF HERSELF. SHE'S COUNTING ON US TO TAKE CARE OF THIS STUFF, OKAY?
OKAY.

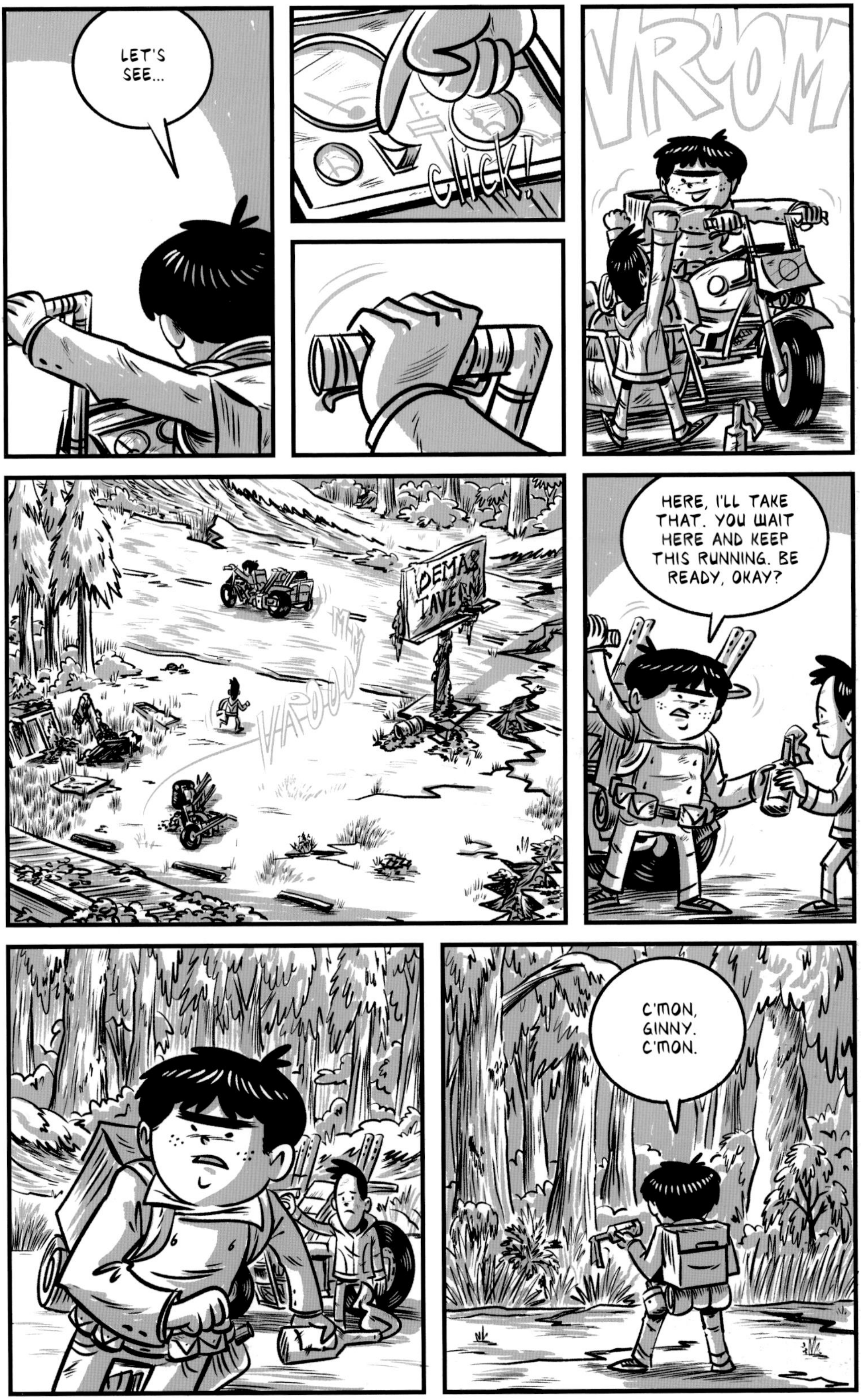
LET'S SEE...
CLICK!
VROOM
DEMAS TAVE
VROOOM
HERE, I'LL TAKE THAT. YOU WAIT HERE AND KEEP THIS RUNNING. BE READY, OKAY?
C'MON, GINNY. C'MON.

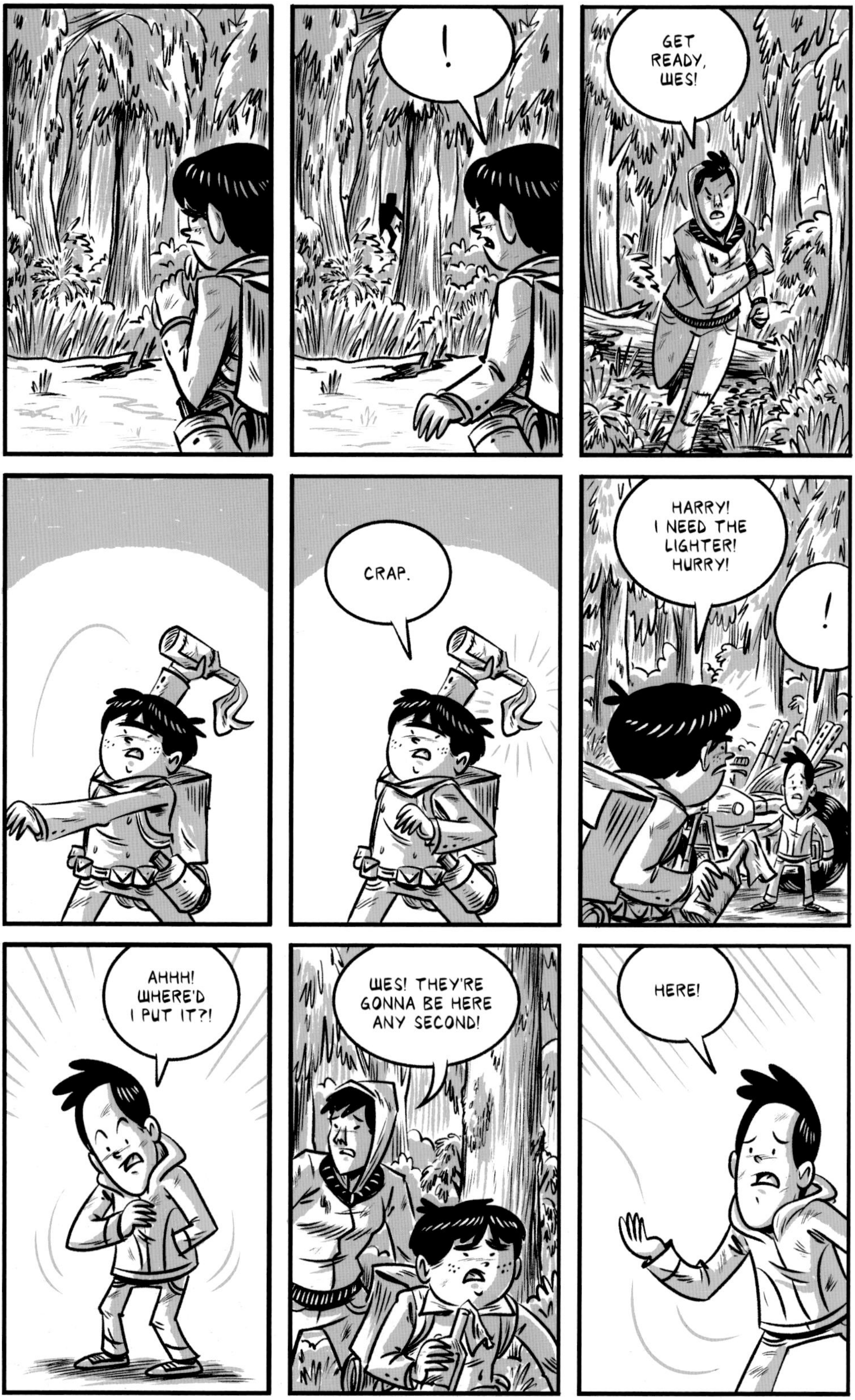
!
GET READY, WES!
CRAP.
HARRY! I NEED THE LIGHTER! HURRY!
!
AHHH! WHERE'D I PUT IT?!
WES! THEY'RE GONNA BE HERE ANY SECOND!
HERE!

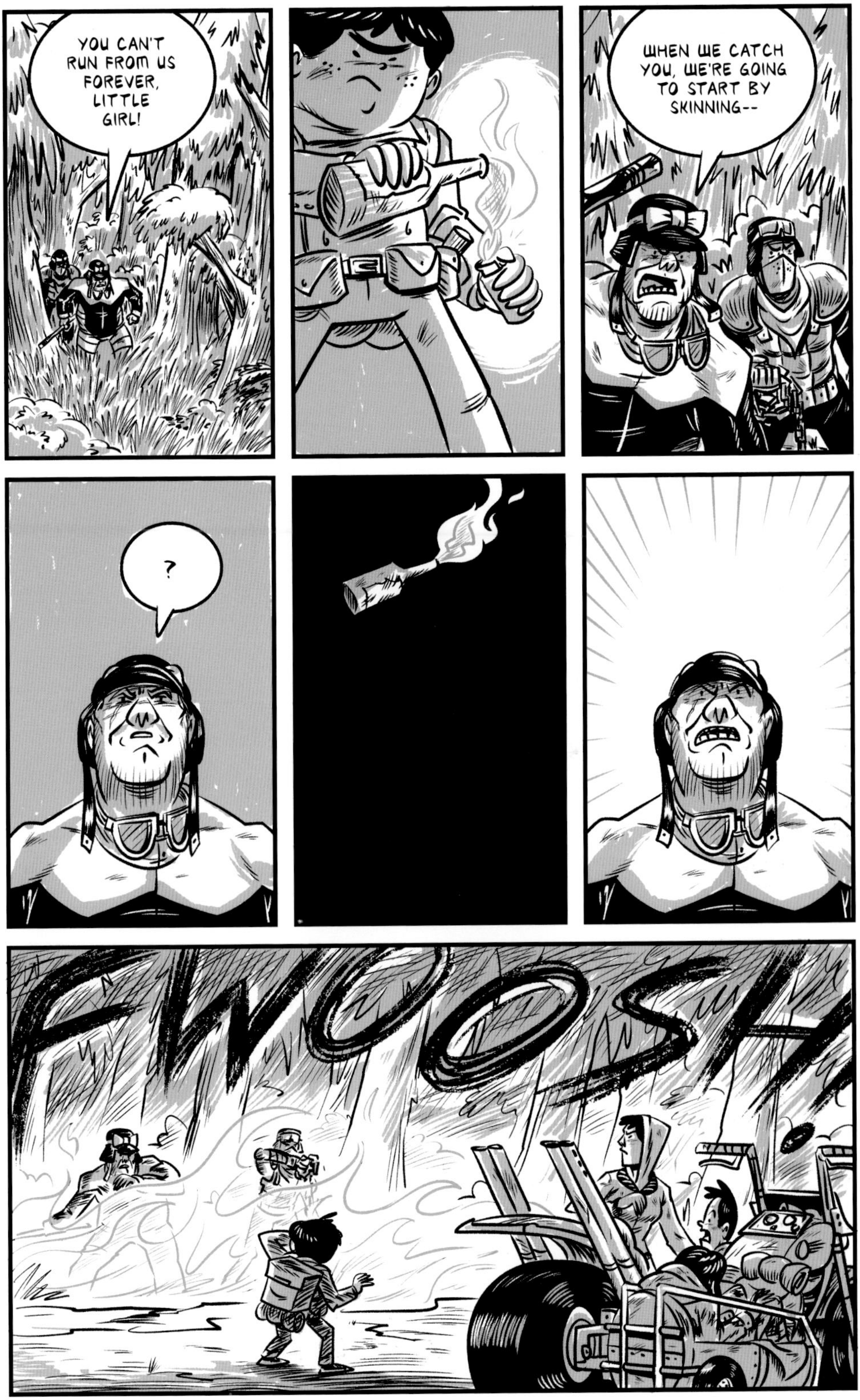
YOU CAN'T RUN FROM US FOREVER, LITTLE GIRL!
WHEN WE CATCH YOU, WE'RE GOING TO START BY SKINNING--
?
FWOOSH

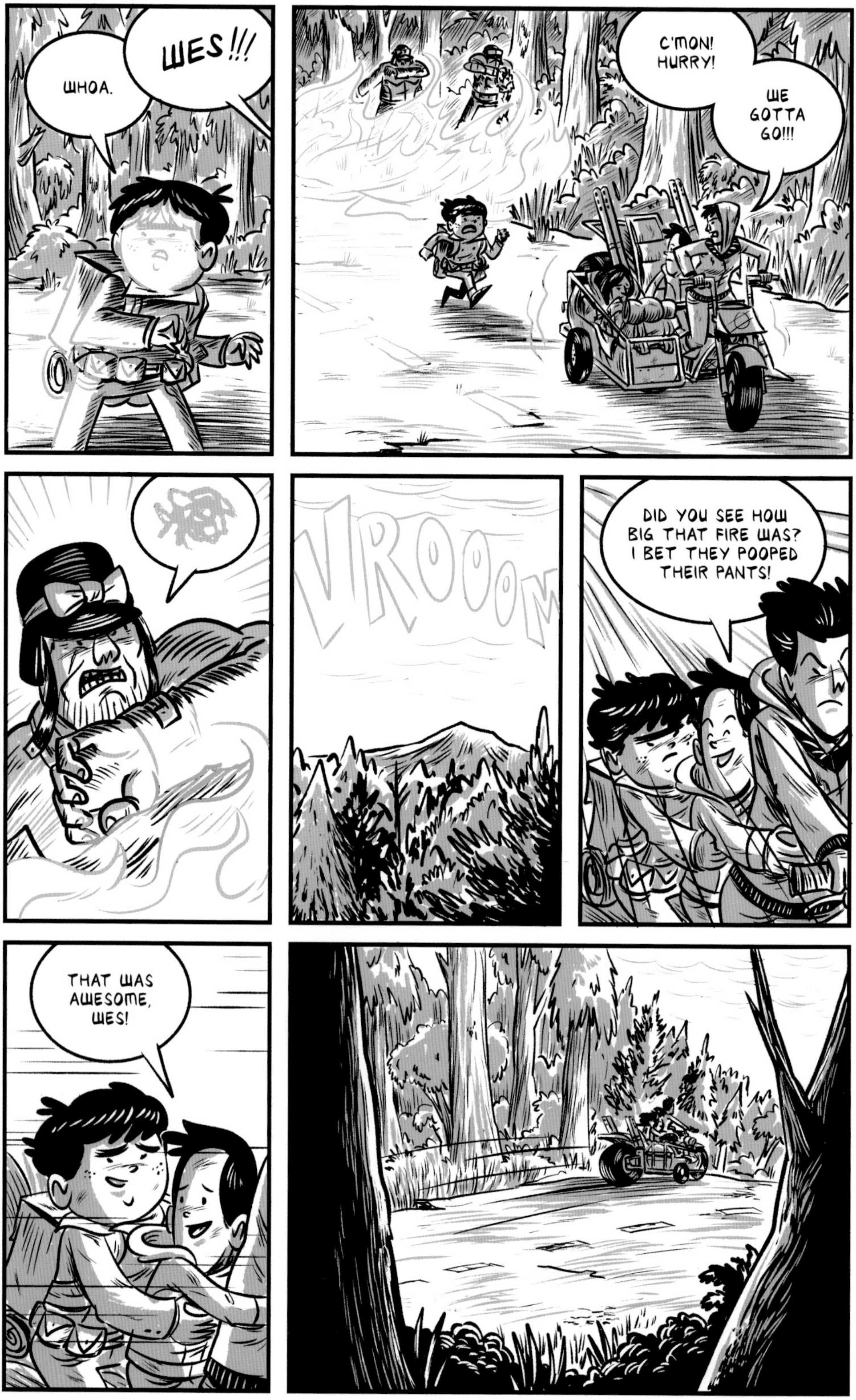
WHOA.
WES!!!
C'MON! HURRY!
WE GOTTA GO!!!
VROOOM
DID YOU SEE HOW BIG THAT FIRE WAS? I BET THEY POOPED THEIR PANTS!
THAT WAS AWESOME, WES!

CHAPTER 5

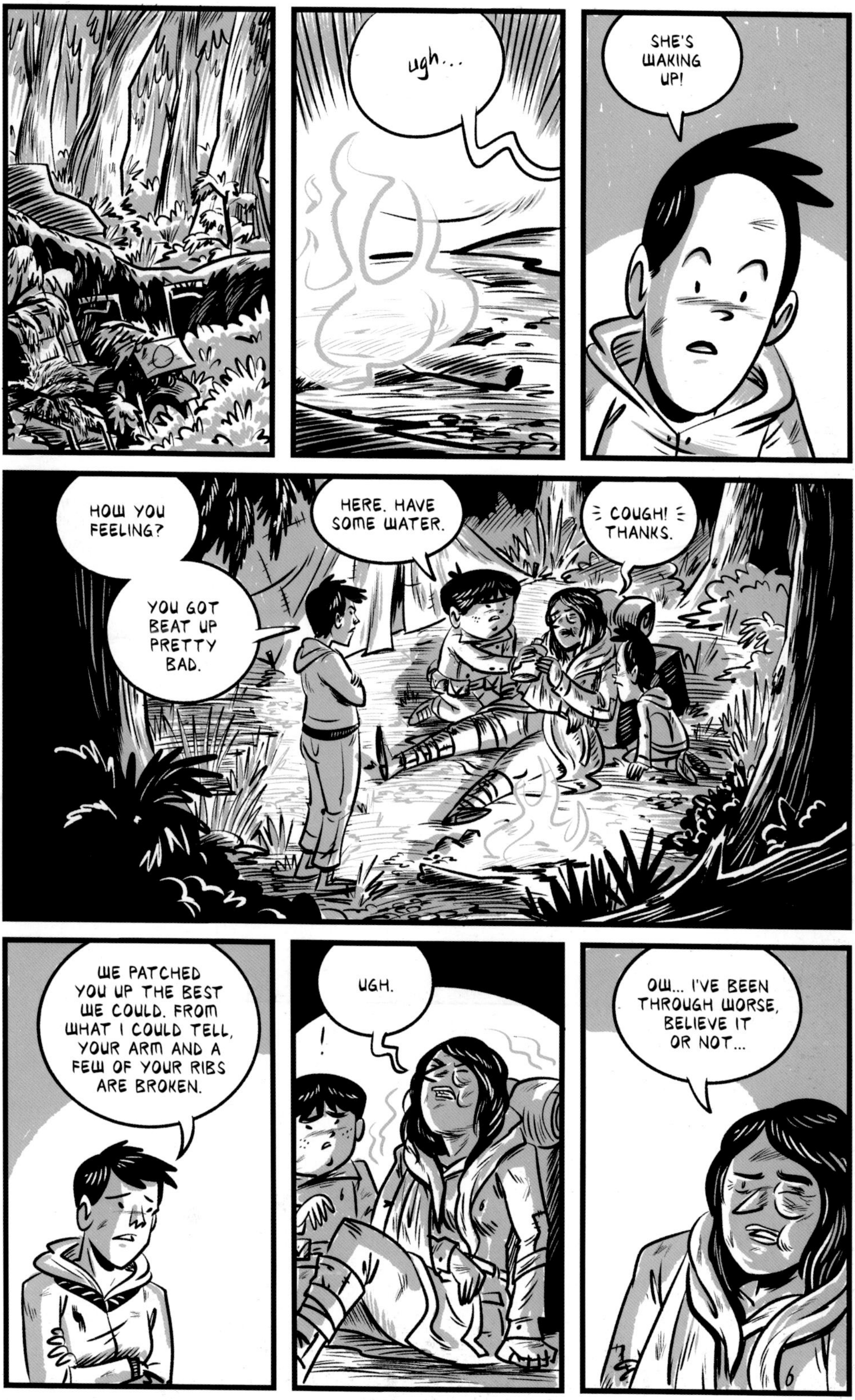
ugh...
SHE'S WAKING UP!
HOW YOU FEELING?
YOU GOT BEAT UP PRETTY BAD.
HERE. HAVE SOME WATER.
COUGH! THANKS.
WE PATCHED YOU UP THE BEST WE COULD. FROM WHAT I COULD TELL, YOUR ARM AND A FEW OF YOUR RIBS ARE BROKEN.
!
UGH.
OW... I'VE BEEN THROUGH WORSE, BELIEVE IT OR NOT...

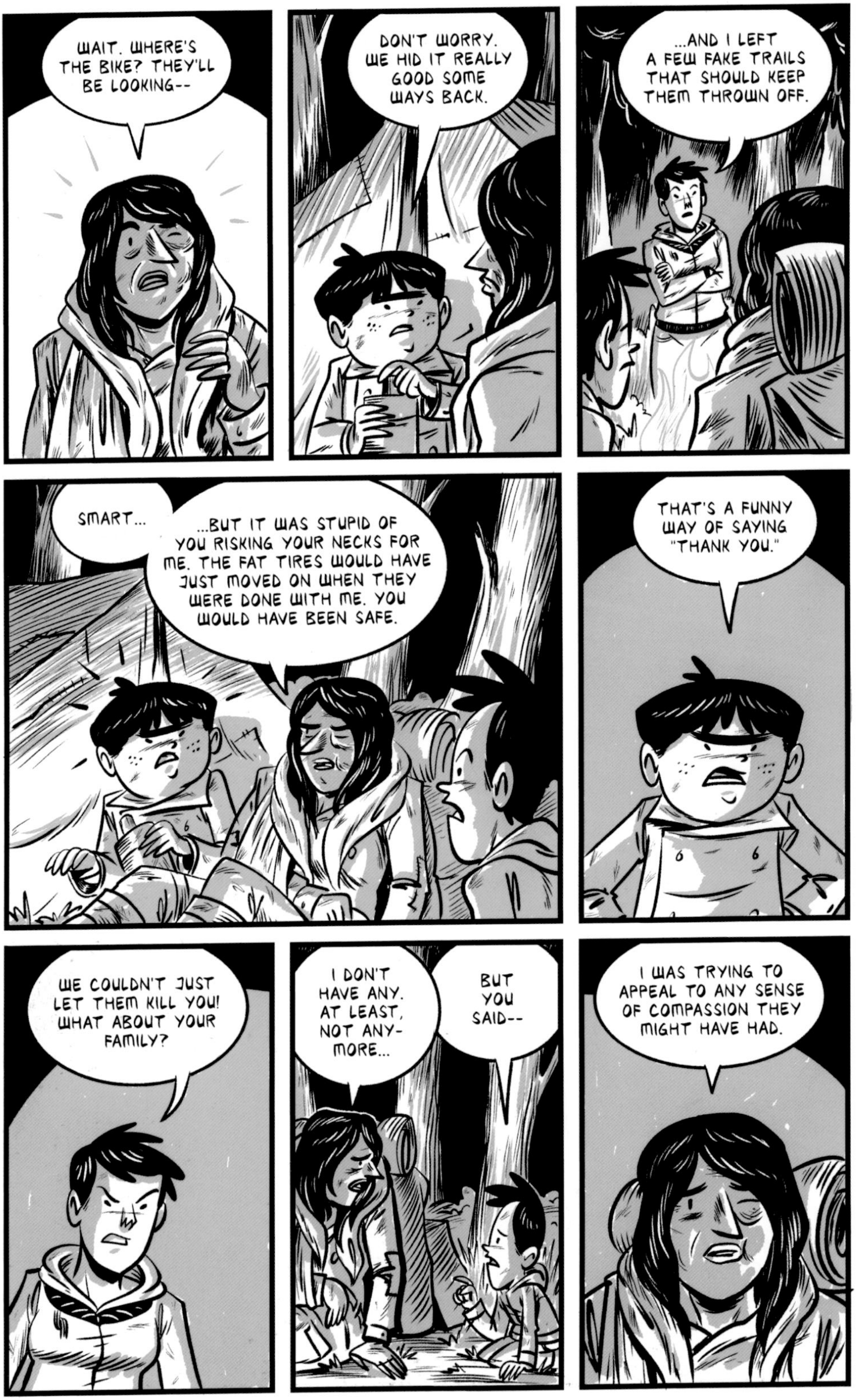
WAIT. WHERE'S THE BIKE? THEY'LL BE LOOKING--
DON'T WORRY. WE HID IT REALLY GOOD SOME WAYS BACK.
...AND I LEFT A FEW FAKE TRAILS THAT SHOULD KEEP THEM THROWN OFF.
SMART...
...BUT IT WAS STUPID OF YOU RISKING YOUR NECKS FOR ME. THE FAT TIRES WOULD HAVE JUST MOVED ON WHEN THEY WERE DONE WITH ME. YOU WOULD HAVE BEEN SAFE.
THAT'S A FUNNY WAY OF SAYING "THANK YOU."
WE COULDN'T JUST LET THEM KILL YOU! WHAT ABOUT YOUR FAMILY?
I DON'T HAVE ANY. AT LEAST, NOT ANY-MORE...
BUT YOU SAID--
I WAS TRYING TO APPEAL TO ANY SENSE OF COMPASSION THEY MIGHT HAVE HAD.

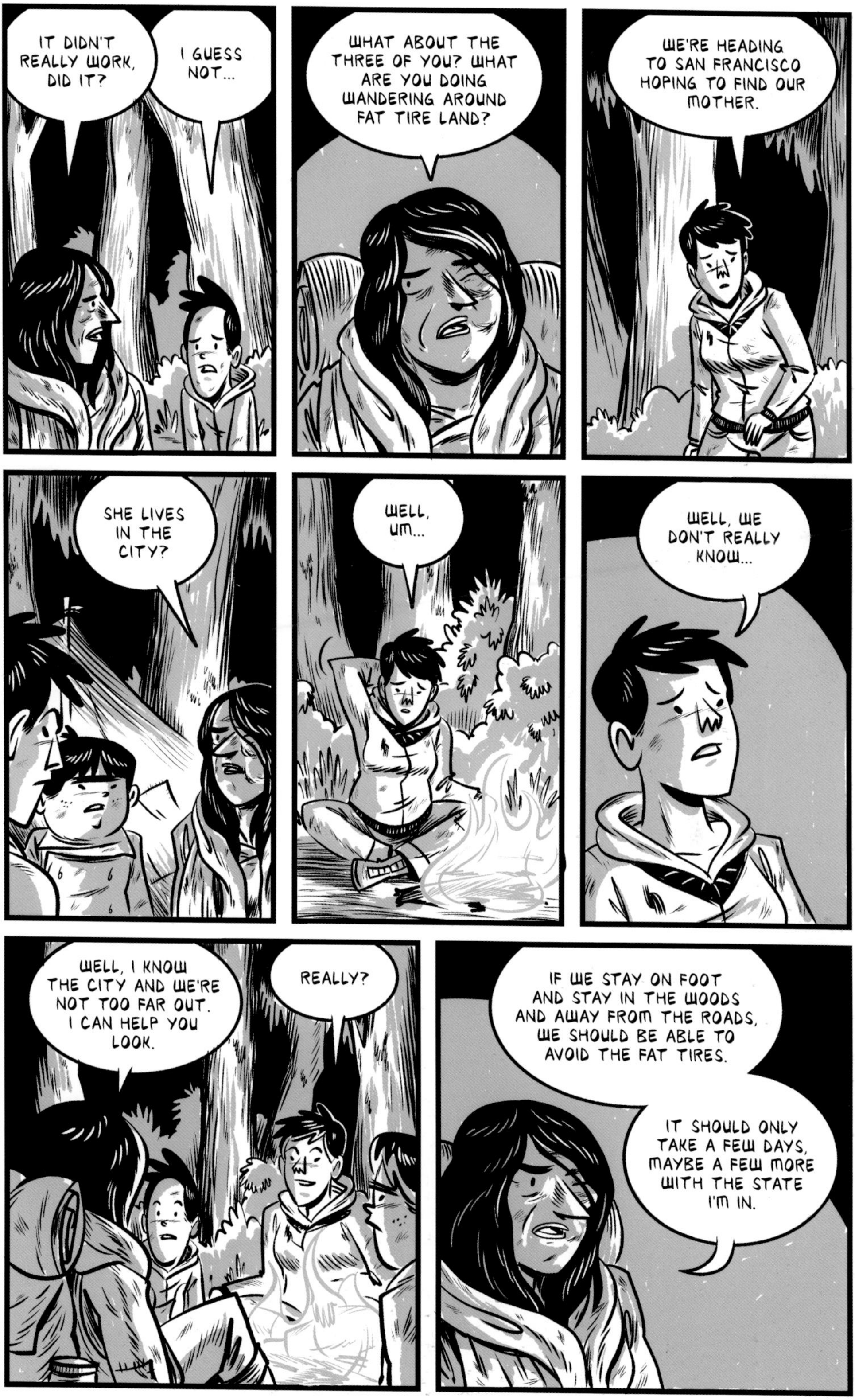
IT DIDN'T REALLY WORK, DID IT?
I GUESS NOT...
WHAT ABOUT THE THREE OF YOU? WHAT ARE YOU DOING WANDERING AROUND FAT TIRE LAND?
WE'RE HEADING TO SAN FRANCISCO HOPING TO FIND OUR MOTHER.
SHE LIVES IN THE CITY?
WELL, UM...
WELL, WE DON'T REALLY KNOW...
WELL, I KNOW THE CITY AND WE'RE NOT TOO FAR OUT. I CAN HELP YOU LOOK.
REALLY?
IF WE STAY ON FOOT AND STAY IN THE WOODS AND AWAY FROM THE ROADS, WE SHOULD BE ABLE TO AVOID THE FAT TIRES.
IT SHOULD ONLY TAKE A FEW DAYS, MAYBE A FEW MORE WITH THE STATE I'M IN.

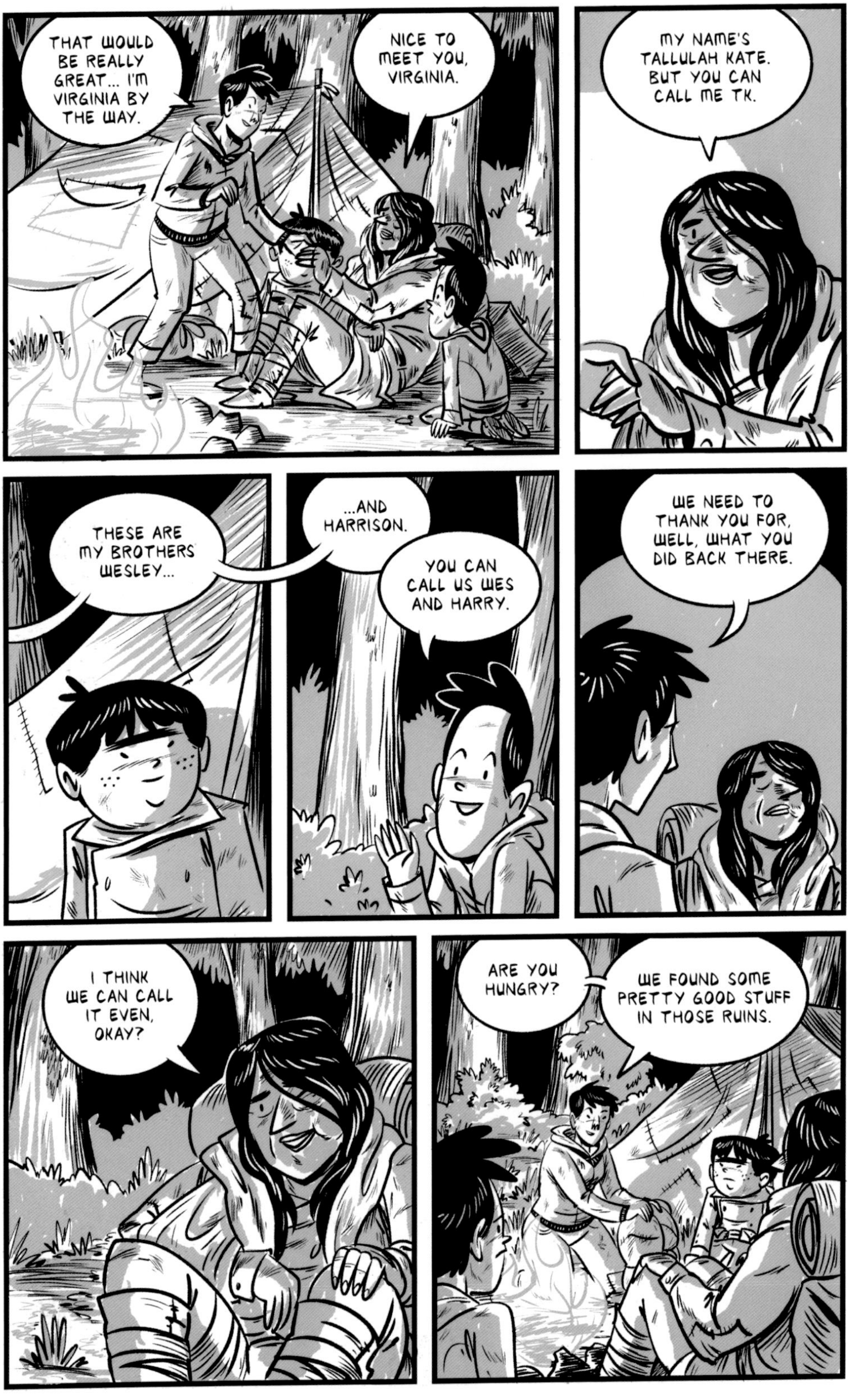
THAT WOULD BE REALLY GREAT... I'M VIRGINIA BY THE WAY.
NICE TO MEET YOU, VIRGINIA.
MY NAME'S TALLULAH KATE. BUT YOU CAN CALL ME TK.
THESE ARE MY BROTHERS WESLEY...
...AND HARRISON.
YOU CAN CALL US WES AND HARRY.
WE NEED TO THANK YOU FOR, WELL, WHAT YOU DID BACK THERE.
I THINK WE CAN CALL IT EVEN, OKAY?
ARE YOU HUNGRY?
WE FOUND SOME PRETTY GOOD STUFF IN THOSE RUINS.

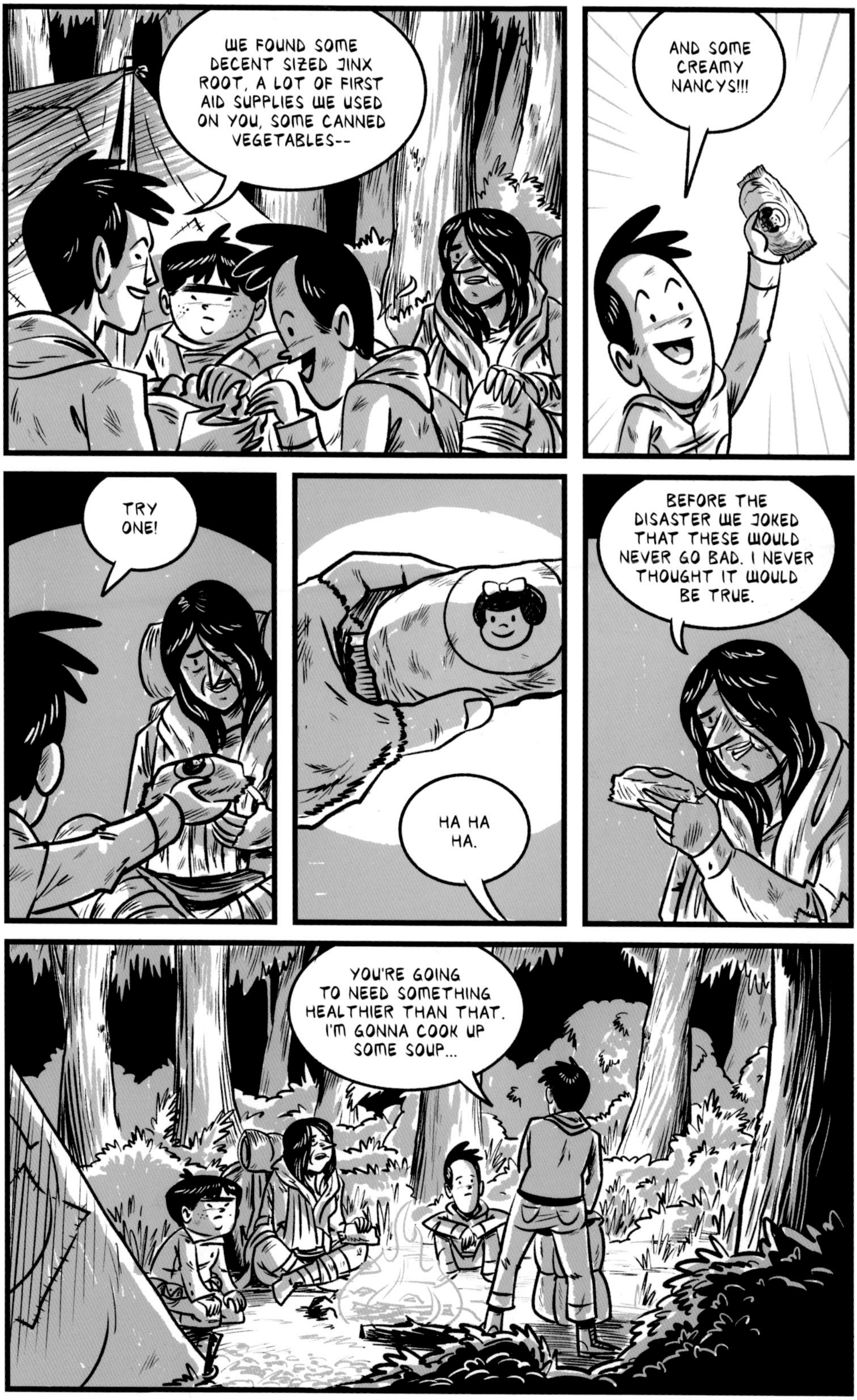
WE FOUND SOME DECENT SIZED JINX ROOT, A LOT OF FIRST AID SUPPLIES WE USED ON YOU, SOME CANNED VEGETABLES--
AND SOME CREAMY NANCYS!!!
TRY ONE!
HA HA HA.
BEFORE THE DISASTER WE JOKED THAT THESE WOULD NEVER GO BAD. I NEVER THOUGHT IT WOULD BE TRUE.
YOU'RE GOING TO NEED SOMETHING HEALTHIER THAN THAT. I'M GONNA COOK UP SOME SOUP...

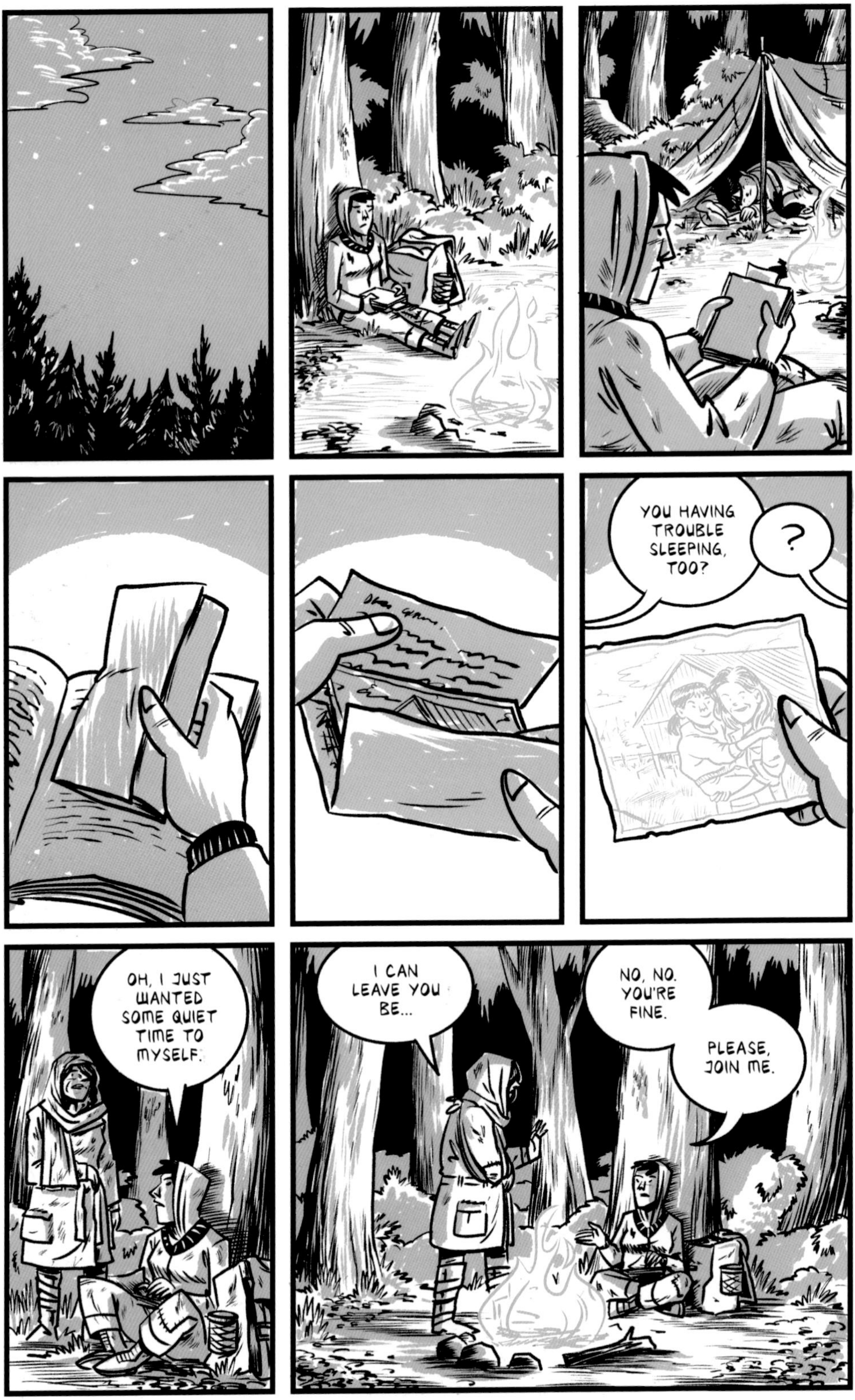
YOU HAVING TROUBLE SLEEPING, TOO?
?
OH, I JUST WANTED SOME QUIET TIME TO MYSELF.
I CAN LEAVE YOU BE...
NO, NO. YOU'RE FINE.
PLEASE, JOIN ME.

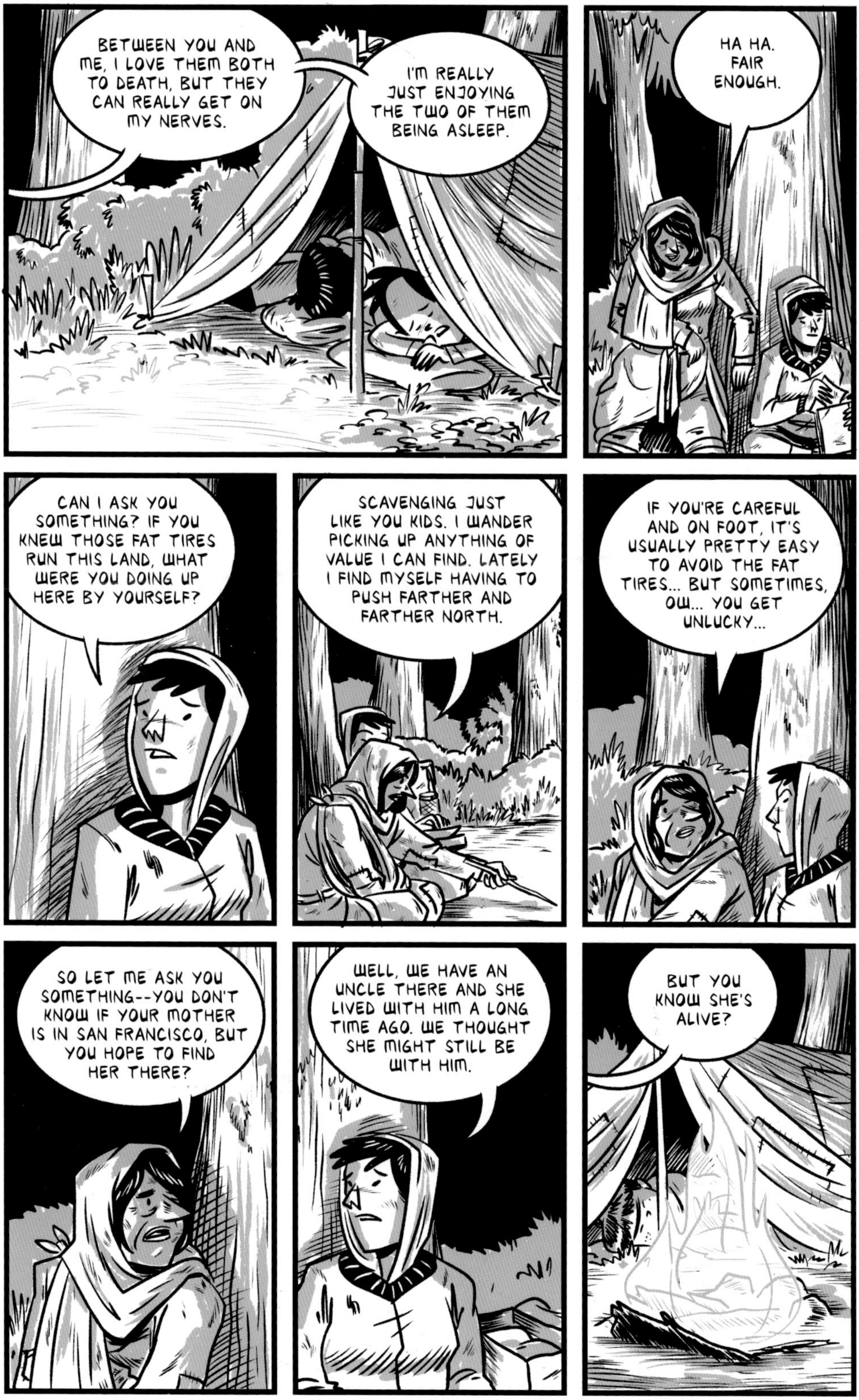
BETWEEN YOU AND ME, I LOVE THEM BOTH TO DEATH, BUT THEY CAN REALLY GET ON MY NERVES.
I'M REALLY JUST ENJOYING THE TWO OF THEM BEING ASLEEP.
HA HA. FAIR ENOUGH.
CAN I ASK YOU SOMETHING? IF YOU KNEW THOSE FAT TIRES RUN THIS LAND, WHAT WERE YOU DOING UP HERE BY YOURSELF?
SCAVENGING JUST LIKE YOU KIDS. I WANDER PICKING UP ANYTHING OF VALUE I CAN FIND. LATELY I FIND MYSELF HAVING TO PUSH FARTHER AND FARTHER NORTH.
IF YOU'RE CAREFUL AND ON FOOT, IT'S USUALLY PRETTY EASY TO AVOID THE FAT TIRES... BUT SOMETIMES, OW... YOU GET UNLUCKY...
SO LET ME ASK YOU SOMETHING--YOU DON'T KNOW IF YOUR MOTHER IS IN SAN FRANCISCO, BUT YOU HOPE TO FIND HER THERE?
WELL, WE HAVE AN UNCLE THERE AND SHE LIVED WITH HIM A LONG TIME AGO. WE THOUGHT SHE MIGHT STILL BE WITH HIM.
BUT YOU KNOW SHE'S ALIVE?

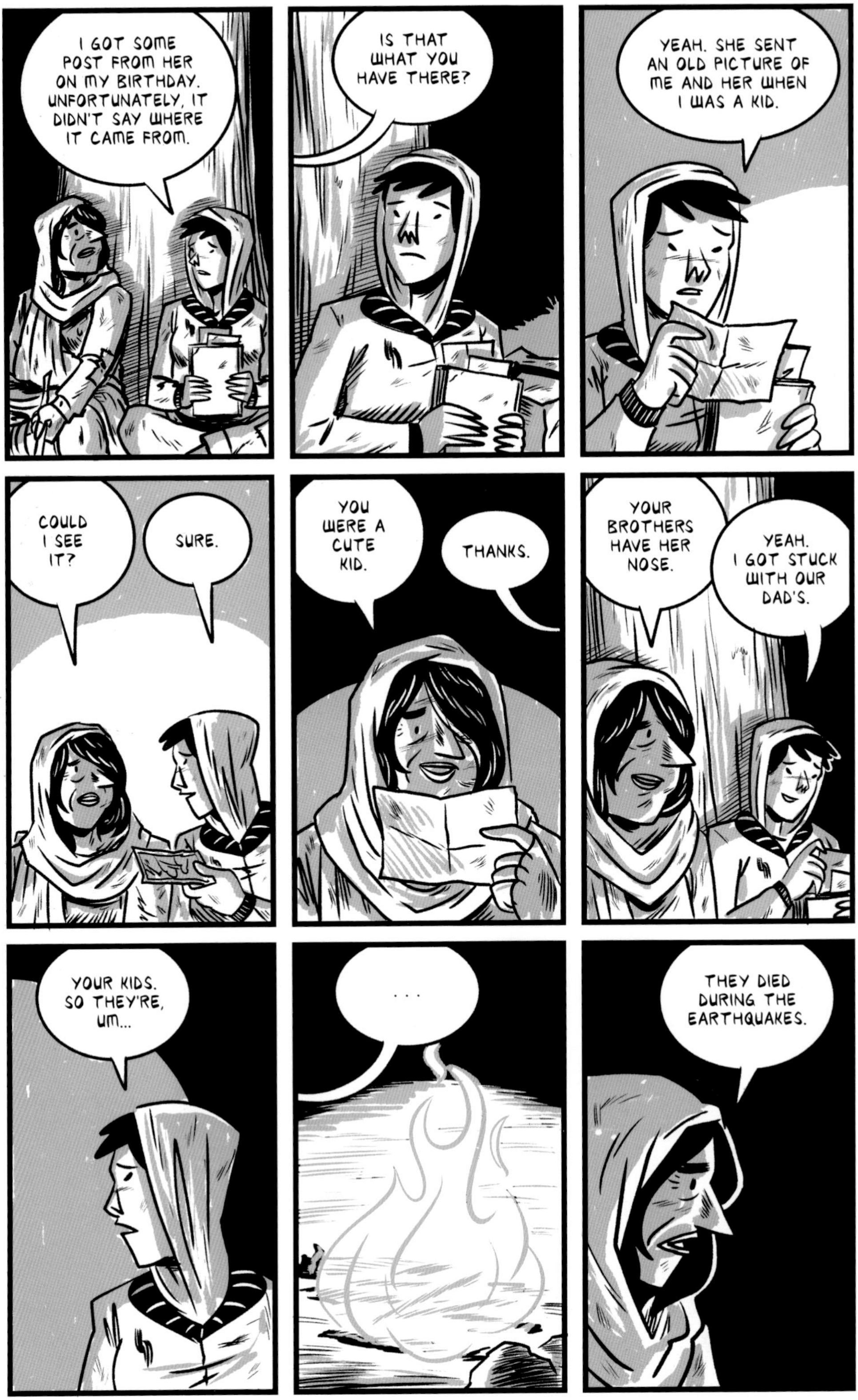
I GOT SOME POST FROM HER ON MY BIRTHDAY. UNFORTUNATELY, IT DIDN'T SAY WHERE IT CAME FROM.
IS THAT WHAT YOU HAVE THERE?
YEAH. SHE SENT AN OLD PICTURE OF ME AND HER WHEN I WAS A KID.
COULD I SEE IT?
SURE.
YOU WERE A CUTE KID.
THANKS.
YOUR BROTHERS HAVE HER NOSE.
YEAH. I GOT STUCK WITH OUR DAD'S.
YOUR KIDS. SO THEY'RE, UM...
. . .
THEY DIED DURING THE EARTHQUAKES.

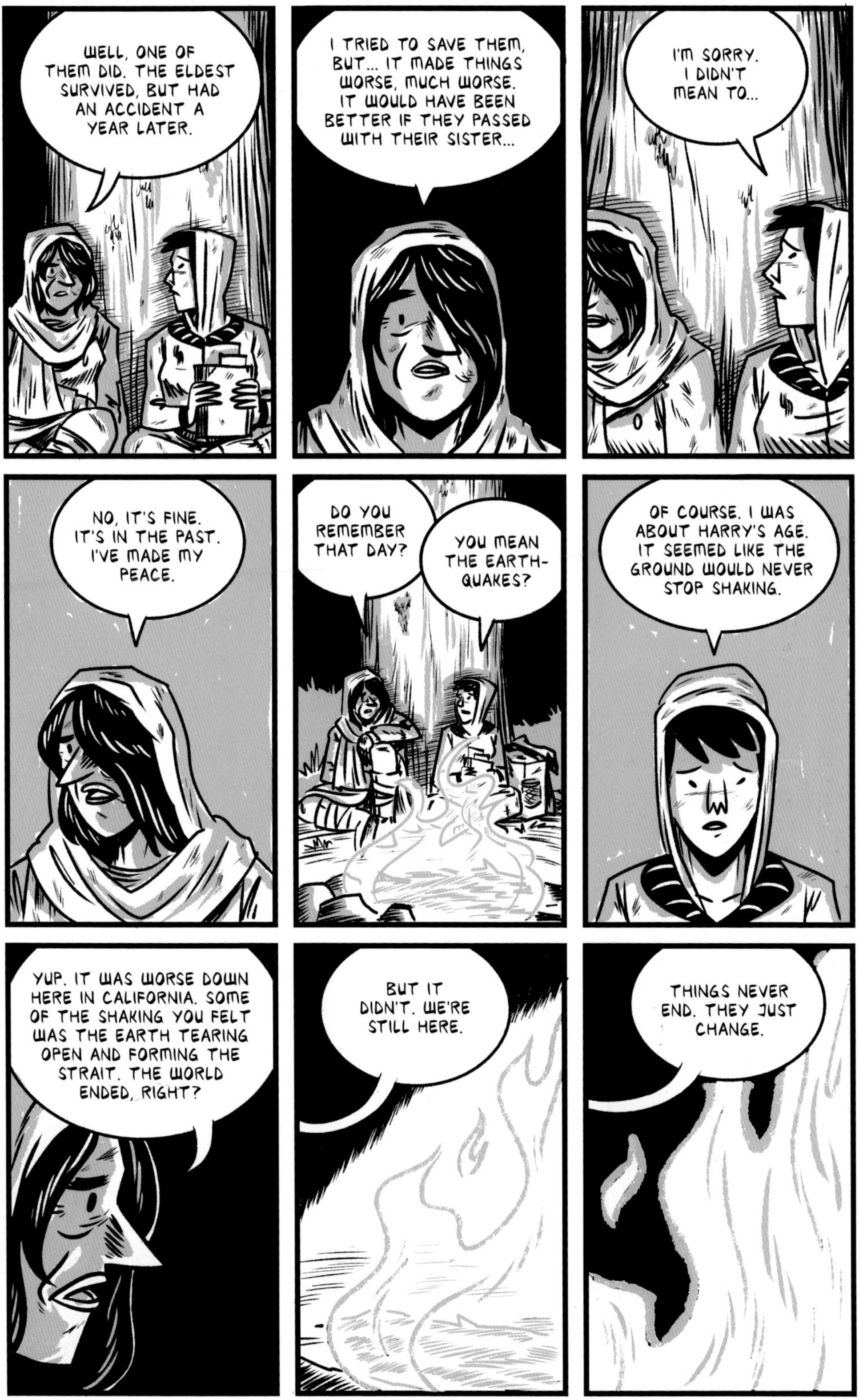
WELL, ONE OF THEM DID. THE ELDEST SURVIVED, BUT HAD AN ACCIDENT A YEAR LATER.
I TRIED TO SAVE THEM, BUT... IT MADE THINGS WORSE, MUCH WORSE. IT WOULD HAVE BEEN BETTER IF THEY PASSED WITH THEIR SISTER...
I'M SORRY. I DIDN'T MEAN TO...
NO, IT'S FINE. IT'S IN THE PAST. I'VE MADE MY PEACE.
DO YOU REMEMBER THAT DAY?
YOU MEAN THE EARTH-QUAKES?
OF COURSE. I WAS ABOUT HARRY'S AGE. IT SEEMED LIKE THE GROUND WOULD NEVER STOP SHAKING.
YUP. IT WAS WORSE DOWN HERE IN CALIFORNIA. SOME OF THE SHAKING YOU FELT WAS THE EARTH TEARING OPEN AND FORMING THE STRAIT. THE WORLD ENDED, RIGHT?
BUT IT DIDN'T. WE'RE STILL HERE.
THINGS NEVER END. THEY JUST CHANGE.

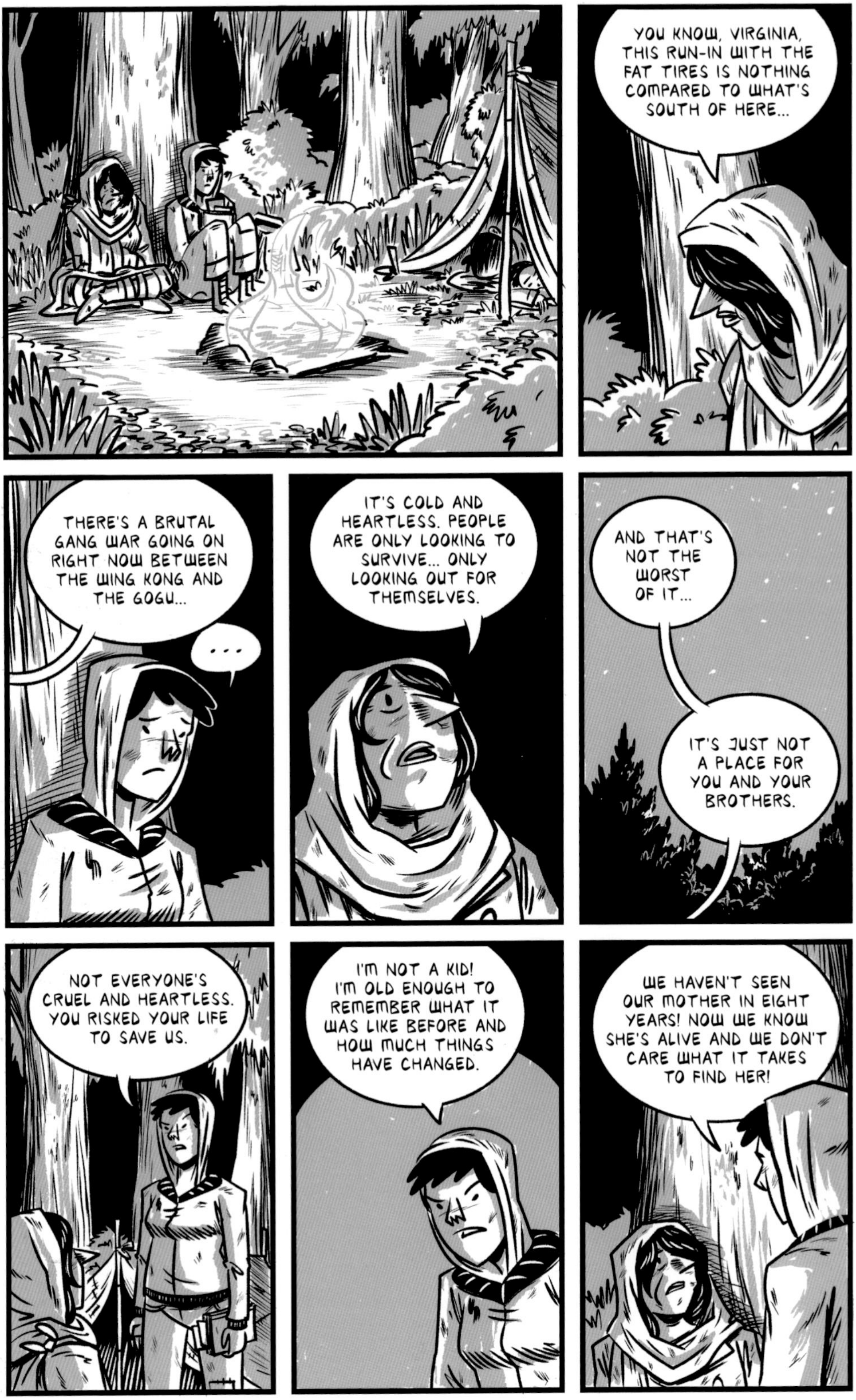

YOU KNOW, VIRGINIA, THIS RUN-IN WITH THE FAT TIRES IS NOTHING COMPARED TO WHAT'S SOUTH OF HERE...
THERE'S A BRUTAL GANG WAR GOING ON RIGHT NOW BETWEEN THE WING KONG AND THE GOGU...
...
IT'S COLD AND HEARTLESS. PEOPLE ARE ONLY LOOKING TO SURVIVE... ONLY LOOKING OUT FOR THEMSELVES.
AND THAT'S NOT THE WORST OF IT...
IT'S JUST NOT A PLACE FOR YOU AND YOUR BROTHERS.
NOT EVERYONE'S CRUEL AND HEARTLESS. YOU RISKED YOUR LIFE TO SAVE US.
I'M NOT A KID! I'M OLD ENOUGH TO REMEMBER WHAT IT WAS LIKE BEFORE AND HOW MUCH THINGS HAVE CHANGED.
WE HAVEN'T SEEN OUR MOTHER IN EIGHT YEARS! NOW WE KNOW SHE'S ALIVE AND WE DON'T CARE WHAT IT TAKES TO FIND HER!

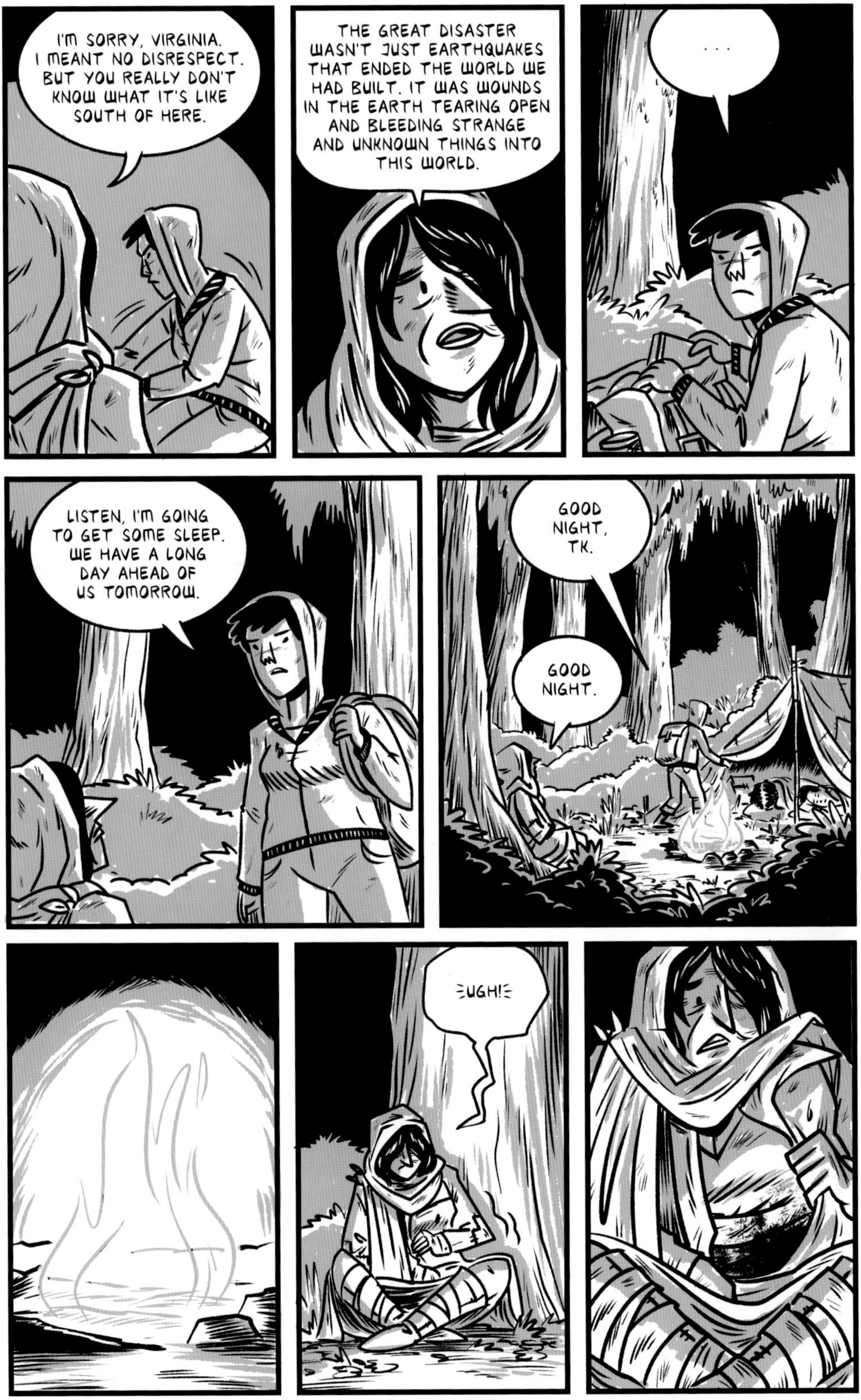
I'M SORRY, VIRGINIA. I MEANT NO DISRESPECT. BUT YOU REALLY DON'T KNOW WHAT IT'S LIKE SOUTH OF HERE.
THE GREAT DISASTER WASN'T JUST EARTHQUAKES THAT ENDED THE WORLD WE HAD BUILT. IT WAS WOUNDS IN THE EARTH TEARING OPEN AND BLEEDING STRANGE AND UNKNOWN THINGS INTO THIS WORLD.
. . .
LISTEN, I'M GOING TO GET SOME SLEEP. WE HAVE A LONG DAY AHEAD OF US TOMORROW.
GOOD NIGHT, TK.
GOOD NIGHT.
UGH!

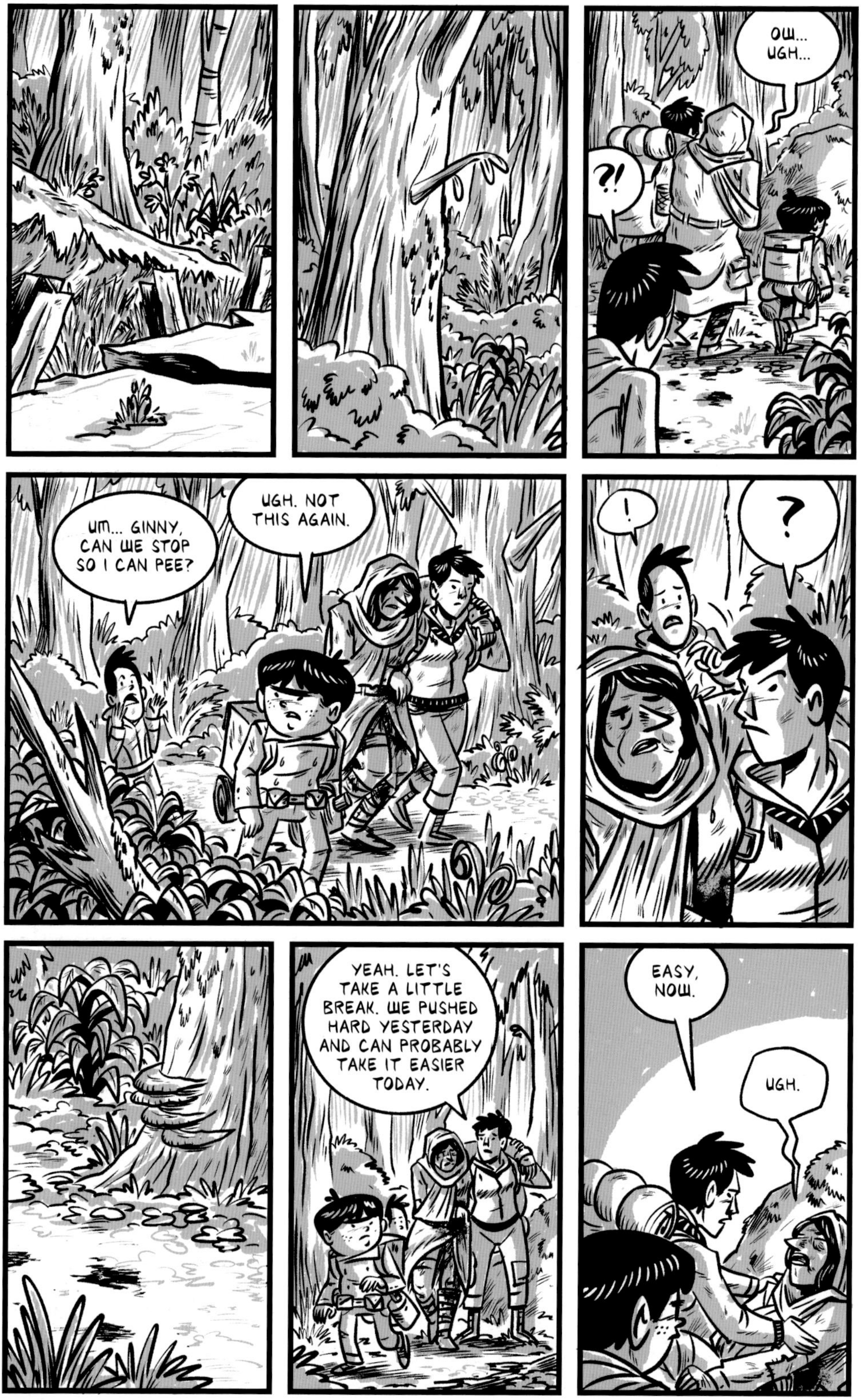

OW...
UGH...
?!
UM... GINNY, CAN WE STOP SO I CAN PEE?
UGH. NOT THIS AGAIN.
!
?
YEAH. LET'S TAKE A LITTLE BREAK. WE PUSHED HARD YESTERDAY AND CAN PROBABLY TAKE IT EASIER TODAY.
EASY, NOW.
UGH.

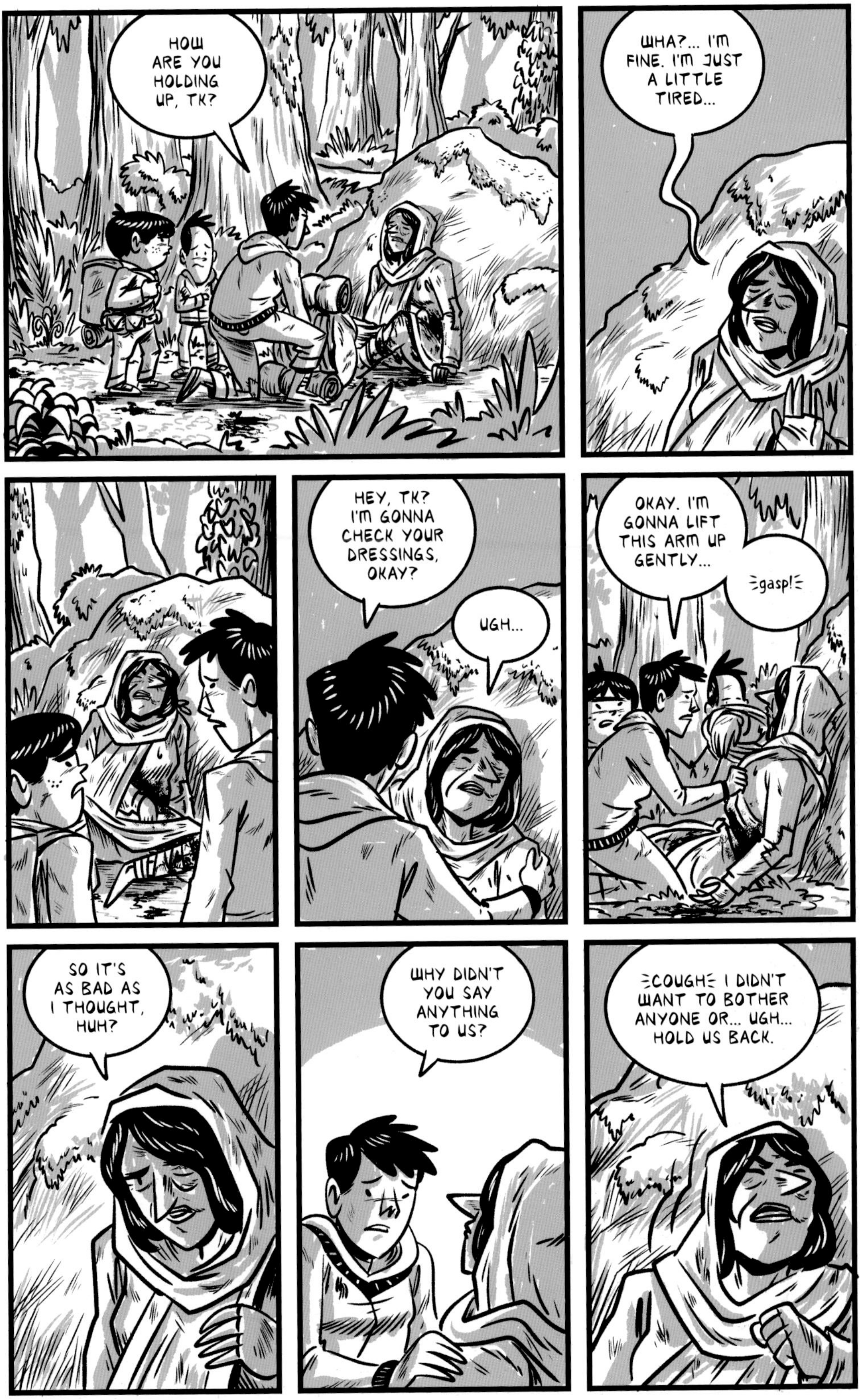
HOW ARE YOU HOLDING UP, TK?
WHA?... I'M FINE. I'M JUST A LITTLE TIRED...
HEY, TK? I'M GONNA CHECK YOUR DRESSINGS, OKAY?
UGH...
OKAY. I'M GONNA LIFT THIS ARM UP GENTLY...
gasp!
SO IT'S AS BAD AS I THOUGHT, HUH?
WHY DIDN'T YOU SAY ANYTHING TO US?
COUGH I DIDN'T WANT TO BOTHER ANYONE OR... UGH... HOLD US BACK.

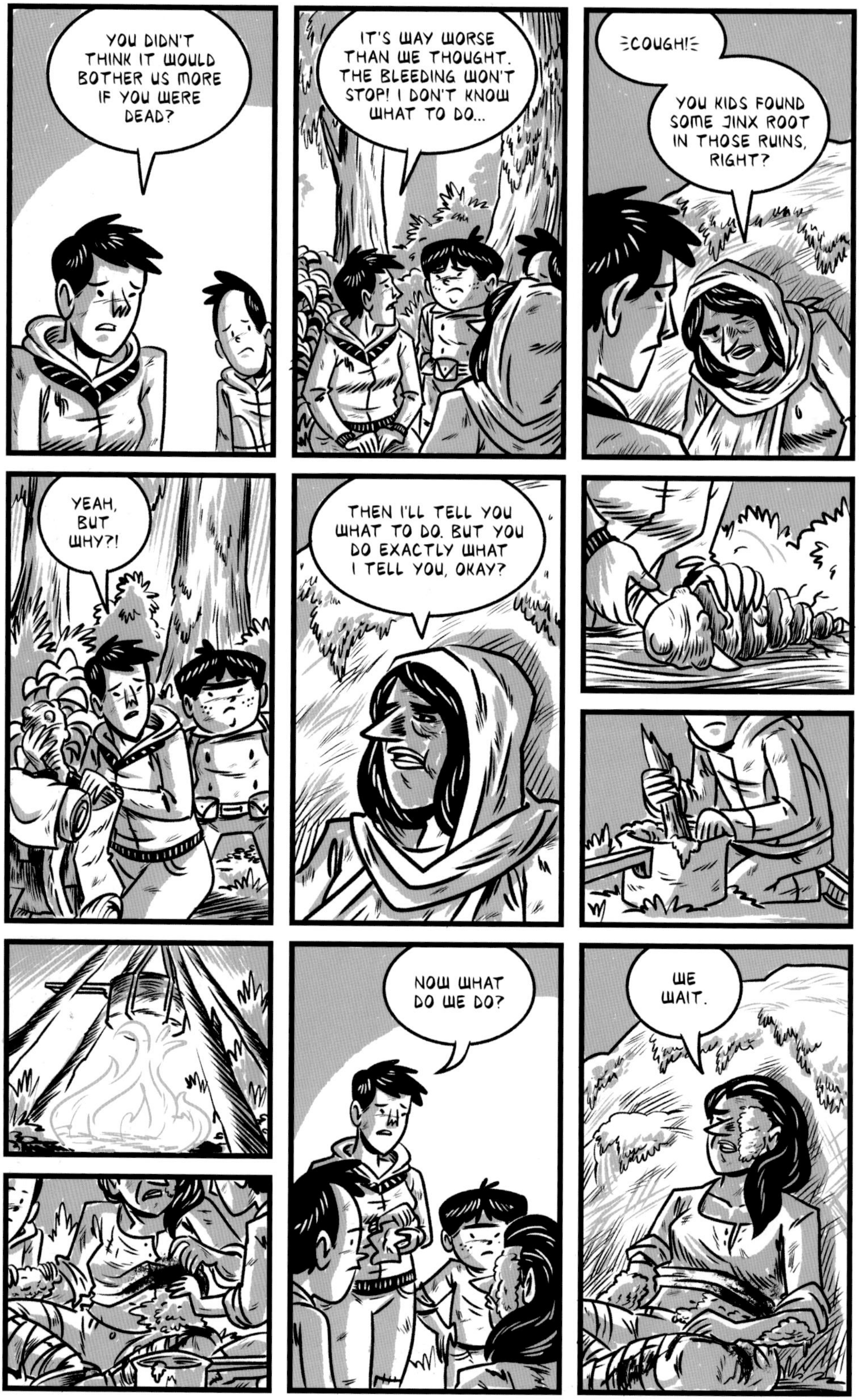
YOU DIDN'T THINK IT WOULD BOTHER US MORE IF YOU WERE DEAD?
IT'S WAY WORSE THAN WE THOUGHT. THE BLEEDING WON'T STOP! I DON'T KNOW WHAT TO DO...
COUGH!
YOU KIDS FOUND SOME JINX ROOT IN THOSE RUINS, RIGHT?
YEAH, BUT WHY?!
THEN I'LL TELL YOU WHAT TO DO. BUT YOU DO EXACTLY WHAT I TELL YOU, OKAY?
NOW WHAT DO WE DO?
WE WAIT.

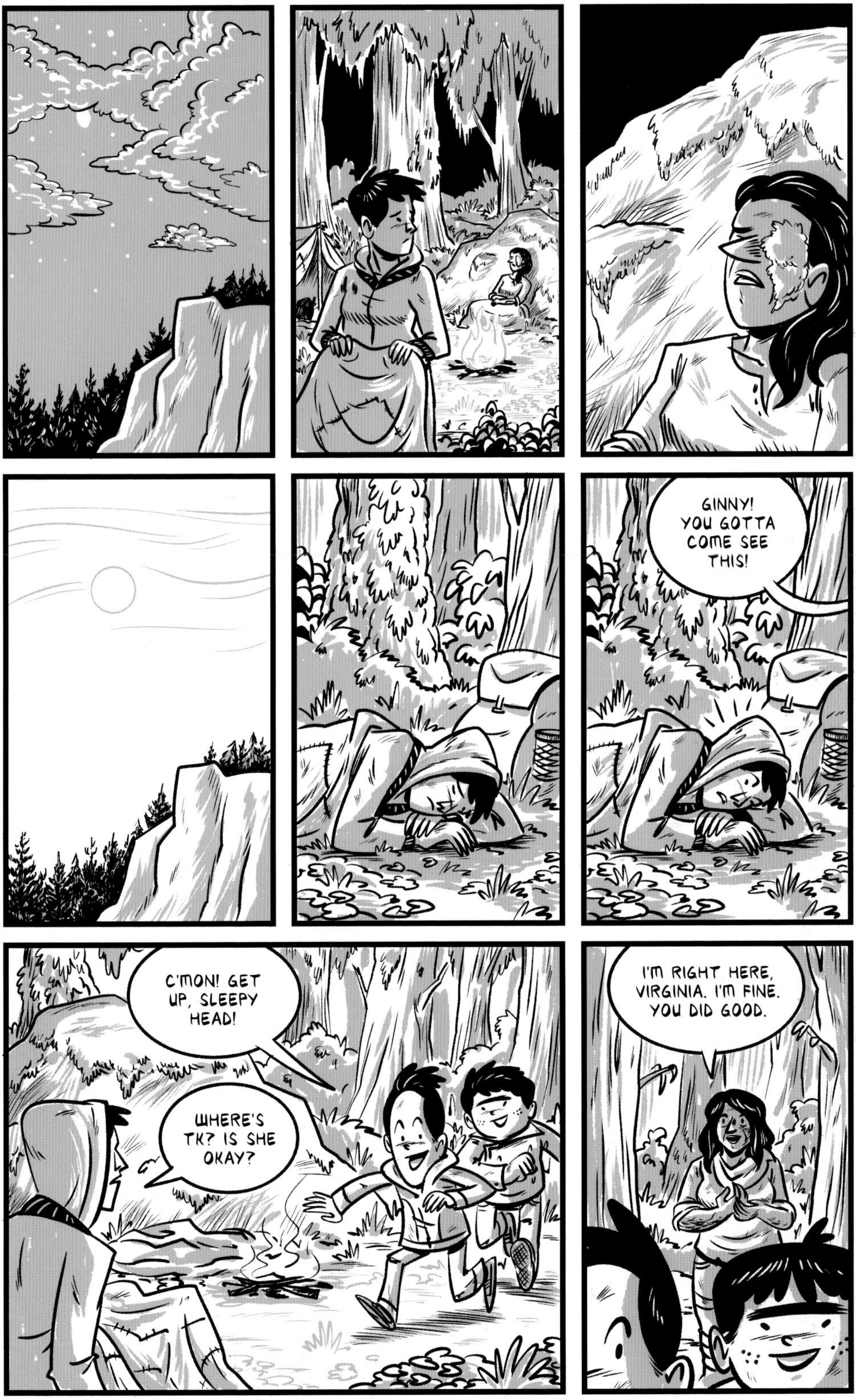
GINNY! YOU GOTTA COME SEE THIS!
C'MON! GET UP, SLEEPY HEAD!
WHERE'S TK? IS SHE OKAY?
I'M RIGHT HERE, VIRGINIA. I'M FINE. YOU DID GOOD.

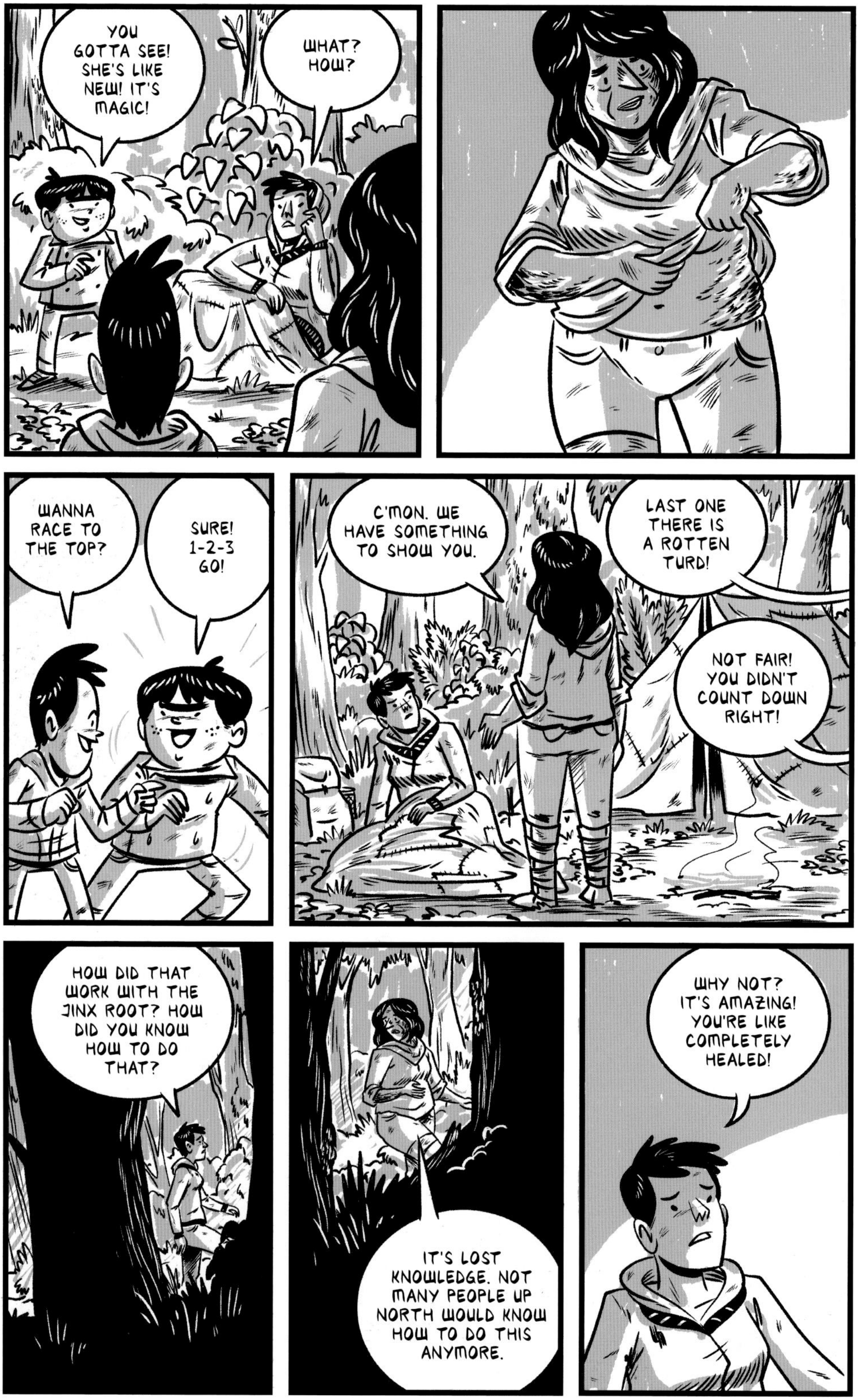
YOU GOTTA SEE! SHE'S LIKE NEW! IT'S MAGIC!
WHAT? HOW?
WANNA RACE TO THE TOP?
SURE! 1-2-3 GO!
C'MON. WE HAVE SOMETHING TO SHOW YOU.
LAST ONE THERE IS A ROTTEN TURD!
NOT FAIR! YOU DIDN'T COUNT DOWN RIGHT!
HOW DID THAT WORK WITH THE JINX ROOT? HOW DID YOU KNOW HOW TO DO THAT?
IT'S LOST KNOWLEDGE. NOT MANY PEOPLE UP NORTH WOULD KNOW HOW TO DO THIS ANYMORE.
WHY NOT? IT'S AMAZING! YOU'RE LIKE COMPLETELY HEALED!

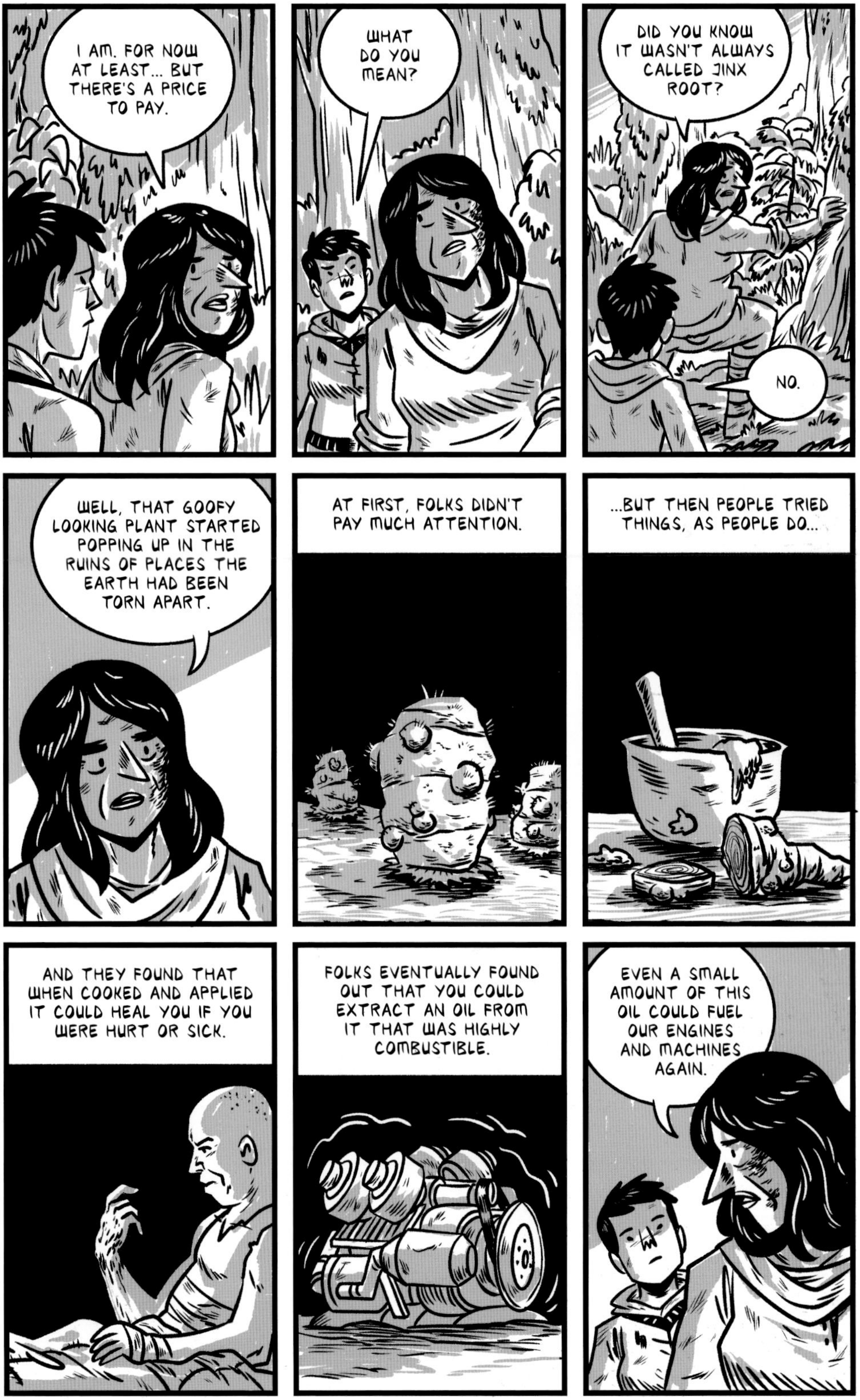
I AM. FOR NOW AT LEAST... BUT THERE'S A PRICE TO PAY.
WHAT DO YOU MEAN?
DID YOU KNOW IT WASN'T ALWAYS CALLED JINX ROOT?
NO.
WELL, THAT GOOFY LOOKING PLANT STARTED POPPING UP IN THE RUINS OF PLACES THE EARTH HAD BEEN TORN APART.
AT FIRST, FOLKS DIDN'T PAY MUCH ATTENTION.
...BUT THEN PEOPLE TRIED THINGS, AS PEOPLE DO...
AND THEY FOUND THAT WHEN COOKED AND APPLIED IT COULD HEAL YOU IF YOU WERE HURT OR SICK.
FOLKS EVENTUALLY FOUND OUT THAT YOU COULD EXTRACT AN OIL FROM IT THAT WAS HIGHLY COMBUSTIBLE.
EVEN A SMALL AMOUNT OF THIS OIL COULD FUEL OUR ENGINES AND MACHINES AGAIN.

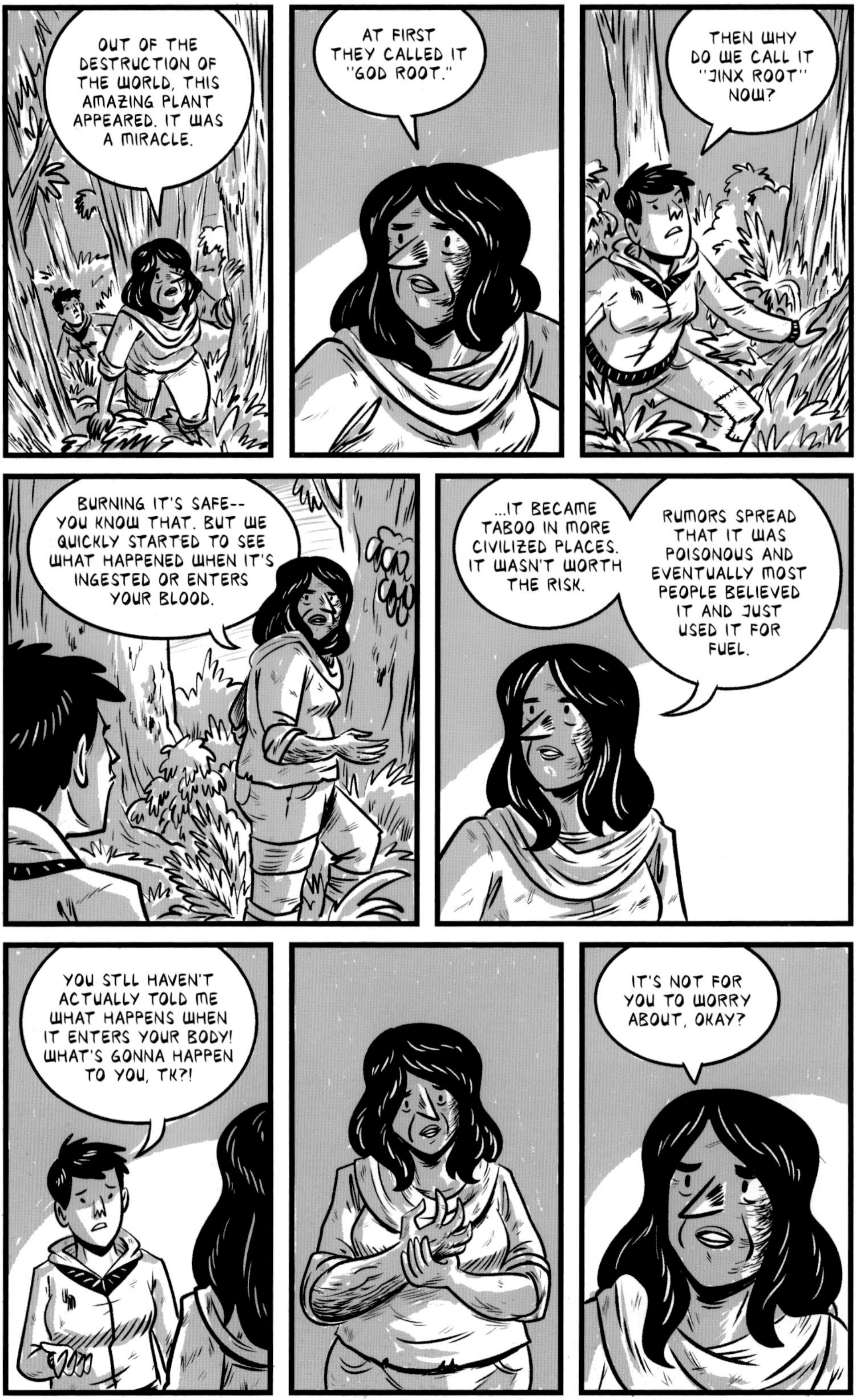
OUT OF THE DESTRUCTION OF THE WORLD, THIS AMAZING PLANT APPEARED. IT WAS A MIRACLE.
AT FIRST THEY CALLED IT "GOD ROOT."
THEN WHY DO WE CALL IT "JINX ROOT" NOW?
BURNING IT'S SAFE-- YOU KNOW THAT. BUT WE QUICKLY STARTED TO SEE WHAT HAPPENED WHEN IT'S INGESTED OR ENTERS YOUR BLOOD.
RUMORS SPREAD THAT IT WAS POISONOUS AND EVENTUALLY MOST PEOPLE BELIEVED IT AND JUST USED IT FOR FUEL.
...IT BECAME TABOO IN MORE CIVILIZED PLACES. IT WASN'T WORTH THE RISK.
YOU STLL HAVEN'T ACTUALLY TOLD ME WHAT HAPPENS WHEN IT ENTERS YOUR BODY! WHAT'S GONNA HAPPEN TO YOU, TK?!
IT'S NOT FOR YOU TO WORRY ABOUT, OKAY?

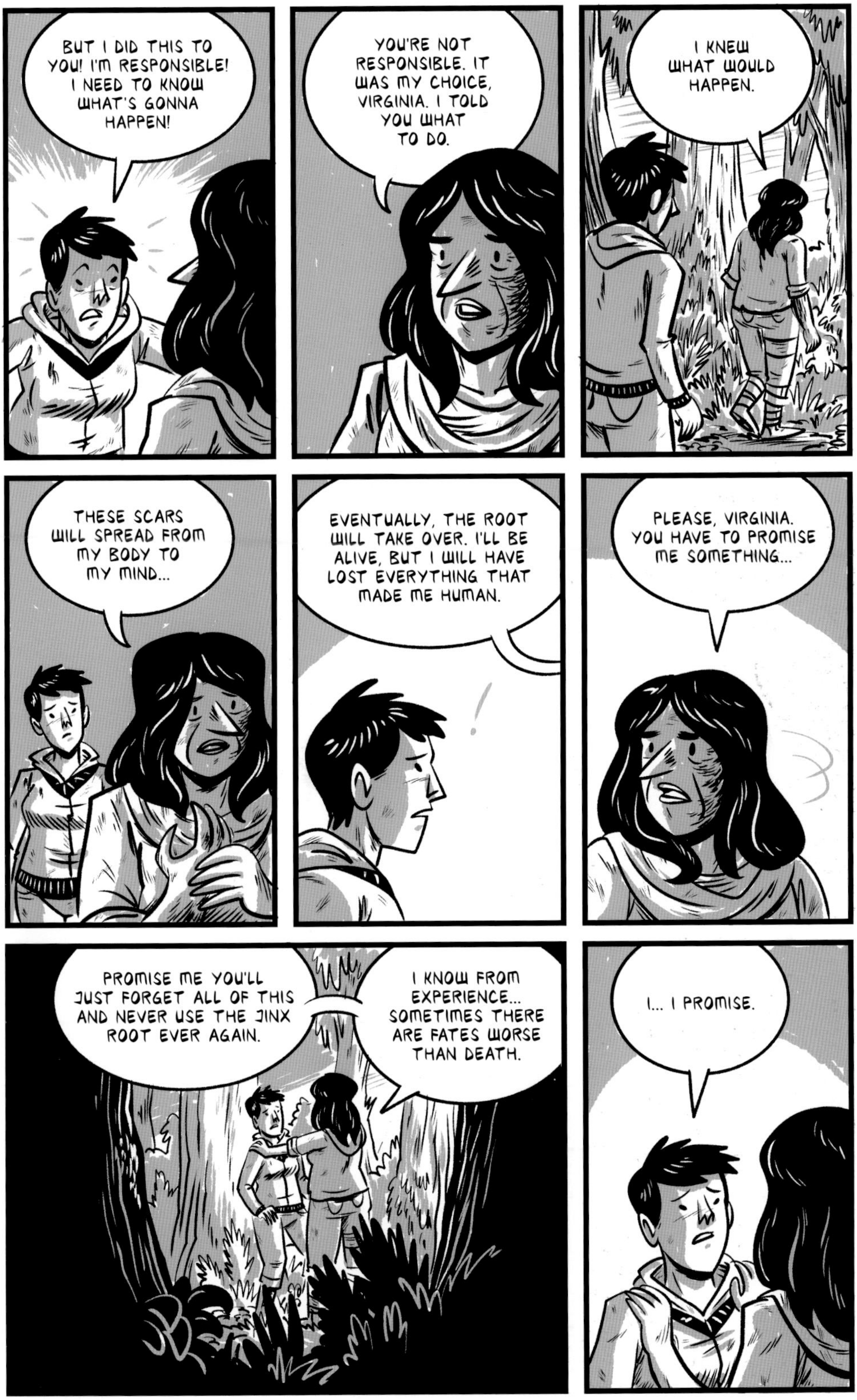
BUT I DID THIS TO YOU! I'M RESPONSIBLE! I NEED TO KNOW WHAT'S GONNA HAPPEN!
YOU'RE NOT RESPONSIBLE. IT WAS MY CHOICE, VIRGINIA. I TOLD YOU WHAT TO DO.
I KNEW WHAT WOULD HAPPEN.
THESE SCARS WILL SPREAD FROM MY BODY TO MY MIND...
EVENTUALLY, THE ROOT WILL TAKE OVER. I'LL BE ALIVE, BUT I WILL HAVE LOST EVERYTHING THAT MADE ME HUMAN.
!
PLEASE, VIRGINIA. YOU HAVE TO PROMISE ME SOMETHING...
PROMISE ME YOU'LL JUST FORGET ALL OF THIS AND NEVER USE THE JINX ROOT EVER AGAIN.
I KNOW FROM EXPERIENCE... SOMETIMES THERE ARE FATES WORSE THAN DEATH.
I... I PROMISE.

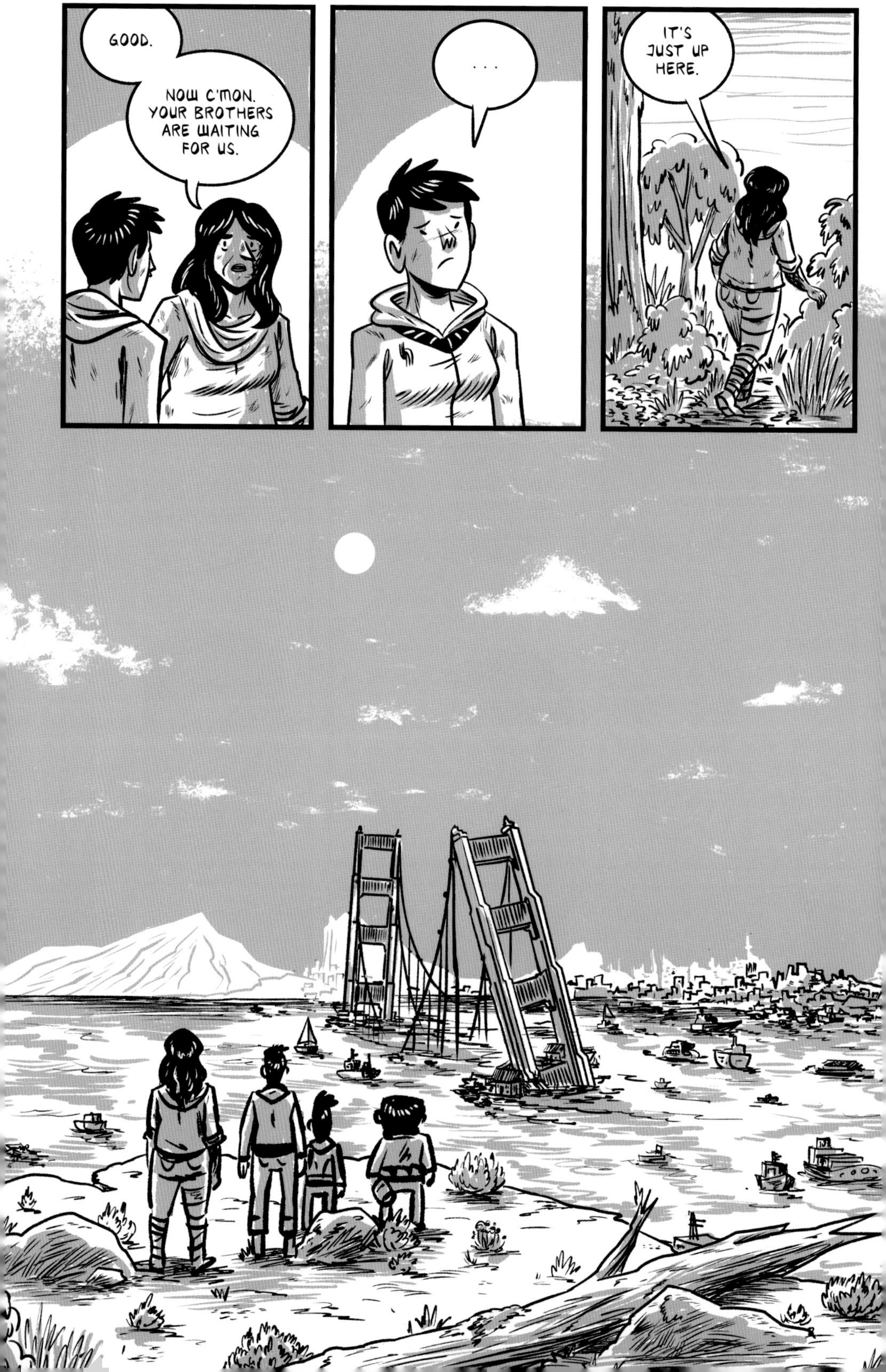
GOOD.
NOW C'MON. YOUR BROTHERS ARE WAITING FOR US.
. . .
IT'S JUST UP HERE.

CHAPTER 6

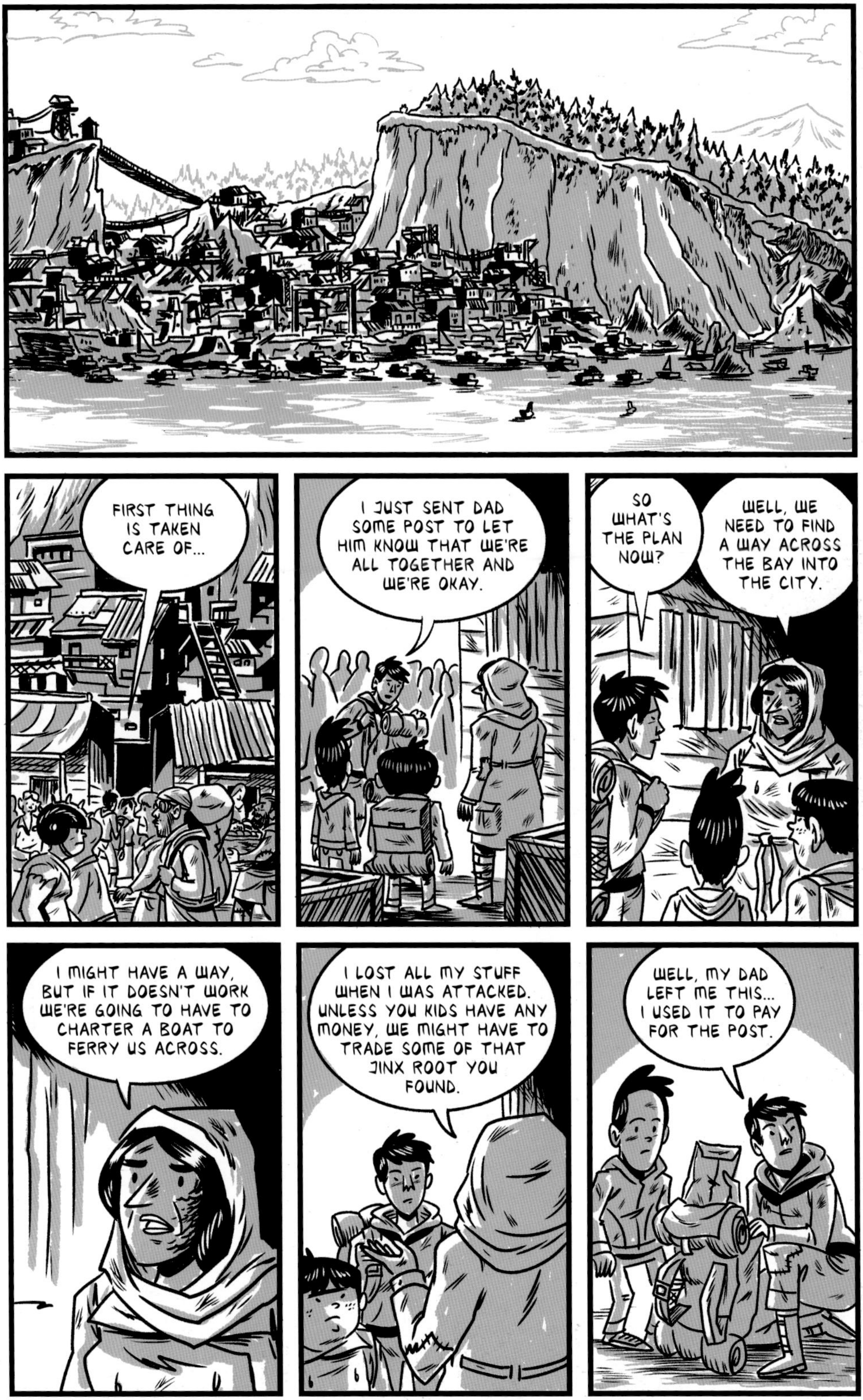
FIRST THING IS TAKEN CARE OF...
I JUST SENT DAD SOME POST TO LET HIM KNOW THAT WE'RE ALL TOGETHER AND WE'RE OKAY.
SO WHAT'S THE PLAN NOW?
WELL, WE NEED TO FIND A WAY ACROSS THE BAY INTO THE CITY.
I MIGHT HAVE A WAY, BUT IF IT DOESN'T WORK WE'RE GOING TO HAVE TO CHARTER A BOAT TO FERRY US ACROSS.
I LOST ALL MY STUFF WHEN I WAS ATTACKED. UNLESS YOU KIDS HAVE ANY MONEY, WE MIGHT HAVE TO TRADE SOME OF THAT JINX ROOT YOU FOUND.
WELL, MY DAD LEFT ME THIS... I USED IT TO PAY FOR THE POST.

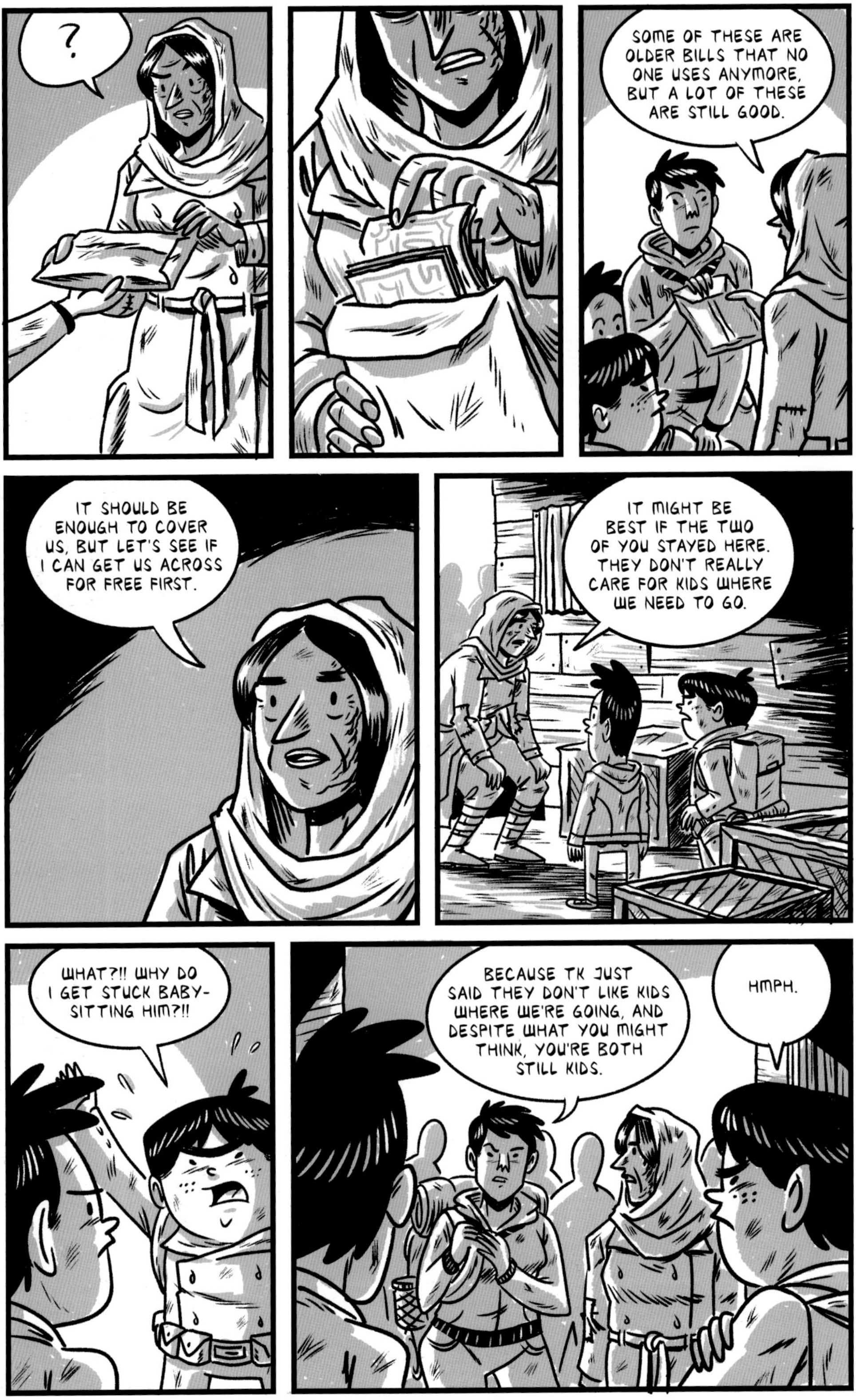
?
SOME OF THESE ARE OLDER BILLS THAT NO ONE USES ANYMORE, BUT A LOT OF THESE ARE STILL GOOD.
IT SHOULD BE ENOUGH TO COVER US, BUT LET'S SEE IF I CAN GET US ACROSS FOR FREE FIRST.
IT MIGHT BE BEST IF THE TWO OF YOU STAYED HERE. THEY DON'T REALLY CARE FOR KIDS WHERE WE NEED TO GO.
WHAT?!! WHY DO I GET STUCK BABY-SITTING HIM?!!
BECAUSE TK JUST SAID THEY DON'T LIKE KIDS WHERE WE'RE GOING, AND DESPITE WHAT YOU MIGHT THINK, YOU'RE BOTH STILL KIDS.
HMPH.

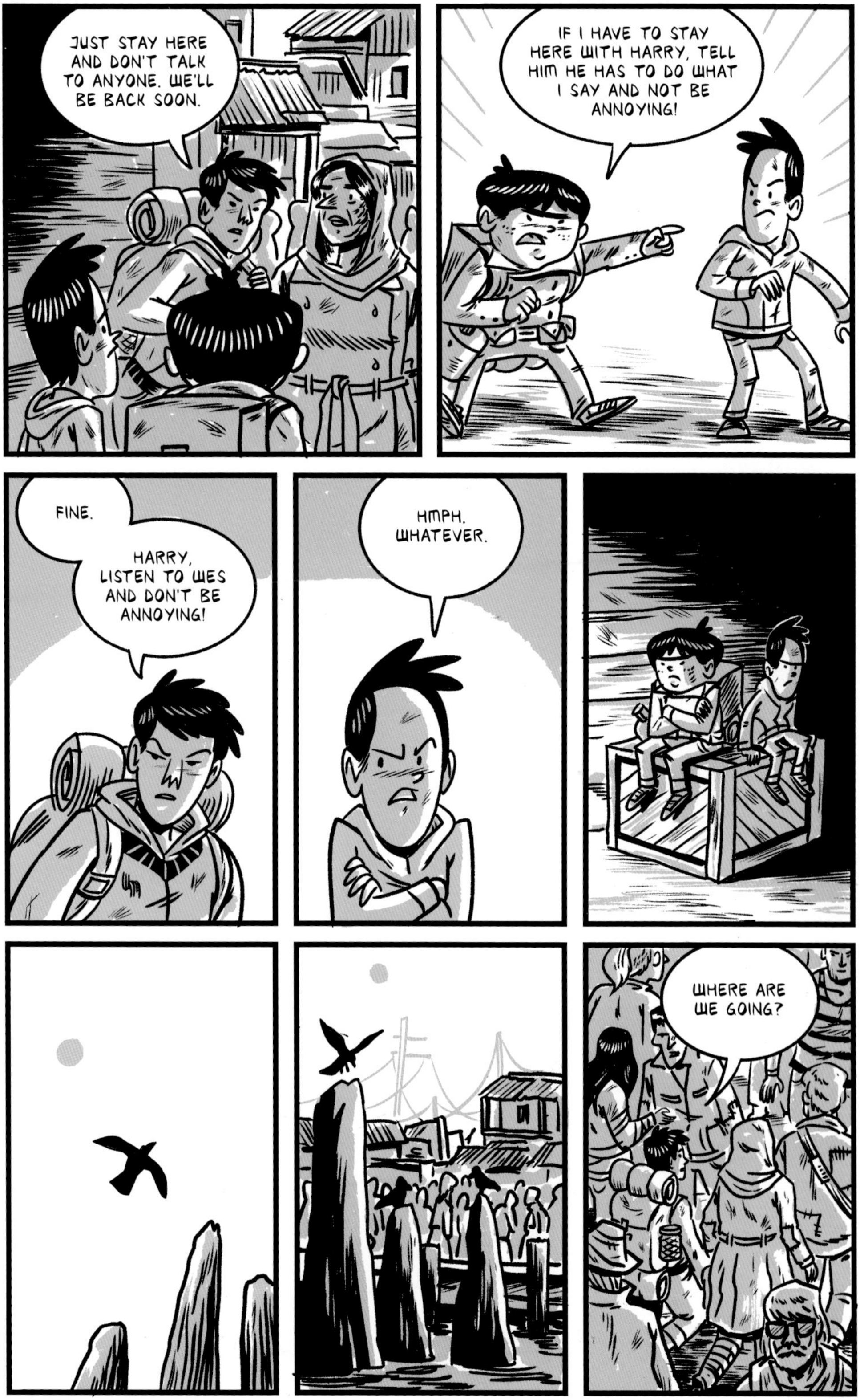
JUST STAY HERE AND DON'T TALK TO ANYONE. WE'LL BE BACK SOON.
IF I HAVE TO STAY HERE WITH HARRY, TELL HIM HE HAS TO DO WHAT I SAY AND NOT BE ANNOYING!
FINE.
HARRY, LISTEN TO WES AND DON'T BE ANNOYING!
HMPH. WHATEVER.
WHERE ARE WE GOING?

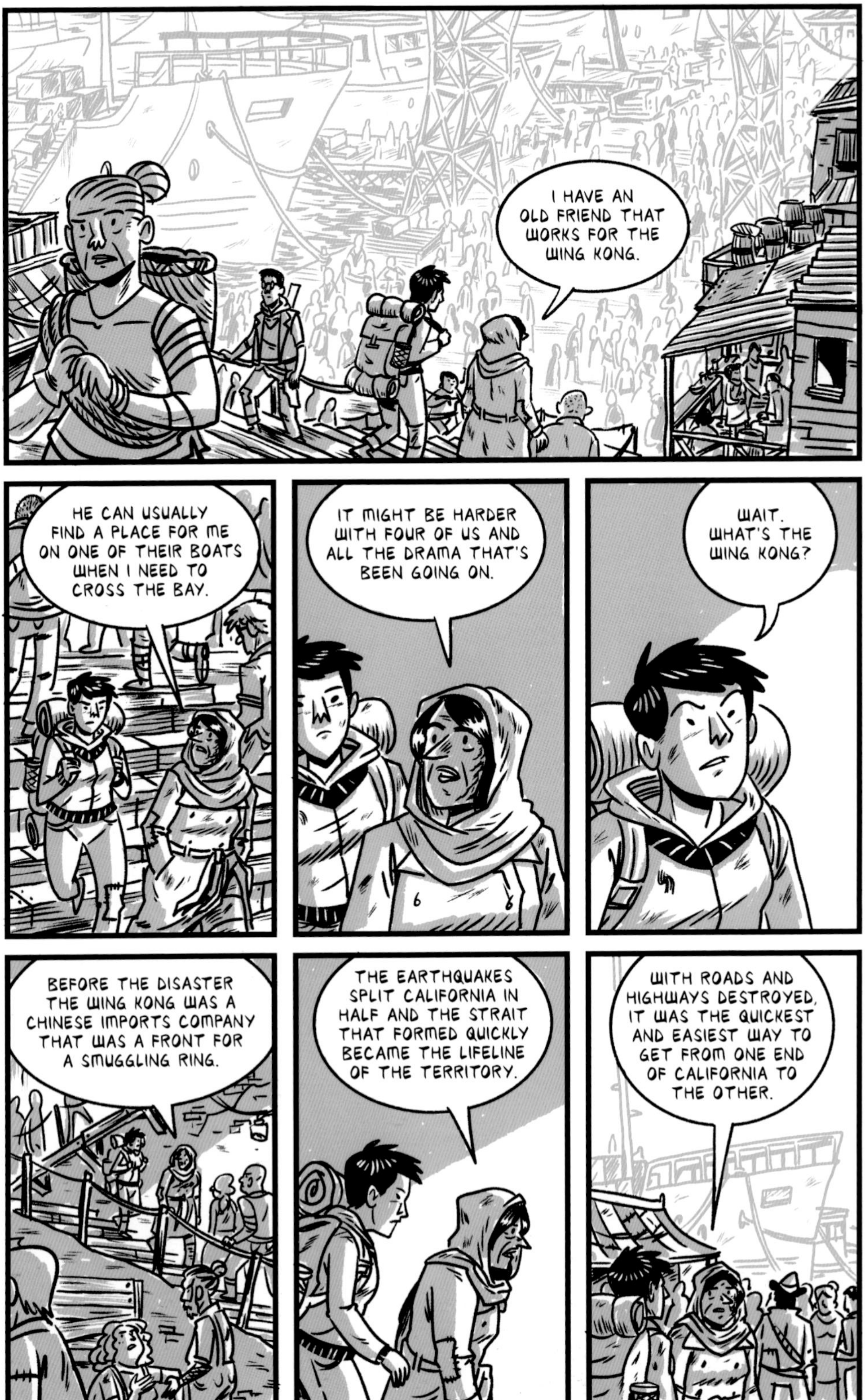
I HAVE AN OLD FRIEND THAT WORKS FOR THE WING KONG.
HE CAN USUALLY FIND A PLACE FOR ME ON ONE OF THEIR BOATS WHEN I NEED TO CROSS THE BAY.
IT MIGHT BE HARDER WITH FOUR OF US AND ALL THE DRAMA THAT'S BEEN GOING ON.
WAIT. WHAT'S THE WING KONG?
BEFORE THE DISASTER THE WING KONG WAS A CHINESE IMPORTS COMPANY THAT WAS A FRONT FOR A SMUGGLING RING.
THE EARTHQUAKES SPLIT CALIFORNIA IN HALF AND THE STRAIT THAT FORMED QUICKLY BECAME THE LIFELINE OF THE TERRITORY.
WITH ROADS AND HIGHWAYS DESTROYED, IT WAS THE QUICKEST AND EASIEST WAY TO GET FROM ONE END OF CALIFORNIA TO THE OTHER.

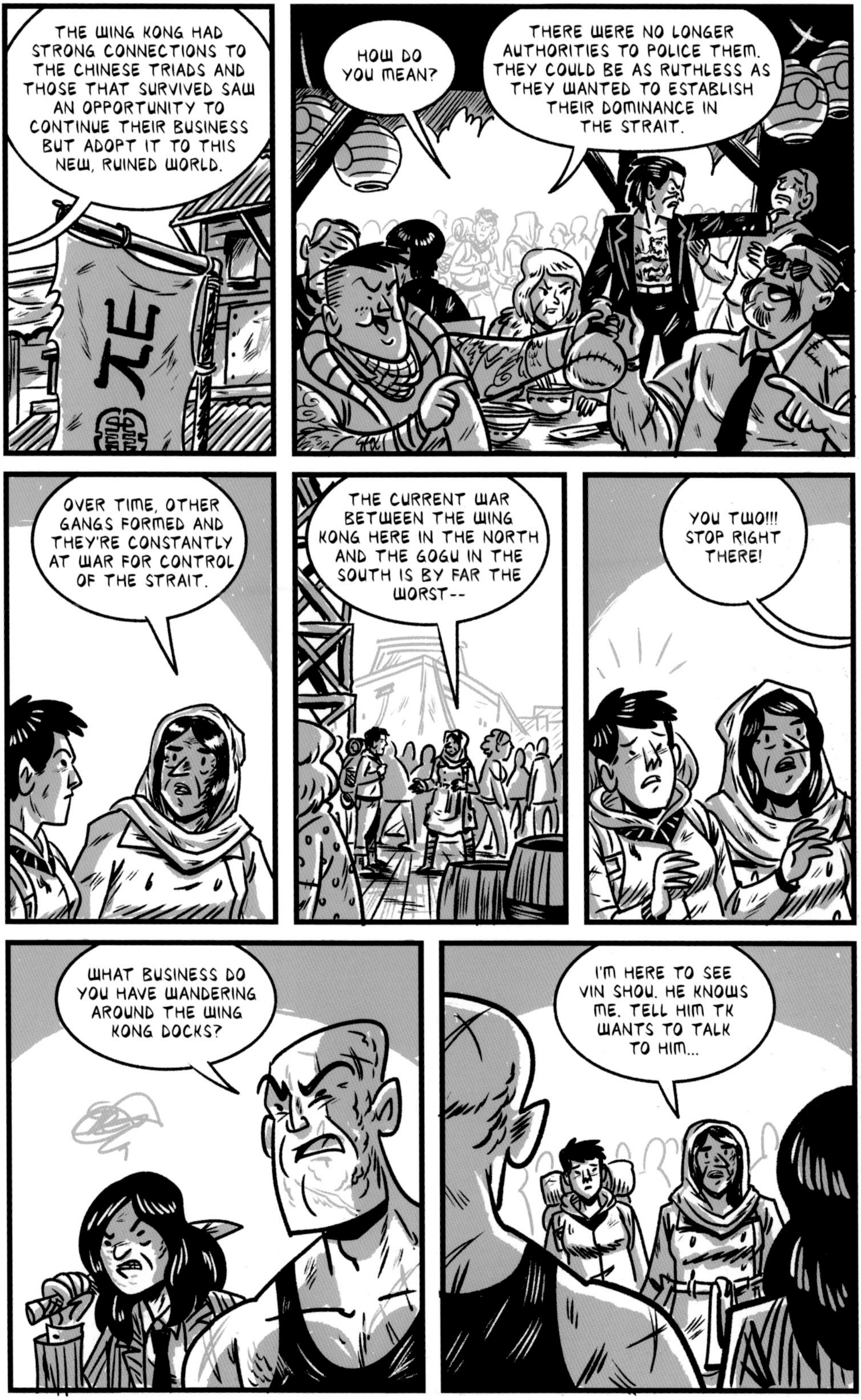
THE WING KONG HAD STRONG CONNECTIONS TO THE CHINESE TRIADS AND THOSE THAT SURVIVED SAW AN OPPORTUNITY TO CONTINUE THEIR BUSINESS BUT ADOPT IT TO THIS NEW, RUINED WORLD.
HOW DO YOU MEAN?
THERE WERE NO LONGER AUTHORITIES TO POLICE THEM. THEY COULD BE AS RUTHLESS AS THEY WANTED TO ESTABLISH THEIR DOMINANCE IN THE STRAIT.
OVER TIME, OTHER GANGS FORMED AND THEY'RE CONSTANTLY AT WAR FOR CONTROL OF THE STRAIT.
THE CURRENT WAR BETWEEN THE WING KONG HERE IN THE NORTH AND THE GOGU IN THE SOUTH IS BY FAR THE WORST--
YOU TWO!!! STOP RIGHT THERE!
WHAT BUSINESS DO YOU HAVE WANDERING AROUND THE WING KONG DOCKS?
I'M HERE TO SEE VIN SHOU. HE KNOWS ME. TELL HIM TK WANTS TO TALK TO HIM...

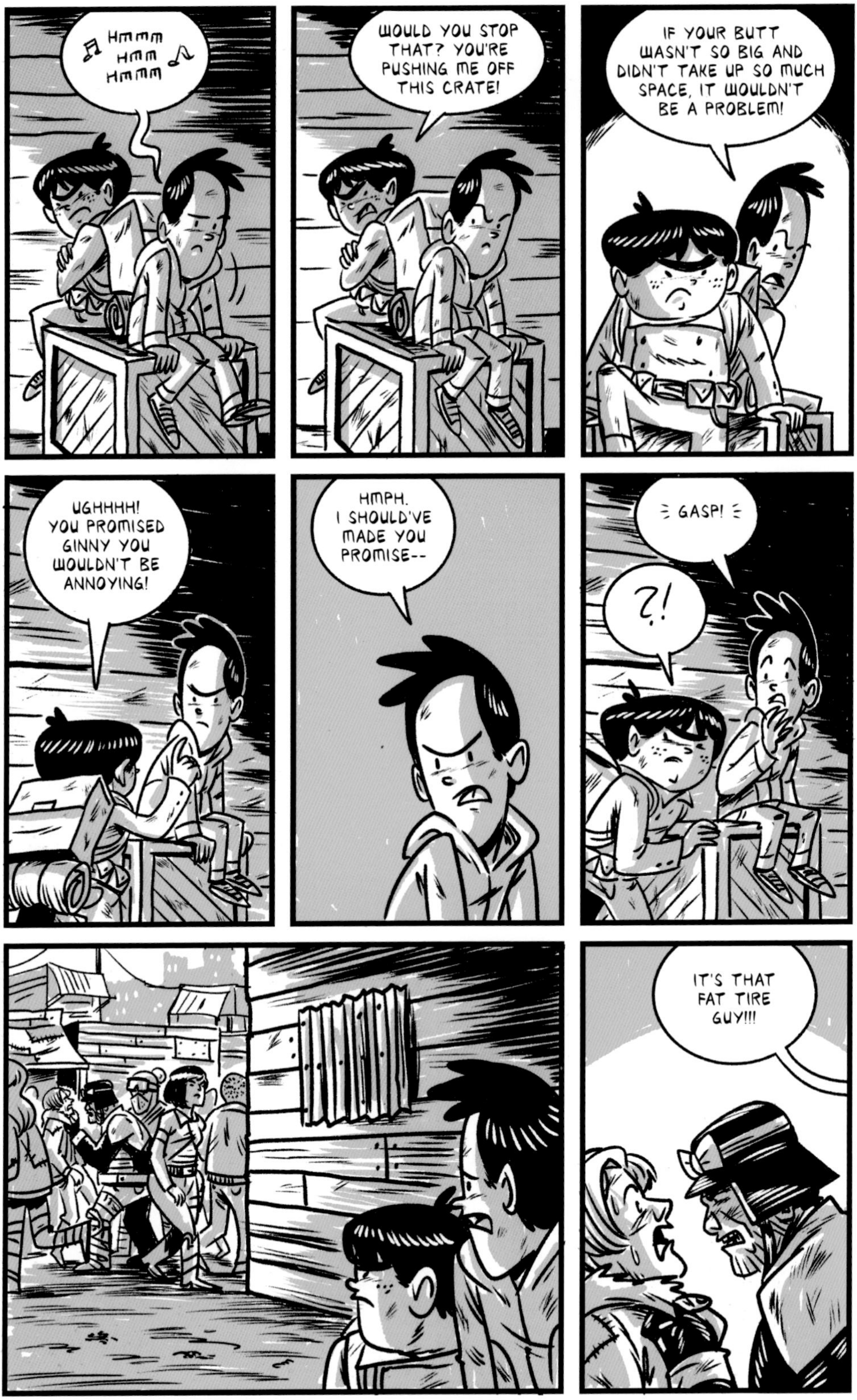
Hmmm Hmm Hmmm
WOULD YOU STOP THAT? YOU'RE PUSHING ME OFF THIS CRATE!
IF YOUR BUTT WASN'T SO BIG AND DIDN'T TAKE UP SO MUCH SPACE, IT WOULDN'T BE A PROBLEM!
UGHHHH! YOU PROMISED GINNY YOU WOULDN'T BE ANNOYING!
HMPH. I SHOULD'VE MADE YOU PROMISE--
GASP!
?!
IT'S THAT FAT TIRE GUY!!!

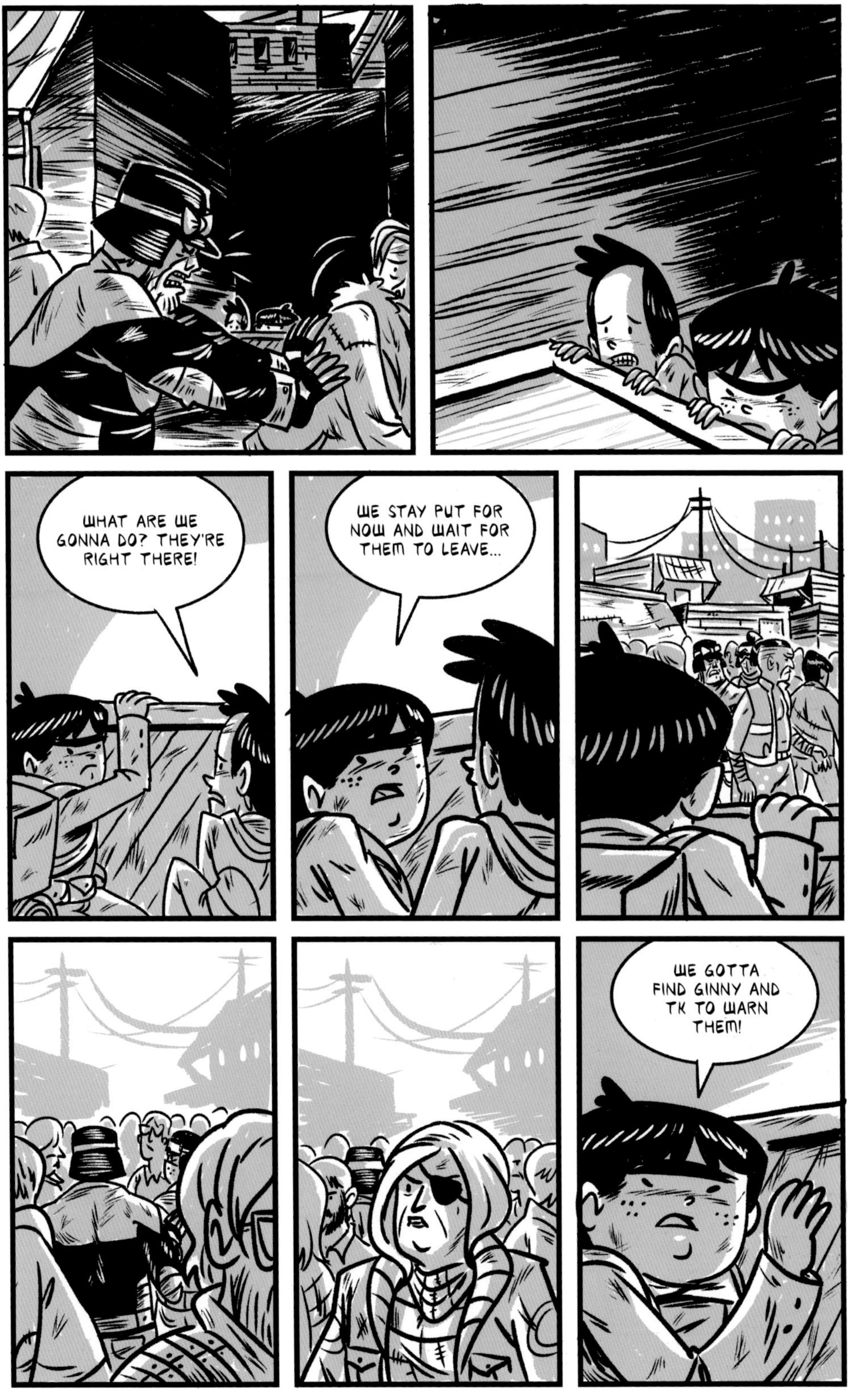
WHAT ARE WE GONNA DO? THEY'RE RIGHT THERE!
WE STAY PUT FOR NOW AND WAIT FOR THEM TO LEAVE...
WE GOTTA FIND GINNY AND TK TO WARN THEM!

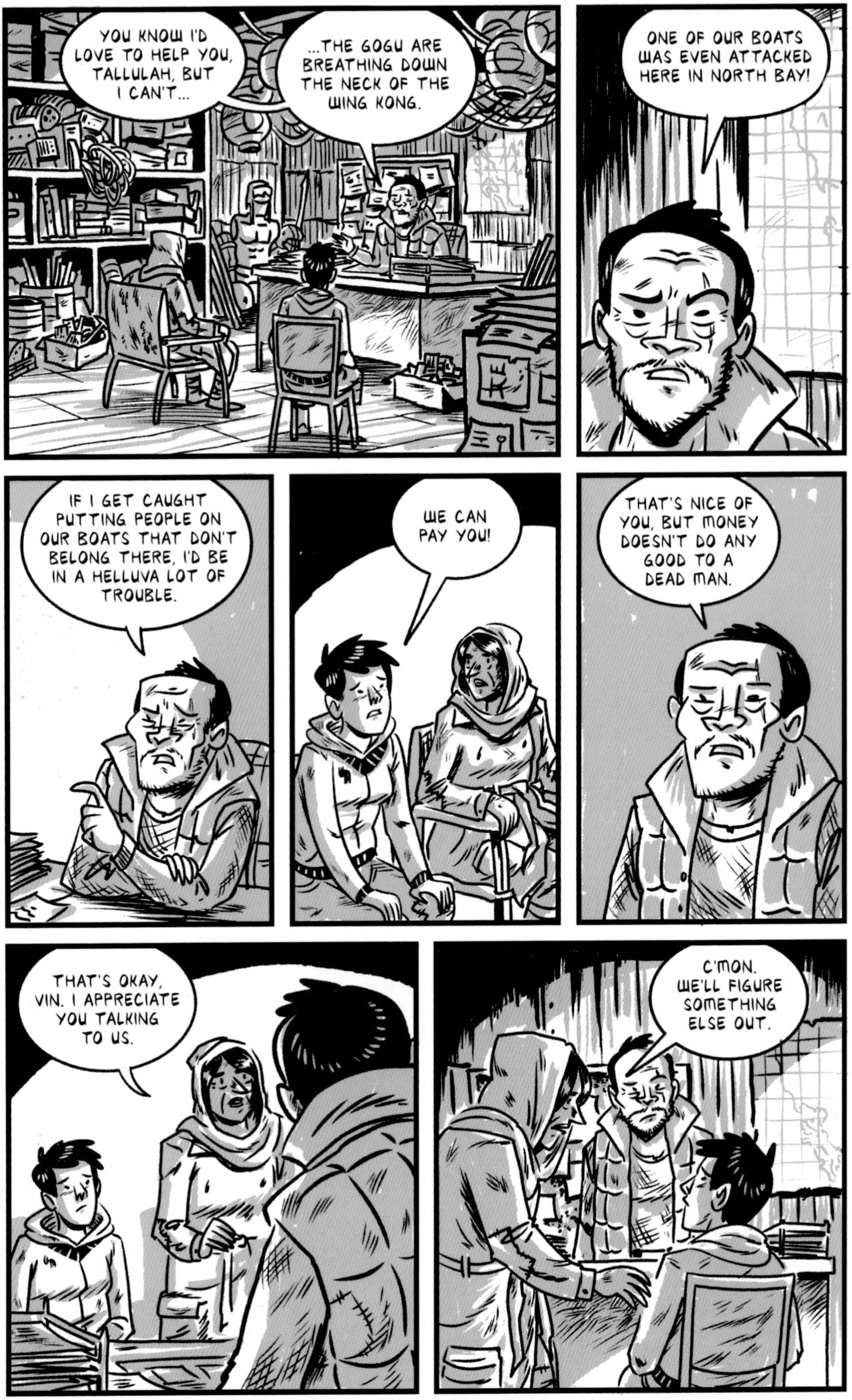
YOU KNOW I'D LOVE TO HELP YOU, TALLULAH, BUT I CAN'T...
...THE GOGU ARE BREATHING DOWN THE NECK OF THE WING KONG.
ONE OF OUR BOATS WAS EVEN ATTACKED HERE IN NORTH BAY!
IF I GET CAUGHT PUTTING PEOPLE ON OUR BOATS THAT DON'T BELONG THERE, I'D BE IN A HELLUVA LOT OF TROUBLE.
WE CAN PAY YOU!
THAT'S NICE OF YOU, BUT MONEY DOESN'T DO ANY GOOD TO A DEAD MAN.
THAT'S OKAY, VIN. I APPRECIATE YOU TALKING TO US.
C'MON. WE'LL FIGURE SOMETHING ELSE OUT.

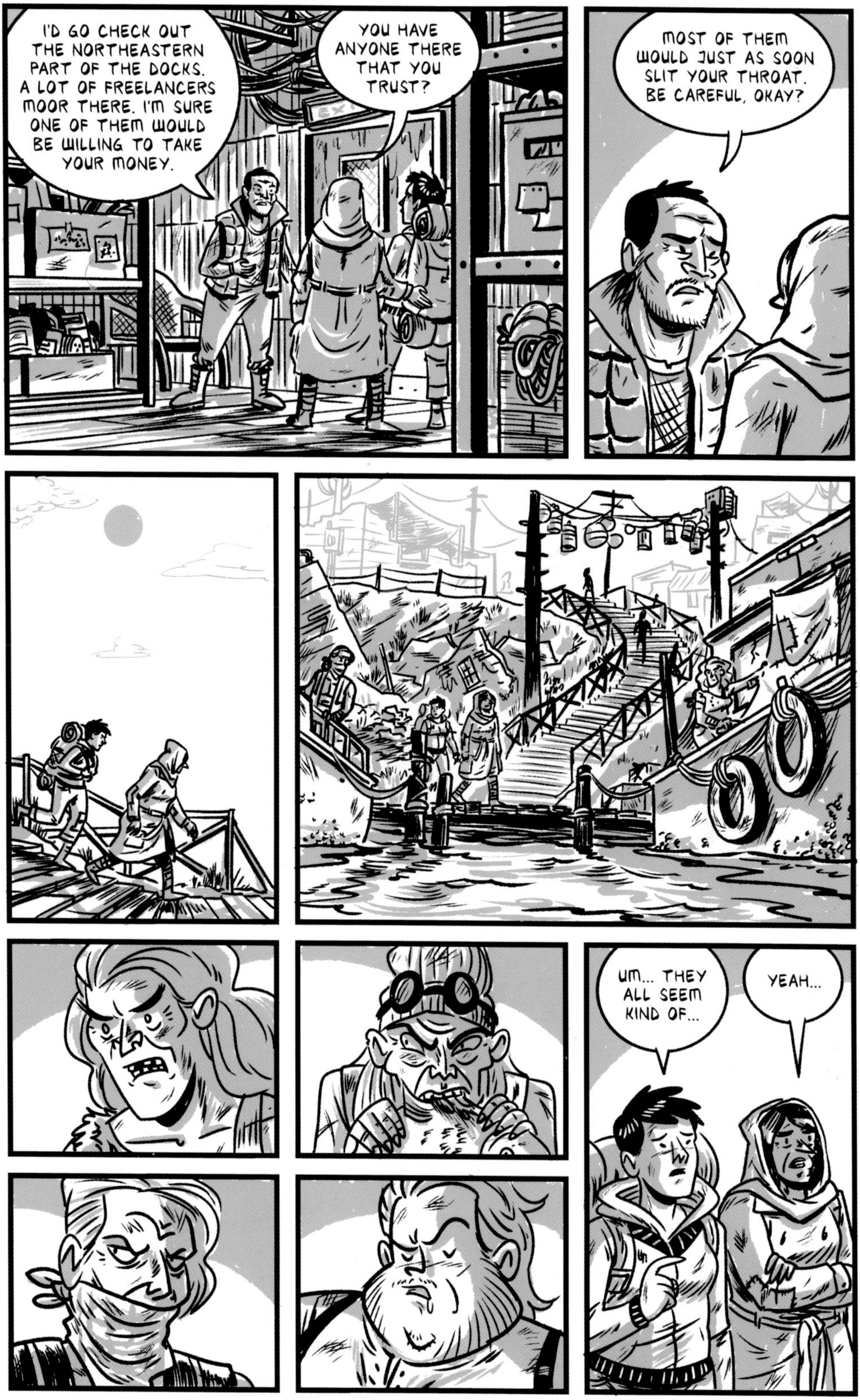
I'D GO CHECK OUT THE NORTHEASTERN PART OF THE DOCKS. A LOT OF FREELANCERS MOOR THERE. I'M SURE ONE OF THEM WOULD BE WILLING TO TAKE YOUR MONEY.
YOU HAVE ANYONE THERE THAT YOU TRUST?
MOST OF THEM WOULD JUST AS SOON SLIT YOUR THROAT. BE CAREFUL, OKAY?
UM... THEY ALL SEEM KIND OF...
YEAH...

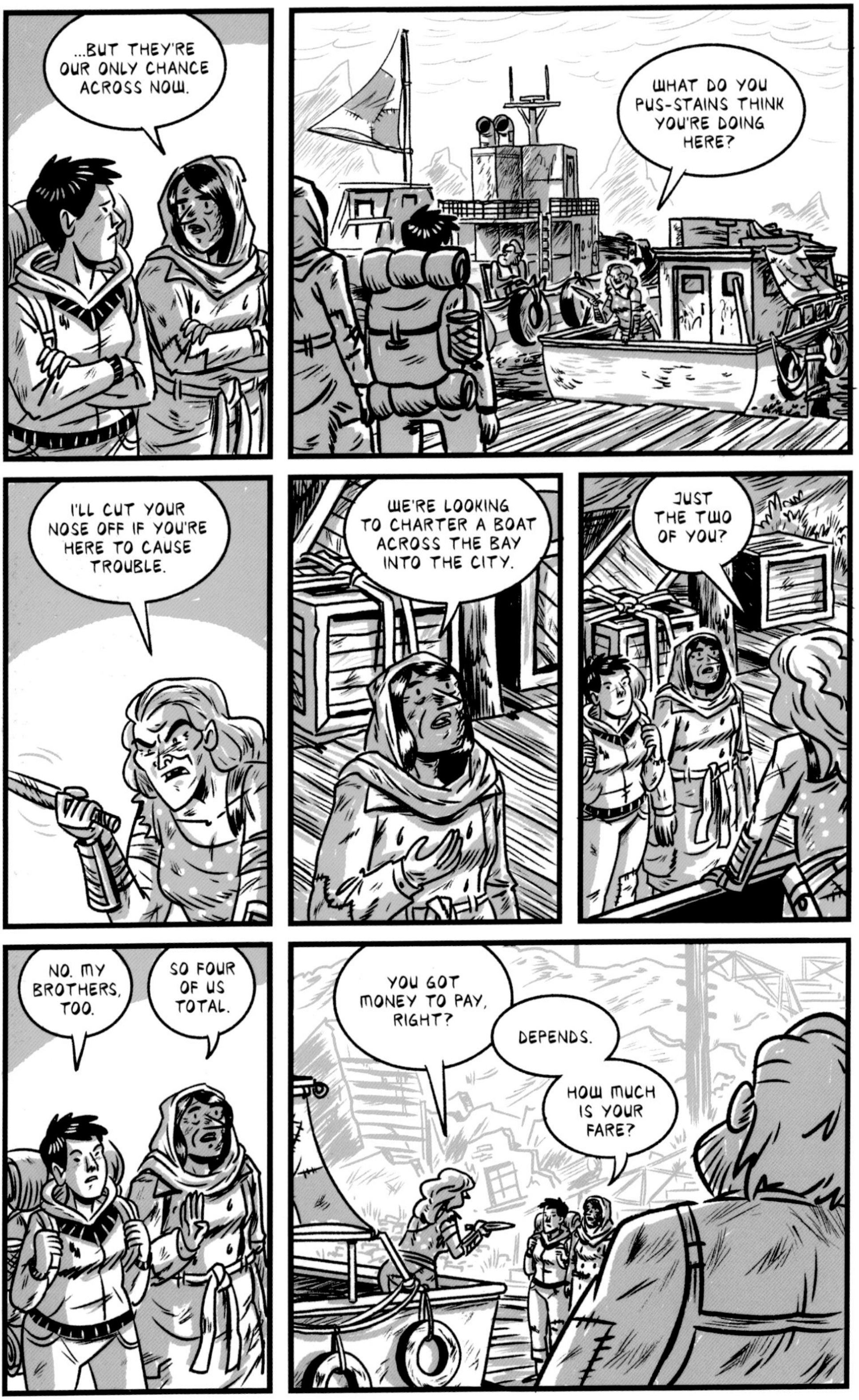
...BUT THEY'RE OUR ONLY CHANCE ACROSS NOW.
WHAT DO YOU PUS-STAINS THINK YOU'RE DOING HERE?
I'LL CUT YOUR NOSE OFF IF YOU'RE HERE TO CAUSE TROUBLE.
WE'RE LOOKING TO CHARTER A BOAT ACROSS THE BAY INTO THE CITY.
JUST THE TWO OF YOU?
NO. MY BROTHERS, TOO.
SO FOUR OF US TOTAL.
YOU GOT MONEY TO PAY, RIGHT?
DEPENDS.
HOW MUCH IS YOUR FARE?

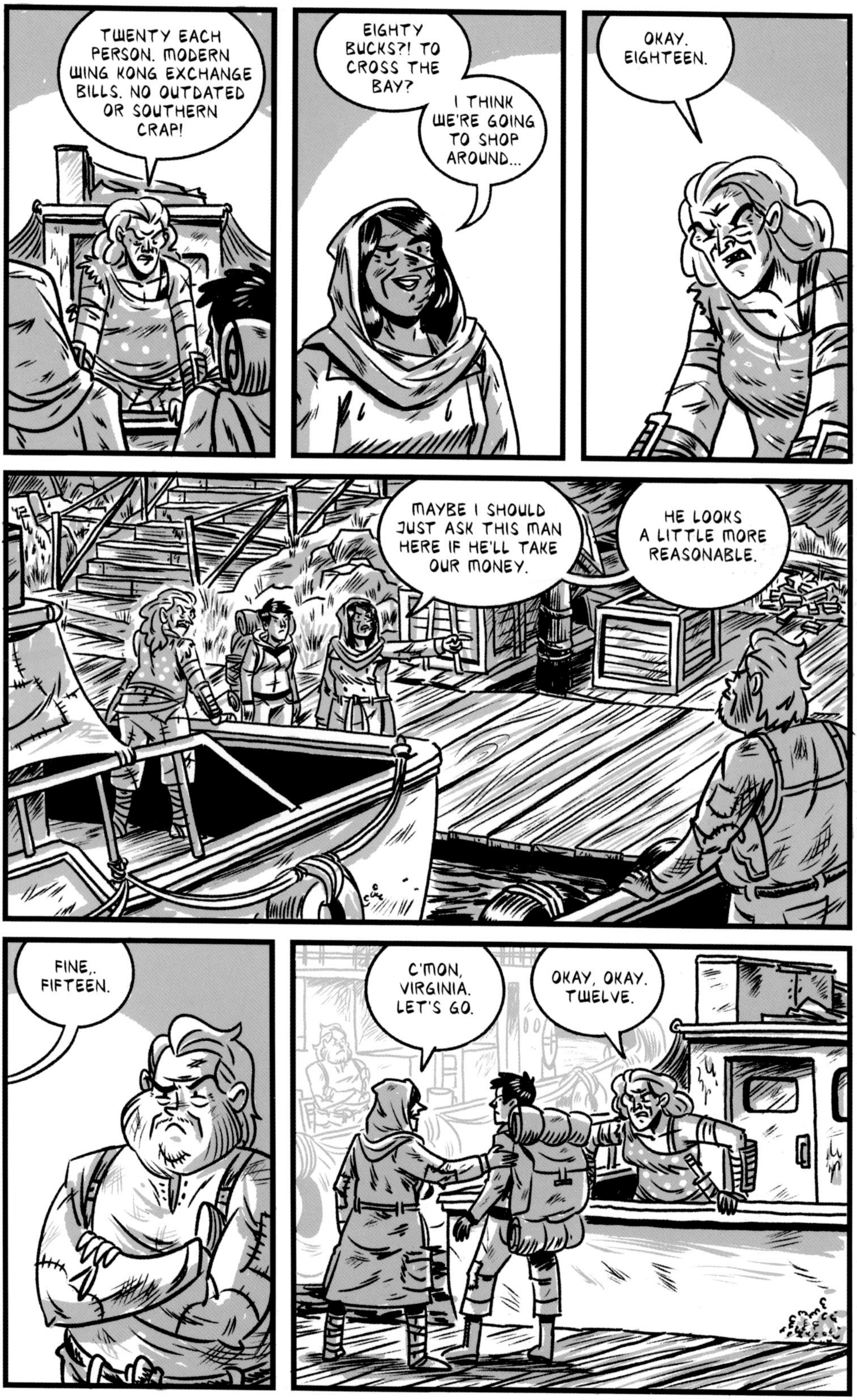
TWENTY EACH PERSON. MODERN WING KONG EXCHANGE BILLS. NO OUTDATED OR SOUTHERN CRAP!
EIGHTY BUCKS?! TO CROSS THE BAY?
I THINK WE'RE GOING TO SHOP AROUND...
OKAY. EIGHTEEN.
MAYBE I SHOULD JUST ASK THIS MAN HERE IF HE'LL TAKE OUR MONEY.
HE LOOKS A LITTLE MORE REASONABLE.
FINE,. FIFTEEN.
C'MON, VIRGINIA. LET'S GO.
OKAY, OKAY. TWELVE.

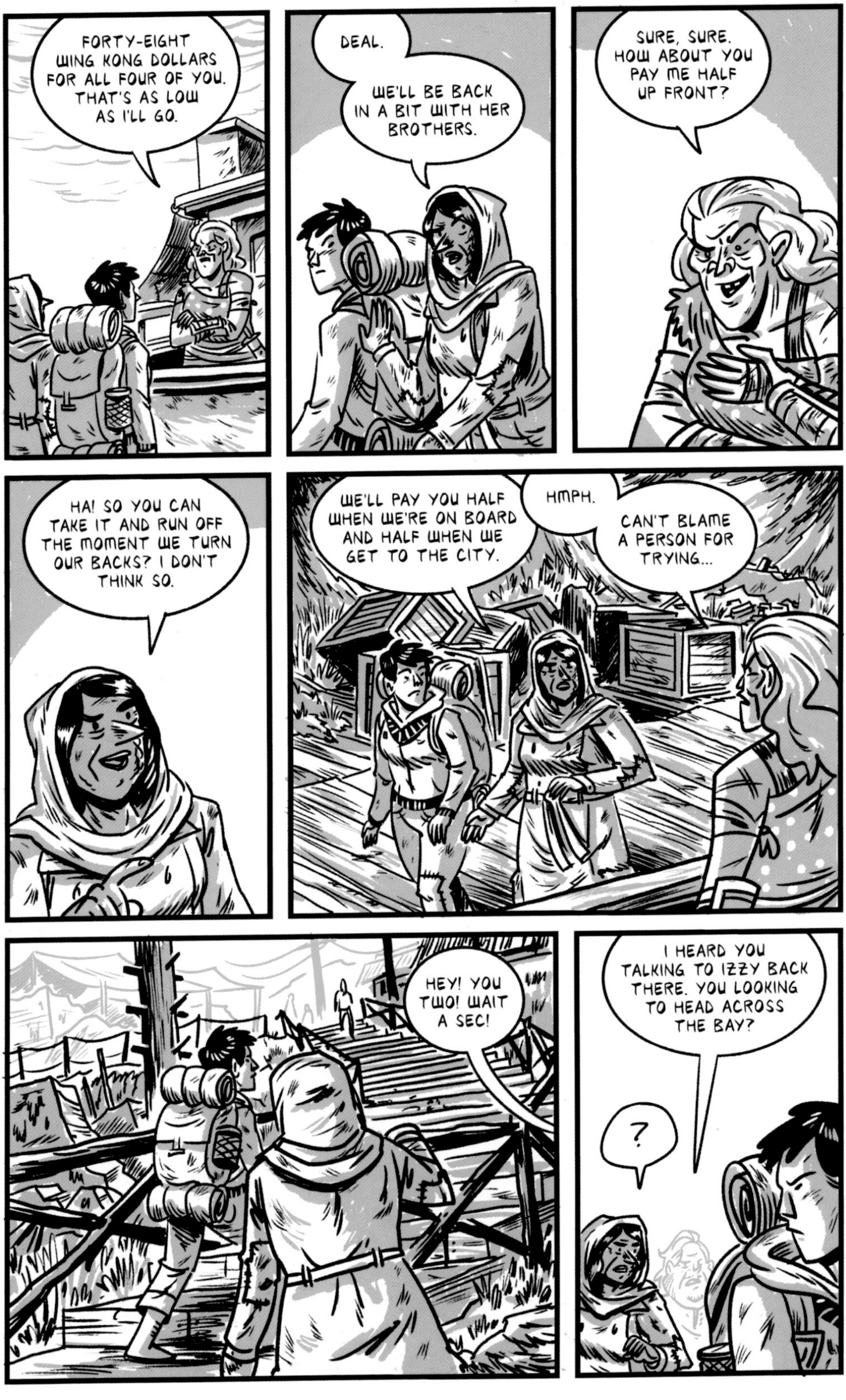
FORTY-EIGHT WING KONG DOLLARS FOR ALL FOUR OF YOU. THAT'S AS LOW AS I'LL GO.
DEAL.
WE'LL BE BACK IN A BIT WITH HER BROTHERS.
SURE, SURE. HOW ABOUT YOU PAY ME HALF UP FRONT?
HA! SO YOU CAN TAKE IT AND RUN OFF THE MOMENT WE TURN OUR BACKS? I DON'T THINK SO.
WE'LL PAY YOU HALF WHEN WE'RE ON BOARD AND HALF WHEN WE GET TO THE CITY.
HMPH.
CAN'T BLAME A PERSON FOR TRYING...
HEY! YOU TWO! WAIT A SEC!
I HEARD YOU TALKING TO IZZY BACK THERE. YOU LOOKING TO HEAD ACROSS THE BAY?
?

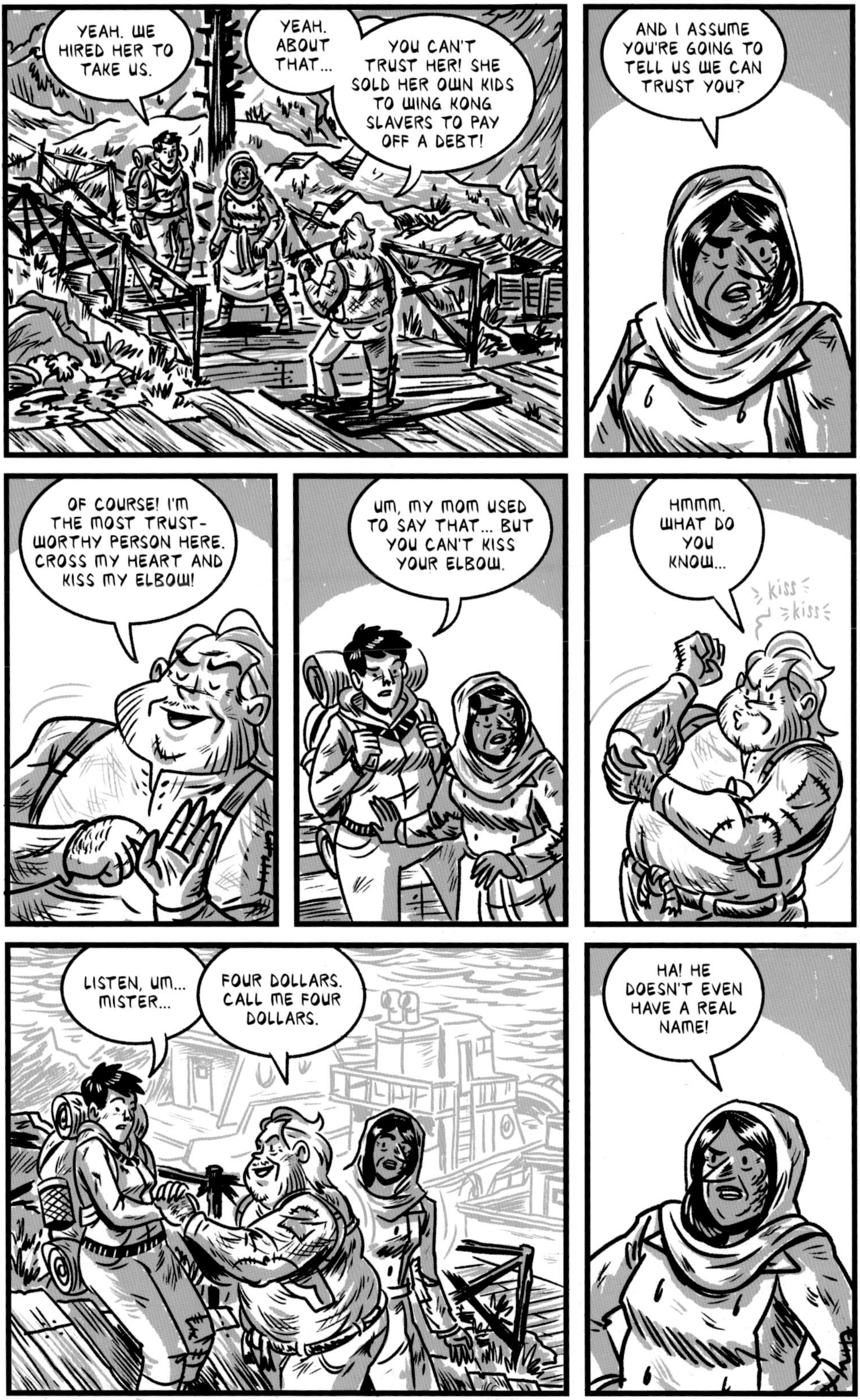

YEAH. WE HIRED HER TO TAKE US.
YEAH. ABOUT THAT...
YOU CAN'T TRUST HER! SHE SOLD HER OWN KIDS TO WING KONG SLAVERS TO PAY OFF A DEBT!
AND I ASSUME YOU'RE GOING TO TELL US WE CAN TRUST YOU?
OF COURSE! I'M THE MOST TRUST-WORTHY PERSON HERE. CROSS MY HEART AND KISS MY ELBOW!
UM, MY MOM USED TO SAY THAT... BUT YOU CAN'T KISS YOUR ELBOW.
HMMM. WHAT DO YOU KNOW...
KISS KISS
LISTEN, UM... MISTER...
FOUR DOLLARS. CALL ME FOUR DOLLARS.
HA! HE DOESN'T EVEN HAVE A REAL NAME!

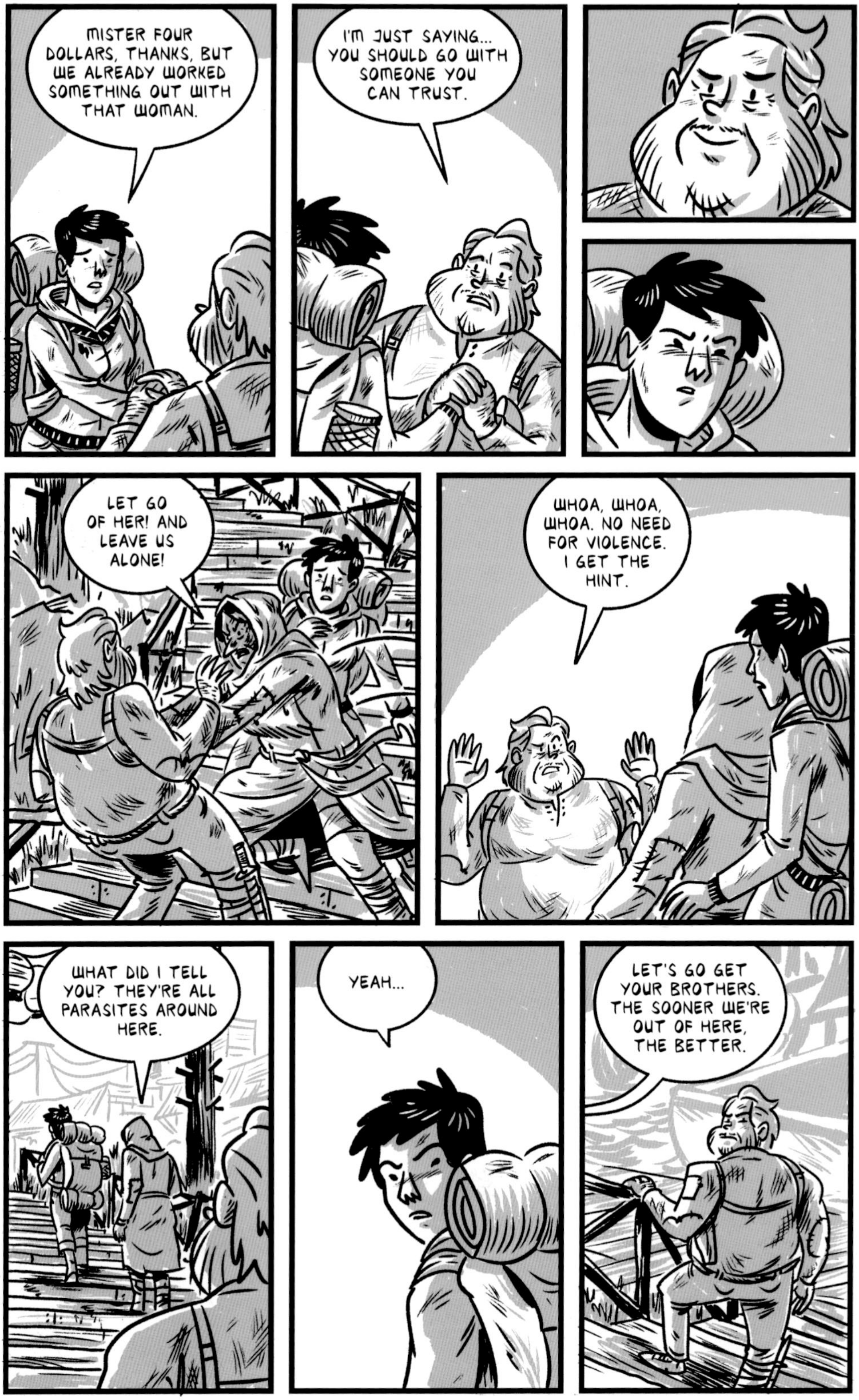
MISTER FOUR DOLLARS, THANKS, BUT WE ALREADY WORKED SOMETHING OUT WITH THAT WOMAN.
I'M JUST SAYING... YOU SHOULD GO WITH SOMEONE YOU CAN TRUST.
LET GO OF HER! AND LEAVE US ALONE!
WHOA, WHOA, WHOA. NO NEED FOR VIOLENCE. I GET THE HINT.
WHAT DID I TELL YOU? THEY'RE ALL PARASITES AROUND HERE.
YEAH...
LET'S GO GET YOUR BROTHERS. THE SOONER WE'RE OUT OF HERE, THE BETTER.

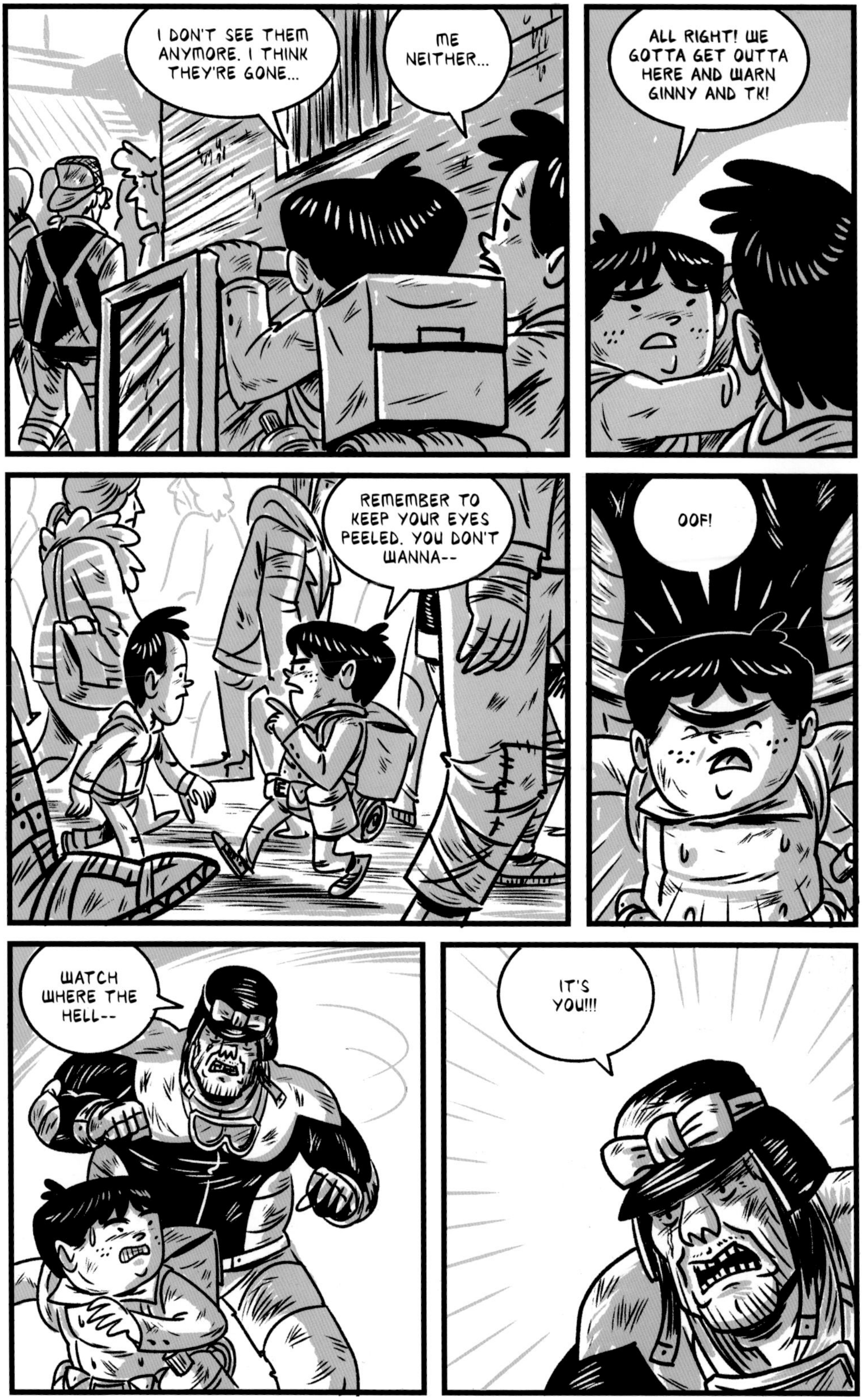
I DON'T SEE THEM ANYMORE. I THINK THEY'RE GONE...
ME NEITHER...
ALL RIGHT! WE GOTTA GET OUTTA HERE AND WARN GINNY AND TK!
REMEMBER TO KEEP YOUR EYES PEELED. YOU DON'T WANNA--
OOF!
WATCH WHERE THE HELL--
IT'S YOU!!!

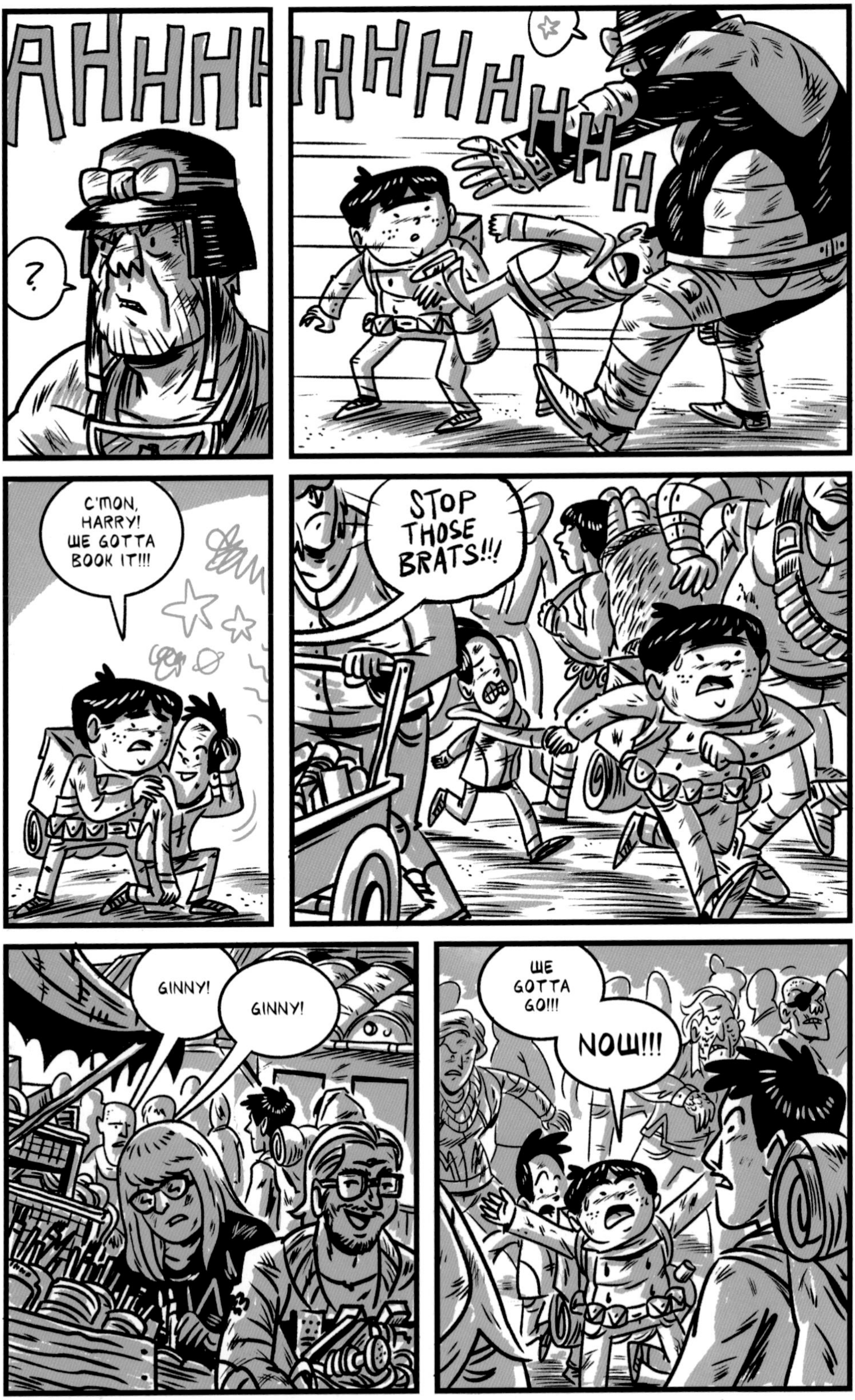
AHHHHHHHHHHHHHH
?
C'MON, HARRY! WE GOTTA BOOK IT!!!
STOP THOSE BRATS!!!
GINNY!
GINNY!
WE GOTTA GO!!!
NOW!!!

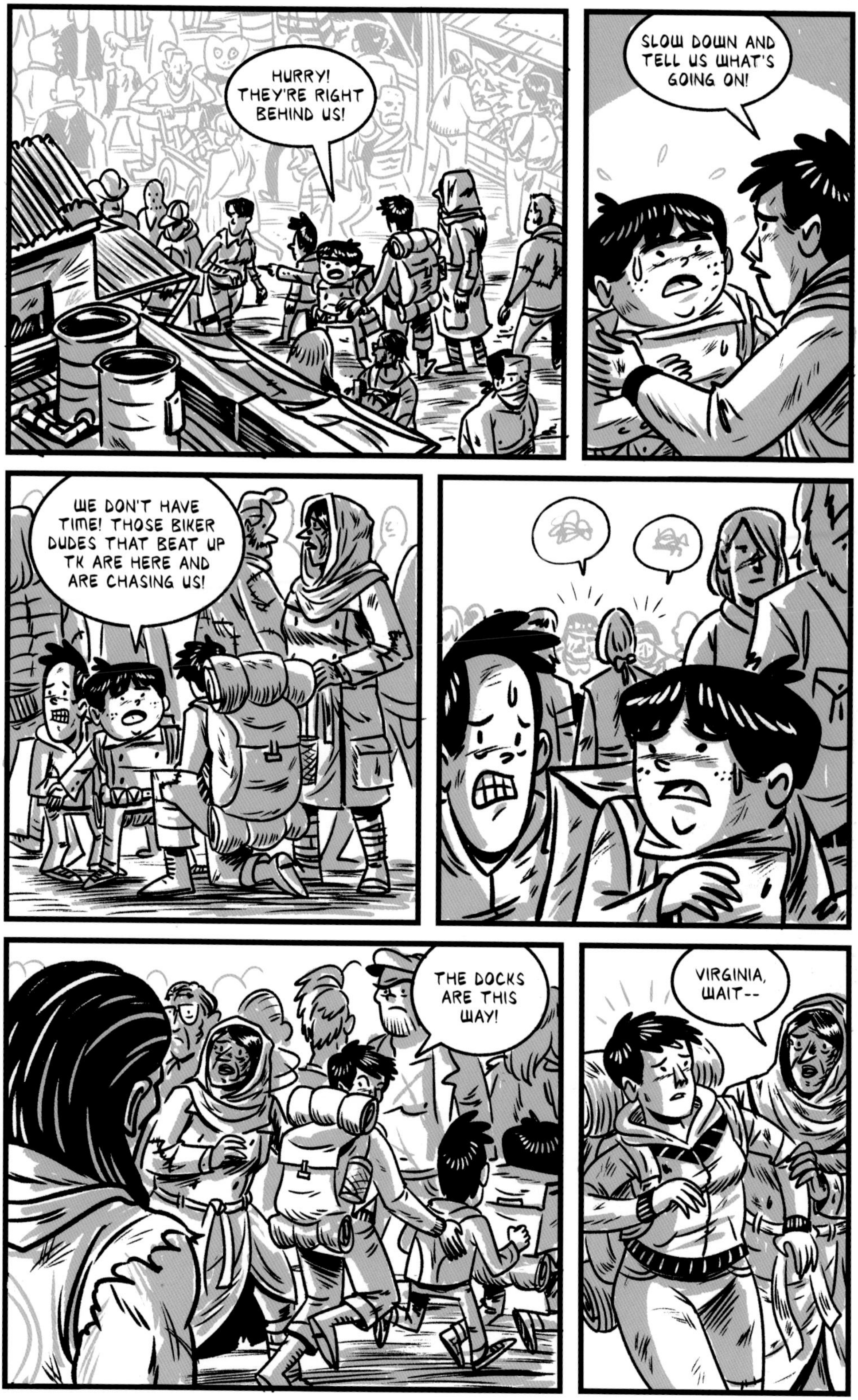
HURRY! THEY'RE RIGHT BEHIND US!
SLOW DOWN AND TELL US WHAT'S GOING ON!
WE DON'T HAVE TIME! THOSE BIKER DUDES THAT BEAT UP TK ARE HERE AND ARE CHASING US!
THE DOCKS ARE THIS WAY!
VIRGINIA, WAIT--

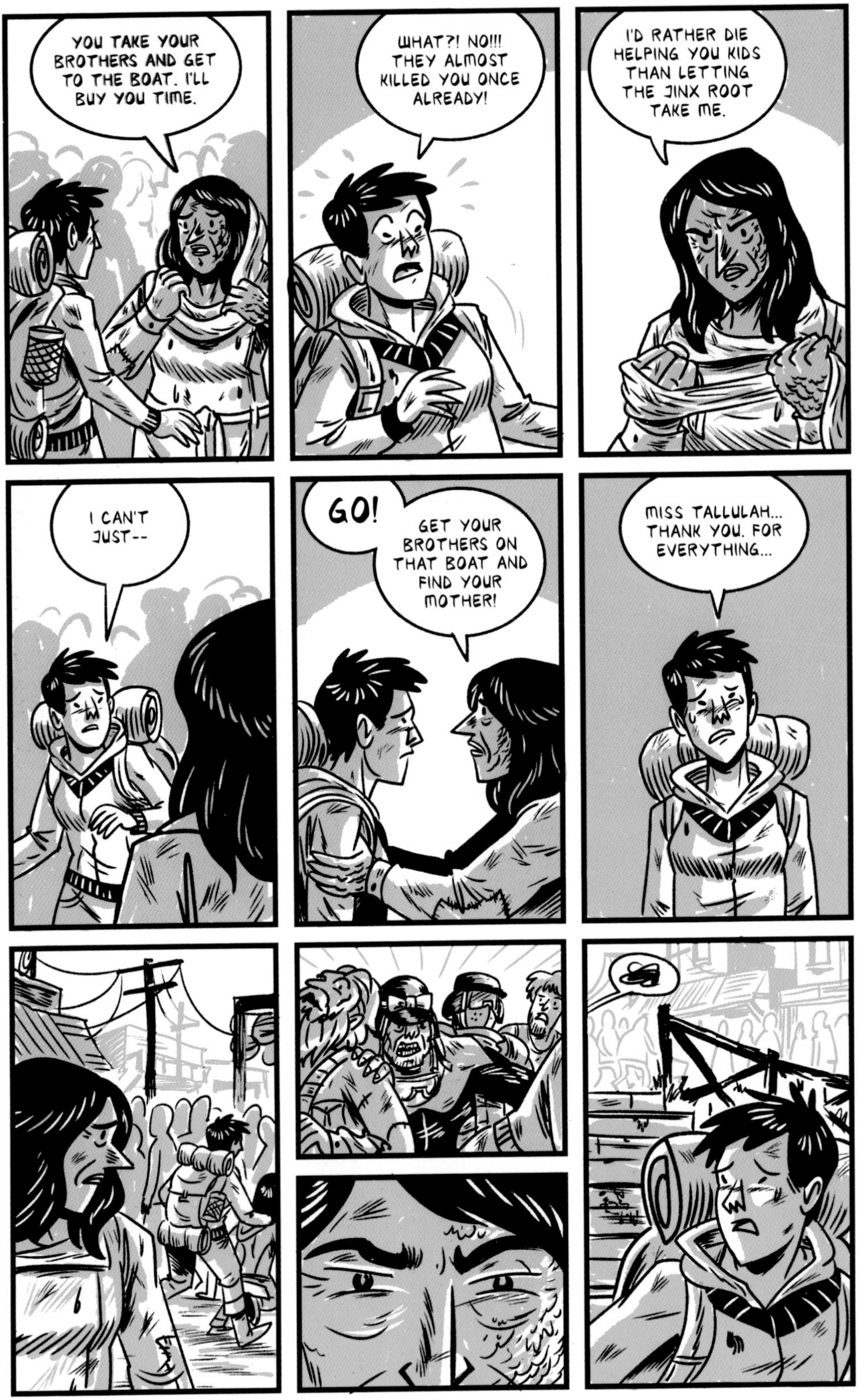
YOU TAKE YOUR BROTHERS AND GET TO THE BOAT. I'LL BUY YOU TIME.
WHAT?! NO!!! THEY ALMOST KILLED YOU ONCE ALREADY!
I'D RATHER DIE HELPING YOU KIDS THAN LETTING THE JINX ROOT TAKE ME.
I CAN'T JUST--
GO!
GET YOUR BROTHERS ON THAT BOAT AND FIND YOUR MOTHER!
MISS TALLULAH... THANK YOU. FOR EVERYTHING...

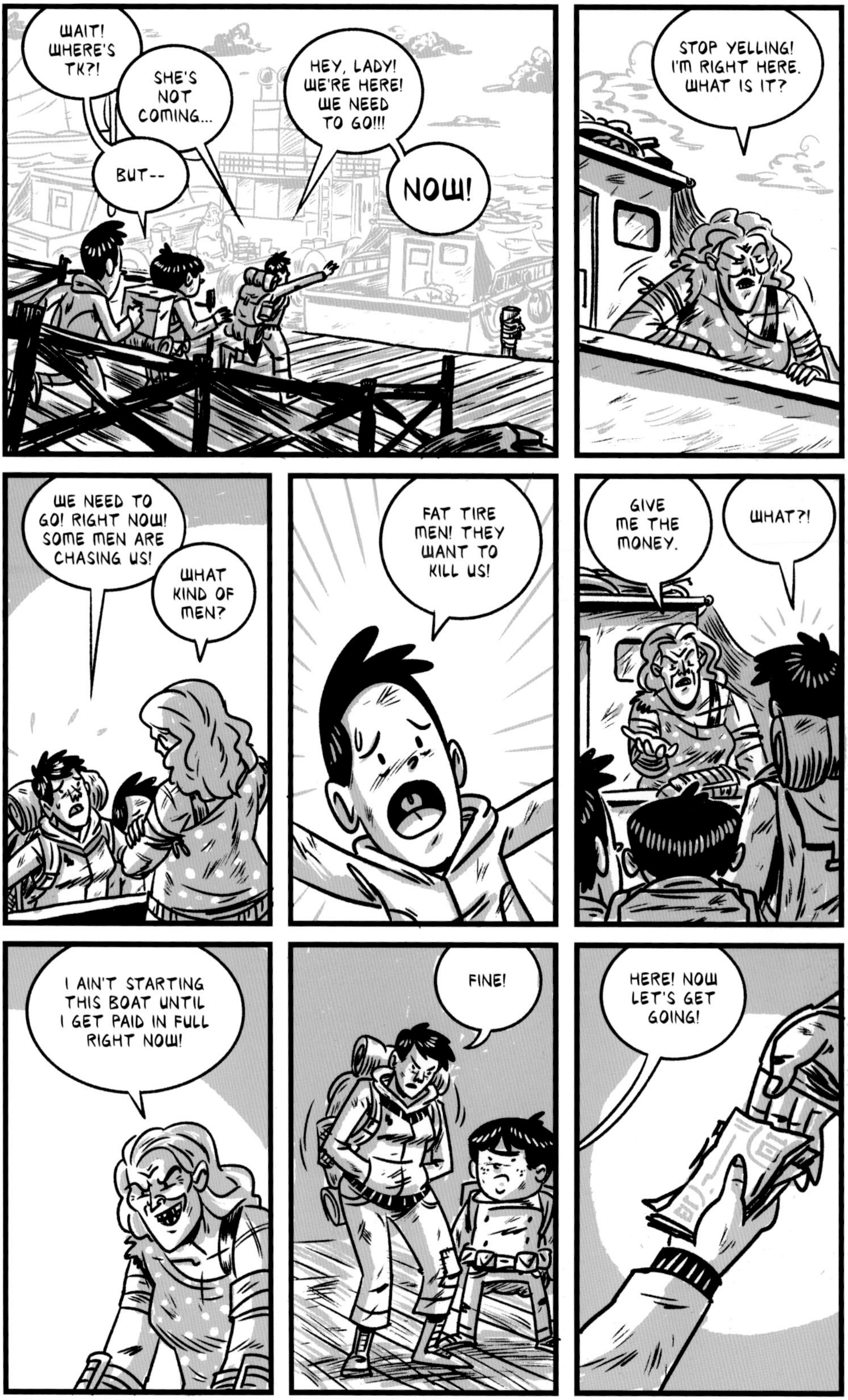

WAIT! WHERE'S TK?!
SHE'S NOT COMING...
BUT--
HEY, LADY! WE'RE HERE! WE NEED TO GO!!!
NOW!
STOP YELLING! I'M RIGHT HERE. WHAT IS IT?
WE NEED TO GO! RIGHT NOW! SOME MEN ARE CHASING US!
WHAT KIND OF MEN?
FAT TIRE MEN! THEY WANT TO KILL US!
GIVE ME THE MONEY.
WHAT?!
I AIN'T STARTING THIS BOAT UNTIL I GET PAID IN FULL RIGHT NOW!
FINE!
HERE! NOW LET'S GET GOING!

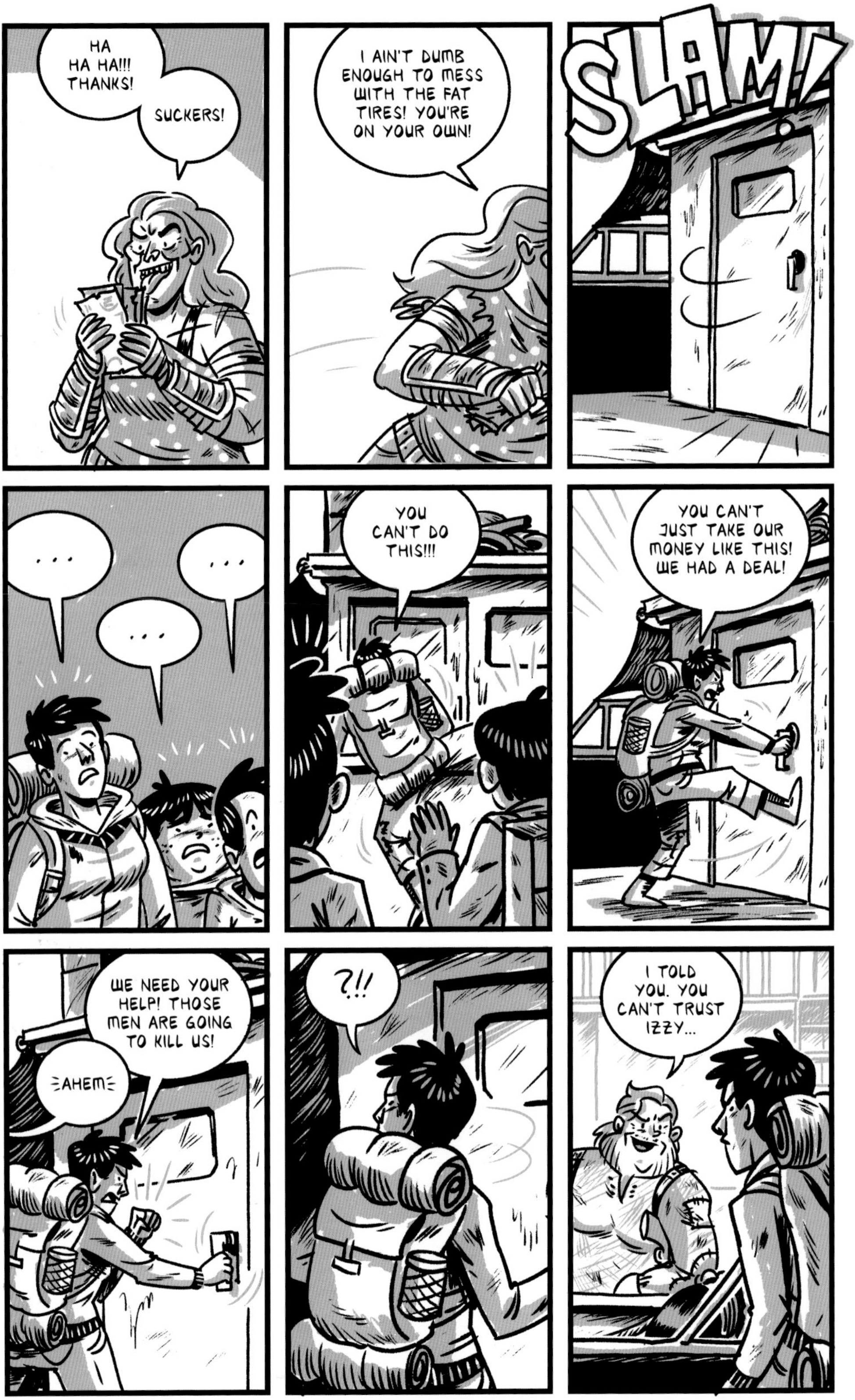
HA HA HA!!! THANKS!
SUCKERS!
I AIN'T DUMB ENOUGH TO MESS WITH THE FAT TIRES! YOU'RE ON YOUR OWN!
SLAM!
...
...
...
YOU CAN'T DO THIS!!!
YOU CAN'T JUST TAKE OUR MONEY LIKE THIS! WE HAD A DEAL!
WE NEED YOUR HELP! THOSE MEN ARE GOING TO KILL US!
AHEM
?!!
I TOLD YOU. YOU CAN'T TRUST IZZY...

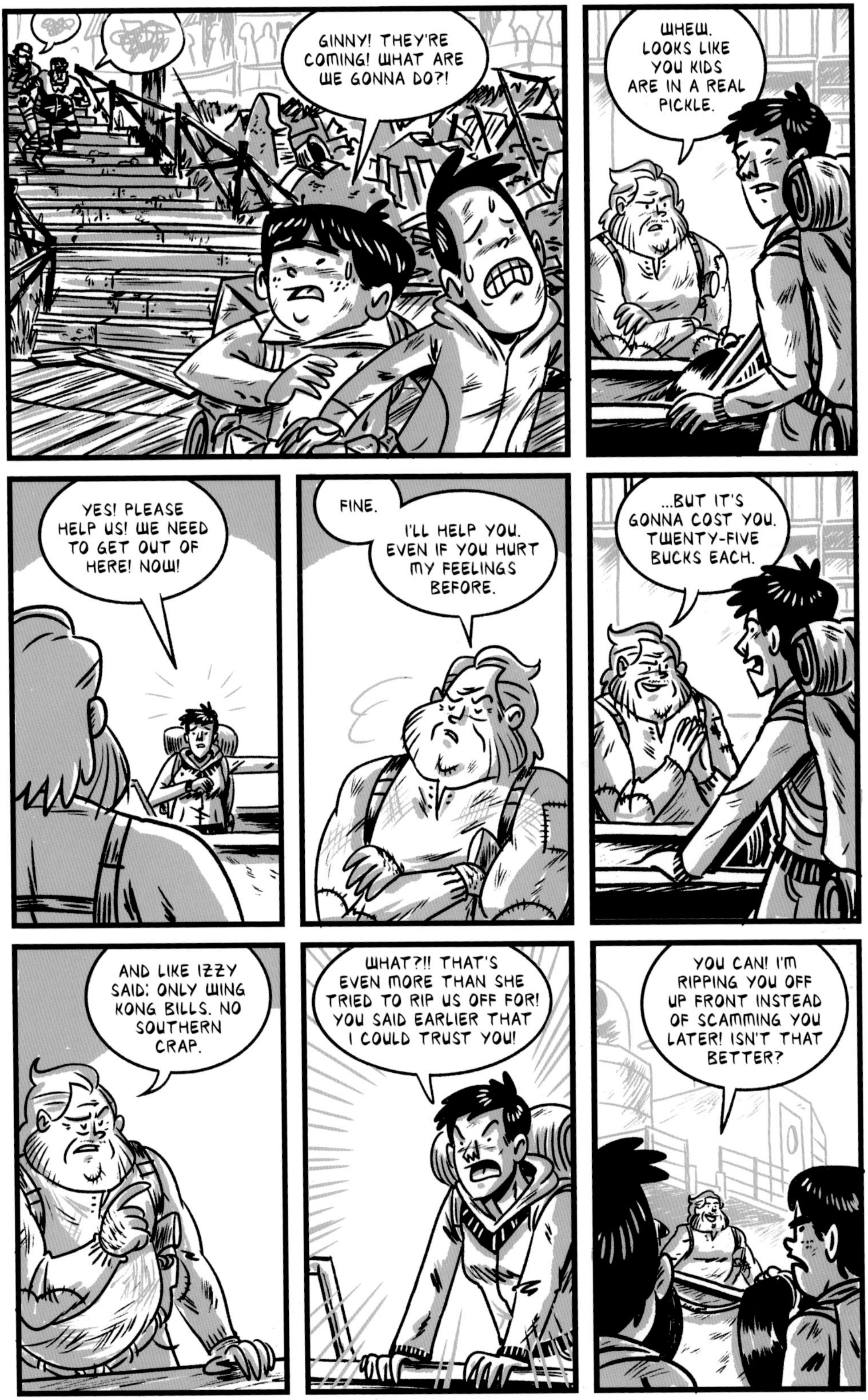
GINNY! THEY'RE COMING! WHAT ARE WE GONNA DO?!
WHEW. LOOKS LIKE YOU KIDS ARE IN A REAL PICKLE.
YES! PLEASE HELP US! WE NEED TO GET OUT OF HERE! NOW!
FINE.
I'LL HELP YOU. EVEN IF YOU HURT MY FEELINGS BEFORE.
...BUT IT'S GONNA COST YOU. TWENTY-FIVE BUCKS EACH.
AND LIKE IZZY SAID: ONLY WING KONG BILLS. NO SOUTHERN CRAP.
WHAT?!! THAT'S EVEN MORE THAN SHE TRIED TO RIP US OFF FOR! YOU SAID EARLIER THAT I COULD TRUST YOU!
YOU CAN! I'M RIPPING YOU OFF UP FRONT INSTEAD OF SCAMMING YOU LATER! ISN'T THAT BETTER?

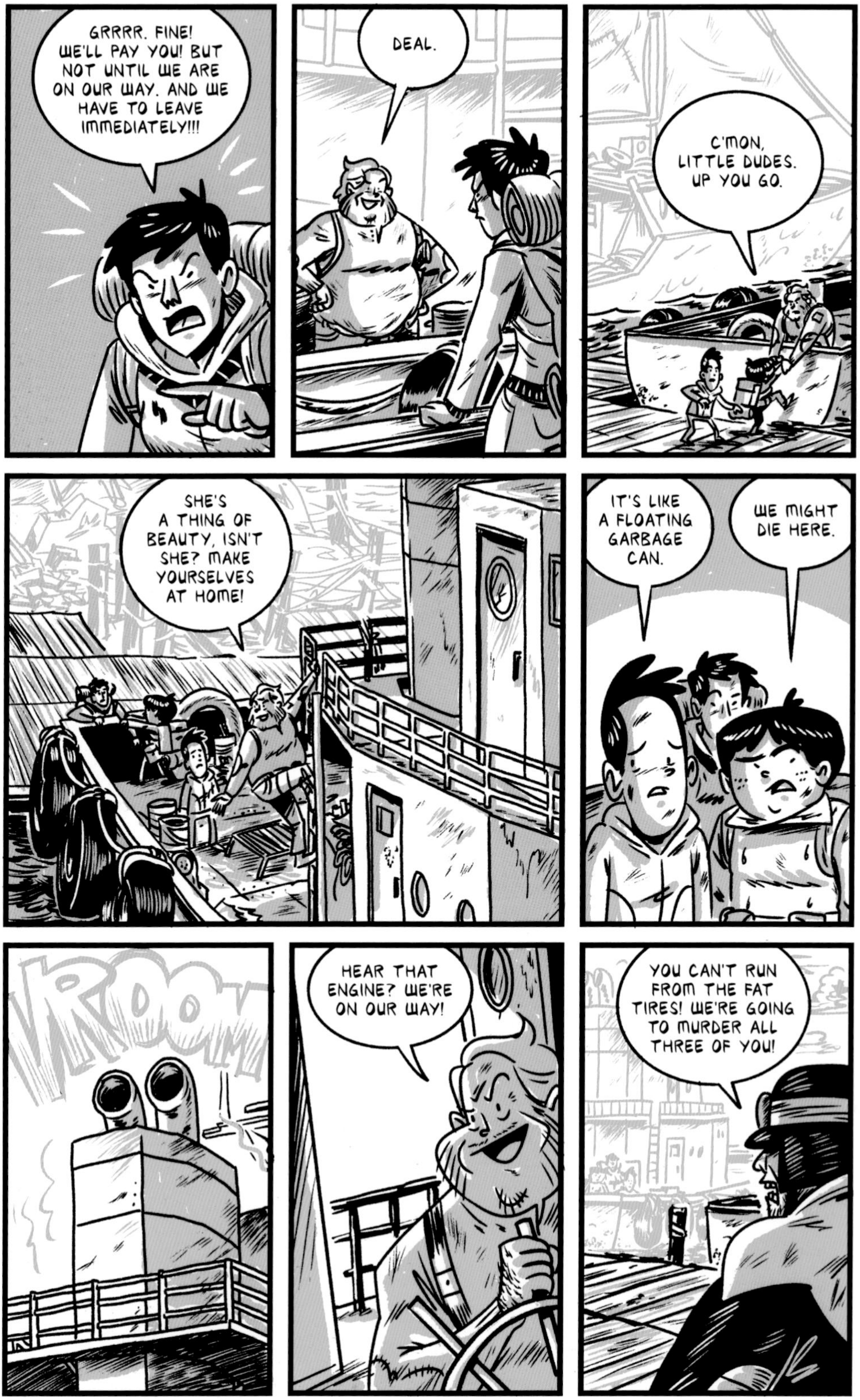
GRRRR. FINE! WE'LL PAY YOU! BUT NOT UNTIL WE ARE ON OUR WAY. AND WE HAVE TO LEAVE IMMEDIATELY!!!
DEAL.
C'MON, LITTLE DUDES. UP YOU GO.
SHE'S A THING OF BEAUTY, ISN'T SHE? MAKE YOURSELVES AT HOME!
IT'S LIKE A FLOATING GARBAGE CAN.
WE MIGHT DIE HERE.
VROOOM
HEAR THAT ENGINE? WE'RE ON OUR WAY!
YOU CAN'T RUN FROM THE FAT TIRES! WE'RE GOING TO MURDER ALL THREE OF YOU!

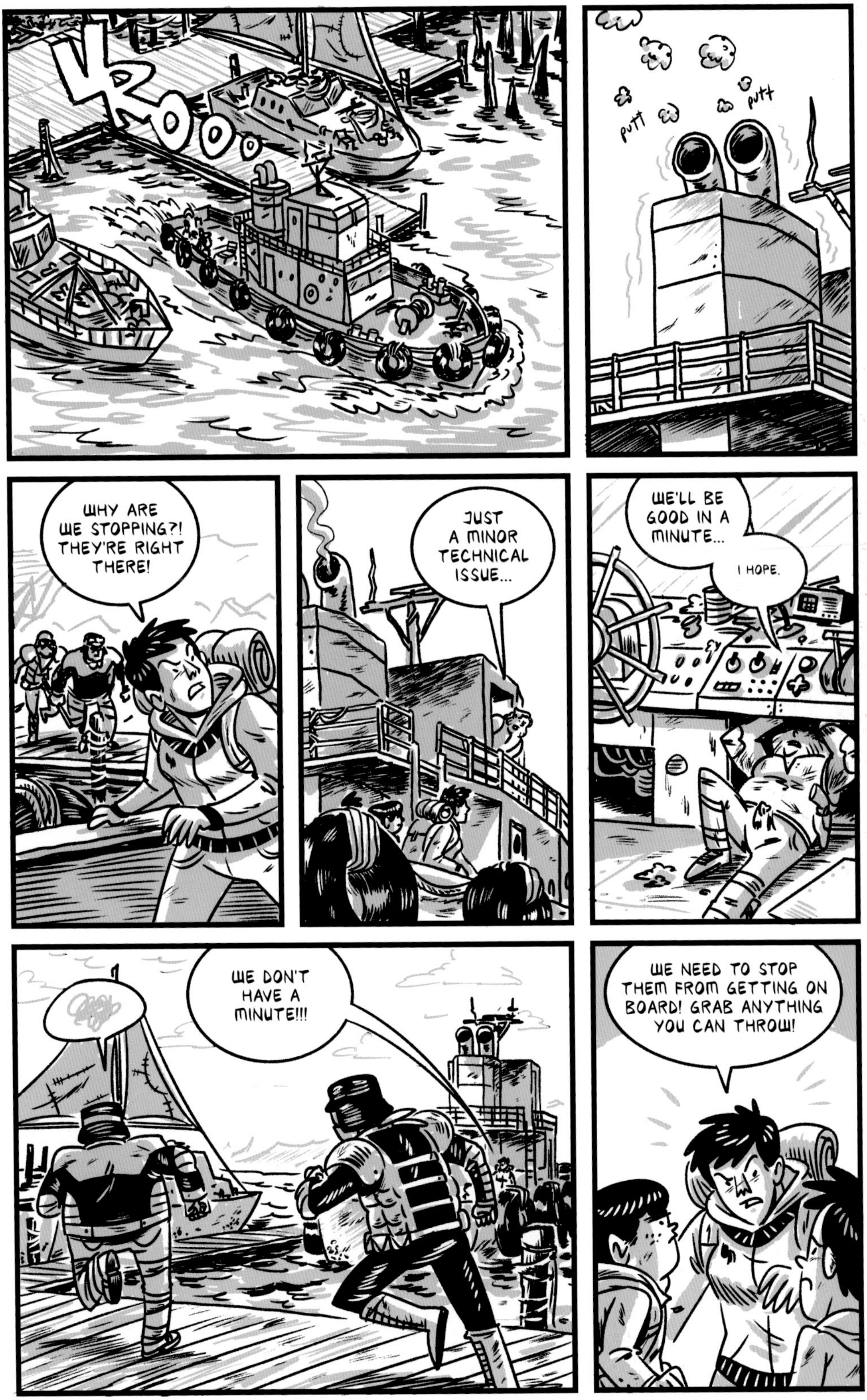
VROOOO
putt
putt
WHY ARE WE STOPPING?! THEY'RE RIGHT THERE!
JUST A MINOR TECHNICAL ISSUE...
WE'LL BE GOOD IN A MINUTE...
I HOPE.
WE DON'T HAVE A MINUTE!!!
WE NEED TO STOP THEM FROM GETTING ON BOARD! GRAB ANYTHING YOU CAN THROW!

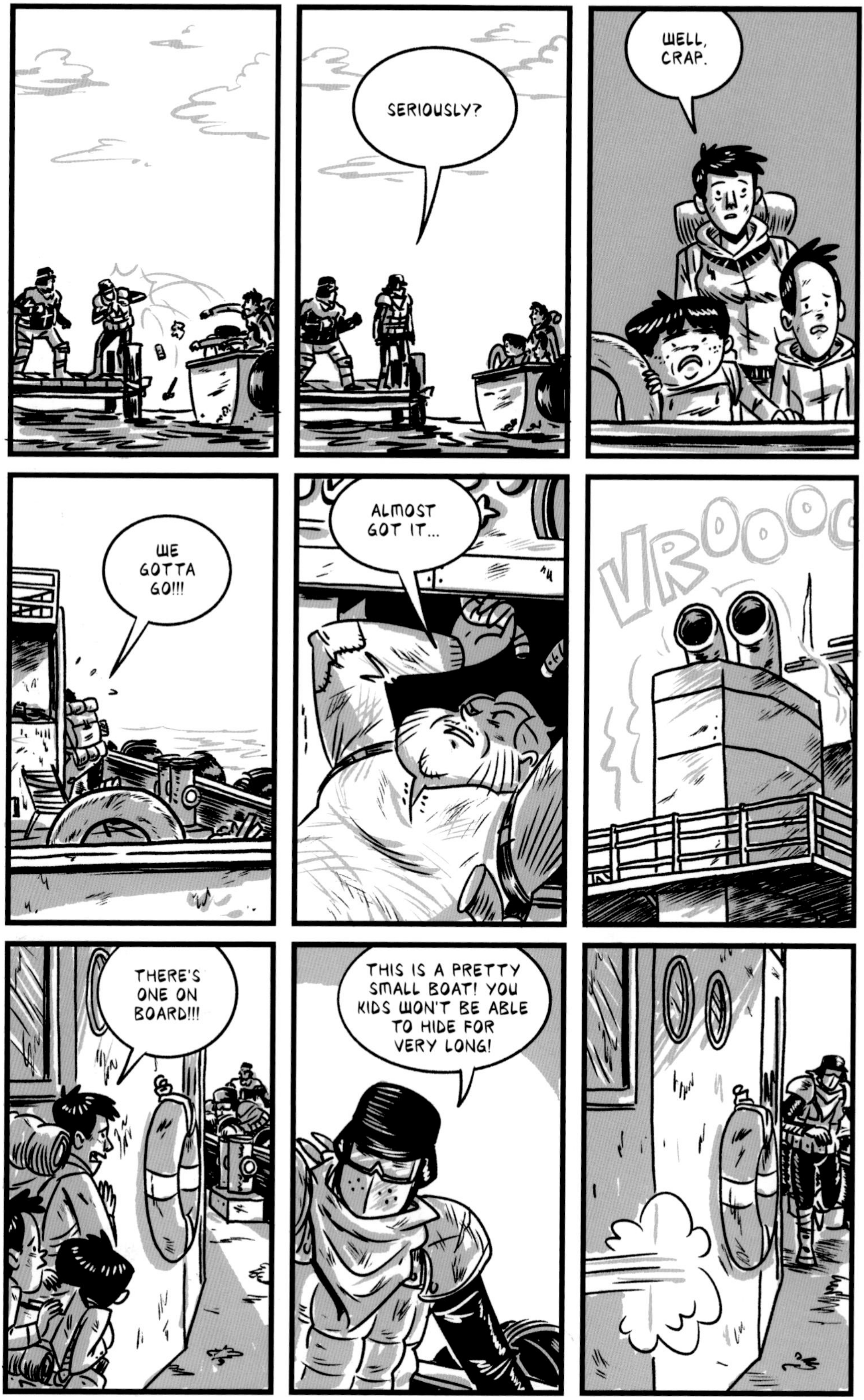
SERIOUSLY?
WELL, CRAP.
WE GOTTA GO!!!
ALMOST GOT IT...
VROOOO
THERE'S ONE ON BOARD!!!
THIS IS A PRETTY SMALL BOAT! YOU KIDS WON'T BE ABLE TO HIDE FOR VERY LONG!

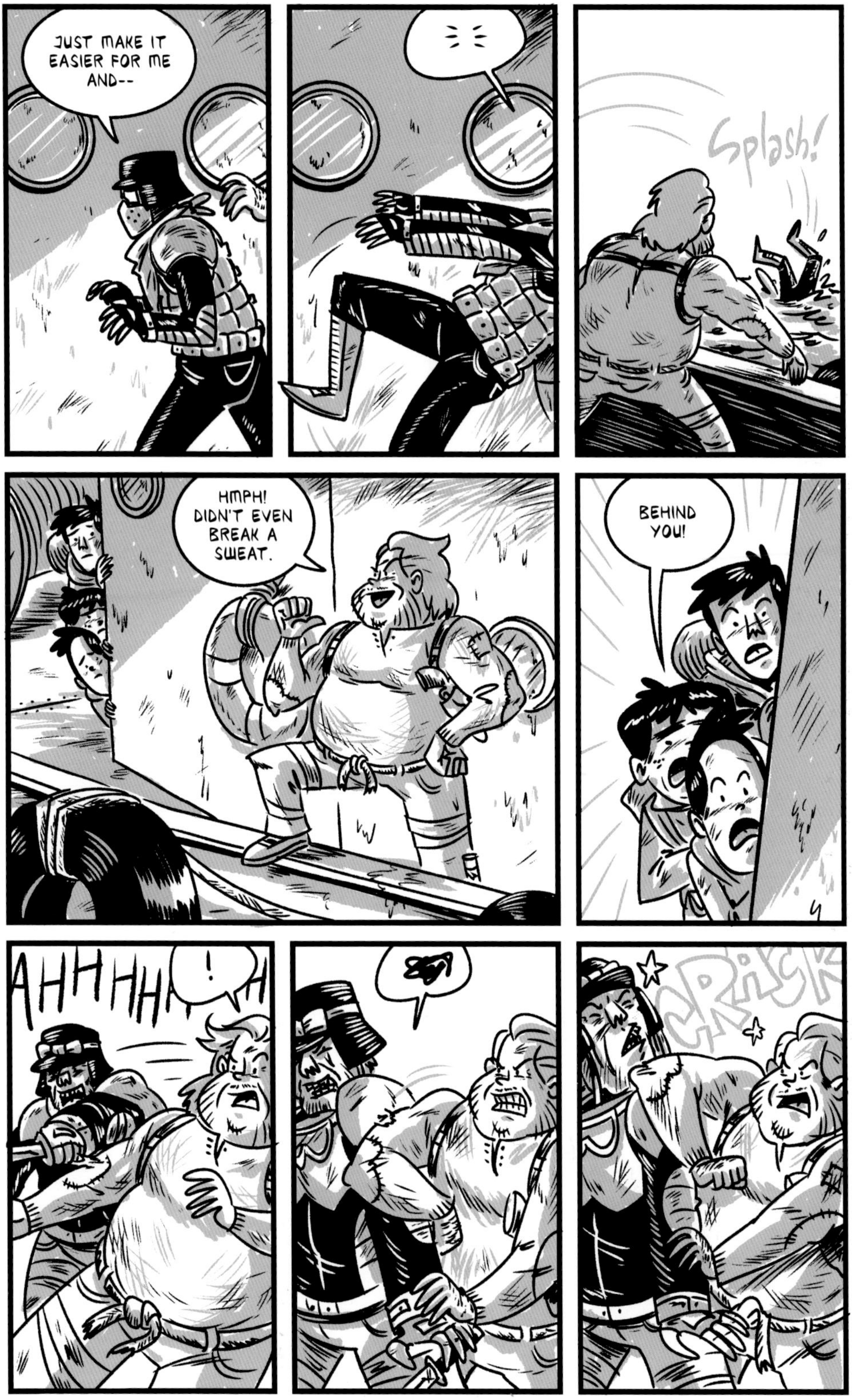
JUST MAKE IT EASIER FOR ME AND--
Splash!
HMPH! DIDN'T EVEN BREAK A SWEAT.
BEHIND YOU!
AHHHHHH
!
CRACK

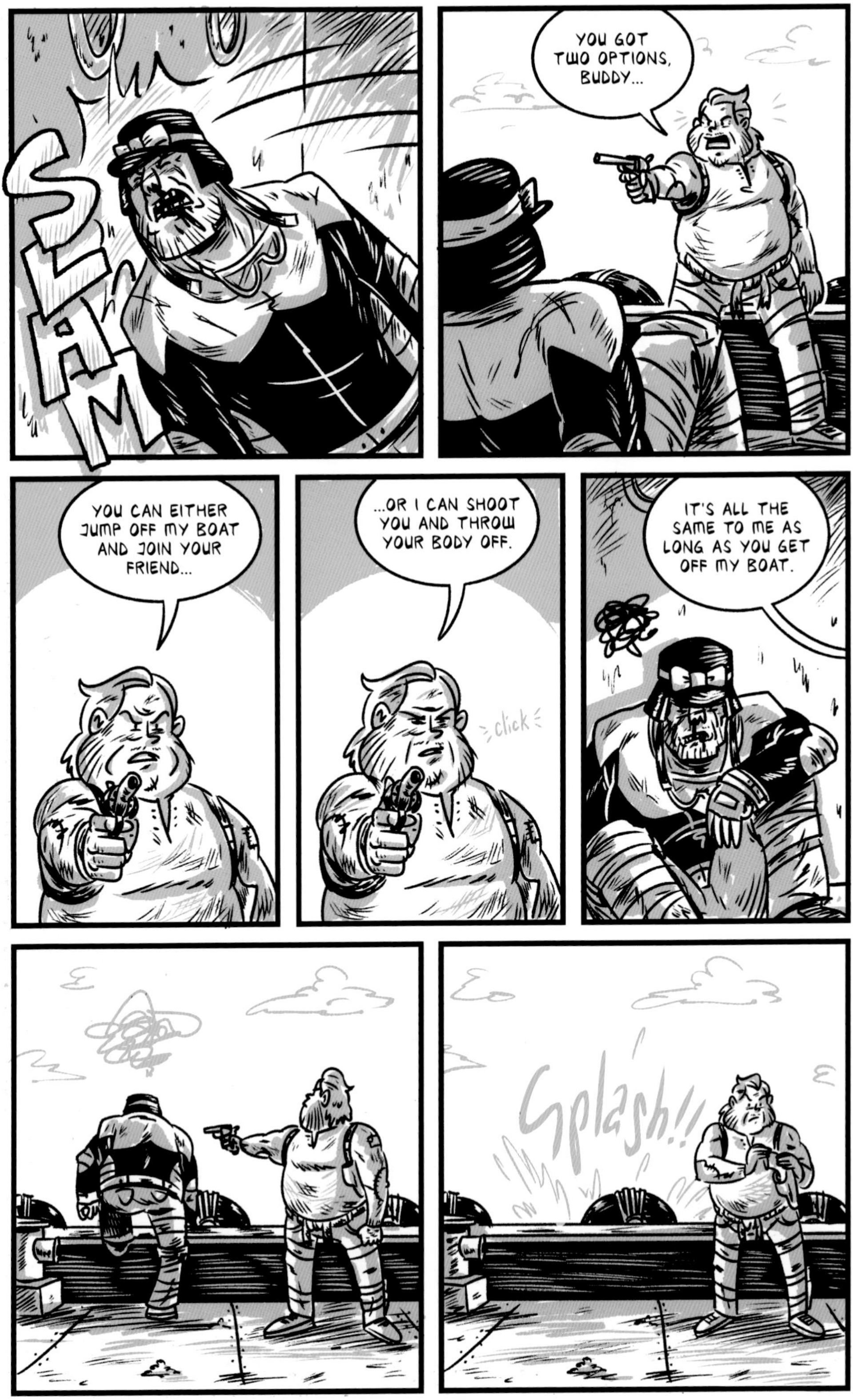
SLAM
YOU GOT TWO OPTIONS, BUDDY...
YOU CAN EITHER JUMP OFF MY BOAT AND JOIN YOUR FRIEND...
...OR I CAN SHOOT YOU AND THROW YOUR BODY OFF.
click
IT'S ALL THE SAME TO ME AS LONG AS YOU GET OFF MY BOAT.
Splash!!

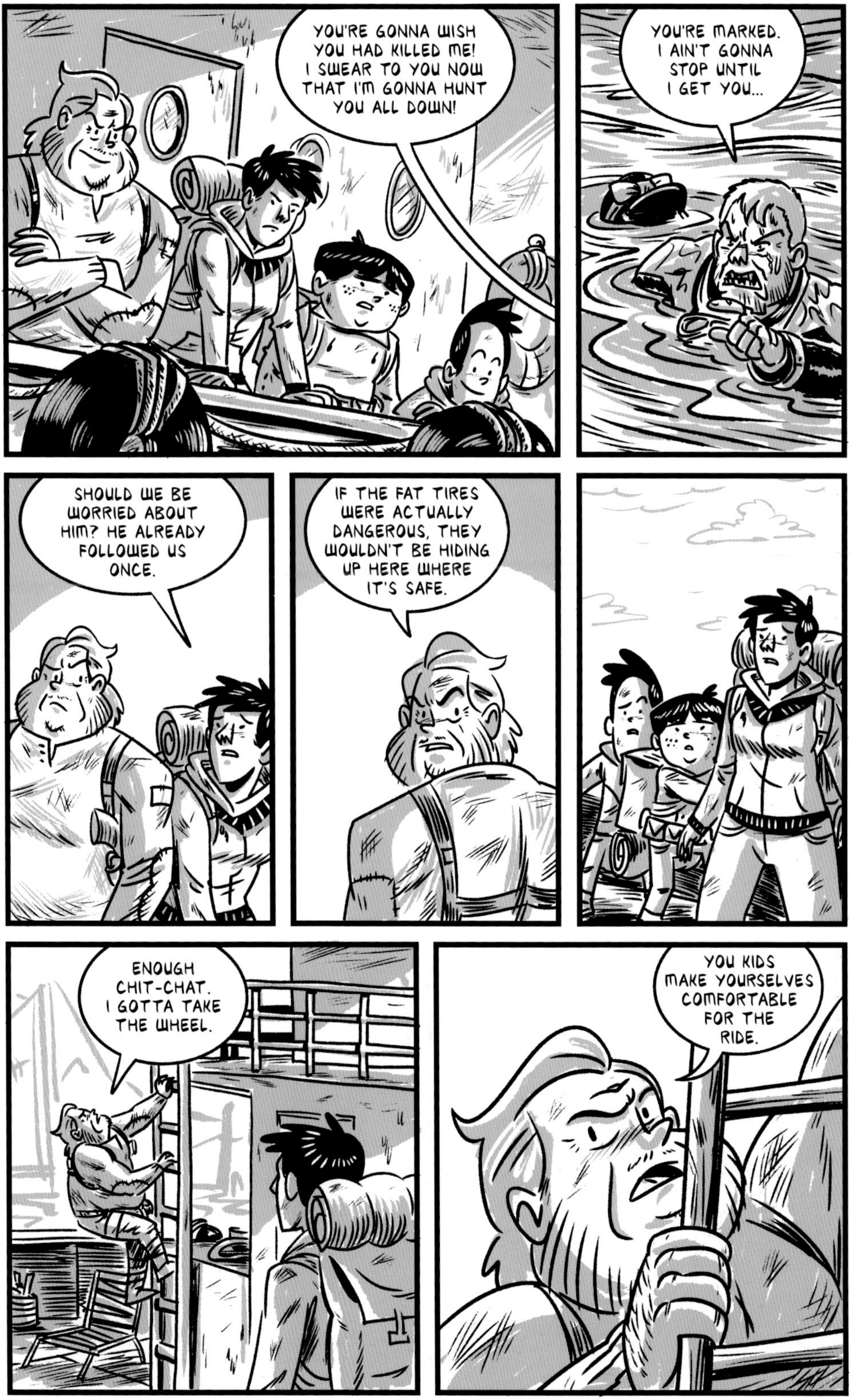
YOU'RE GONNA WISH YOU HAD KILLED ME! I SWEAR TO YOU NOW THAT I'M GONNA HUNT YOU ALL DOWN!
YOU'RE MARKED. I AIN'T GONNA STOP UNTIL I GET YOU...
SHOULD WE BE WORRIED ABOUT HIM? HE ALREADY FOLLOWED US ONCE.
IF THE FAT TIRES WERE ACTUALLY DANGEROUS, THEY WOULDN'T BE HIDING UP HERE WHERE IT'S SAFE.
ENOUGH CHIT-CHAT. I GOTTA TAKE THE WHEEL.
YOU KIDS MAKE YOURSELVES COMFORTABLE FOR THE RIDE.

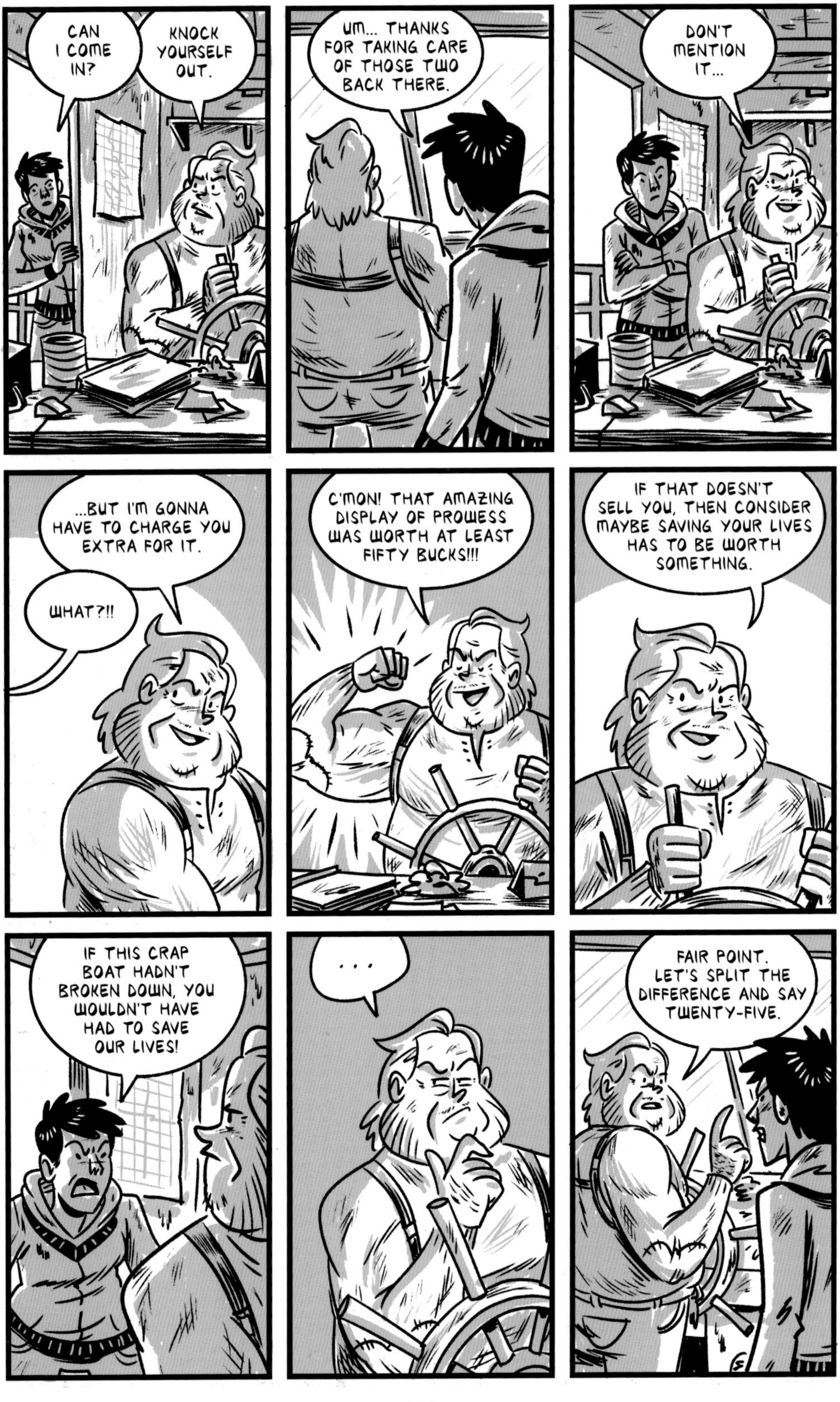

CAN I COME IN?
KNOCK YOURSELF OUT.
UM... THANKS FOR TAKING CARE OF THOSE TWO BACK THERE.
DON'T MENTION IT...
...BUT I'M GONNA HAVE TO CHARGE YOU EXTRA FOR IT.
WHAT?!!
C'MON! THAT AMAZING DISPLAY OF PROWESS WAS WORTH AT LEAST FIFTY BUCKS!!!
IF THAT DOESN'T SELL YOU, THEN CONSIDER MAYBE SAVING YOUR LIVES HAS TO BE WORTH SOMETHING.
IF THIS CRAP BOAT HADN'T BROKEN DOWN, YOU WOULDN'T HAVE HAD TO SAVE OUR LIVES!
. . .
FAIR POINT. LET'S SPLIT THE DIFFERENCE AND SAY TWENTY-FIVE.

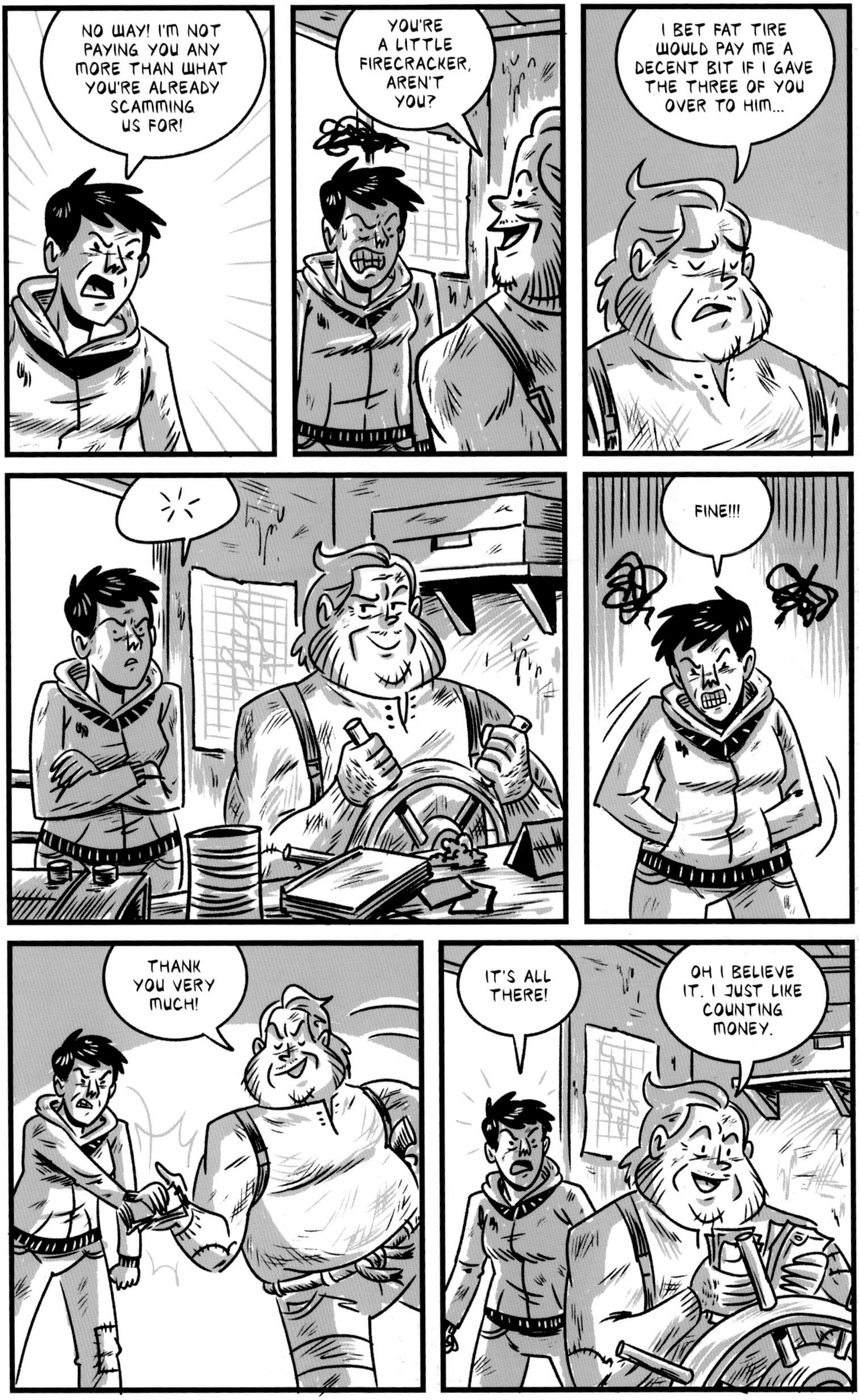
NO WAY! I'M NOT PAYING YOU ANY MORE THAN WHAT YOU'RE ALREADY SCAMMING US FOR!
YOU'RE A LITTLE FIRECRACKER, AREN'T YOU?
I BET FAT TIRE WOULD PAY ME A DECENT BIT IF I GAVE THE THREE OF YOU OVER TO HIM...
FINE!!!
THANK YOU VERY MUCH!
IT'S ALL THERE!
OH I BELIEVE IT. I JUST LIKE COUNTING MONEY.

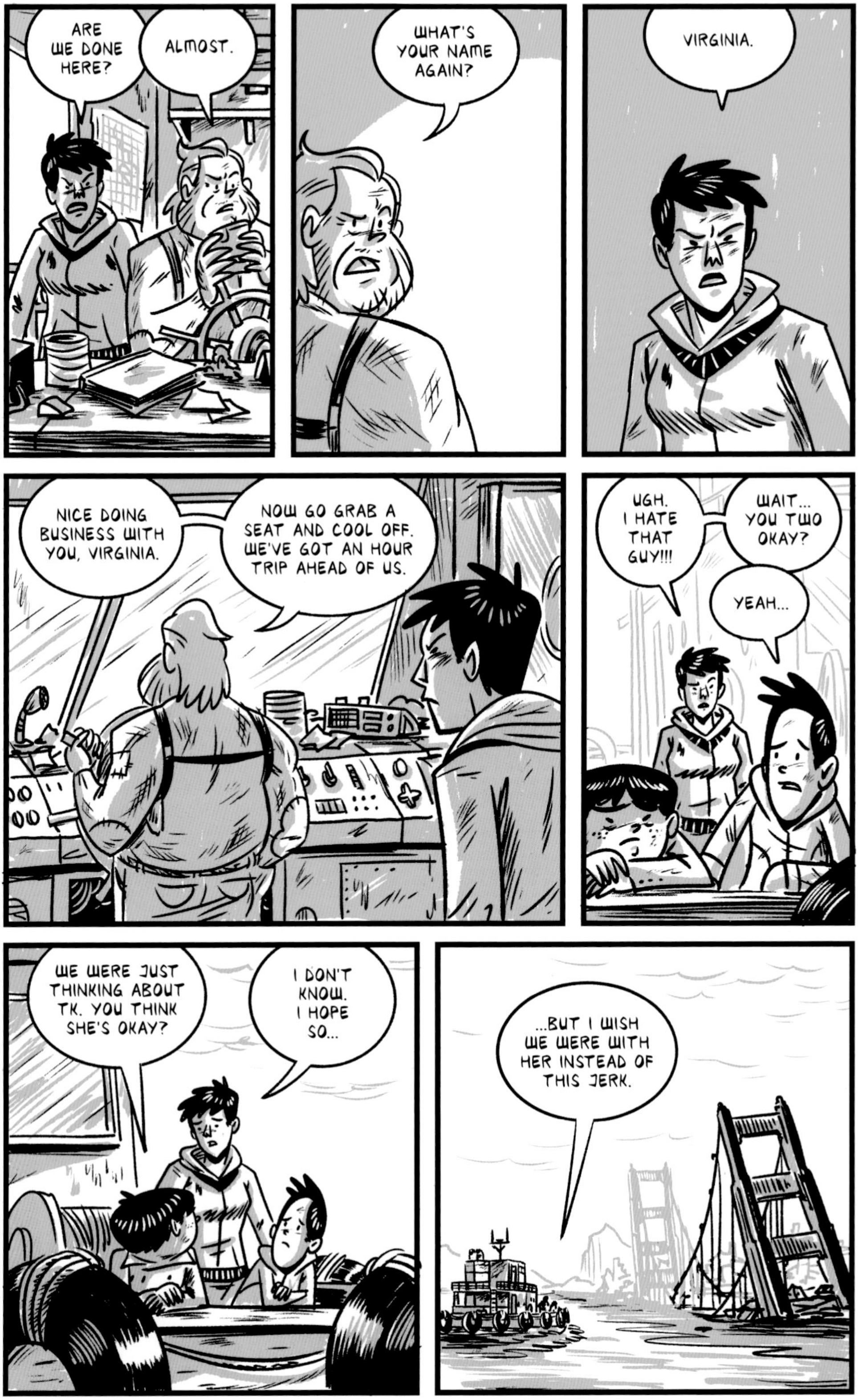
ARE WE DONE HERE?
ALMOST.
WHAT'S YOUR NAME AGAIN?
VIRGINIA.
NICE DOING BUSINESS WITH YOU, VIRGINIA.
NOW GO GRAB A SEAT AND COOL OFF. WE'VE GOT AN HOUR TRIP AHEAD OF US.
UGH. I HATE THAT GUY!!!
WAIT... YOU TWO OKAY?
YEAH...
WE WERE JUST THINKING ABOUT TK. YOU THINK SHE'S OKAY?
I DON'T KNOW. I HOPE SO...
...BUT I WISH WE WERE WITH HER INSTEAD OF THIS JERK.

CHAPTER 7

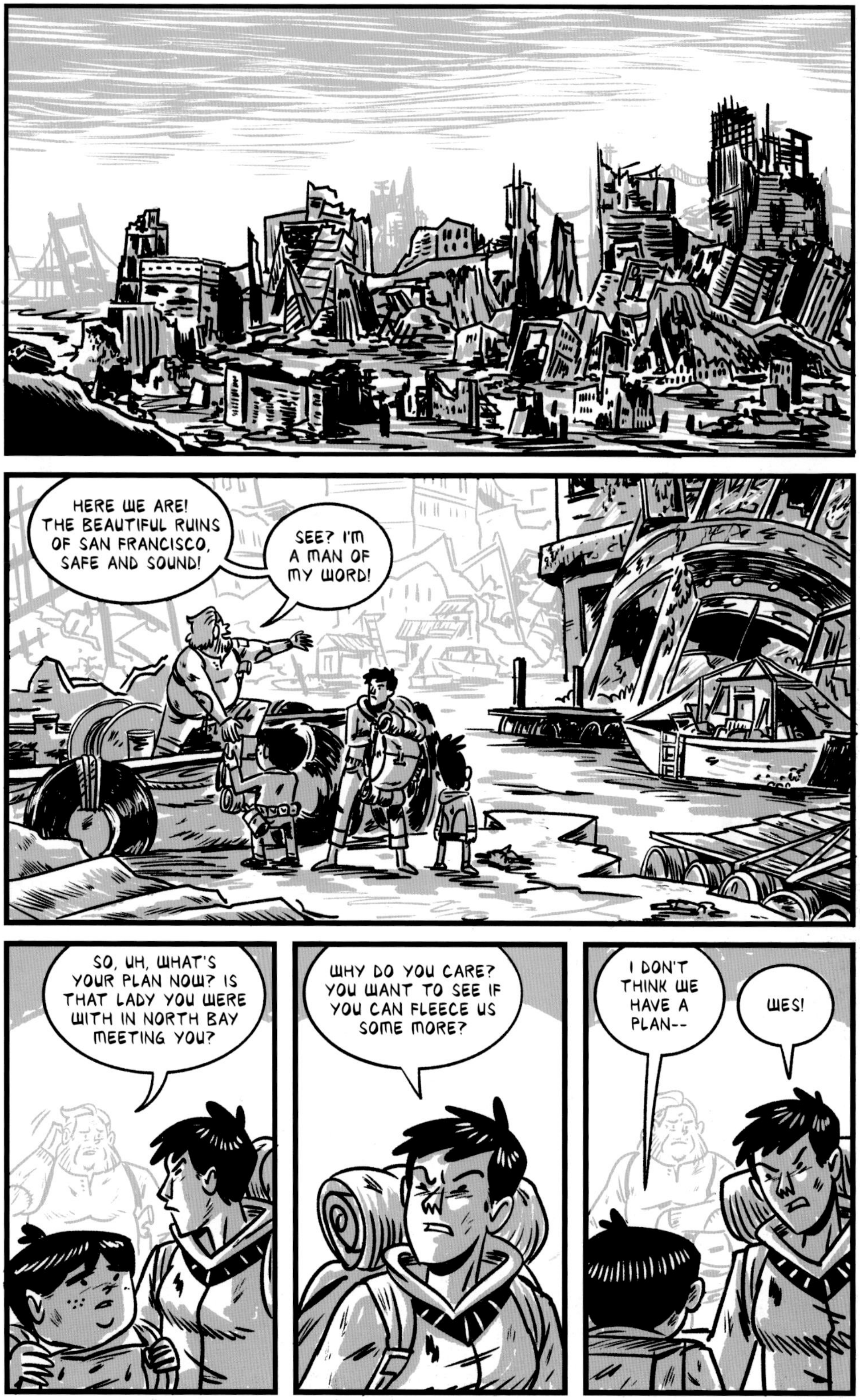
HERE WE ARE! THE BEAUTIFUL RUINS OF SAN FRANCISCO, SAFE AND SOUND!
SEE? I'M A MAN OF MY WORD!
SO, UH, WHAT'S YOUR PLAN NOW? IS THAT LADY YOU WERE WITH IN NORTH BAY MEETING YOU?
WHY DO YOU CARE? YOU WANT TO SEE IF YOU CAN FLEECE US SOME MORE?
I DON'T THINK WE HAVE A PLAN--
WES!

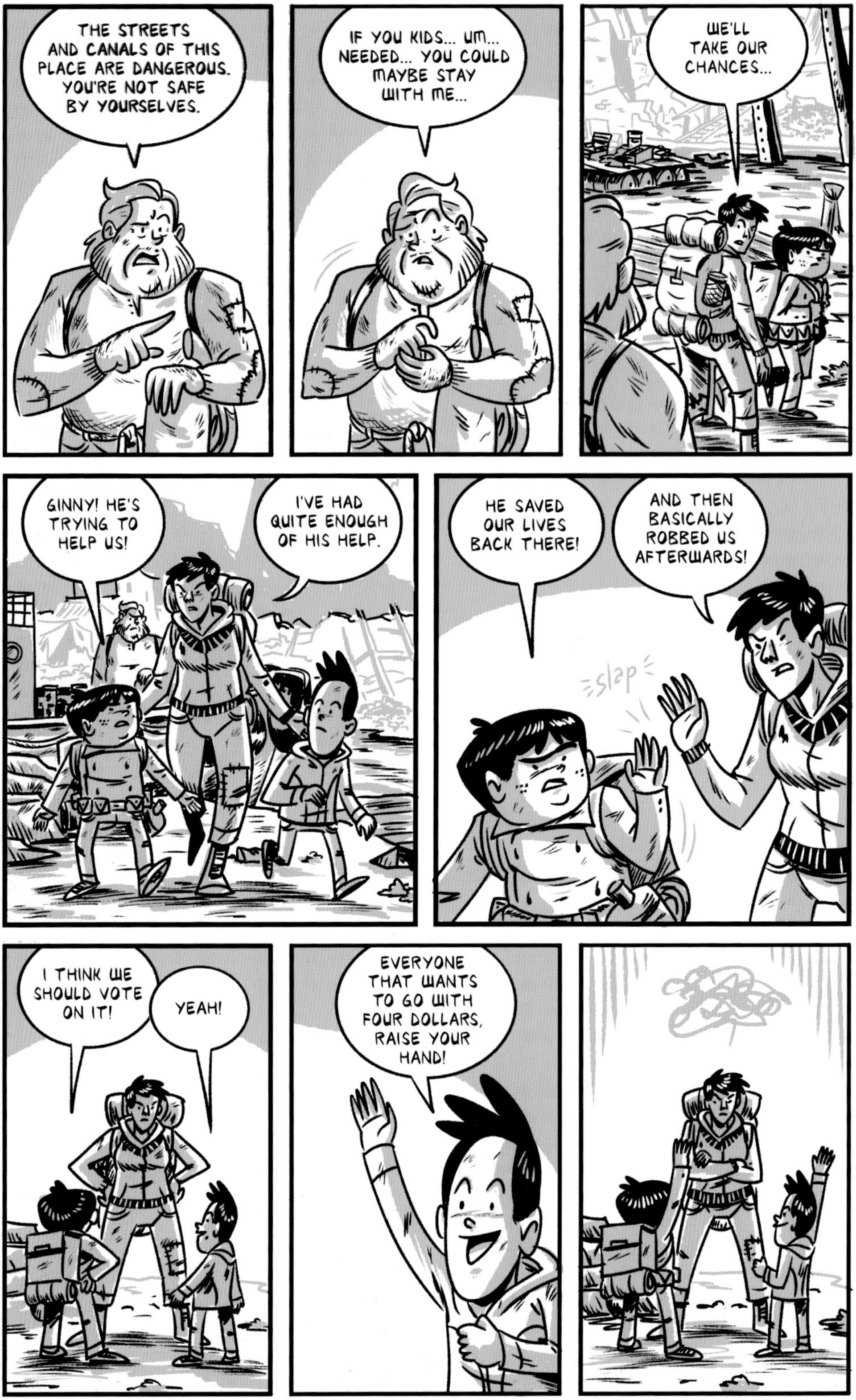
THE STREETS AND CANALS OF THIS PLACE ARE DANGEROUS. YOU'RE NOT SAFE BY YOURSELVES.
IF YOU KIDS... UM... NEEDED... YOU COULD MAYBE STAY WITH ME...
WE'LL TAKE OUR CHANCES...
GINNY! HE'S TRYING TO HELP US!
I'VE HAD QUITE ENOUGH OF HIS HELP.
HE SAVED OUR LIVES BACK THERE!
AND THEN BASICALLY ROBBED US AFTERWARDS!
slap
I THINK WE SHOULD VOTE ON IT!
YEAH!
EVERYONE THAT WANTS TO GO WITH FOUR DOLLARS, RAISE YOUR HAND!

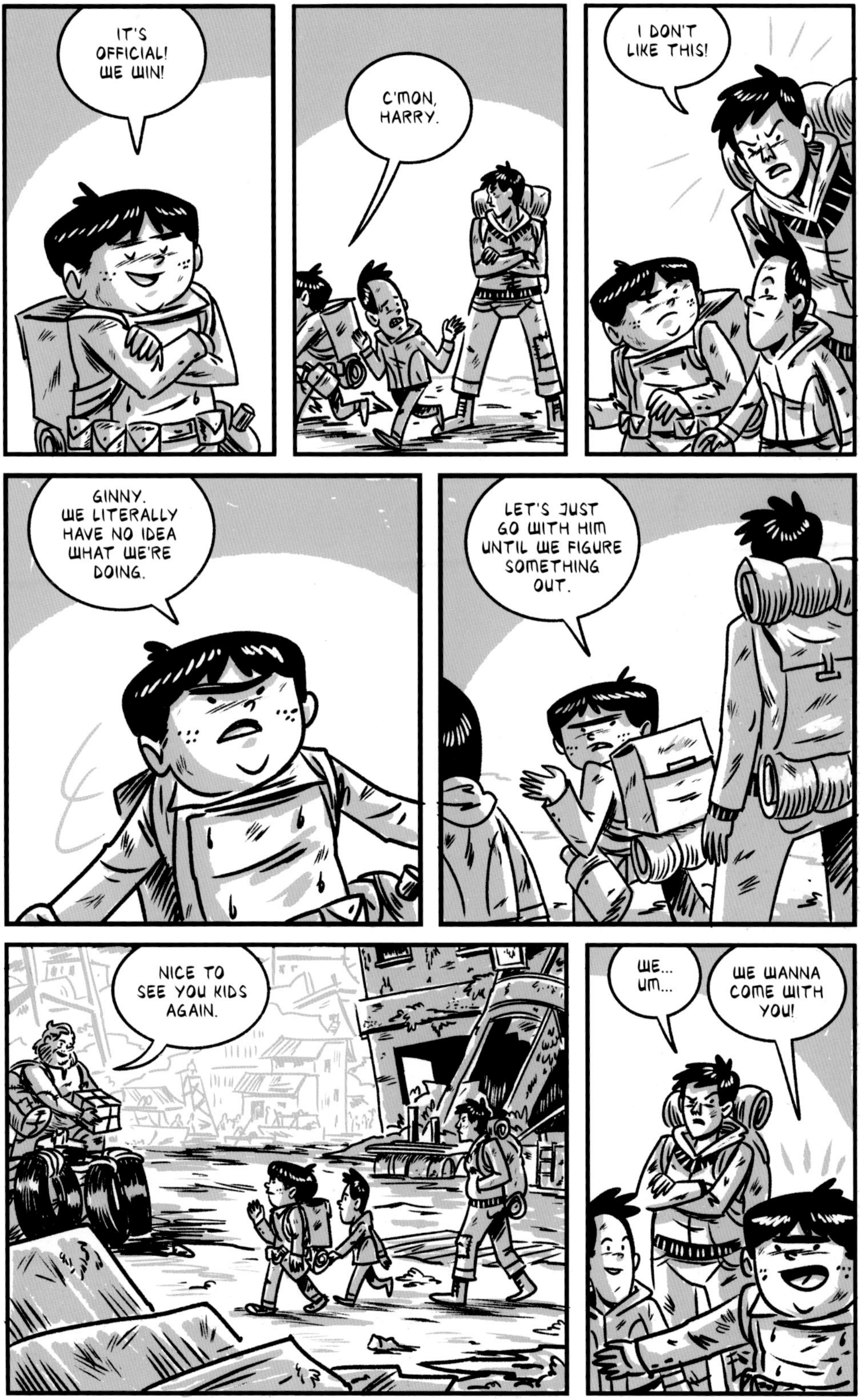
IT'S OFFICIAL! WE WIN!
C'MON, HARRY.
I DON'T LIKE THIS!
GINNY. WE LITERALLY HAVE NO IDEA WHAT WE'RE DOING.
LET'S JUST GO WITH HIM UNTIL WE FIGURE SOMETHING OUT.
NICE TO SEE YOU KIDS AGAIN.
WE... UM...
WE WANNA COME WITH YOU!

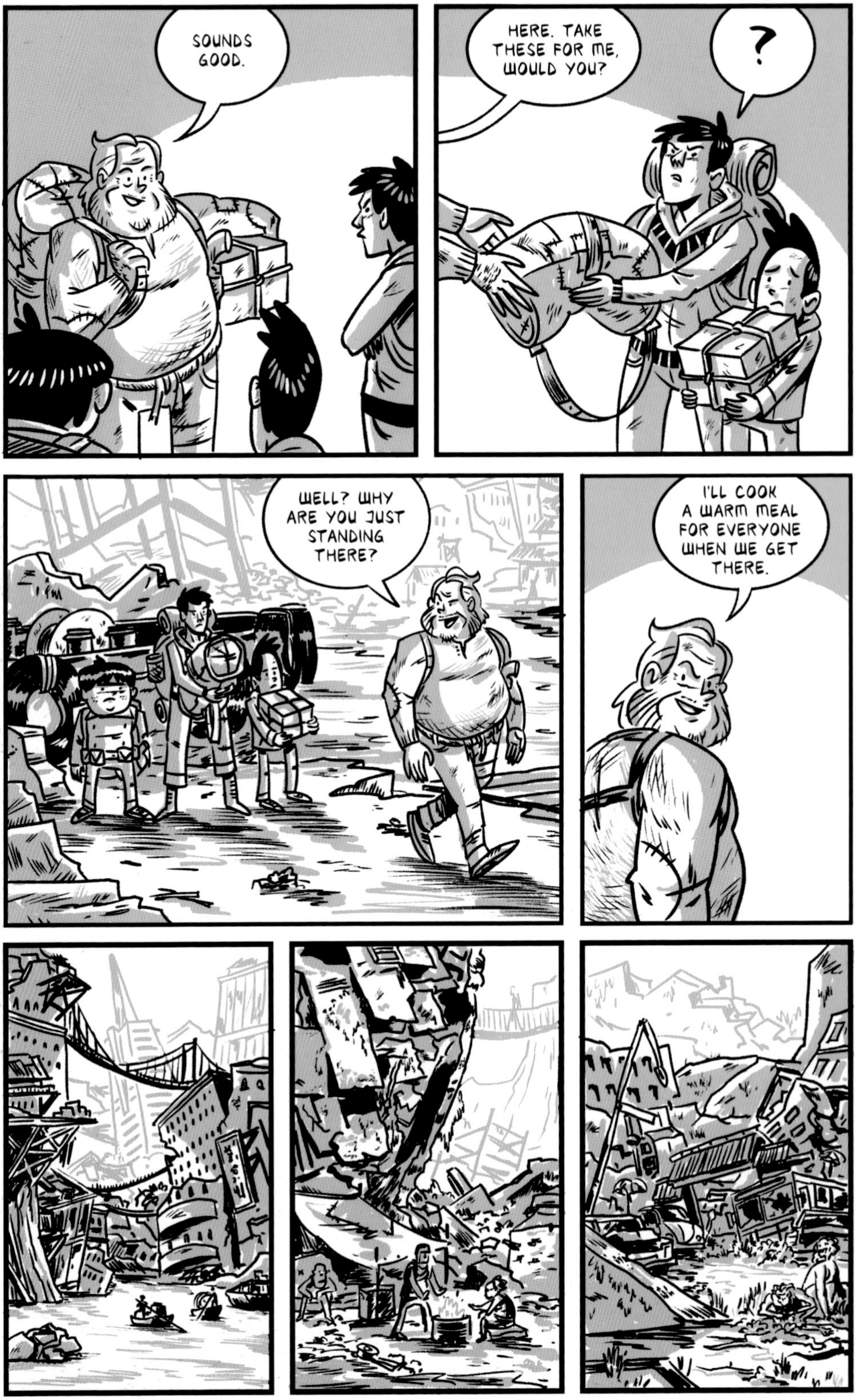
SOUNDS GOOD.
HERE. TAKE THESE FOR ME, WOULD YOU?
?
WELL? WHY ARE YOU JUST STANDING THERE?
I'LL COOK A WARM MEAL FOR EVERYONE WHEN WE GET THERE.

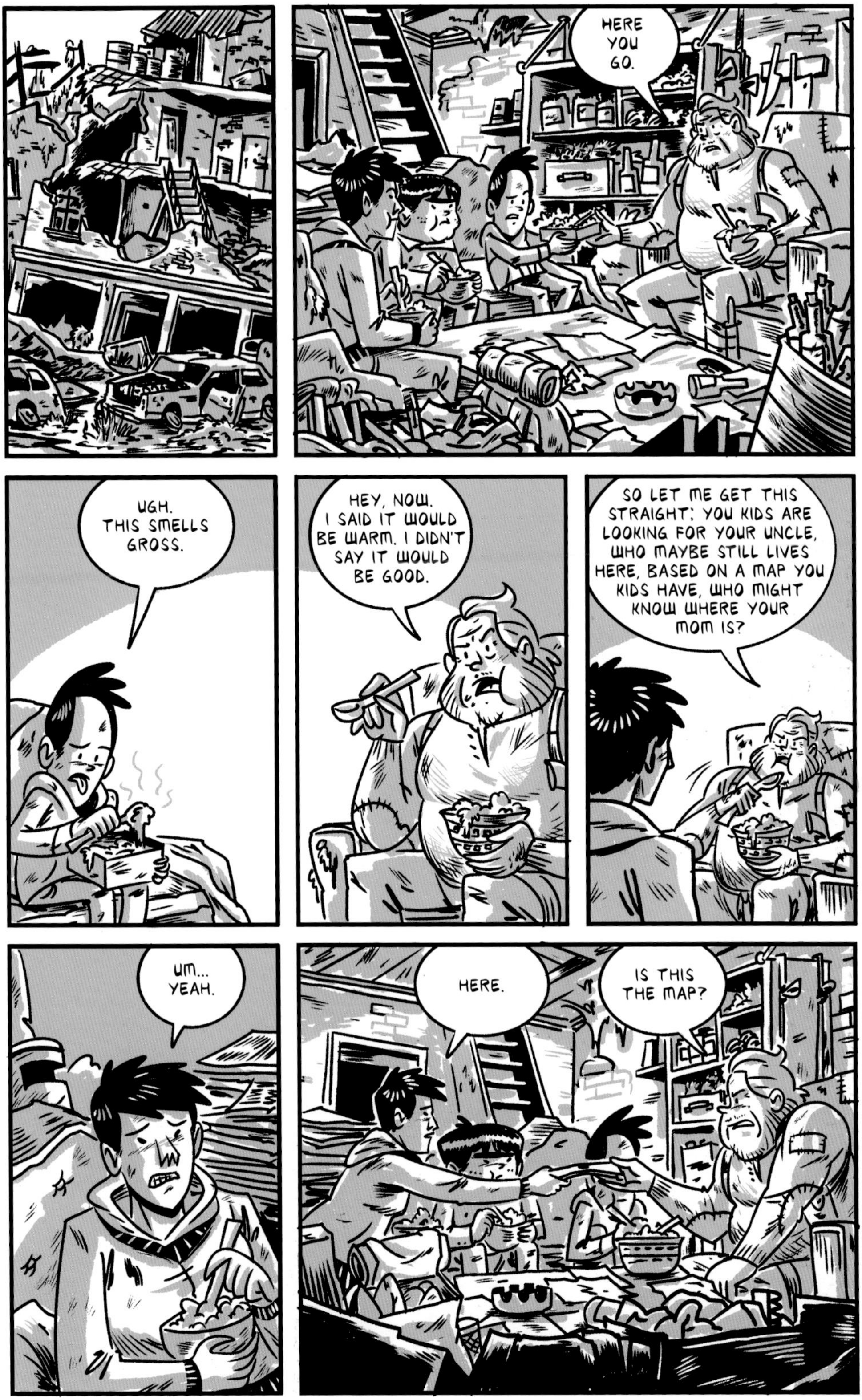
HERE YOU GO.
UGH. THIS SMELLS GROSS.
HEY, NOW. I SAID IT WOULD BE WARM. I DIDN'T SAY IT WOULD BE GOOD.
SO LET ME GET THIS STRAIGHT: YOU KIDS ARE LOOKING FOR YOUR UNCLE, WHO MAYBE STILL LIVES HERE, BASED ON A MAP YOU KIDS HAVE, WHO MIGHT KNOW WHERE YOUR MOM IS?
UM... YEAH.
HERE.
IS THIS THE MAP?

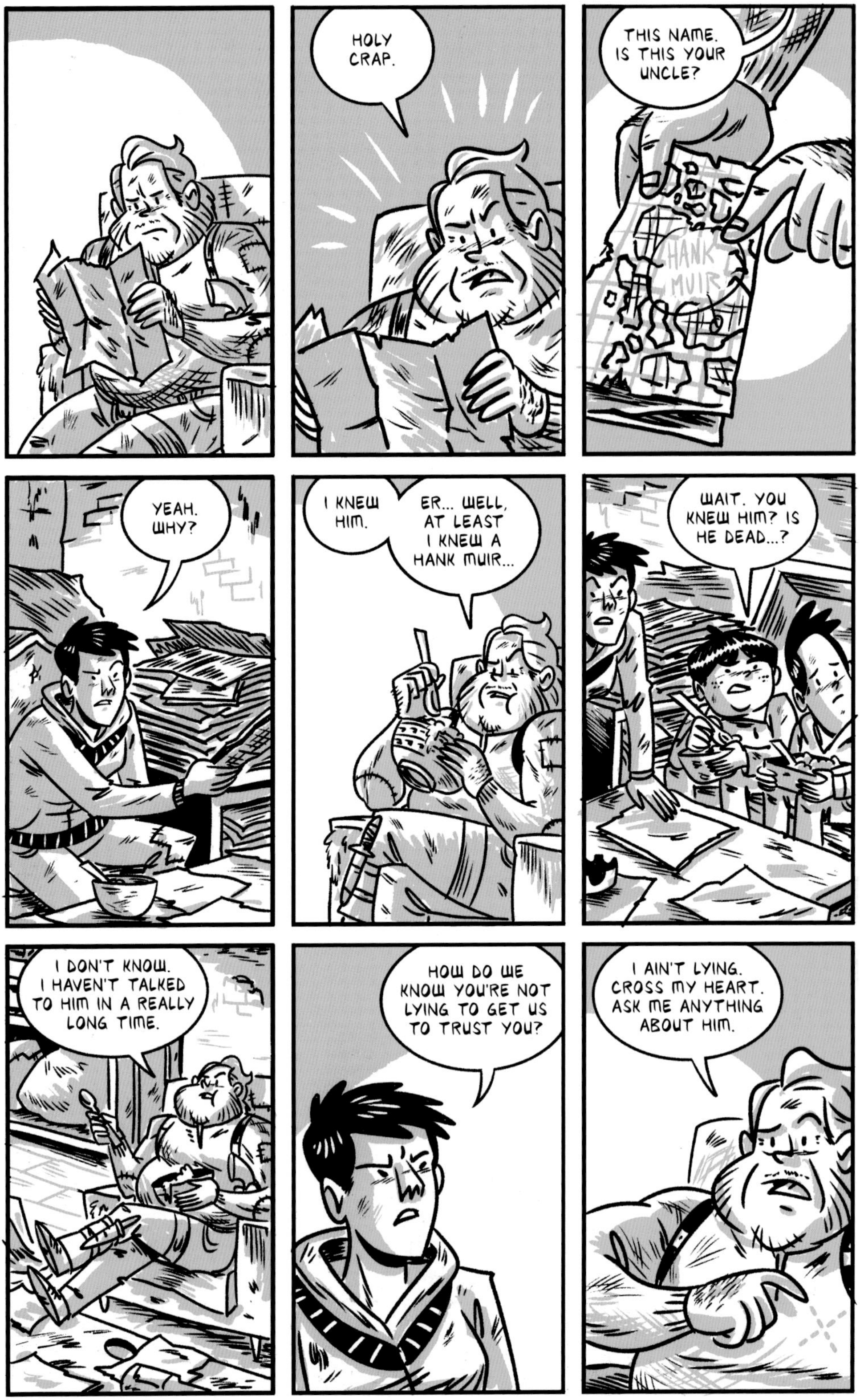
HOLY CRAP.
THIS NAME. IS THIS YOUR UNCLE?
HANK MUIR
YEAH. WHY?
I KNEW HIM.
ER... WELL, AT LEAST I KNEW A HANK MUIR...
WAIT. YOU KNEW HIM? IS HE DEAD...?
I DON'T KNOW. I HAVEN'T TALKED TO HIM IN A REALLY LONG TIME.
HOW DO WE KNOW YOU'RE NOT LYING TO GET US TO TRUST YOU?
I AIN'T LYING. CROSS MY HEART. ASK ME ANYTHING ABOUT HIM.

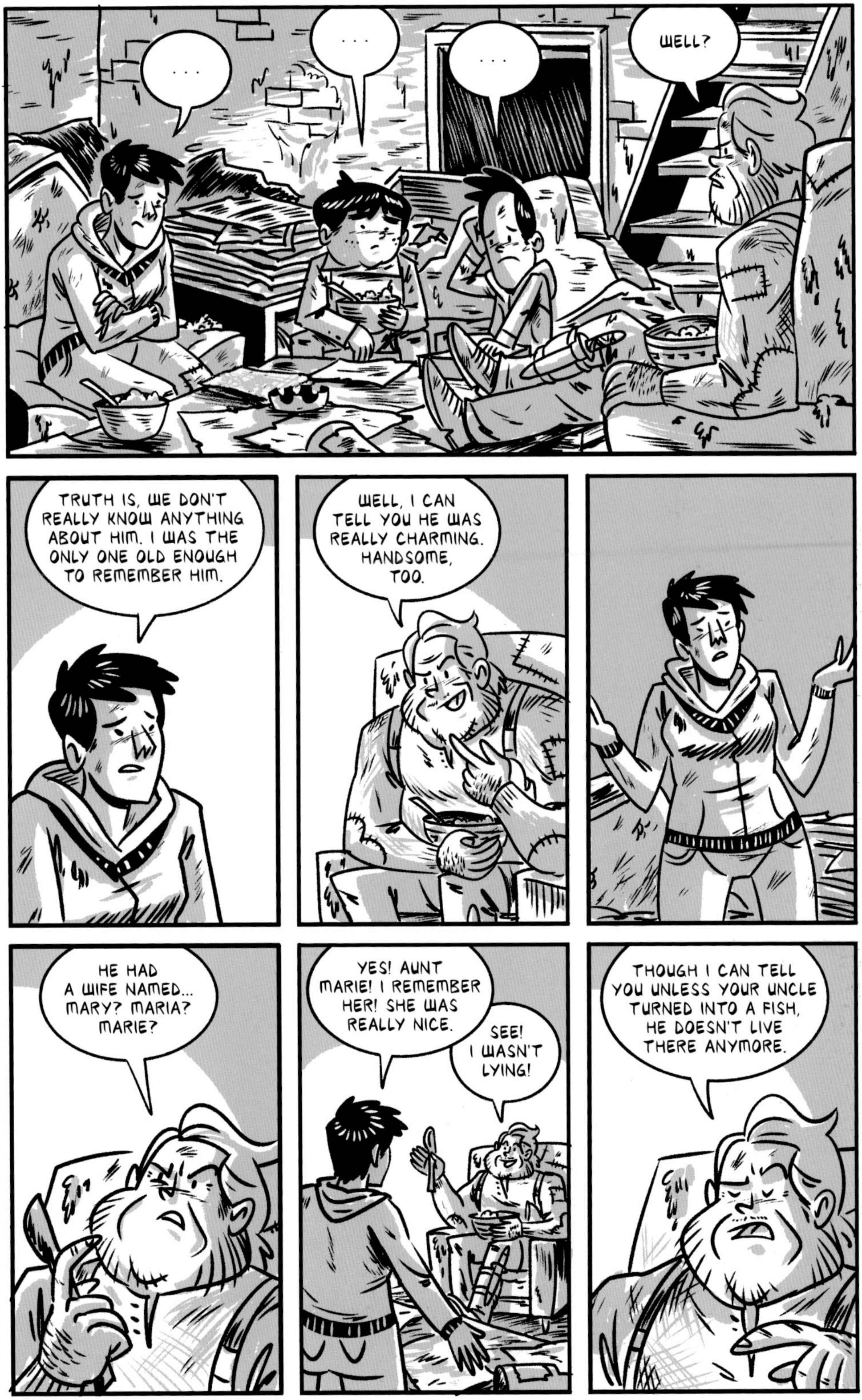
...
...
...
WELL?
TRUTH IS, WE DON'T REALLY KNOW ANYTHING ABOUT HIM. I WAS THE ONLY ONE OLD ENOUGH TO REMEMBER HIM.
WELL, I CAN TELL YOU HE WAS REALLY CHARMING. HANDSOME, TOO.
HE HAD A WIFE NAMED... MARY? MARIA? MARIE?
YES! AUNT MARIE! I REMEMBER HER! SHE WAS REALLY NICE.
SEE! I WASN'T LYING!
THOUGH I CAN TELL YOU UNLESS YOUR UNCLE TURNED INTO A FISH, HE DOESN'T LIVE THERE ANYMORE.

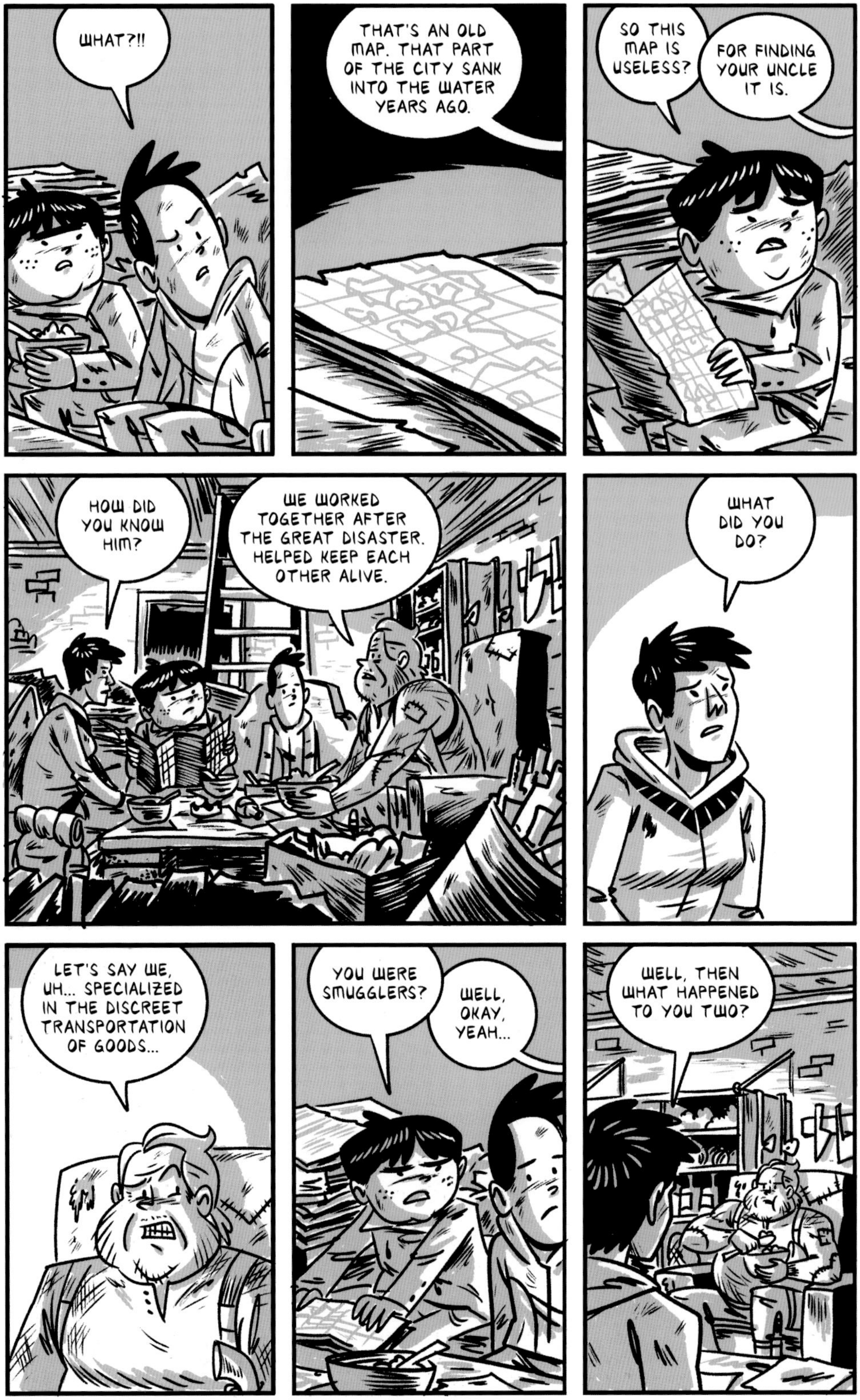
WHAT?!!
THAT'S AN OLD MAP. THAT PART OF THE CITY SANK INTO THE WATER YEARS AGO.
SO THIS MAP IS USELESS?
FOR FINDING YOUR UNCLE IT IS.
HOW DID YOU KNOW HIM?
WE WORKED TOGETHER AFTER THE GREAT DISASTER. HELPED KEEP EACH OTHER ALIVE.
WHAT DID YOU DO?
LET'S SAY WE, UH... SPECIALIZED IN THE DISCREET TRANSPORTATION OF GOODS...
YOU WERE SMUGGLERS?
WELL, OKAY, YEAH...
WELL, THEN WHAT HAPPENED TO YOU TWO?

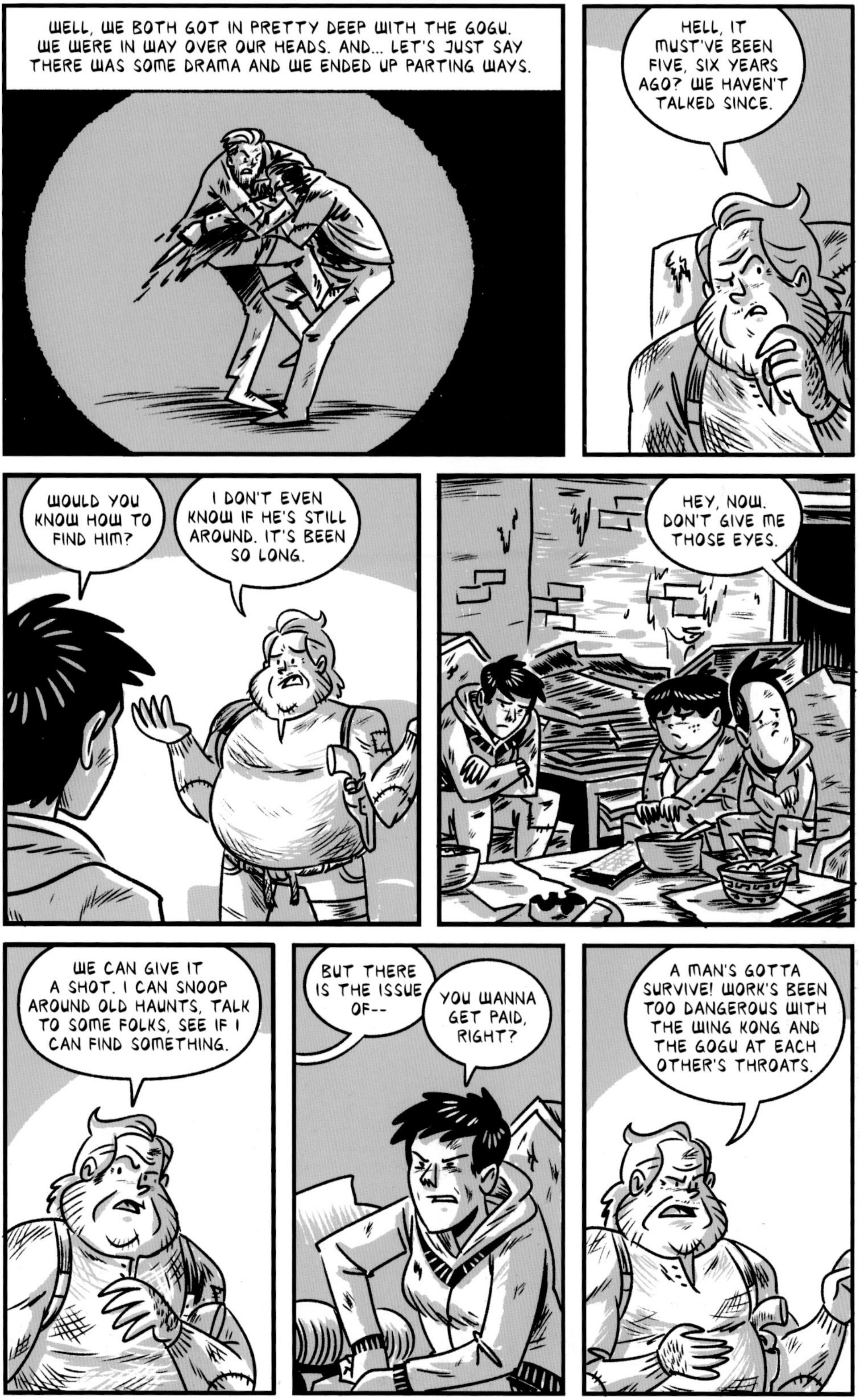
WELL, WE BOTH GOT IN PRETTY DEEP WITH THE GOGU. WE WERE IN WAY OVER OUR HEADS. AND... LET'S JUST SAY THERE WAS SOME DRAMA AND WE ENDED UP PARTING WAYS.
HELL, IT MUST'VE BEEN FIVE, SIX YEARS AGO? WE HAVEN'T TALKED SINCE.
WOULD YOU KNOW HOW TO FIND HIM?
I DON'T EVEN KNOW IF HE'S STILL AROUND. IT'S BEEN SO LONG.
HEY, NOW. DON'T GIVE ME THOSE EYES.
WE CAN GIVE IT A SHOT. I CAN SNOOP AROUND OLD HAUNTS, TALK TO SOME FOLKS, SEE IF I CAN FIND SOMETHING.
BUT THERE IS THE ISSUE OF--
YOU WANNA GET PAID, RIGHT?
A MAN'S GOTTA SURVIVE! WORK'S BEEN TOO DANGEROUS WITH THE WING KONG AND THE GOGU AT EACH OTHER'S THROATS.

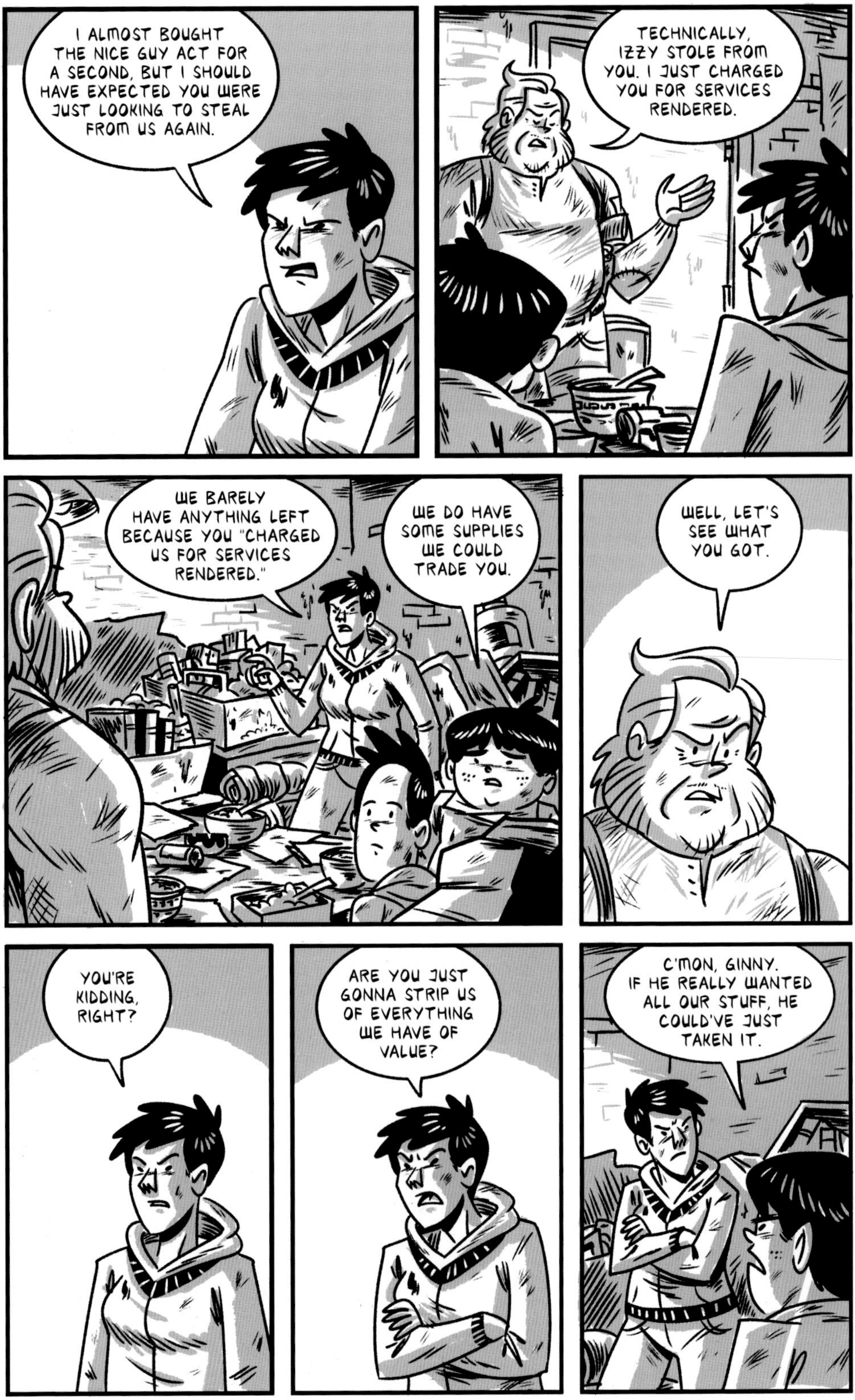
I ALMOST BOUGHT THE NICE GUY ACT FOR A SECOND, BUT I SHOULD HAVE EXPECTED YOU WERE JUST LOOKING TO STEAL FROM US AGAIN.
TECHNICALLY, IZZY STOLE FROM YOU. I JUST CHARGED YOU FOR SERVICES RENDERED.
WE BARELY HAVE ANYTHING LEFT BECAUSE YOU "CHARGED US FOR SERVICES RENDERED."
WE DO HAVE SOME SUPPLIES WE COULD TRADE YOU.
WELL, LET'S SEE WHAT YOU GOT.
YOU'RE KIDDING, RIGHT?
ARE YOU JUST GONNA STRIP US OF EVERYTHING WE HAVE OF VALUE?
C'MON, GINNY. IF HE REALLY WANTED ALL OUR STUFF, HE COULD'VE JUST TAKEN IT.

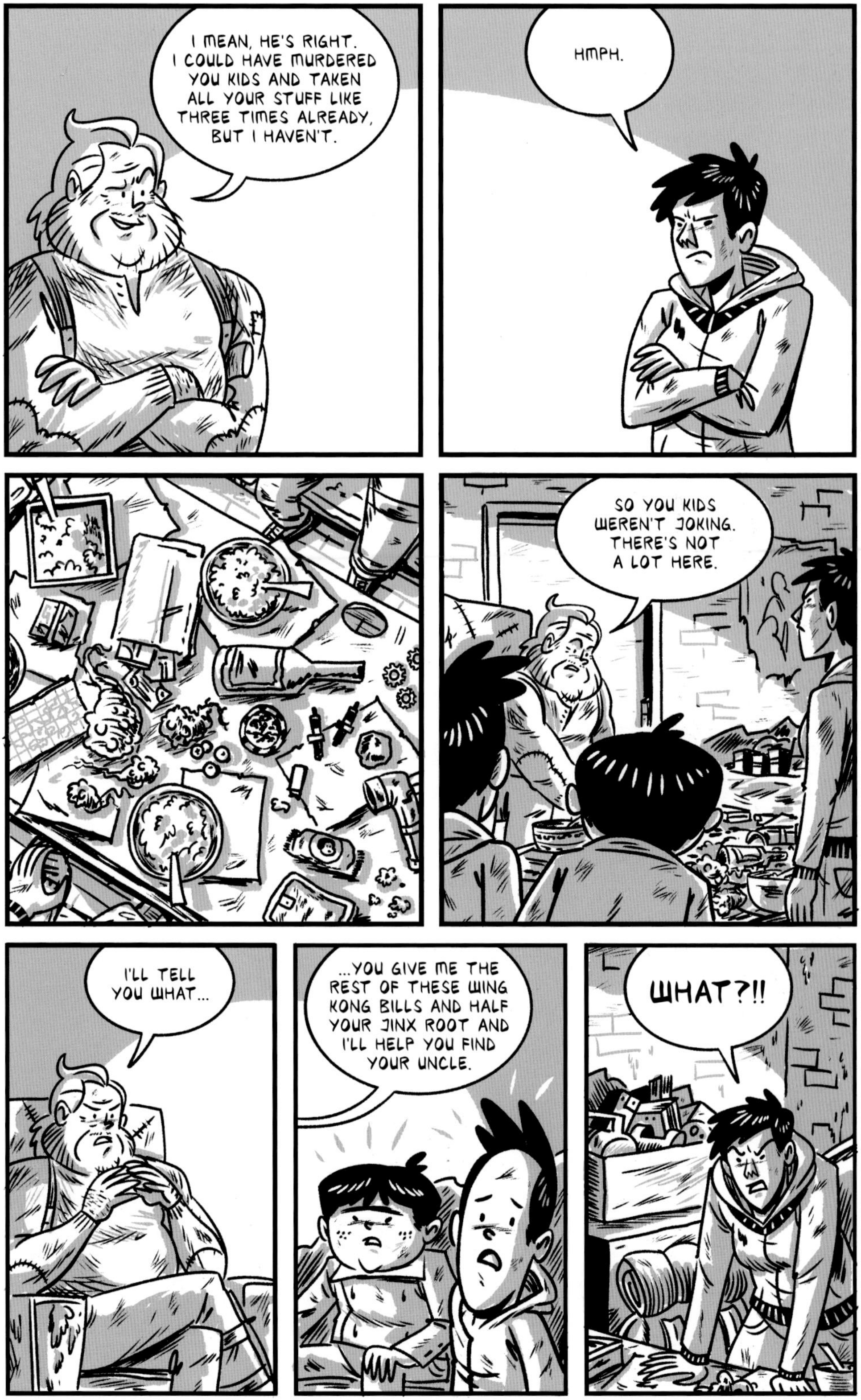
I MEAN, HE'S RIGHT. I COULD HAVE MURDERED YOU KIDS AND TAKEN ALL YOUR STUFF LIKE THREE TIMES ALREADY, BUT I HAVEN'T.
HMPH.
SO YOU KIDS WEREN'T JOKING. THERE'S NOT A LOT HERE.
I'LL TELL YOU WHAT...
...YOU GIVE ME THE REST OF THESE WING KONG BILLS AND HALF YOUR JINX ROOT AND I'LL HELP YOU FIND YOUR UNCLE.
WHAT?!!

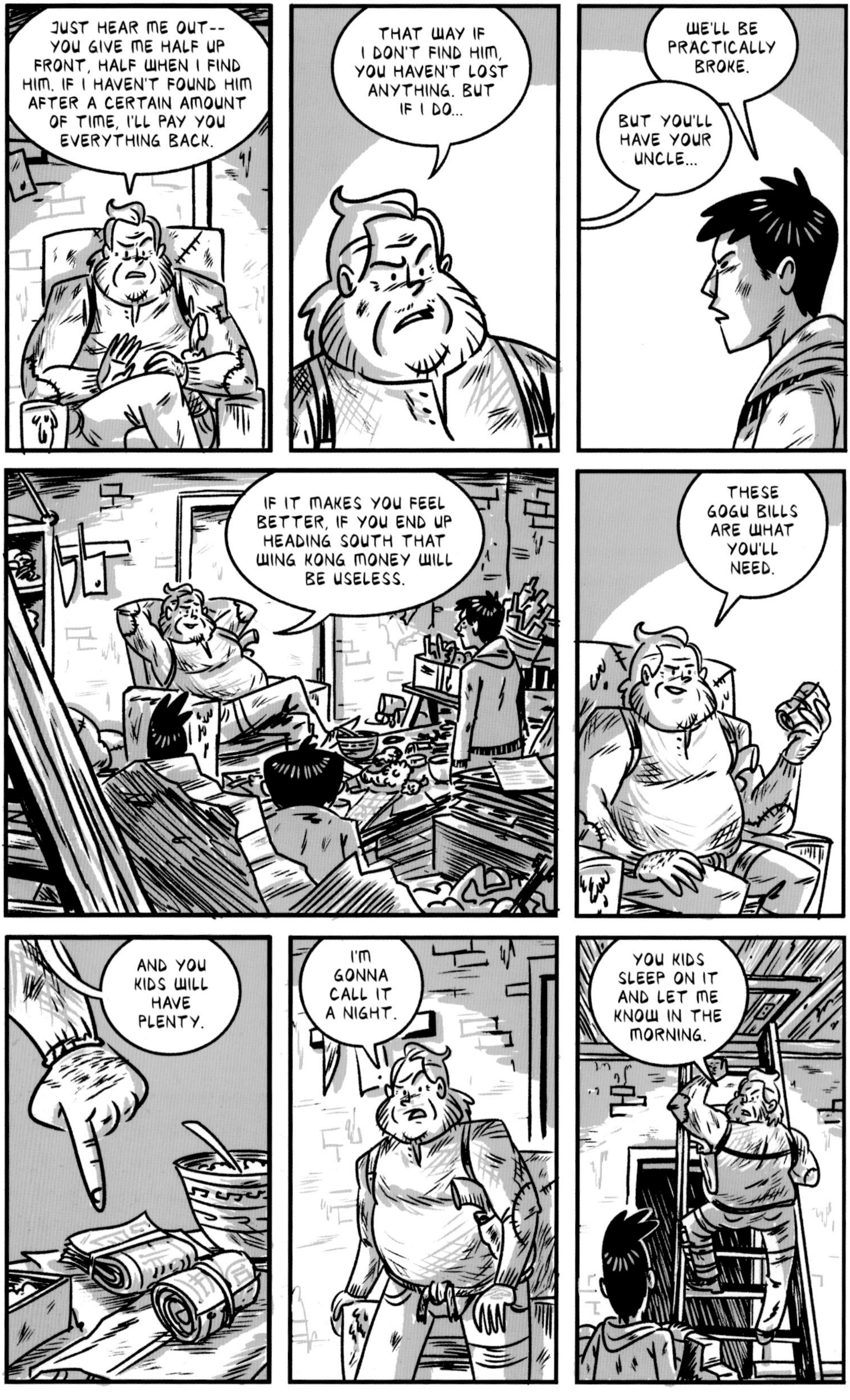
JUST HEAR ME OUT-- YOU GIVE ME HALF UP FRONT, HALF WHEN I FIND HIM. IF I HAVEN'T FOUND HIM AFTER A CERTAIN AMOUNT OF TIME, I'LL PAY YOU EVERYTHING BACK.
THAT WAY IF I DON'T FIND HIM, YOU HAVEN'T LOST ANYTHING. BUT IF I DO...
WE'LL BE PRACTICALLY BROKE.
BUT YOU'LL HAVE YOUR UNCLE...
IF IT MAKES YOU FEEL BETTER, IF YOU END UP HEADING SOUTH THAT WING KONG MONEY WILL BE USELESS.
THESE GOGU BILLS ARE WHAT YOU'LL NEED.
AND YOU KIDS WILL HAVE PLENTY.
I'M GONNA CALL IT A NIGHT.
YOU KIDS SLEEP ON IT AND LET ME KNOW IN THE MORNING.

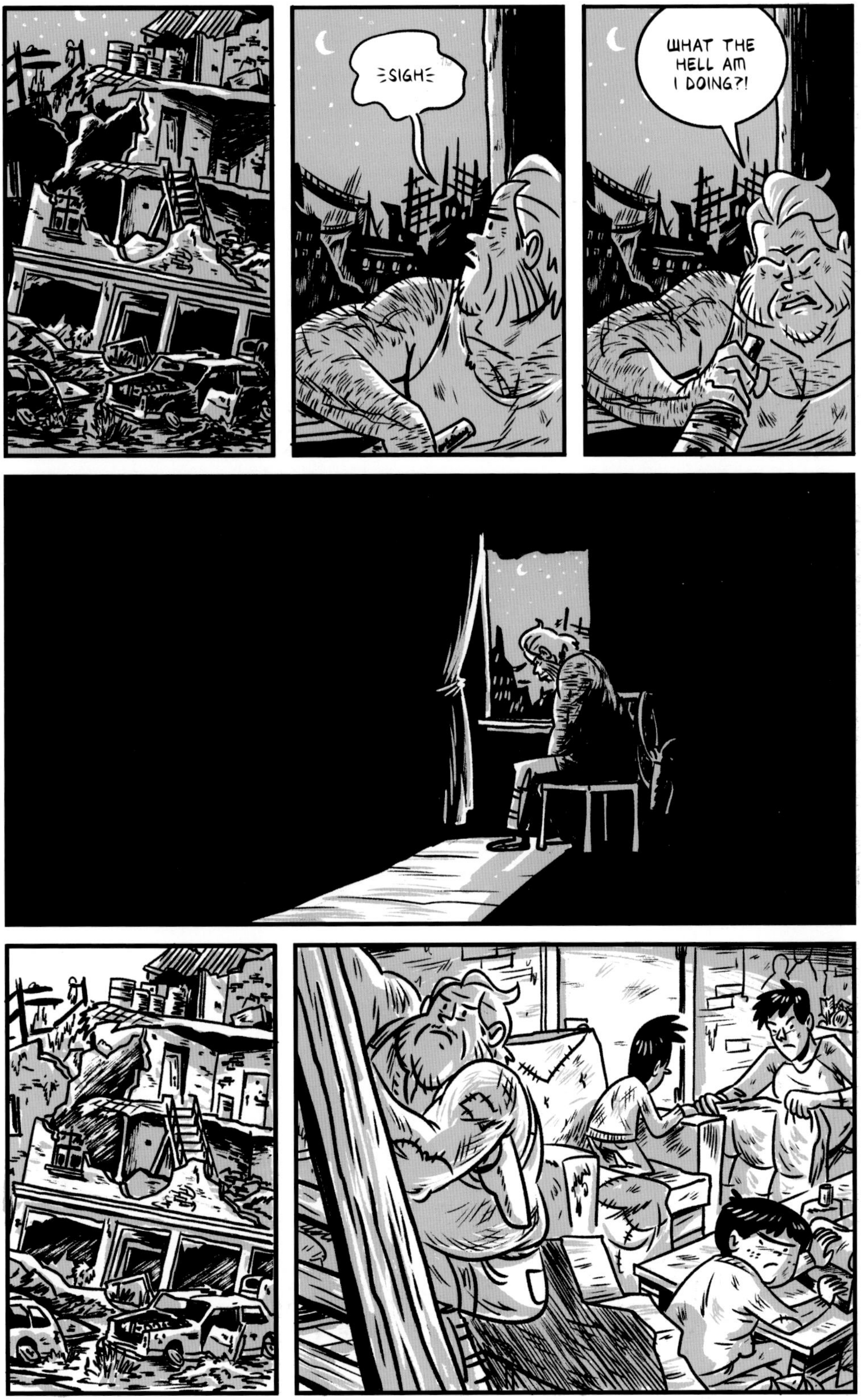
SIGH
WHAT THE HELL AM I DOING?!

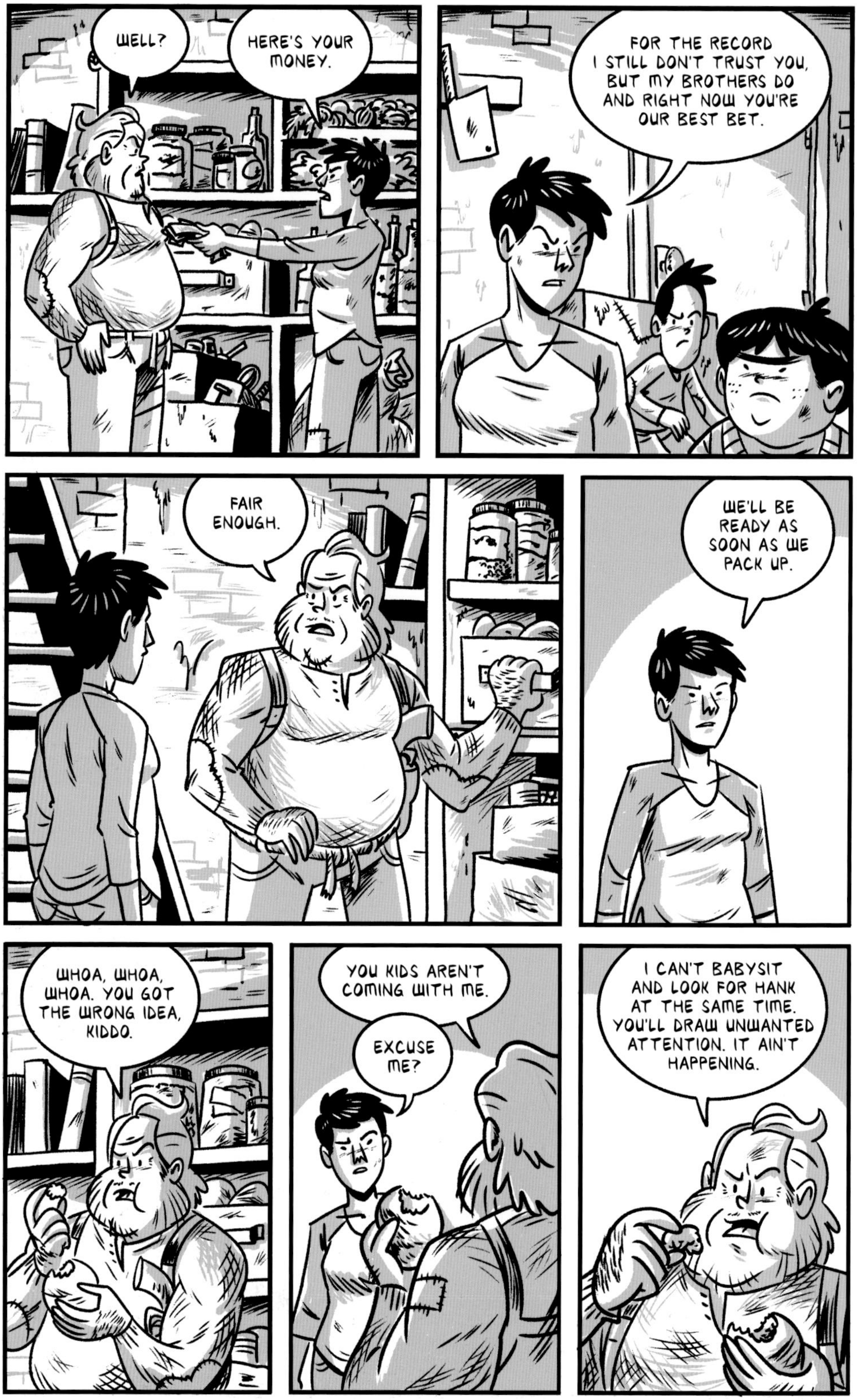

WELL?
HERE'S YOUR MONEY.
FOR THE RECORD I STILL DON'T TRUST YOU, BUT MY BROTHERS DO AND RIGHT NOW YOU'RE OUR BEST BET.
FAIR ENOUGH.
WE'LL BE READY AS SOON AS WE PACK UP.
WHOA, WHOA, WHOA. YOU GOT THE WRONG IDEA, KIDDO.
YOU KIDS AREN'T COMING WITH ME.
EXCUSE ME?
I CAN'T BABYSIT AND LOOK FOR HANK AT THE SAME TIME. YOU'LL DRAW UNWANTED ATTENTION. IT AIN'T HAPPENING.

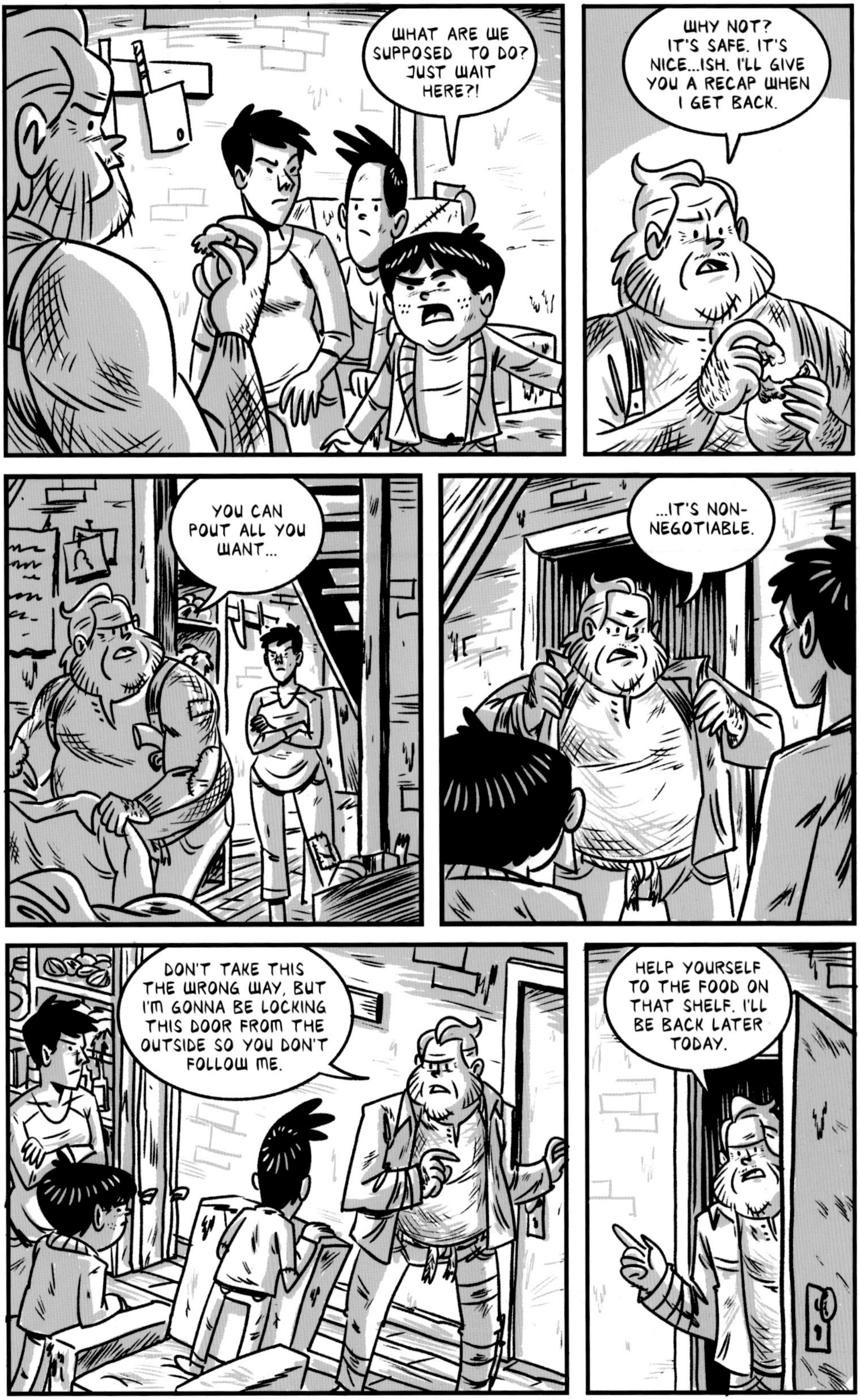
WHAT ARE WE SUPPOSED TO DO? JUST WAIT HERE?!
WHY NOT? IT'S SAFE. IT'S NICE...ISH. I'LL GIVE YOU A RECAP WHEN I GET BACK.
YOU CAN POUT ALL YOU WANT...
...IT'S NON-NEGOTIABLE.
DON'T TAKE THIS THE WRONG WAY, BUT I'M GONNA BE LOCKING THIS DOOR FROM THE OUTSIDE SO YOU DON'T FOLLOW ME.
HELP YOURSELF TO THE FOOD ON THAT SHELF. I'LL BE BACK LATER TODAY.

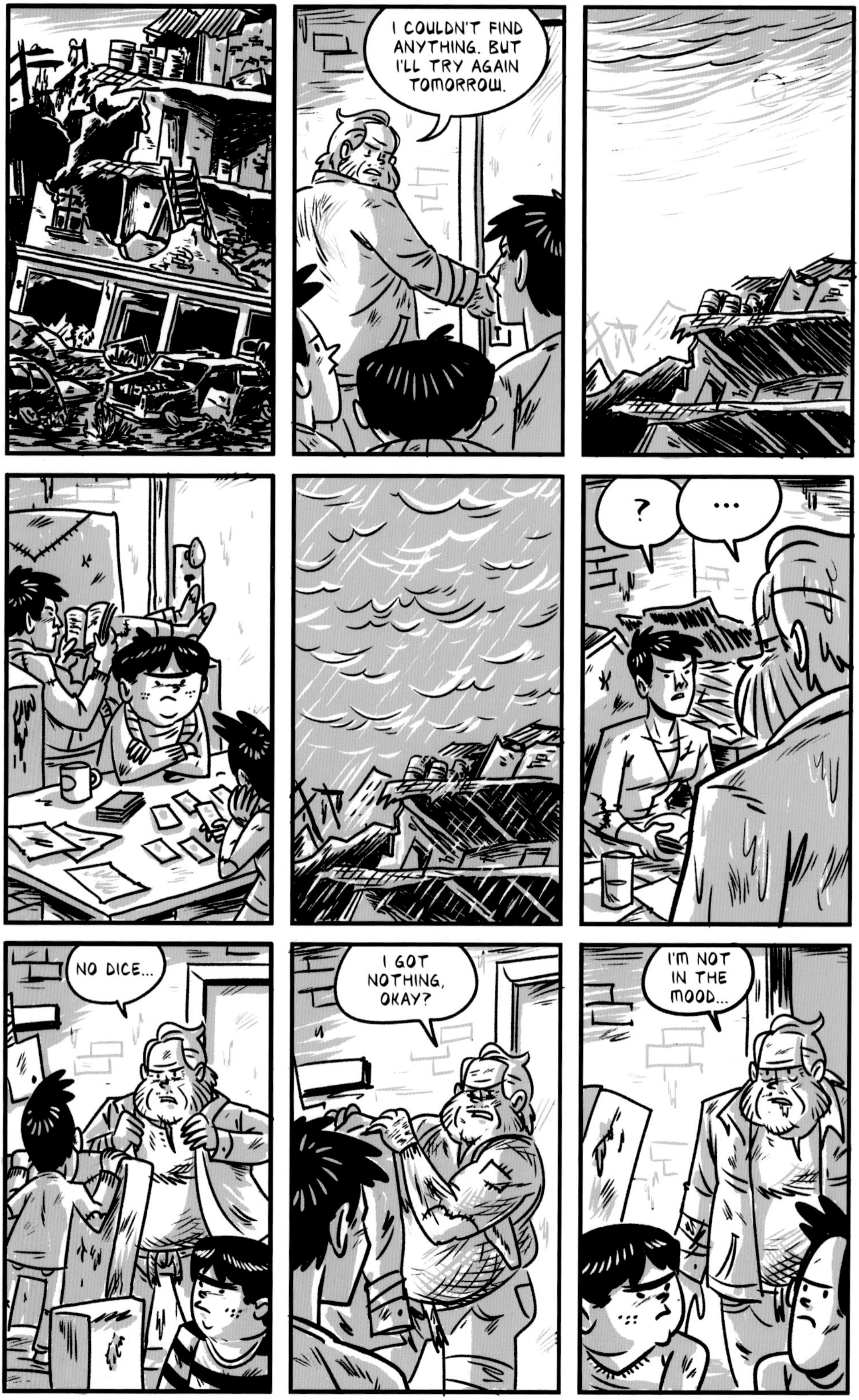
I COULDN'T FIND ANYTHING. BUT I'LL TRY AGAIN TOMORROW.
?
...
NO DICE...
I GOT NOTHING, OKAY?
I'M NOT IN THE MOOD...

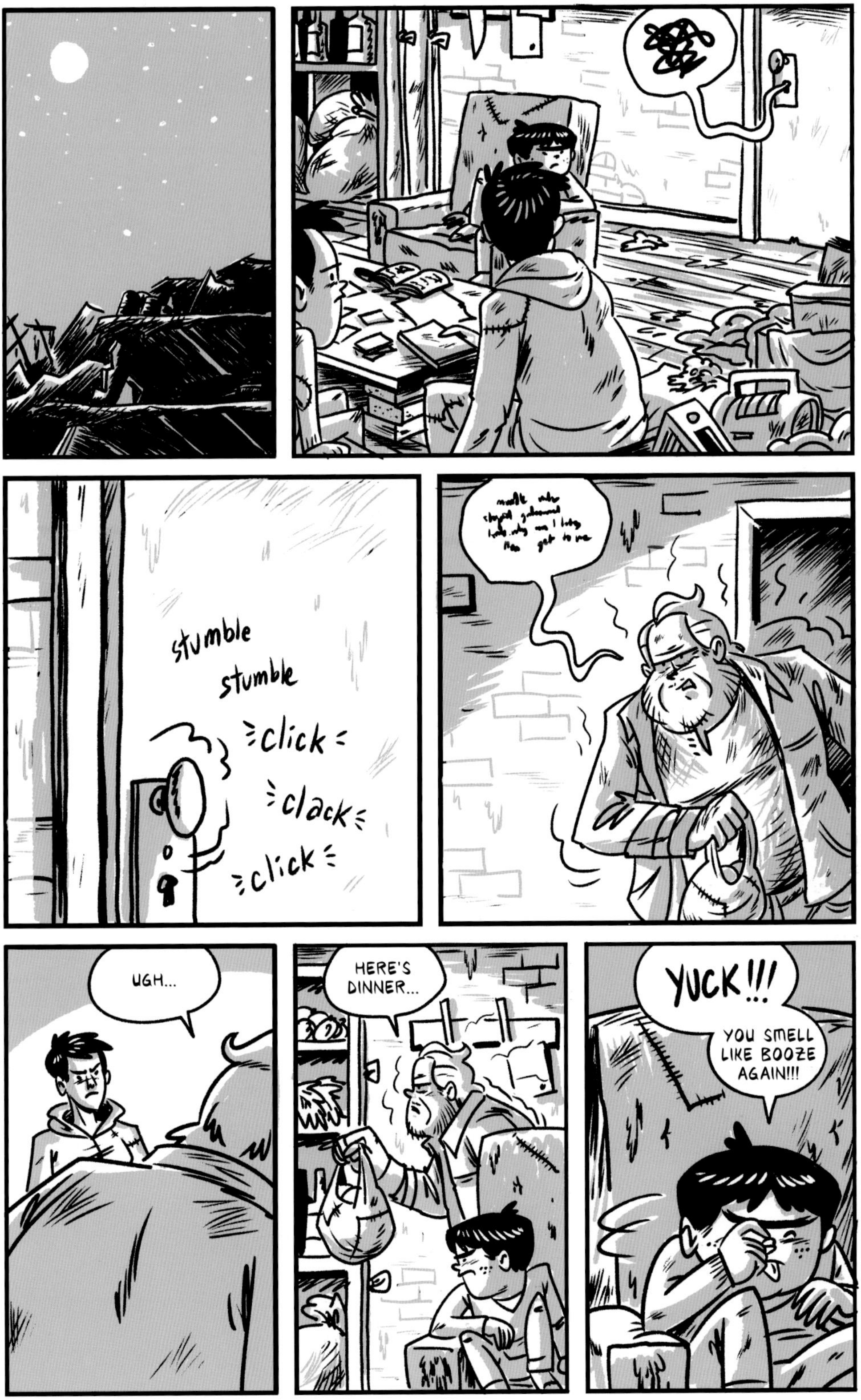
stumble
stumble
click
clack
click
UGH...
HERE'S DINNER...
YUCK!!!
YOU SMELL LIKE BOOZE AGAIN!!!

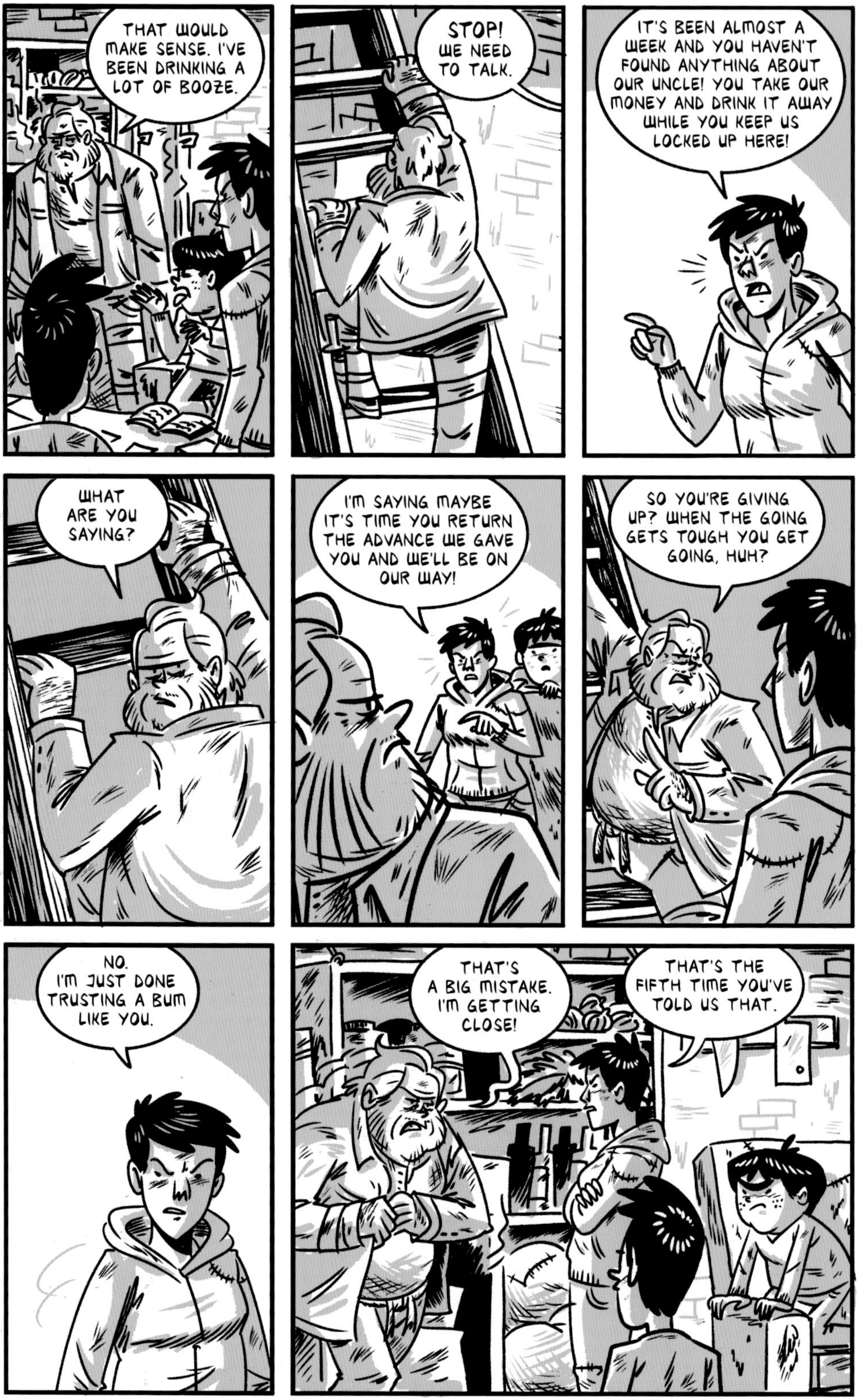
THAT WOULD MAKE SENSE. I'VE BEEN DRINKING A LOT OF BOOZE.
STOP! WE NEED TO TALK.
IT'S BEEN ALMOST A WEEK AND YOU HAVEN'T FOUND ANYTHING ABOUT OUR UNCLE! YOU TAKE OUR MONEY AND DRINK IT AWAY WHILE YOU KEEP US LOCKED UP HERE!
WHAT ARE YOU SAYING?
I'M SAYING MAYBE IT'S TIME YOU RETURN THE ADVANCE WE GAVE YOU AND WE'LL BE ON OUR WAY!
SO YOU'RE GIVING UP? WHEN THE GOING GETS TOUGH YOU GET GOING, HUH?
NO. I'M JUST DONE TRUSTING A BUM LIKE YOU.
THAT'S A BIG MISTAKE. I'M GETTING CLOSE!
THAT'S THE FIFTH TIME YOU'VE TOLD US THAT.

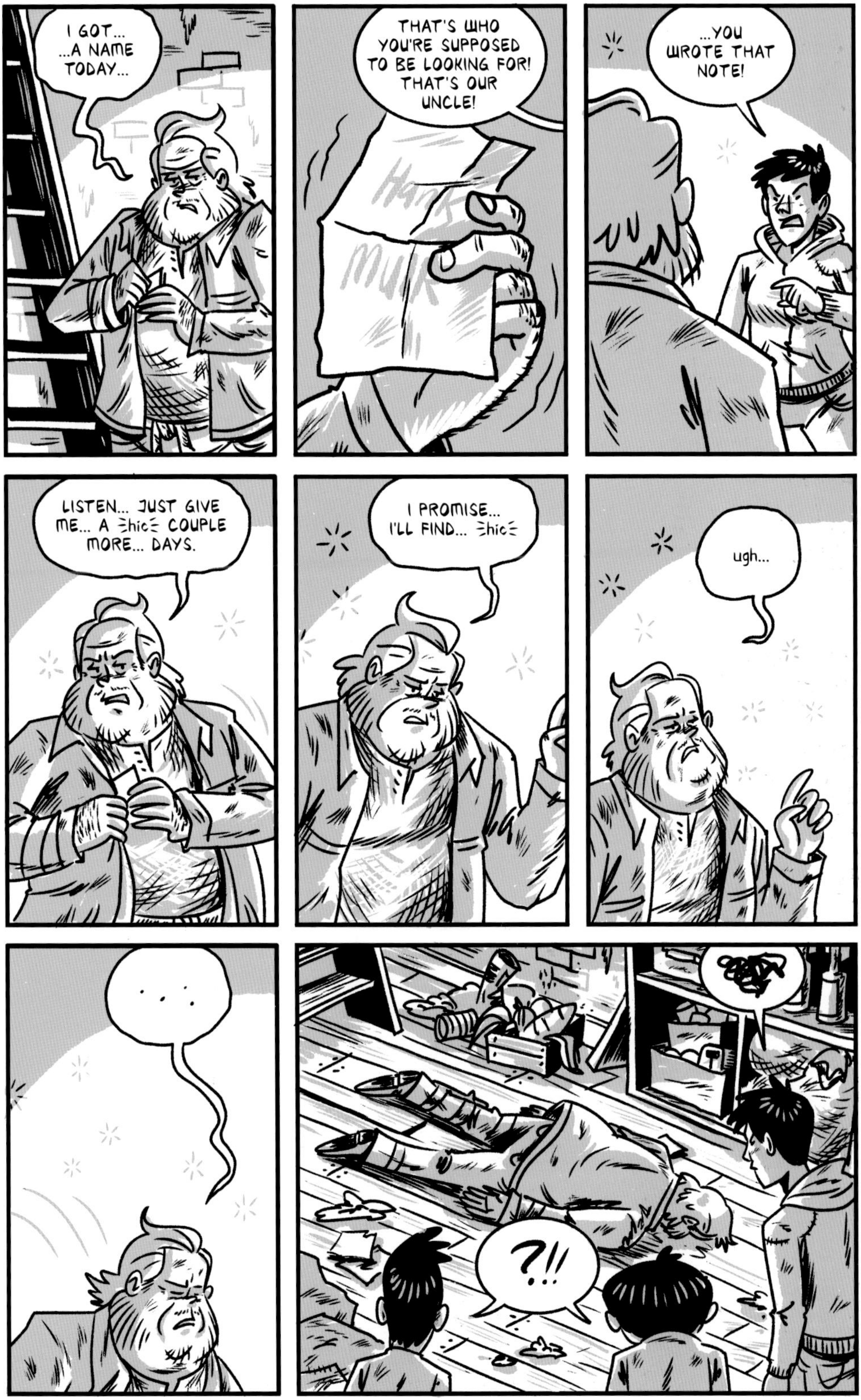
I GOT...
...A NAME TODAY...
THAT'S WHO YOU'RE SUPPOSED TO BE LOOKING FOR! THAT'S OUR UNCLE!
...YOU WROTE THAT NOTE!
LISTEN... JUST GIVE ME... A hic COUPLE MORE... DAYS.
I PROMISE... I'LL FIND... hic
ugh...
. . .
?!!

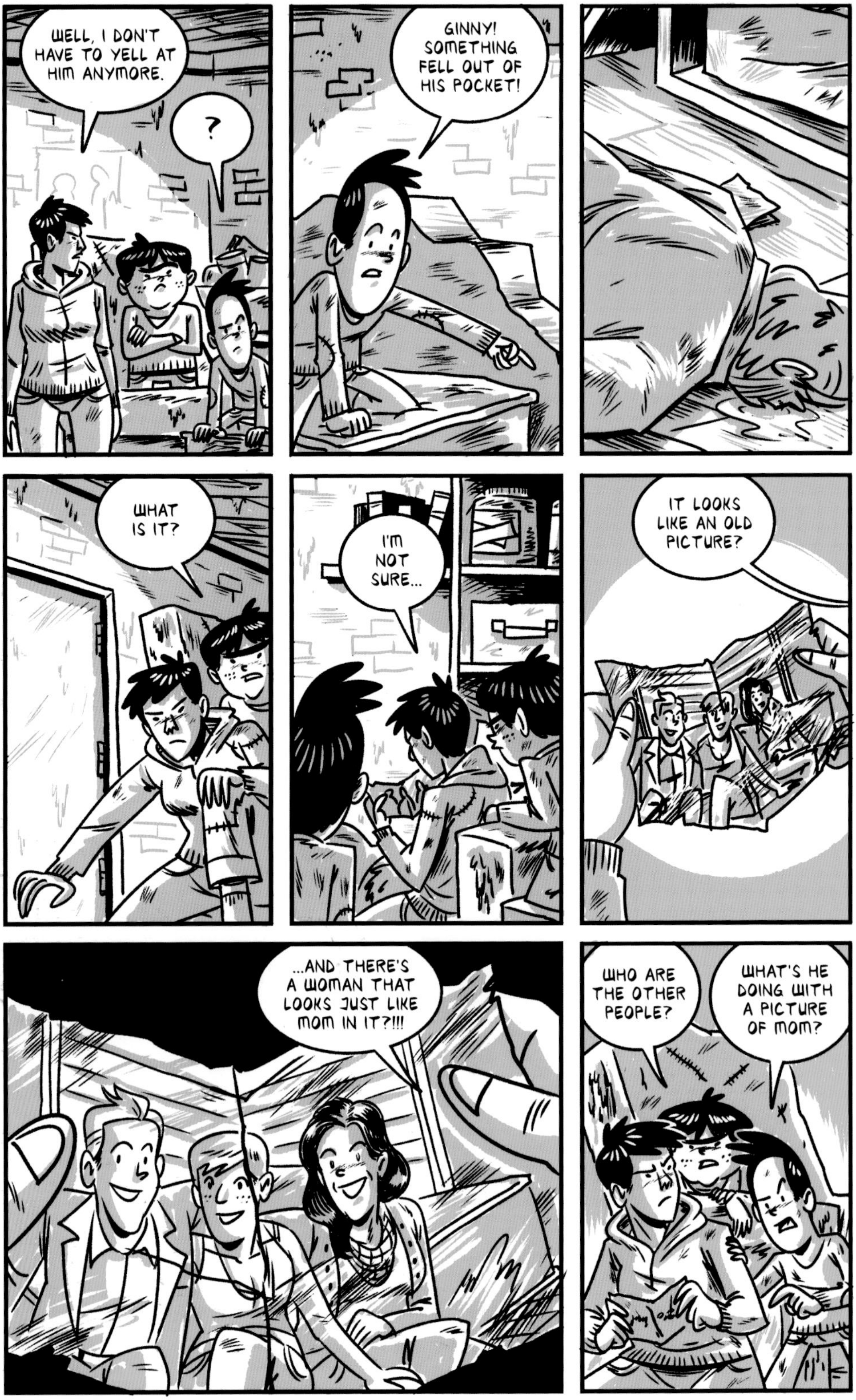
WELL, I DON'T HAVE TO YELL AT HIM ANYMORE.
?
GINNY! SOMETHING FELL OUT OF HIS POCKET!
WHAT IS IT?
I'M NOT SURE...
IT LOOKS LIKE AN OLD PICTURE?
...AND THERE'S A WOMAN THAT LOOKS JUST LIKE MOM IN IT?!!!
WHO ARE THE OTHER PEOPLE?
WHAT'S HE DOING WITH A PICTURE OF MOM?

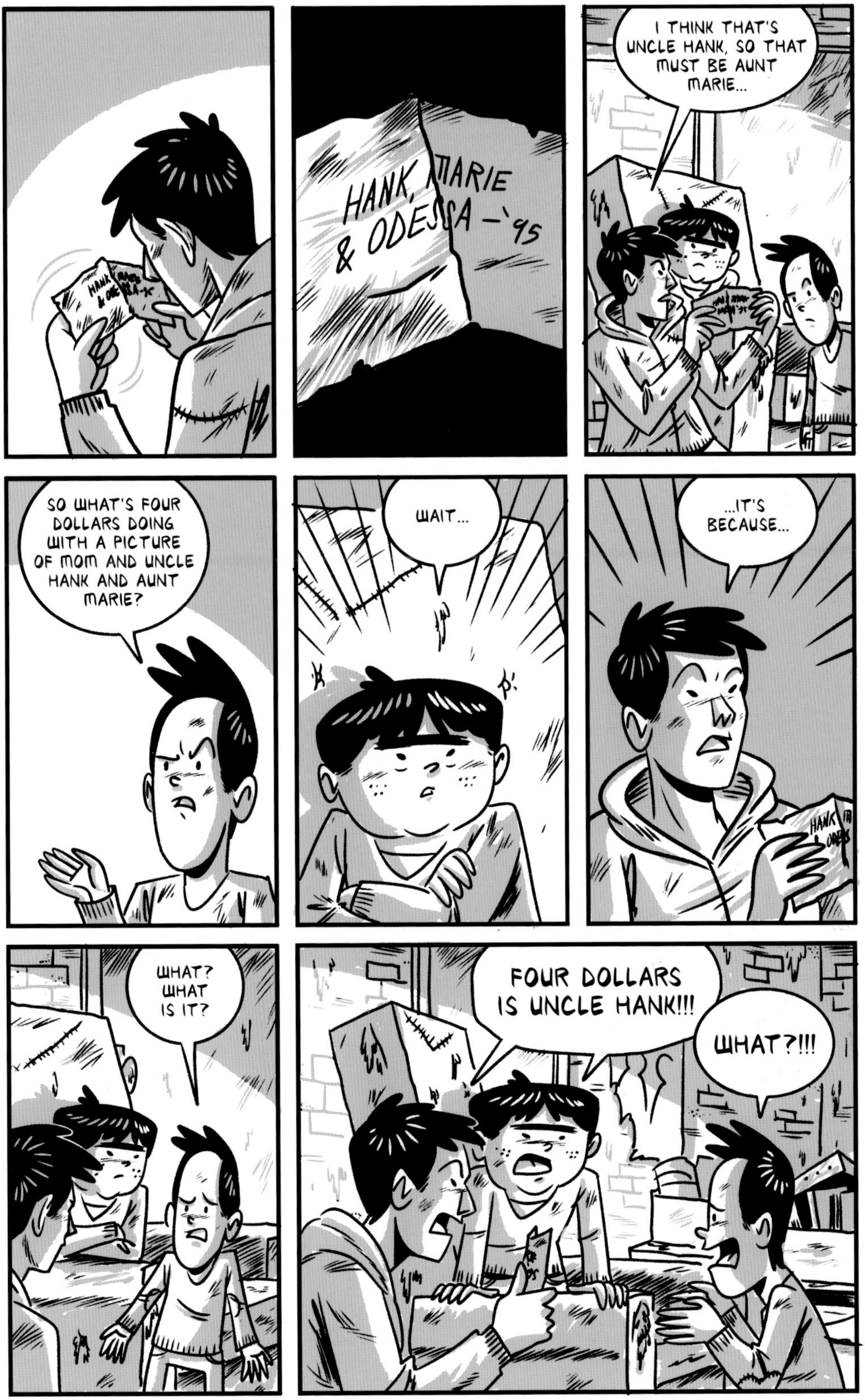

HANK, MARIE & ODESSA —'95
I THINK THAT'S UNCLE HANK, SO THAT MUST BE AUNT MARIE...
SO WHAT'S FOUR DOLLARS DOING WITH A PICTURE OF MOM AND UNCLE HANK AND AUNT MARIE?
WAIT...
...IT'S BECAUSE...
WHAT? WHAT IS IT?
FOUR DOLLARS IS UNCLE HANK!!!
WHAT?!!!

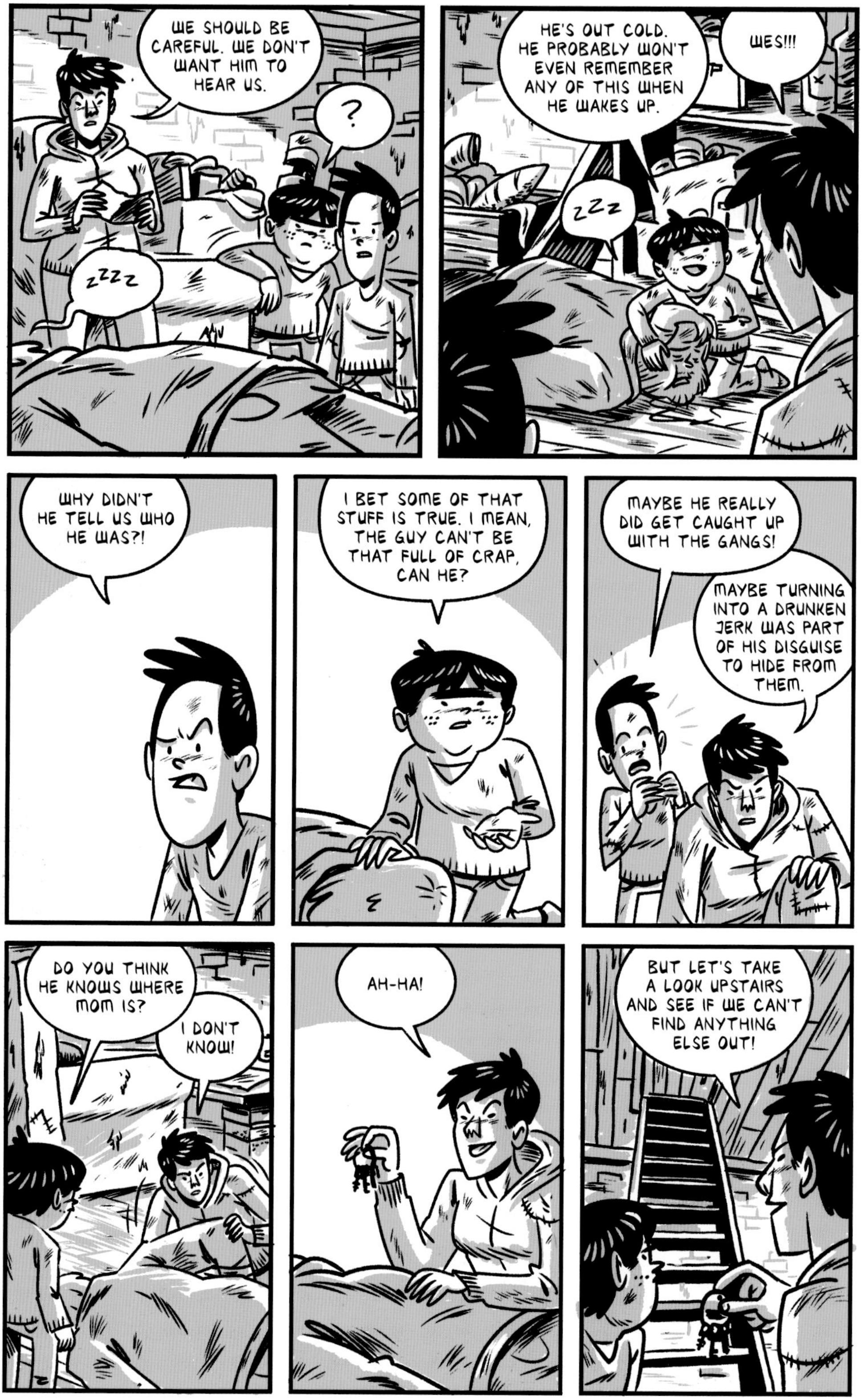
WE SHOULD BE CAREFUL. WE DON'T WANT HIM TO HEAR US.
?
ZZZZ
HE'S OUT COLD. HE PROBABLY WON'T EVEN REMEMBER ANY OF THIS WHEN HE WAKES UP.
WES!!!
ZZZ
WHY DIDN'T HE TELL US WHO HE WAS?!
I BET SOME OF THAT STUFF IS TRUE. I MEAN, THE GUY CAN'T BE THAT FULL OF CRAP, CAN HE?
MAYBE HE REALLY DID GET CAUGHT UP WITH THE GANGS!
MAYBE TURNING INTO A DRUNKEN JERK WAS PART OF HIS DISGUISE TO HIDE FROM THEM.
DO YOU THINK HE KNOWS WHERE MOM IS?
I DON'T KNOW!
AH-HA!
BUT LET'S TAKE A LOOK UPSTAIRS AND SEE IF WE CAN'T FIND ANYTHING ELSE OUT!

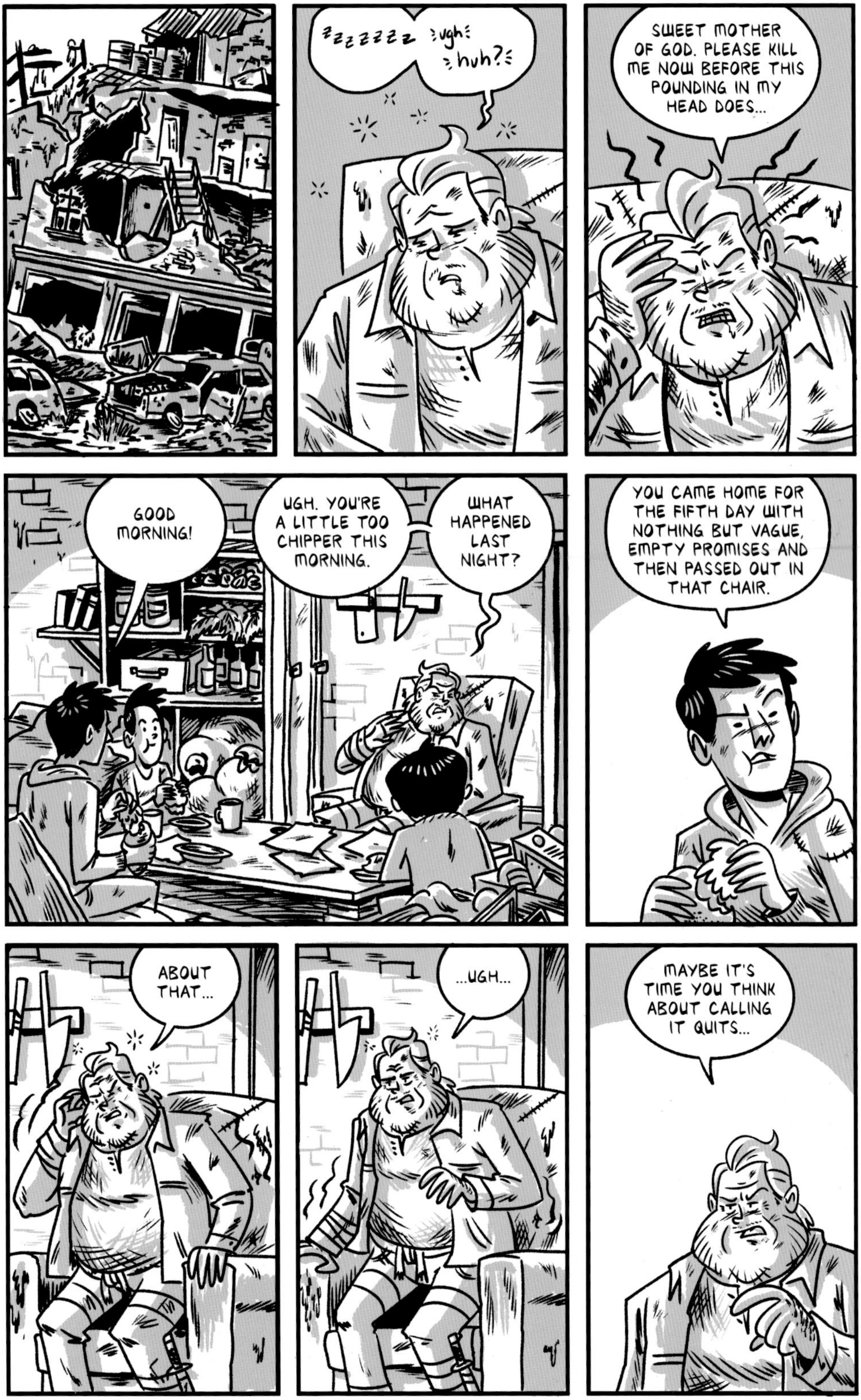
ZZZZZZZZ
ugh
huh?
SWEET MOTHER OF GOD. PLEASE KILL ME NOW BEFORE THIS POUNDING IN MY HEAD DOES...
GOOD MORNING!
UGH. YOU'RE A LITTLE TOO CHIPPER THIS MORNING.
WHAT HAPPENED LAST NIGHT?
YOU CAME HOME FOR THE FIFTH DAY WITH NOTHING BUT VAGUE, EMPTY PROMISES AND THEN PASSED OUT IN THAT CHAIR.
ABOUT THAT...
...UGH...
MAYBE IT'S TIME YOU THINK ABOUT CALLING IT QUITS...

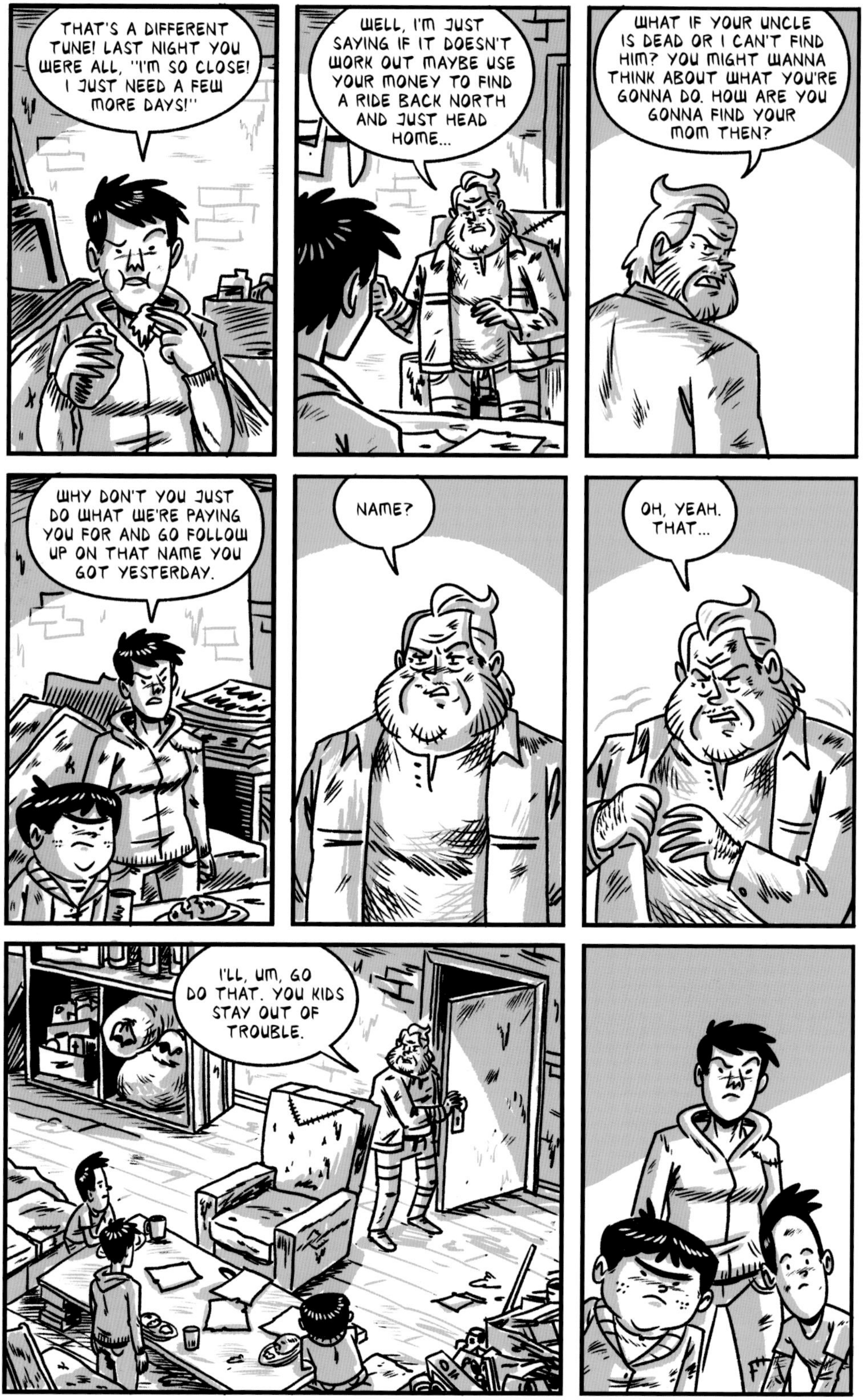
THAT'S A DIFFERENT TUNE! LAST NIGHT YOU WERE ALL, "I'M SO CLOSE! I JUST NEED A FEW MORE DAYS!"
WELL, I'M JUST SAYING IF IT DOESN'T WORK OUT MAYBE USE YOUR MONEY TO FIND A RIDE BACK NORTH AND JUST HEAD HOME...
WHAT IF YOUR UNCLE IS DEAD OR I CAN'T FIND HIM? YOU MIGHT WANNA THINK ABOUT WHAT YOU'RE GONNA DO. HOW ARE YOU GONNA FIND YOUR MOM THEN?
WHY DON'T YOU JUST DO WHAT WE'RE PAYING YOU FOR AND GO FOLLOW UP ON THAT NAME YOU GOT YESTERDAY.
NAME?
OH, YEAH. THAT...
I'LL, UM, GO DO THAT. YOU KIDS STAY OUT OF TROUBLE.

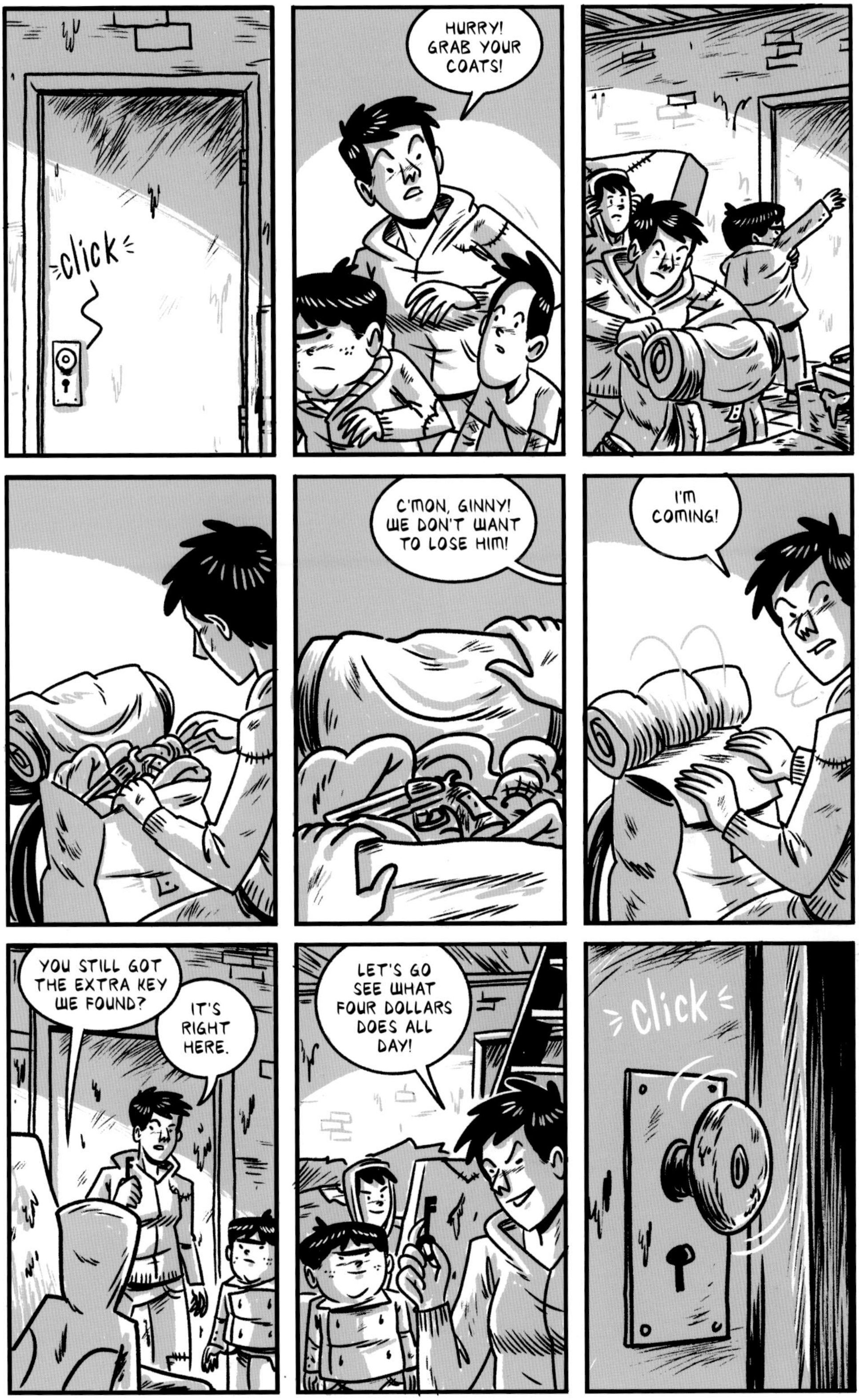
click
HURRY! GRAB YOUR COATS!
C'MON, GINNY! WE DON'T WANT TO LOSE HIM!
I'M COMING!
YOU STILL GOT THE EXTRA KEY WE FOUND?
IT'S RIGHT HERE.
LET'S GO SEE WHAT FOUR DOLLARS DOES ALL DAY!
click

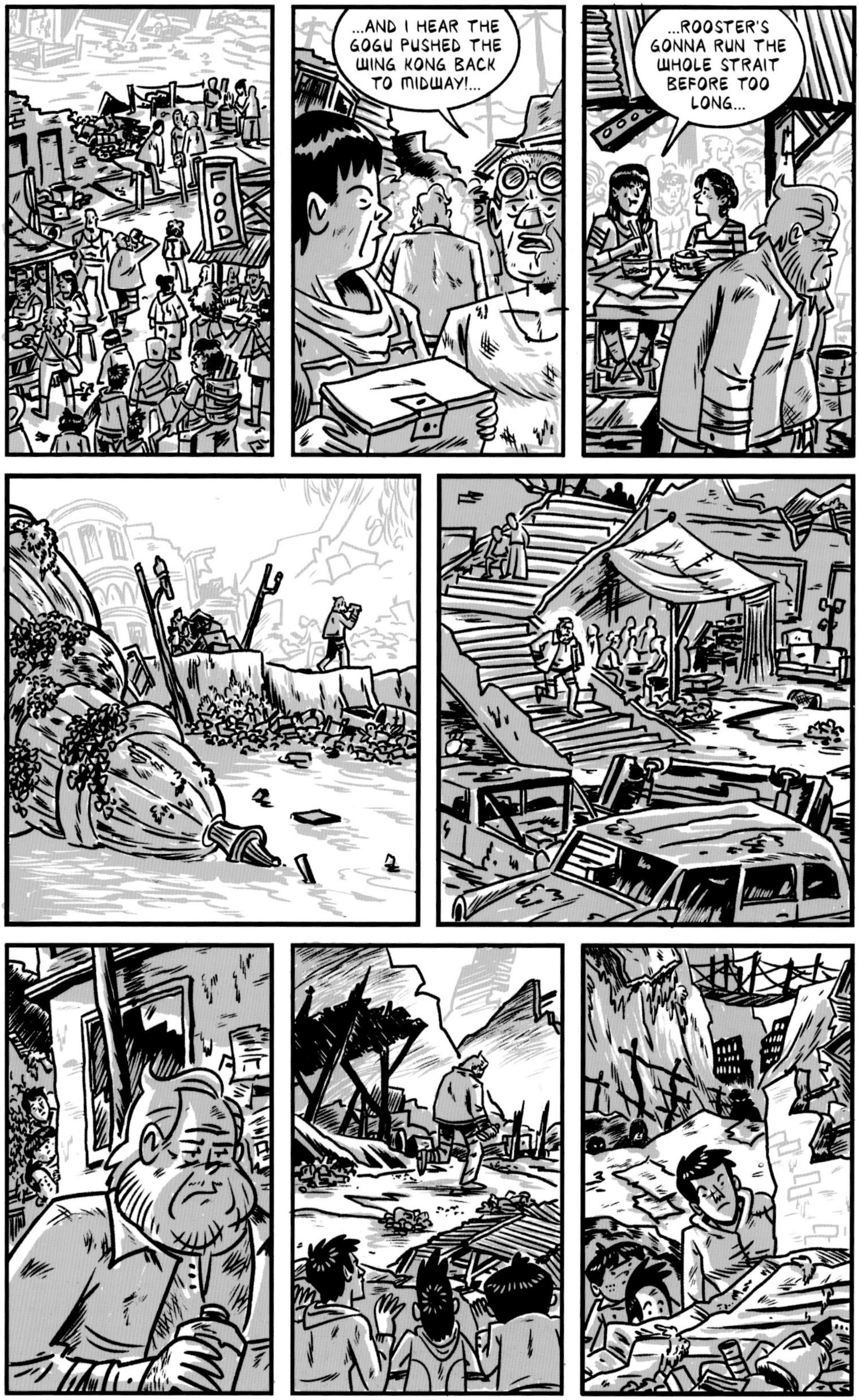
FOOD
...AND I HEAR THE GOGU PUSHED THE WING KONG BACK TO MIDWAY!...
...ROOSTER'S GONNA RUN THE WHOLE STRAIT BEFORE TOO LONG...

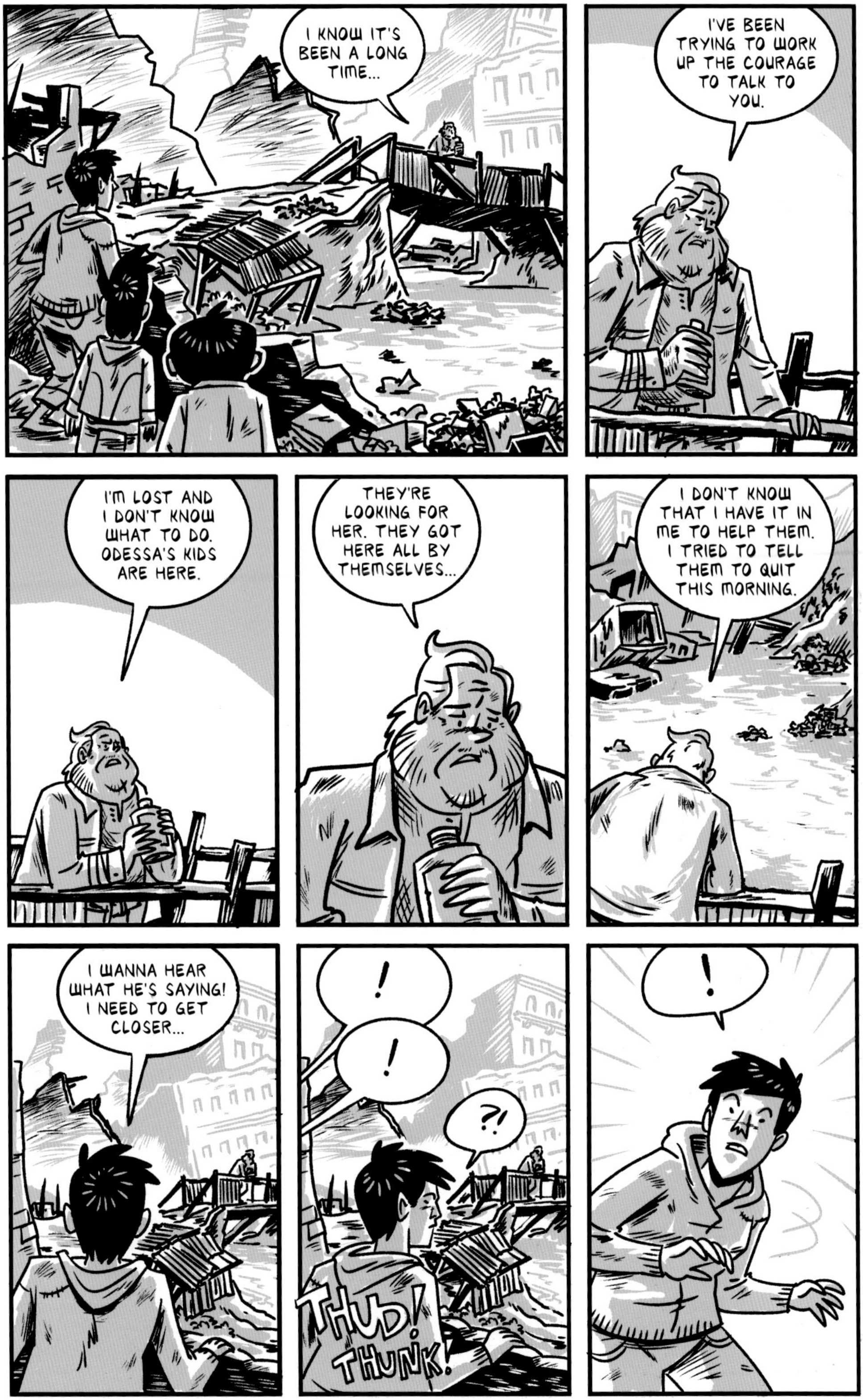
I KNOW IT'S BEEN A LONG TIME...
I'VE BEEN TRYING TO WORK UP THE COURAGE TO TALK TO YOU.
I'M LOST AND I DON'T KNOW WHAT TO DO. ODESSA'S KIDS ARE HERE.
THEY'RE LOOKING FOR HER. THEY GOT HERE ALL BY THEMSELVES...
I DON'T KNOW THAT I HAVE IT IN ME TO HELP THEM. I TRIED TO TELL THEM TO QUIT THIS MORNING.
I WANNA HEAR WHAT HE'S SAYING! I NEED TO GET CLOSER...
!
!
?!
THUD! THUNK!
!

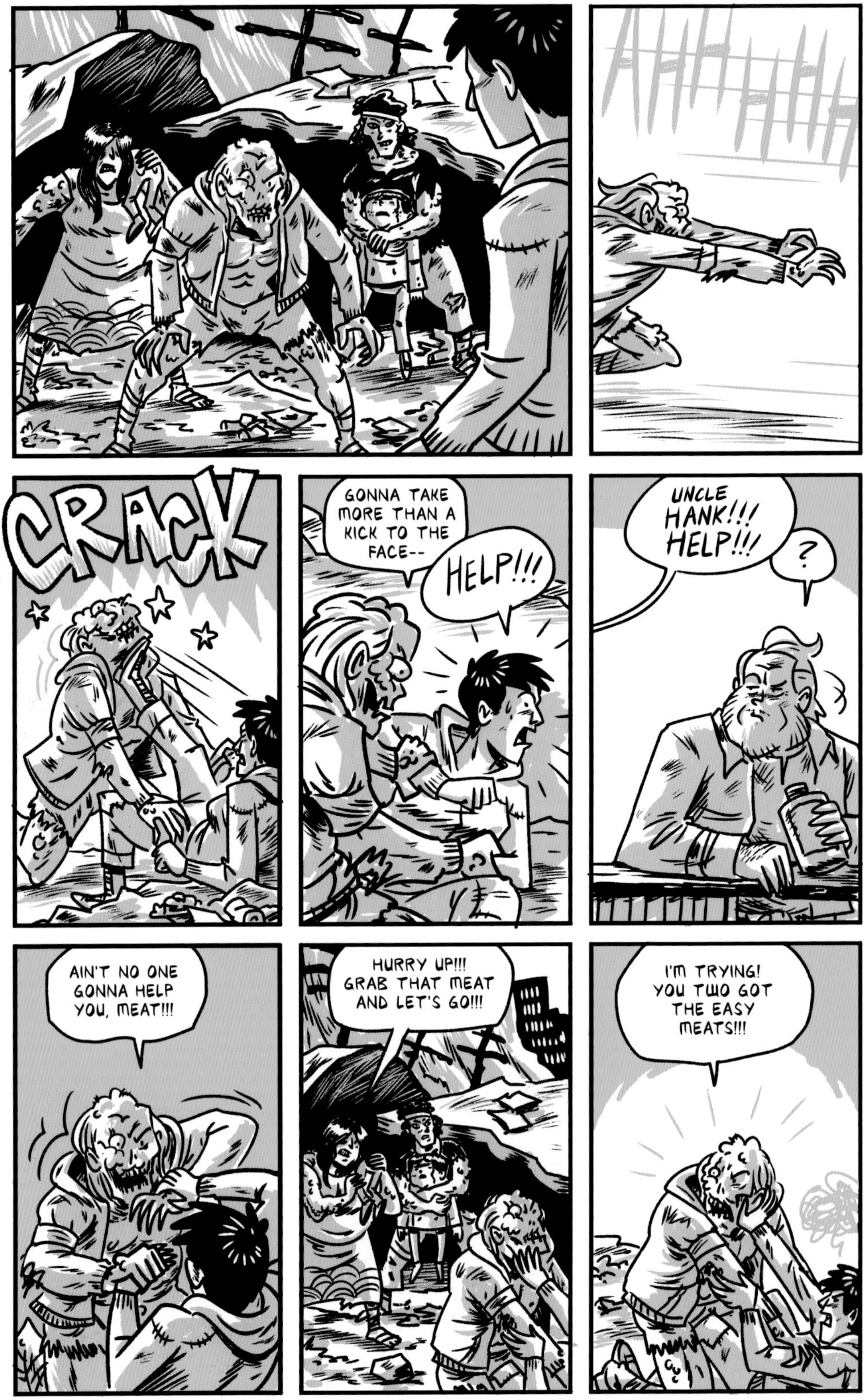
AHHHHH
CRACK
GONNA TAKE MORE THAN A KICK TO THE FACE--
HELP!!!
UNCLE HANK!!! HELP!!!
?
AIN'T NO ONE GONNA HELP YOU, MEAT!!!
HURRY UP!!! GRAB THAT MEAT AND LET'S GO!!!
I'M TRYING! YOU TWO GOT THE EASY MEATS!!!

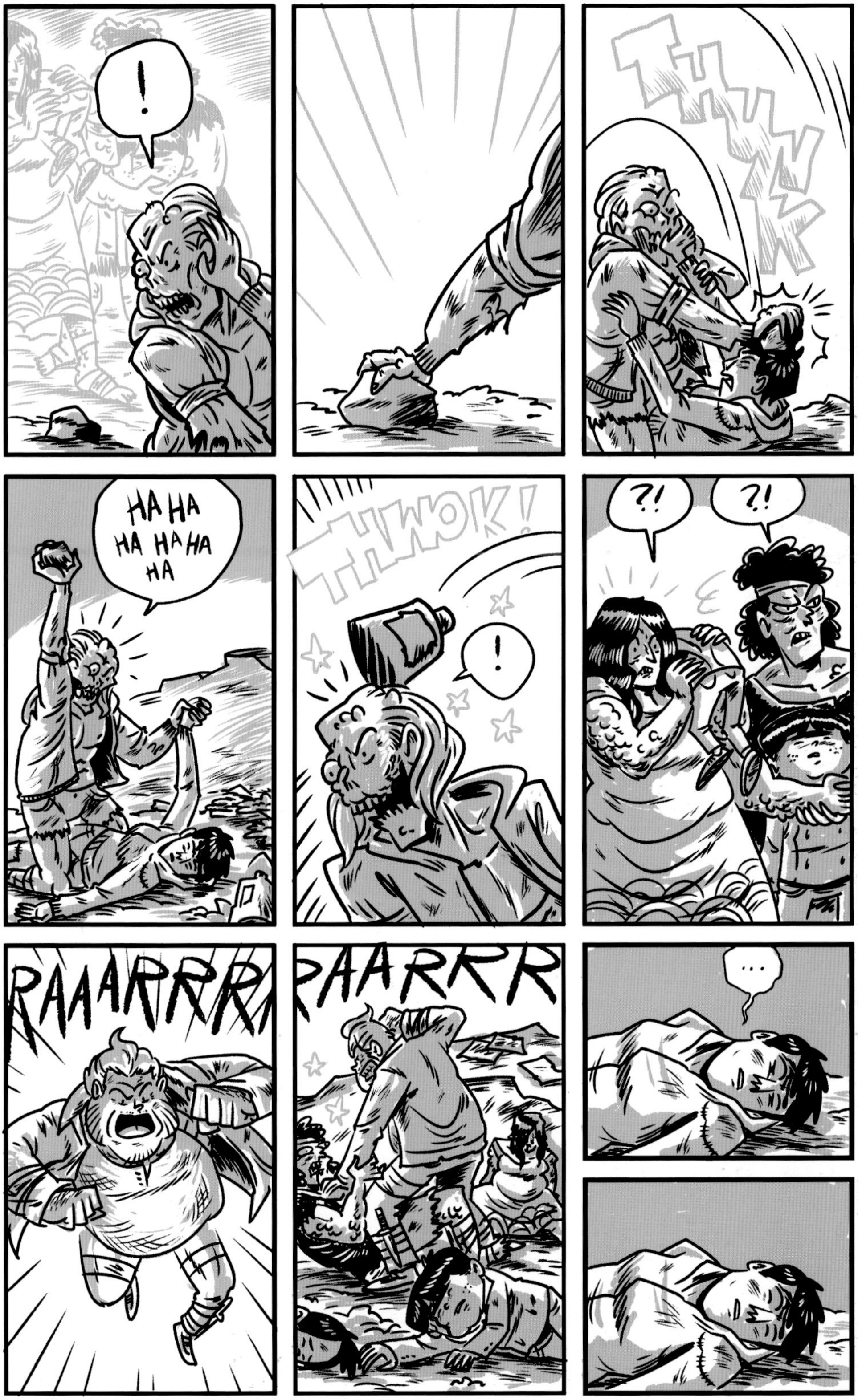
!
THUNK
HA HA HA HA HA HA HA
THWOK!
!
?!
?!
RAAARRRR
RAARRR
...

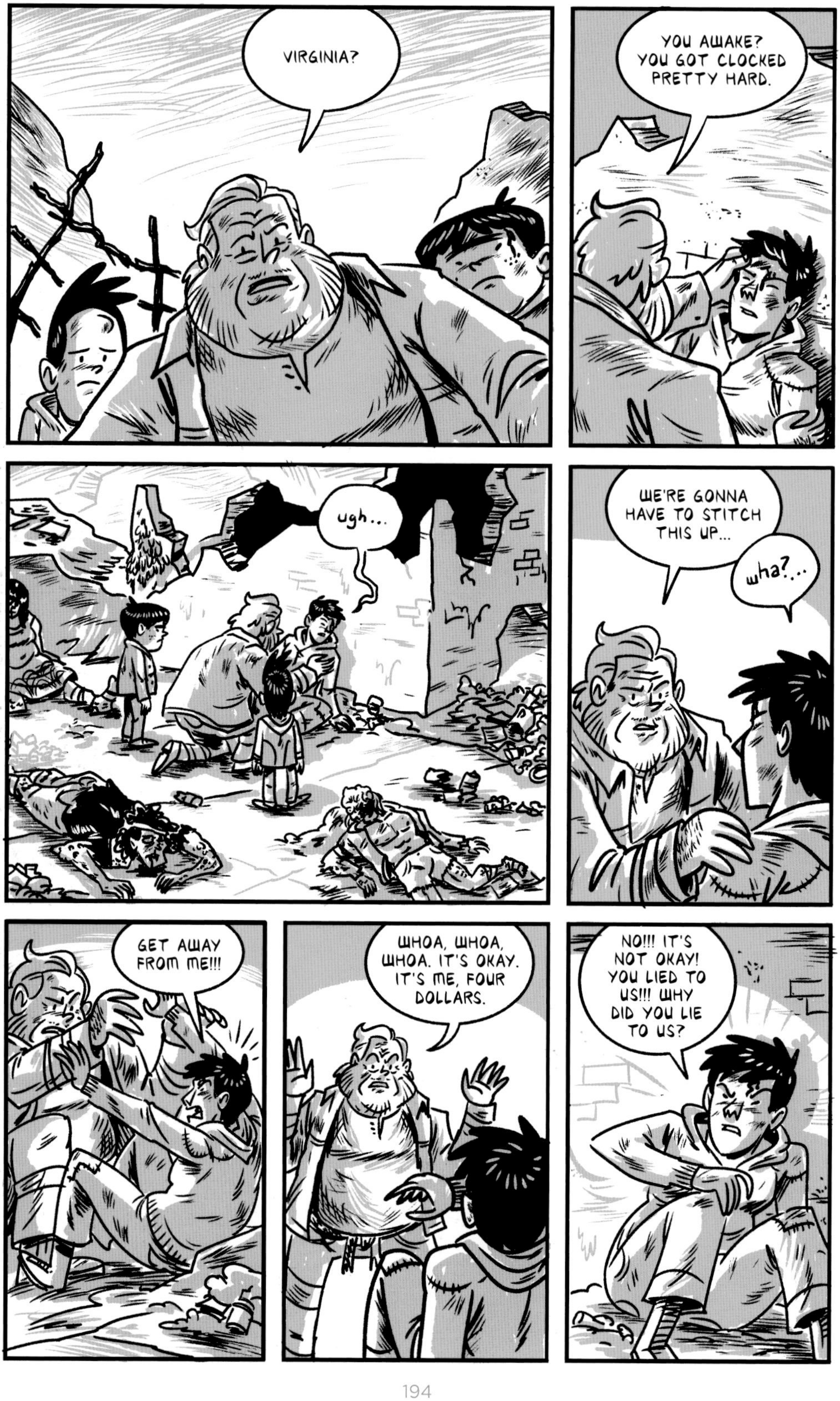

VIRGINIA?
YOU AWAKE? YOU GOT CLOCKED PRETTY HARD.
ugh...
WE'RE GONNA HAVE TO STITCH THIS UP...
wha?...
GET AWAY FROM ME!!!
WHOA, WHOA, WHOA. IT'S OKAY. IT'S ME, FOUR DOLLARS.
NO!!! IT'S NOT OKAY! YOU LIED TO US!!! WHY DID YOU LIE TO US?

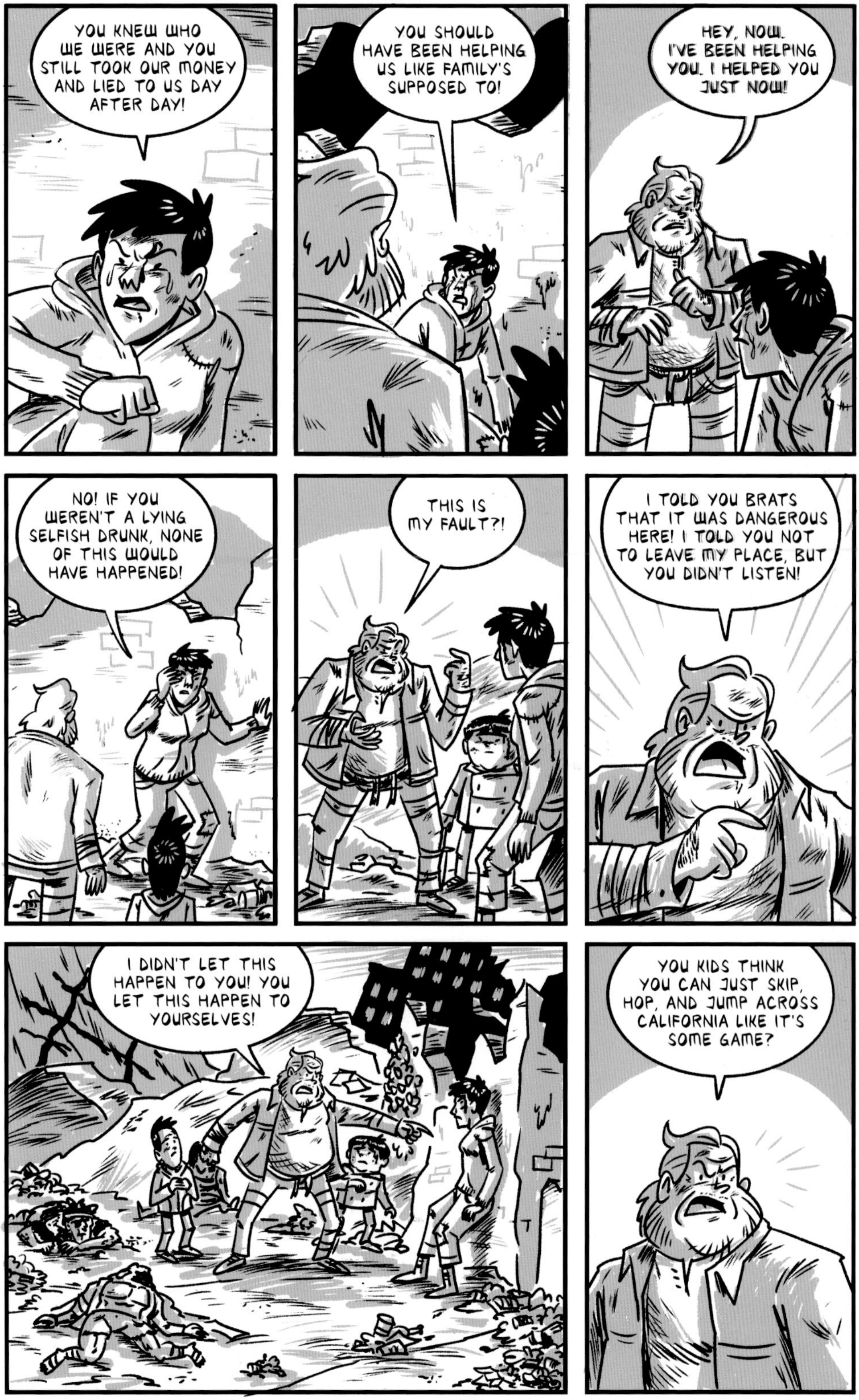
YOU KNEW WHO WE WERE AND YOU STILL TOOK OUR MONEY AND LIED TO US DAY AFTER DAY!
YOU SHOULD HAVE BEEN HELPING US LIKE FAMILY'S SUPPOSED TO!
HEY, NOW. I'VE BEEN HELPING YOU. I HELPED YOU JUST NOW!
NO! IF YOU WEREN'T A LYING SELFISH DRUNK, NONE OF THIS WOULD HAVE HAPPENED!
THIS IS MY FAULT?!
I TOLD YOU BRATS THAT IT WAS DANGEROUS HERE! I TOLD YOU NOT TO LEAVE MY PLACE, BUT YOU DIDN'T LISTEN!
I DIDN'T LET THIS HAPPEN TO YOU! YOU LET THIS HAPPEN TO YOURSELVES!
YOU KIDS THINK YOU CAN JUST SKIP, HOP, AND JUMP ACROSS CALIFORNIA LIKE IT'S SOME GAME?

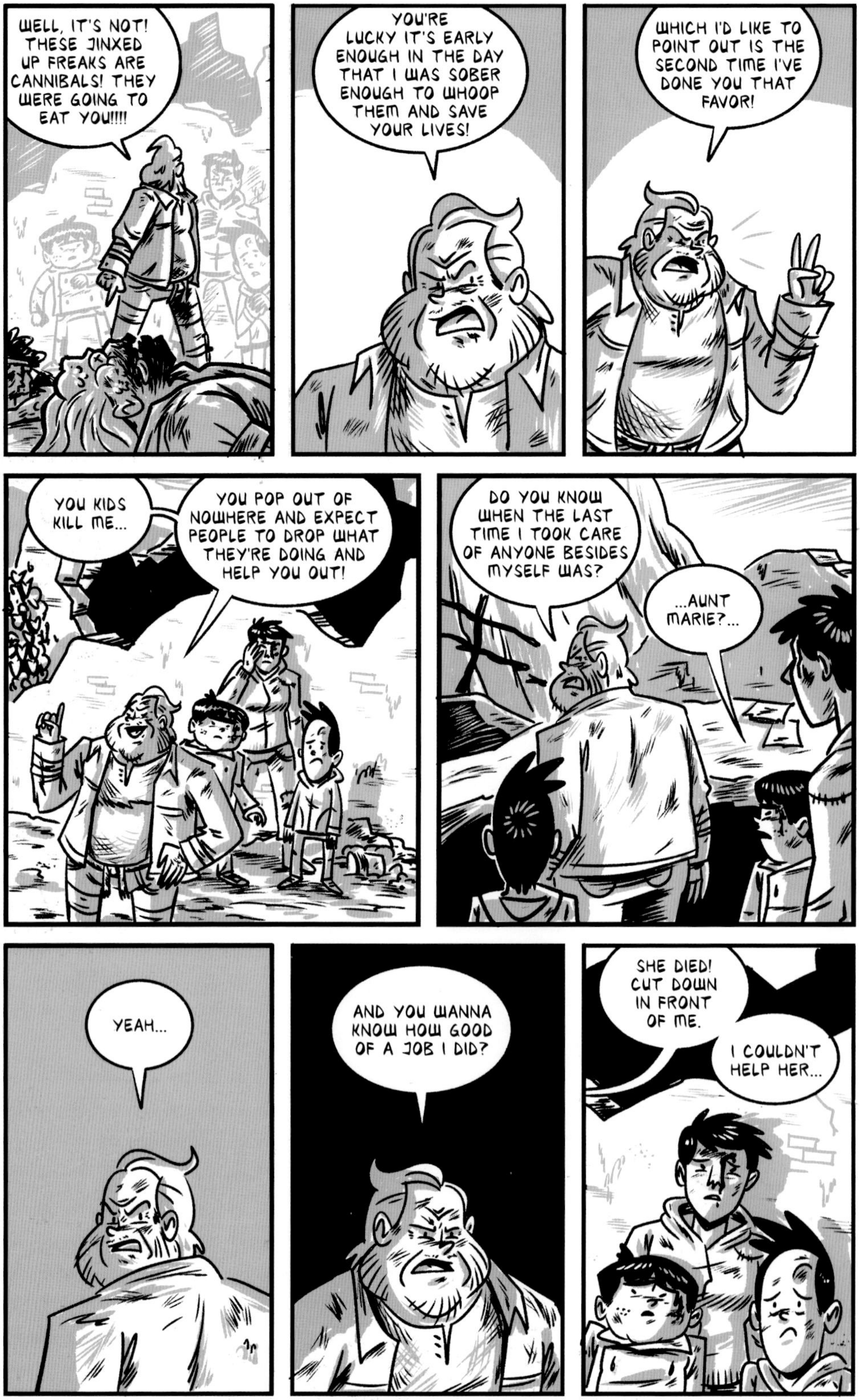
WELL, IT'S NOT! THESE JINXED UP FREAKS ARE CANNIBALS! THEY WERE GOING TO EAT YOU!!!!
YOU'RE LUCKY IT'S EARLY ENOUGH IN THE DAY THAT I WAS SOBER ENOUGH TO WHOOP THEM AND SAVE YOUR LIVES!
WHICH I'D LIKE TO POINT OUT IS THE SECOND TIME I'VE DONE YOU THAT FAVOR!
YOU KIDS KILL ME...
YOU POP OUT OF NOWHERE AND EXPECT PEOPLE TO DROP WHAT THEY'RE DOING AND HELP YOU OUT!
DO YOU KNOW WHEN THE LAST TIME I TOOK CARE OF ANYONE BESIDES MYSELF WAS?
...AUNT MARIE?...
YEAH...
AND YOU WANNA KNOW HOW GOOD OF A JOB I DID?
SHE DIED! CUT DOWN IN FRONT OF ME.
I COULDN'T HELP HER...

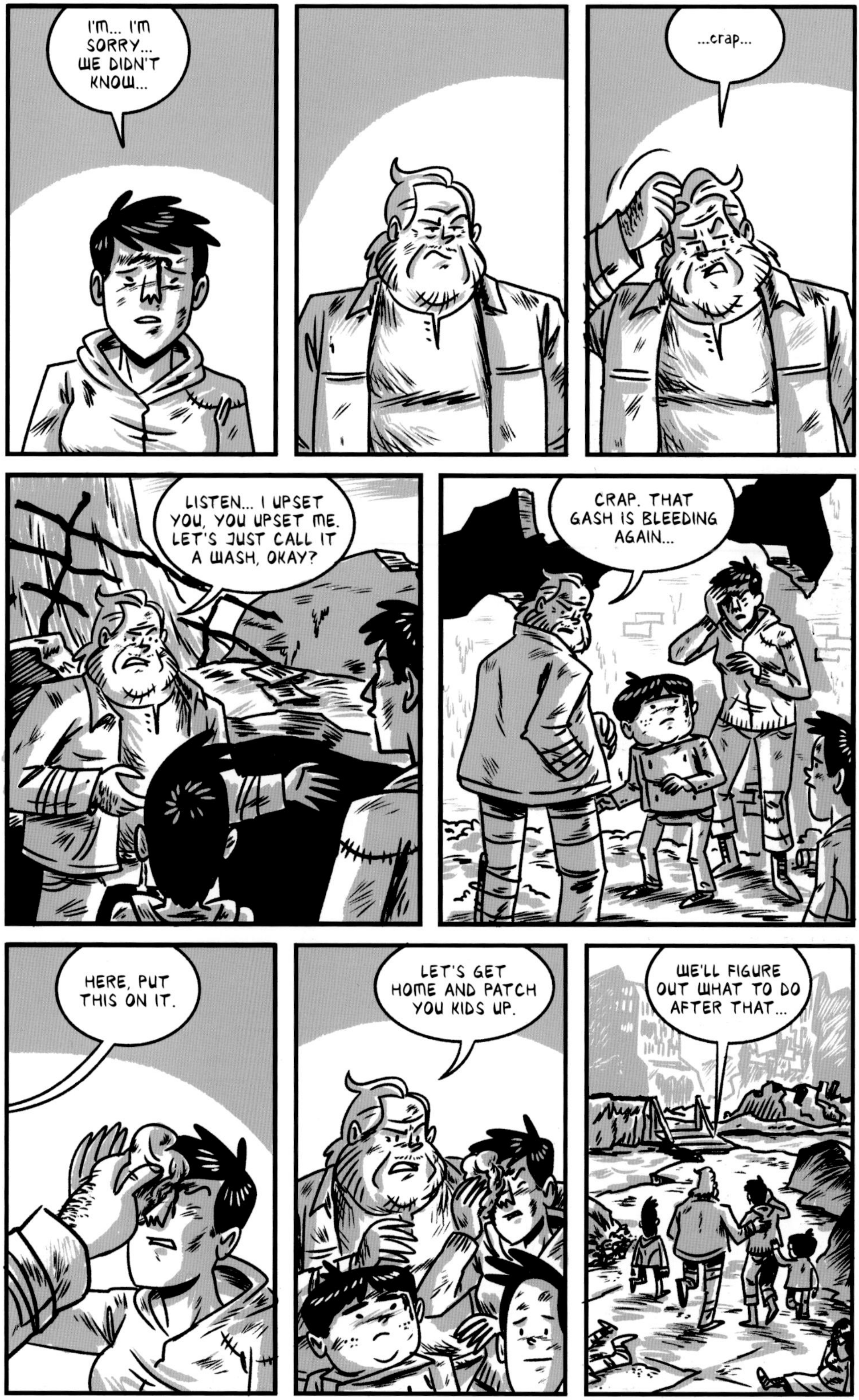
I'M... I'M SORRY... WE DIDN'T KNOW...
...crap...
LISTEN... I UPSET YOU, YOU UPSET ME. LET'S JUST CALL IT A WASH, OKAY?
CRAP. THAT GASH IS BLEEDING AGAIN...
HERE, PUT THIS ON IT.
LET'S GET HOME AND PATCH YOU KIDS UP.
WE'LL FIGURE OUT WHAT TO DO AFTER THAT...

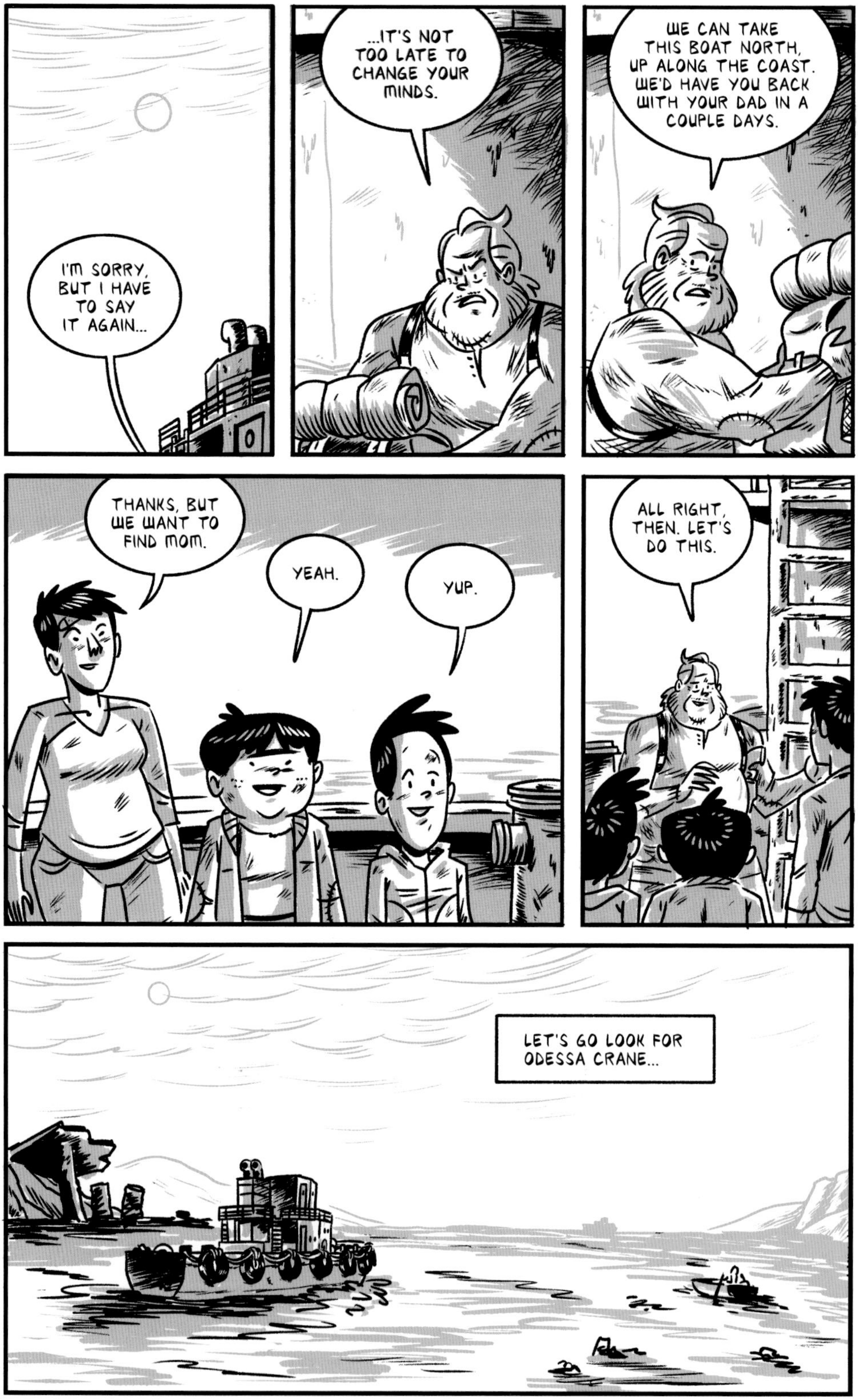
I'M SORRY, BUT I HAVE TO SAY IT AGAIN...
...IT'S NOT TOO LATE TO CHANGE YOUR MINDS.
WE CAN TAKE THIS BOAT NORTH, UP ALONG THE COAST. WE'D HAVE YOU BACK WITH YOUR DAD IN A COUPLE DAYS.
THANKS, BUT WE WANT TO FIND MOM.
YEAH.
YUP.
ALL RIGHT, THEN. LET'S DO THIS.
LET'S GO LOOK FOR ODESSA CRANE...

CHAPTER 8

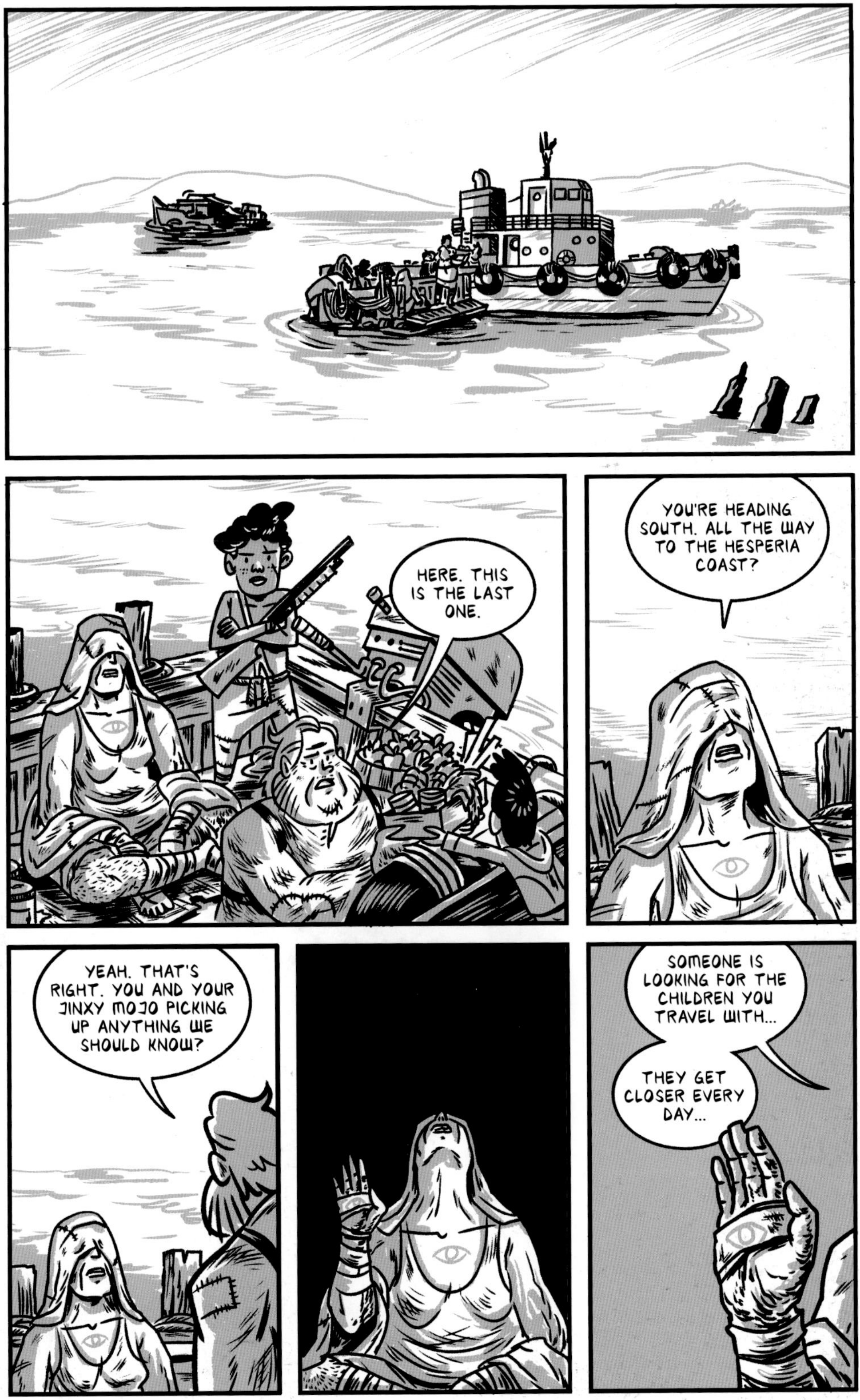
HERE. THIS IS THE LAST ONE.
YOU'RE HEADING SOUTH. ALL THE WAY TO THE HESPERIA COAST?
YEAH. THAT'S RIGHT. YOU AND YOUR JINXY MOJO PICKING UP ANYTHING WE SHOULD KNOW?
SOMEONE IS LOOKING FOR THE CHILDREN YOU TRAVEL WITH...
THEY GET CLOSER EVERY DAY...

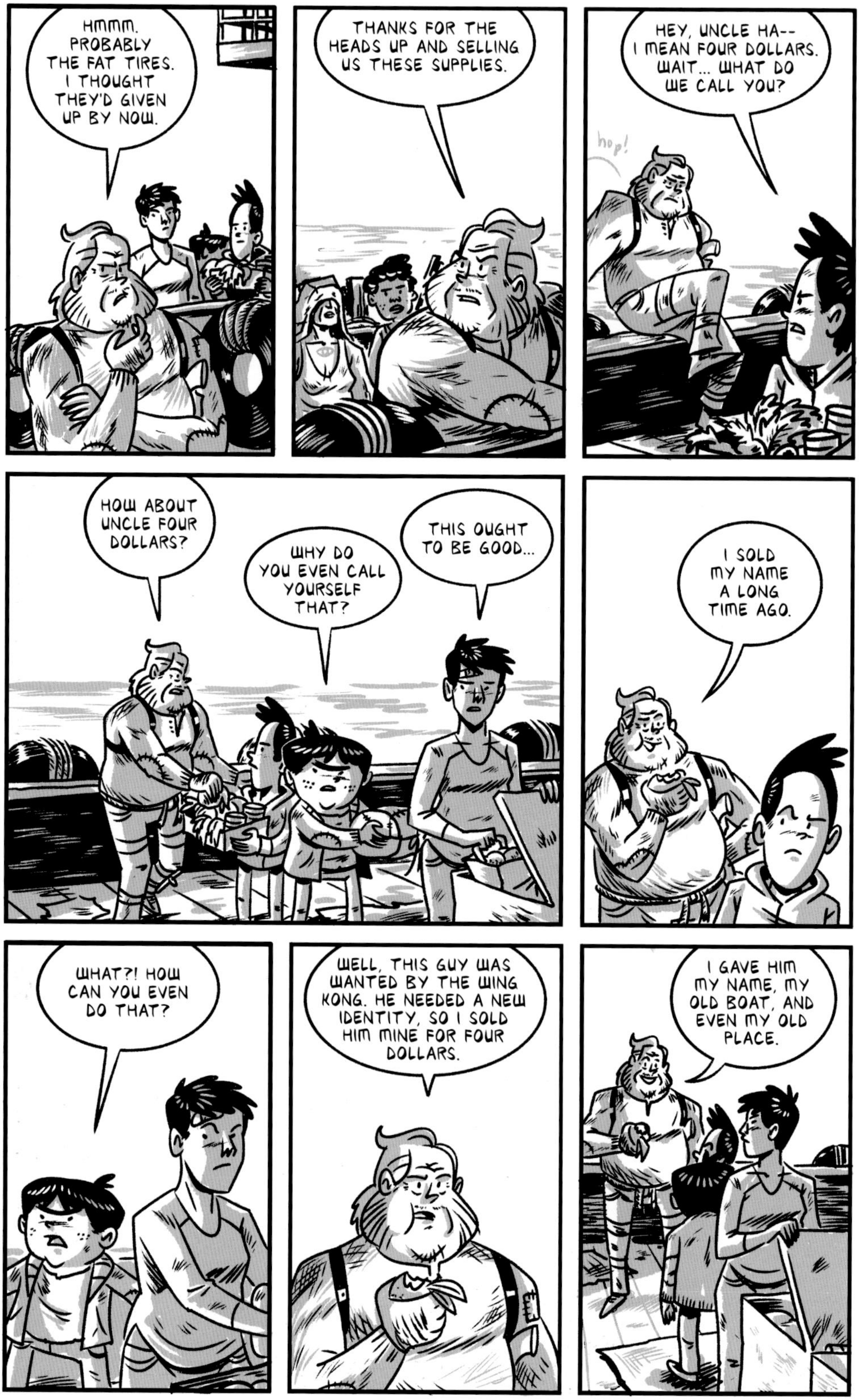
HMMM. PROBABLY THE FAT TIRES. I THOUGHT THEY'D GIVEN UP BY NOW.
THANKS FOR THE HEADS UP AND SELLING US THESE SUPPLIES.
HEY, UNCLE HA-- I MEAN FOUR DOLLARS. WAIT... WHAT DO WE CALL YOU?
hop!
HOW ABOUT UNCLE FOUR DOLLARS?
WHY DO YOU EVEN CALL YOURSELF THAT?
THIS OUGHT TO BE GOOD...
I SOLD MY NAME A LONG TIME AGO.
WHAT?! HOW CAN YOU EVEN DO THAT?
WELL, THIS GUY WAS WANTED BY THE WING KONG. HE NEEDED A NEW IDENTITY, SO I SOLD HIM MINE FOR FOUR DOLLARS.
I GAVE HIM MY NAME, MY OLD BOAT, AND EVEN MY OLD PLACE.

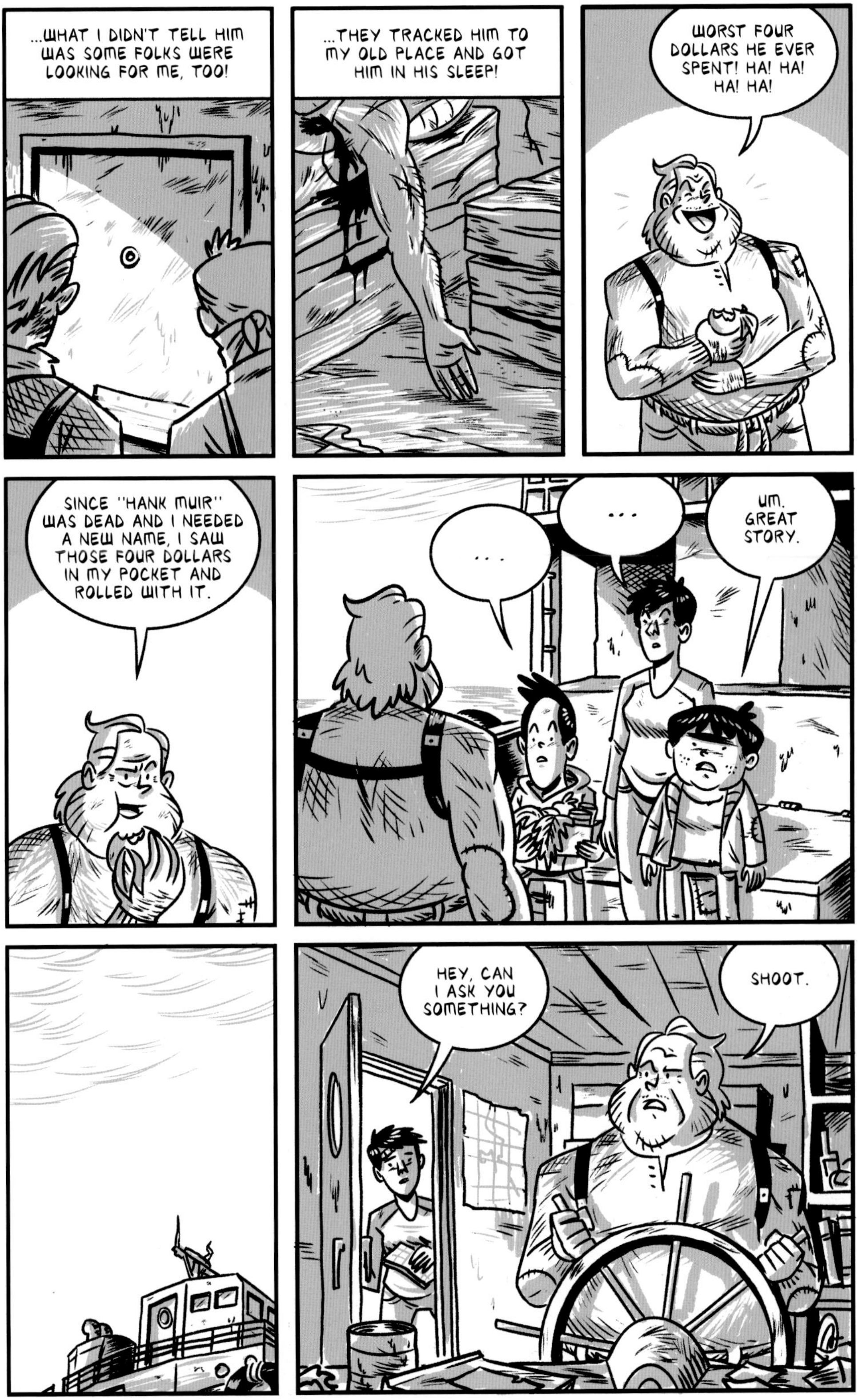
...WHAT I DIDN'T TELL HIM WAS SOME FOLKS WERE LOOKING FOR ME, TOO!
...THEY TRACKED HIM TO MY OLD PLACE AND GOT HIM IN HIS SLEEP!
WORST FOUR DOLLARS HE EVER SPENT! HA! HA! HA! HA!
SINCE "HANK MUIR" WAS DEAD AND I NEEDED A NEW NAME, I SAW THOSE FOUR DOLLARS IN MY POCKET AND ROLLED WITH IT.
. . .
. . .
UM. GREAT STORY.
HEY, CAN I ASK YOU SOMETHING?
SHOOT.

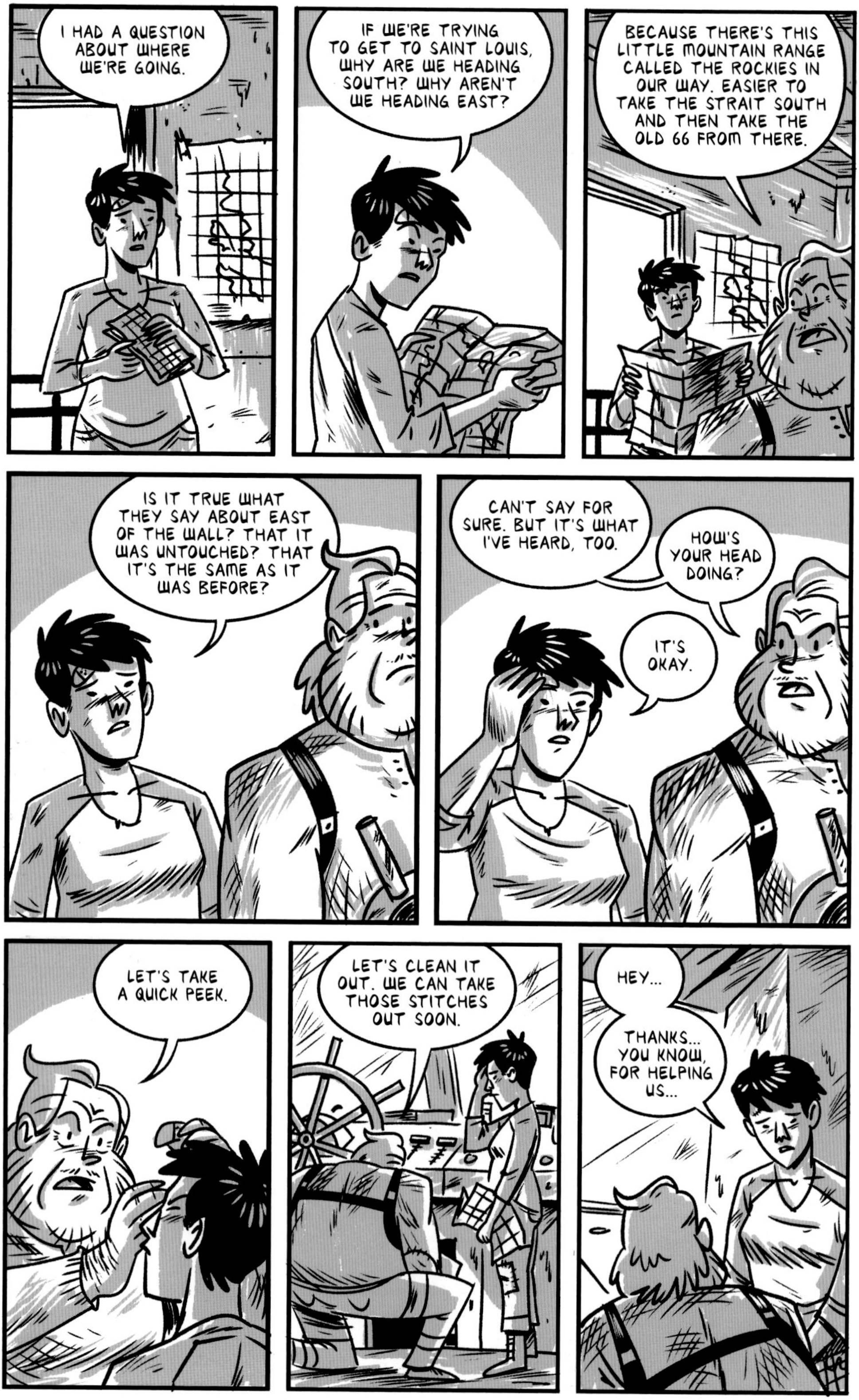
I HAD A QUESTION ABOUT WHERE WE'RE GOING.
IF WE'RE TRYING TO GET TO SAINT LOUIS, WHY ARE WE HEADING SOUTH? WHY AREN'T WE HEADING EAST?
BECAUSE THERE'S THIS LITTLE MOUNTAIN RANGE CALLED THE ROCKIES IN OUR WAY. EASIER TO TAKE THE STRAIT SOUTH AND THEN TAKE THE OLD 66 FROM THERE.
IS IT TRUE WHAT THEY SAY ABOUT EAST OF THE WALL? THAT IT WAS UNTOUCHED? THAT IT'S THE SAME AS IT WAS BEFORE?
CAN'T SAY FOR SURE. BUT IT'S WHAT I'VE HEARD, TOO.
HOW'S YOUR HEAD DOING?
IT'S OKAY.
LET'S TAKE A QUICK PEEK.
LET'S CLEAN IT OUT. WE CAN TAKE THOSE STITCHES OUT SOON.
HEY...
THANKS... YOU KNOW, FOR HELPING US...

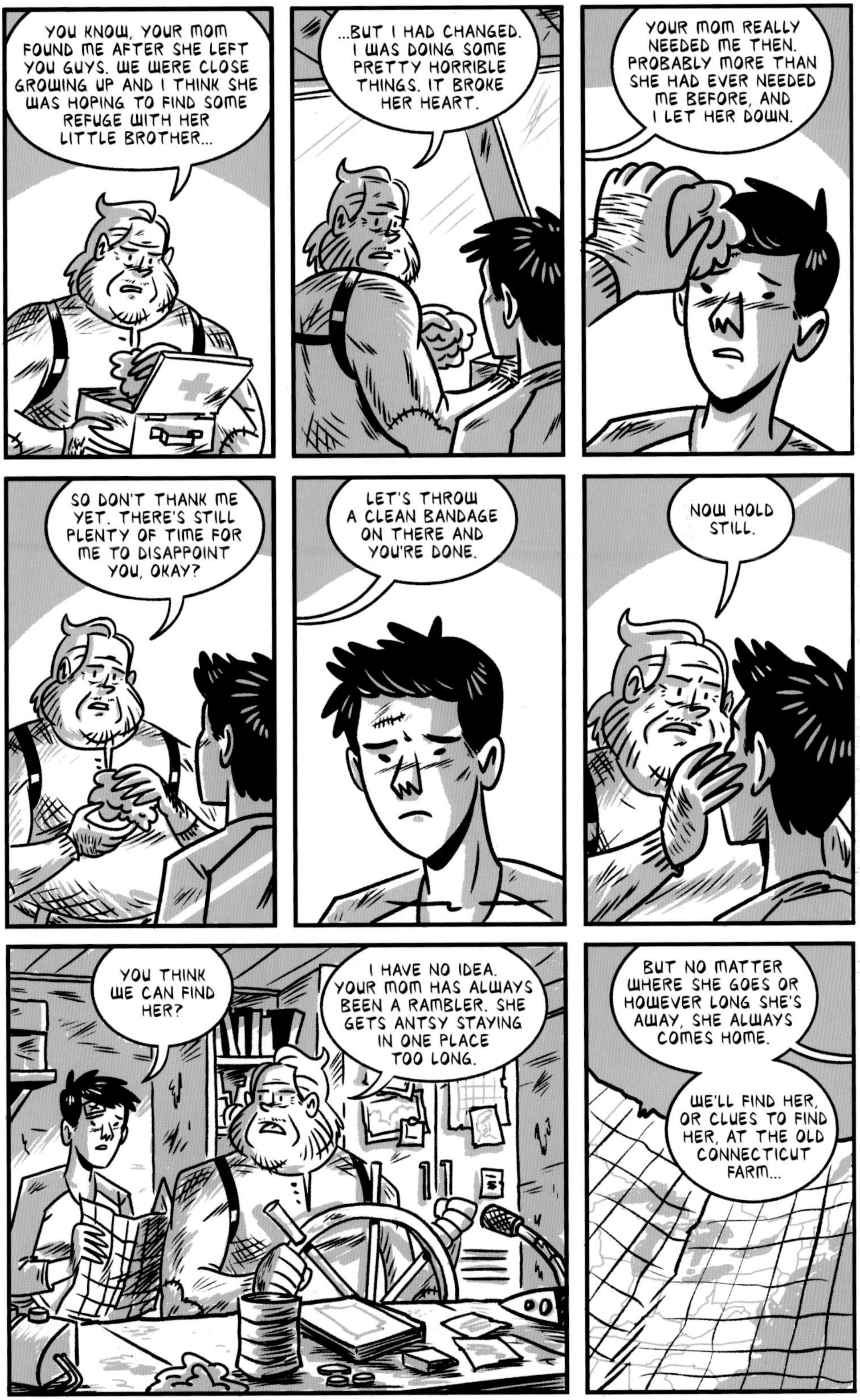
YOU KNOW, YOUR MOM FOUND ME AFTER SHE LEFT YOU GUYS. WE WERE CLOSE GROWING UP AND I THINK SHE WAS HOPING TO FIND SOME REFUGE WITH HER LITTLE BROTHER...
...BUT I HAD CHANGED. I WAS DOING SOME PRETTY HORRIBLE THINGS. IT BROKE HER HEART.
YOUR MOM REALLY NEEDED ME THEN. PROBABLY MORE THAN SHE HAD EVER NEEDED ME BEFORE, AND I LET HER DOWN.
SO DON'T THANK ME YET. THERE'S STILL PLENTY OF TIME FOR ME TO DISAPPOINT YOU, OKAY?
LET'S THROW A CLEAN BANDAGE ON THERE AND YOU'RE DONE.
NOW HOLD STILL.
YOU THINK WE CAN FIND HER?
I HAVE NO IDEA. YOUR MOM HAS ALWAYS BEEN A RAMBLER. SHE GETS ANTSY STAYING IN ONE PLACE TOO LONG.
BUT NO MATTER WHERE SHE GOES OR HOWEVER LONG SHE'S AWAY, SHE ALWAYS COMES HOME.
WE'LL FIND HER, OR CLUES TO FIND HER, AT THE OLD CONNECTICUT FARM...

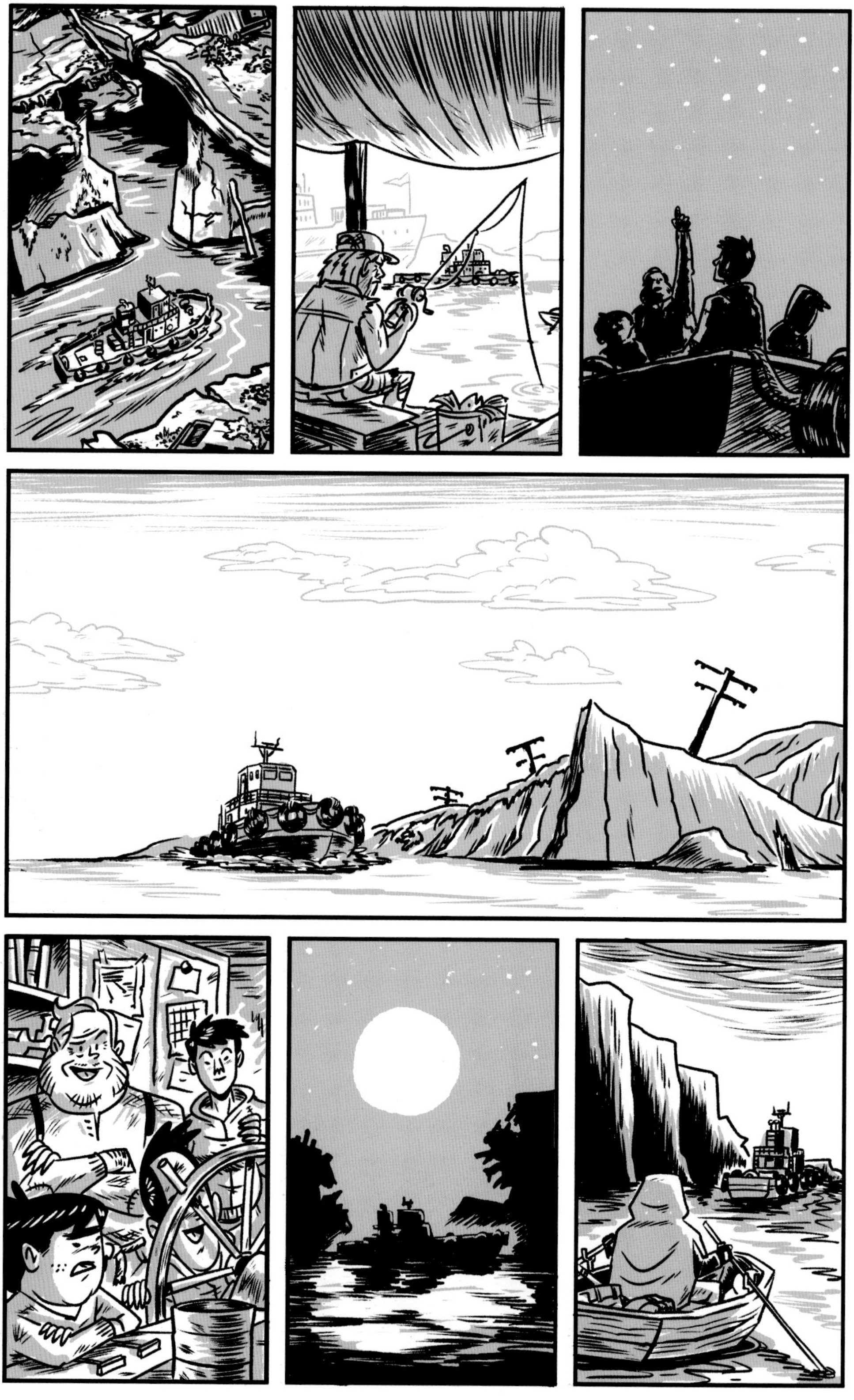

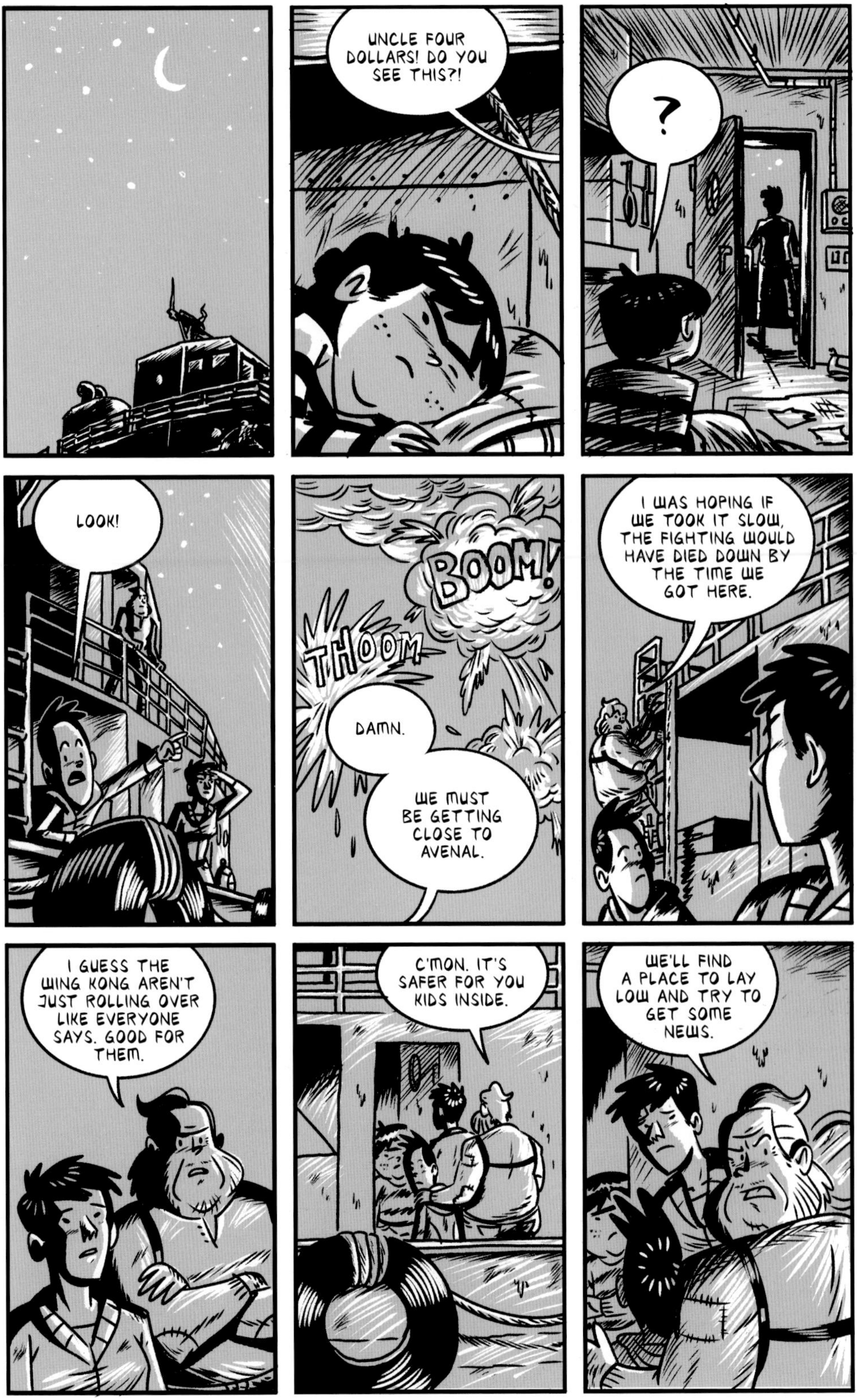
UNCLE FOUR DOLLARS! DO YOU SEE THIS?!
?
LOOK!
BOOM!
THOOM
DAMN.
WE MUST BE GETTING CLOSE TO AVENAL.
I WAS HOPING IF WE TOOK IT SLOW, THE FIGHTING WOULD HAVE DIED DOWN BY THE TIME WE GOT HERE.
I GUESS THE WING KONG AREN'T JUST ROLLING OVER LIKE EVERYONE SAYS. GOOD FOR THEM.
C'MON. IT'S SAFER FOR YOU KIDS INSIDE.
WE'LL FIND A PLACE TO LAY LOW AND TRY TO GET SOME NEWS.

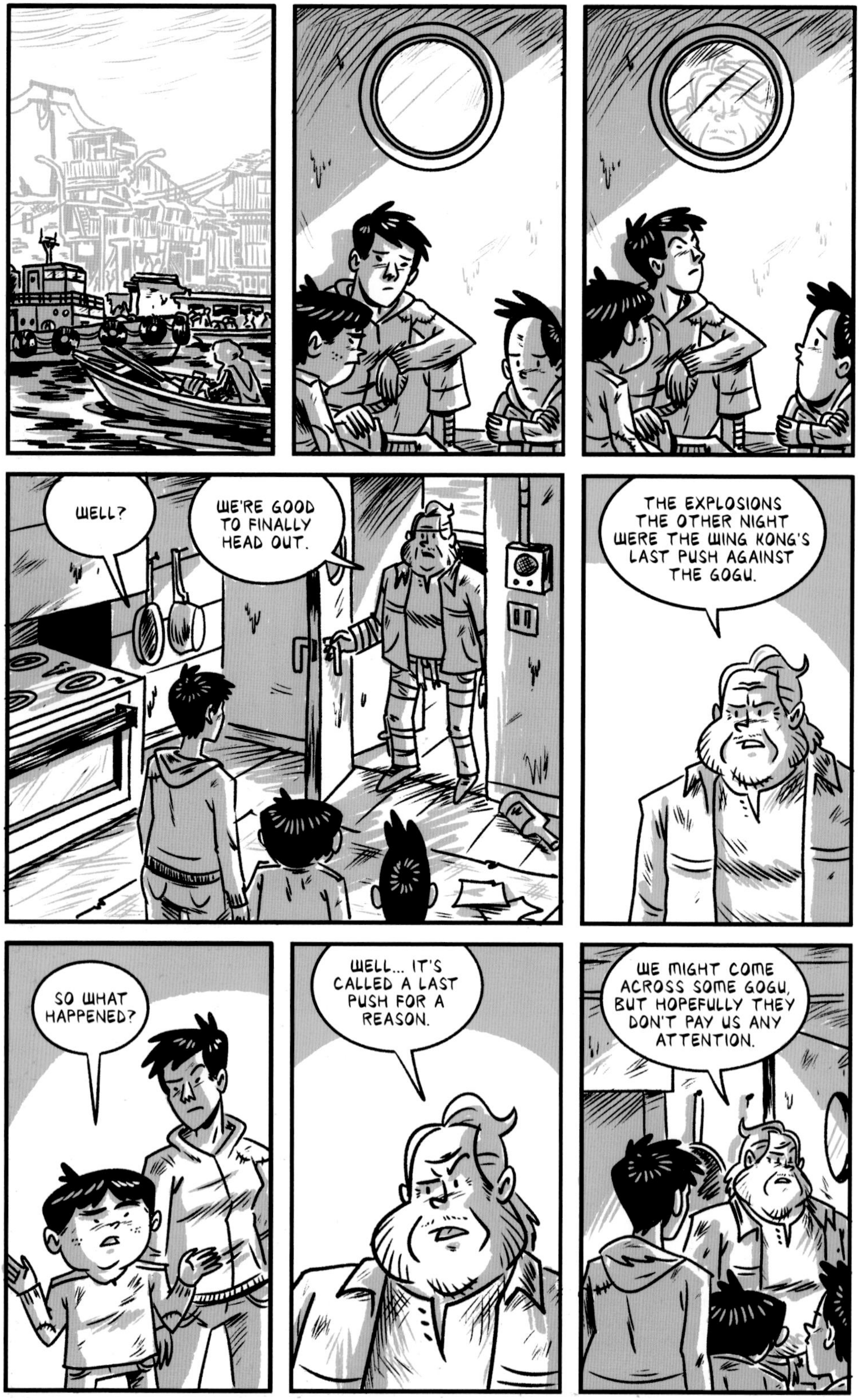
WELL?
WE'RE GOOD TO FINALLY HEAD OUT.
THE EXPLOSIONS THE OTHER NIGHT WERE THE WING KONG'S LAST PUSH AGAINST THE GOGU.
SO WHAT HAPPENED?
WELL... IT'S CALLED A LAST PUSH FOR A REASON.
WE MIGHT COME ACROSS SOME GOGU, BUT HOPEFULLY THEY DON'T PAY US ANY ATTENTION.

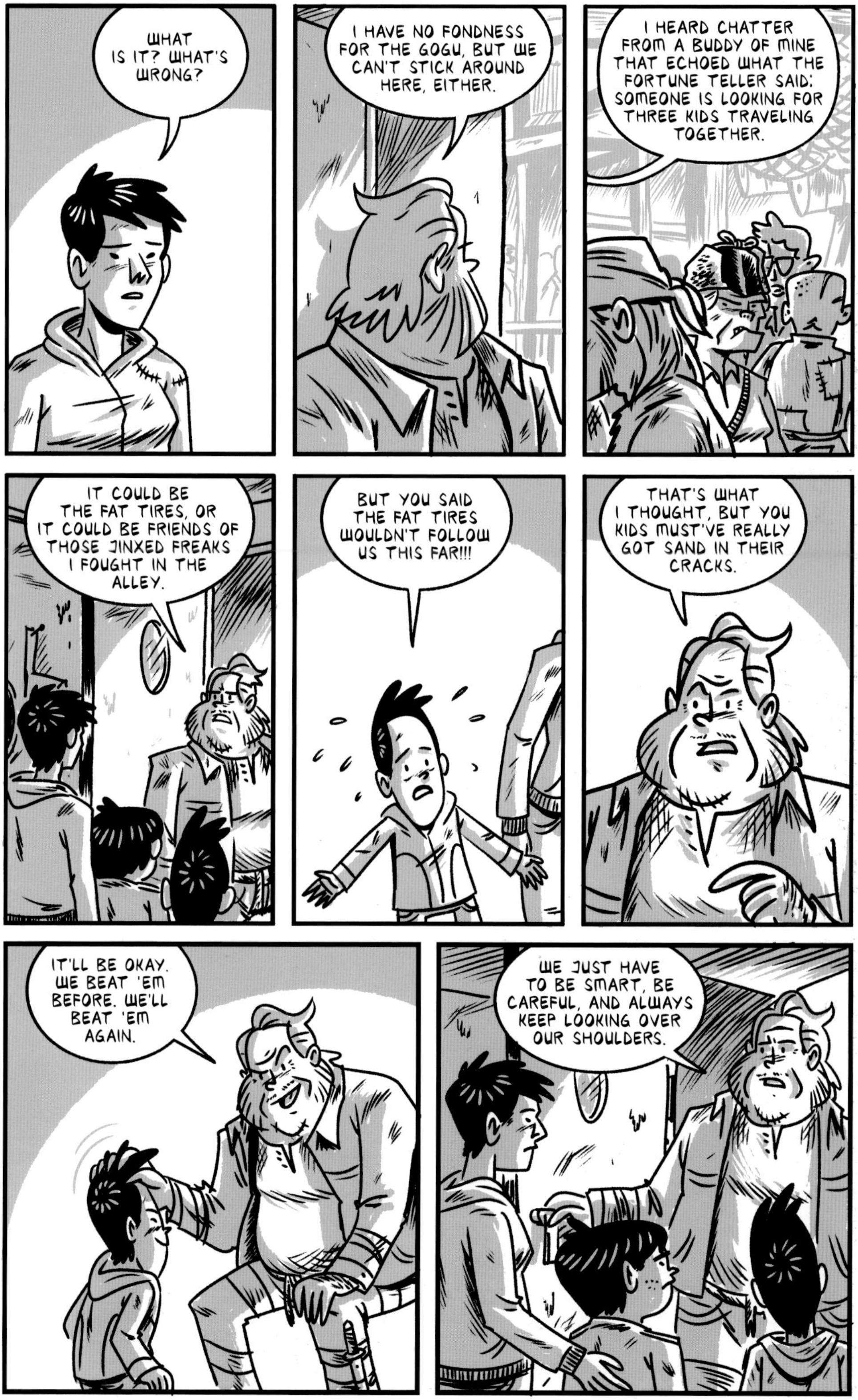
WHAT IS IT? WHAT'S WRONG?
I HAVE NO FONDNESS FOR THE GOGU, BUT WE CAN'T STICK AROUND HERE, EITHER.
I HEARD CHATTER FROM A BUDDY OF MINE THAT ECHOED WHAT THE FORTUNE TELLER SAID: SOMEONE IS LOOKING FOR THREE KIDS TRAVELING TOGETHER.
IT COULD BE THE FAT TIRES, OR IT COULD BE FRIENDS OF THOSE JINXED FREAKS I FOUGHT IN THE ALLEY.
BUT YOU SAID THE FAT TIRES WOULDN'T FOLLOW US THIS FAR!!!
THAT'S WHAT I THOUGHT, BUT YOU KIDS MUST'VE REALLY GOT SAND IN THEIR CRACKS.
IT'LL BE OKAY. WE BEAT 'EM BEFORE. WE'LL BEAT 'EM AGAIN.
WE JUST HAVE TO BE SMART, BE CAREFUL, AND ALWAYS KEEP LOOKING OVER OUR SHOULDERS.

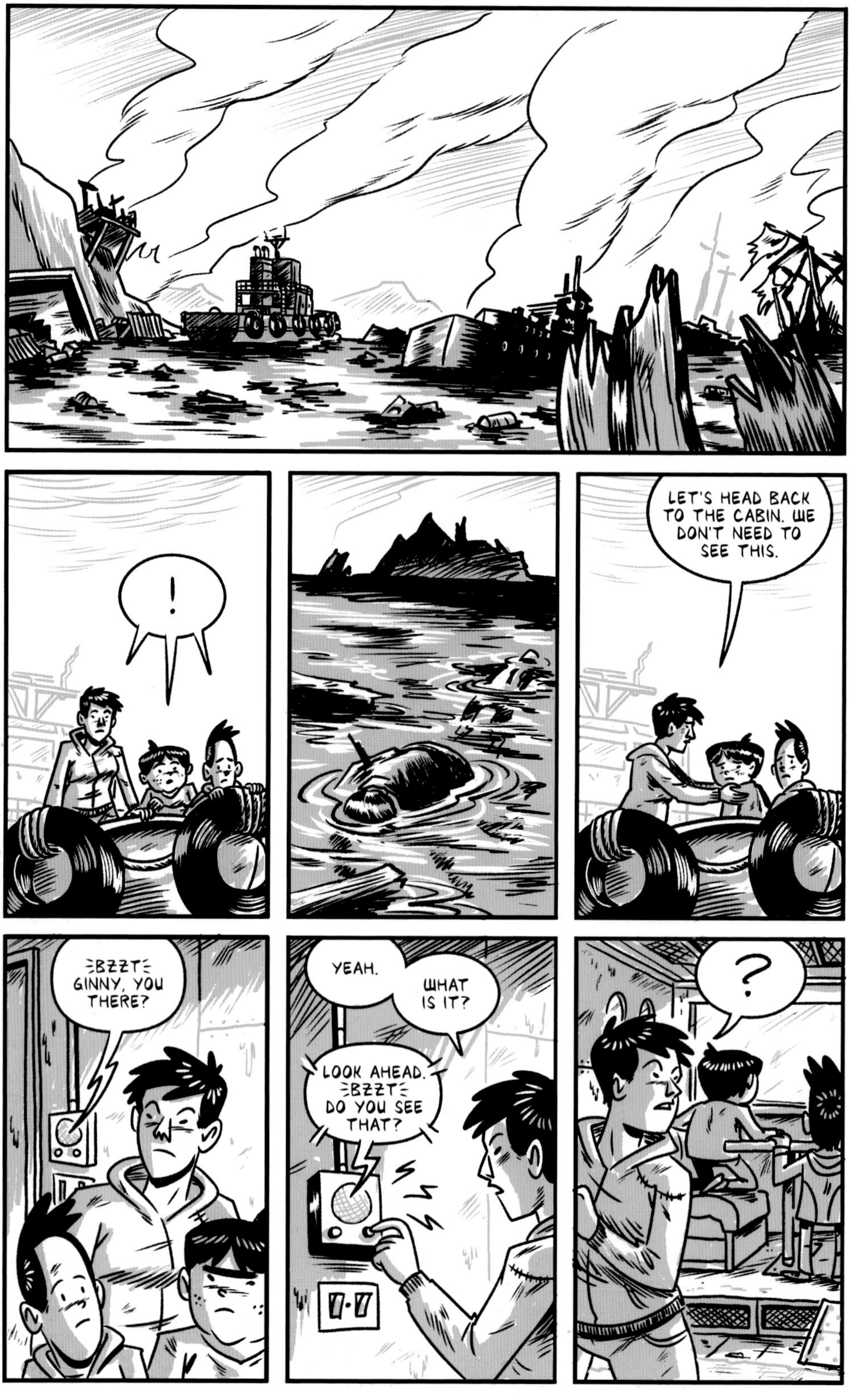
!
LET'S HEAD BACK TO THE CABIN. WE DON'T NEED TO SEE THIS.
BZZT GINNY, YOU THERE?
YEAH.
WHAT IS IT?
LOOK AHEAD. BZZT DO YOU SEE THAT?
?

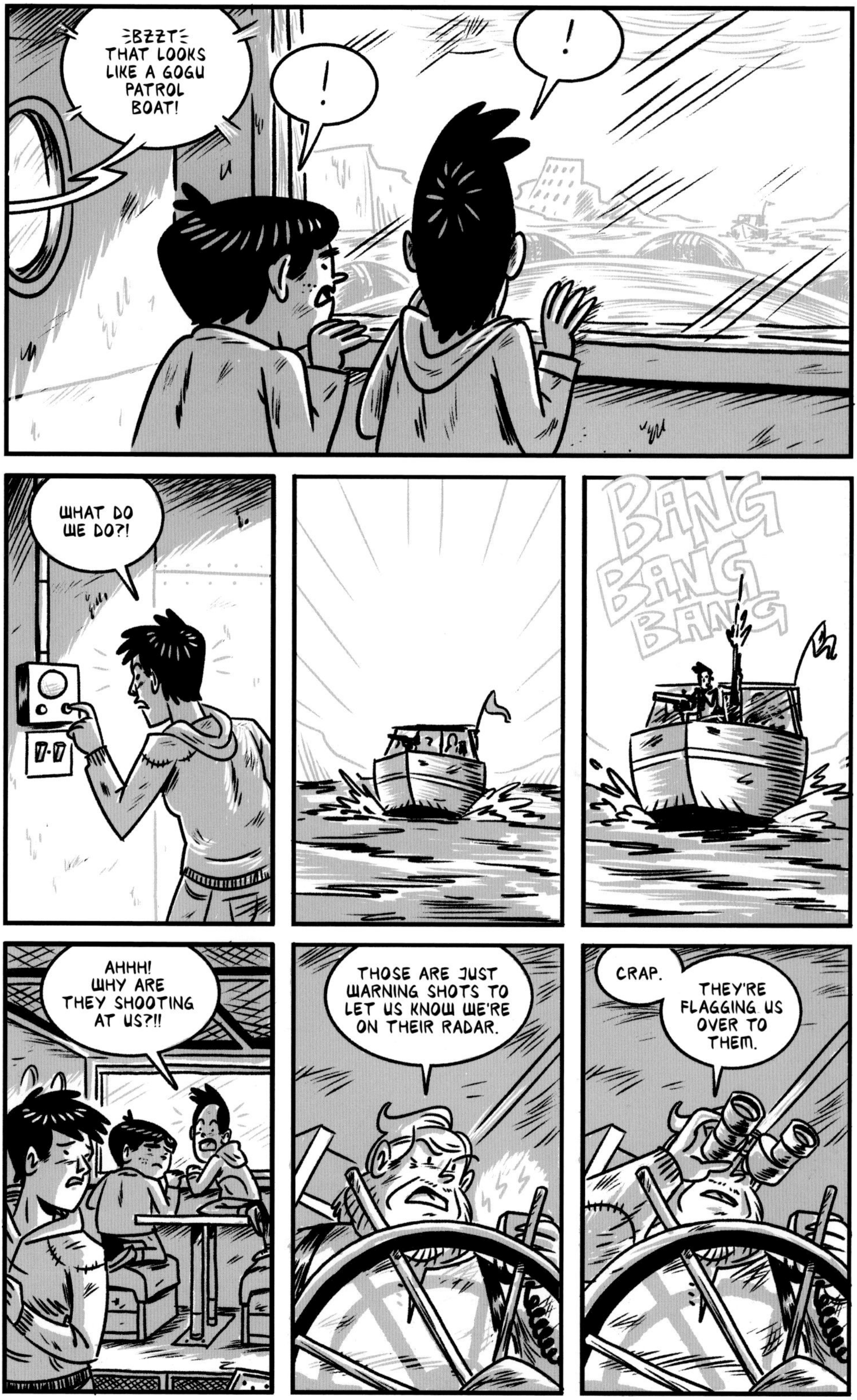

BZZT THAT LOOKS LIKE A GOGU PATROL BOAT!
!
!
WHAT DO WE DO?!
BANG
BANG
BANG
AHHH! WHY ARE THEY SHOOTING AT US?!!
THOSE ARE JUST WARNING SHOTS TO LET US KNOW WE'RE ON THEIR RADAR.
CRAP.
THEY'RE FLAGGING US OVER TO THEM.

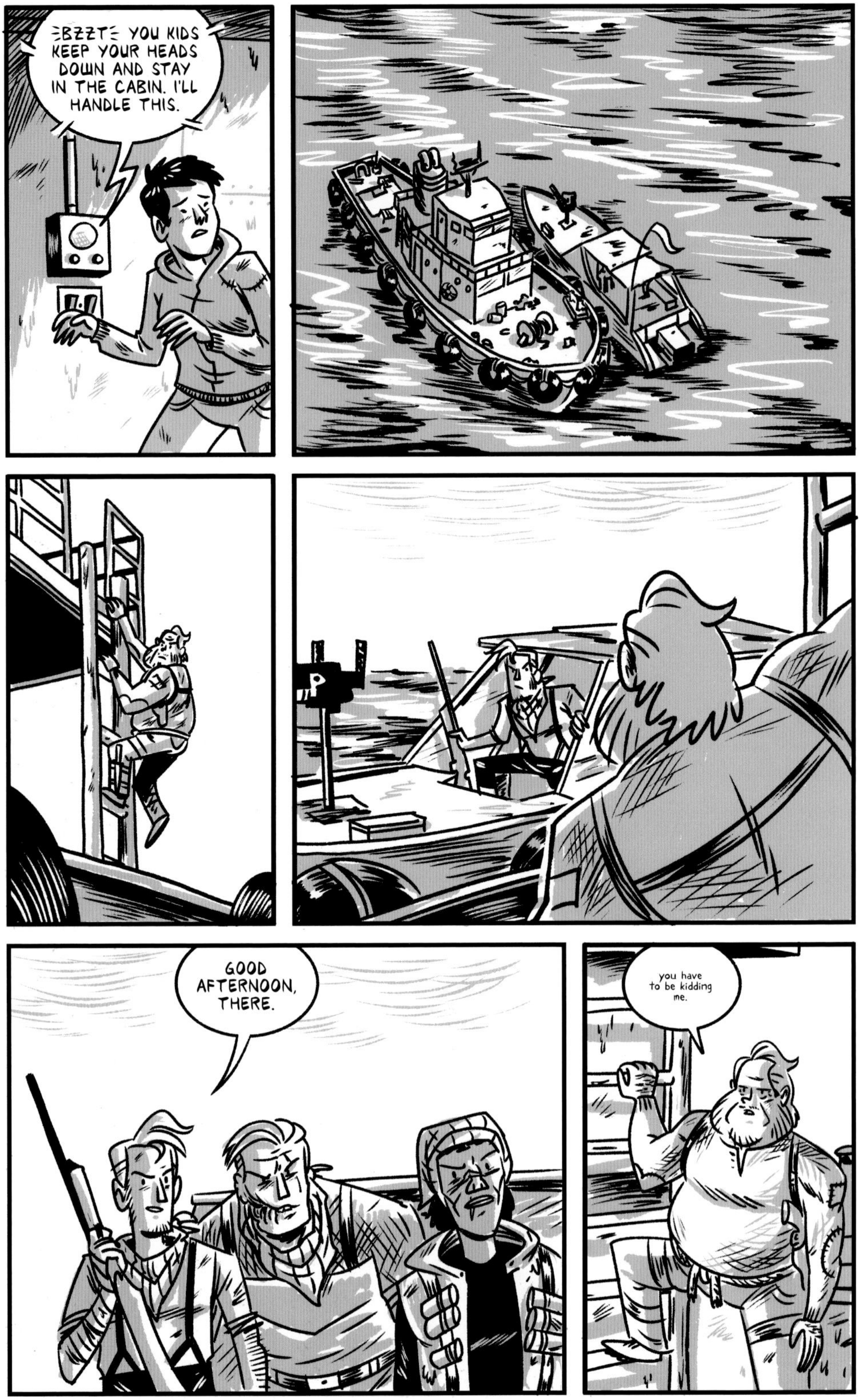
ƎBZZTƎ YOU KIDS KEEP YOUR HEADS DOWN AND STAY IN THE CABIN. I'LL HANDLE THIS.
GOOD AFTERNOON, THERE.
you have to be kidding me.

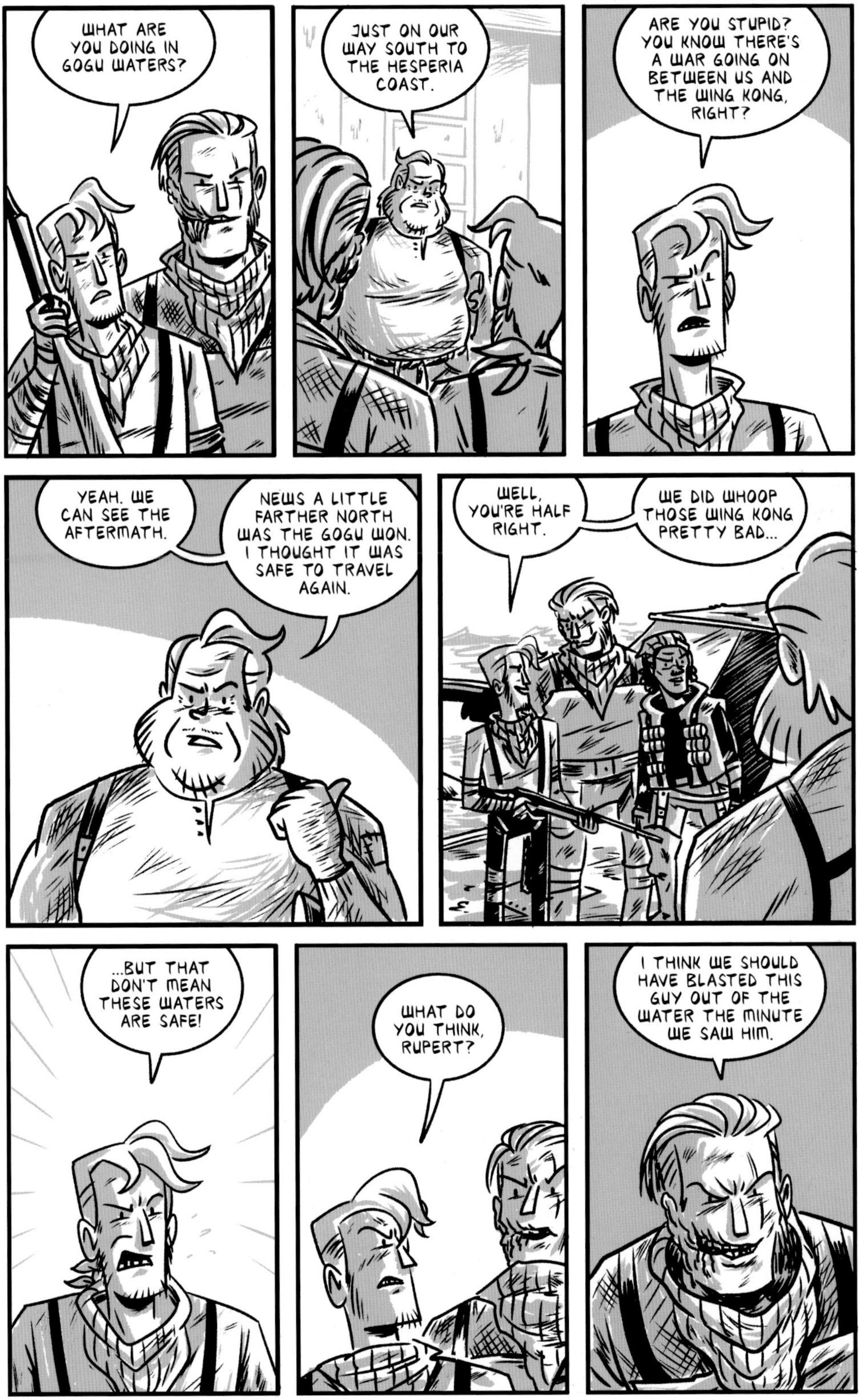
WHAT ARE YOU DOING IN GOGU WATERS?
JUST ON OUR WAY SOUTH TO THE HESPERIA COAST.
ARE YOU STUPID? YOU KNOW THERE'S A WAR GOING ON BETWEEN US AND THE WING KONG, RIGHT?
YEAH. WE CAN SEE THE AFTERMATH.
NEWS A LITTLE FARTHER NORTH WAS THE GOGU WON. I THOUGHT IT WAS SAFE TO TRAVEL AGAIN.
WELL, YOU'RE HALF RIGHT.
WE DID WHOOP THOSE WING KONG PRETTY BAD...
...BUT THAT DON'T MEAN THESE WATERS ARE SAFE!
WHAT DO YOU THINK, RUPERT?
I THINK WE SHOULD HAVE BLASTED THIS GUY OUT OF THE WATER THE MINUTE WE SAW HIM.

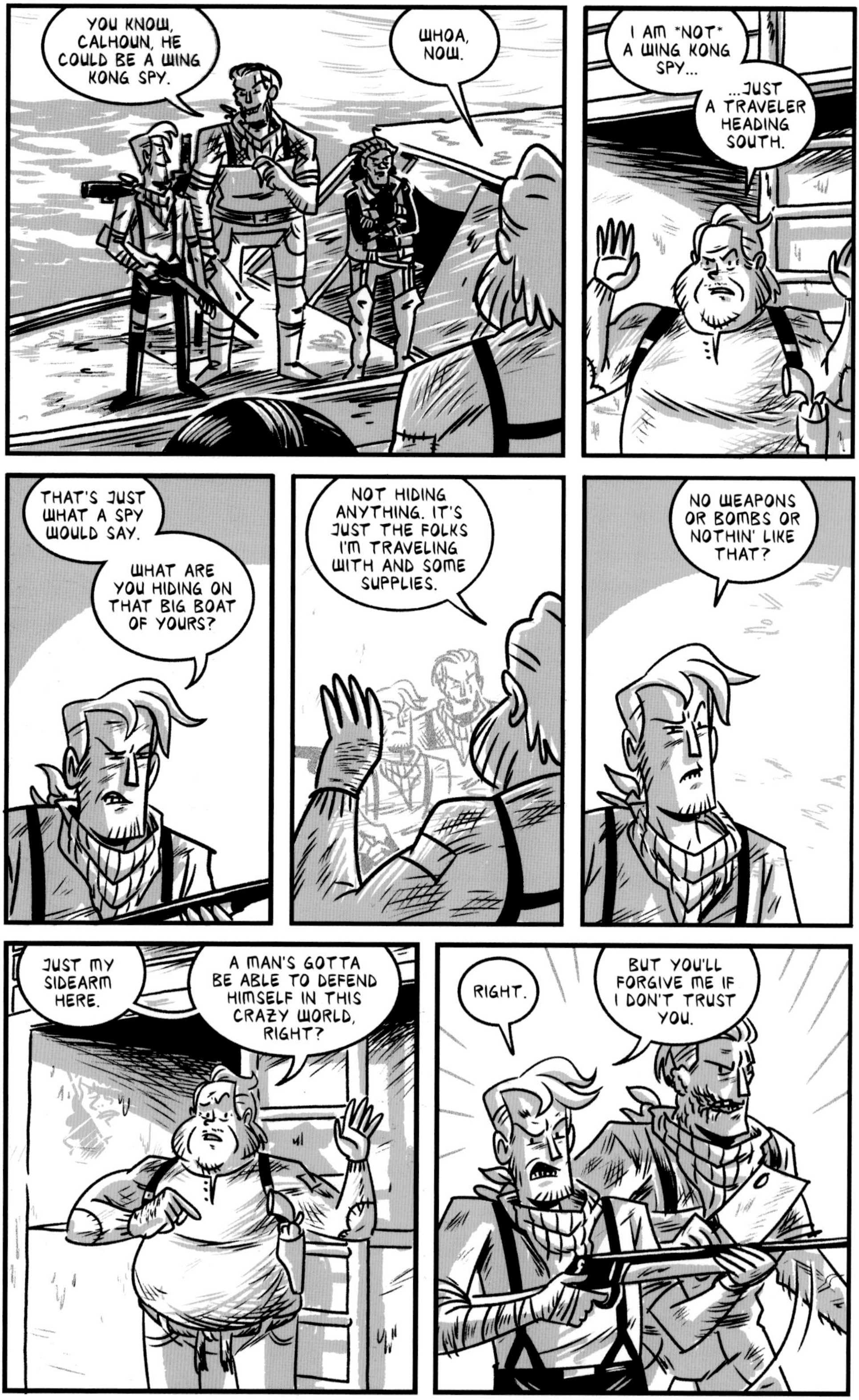
YOU KNOW, CALHOUN, HE COULD BE A WING KONG SPY.
WHOA, NOW.
I AM *NOT* A WING KONG SPY...
...JUST A TRAVELER HEADING SOUTH.
THAT'S JUST WHAT A SPY WOULD SAY.
WHAT ARE YOU HIDING ON THAT BIG BOAT OF YOURS?
NOT HIDING ANYTHING. IT'S JUST THE FOLKS I'M TRAVELING WITH AND SOME SUPPLIES.
NO WEAPONS OR BOMBS OR NOTHIN' LIKE THAT?
JUST MY SIDEARM HERE.
A MAN'S GOTTA BE ABLE TO DEFEND HIMSELF IN THIS CRAZY WORLD, RIGHT?
RIGHT.
BUT YOU'LL FORGIVE ME IF I DON'T TRUST YOU.

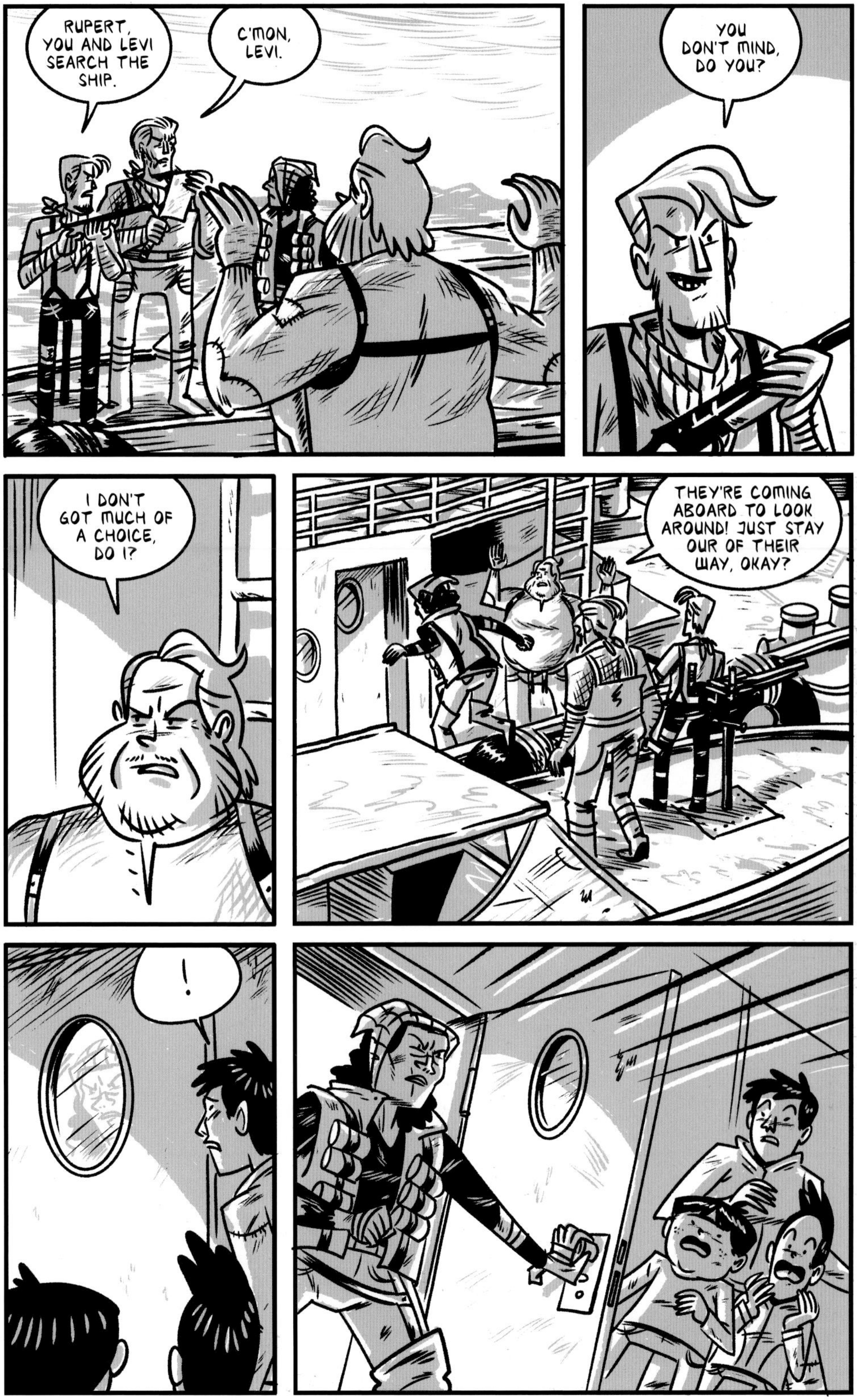
RUPERT, YOU AND LEVI SEARCH THE SHIP.
C'MON, LEVI.
YOU DON'T MIND, DO YOU?
I DON'T GOT MUCH OF A CHOICE, DO I?
THEY'RE COMING ABOARD TO LOOK AROUND! JUST STAY OUR OF THEIR WAY, OKAY?
!

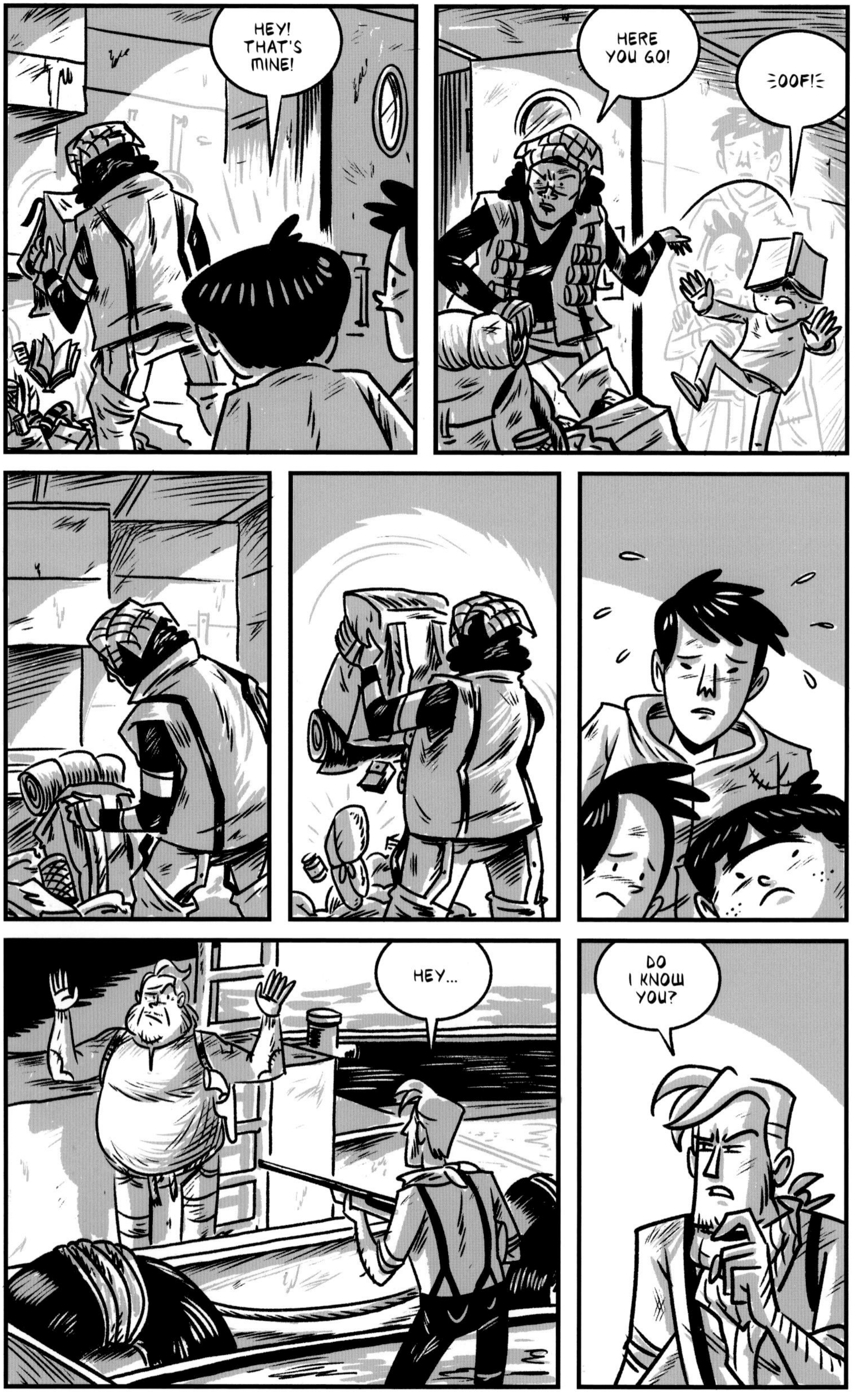
HEY! THAT'S MINE!
HERE YOU GO!
OOF!
HEY...
DO I KNOW YOU?

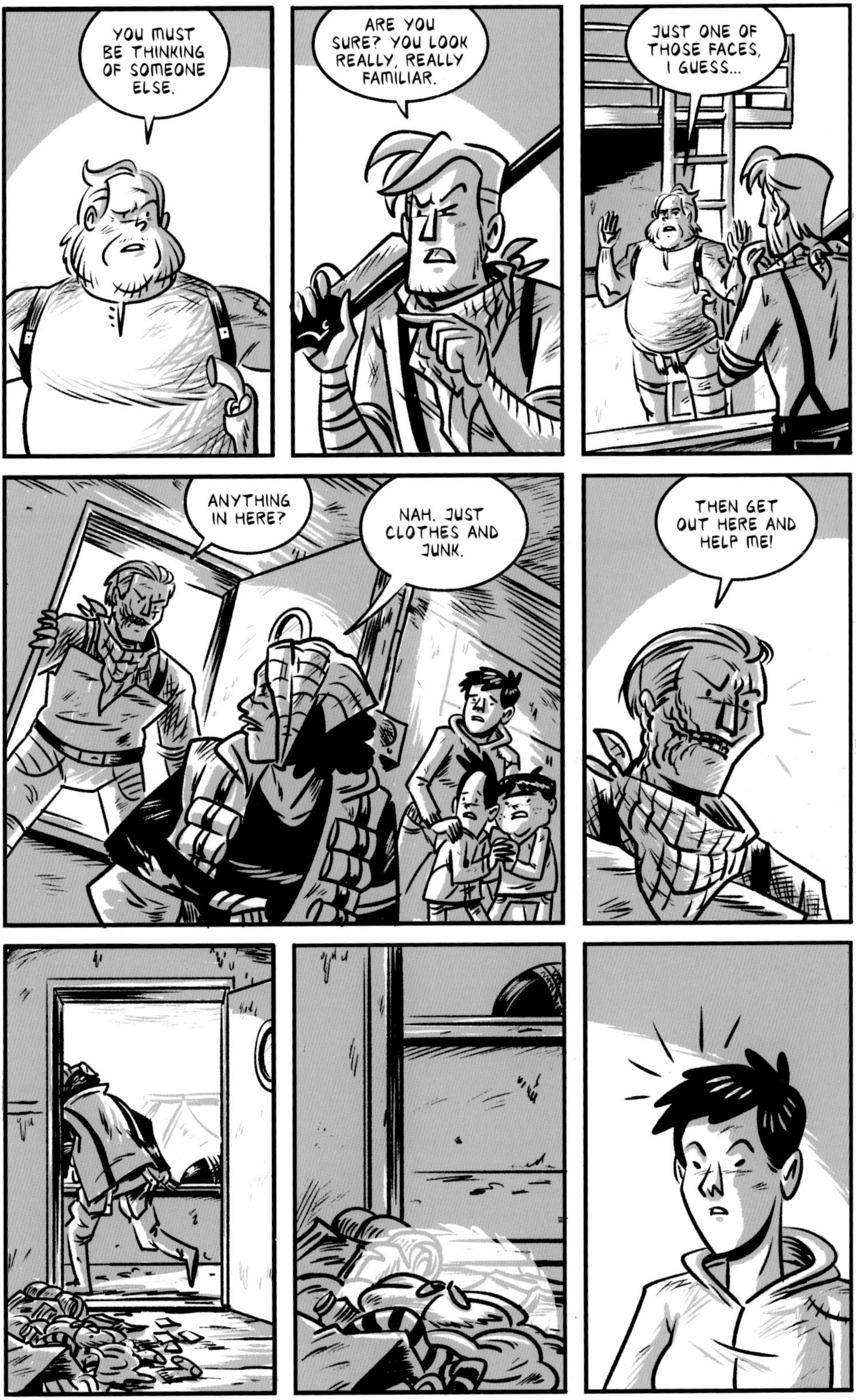
YOU MUST BE THINKING OF SOMEONE ELSE.
ARE YOU SURE? YOU LOOK REALLY, REALLY FAMILIAR.
JUST ONE OF THOSE FACES, I GUESS...
ANYTHING IN HERE?
NAH. JUST CLOTHES AND JUNK.
THEN GET OUT HERE AND HELP ME!

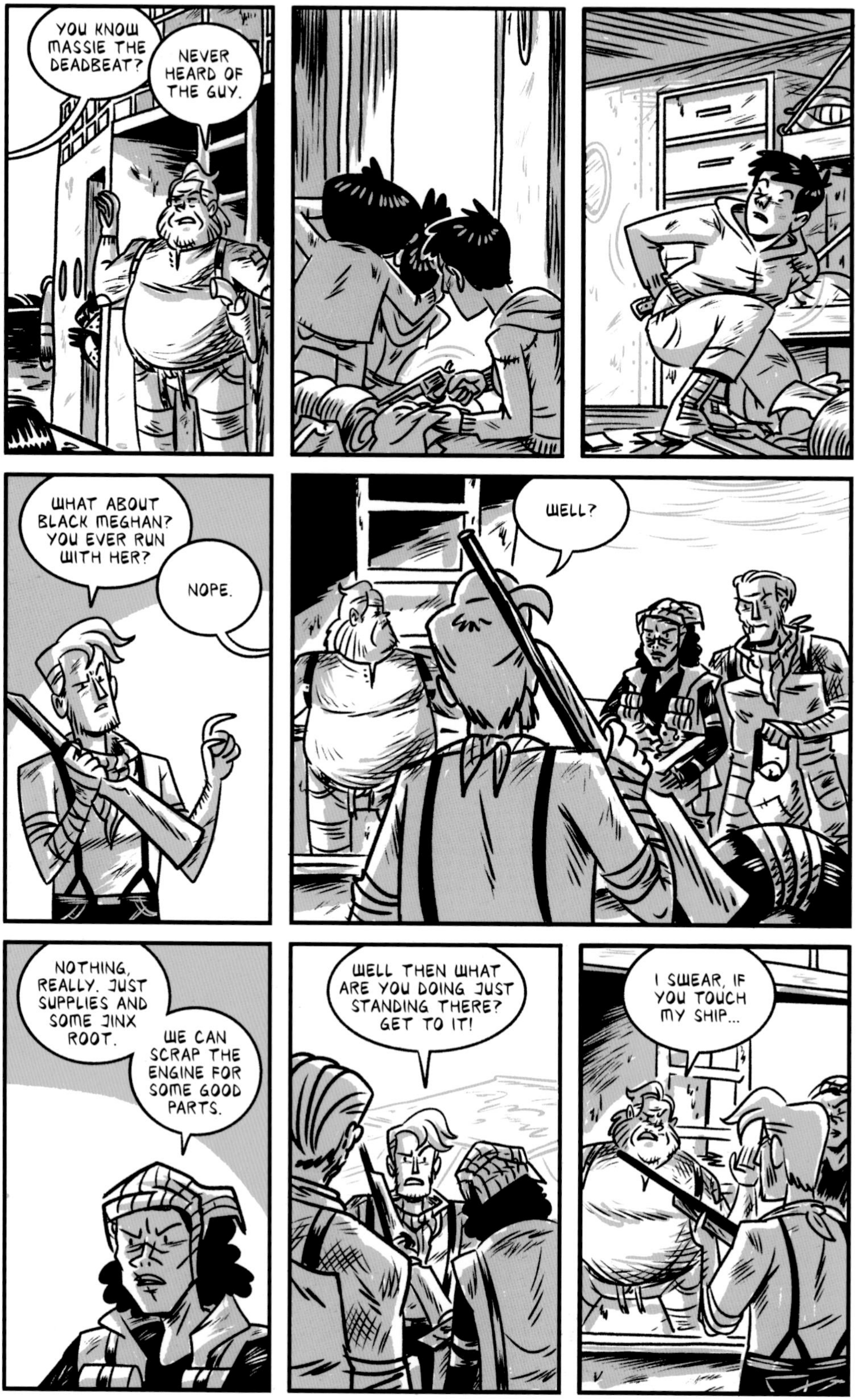
YOU KNOW MASSIE THE DEADBEAT?
NEVER HEARD OF THE GUY.
WHAT ABOUT BLACK MEGHAN? YOU EVER RUN WITH HER?
NOPE.
WELL?
NOTHING, REALLY. JUST SUPPLIES AND SOME JINX ROOT.
WE CAN SCRAP THE ENGINE FOR SOME GOOD PARTS.
WELL THEN WHAT ARE YOU DOING JUST STANDING THERE? GET TO IT!
I SWEAR, IF YOU TOUCH MY SHIP...

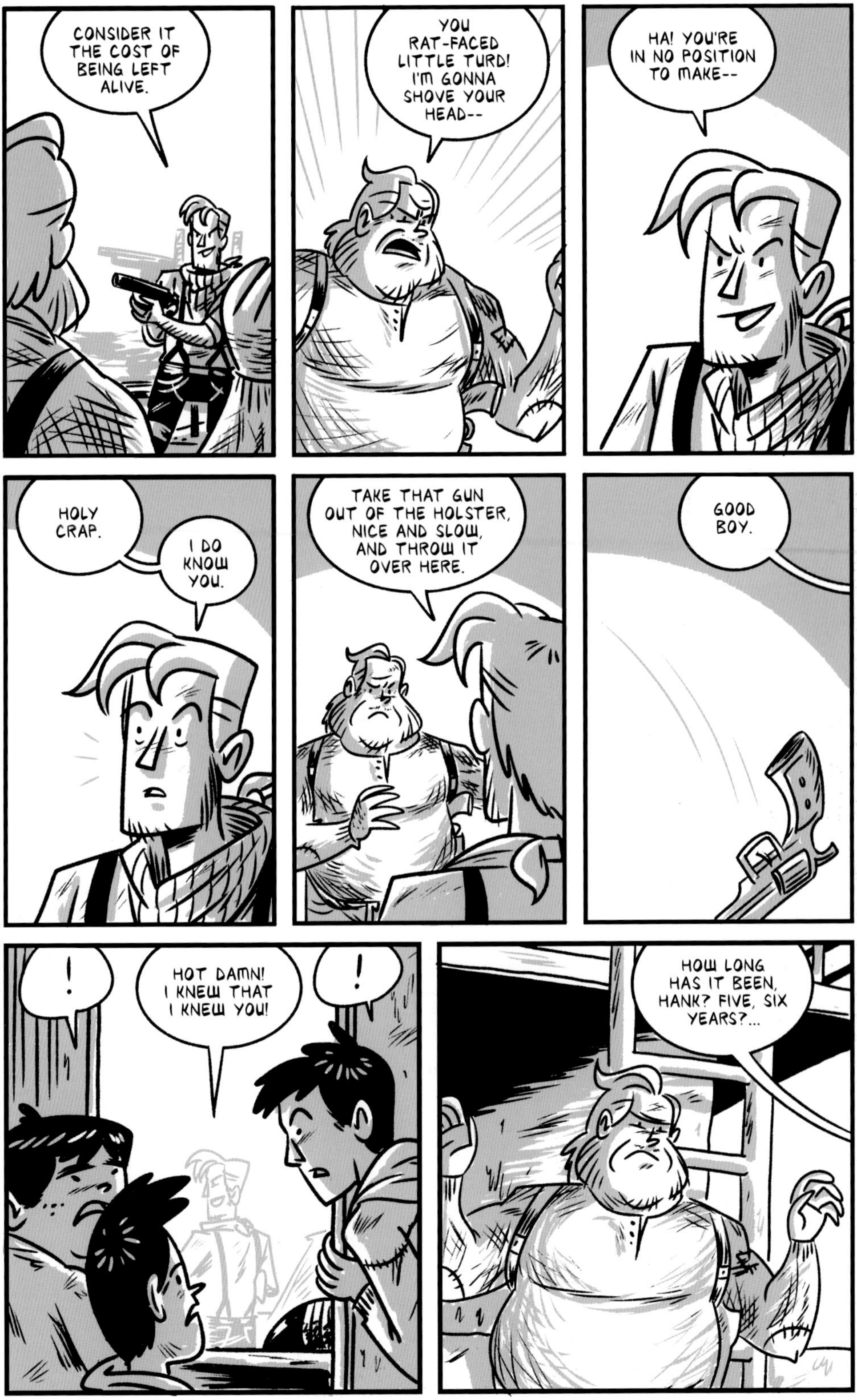
CONSIDER IT THE COST OF BEING LEFT ALIVE.
YOU RAT-FACED LITTLE TURD! I'M GONNA SHOVE YOUR HEAD--
HA! YOU'RE IN NO POSITION TO MAKE--
HOLY CRAP.
I DO KNOW YOU.
TAKE THAT GUN OUT OF THE HOLSTER, NICE AND SLOW, AND THROW IT OVER HERE.
GOOD BOY.
!
HOT DAMN! I KNEW THAT I KNEW YOU!
!
HOW LONG HAS IT BEEN, HANK? FIVE, SIX YEARS?...

CHAPTER 9

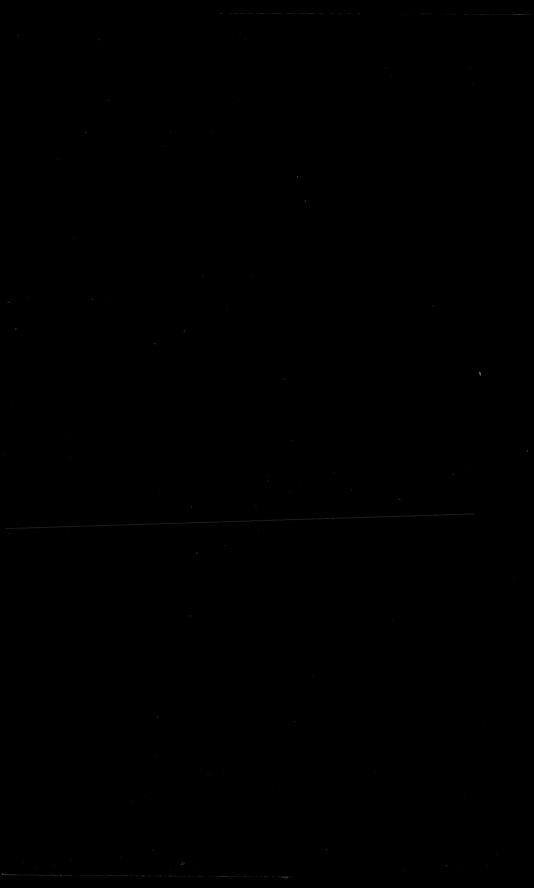

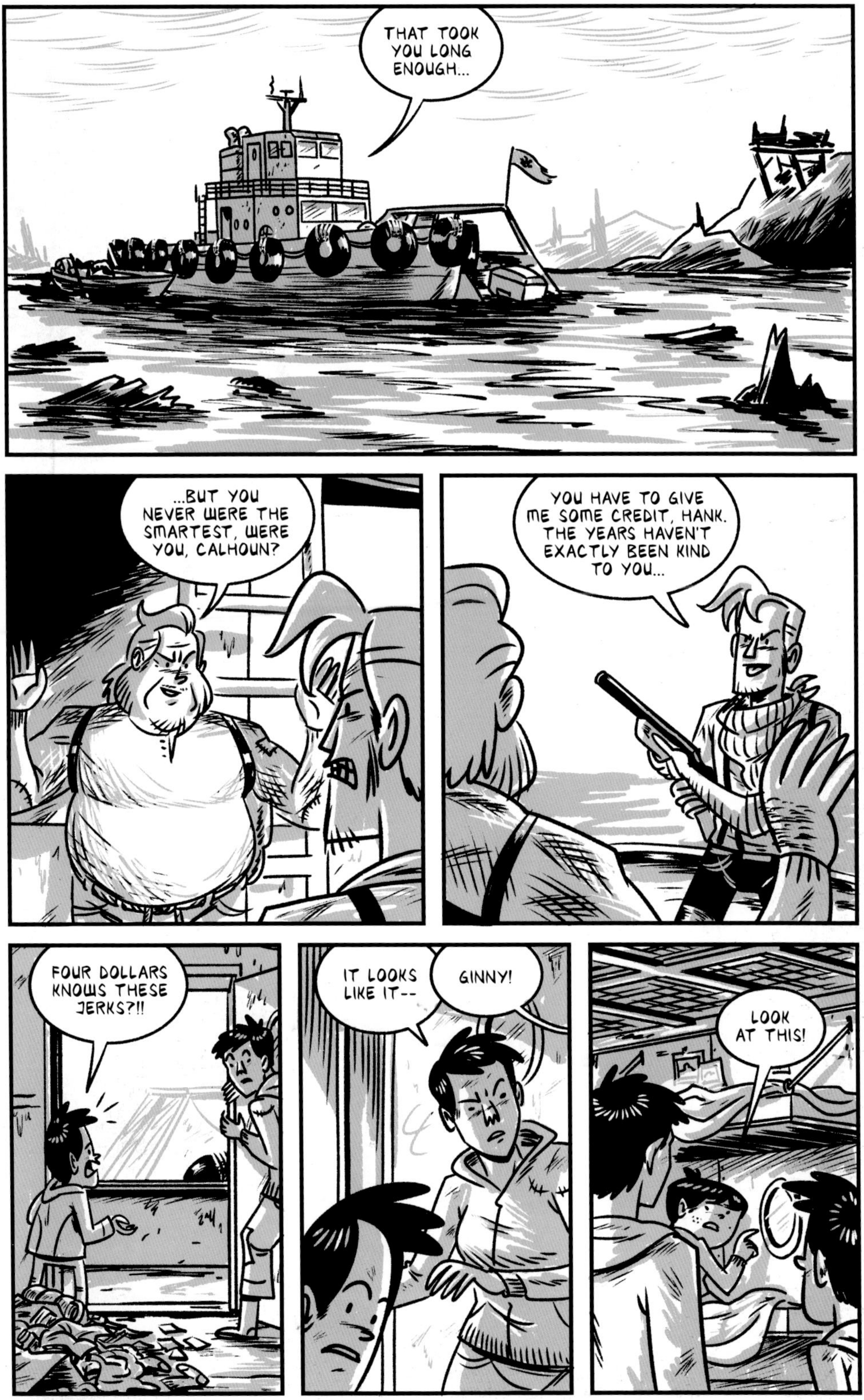
THAT TOOK YOU LONG ENOUGH...
...BUT YOU NEVER WERE THE SMARTEST, WERE YOU, CALHOUN?
YOU HAVE TO GIVE ME SOME CREDIT, HANK. THE YEARS HAVEN'T EXACTLY BEEN KIND TO YOU...
FOUR DOLLARS KNOWS THESE JERKS?!!
IT LOOKS LIKE IT--
GINNY!
LOOK AT THIS!

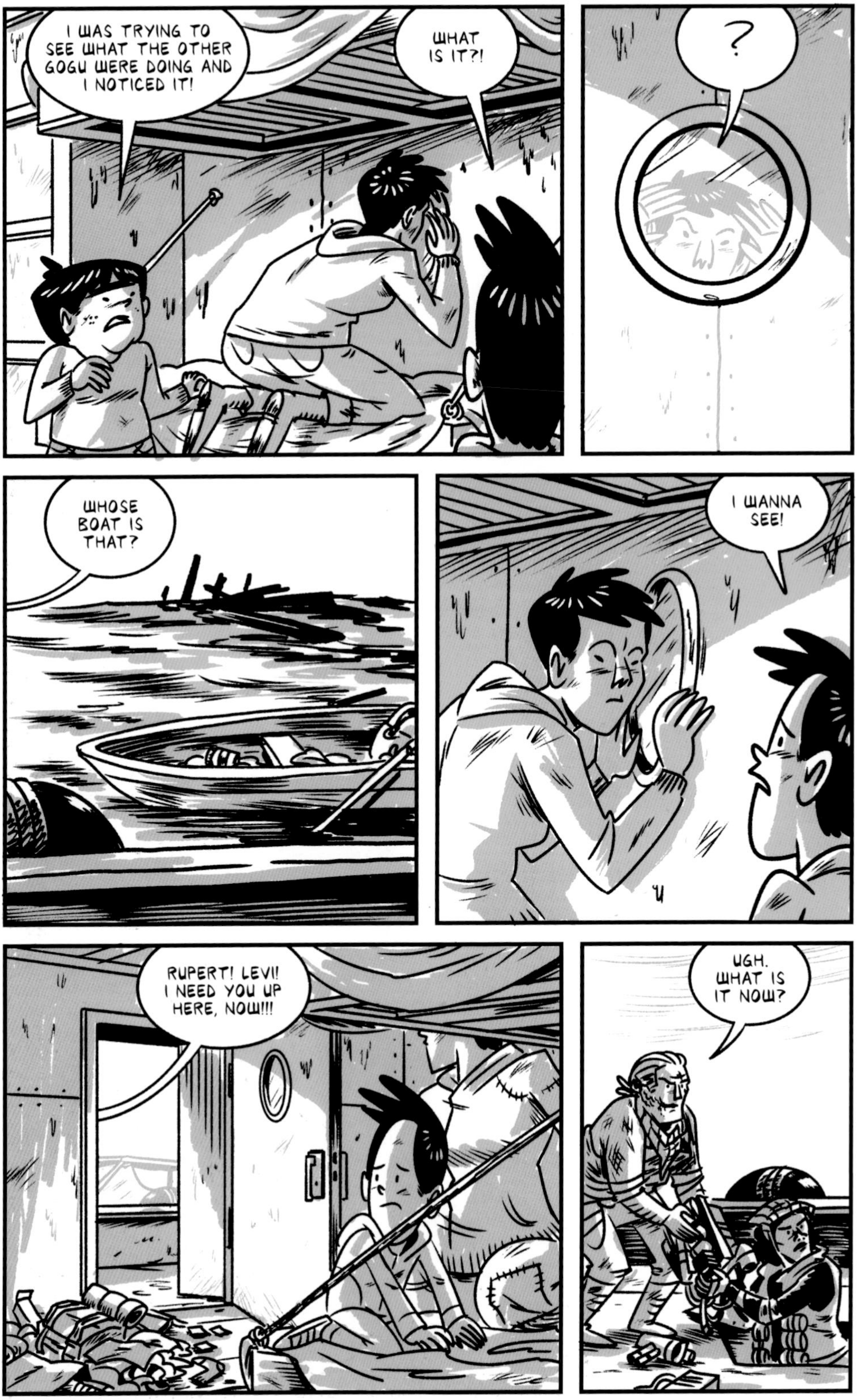
I WAS TRYING TO SEE WHAT THE OTHER GOGU WERE DOING AND I NOTICED IT!
WHAT IS IT?!
?
WHOSE BOAT IS THAT?
I WANNA SEE!
RUPERT! LEVI! I NEED YOU UP HERE, NOW!!!
UGH. WHAT IS IT NOW?

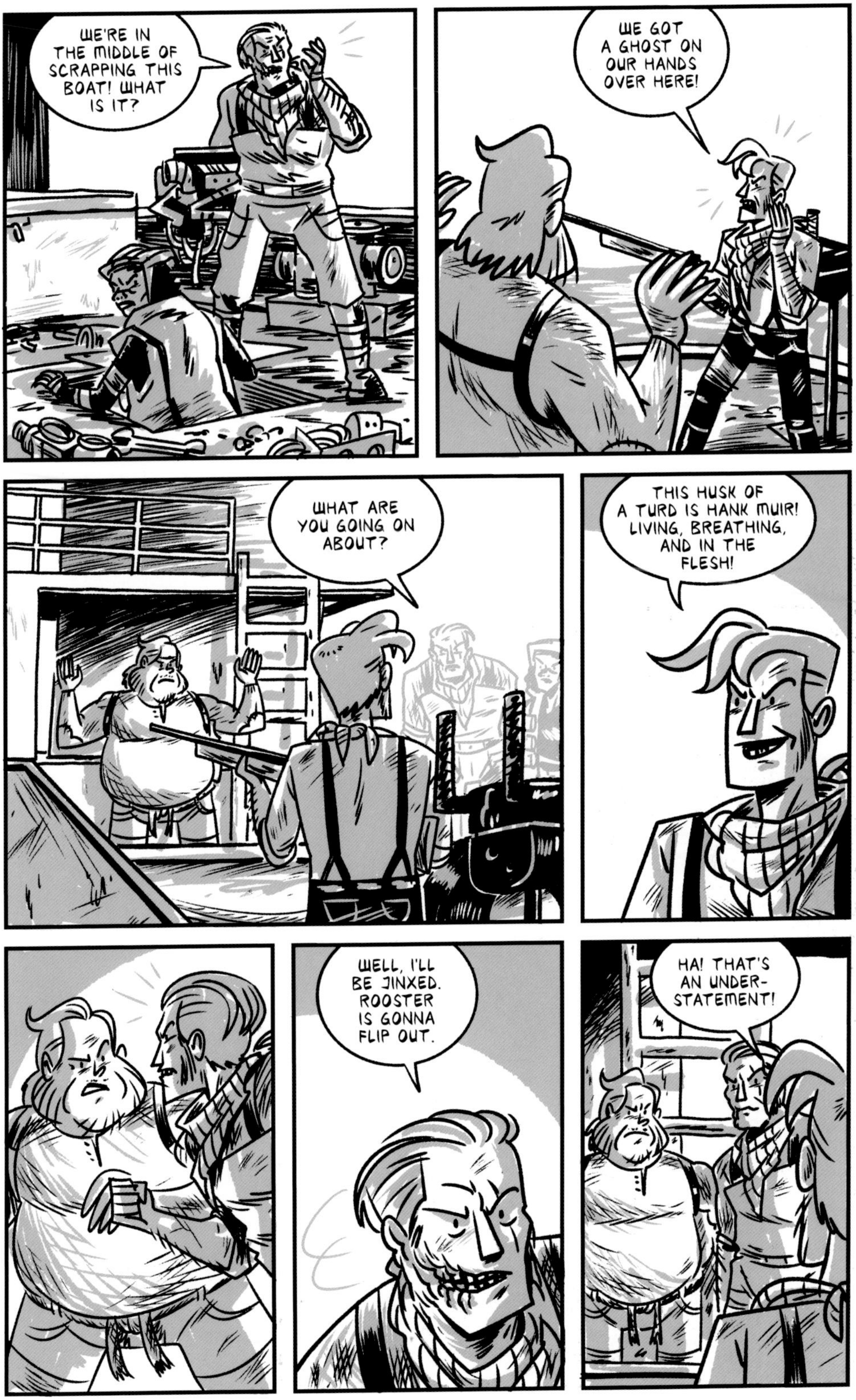
WE'RE IN THE MIDDLE OF SCRAPPING THIS BOAT! WHAT IS IT?
WE GOT A GHOST ON OUR HANDS OVER HERE!
WHAT ARE YOU GOING ON ABOUT?
THIS HUSK OF A TURD IS HANK MUIR! LIVING, BREATHING, AND IN THE FLESH!
WELL, I'LL BE JINXED. ROOSTER IS GONNA FLIP OUT.
HA! THAT'S AN UNDER-STATEMENT!

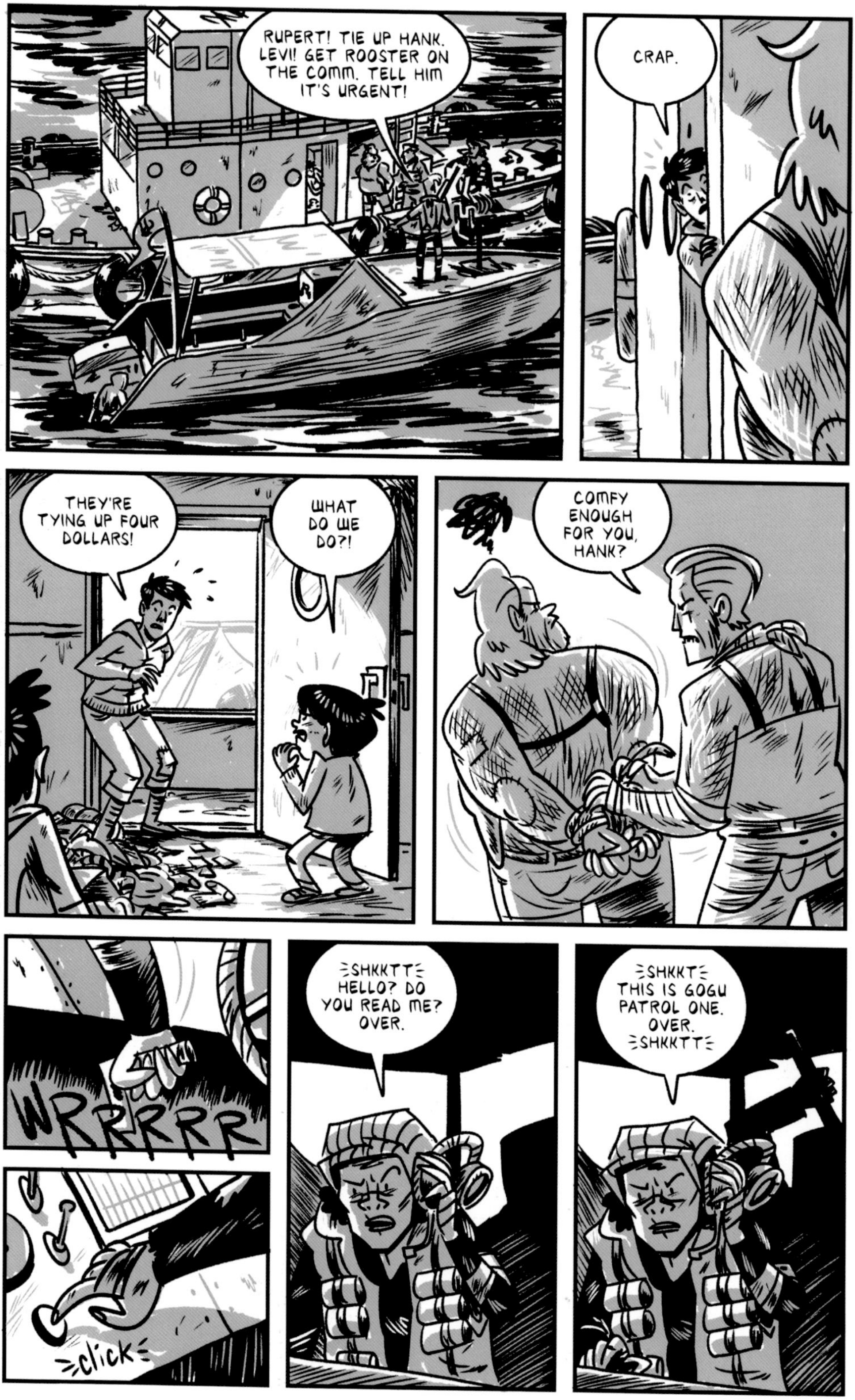
RUPERT! TIE UP HANK. LEVI! GET ROOSTER ON THE COMM. TELL HIM IT'S URGENT!
CRAP.
THEY'RE TYING UP FOUR DOLLARS!
WHAT DO WE DO?!
COMFY ENOUGH FOR YOU, HANK?
WRRRRRR
CLICK
SHKKTT HELLO? DO YOU READ ME? OVER.
SHKKT THIS IS GOGU PATROL ONE. OVER. SHKKTT

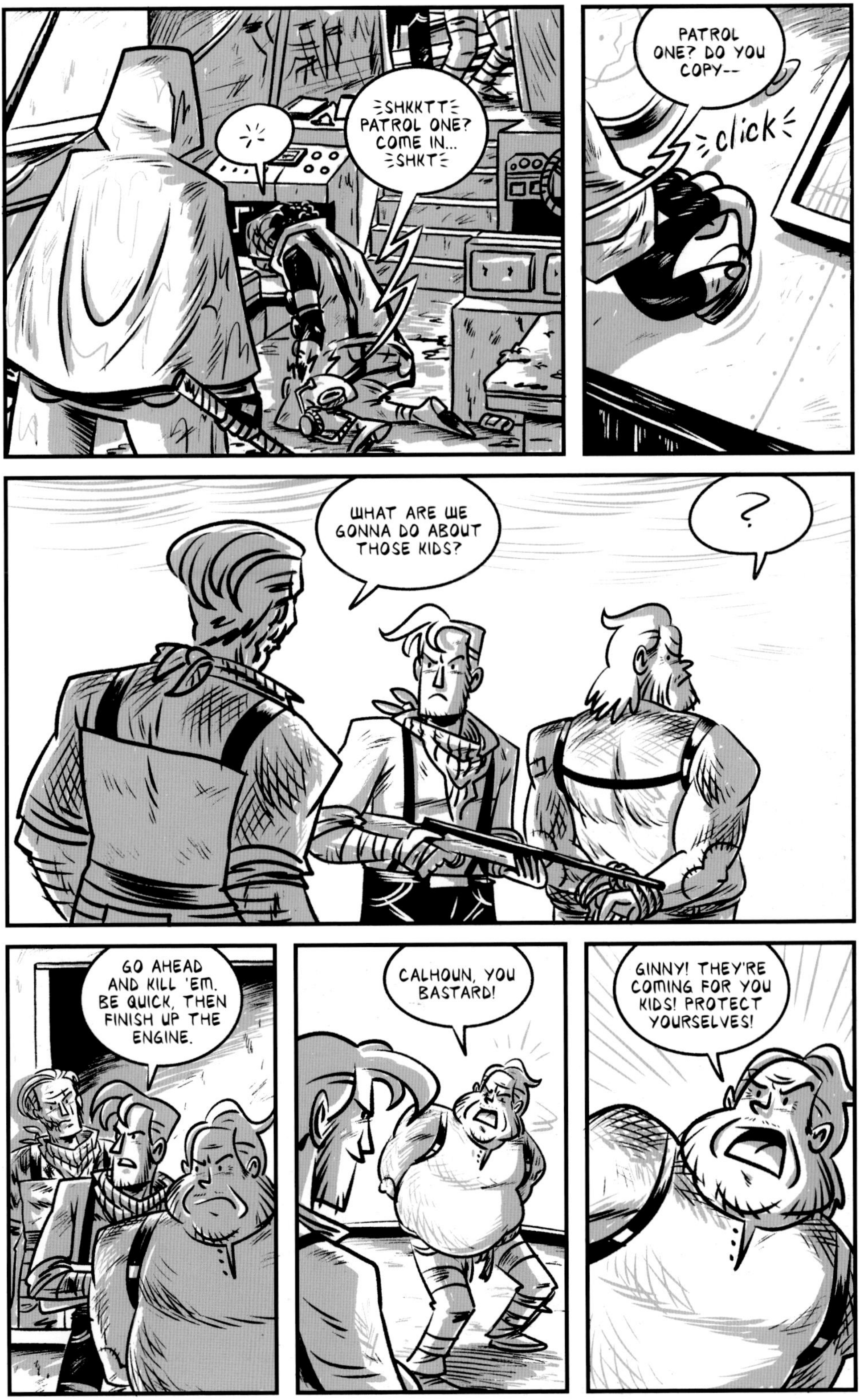

=SHKKTT=
PATROL ONE? COME IN... =SHKT=
PATROL ONE? DO YOU COPY--
click
WHAT ARE WE GONNA DO ABOUT THOSE KIDS?
?
GO AHEAD AND KILL 'EM. BE QUICK, THEN FINISH UP THE ENGINE.
CALHOUN, YOU BASTARD!
GINNY! THEY'RE COMING FOR YOU KIDS! PROTECT YOURSELVES!

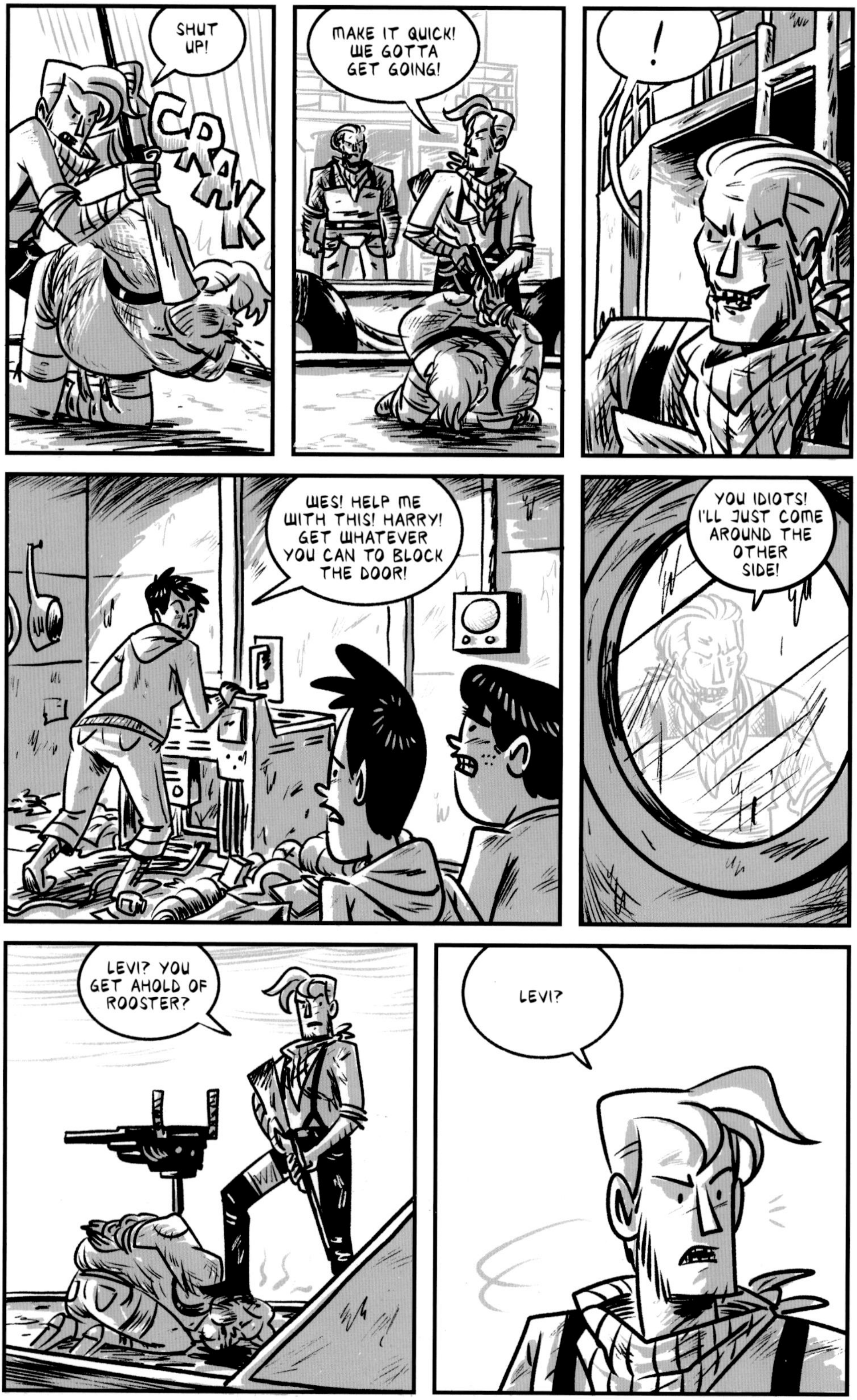
SHUT UP!
CRAAAK
MAKE IT QUICK! WE GOTTA GET GOING!
!
WES! HELP ME WITH THIS! HARRY! GET WHATEVER YOU CAN TO BLOCK THE DOOR!
YOU IDIOTS! I'LL JUST COME AROUND THE OTHER SIDE!
LEVI? YOU GET AHOLD OF ROOSTER?
LEVI?

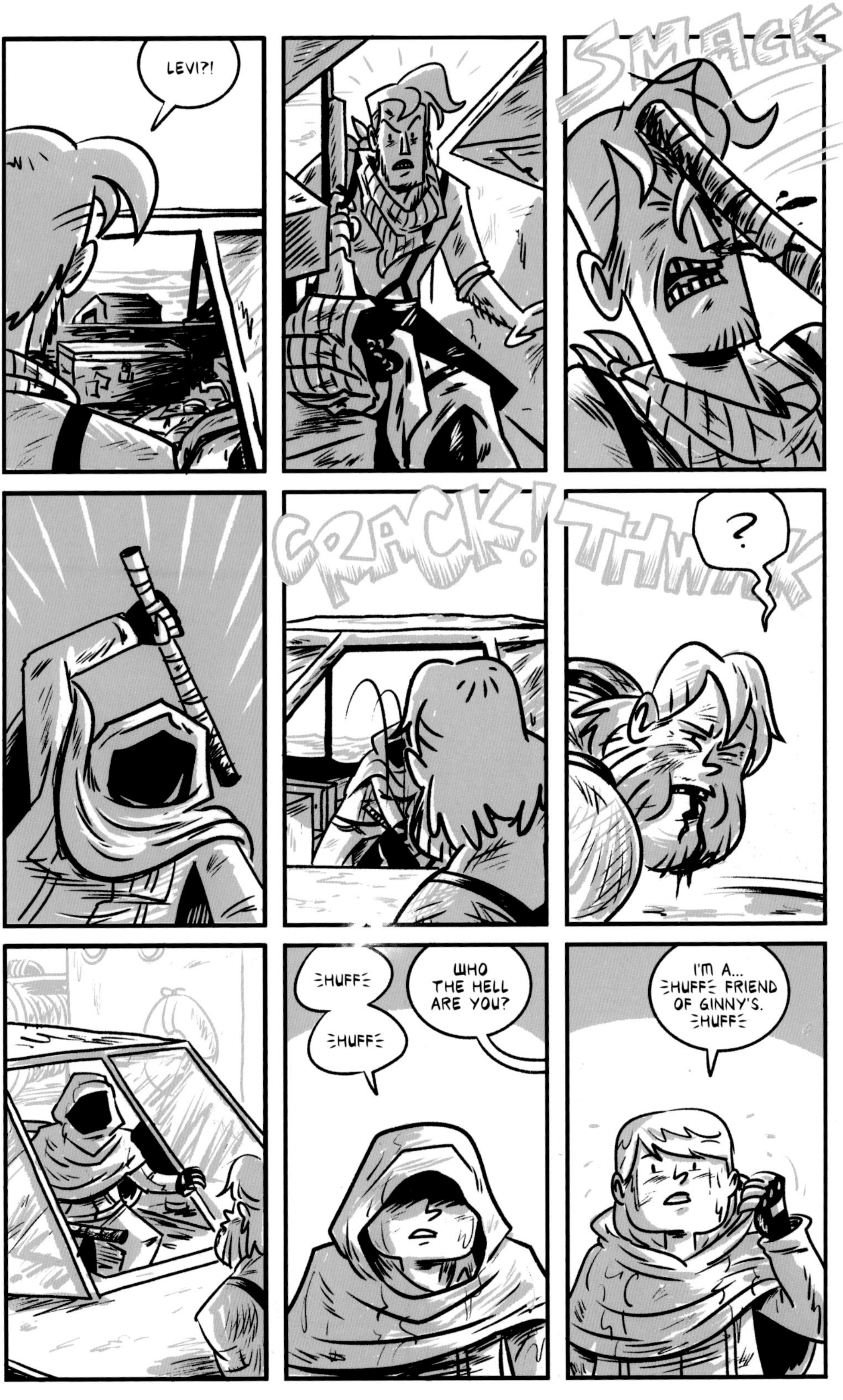
LEVI?!
SMACK
CRACK!
THWACK
?
HUFF
HUFF
WHO THE HELL ARE YOU?
I'M A... HUFF FRIEND OF GINNY'S. HUFF

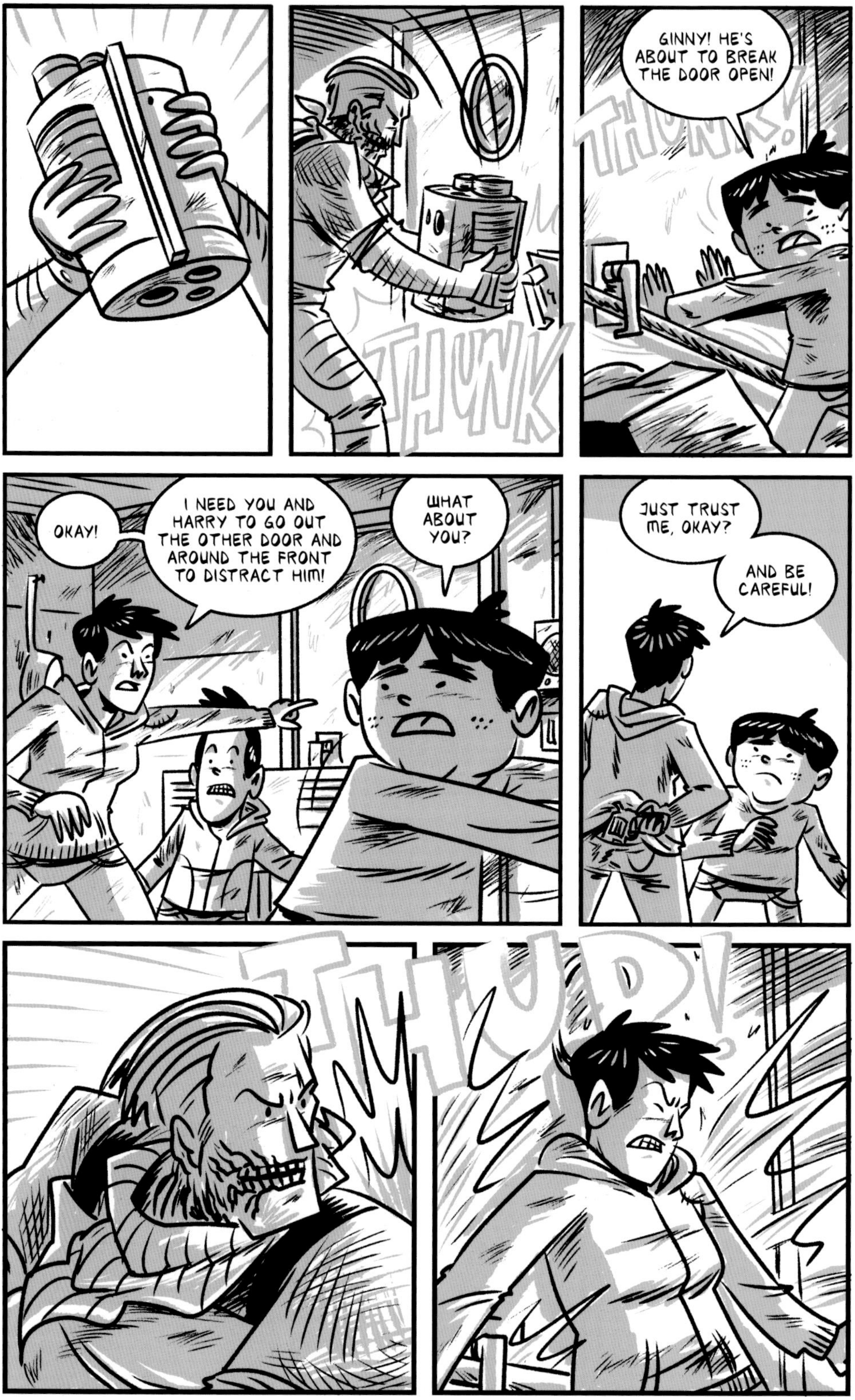
THUNK
GINNY! HE'S ABOUT TO BREAK THE DOOR OPEN!
THUNK!
OKAY!
I NEED YOU AND HARRY TO GO OUT THE OTHER DOOR AND AROUND THE FRONT TO DISTRACT HIM!
WHAT ABOUT YOU?
JUST TRUST ME, OKAY?
AND BE CAREFUL!
THUD!

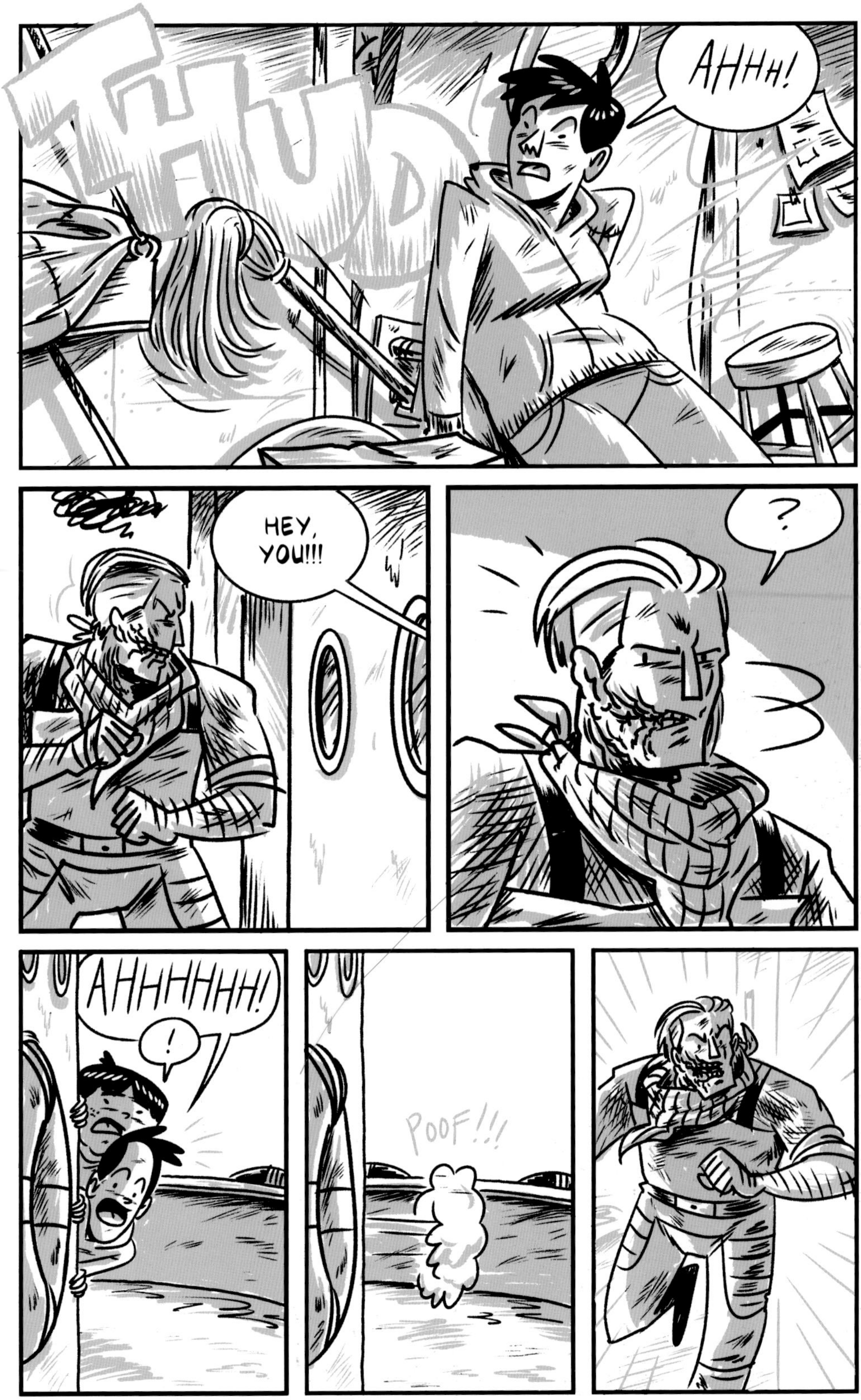
THUD
AHHH!
HEY, YOU!!!
?
AHHHHHH!
!
POOF!!!

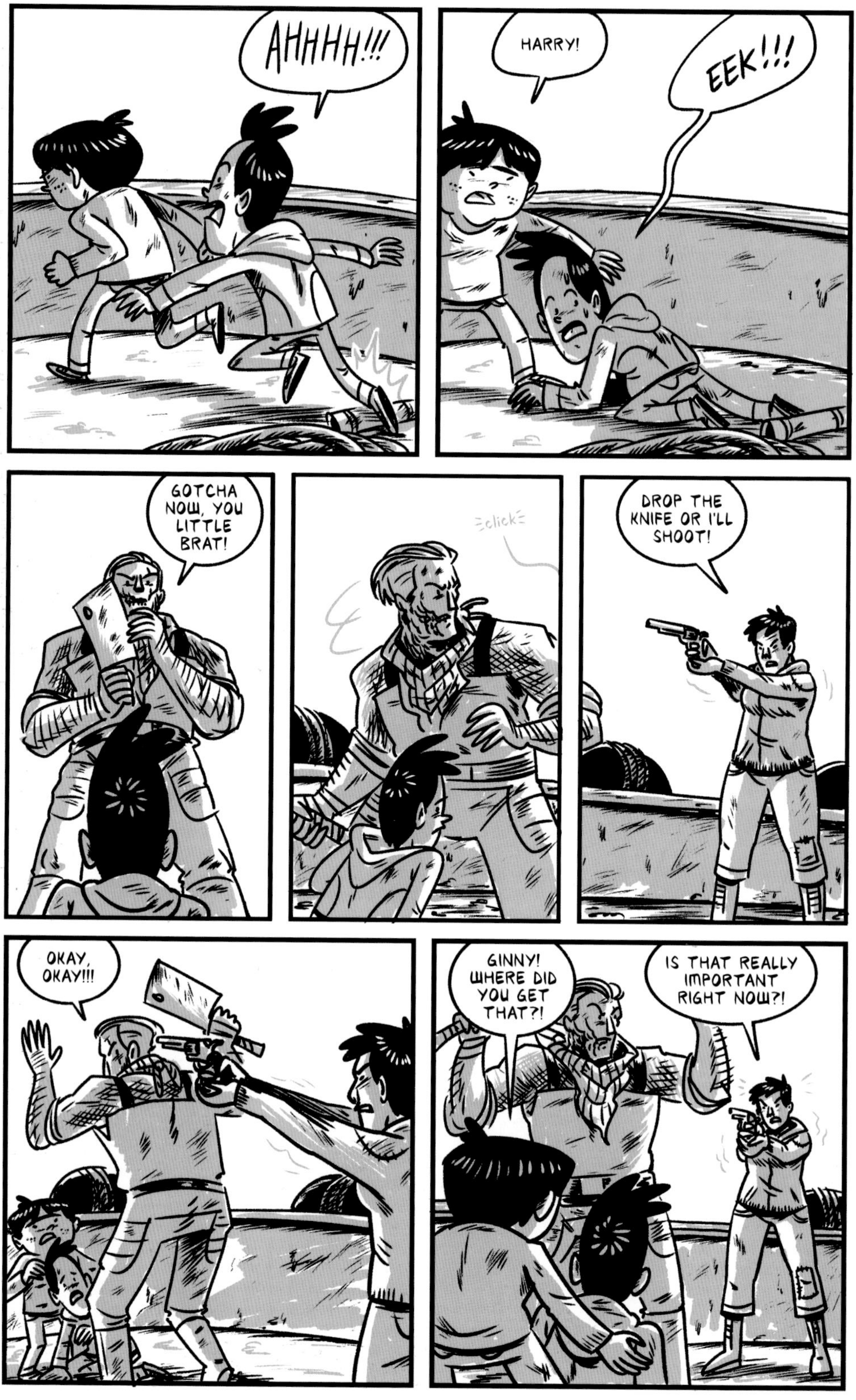
AHHHH!!!
HARRY!
EEK!!!
GOTCHA NOW, YOU LITTLE BRAT!
click
DROP THE KNIFE OR I'LL SHOOT!
OKAY, OKAY!!!
GINNY! WHERE DID YOU GET THAT?!
IS THAT REALLY IMPORTANT RIGHT NOW?!

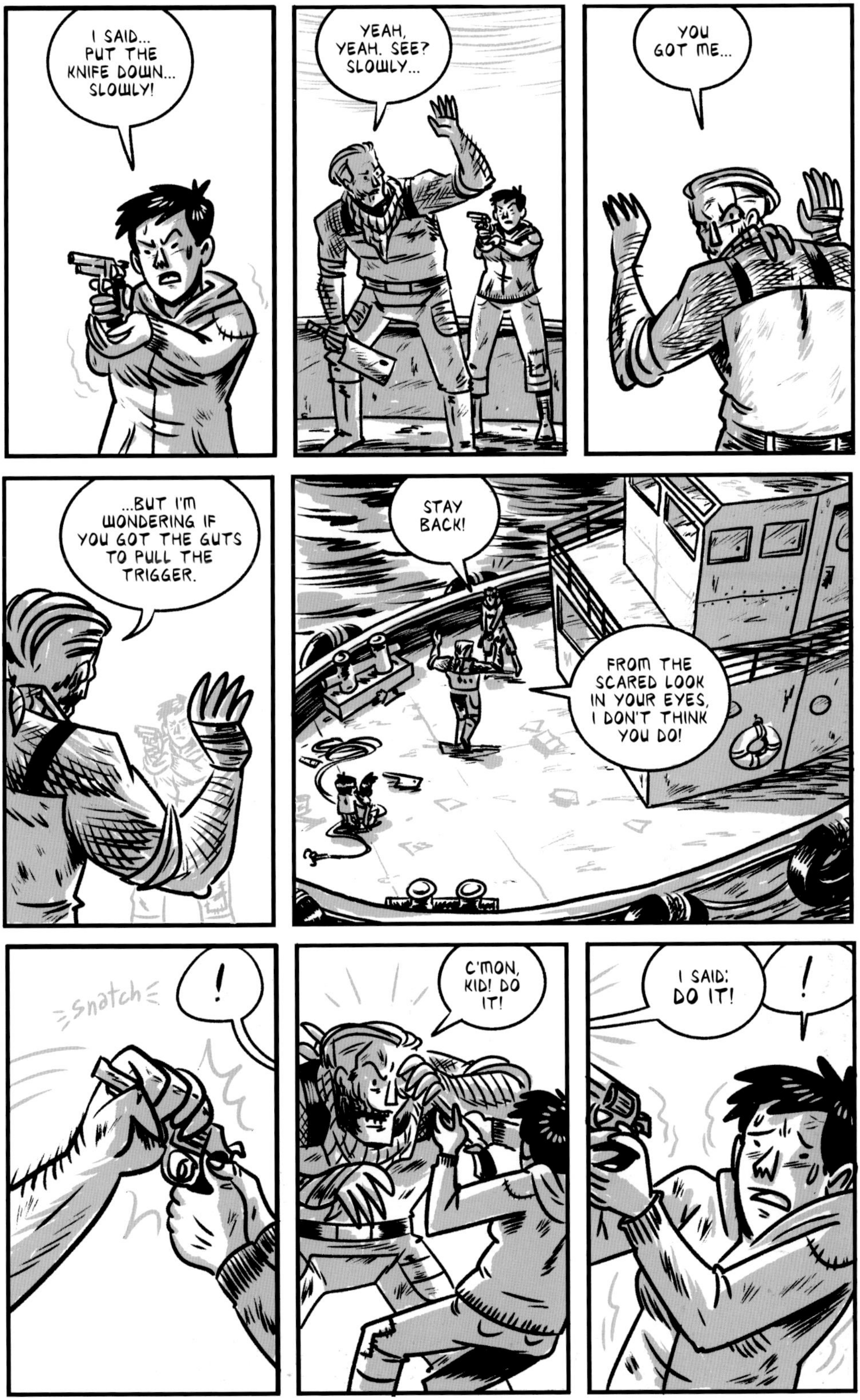
I SAID... PUT THE KNIFE DOWN... SLOWLY!
YEAH, YEAH. SEE? SLOWLY...
YOU GOT ME...
...BUT I'M WONDERING IF YOU GOT THE GUTS TO PULL THE TRIGGER.
STAY BACK!
FROM THE SCARED LOOK IN YOUR EYES, I DON'T THINK YOU DO!
snatch
!
C'MON, KID! DO IT!
I SAID: DO IT!
!

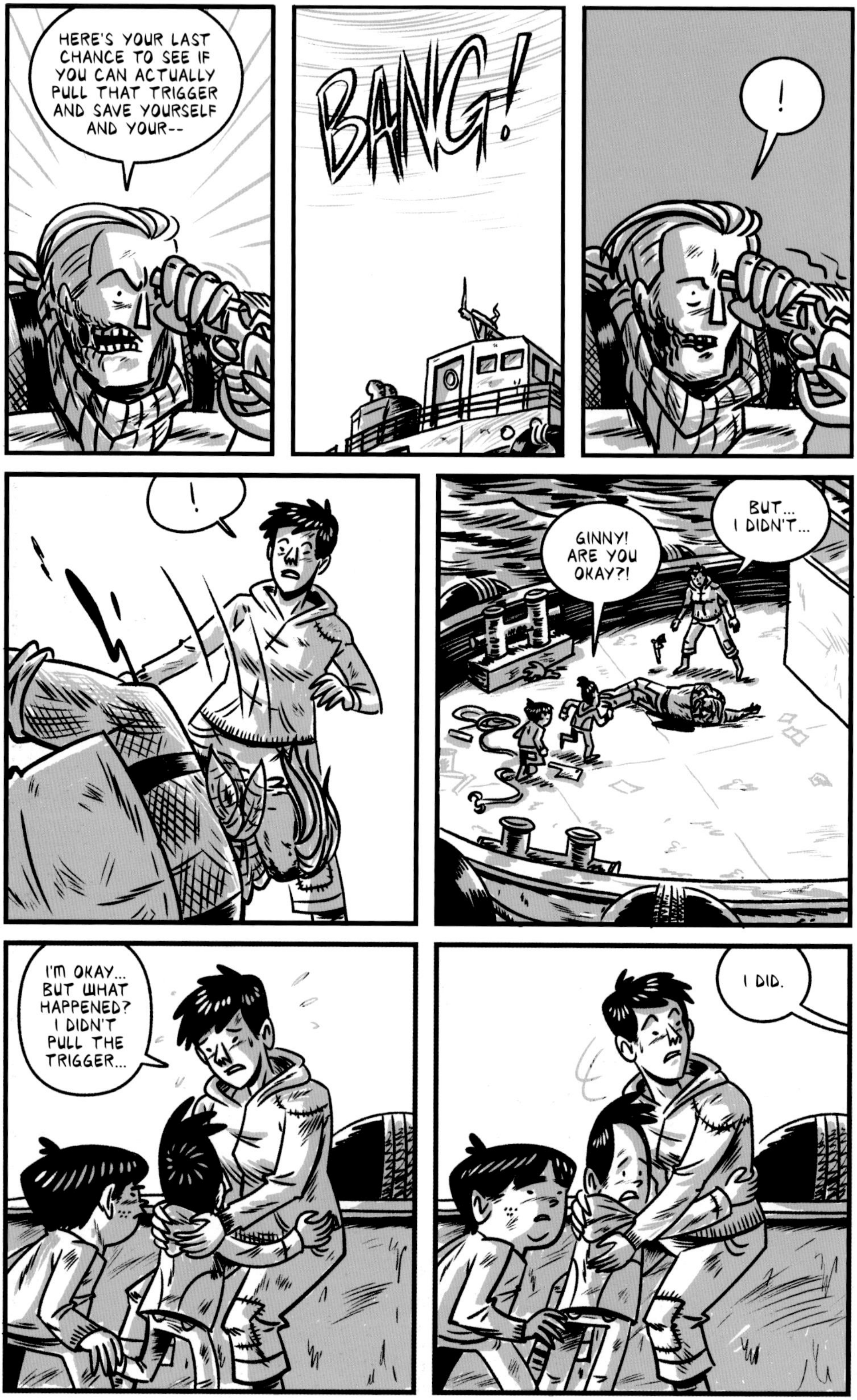
HERE'S YOUR LAST CHANCE TO SEE IF YOU CAN ACTUALLY PULL THAT TRIGGER AND SAVE YOURSELF AND YOUR--
BANG!
!
!
GINNY! ARE YOU OKAY?!
BUT... I DIDN'T...
I'M OKAY... BUT WHAT HAPPENED? I DIDN'T PULL THE TRIGGER...
I DID.

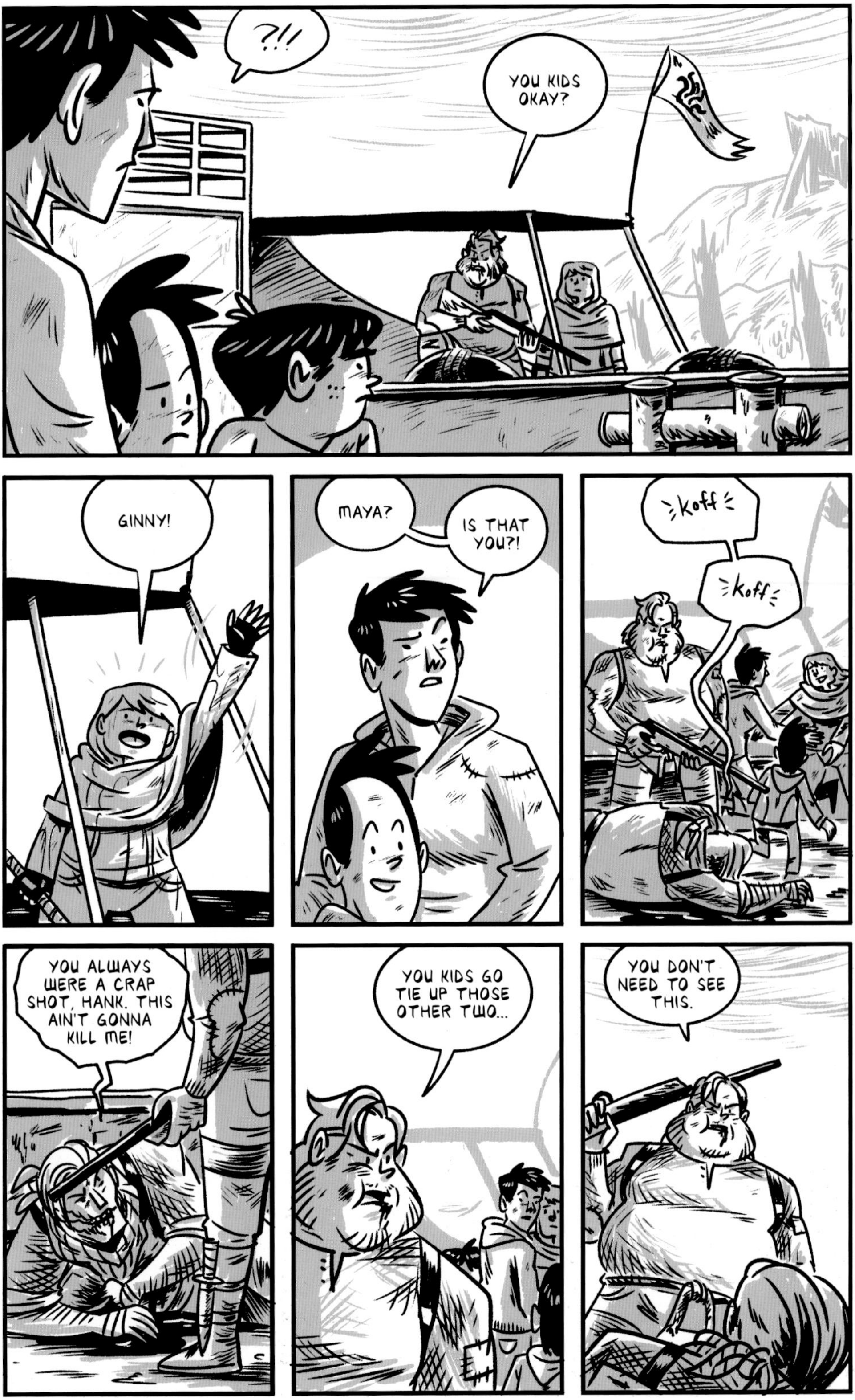
?!!
YOU KIDS OKAY?
GINNY!
MAYA?
IS THAT YOU?!
koff
koff
YOU ALWAYS WERE A CRAP SHOT, HANK. THIS AIN'T GONNA KILL ME!
YOU KIDS GO TIE UP THOSE OTHER TWO...
YOU DON'T NEED TO SEE THIS.

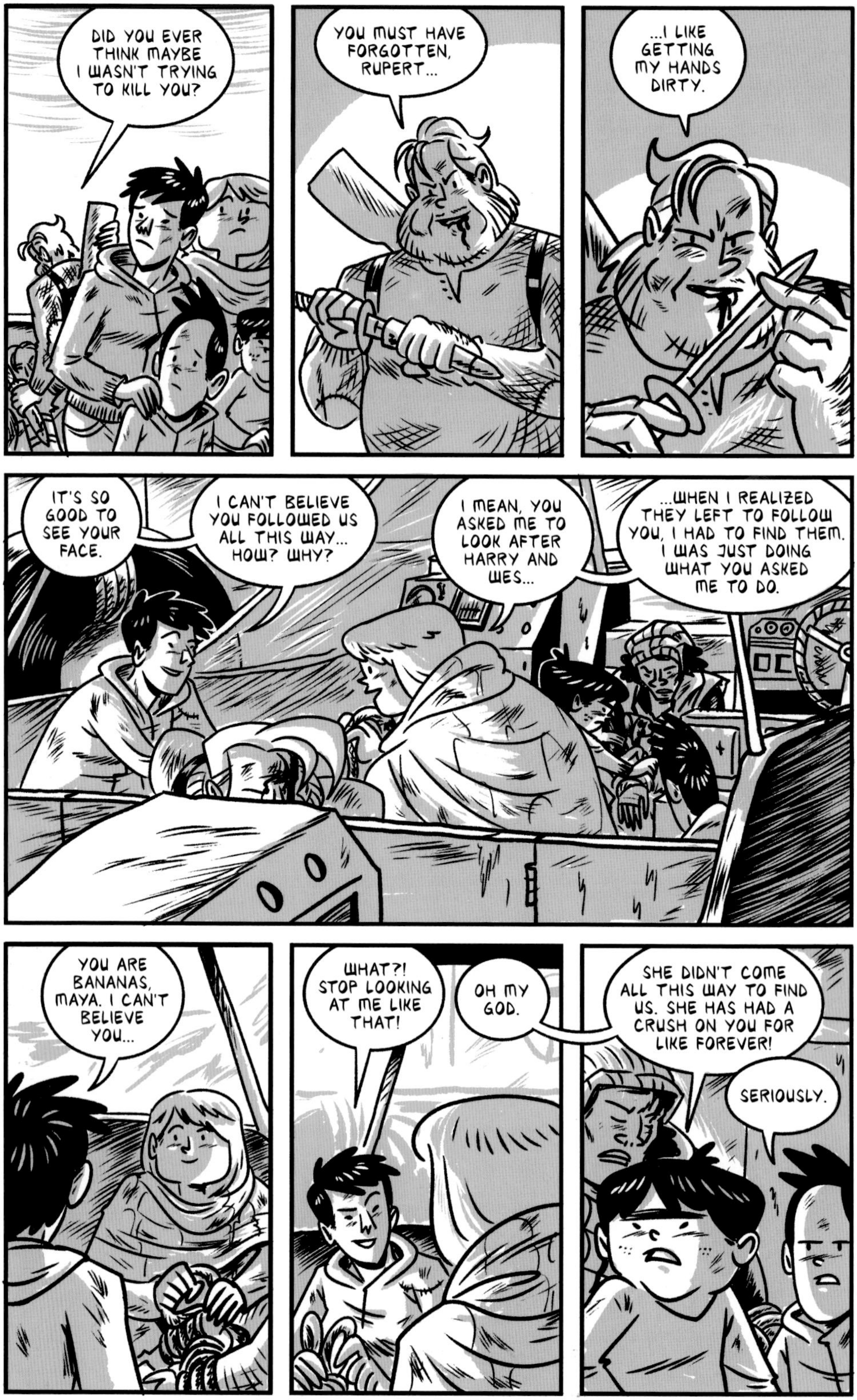
DID YOU EVER THINK MAYBE I WASN'T TRYING TO KILL YOU?
YOU MUST HAVE FORGOTTEN, RUPERT...
...I LIKE GETTING MY HANDS DIRTY.
IT'S SO GOOD TO SEE YOUR FACE.
I CAN'T BELIEVE YOU FOLLOWED US ALL THIS WAY... HOW? WHY?
I MEAN, YOU ASKED ME TO LOOK AFTER HARRY AND WES...
...WHEN I REALIZED THEY LEFT TO FOLLOW YOU, I HAD TO FIND THEM. I WAS JUST DOING WHAT YOU ASKED ME TO DO.
YOU ARE BANANAS, MAYA. I CAN'T BELIEVE YOU...
WHAT?! STOP LOOKING AT ME LIKE THAT!
OH MY GOD.
SHE DIDN'T COME ALL THIS WAY TO FIND US. SHE HAS HAD A CRUSH ON YOU FOR LIKE FOREVER!
SERIOUSLY.

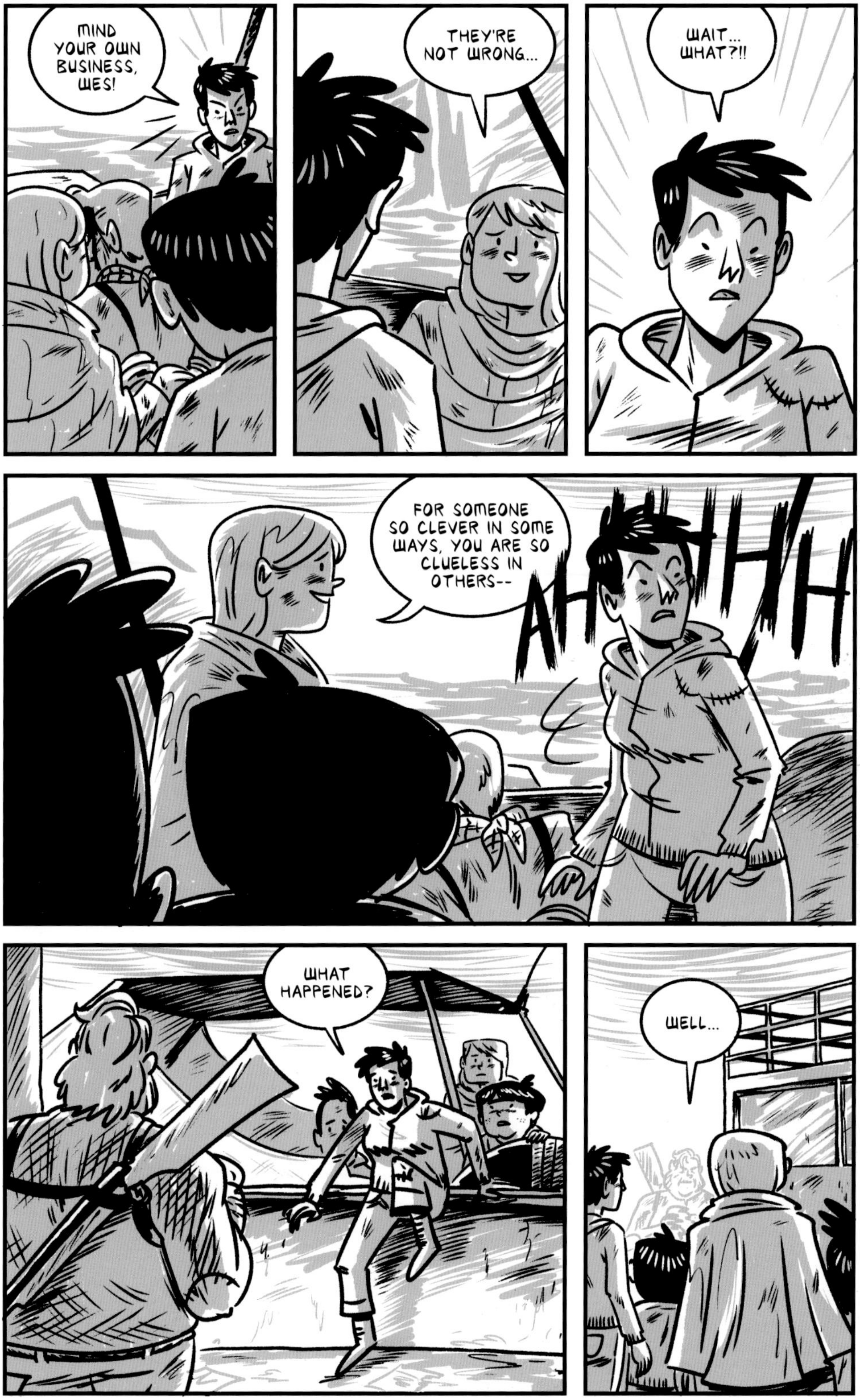
MIND YOUR OWN BUSINESS, WES!
THEY'RE NOT WRONG...
WAIT... WHAT?!!
FOR SOMEONE SO CLEVER IN SOME WAYS, YOU ARE SO CLUELESS IN OTHERS--
AHHHH
WHAT HAPPENED?
WELL...

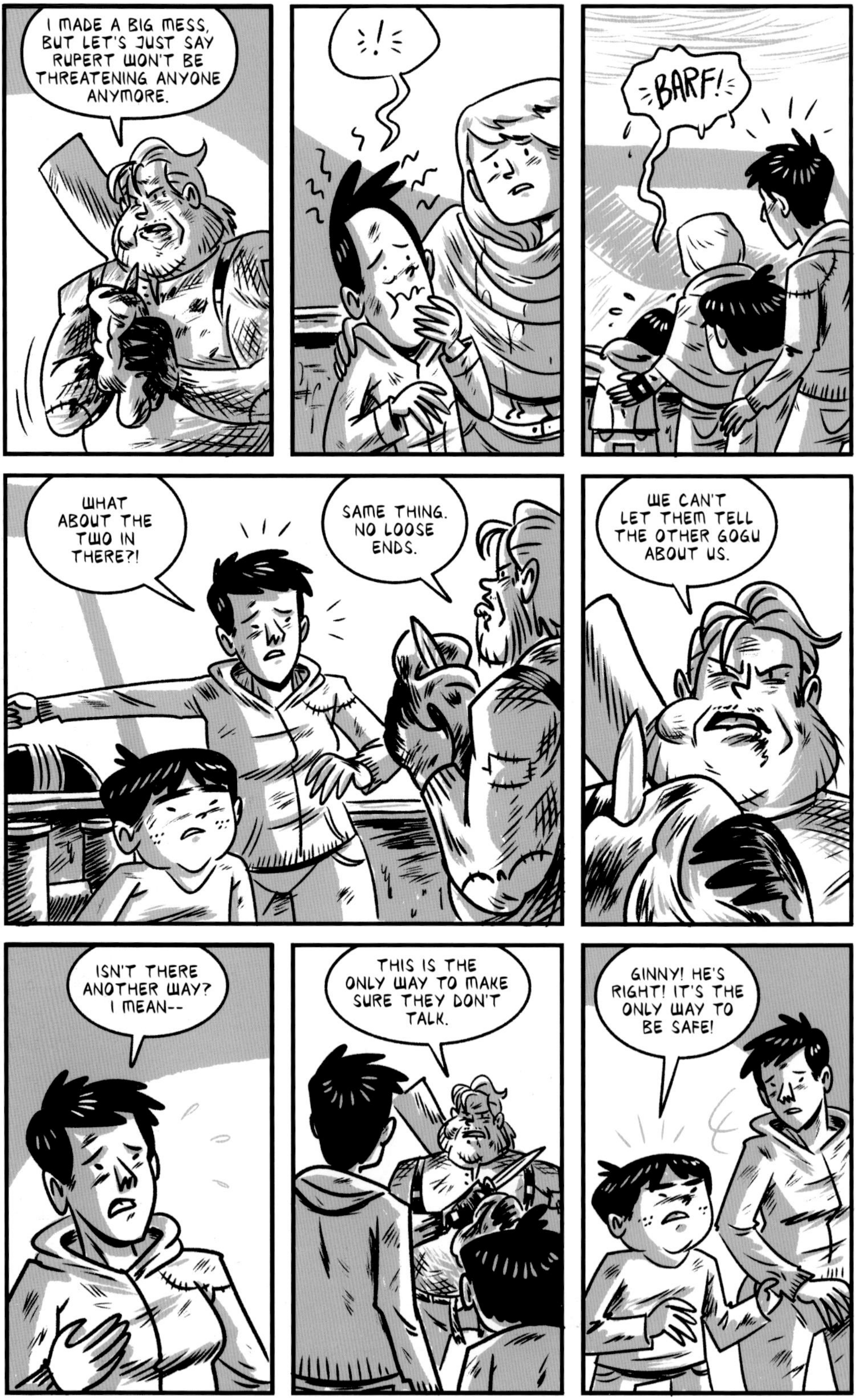
I MADE A BIG MESS, BUT LET'S JUST SAY RUPERT WON'T BE THREATENING ANYONE ANYMORE.
!
BARF!
WHAT ABOUT THE TWO IN THERE?!
SAME THING. NO LOOSE ENDS.
WE CAN'T LET THEM TELL THE OTHER GOGU ABOUT US.
ISN'T THERE ANOTHER WAY? I MEAN--
THIS IS THE ONLY WAY TO MAKE SURE THEY DON'T TALK.
GINNY! HE'S RIGHT! IT'S THE ONLY WAY TO BE SAFE!

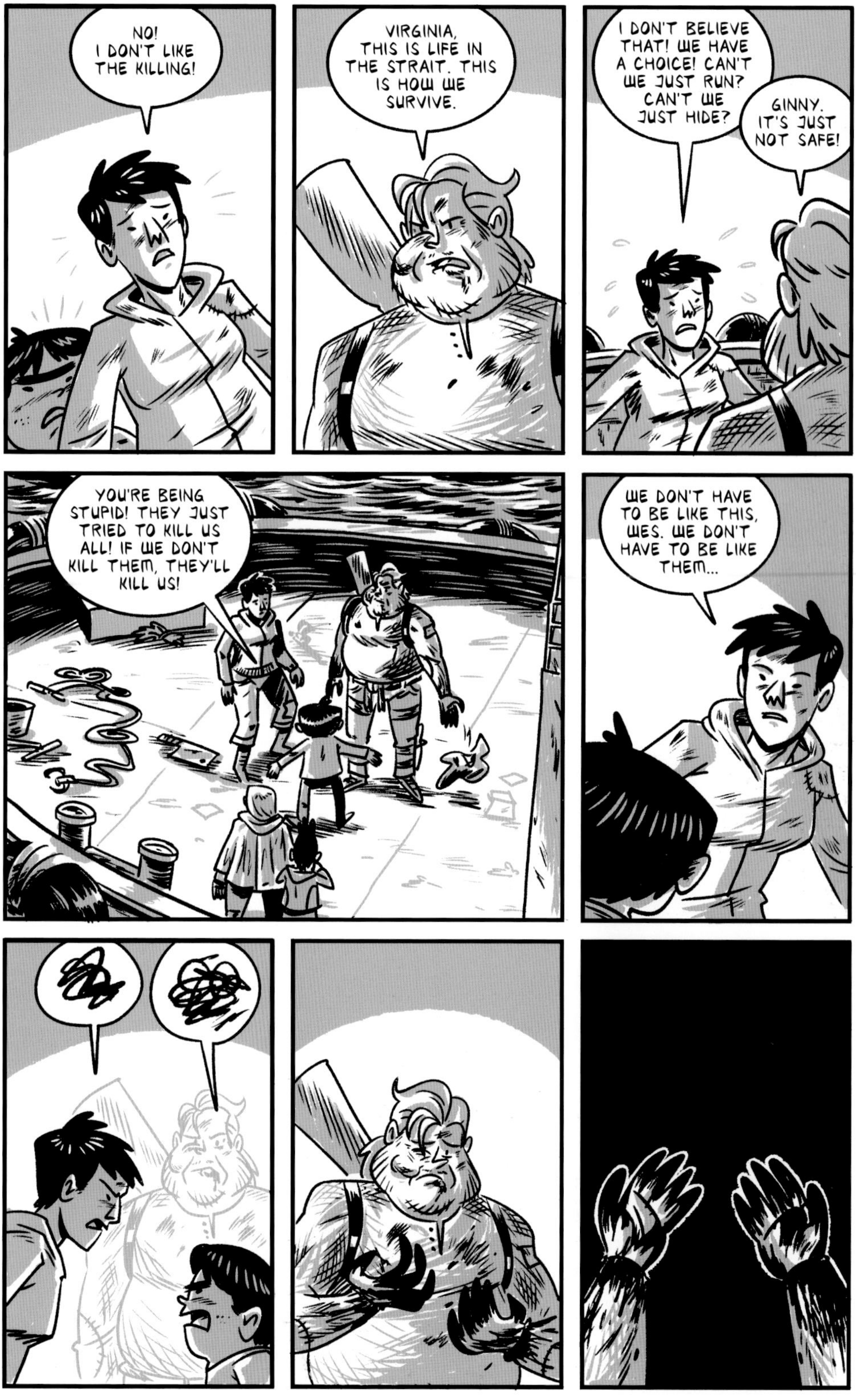
NO! I DON'T LIKE THE KILLING!
VIRGINIA, THIS IS LIFE IN THE STRAIT. THIS IS HOW WE SURVIVE.
I DON'T BELIEVE THAT! WE HAVE A CHOICE! CAN'T WE JUST RUN? CAN'T WE JUST HIDE?
GINNY. IT'S JUST NOT SAFE!
YOU'RE BEING STUPID! THEY JUST TRIED TO KILL US ALL! IF WE DON'T KILL THEM, THEY'LL KILL US!
WE DON'T HAVE TO BE LIKE THIS, WES. WE DON'T HAVE TO BE LIKE THEM...

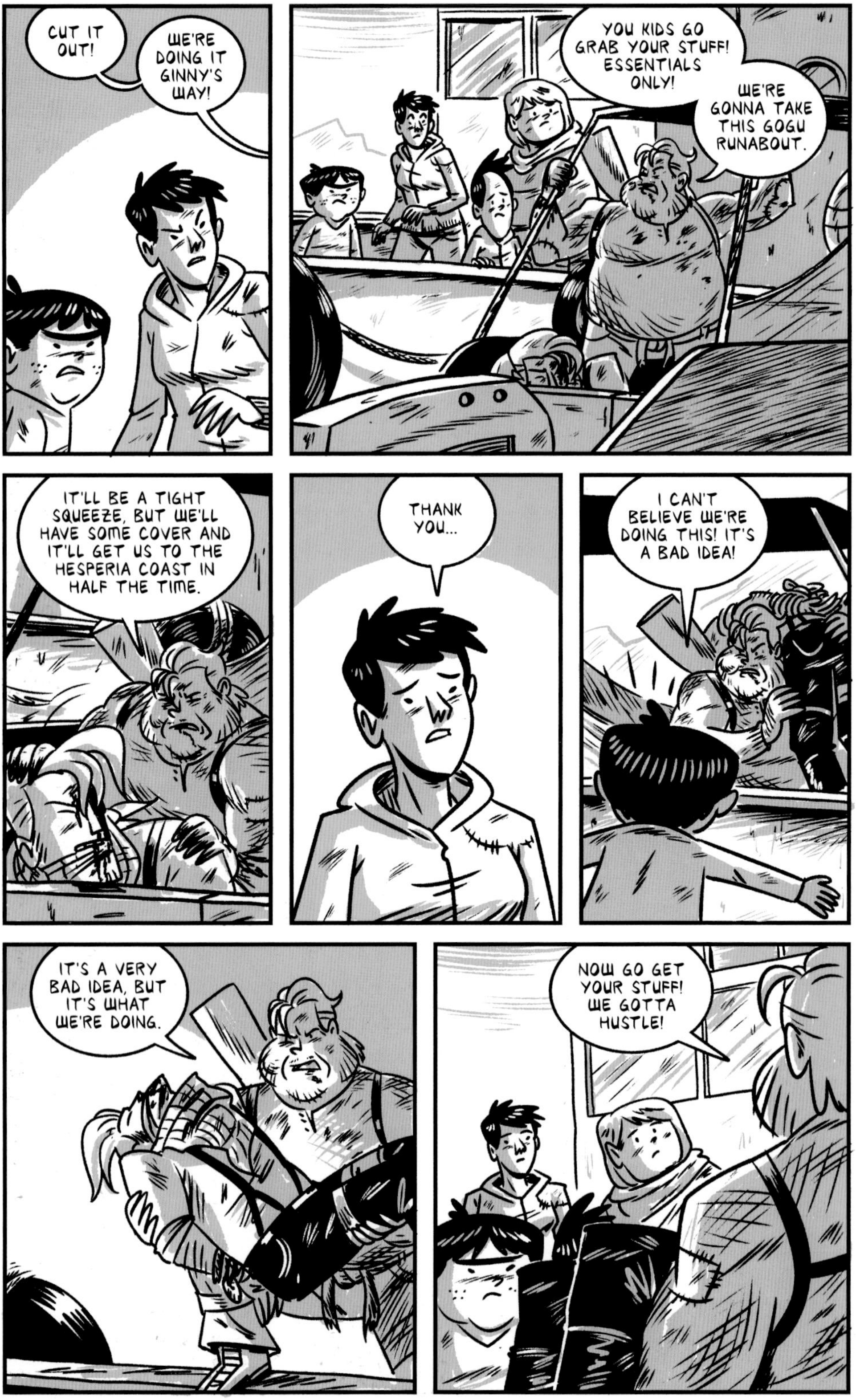
CUT IT OUT!
WE'RE DOING IT GINNY'S WAY!
YOU KIDS GO GRAB YOUR STUFF! ESSENTIALS ONLY!
WE'RE GONNA TAKE THIS GOGU RUNABOUT.
IT'LL BE A TIGHT SQUEEZE, BUT WE'LL HAVE SOME COVER AND IT'LL GET US TO THE HESPERIA COAST IN HALF THE TIME.
THANK YOU...
I CAN'T BELIEVE WE'RE DOING THIS! IT'S A BAD IDEA!
IT'S A VERY BAD IDEA, BUT IT'S WHAT WE'RE DOING.
NOW GO GET YOUR STUFF! WE GOTTA HUSTLE!

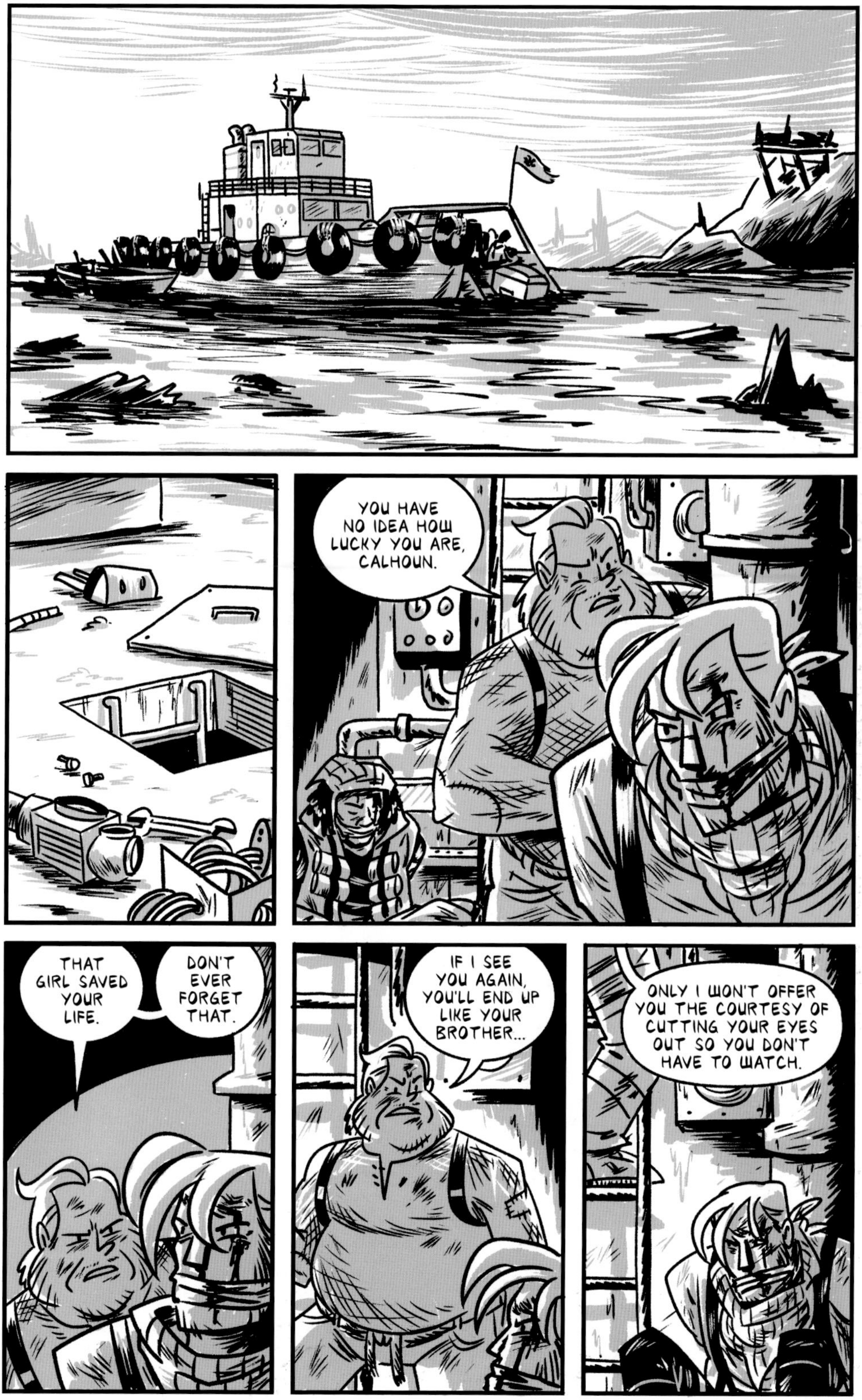
YOU HAVE NO IDEA HOW LUCKY YOU ARE, CALHOUN.
THAT GIRL SAVED YOUR LIFE.
DON'T EVER FORGET THAT.
IF I SEE YOU AGAIN, YOU'LL END UP LIKE YOUR BROTHER...
ONLY I WON'T OFFER YOU THE COURTESY OF CUTTING YOUR EYES OUT SO YOU DON'T HAVE TO WATCH.

CHAPTER 10

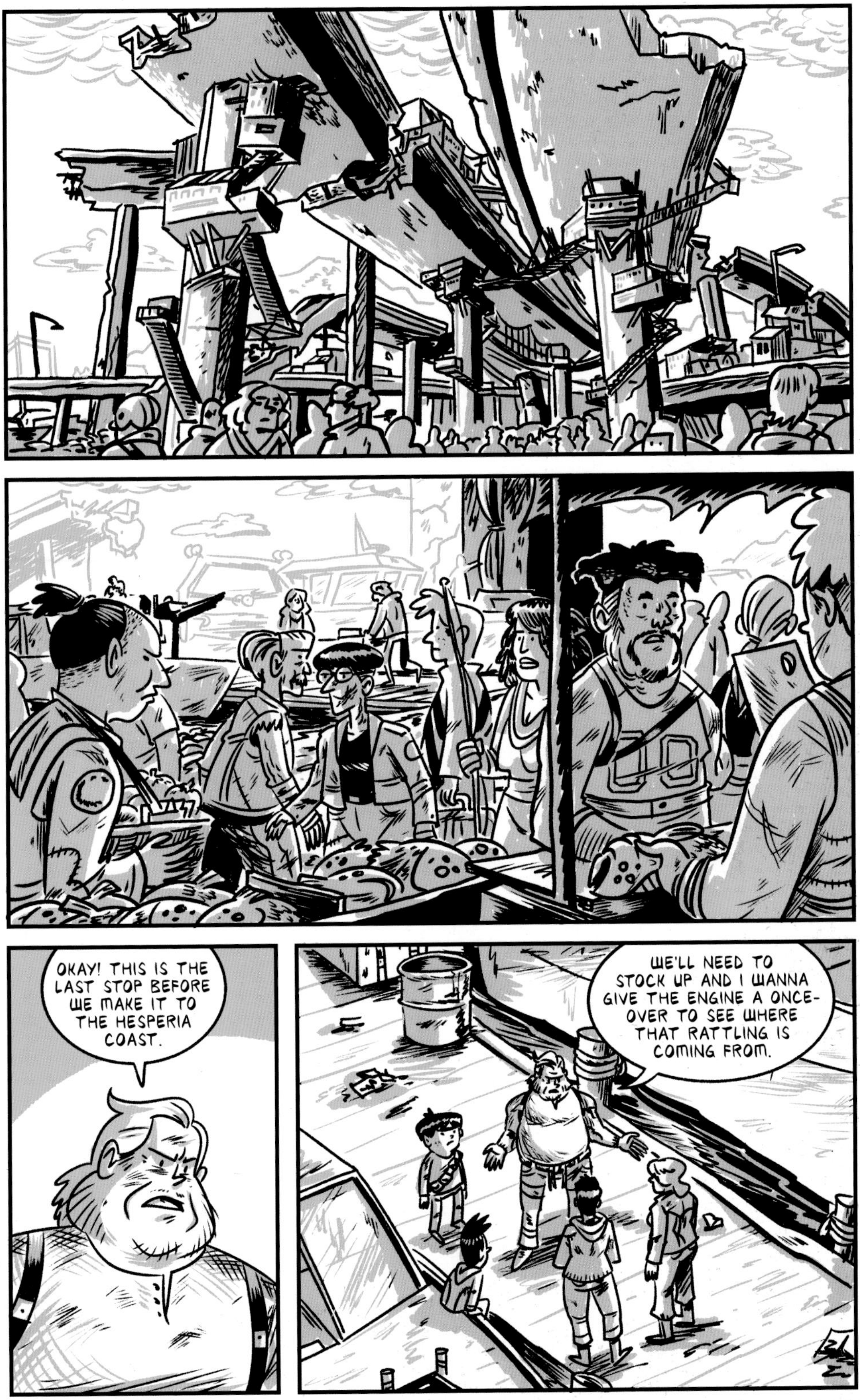
OKAY! THIS IS THE LAST STOP BEFORE WE MAKE IT TO THE HESPERIA COAST.
WE'LL NEED TO STOCK UP AND I WANNA GIVE THE ENGINE A ONCE-OVER TO SEE WHERE THAT RATTLING IS COMING FROM.

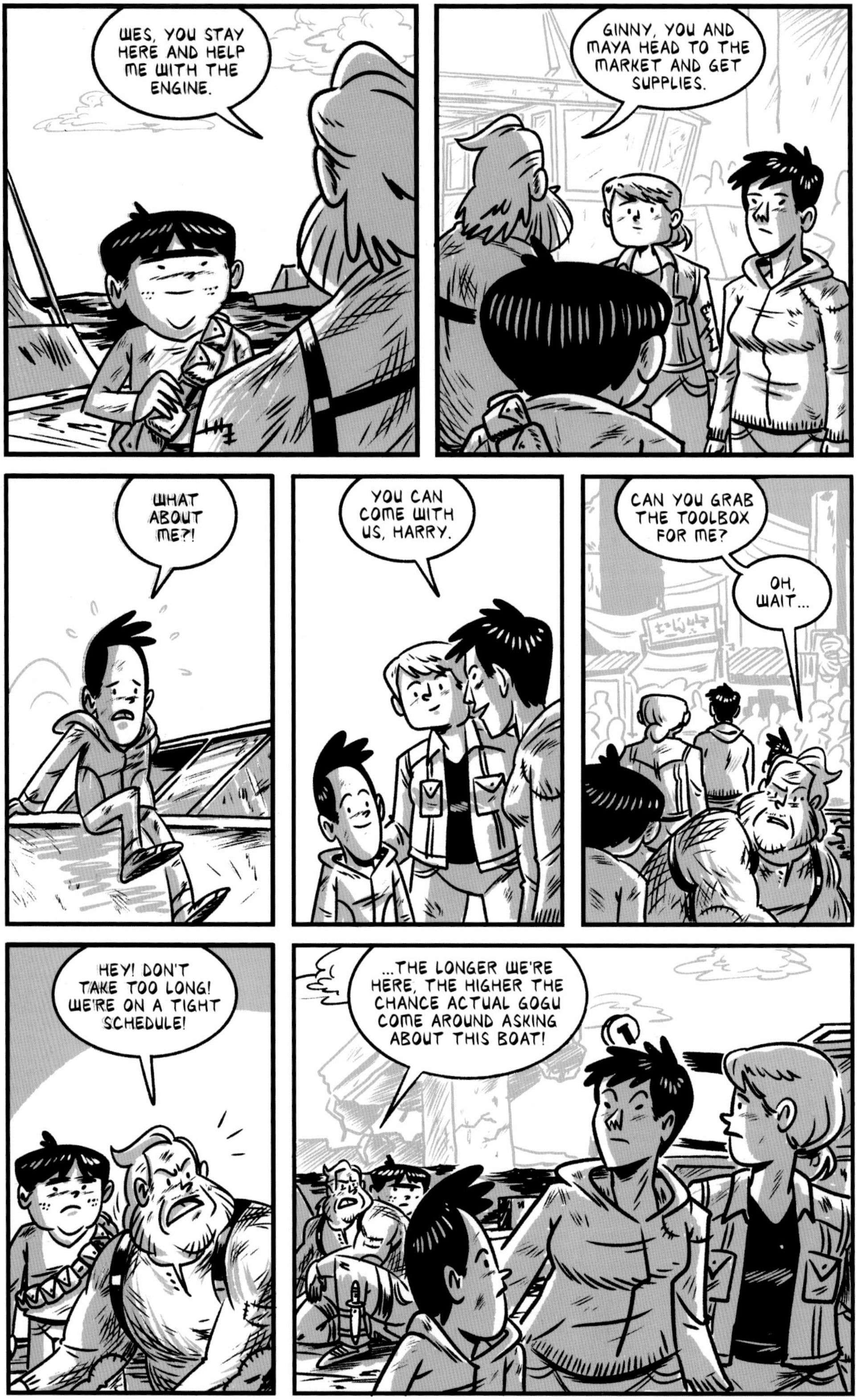
WES, YOU STAY HERE AND HELP ME WITH THE ENGINE.
GINNY, YOU AND MAYA HEAD TO THE MARKET AND GET SUPPLIES.
WHAT ABOUT ME?!
YOU CAN COME WITH US, HARRY.
CAN YOU GRAB THE TOOLBOX FOR ME?
OH, WAIT...
HEY! DON'T TAKE TOO LONG! WE'RE ON A TIGHT SCHEDULE!
...THE LONGER WE'RE HERE, THE HIGHER THE CHANCE ACTUAL GOGU COME AROUND ASKING ABOUT THIS BOAT!

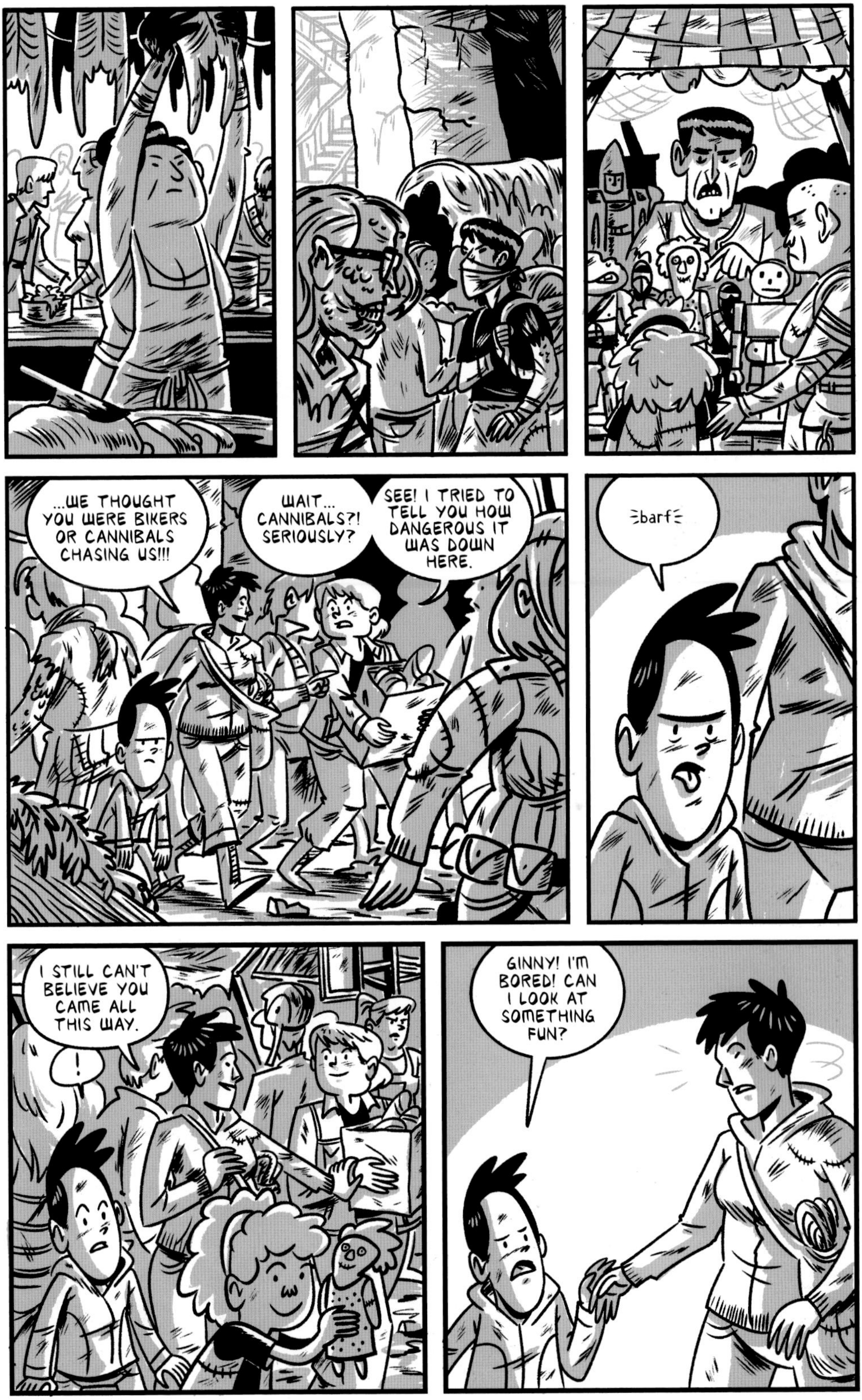
...WE THOUGHT YOU WERE BIKERS OR CANNIBALS CHASING US!!!
WAIT... CANNIBALS?! SERIOUSLY?
SEE! I TRIED TO TELL YOU HOW DANGEROUS IT WAS DOWN HERE.
barf
I STILL CAN'T BELIEVE YOU CAME ALL THIS WAY.
!
GINNY! I'M BORED! CAN I LOOK AT SOMETHING FUN?

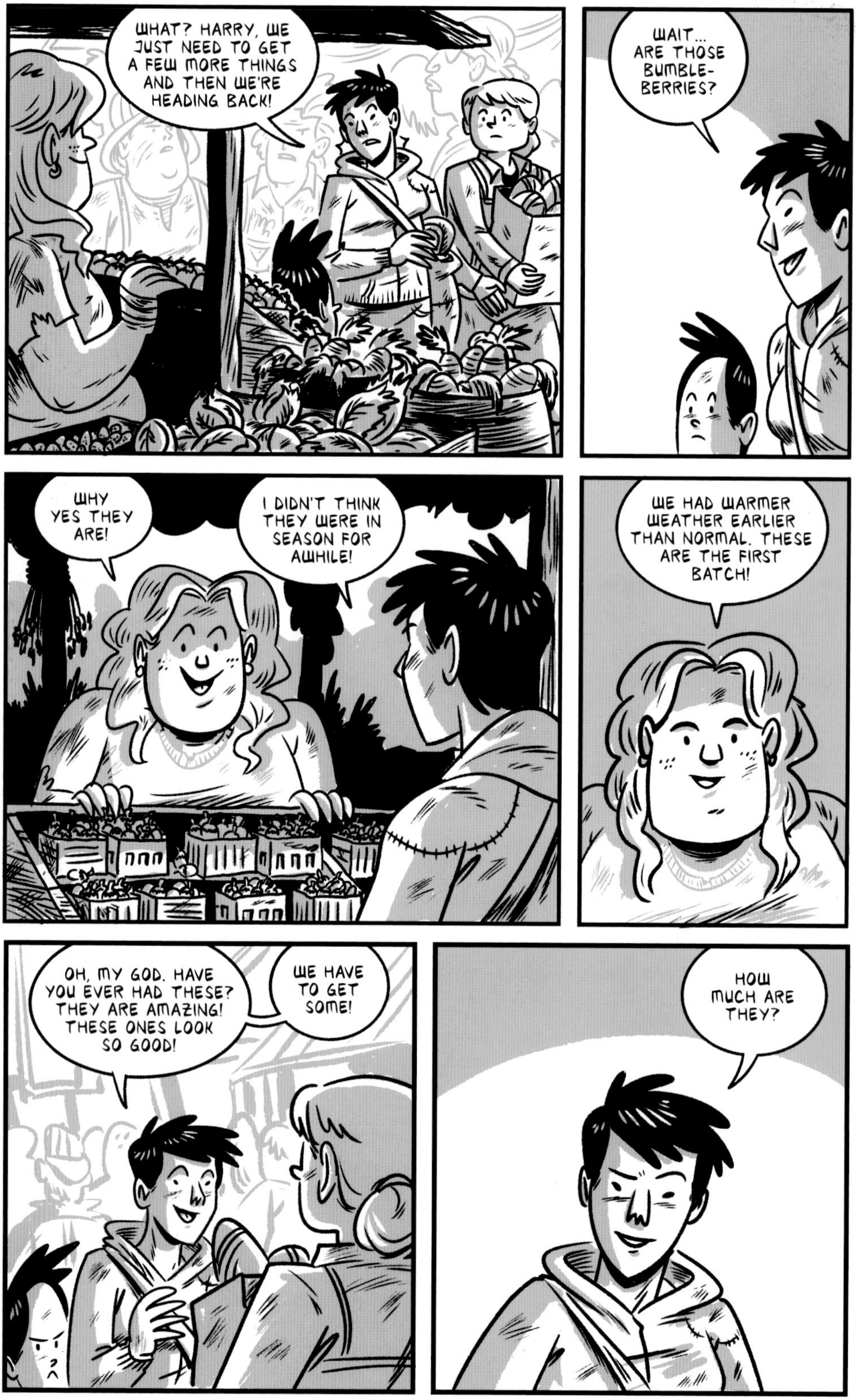
WHAT? HARRY, WE JUST NEED TO GET A FEW MORE THINGS AND THEN WE'RE HEADING BACK!
WAIT... ARE THOSE BUMBLE-BERRIES?
WHY YES THEY ARE!
I DIDN'T THINK THEY WERE IN SEASON FOR AWHILE!
WE HAD WARMER WEATHER EARLIER THAN NORMAL. THESE ARE THE FIRST BATCH!
OH, MY GOD. HAVE YOU EVER HAD THESE? THEY ARE AMAZING! THESE ONES LOOK SO GOOD!
WE HAVE TO GET SOME!
HOW MUCH ARE THEY?

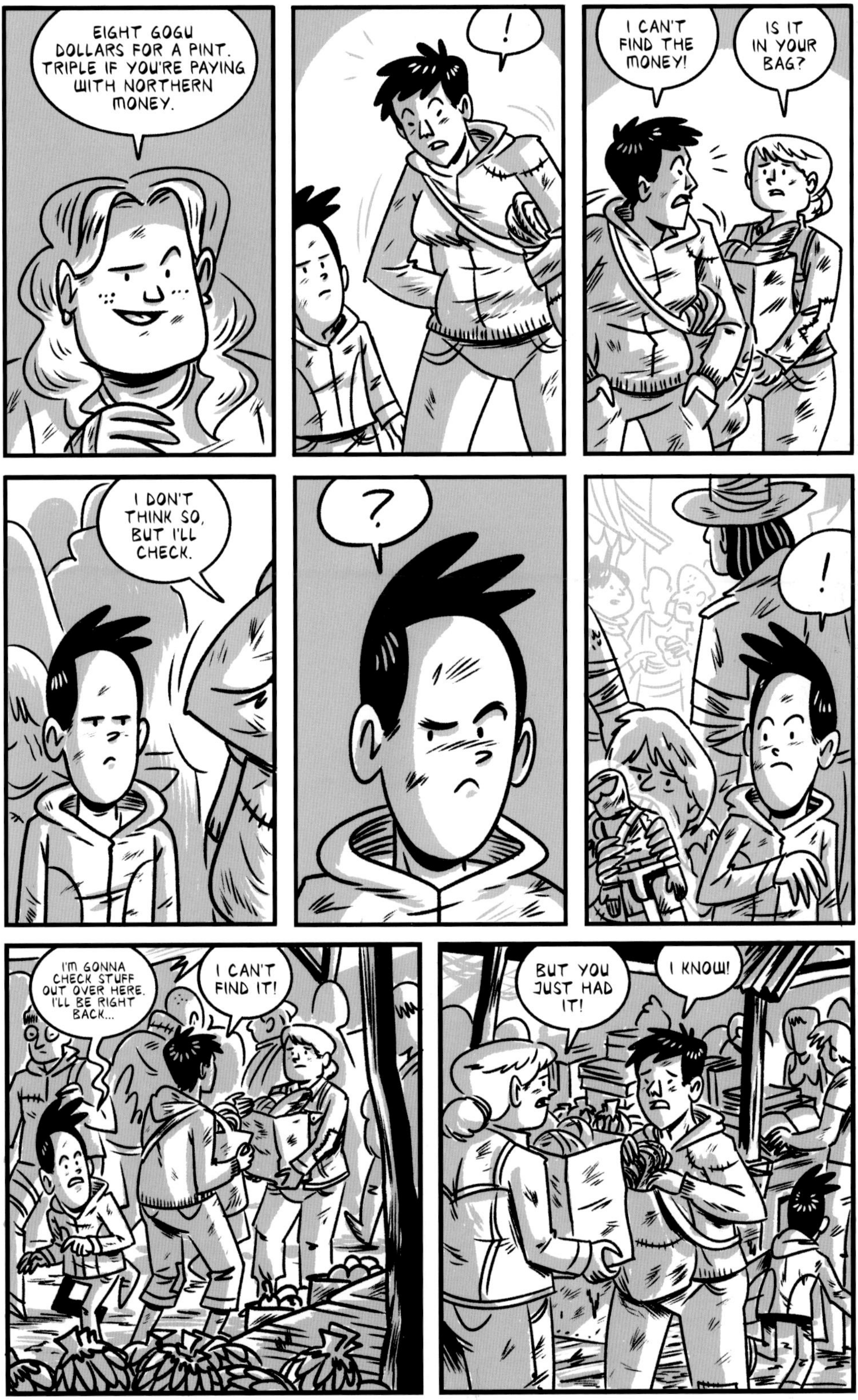
EIGHT GOGU DOLLARS FOR A PINT. TRIPLE IF YOU'RE PAYING WITH NORTHERN MONEY.
!
I CAN'T FIND THE MONEY!
IS IT IN YOUR BAG?
I DON'T THINK SO, BUT I'LL CHECK.
?
!
I'M GONNA CHECK STUFF OUT OVER HERE. I'LL BE RIGHT BACK...
I CAN'T FIND IT!
BUT YOU JUST HAD IT!
I KNOW!

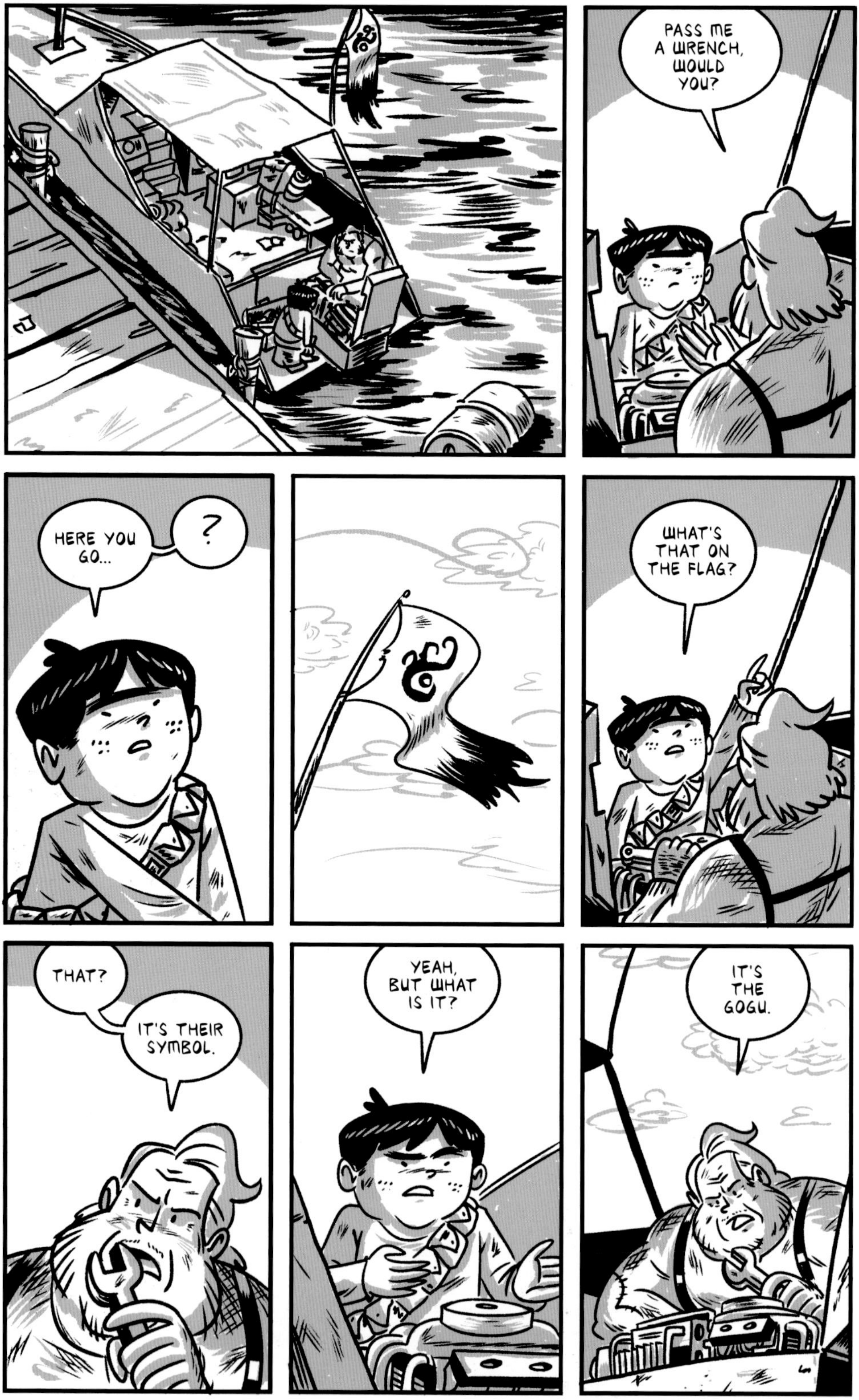
PASS ME A WRENCH, WOULD YOU?
HERE YOU GO...
?
WHAT'S THAT ON THE FLAG?
THAT?
IT'S THEIR SYMBOL.
YEAH, BUT WHAT IS IT?
IT'S THE GOGU.

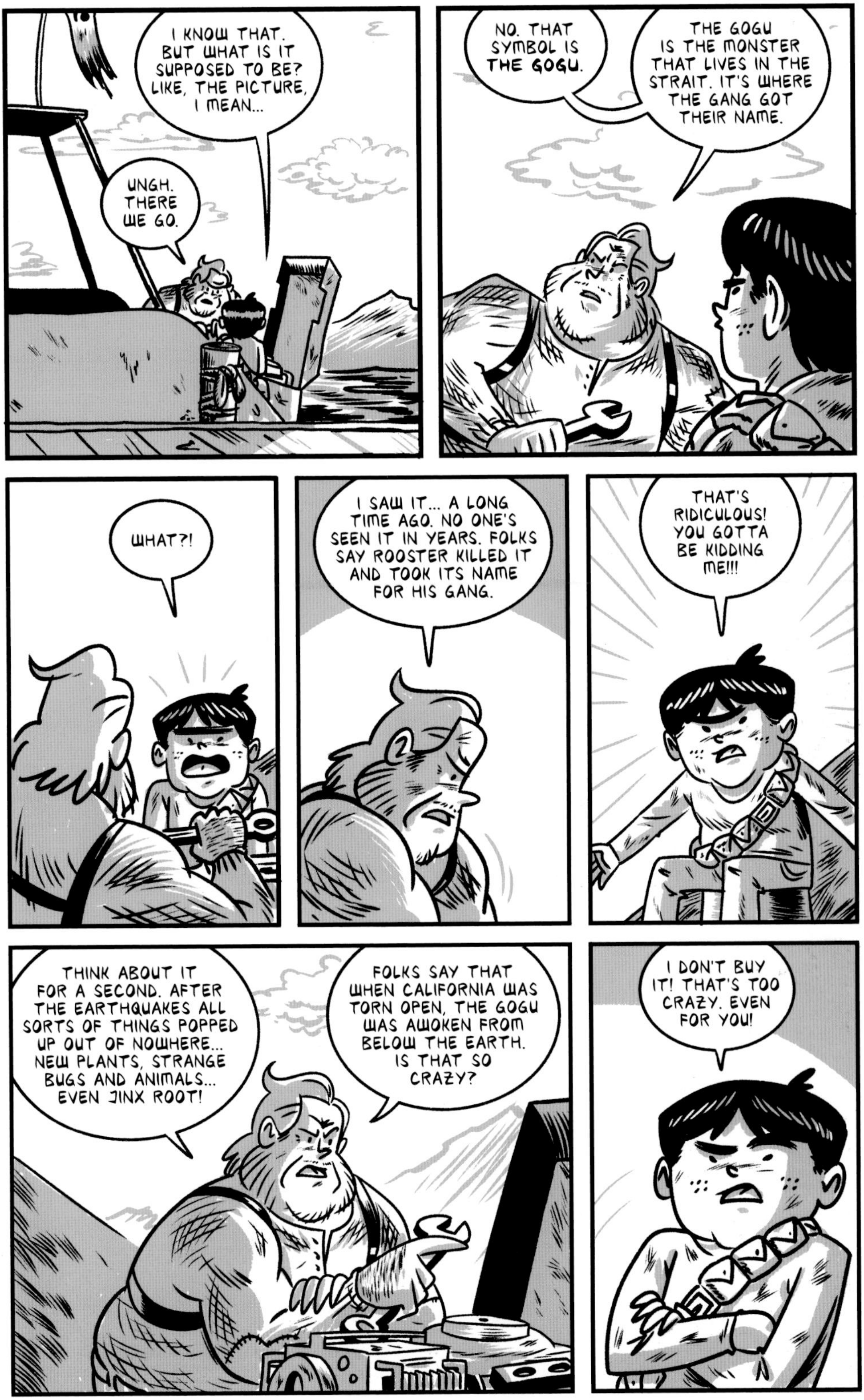
I KNOW THAT. BUT WHAT IS IT SUPPOSED TO BE? LIKE, THE PICTURE, I MEAN...
UNGH. THERE WE GO.
NO. THAT SYMBOL IS THE GOGU.
THE GOGU IS THE MONSTER THAT LIVES IN THE STRAIT. IT'S WHERE THE GANG GOT THEIR NAME.
WHAT?!
I SAW IT... A LONG TIME AGO. NO ONE'S SEEN IT IN YEARS. FOLKS SAY ROOSTER KILLED IT AND TOOK ITS NAME FOR HIS GANG.
THAT'S RIDICULOUS! YOU GOTTA BE KIDDING ME!!!
THINK ABOUT IT FOR A SECOND. AFTER THE EARTHQUAKES ALL SORTS OF THINGS POPPED UP OUT OF NOWHERE... NEW PLANTS, STRANGE BUGS AND ANIMALS... EVEN JINX ROOT!
FOLKS SAY THAT WHEN CALIFORNIA WAS TORN OPEN, THE GOGU WAS AWOKEN FROM BELOW THE EARTH. IS THAT SO CRAZY?
I DON'T BUY IT! THAT'S TOO CRAZY. EVEN FOR YOU!

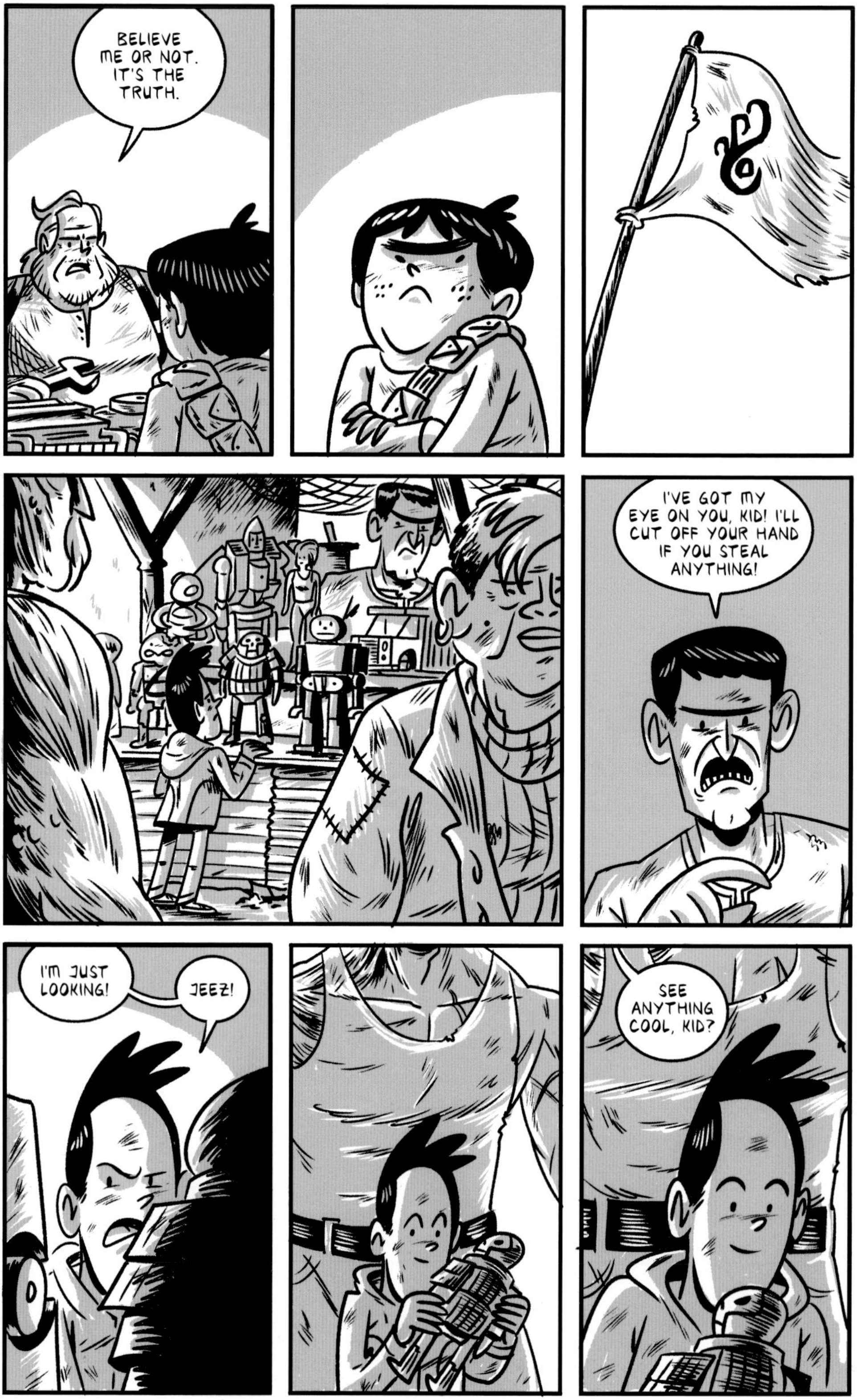
BELIEVE ME OR NOT. IT'S THE TRUTH.
I'VE GOT MY EYE ON YOU, KID! I'LL CUT OFF YOUR HAND IF YOU STEAL ANYTHING!
I'M JUST LOOKING!
JEEZ!
SEE ANYTHING COOL, KID?

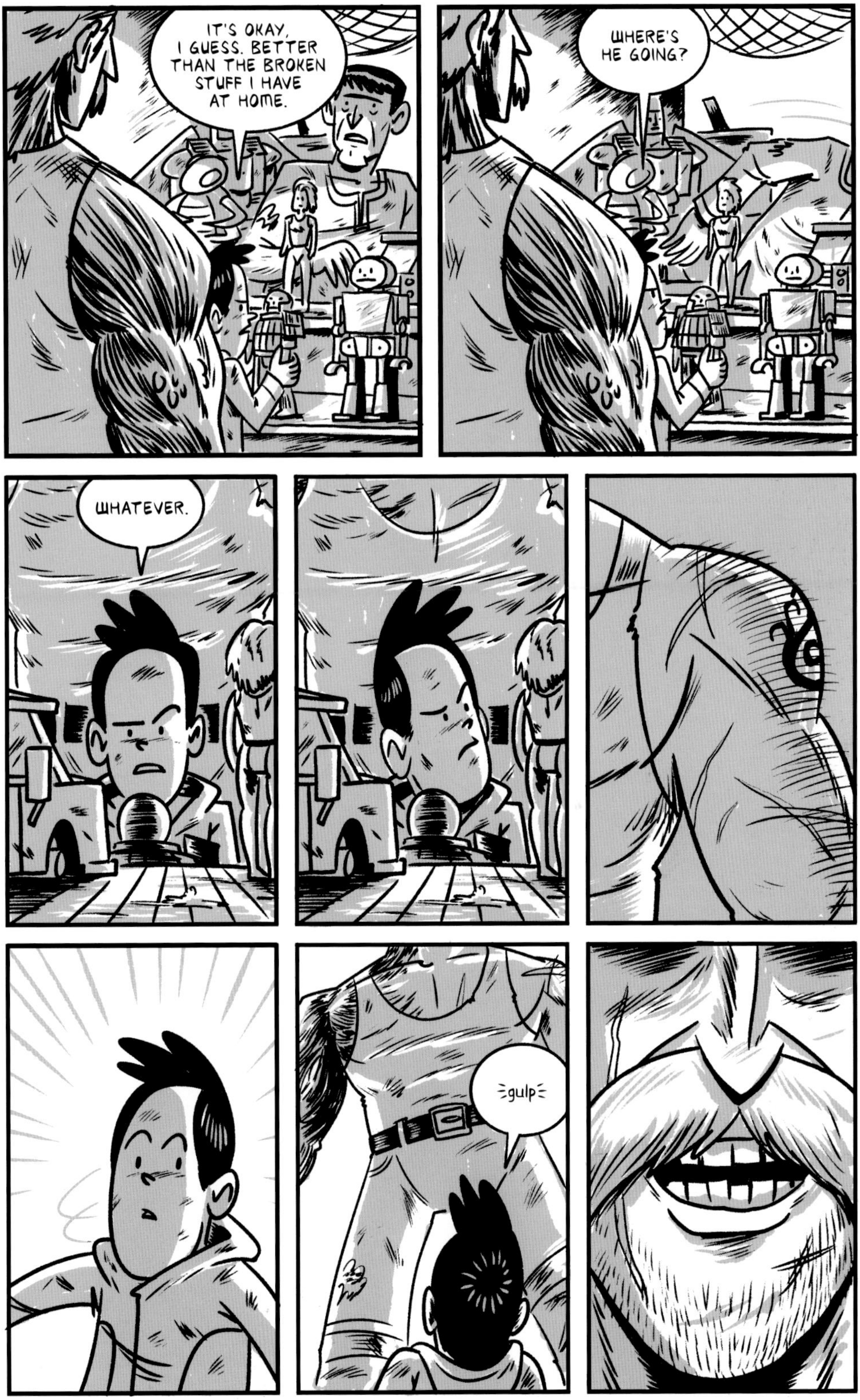
IT'S OKAY, I GUESS. BETTER THAN THE BROKEN STUFF I HAVE AT HOME.
WHERE'S HE GOING?
WHATEVER.
gulp

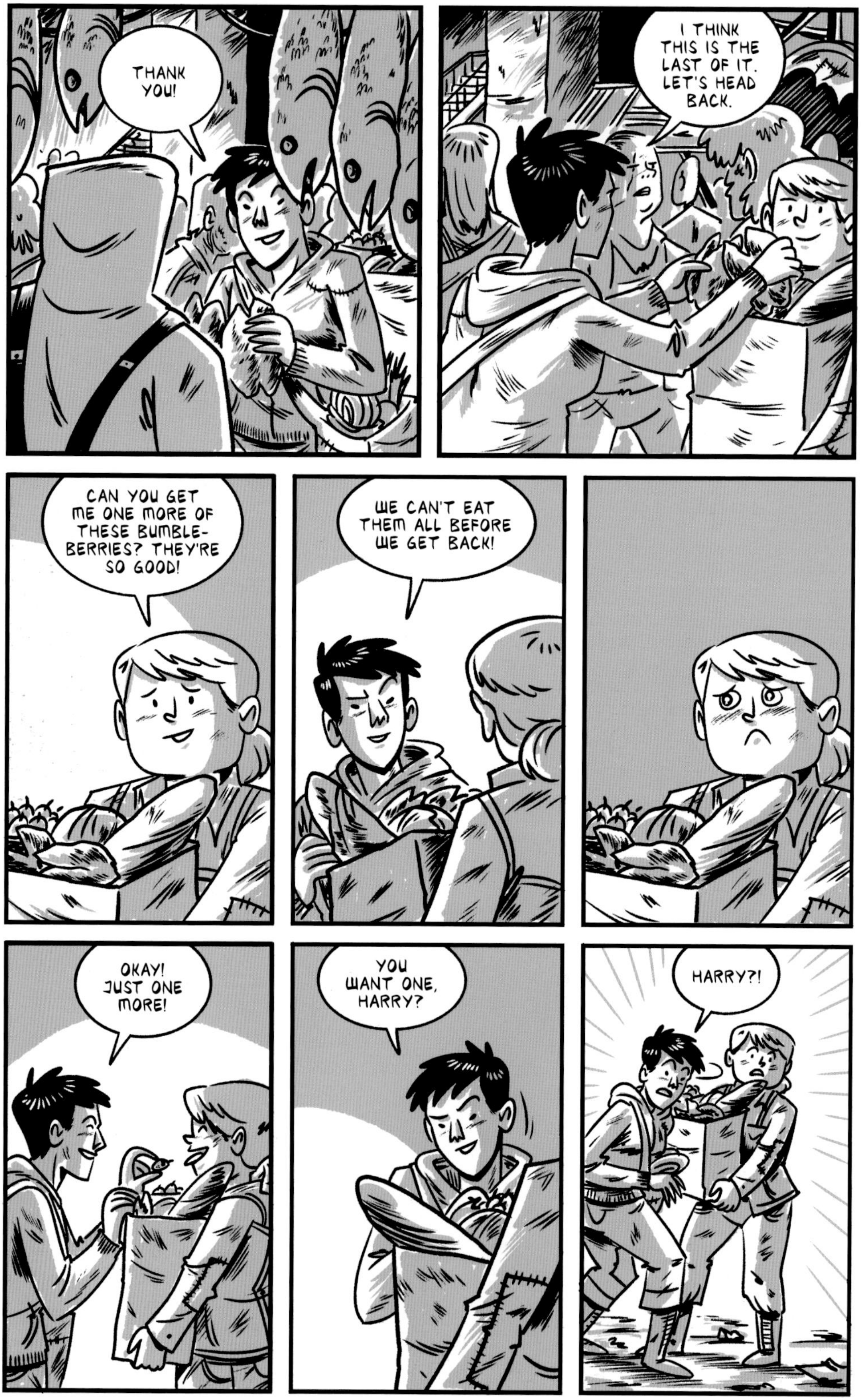
THANK YOU!
I THINK THIS IS THE LAST OF IT. LET'S HEAD BACK.
CAN YOU GET ME ONE MORE OF THESE BUMBLE-BERRIES? THEY'RE SO GOOD!
WE CAN'T EAT THEM ALL BEFORE WE GET BACK!
OKAY! JUST ONE MORE!
YOU WANT ONE, HARRY?
HARRY?!

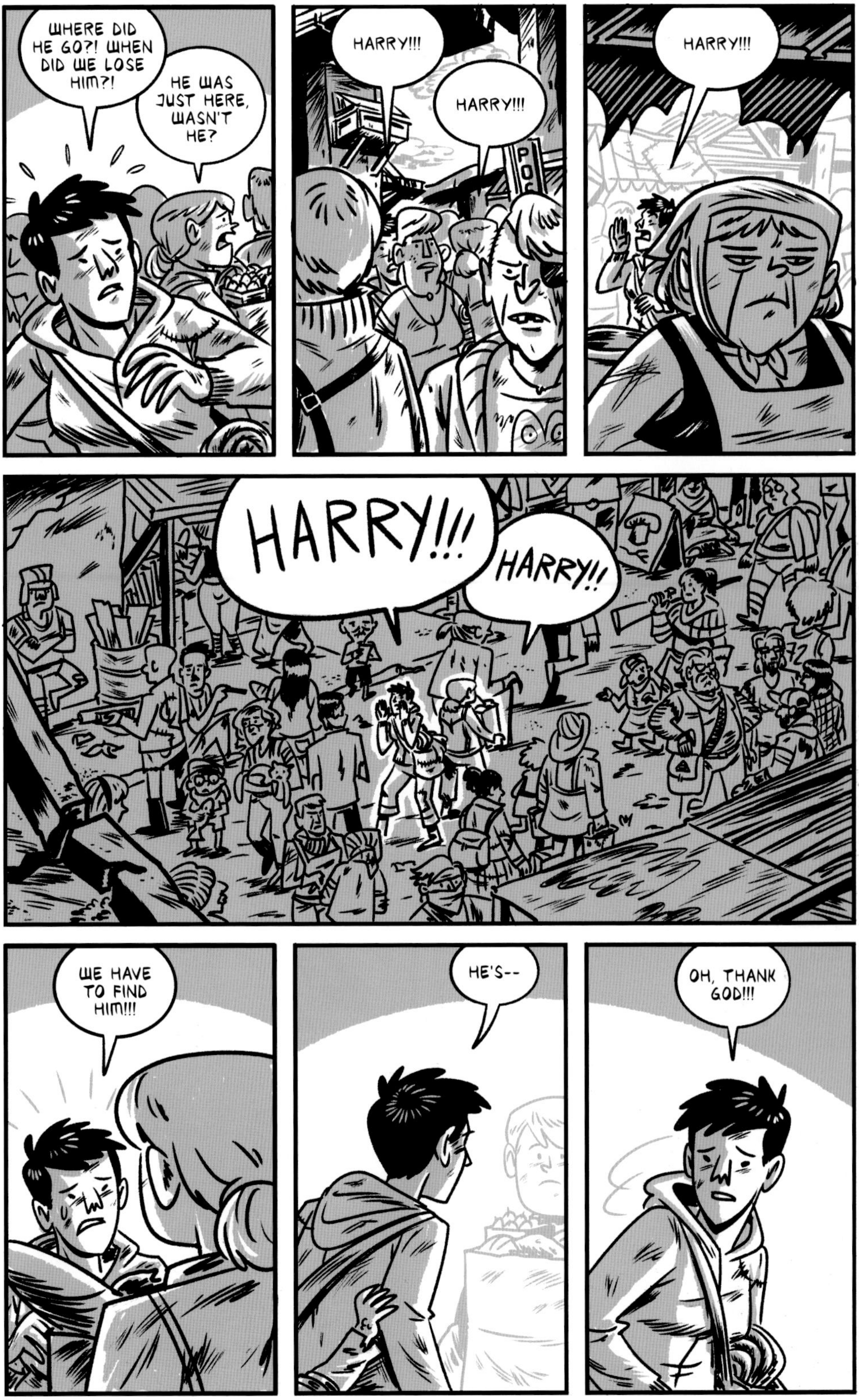
WHERE DID HE GO?! WHEN DID WE LOSE HIM?!
HE WAS JUST HERE, WASN'T HE?
HARRY!!!
HARRY!!!
HARRY!!!
HARRY!!!
HARRY!!
WE HAVE TO FIND HIM!!!
HE'S--
OH, THANK GOD!!!

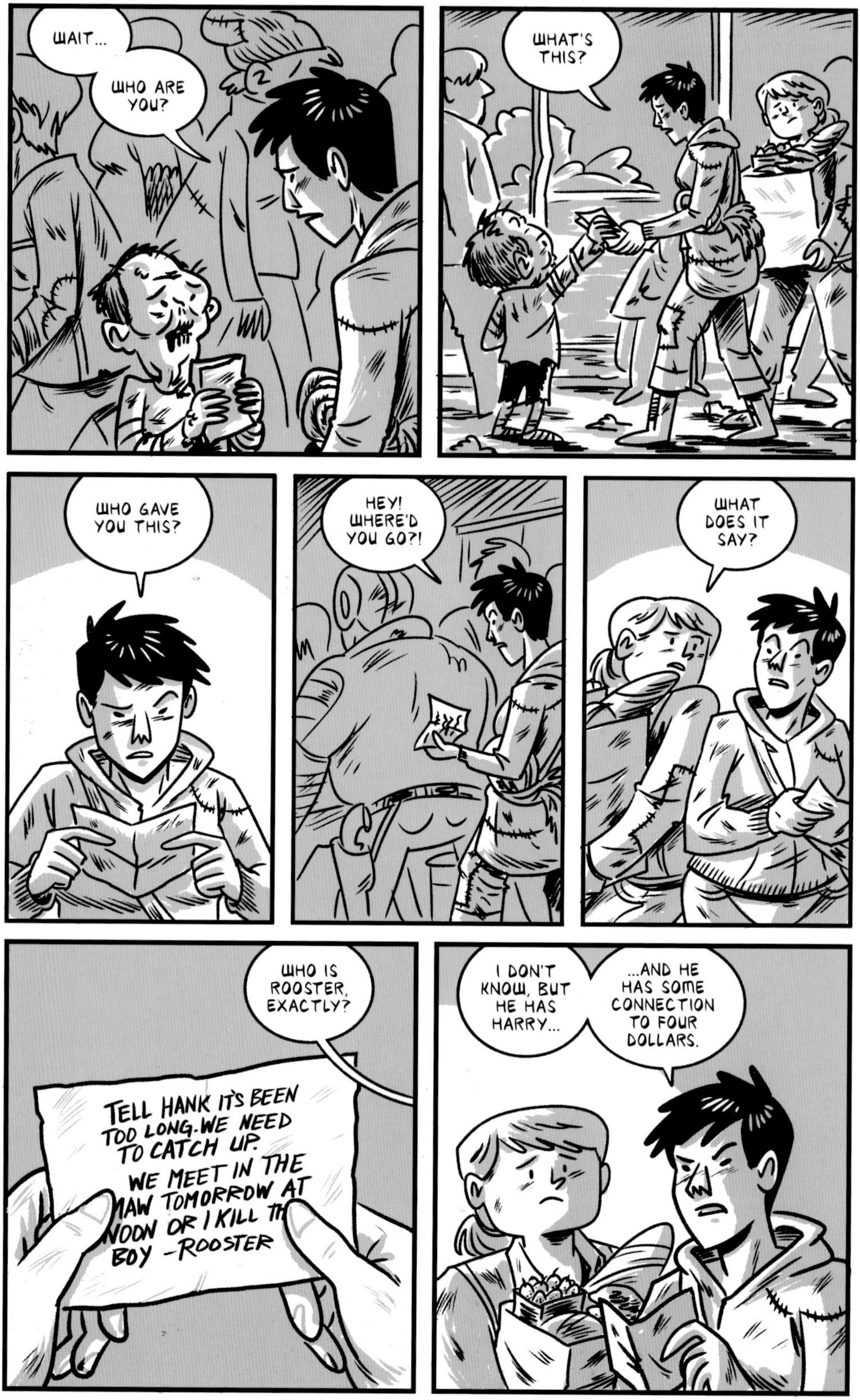
WAIT...
WHO ARE YOU?
WHAT'S THIS?
WHO GAVE YOU THIS?
HEY! WHERE'D YOU GO?!
WHAT DOES IT SAY?
WHO IS ROOSTER, EXACTLY?
TELL HANK IT'S BEEN TOO LONG. WE NEED TO CATCH UP. WE MEET IN THE MAW TOMORROW AT NOON OR I KILL TH BOY -ROOSTER
I DON'T KNOW, BUT HE HAS HARRY...
...AND HE HAS SOME CONNECTION TO FOUR DOLLARS.

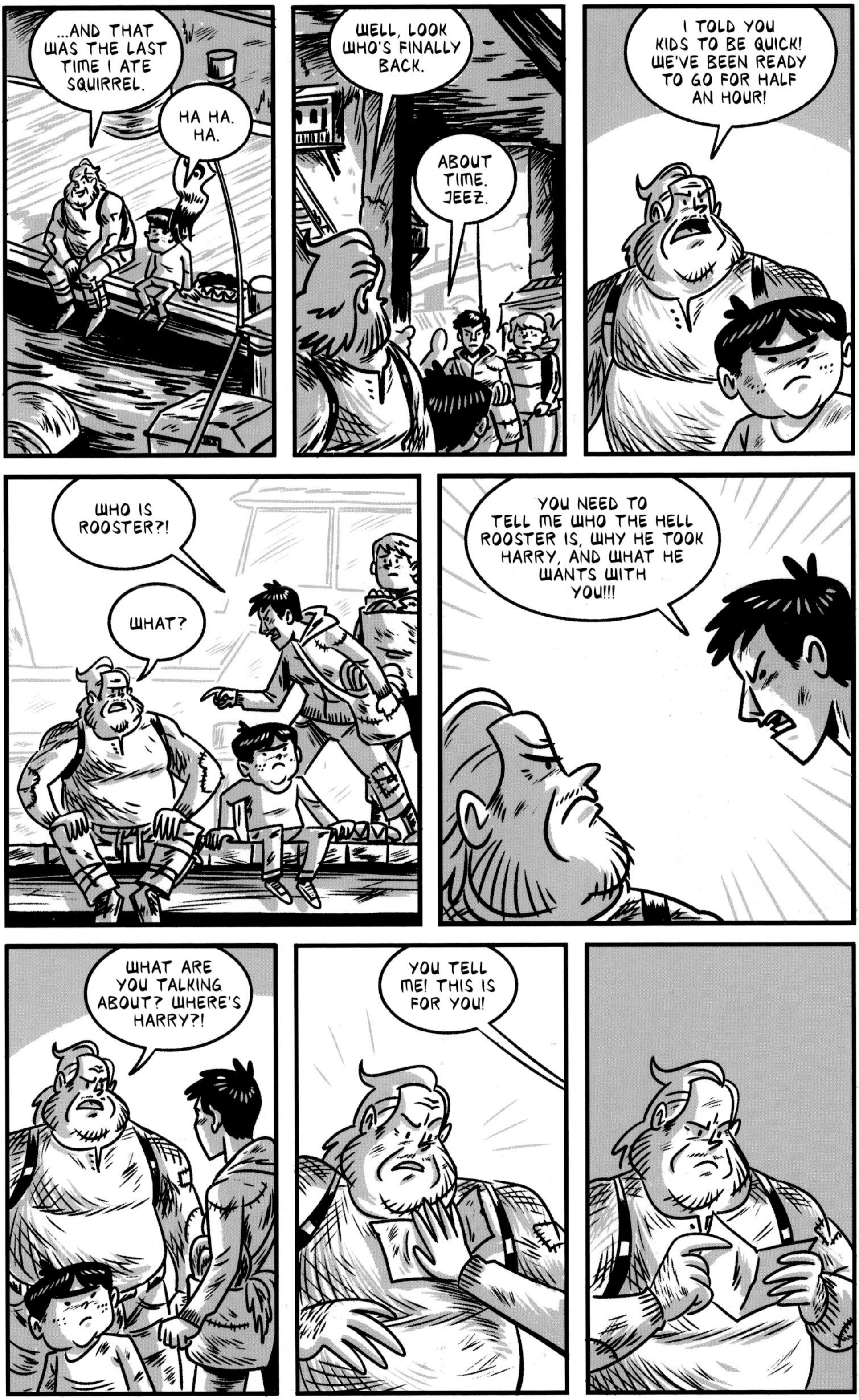
...AND THAT WAS THE LAST TIME I ATE SQUIRREL.
HA HA. HA.
WELL, LOOK WHO'S FINALLY BACK.
ABOUT TIME. JEEZ.
I TOLD YOU KIDS TO BE QUICK! WE'VE BEEN READY TO GO FOR HALF AN HOUR!
WHO IS ROOSTER?!
WHAT?
YOU NEED TO TELL ME WHO THE HELL ROOSTER IS, WHY HE TOOK HARRY, AND WHAT HE WANTS WITH YOU!!!
WHAT ARE YOU TALKING ABOUT? WHERE'S HARRY?!
YOU TELL ME! THIS IS FOR YOU!

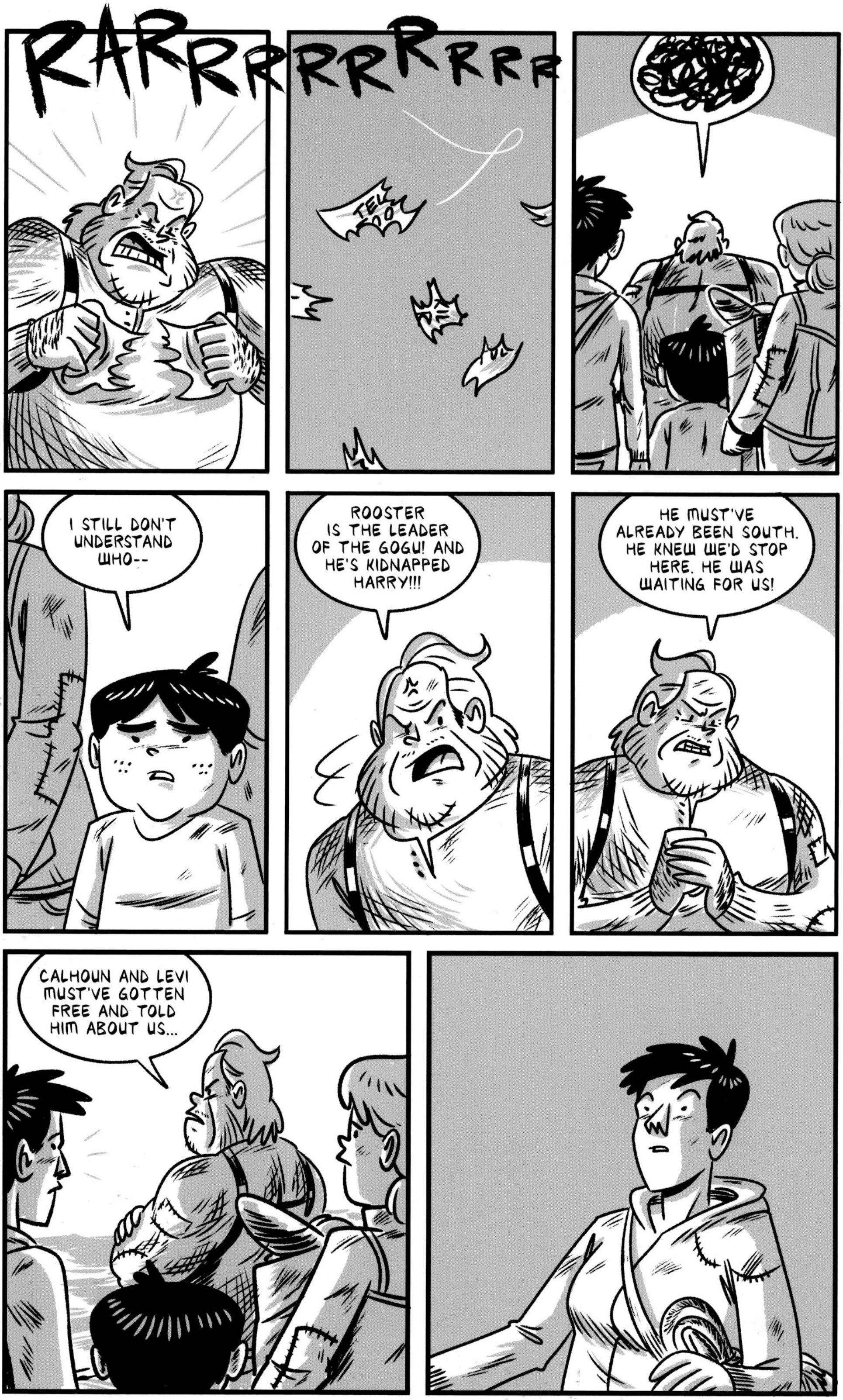
RARRRRRRRRR
I STILL DON'T UNDERSTAND WHO--
ROOSTER IS THE LEADER OF THE GOGU! AND HE'S KIDNAPPED HARRY!!!
HE MUST'VE ALREADY BEEN SOUTH. HE KNEW WE'D STOP HERE. HE WAS WAITING FOR US!
CALHOUN AND LEVI MUST'VE GOTTEN FREE AND TOLD HIM ABOUT US...

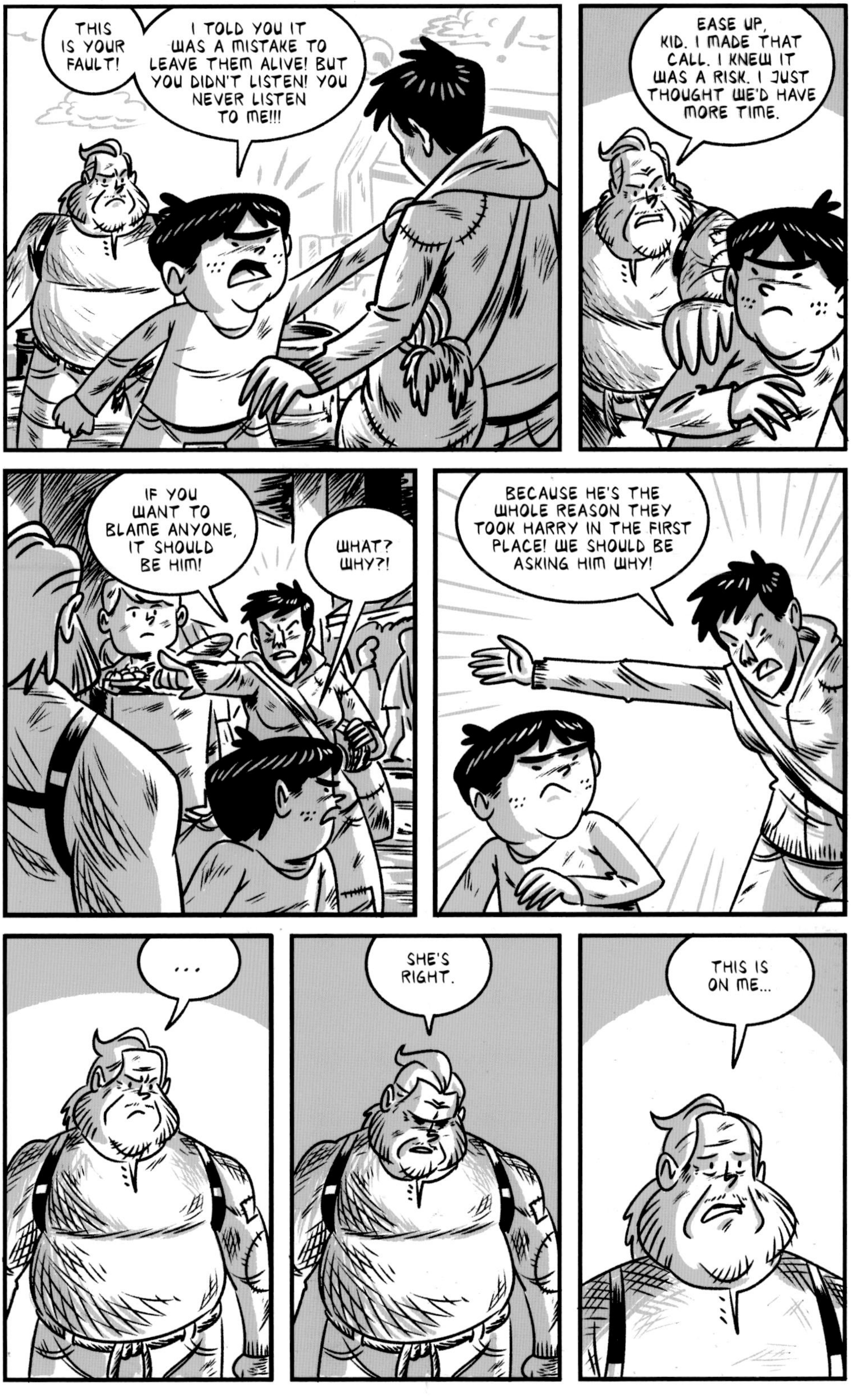
THIS IS YOUR FAULT!
I TOLD YOU IT WAS A MISTAKE TO LEAVE THEM ALIVE! BUT YOU DIDN'T LISTEN! YOU NEVER LISTEN TO ME!!!
EASE UP, KID. I MADE THAT CALL. I KNEW IT WAS A RISK. I JUST THOUGHT WE'D HAVE MORE TIME.
IF YOU WANT TO BLAME ANYONE, IT SHOULD BE HIM!
WHAT? WHY?!
BECAUSE HE'S THE WHOLE REASON THEY TOOK HARRY IN THE FIRST PLACE! WE SHOULD BE ASKING HIM WHY!
...
SHE'S RIGHT.
THIS IS ON ME...

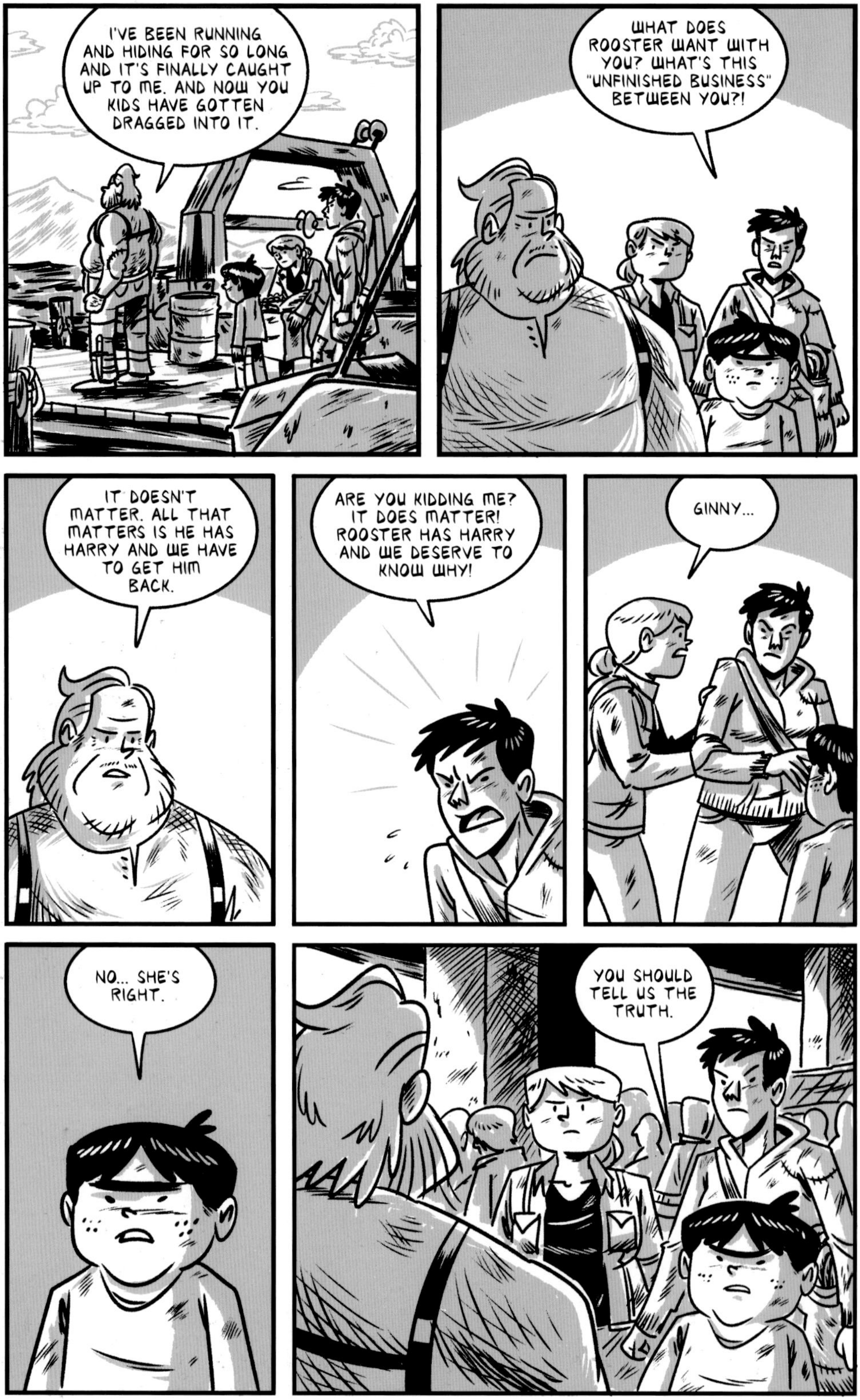

I'VE BEEN RUNNING AND HIDING FOR SO LONG AND IT'S FINALLY CAUGHT UP TO ME. AND NOW YOU KIDS HAVE GOTTEN DRAGGED INTO IT.
WHAT DOES ROOSTER WANT WITH YOU? WHAT'S THIS "UNFINISHED BUSINESS" BETWEEN YOU?!
IT DOESN'T MATTER. ALL THAT MATTERS IS HE HAS HARRY AND WE HAVE TO GET HIM BACK.
ARE YOU KIDDING ME? IT DOES MATTER! ROOSTER HAS HARRY AND WE DESERVE TO KNOW WHY!
GINNY...
NO... SHE'S RIGHT.
YOU SHOULD TELL US THE TRUTH.

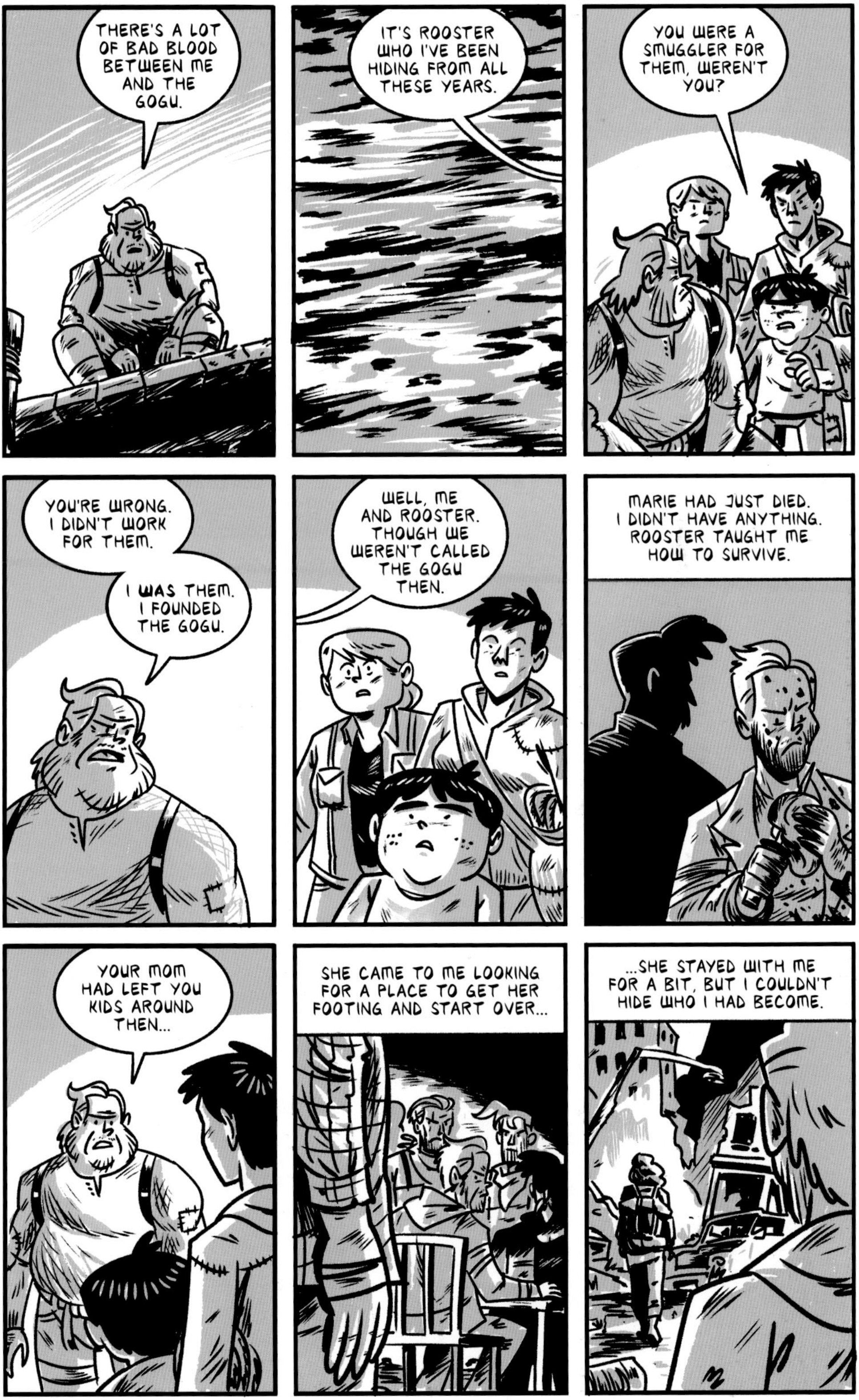
THERE'S A LOT OF BAD BLOOD BETWEEN ME AND THE GOGU.
IT'S ROOSTER WHO I'VE BEEN HIDING FROM ALL THESE YEARS.
YOU WERE A SMUGGLER FOR THEM, WEREN'T YOU?
YOU'RE WRONG. I DIDN'T WORK FOR THEM.
I WAS THEM. I FOUNDED THE GOGU.
WELL, ME AND ROOSTER. THOUGH WE WEREN'T CALLED THE GOGU THEN.
MARIE HAD JUST DIED. I DIDN'T HAVE ANYTHING. ROOSTER TAUGHT ME HOW TO SURVIVE.
YOUR MOM HAD LEFT YOU KIDS AROUND THEN...
SHE CAME TO ME LOOKING FOR A PLACE TO GET HER FOOTING AND START OVER...
...SHE STAYED WITH ME FOR A BIT, BUT I COULDN'T HIDE WHO I HAD BECOME.

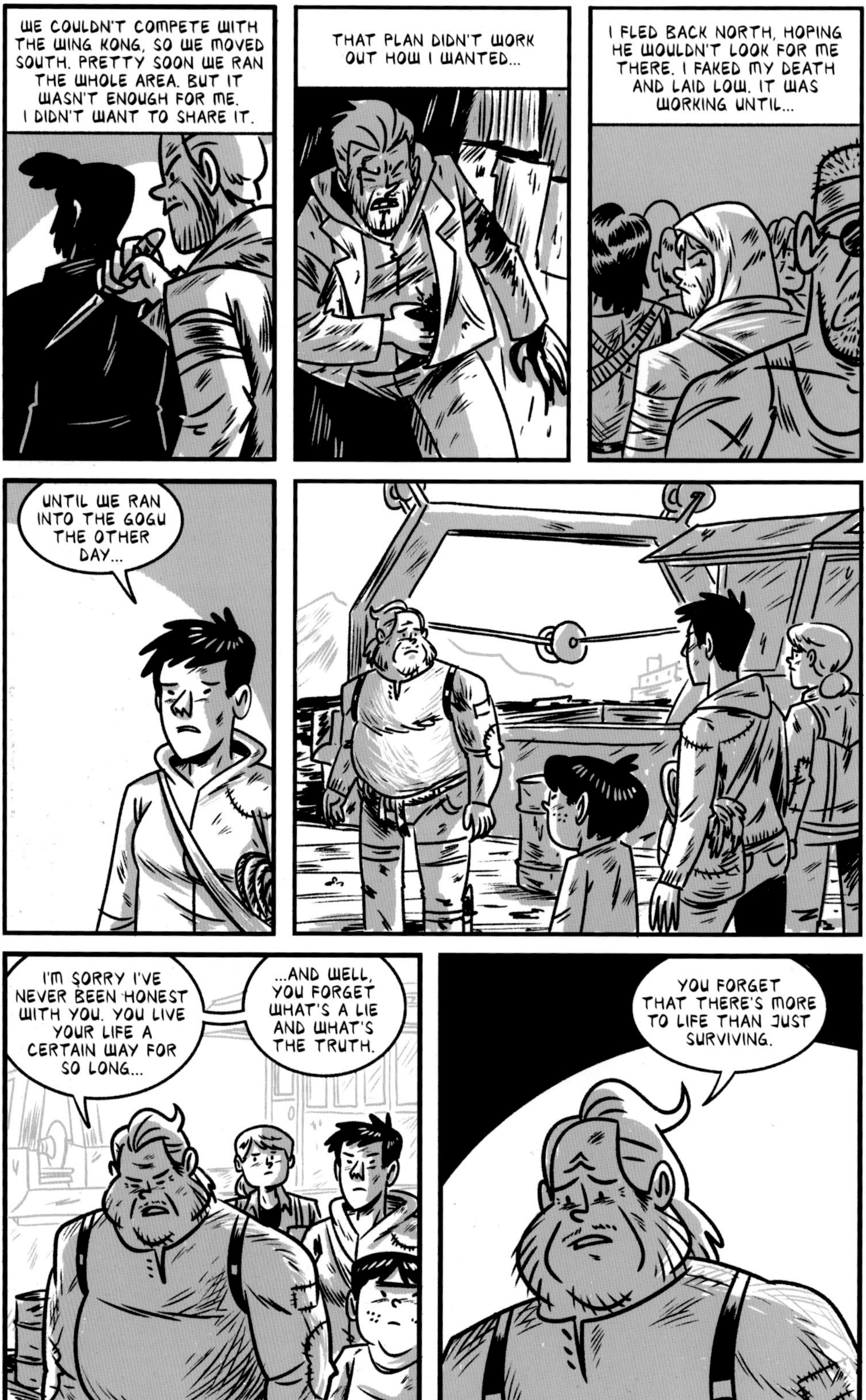
WE COULDN'T COMPETE WITH THE WING KONG, SO WE MOVED SOUTH. PRETTY SOON WE RAN THE WHOLE AREA. BUT IT WASN'T ENOUGH FOR ME. I DIDN'T WANT TO SHARE IT.
THAT PLAN DIDN'T WORK OUT HOW I WANTED...
I FLED BACK NORTH, HOPING HE WOULDN'T LOOK FOR ME THERE. I FAKED MY DEATH AND LAID LOW. IT WAS WORKING UNTIL...
UNTIL WE RAN INTO THE GOGU THE OTHER DAY...
I'M SORRY I'VE NEVER BEEN HONEST WITH YOU. YOU LIVE YOUR LIFE A CERTAIN WAY FOR SO LONG...
...AND WELL, YOU FORGET WHAT'S A LIE AND WHAT'S THE TRUTH.
YOU FORGET THAT THERE'S MORE TO LIFE THAN JUST SURVIVING.

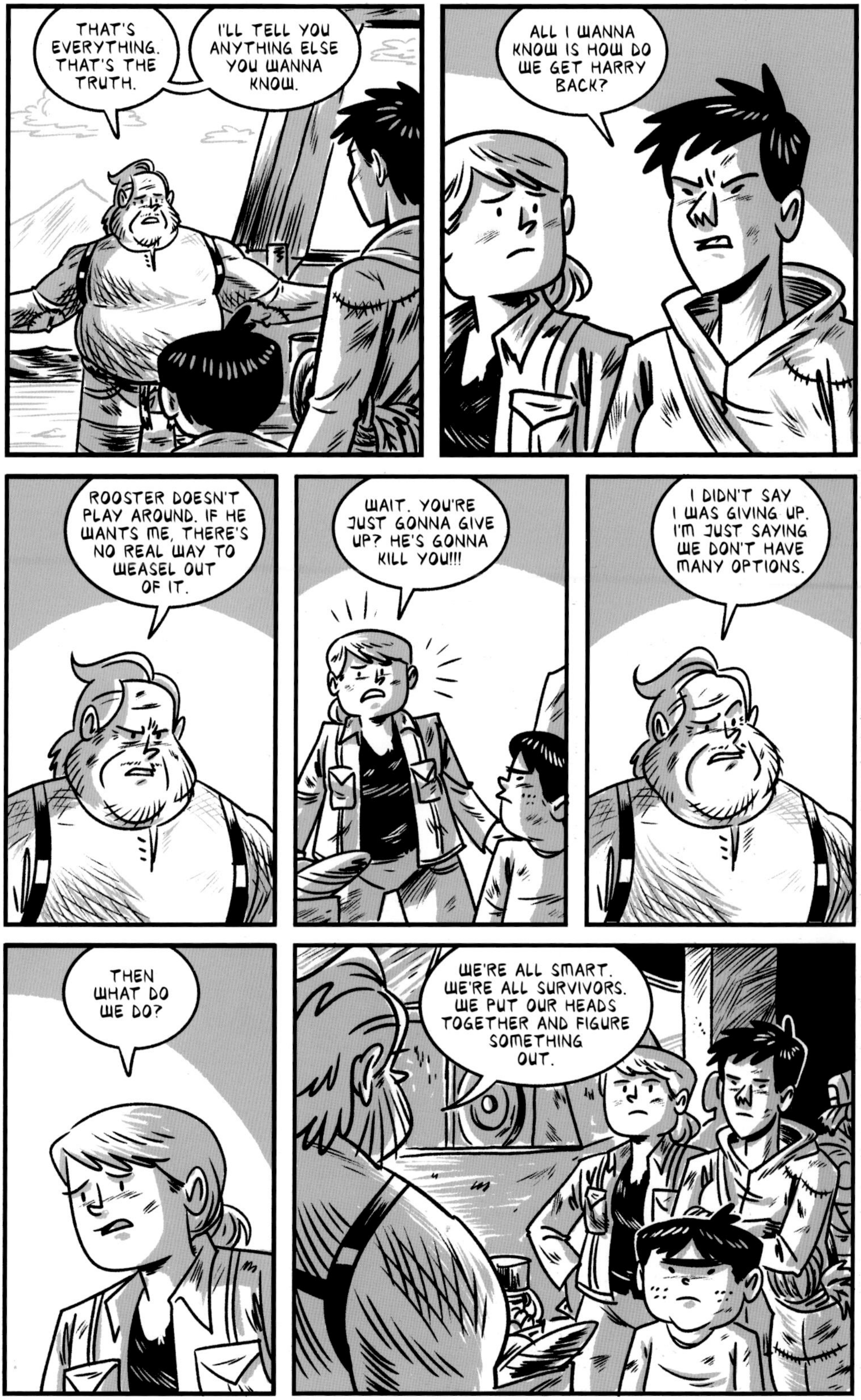
THAT'S EVERYTHING. THAT'S THE TRUTH.
I'LL TELL YOU ANYTHING ELSE YOU WANNA KNOW.
ALL I WANNA KNOW IS HOW DO WE GET HARRY BACK?
ROOSTER DOESN'T PLAY AROUND. IF HE WANTS ME, THERE'S NO REAL WAY TO WEASEL OUT OF IT.
WAIT. YOU'RE JUST GONNA GIVE UP? HE'S GONNA KILL YOU!!!
I DIDN'T SAY I WAS GIVING UP. I'M JUST SAYING WE DON'T HAVE MANY OPTIONS.
THEN WHAT DO WE DO?
WE'RE ALL SMART. WE'RE ALL SURVIVORS. WE PUT OUR HEADS TOGETHER AND FIGURE SOMETHING OUT.

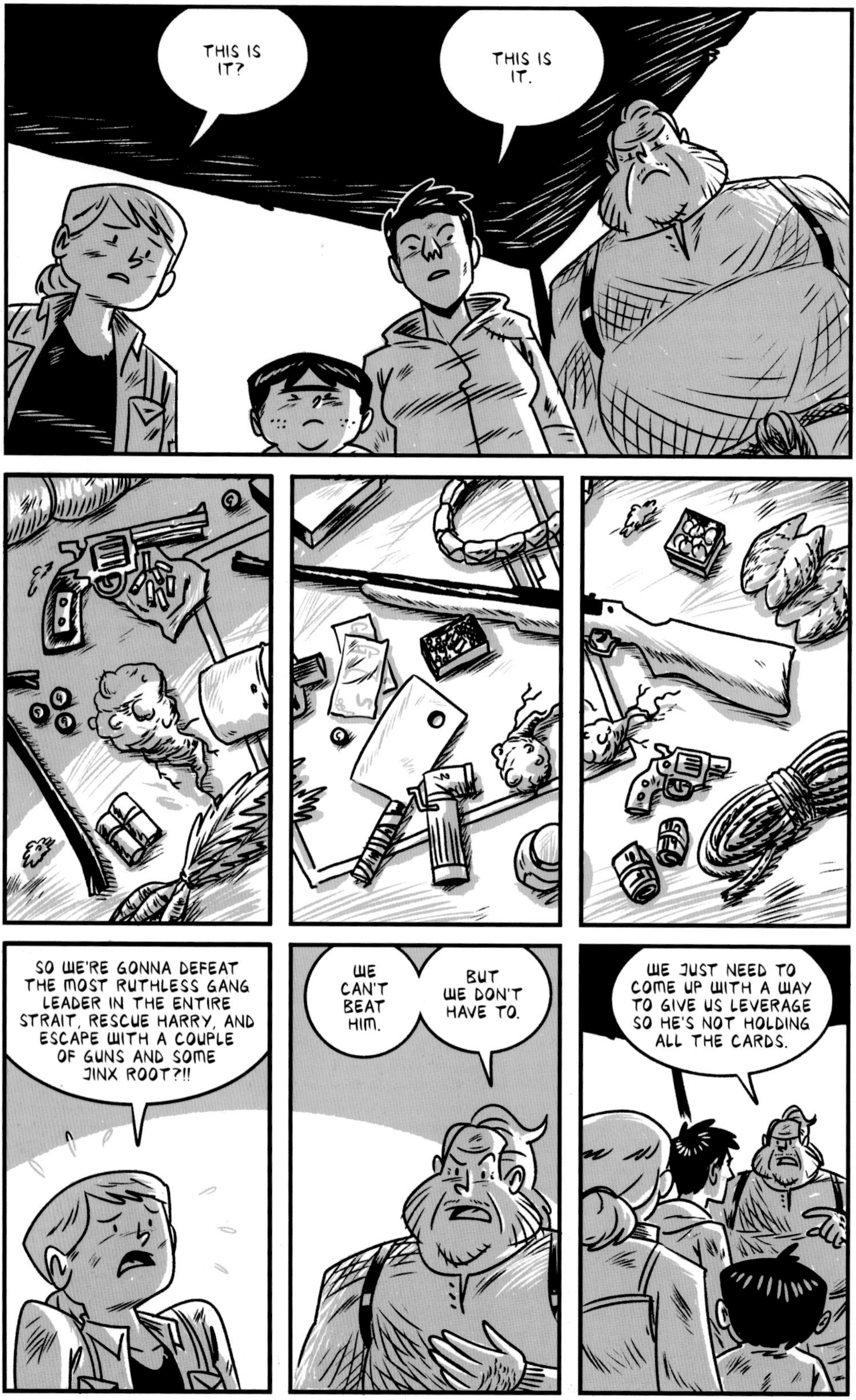
THIS IS IT?
THIS IS IT.
SO WE'RE GONNA DEFEAT THE MOST RUTHLESS GANG LEADER IN THE ENTIRE STRAIT, RESCUE HARRY, AND ESCAPE WITH A COUPLE OF GUNS AND SOME JINX ROOT?!!
WE CAN'T BEAT HIM.
BUT WE DON'T HAVE TO.
WE JUST NEED TO COME UP WITH A WAY TO GIVE US LEVERAGE SO HE'S NOT HOLDING ALL THE CARDS.

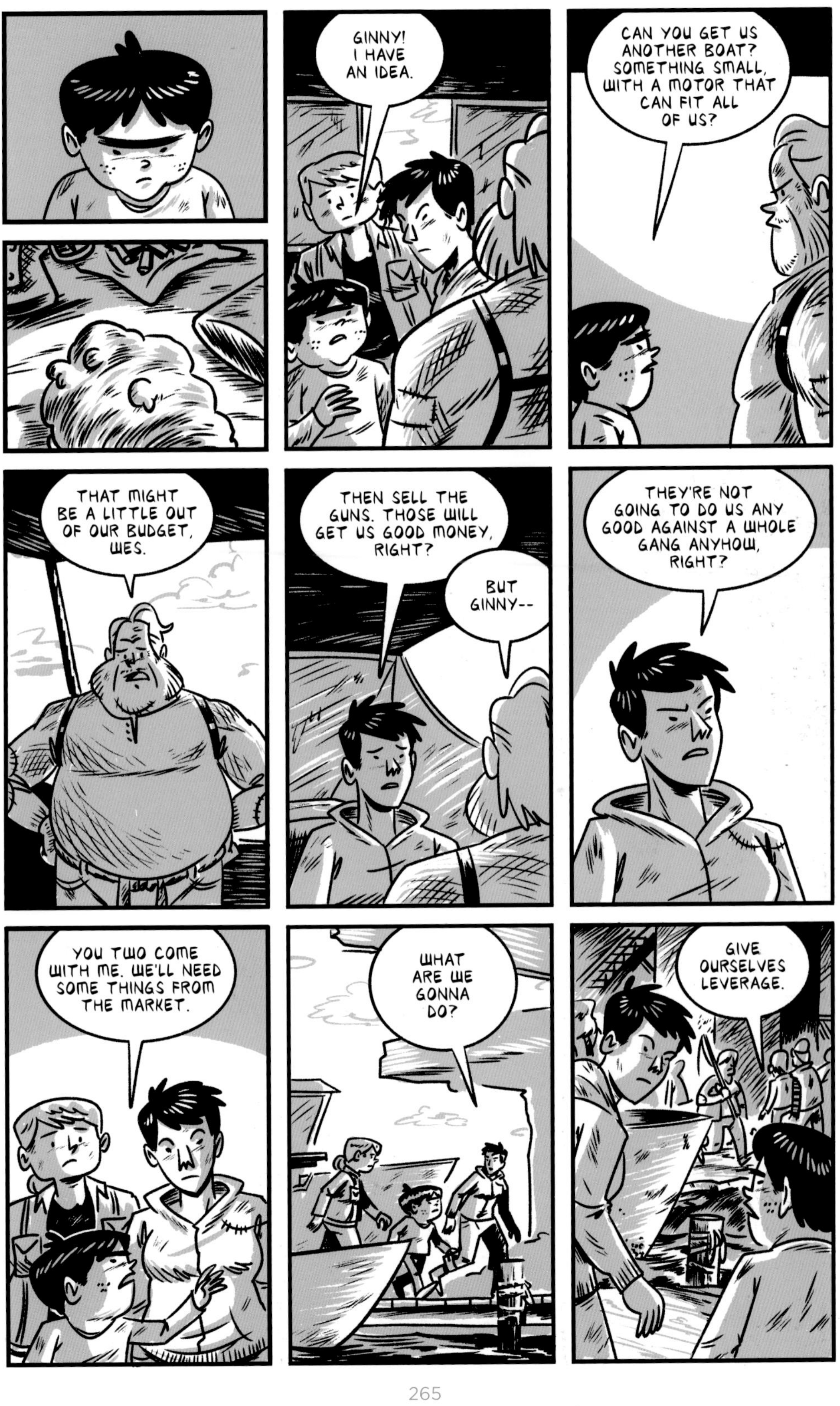
GINNY! I HAVE AN IDEA.
CAN YOU GET US ANOTHER BOAT? SOMETHING SMALL, WITH A MOTOR THAT CAN FIT ALL OF US?
THAT MIGHT BE A LITTLE OUT OF OUR BUDGET, WES.
THEN SELL THE GUNS. THOSE WILL GET US GOOD MONEY, RIGHT?
BUT GINNY--
THEY'RE NOT GOING TO DO US ANY GOOD AGAINST A WHOLE GANG ANYHOW, RIGHT?
YOU TWO COME WITH ME. WE'LL NEED SOME THINGS FROM THE MARKET.
WHAT ARE WE GONNA DO?
GIVE OURSELVES LEVERAGE.

CHAPTER 11

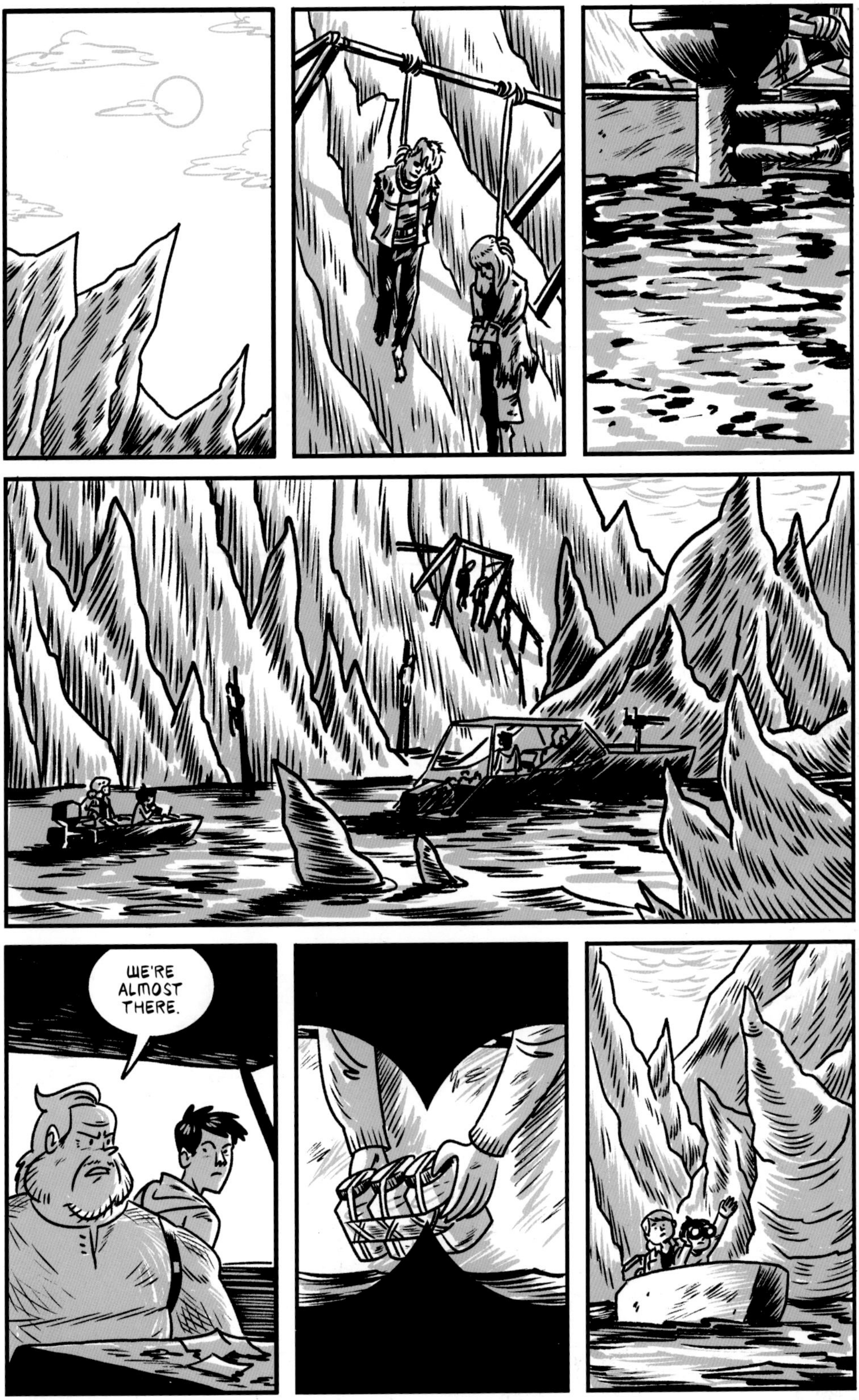
WE'RE ALMOST THERE.

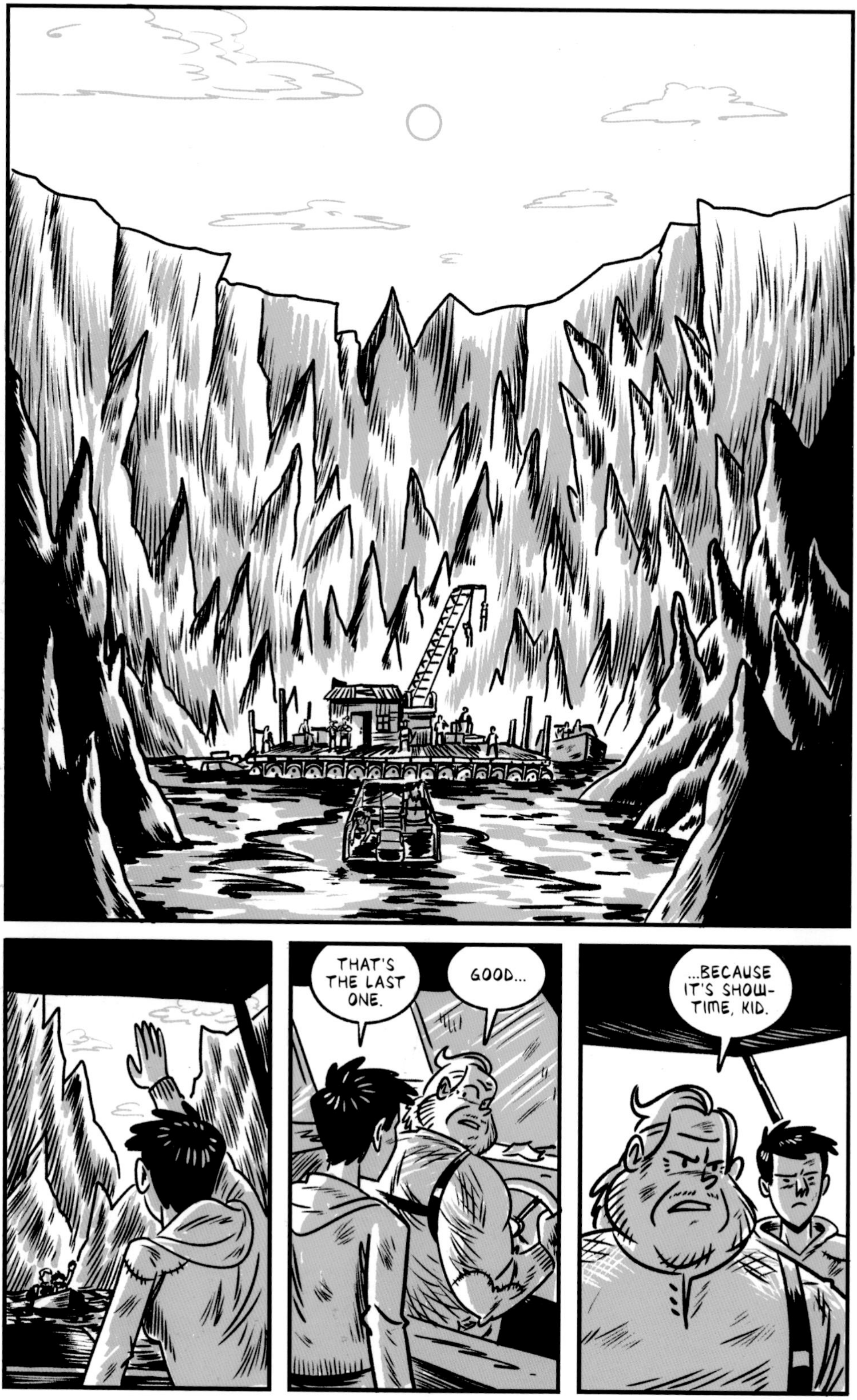
THAT'S THE LAST ONE.
GOOD...
...BECAUSE IT'S SHOW-TIME, KID.

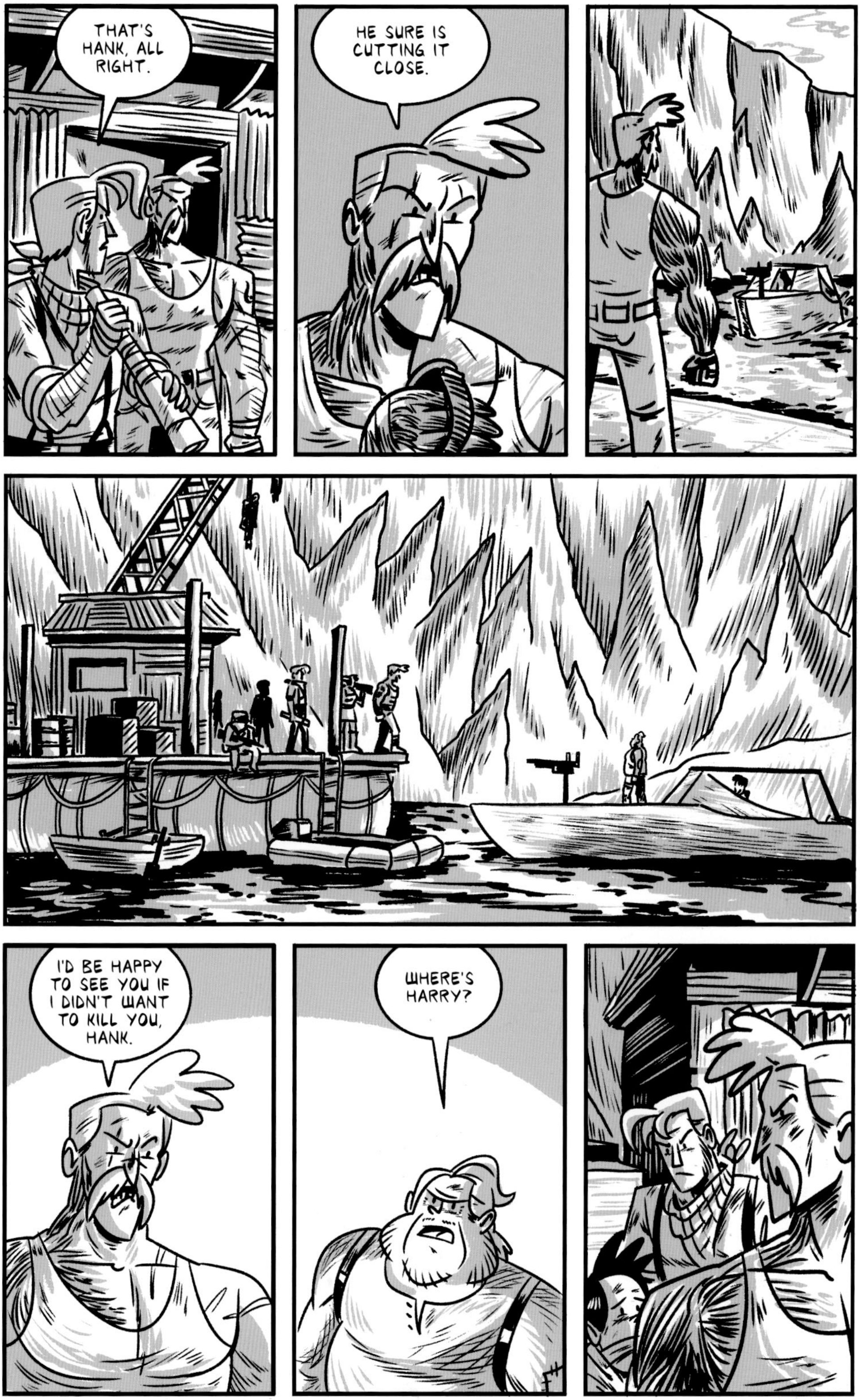
THAT'S HANK, ALL RIGHT.
HE SURE IS CUTTING IT CLOSE.
I'D BE HAPPY TO SEE YOU IF I DIDN'T WANT TO KILL YOU, HANK.
WHERE'S HARRY?

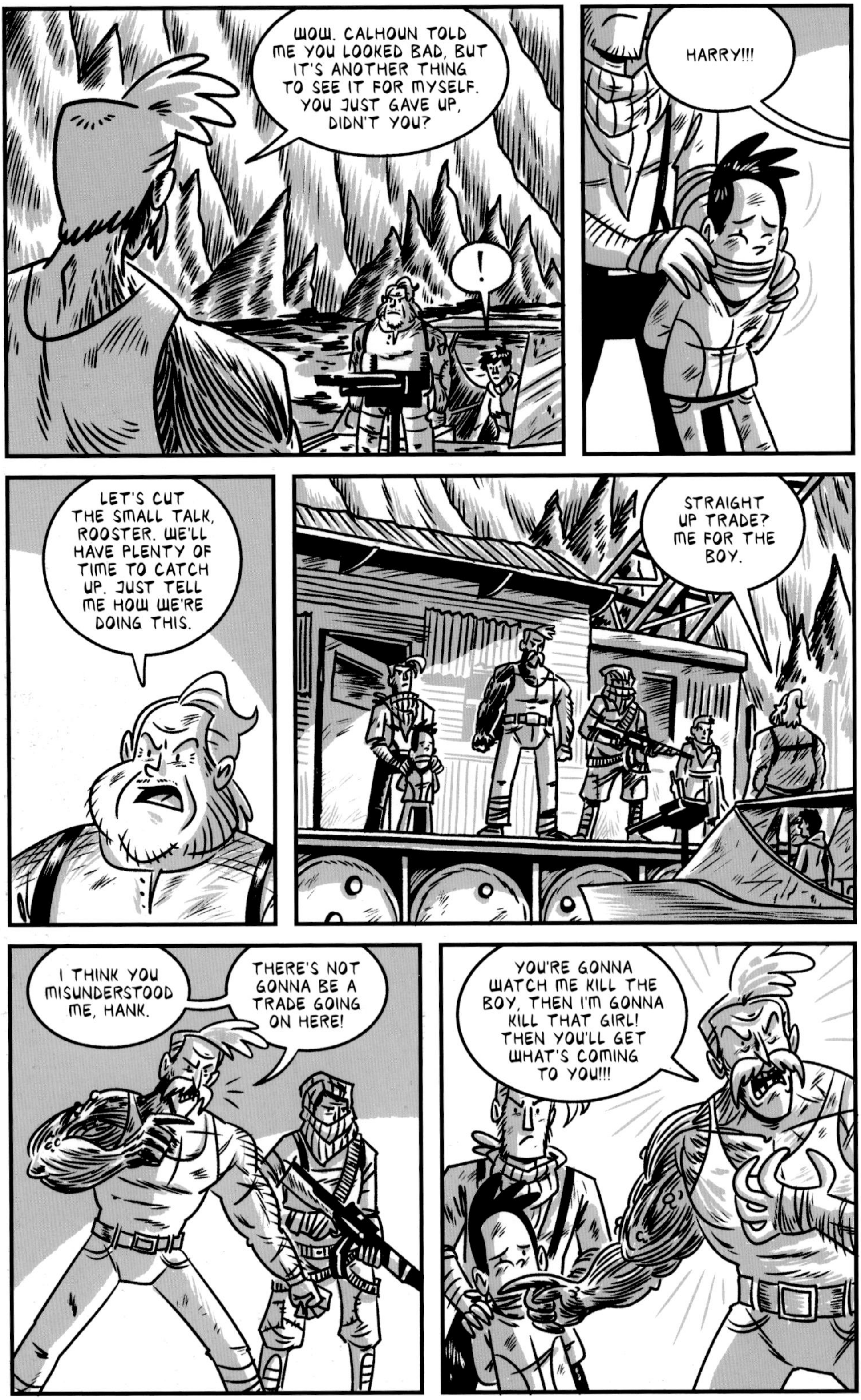
WOW. CALHOUN TOLD ME YOU LOOKED BAD, BUT IT'S ANOTHER THING TO SEE IT FOR MYSELF. YOU JUST GAVE UP, DIDN'T YOU?
!
HARRY!!!
LET'S CUT THE SMALL TALK, ROOSTER. WE'LL HAVE PLENTY OF TIME TO CATCH UP. JUST TELL ME HOW WE'RE DOING THIS.
STRAIGHT UP TRADE? ME FOR THE BOY.
I THINK YOU MISUNDERSTOOD ME, HANK.
THERE'S NOT GONNA BE A TRADE GOING ON HERE!
YOU'RE GONNA WATCH ME KILL THE BOY, THEN I'M GONNA KILL THAT GIRL! THEN YOU'LL GET WHAT'S COMING TO YOU!!!

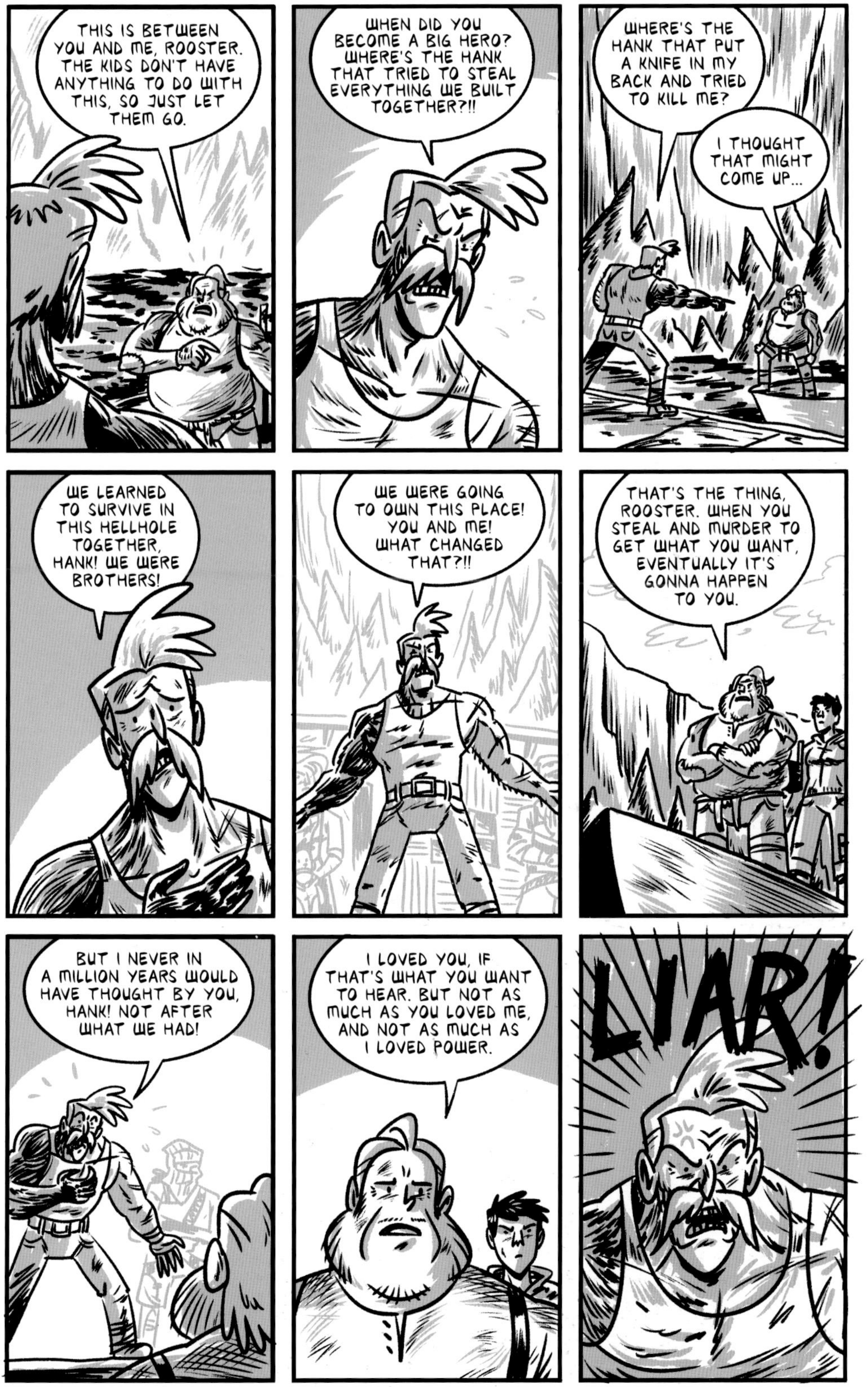
THIS IS BETWEEN YOU AND ME, ROOSTER. THE KIDS DON'T HAVE ANYTHING TO DO WITH THIS, SO JUST LET THEM GO.
WHEN DID YOU BECOME A BIG HERO? WHERE'S THE HANK THAT TRIED TO STEAL EVERYTHING WE BUILT TOGETHER?!!
WHERE'S THE HANK THAT PUT A KNIFE IN MY BACK AND TRIED TO KILL ME?
I THOUGHT THAT MIGHT COME UP...
WE LEARNED TO SURVIVE IN THIS HELLHOLE TOGETHER, HANK! WE WERE BROTHERS!
WE WERE GOING TO OWN THIS PLACE! YOU AND ME! WHAT CHANGED THAT?!!
THAT'S THE THING, ROOSTER. WHEN YOU STEAL AND MURDER TO GET WHAT YOU WANT, EVENTUALLY IT'S GONNA HAPPEN TO YOU.
BUT I NEVER IN A MILLION YEARS WOULD HAVE THOUGHT BY YOU, HANK! NOT AFTER WHAT WE HAD!
I LOVED YOU, IF THAT'S WHAT YOU WANT TO HEAR. BUT NOT AS MUCH AS YOU LOVED ME, AND NOT AS MUCH AS I LOVED POWER.
LIAR!

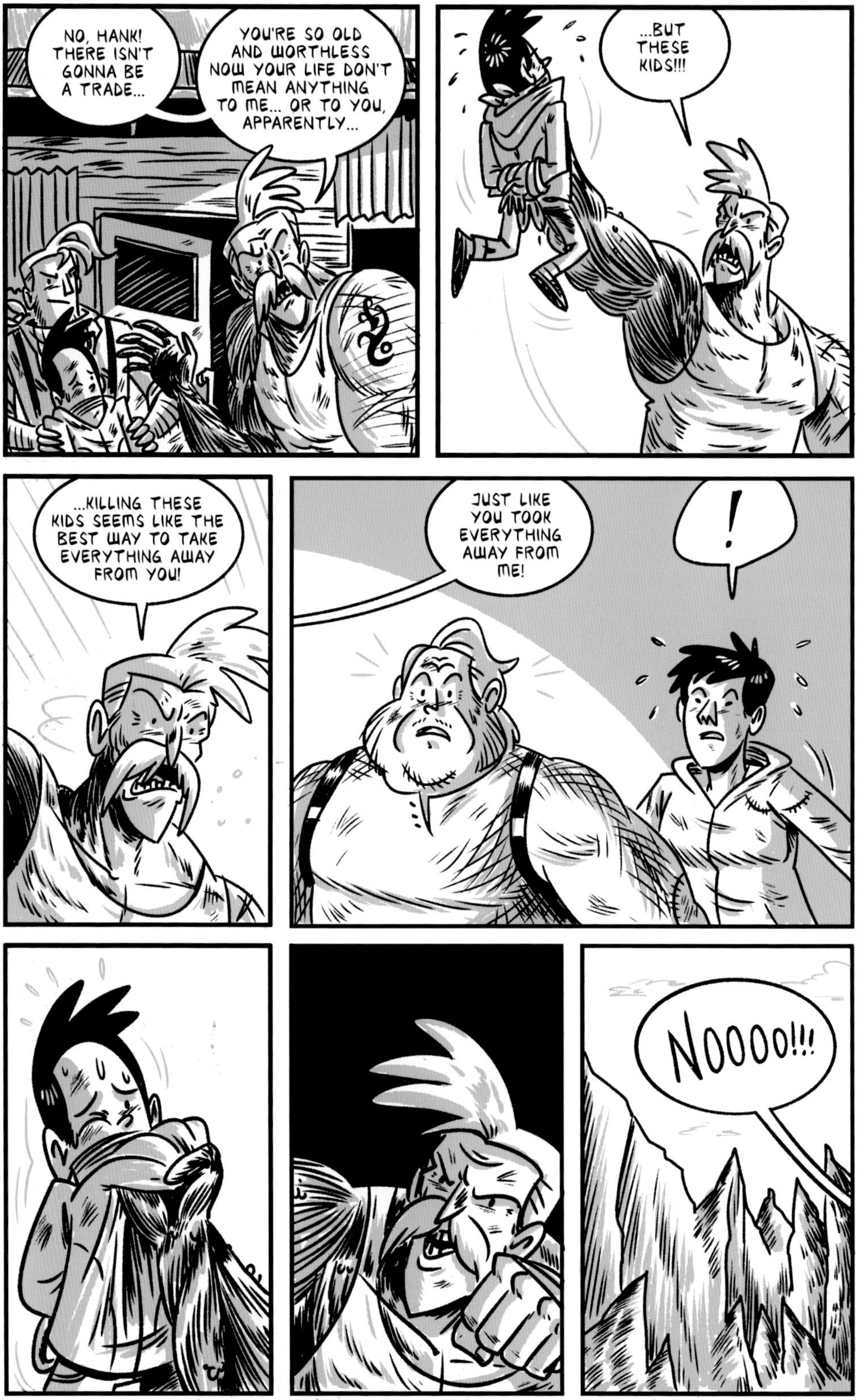
NO, HANK! THERE ISN'T GONNA BE A TRADE...
YOU'RE SO OLD AND WORTHLESS NOW YOUR LIFE DON'T MEAN ANYTHING TO ME... OR TO YOU, APPARENTLY...
...BUT THESE KIDS!!!
...KILLING THESE KIDS SEEMS LIKE THE BEST WAY TO TAKE EVERYTHING AWAY FROM YOU!
JUST LIKE YOU TOOK EVERYTHING AWAY FROM ME!
!
NOOOO!!!

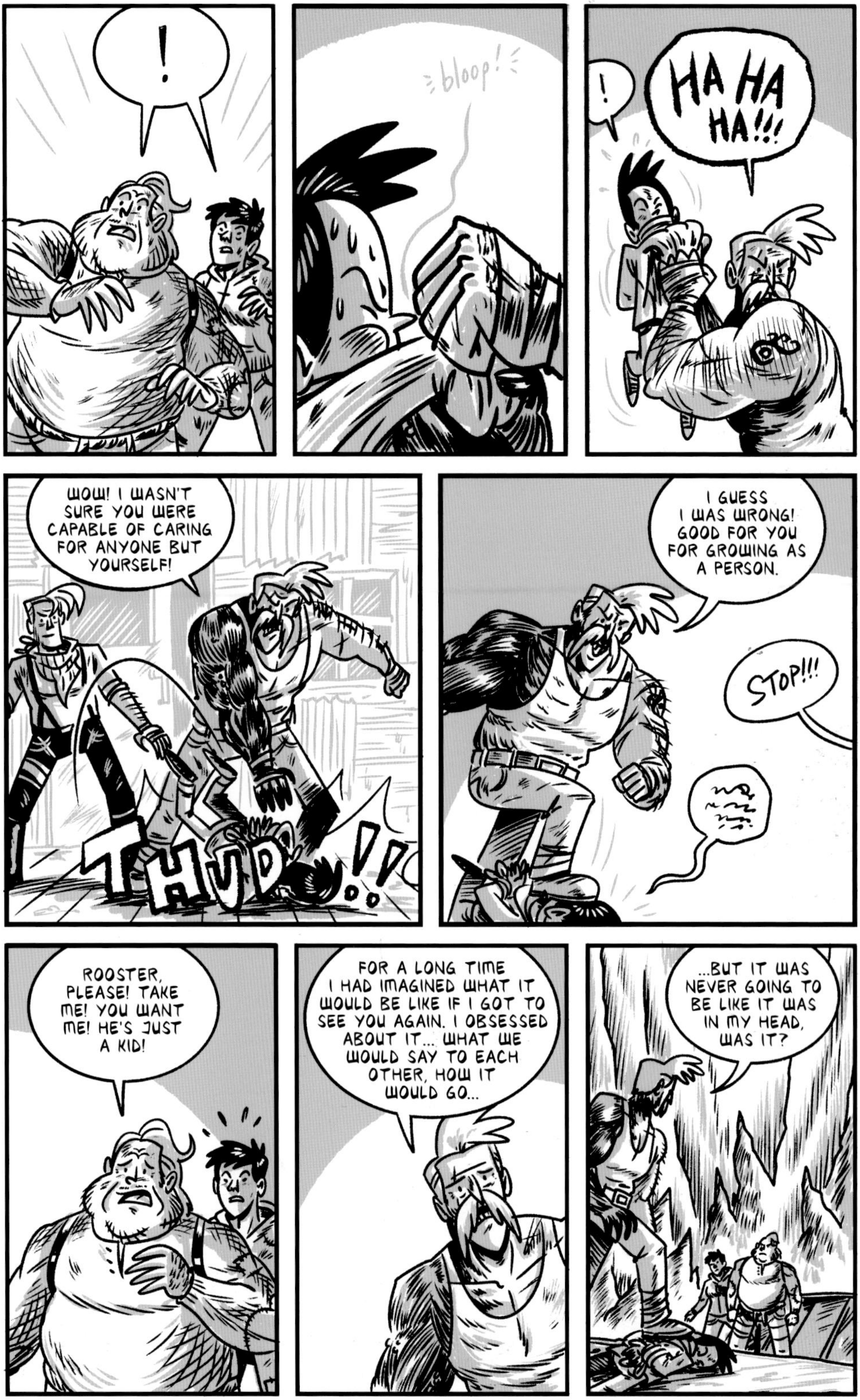
!
bloop!
!
HA HA HA!!!
WOW! I WASN'T SURE YOU WERE CAPABLE OF CARING FOR ANYONE BUT YOURSELF!
THUD!!
I GUESS I WAS WRONG! GOOD FOR YOU FOR GROWING AS A PERSON.
STOP!!!
ROOSTER, PLEASE! TAKE ME! YOU WANT ME! HE'S JUST A KID!
FOR A LONG TIME I HAD IMAGINED WHAT IT WOULD BE LIKE IF I GOT TO SEE YOU AGAIN. I OBSESSED ABOUT IT... WHAT WE WOULD SAY TO EACH OTHER, HOW IT WOULD GO...
...BUT IT WAS NEVER GOING TO BE LIKE IT WAS IN MY HEAD, WAS IT?

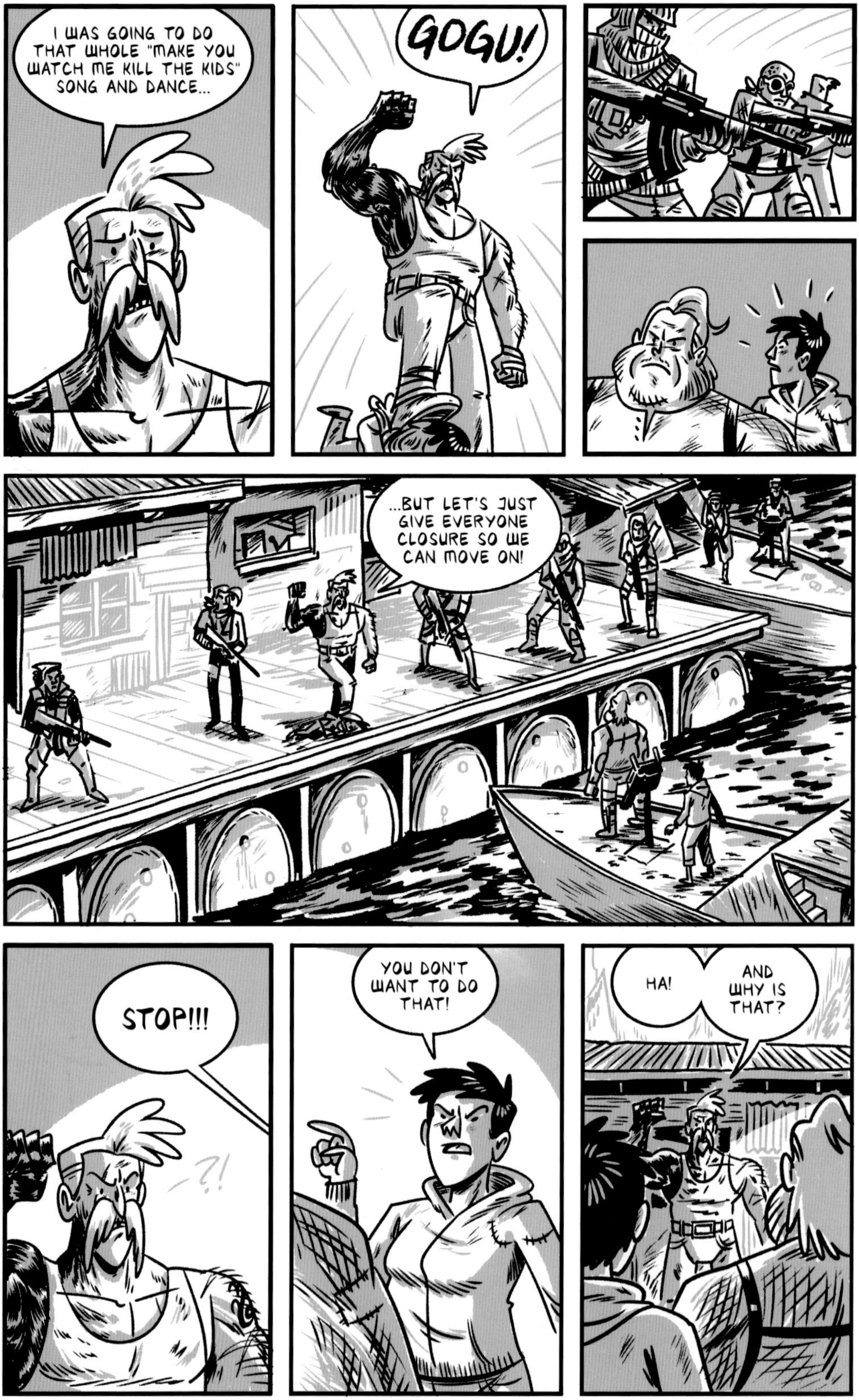
I WAS GOING TO DO THAT WHOLE "MAKE YOU WATCH ME KILL THE KIDS" SONG AND DANCE...
GOGU!
...BUT LET'S JUST GIVE EVERYONE CLOSURE SO WE CAN MOVE ON!
STOP!!!
?!
YOU DON'T WANT TO DO THAT!
HA!
AND WHY IS THAT?

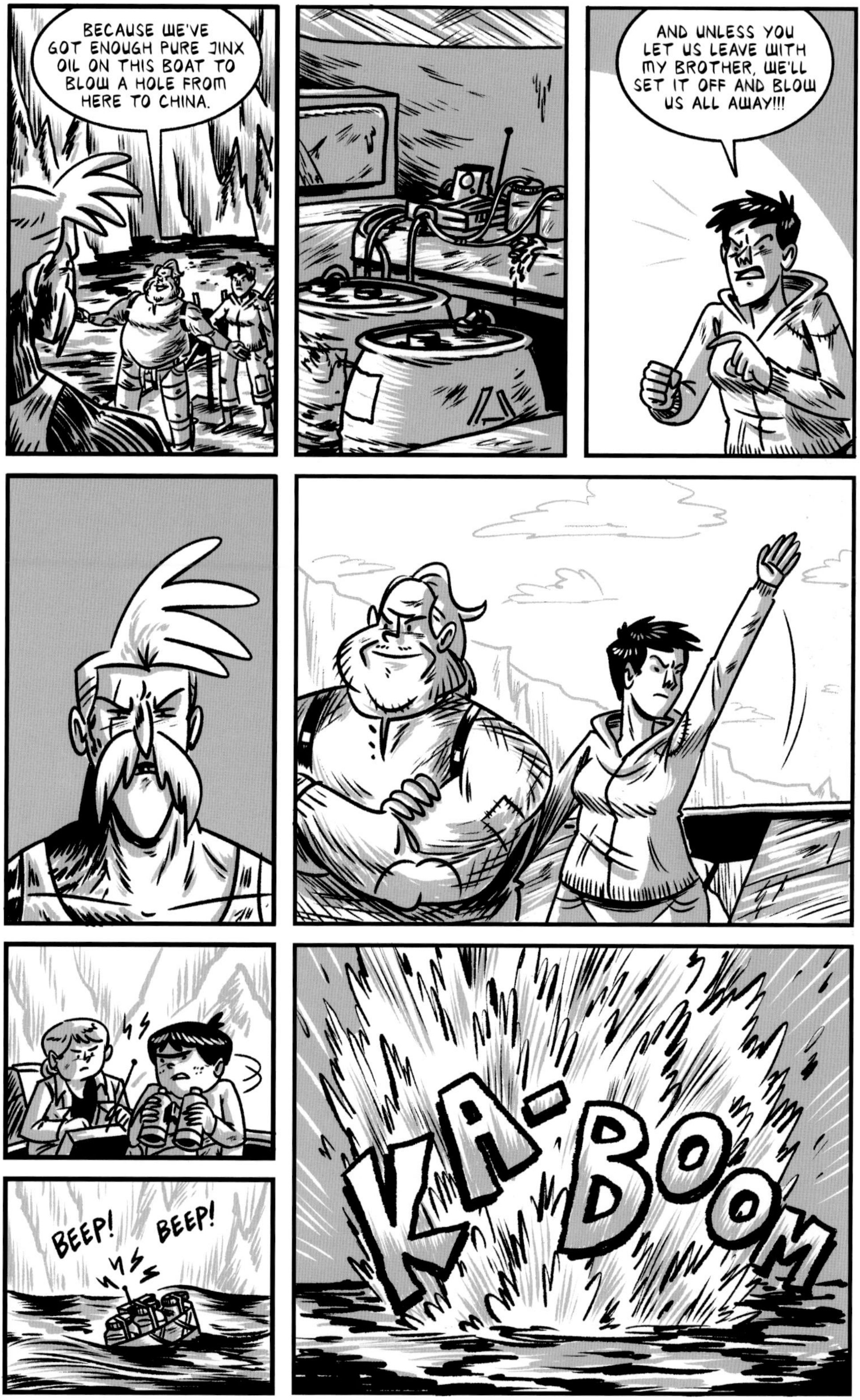
BECAUSE WE'VE GOT ENOUGH PURE JINX OIL ON THIS BOAT TO BLOW A HOLE FROM HERE TO CHINA.
AND UNLESS YOU LET US LEAVE WITH MY BROTHER, WE'LL SET IT OFF AND BLOW US ALL AWAY!!!
BEEP!
BEEP!
KA-BOOM

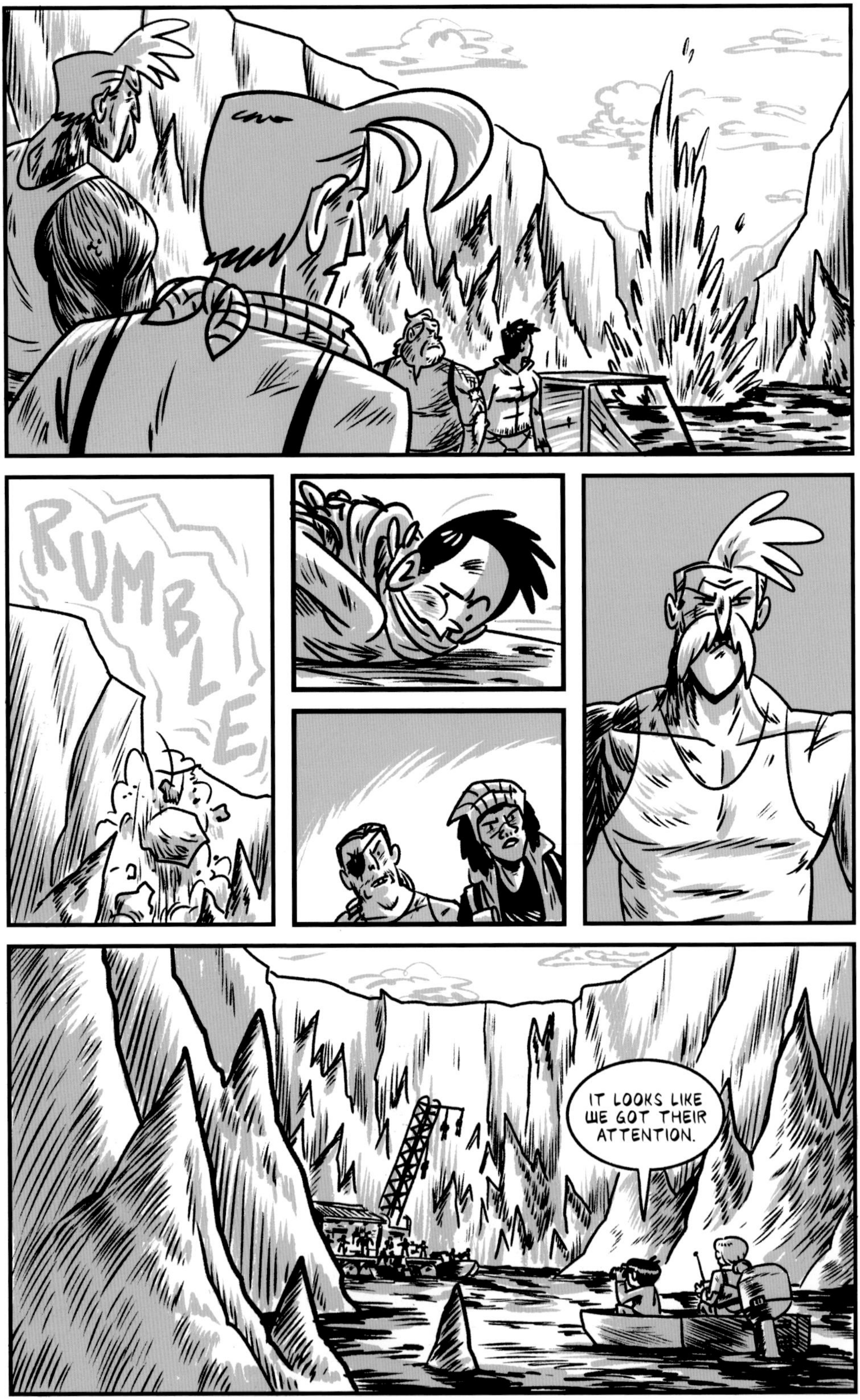
RUMBLE
IT LOOKS LIKE WE GOT THEIR ATTENTION.

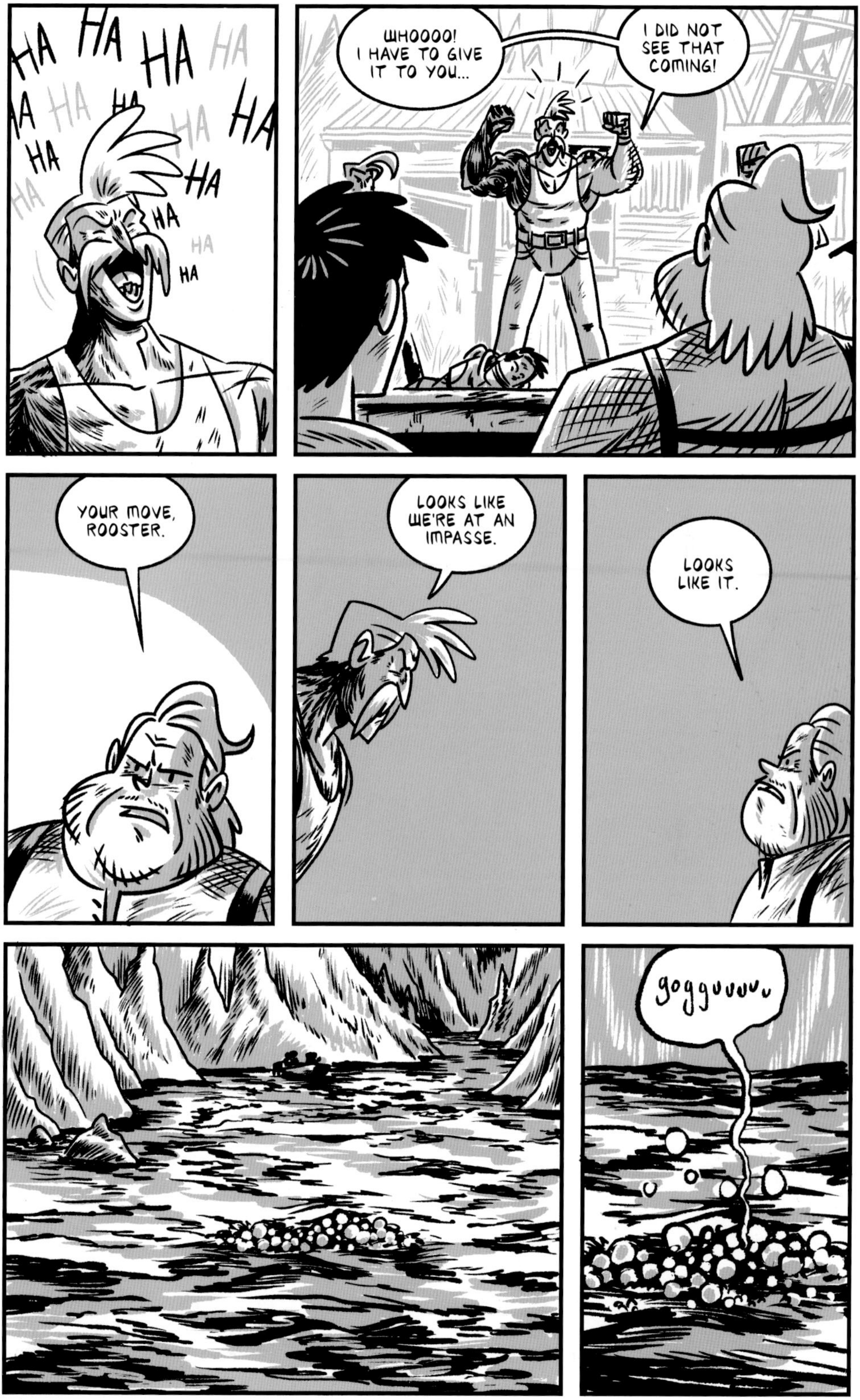
HA HA HA HA HA HA HA HA HA HA HA HA HA HA HA
WHOOOO! I HAVE TO GIVE IT TO YOU...
I DID NOT SEE THAT COMING!
YOUR MOVE, ROOSTER.
LOOKS LIKE WE'RE AT AN IMPASSE.
LOOKS LIKE IT.
gogguuuu

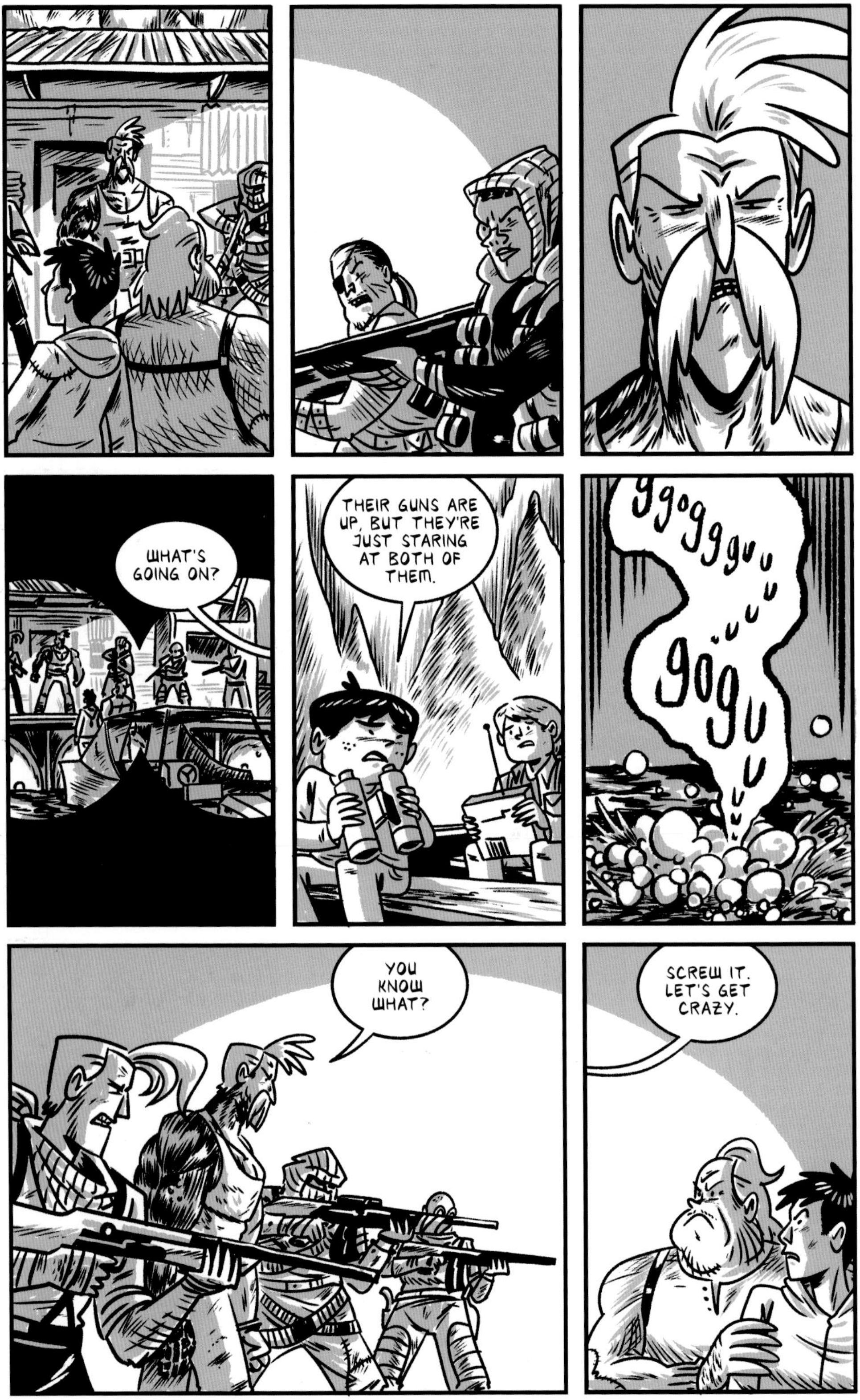
WHAT'S GOING ON?
THEIR GUNS ARE UP, BUT THEY'RE JUST STARING AT BOTH OF THEM.
ggogggu
gogu
YOU KNOW WHAT?
SCREW IT. LET'S GET CRAZY.

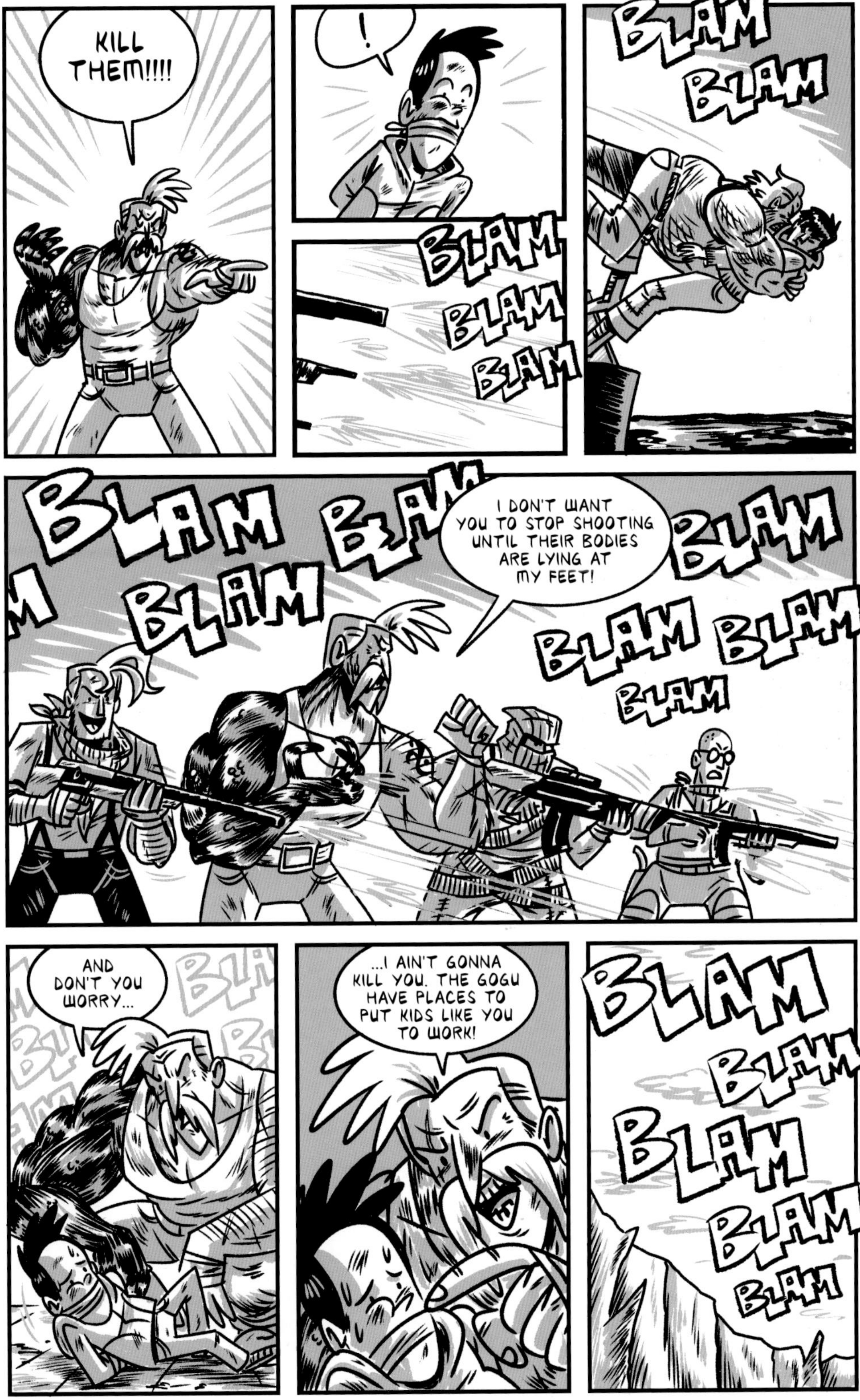
KILL THEM!!!!
!
BLAM
BLAM
BLAM
BLAM
BLAM
BLAM
BLAM
BLAM
BLAM
I DON'T WANT YOU TO STOP SHOOTING UNTIL THEIR BODIES ARE LYING AT MY FEET!
BLAM
BLAM
BLAM
BLAM
AND DON'T YOU WORRY...
...I AIN'T GONNA KILL YOU. THE GOGU HAVE PLACES TO PUT KIDS LIKE YOU TO WORK!
BLAM
BLAM
BLAM
BLAM
BLAM

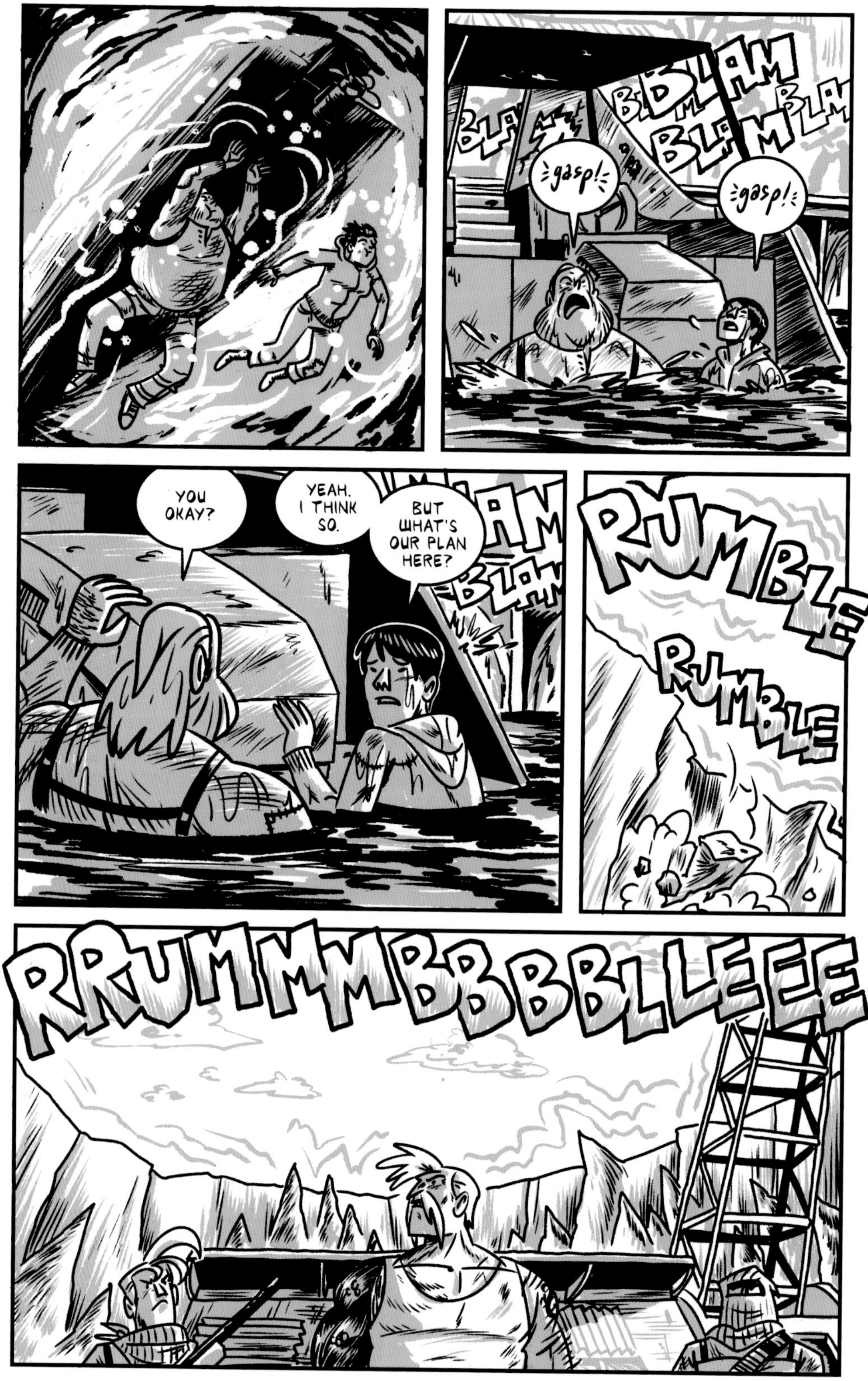
BLAM
BLAM
BLAM
BLAM
gasp!
gasp!
YOU OKAY?
YEAH. I THINK SO.
BUT WHAT'S OUR PLAN HERE?
BLAM
RUMBLE
RUMBLE
RRUMMMBBBBLLEEE

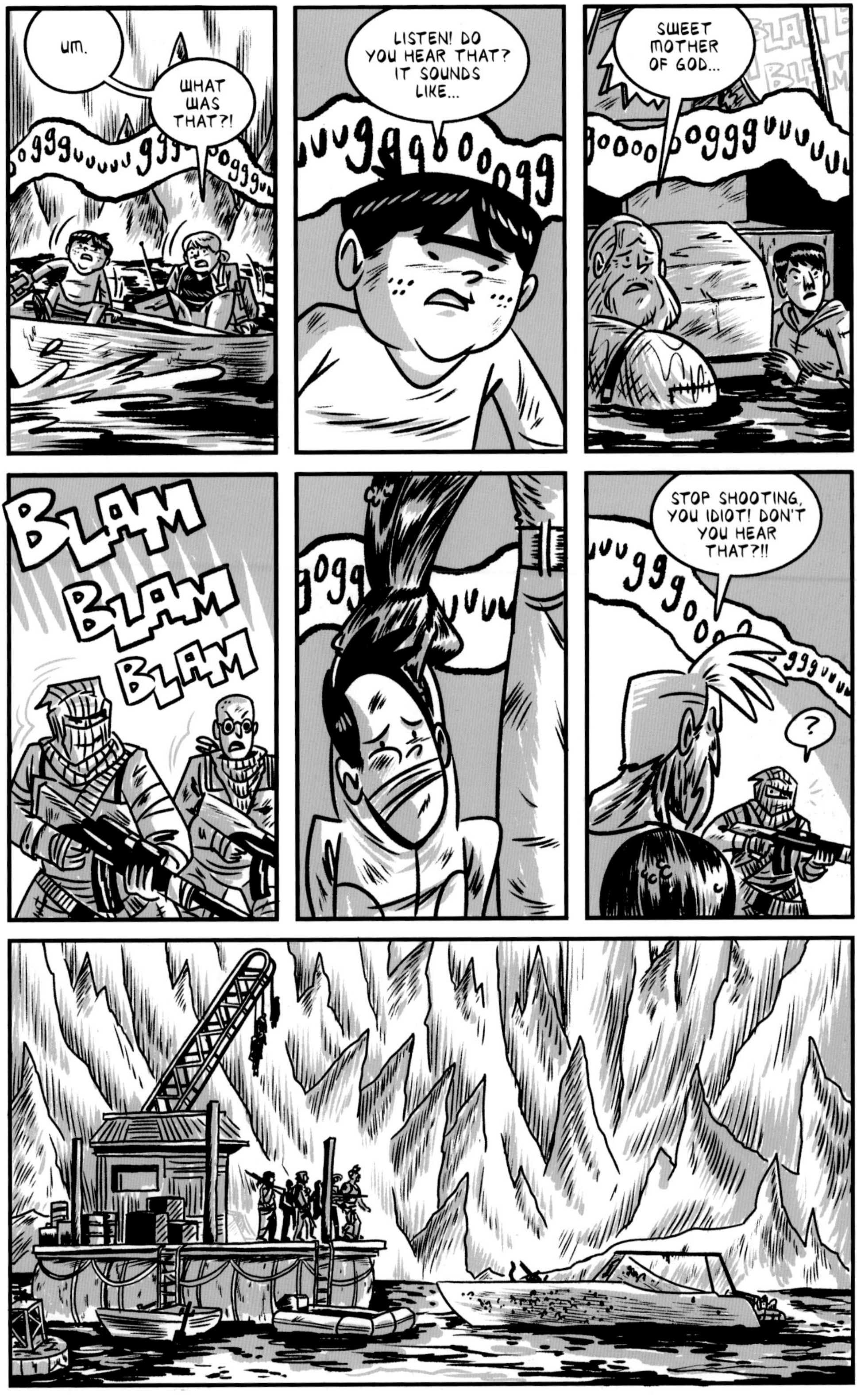

UM.
WHAT WAS THAT?!
LISTEN! DO YOU HEAR THAT? IT SOUNDS LIKE...
SWEET MOTHER OF GOD...
BLAM BLAM BLAM
STOP SHOOTING, YOU IDIOT! DON'T YOU HEAR THAT?!!
?

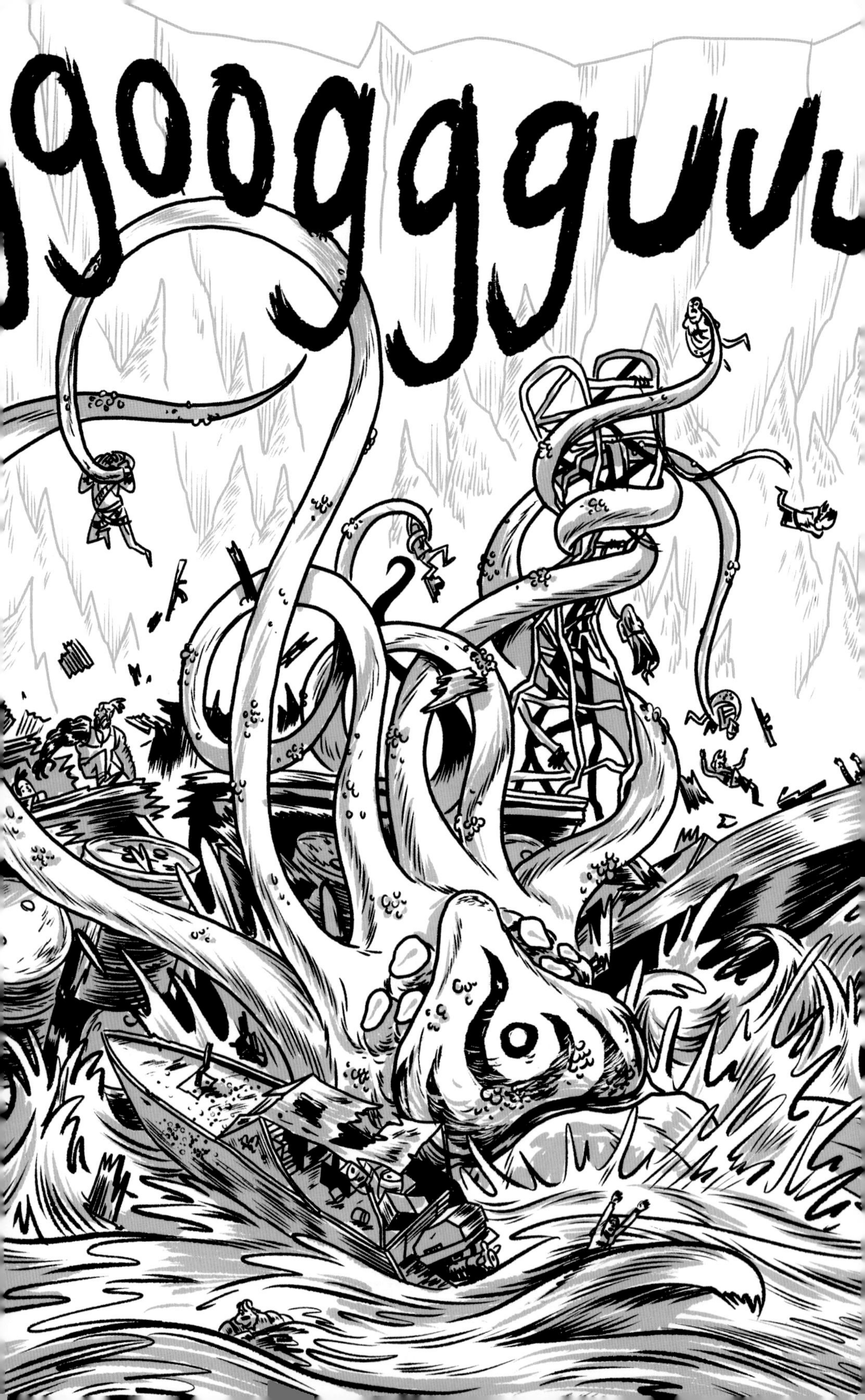
googgguu

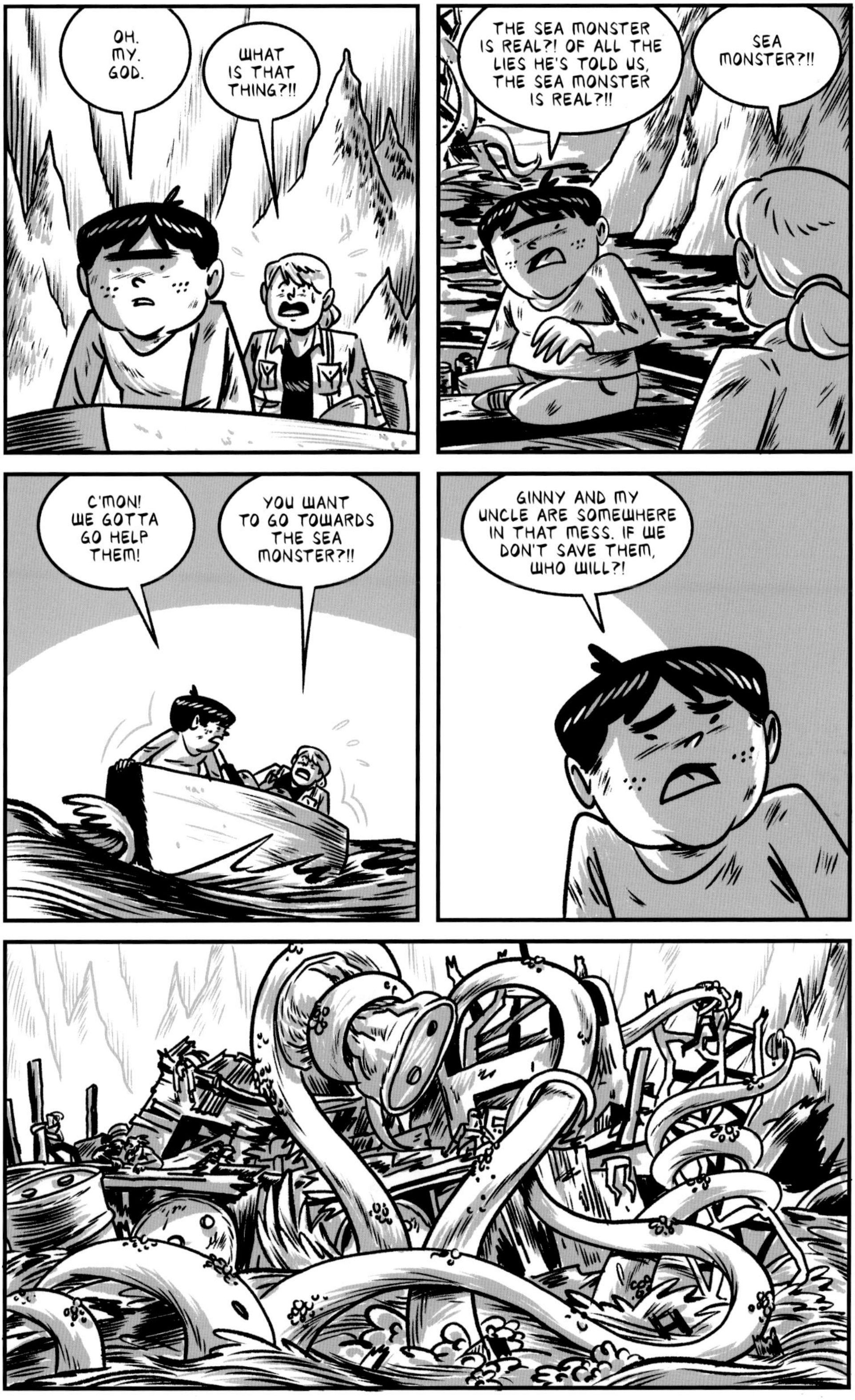
OH. MY. GOD.
WHAT IS THAT THING?!!
THE SEA MONSTER IS REAL?! OF ALL THE LIES HE'S TOLD US, THE SEA MONSTER IS REAL?!!
SEA MONSTER?!!
C'MON! WE GOTTA GO HELP THEM!
YOU WANT TO GO TOWARDS THE SEA MONSTER?!!
GINNY AND MY UNCLE ARE SOMEWHERE IN THAT MESS. IF WE DON'T SAVE THEM, WHO WILL?!

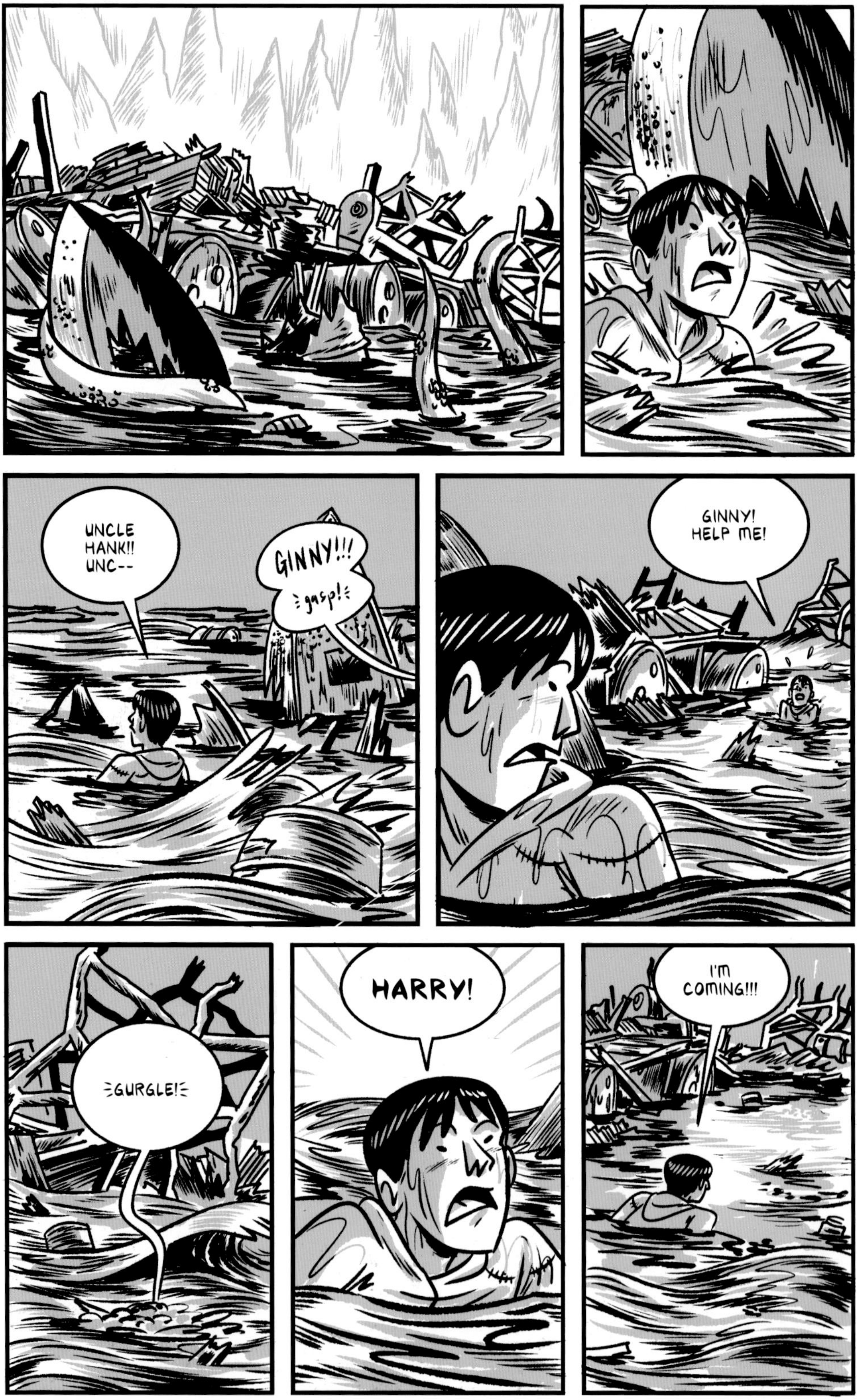
UNCLE HANK!! UNC--
GINNY!!!
gasp!
GINNY! HELP ME!
GURGLE!
HARRY!
I'M COMING!!!

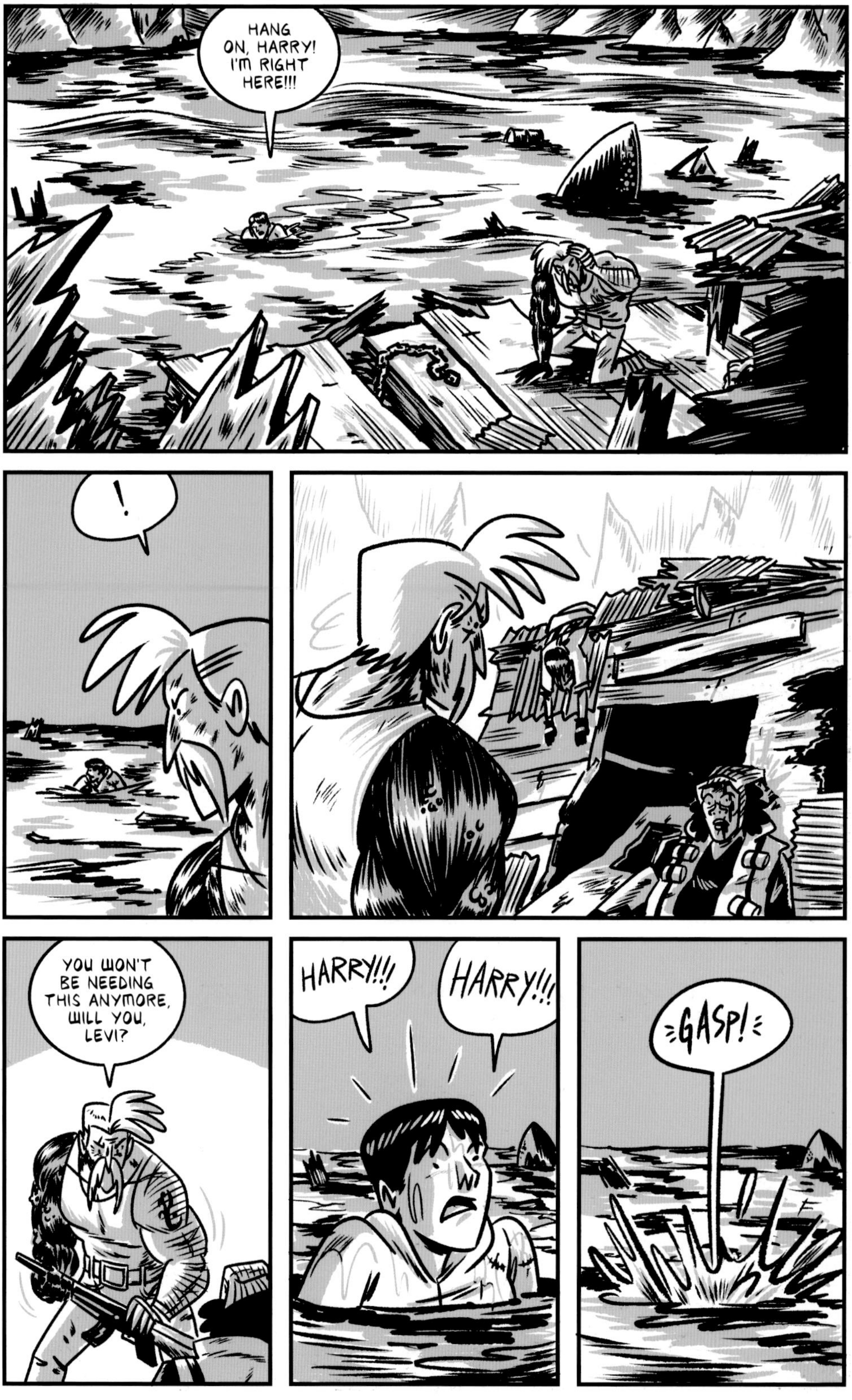
HANG ON, HARRY! I'M RIGHT HERE!!!
!
YOU WON'T BE NEEDING THIS ANYMORE, WILL YOU, LEVI?
HARRY!!!
HARRY!!!
GASP!

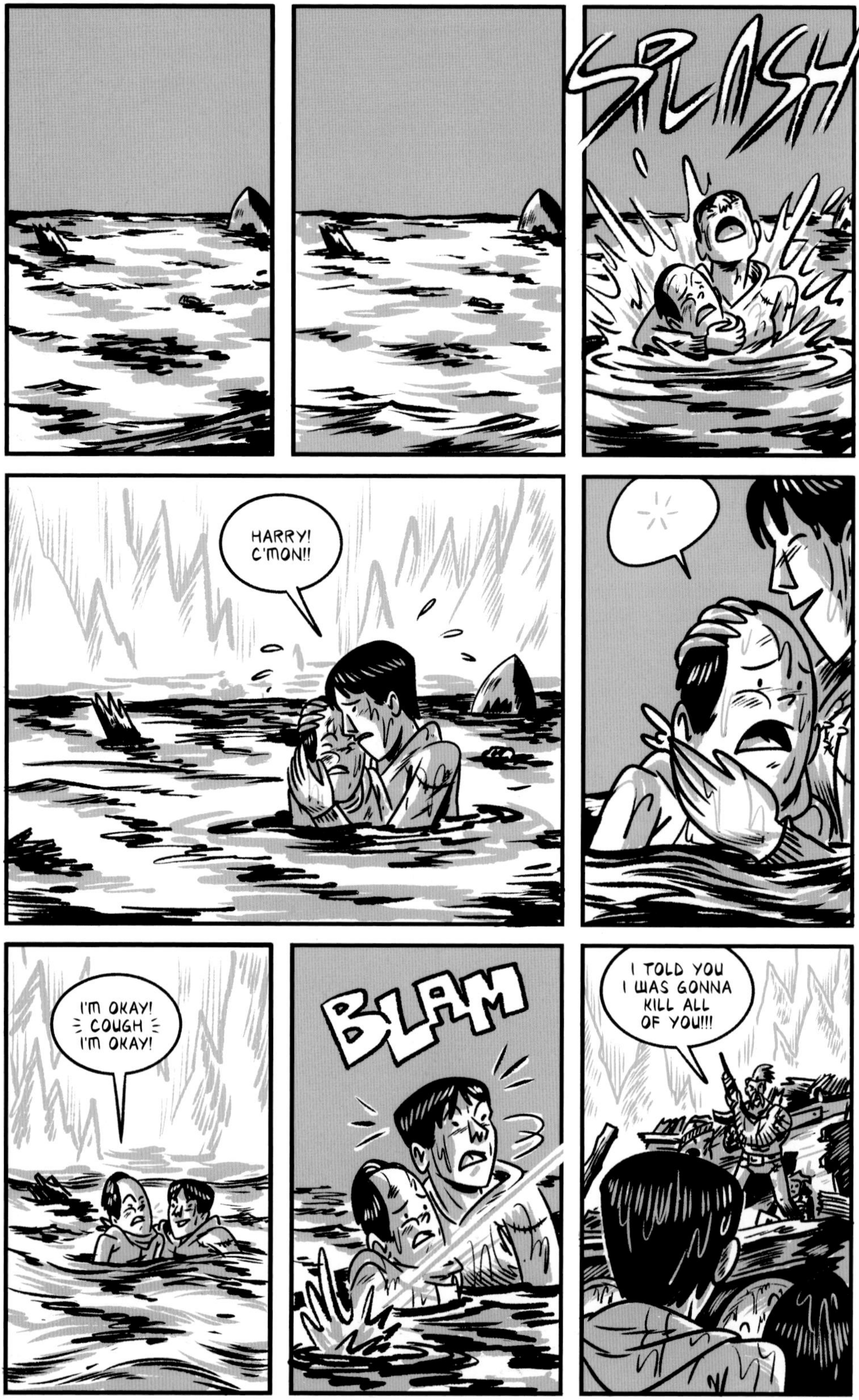
SPLASH
HARRY! C'MON!!
I'M OKAY! COUGH I'M OKAY!
BLAM
I TOLD YOU I WAS GONNA KILL ALL OF YOU!!!

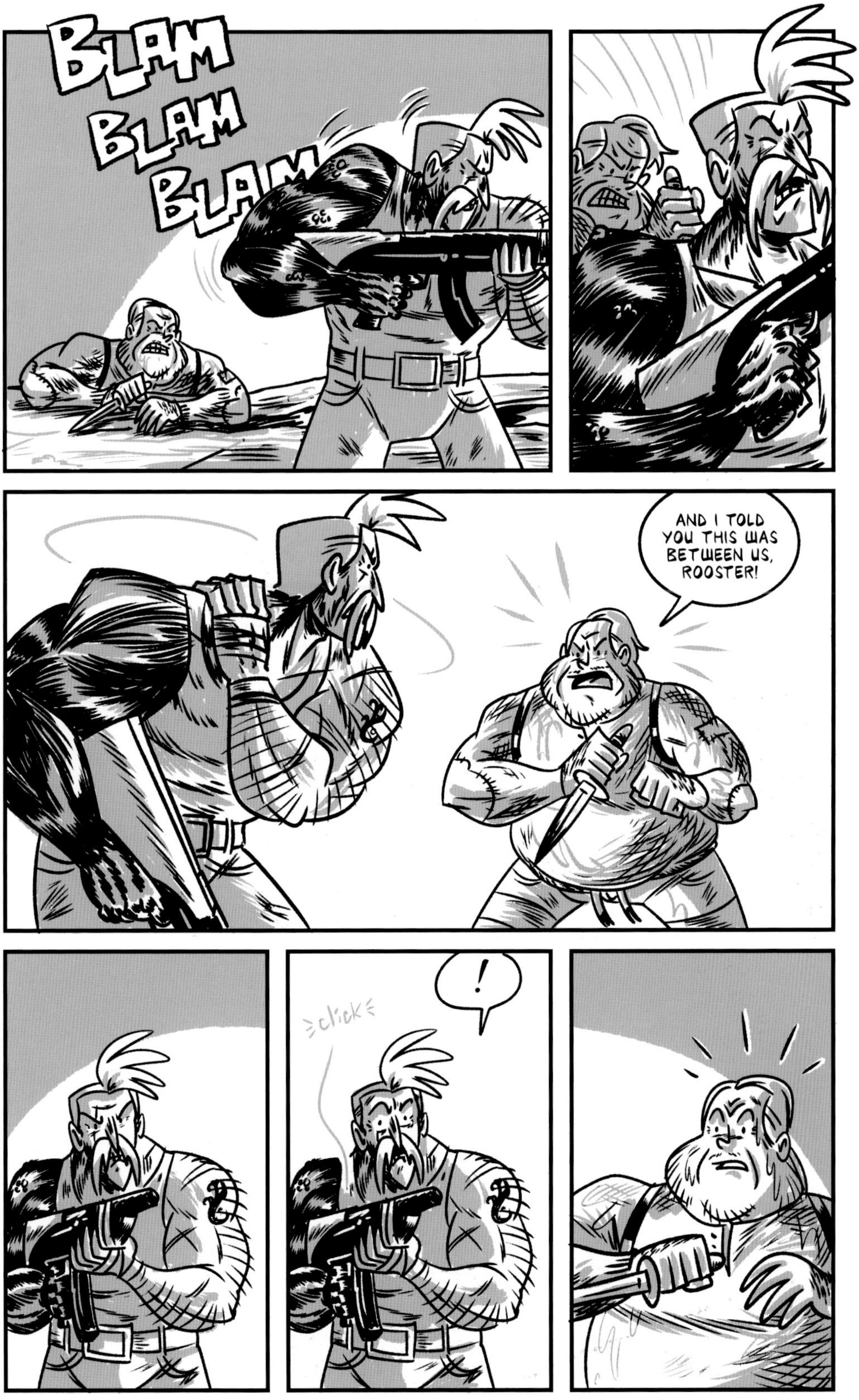
BLAM
BLAM
BLAM
AND I TOLD YOU THIS WAS BETWEEN US, ROOSTER!
click
!

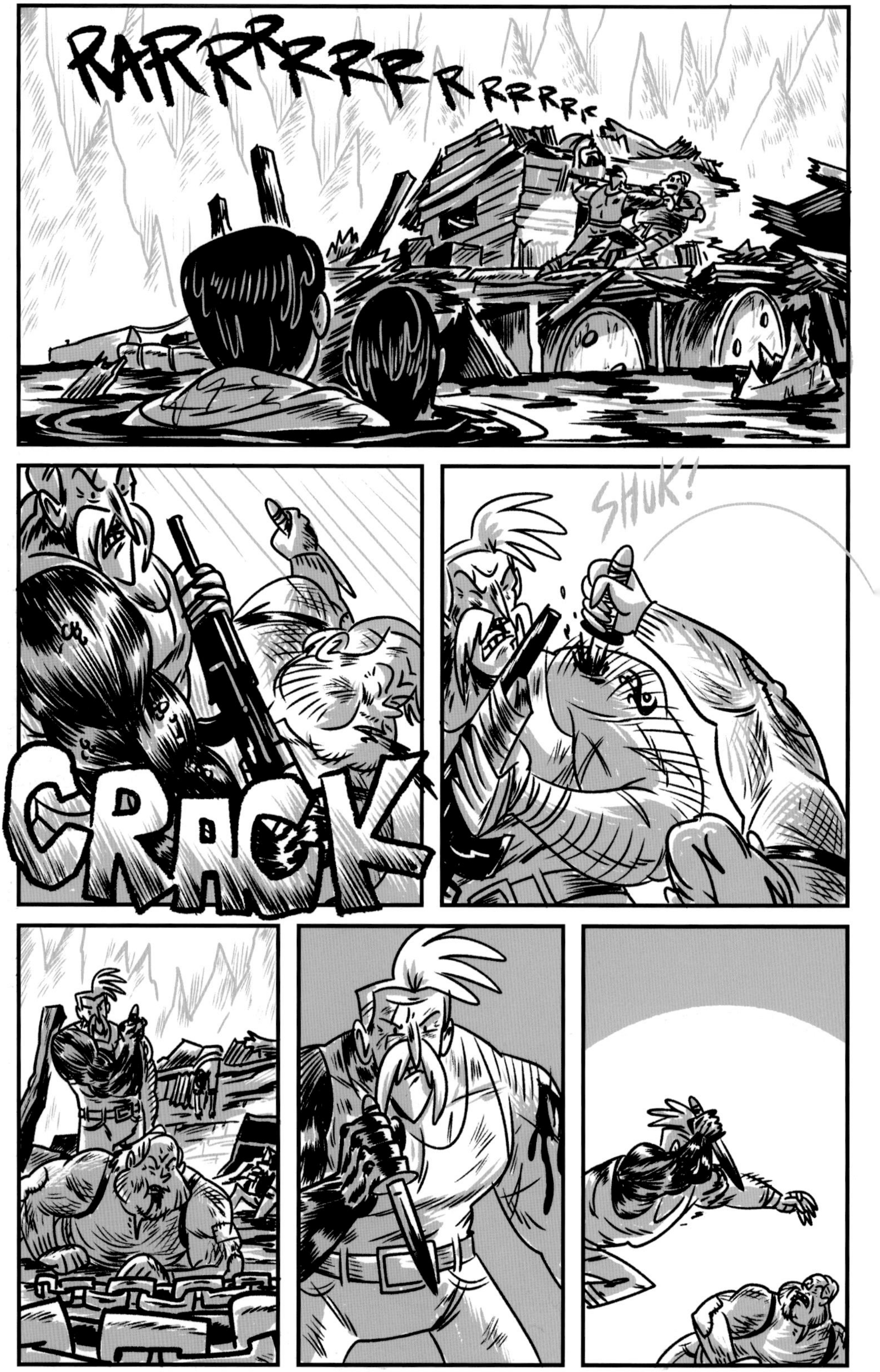
RARRRRRRRRRRRRRR
CRACK
SHUK!

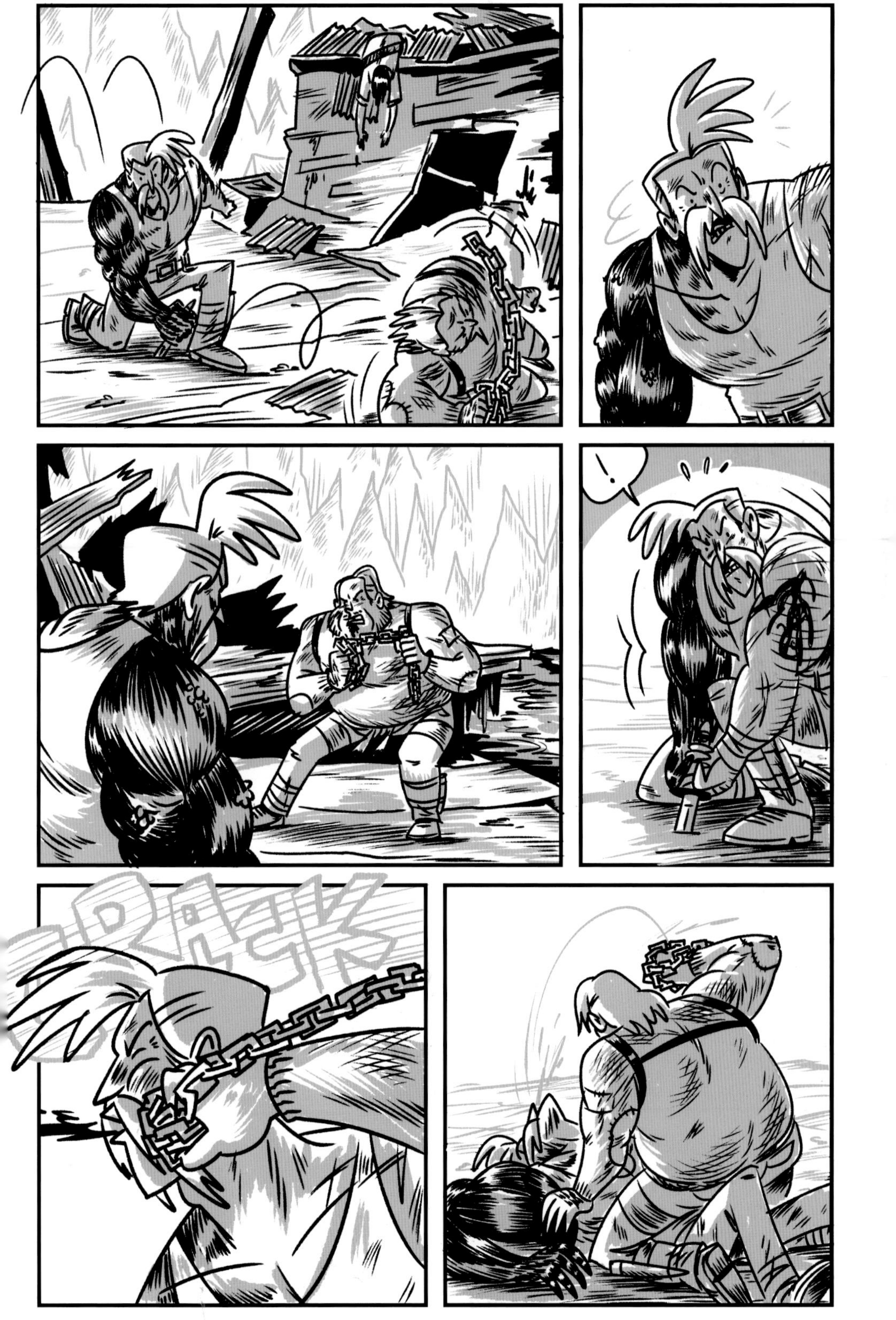
!

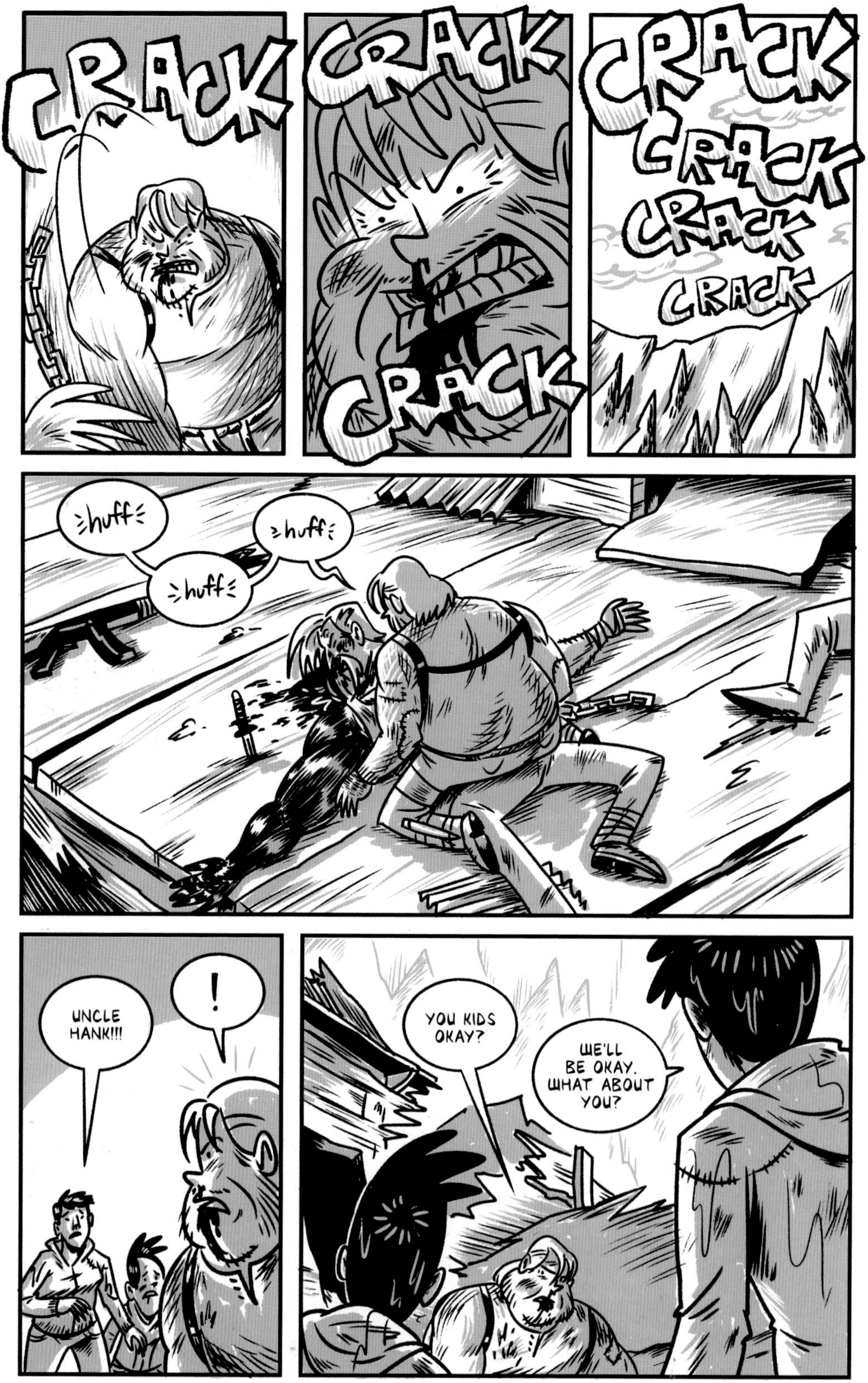
CRACK
CRACK
CRACK
CRACK
CRACK
CRACK
CRACK
huff
huff
huff
UNCLE HANK!!!
!
YOU KIDS OKAY?
WE'LL BE OKAY. WHAT ABOUT YOU?

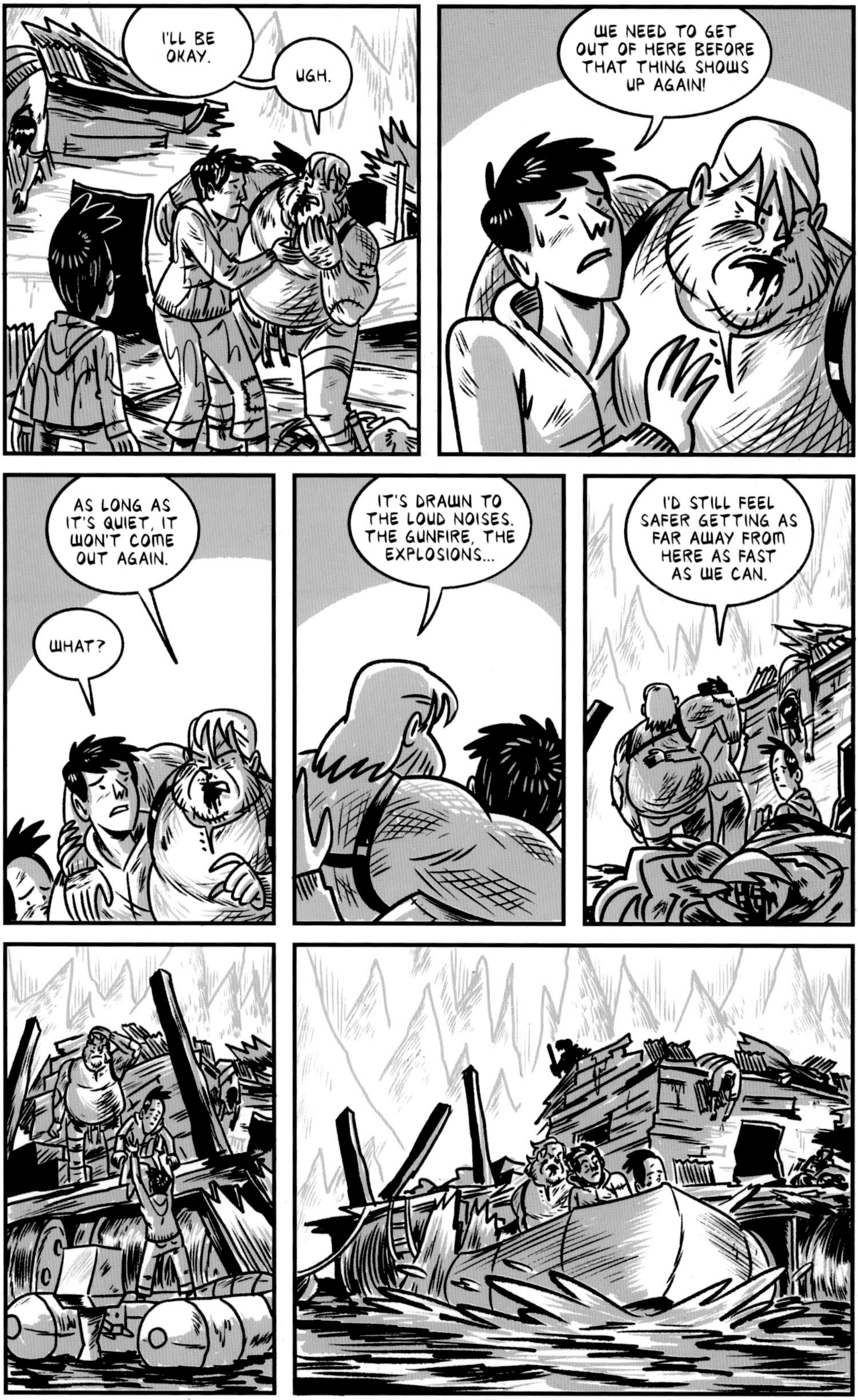
I'LL BE OKAY.
UGH.
WE NEED TO GET OUT OF HERE BEFORE THAT THING SHOWS UP AGAIN!
AS LONG AS IT'S QUIET, IT WON'T COME OUT AGAIN.
WHAT?
IT'S DRAWN TO THE LOUD NOISES. THE GUNFIRE, THE EXPLOSIONS...
I'D STILL FEEL SAFER GETTING AS FAR AWAY FROM HERE AS FAST AS WE CAN.

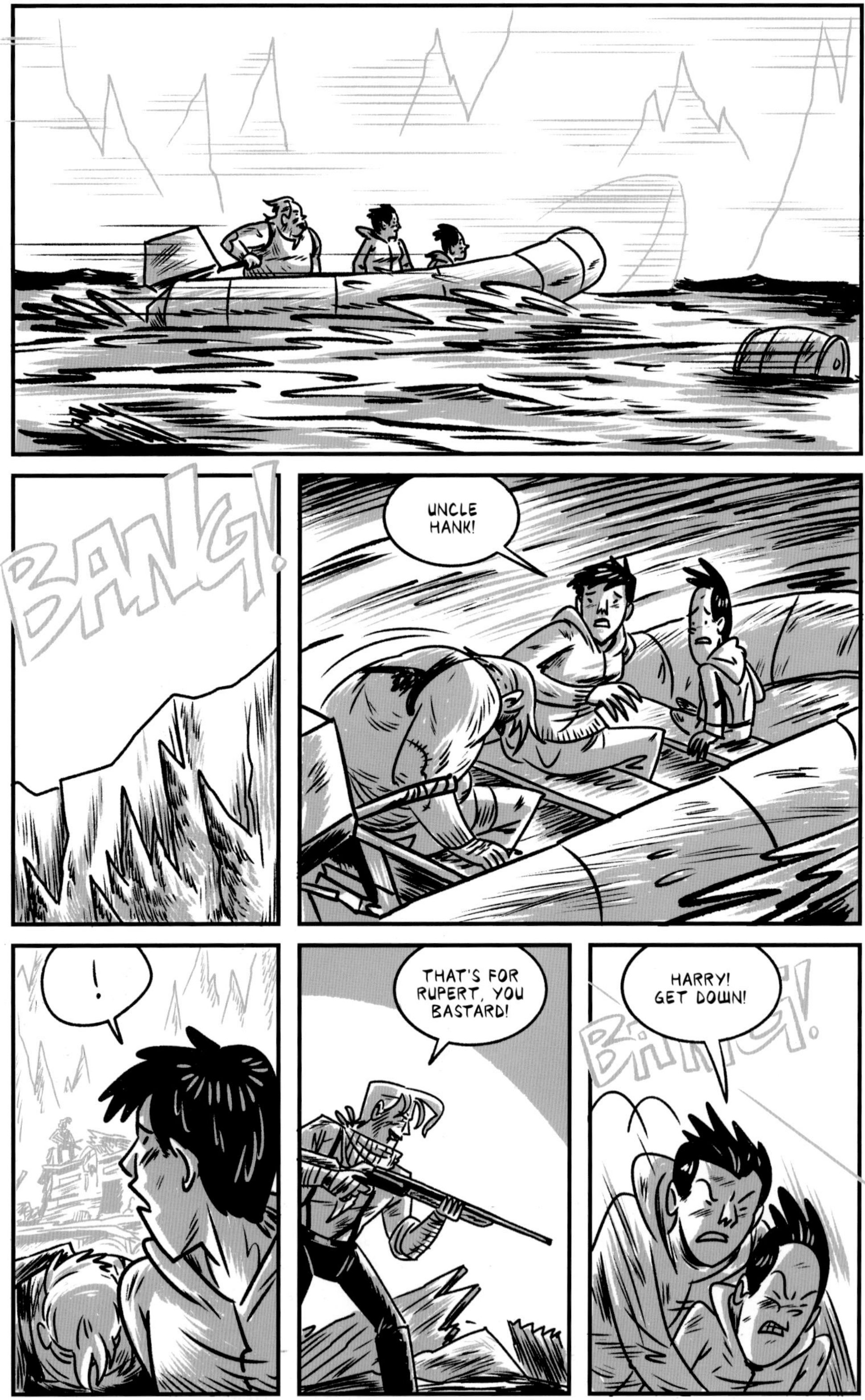
BANG!
UNCLE HANK!
!
THAT'S FOR RUPERT, YOU BASTARD!
HARRY! GET DOWN!
BANG!

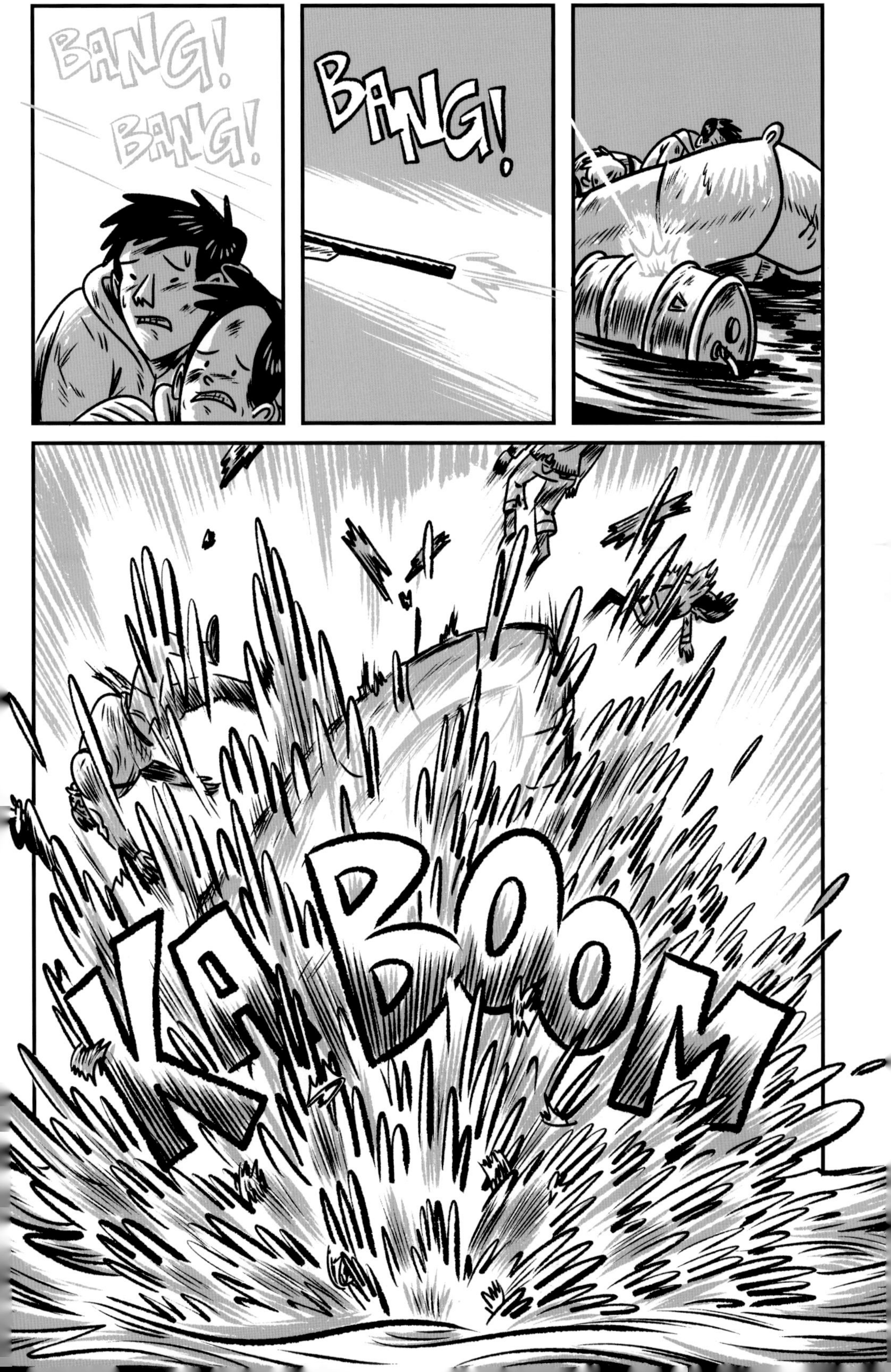
BANG!
BANG!
BANG!
KA-BOOM

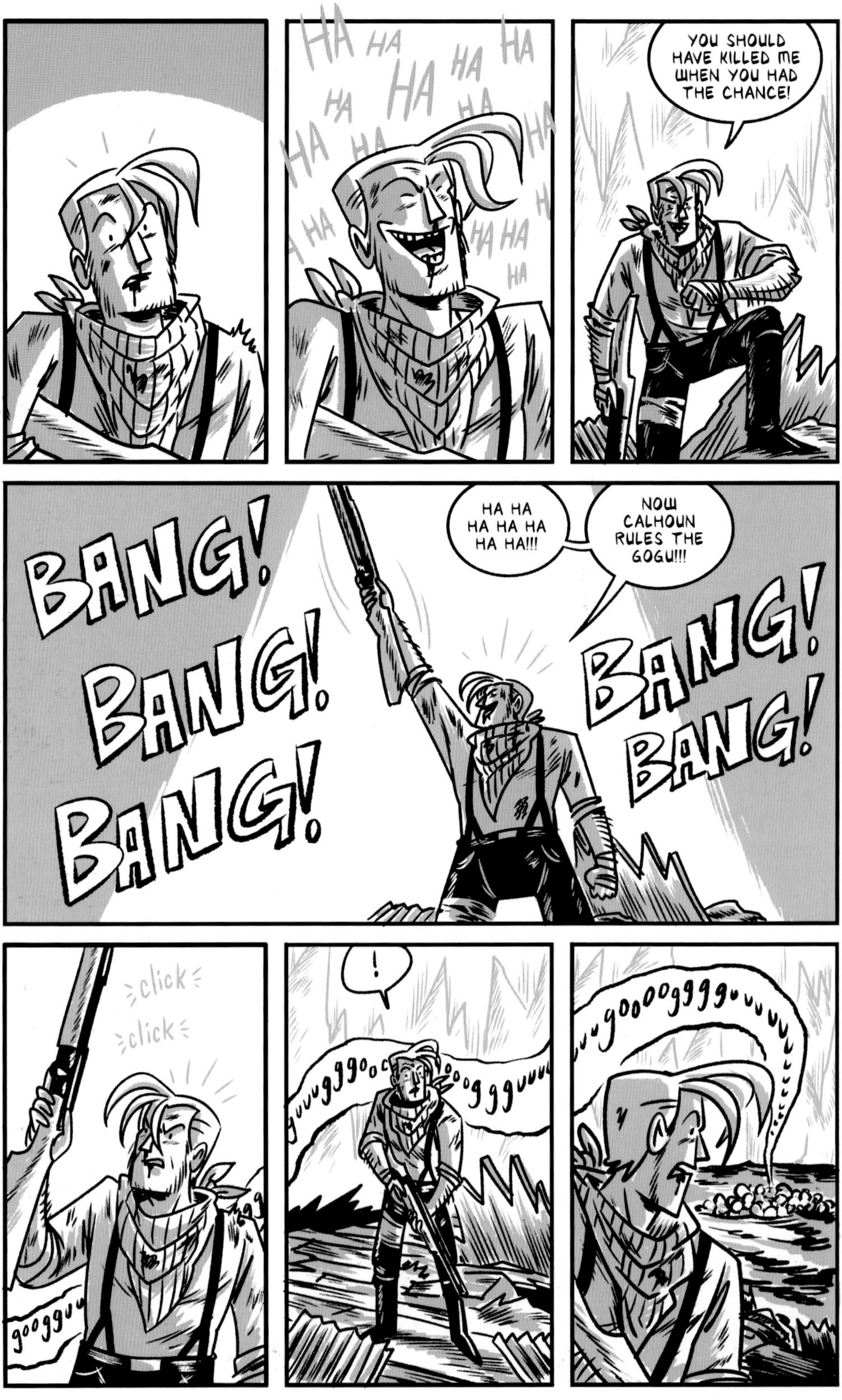
HA HA HA HA HA HA HA HA HA HA HA HA HA HA HA
YOU SHOULD HAVE KILLED ME WHEN YOU HAD THE CHANCE!
BANG! BANG! BANG!
HA HA HA HA HA HA HA!!!
NOW CALHOUN RULES THE GOGU!!!
BANG! BANG!
click
click
googgu
!
guuuggggooo oooggguuuu
uugoooggggguuuu

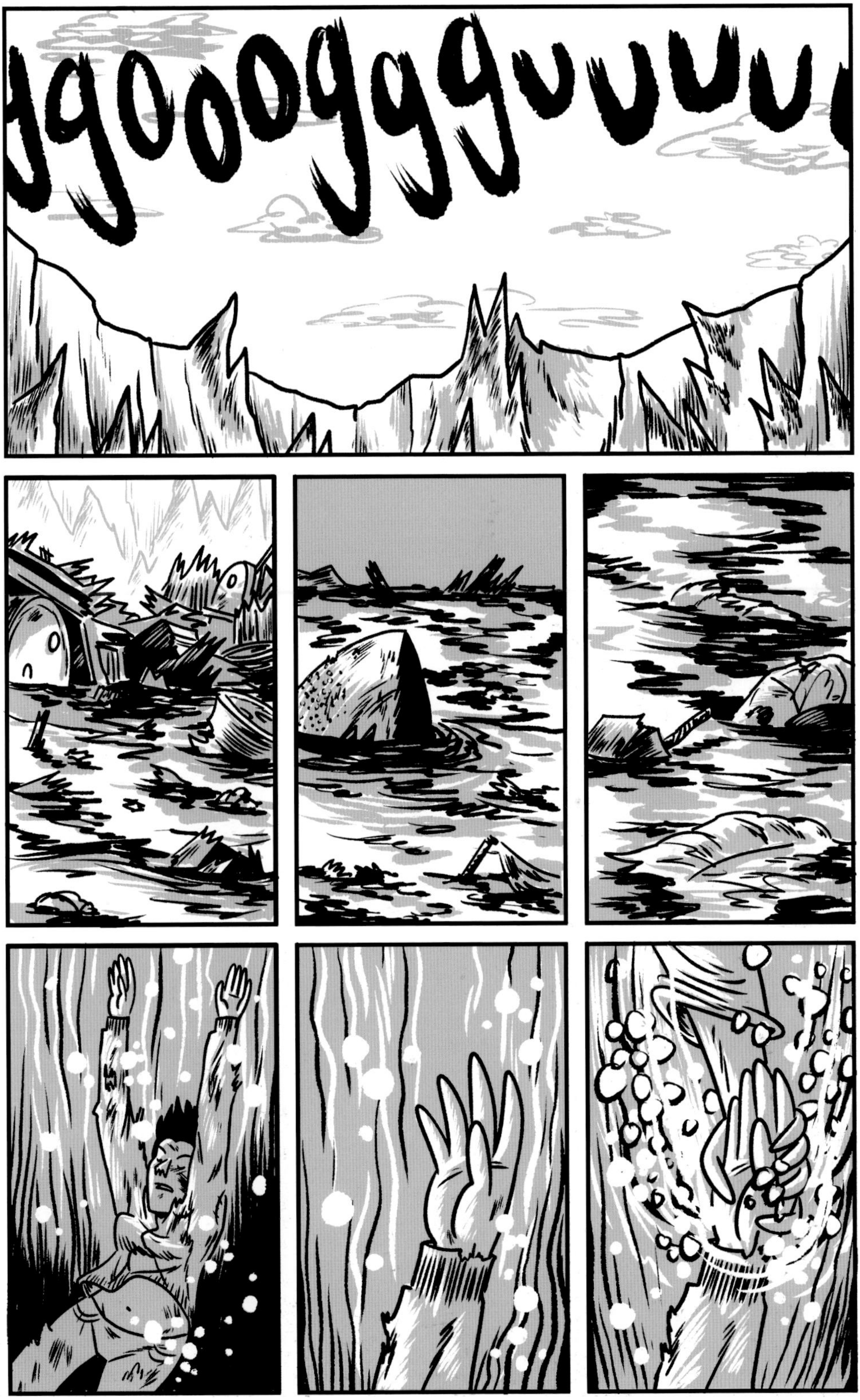
goooggguuuu

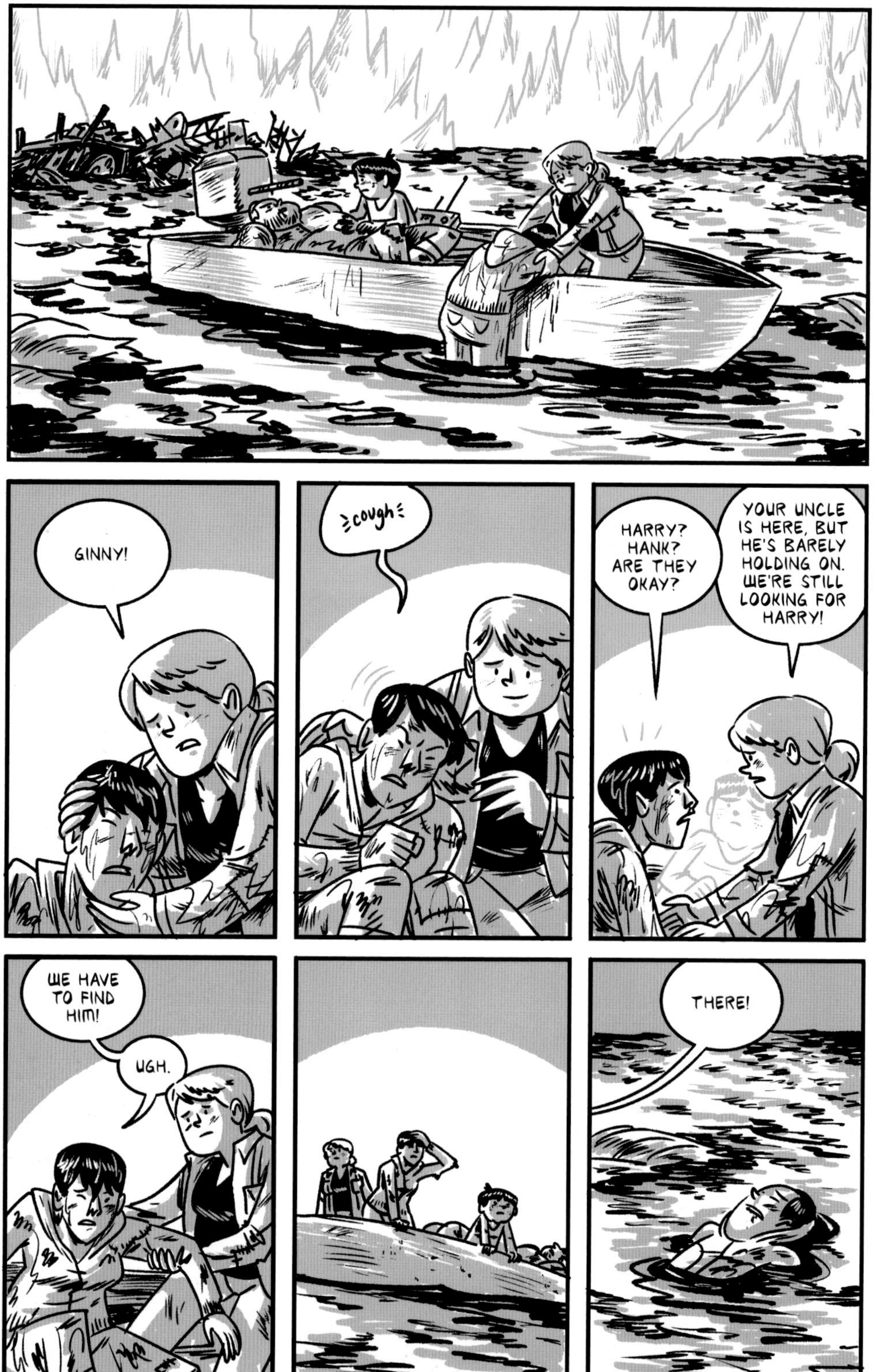
GINNY!
cough
HARRY? HANK? ARE THEY OKAY?
YOUR UNCLE IS HERE, BUT HE'S BARELY HOLDING ON. WE'RE STILL LOOKING FOR HARRY!
WE HAVE TO FIND HIM!
UGH.
THERE!

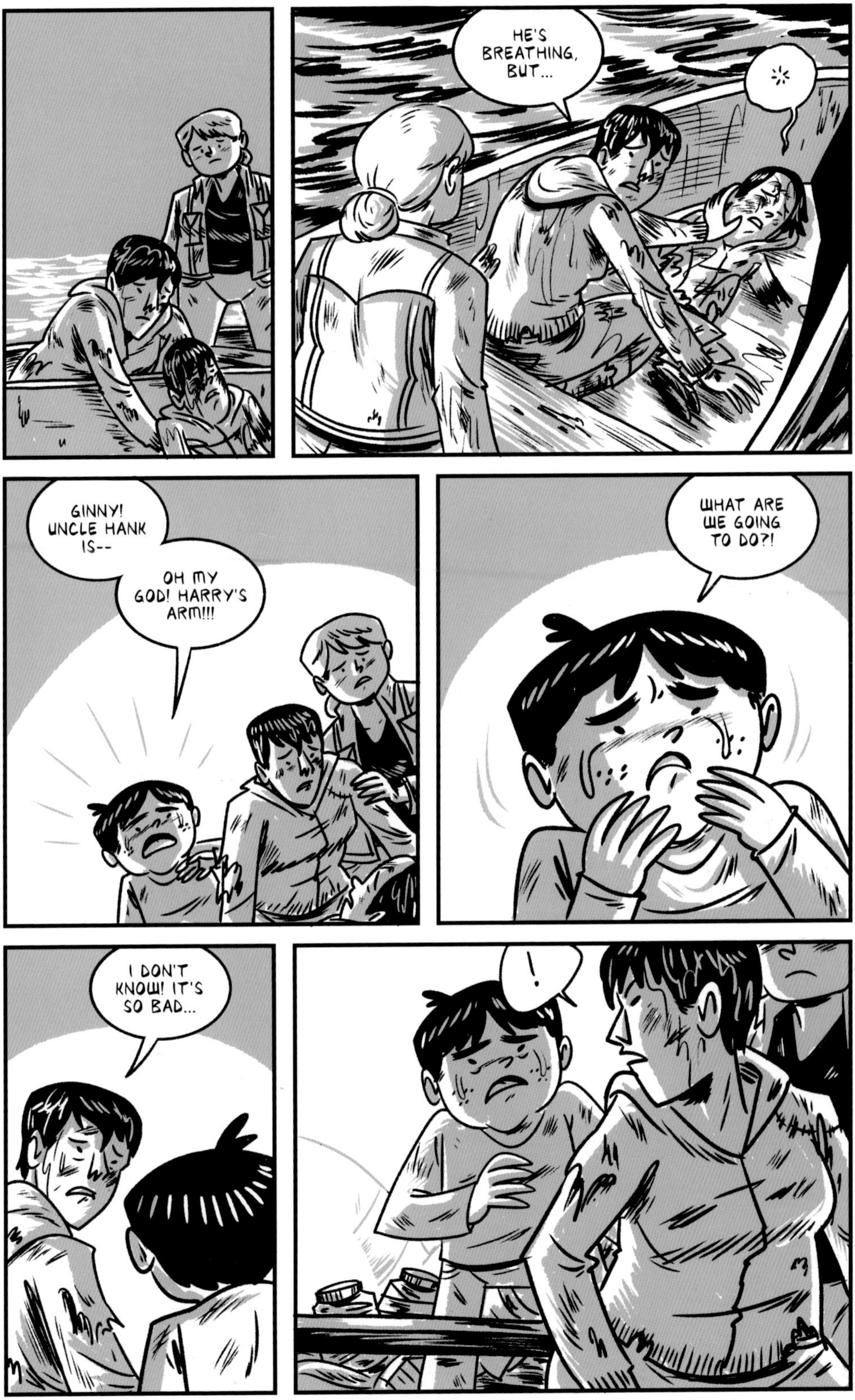

HE'S BREATHING, BUT...
GINNY! UNCLE HANK IS--
OH MY GOD! HARRY'S ARM!!!
WHAT ARE WE GOING TO DO?!
I DON'T KNOW! IT'S SO BAD...
!

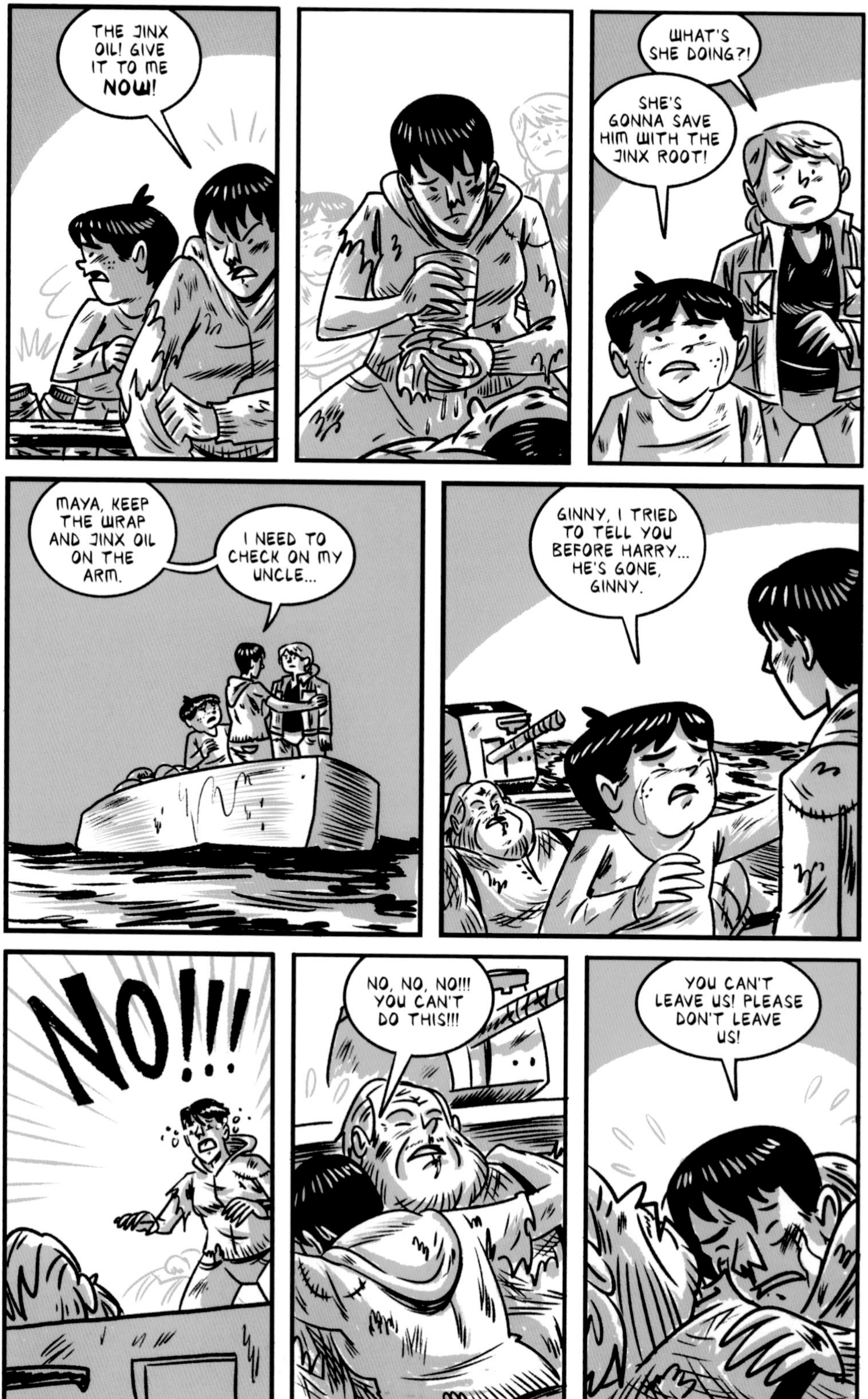
THE JINX OIL! GIVE IT TO ME NOW!
WHAT'S SHE DOING?!
SHE'S GONNA SAVE HIM WITH THE JINX ROOT!
MAYA, KEEP THE WRAP AND JINX OIL ON THE ARM.
I NEED TO CHECK ON MY UNCLE...
GINNY, I TRIED TO TELL YOU BEFORE HARRY... HE'S GONE, GINNY.
NO!!!
NO, NO, NO!!! YOU CAN'T DO THIS!!!
YOU CAN'T LEAVE US! PLEASE DON'T LEAVE US!

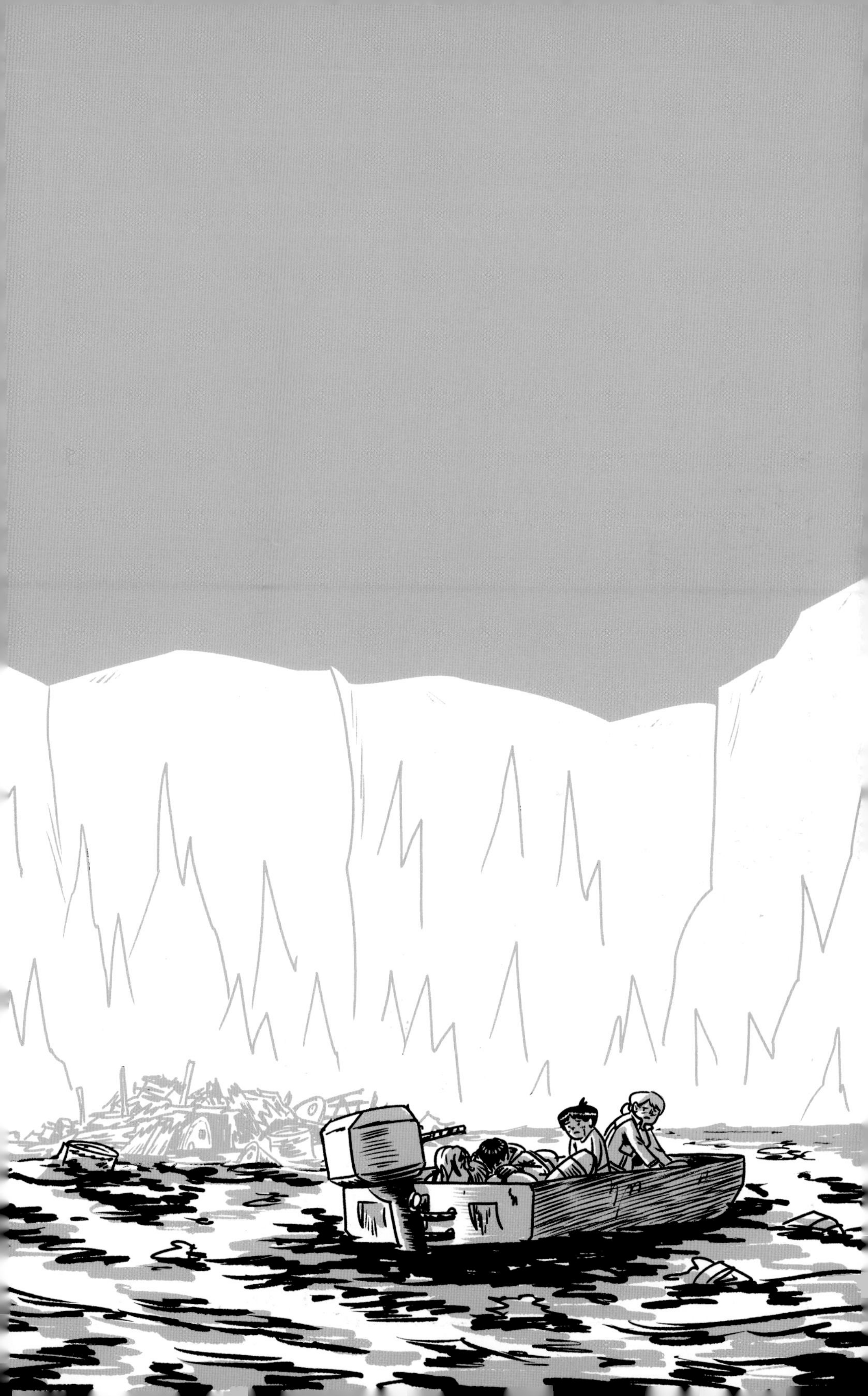

CHAPTER 12

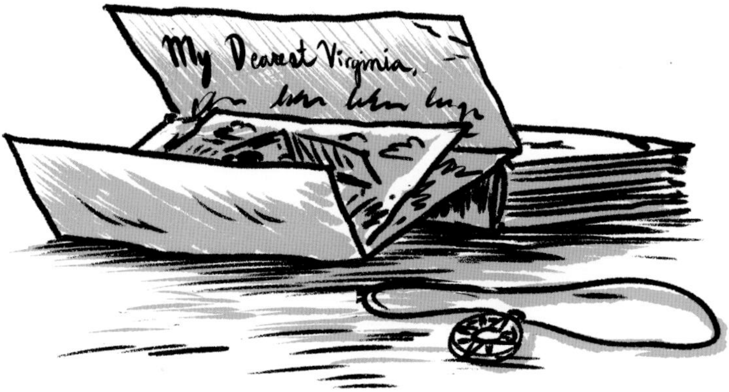
My Dearest Virginia,

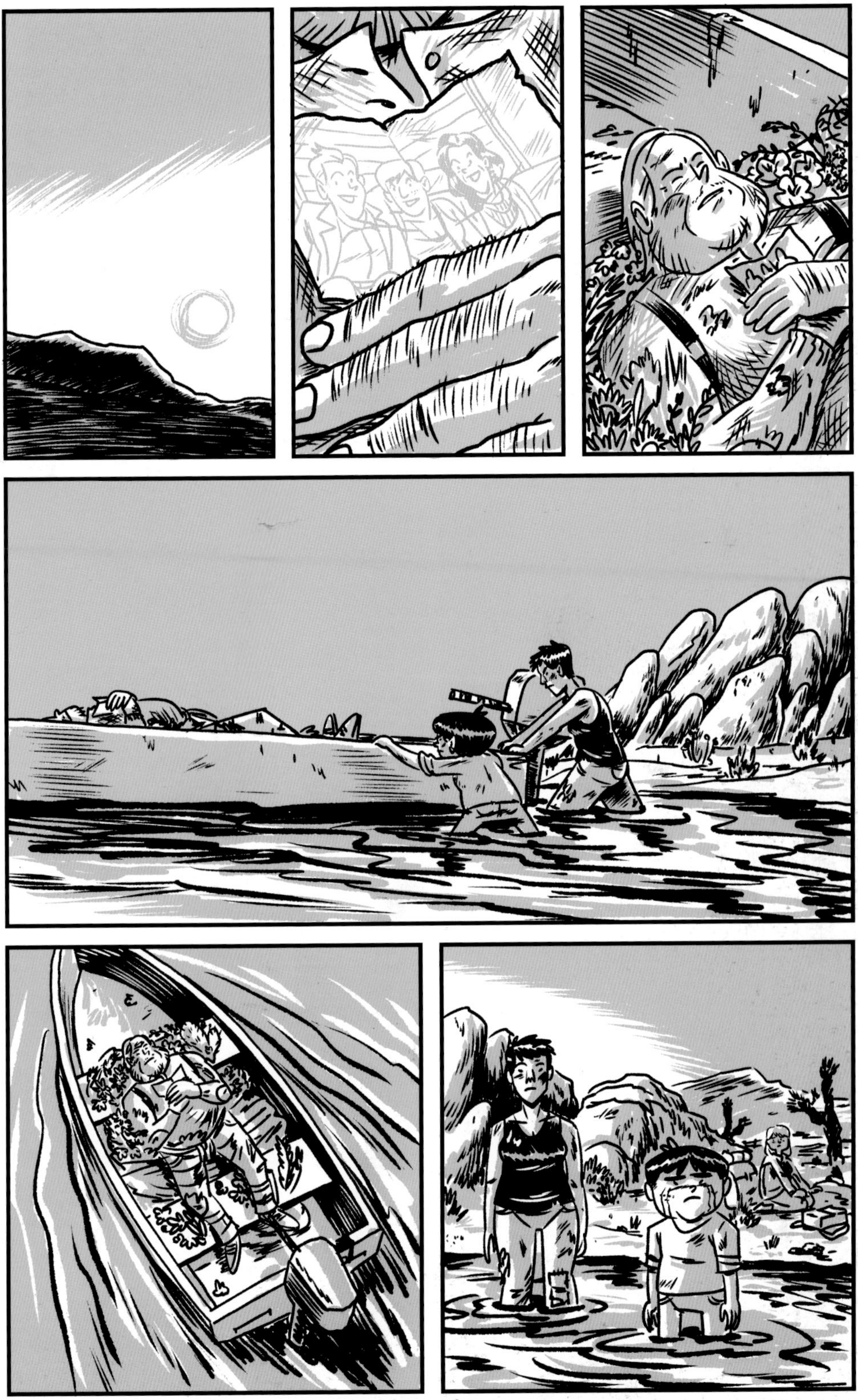

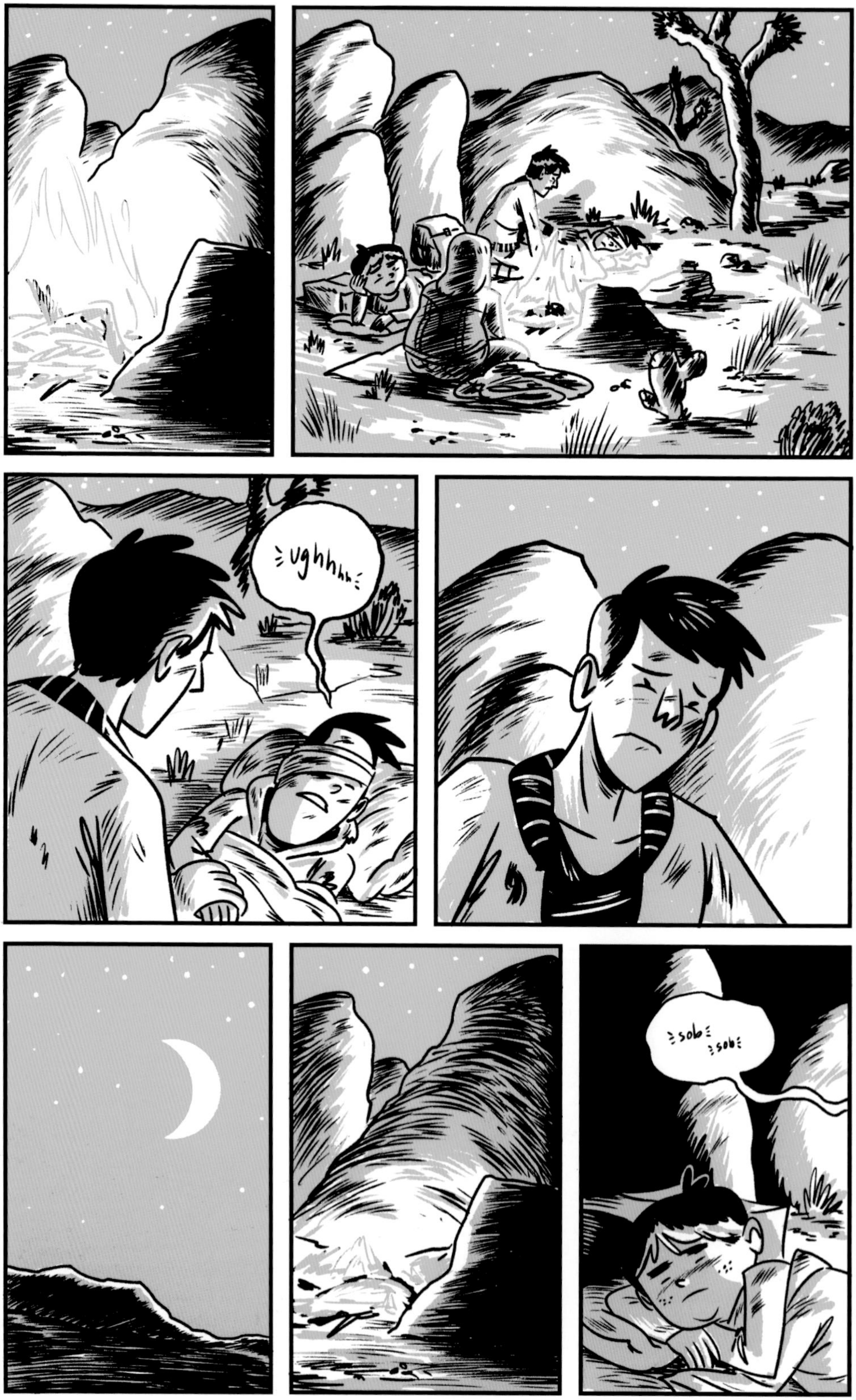
ughhhh
sob sob

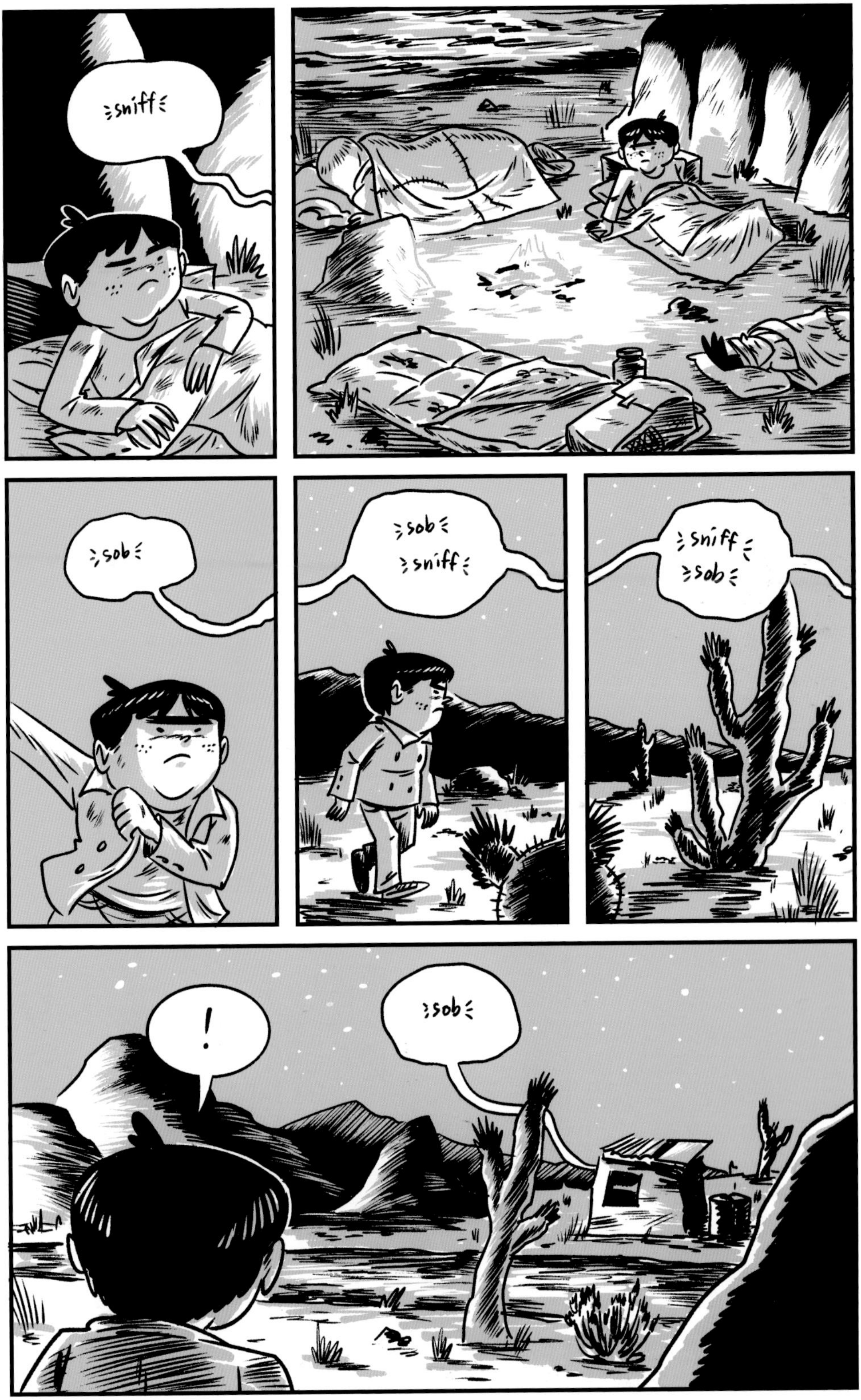

sniff
sob
sob
sniff
sniff
sob
!
sob

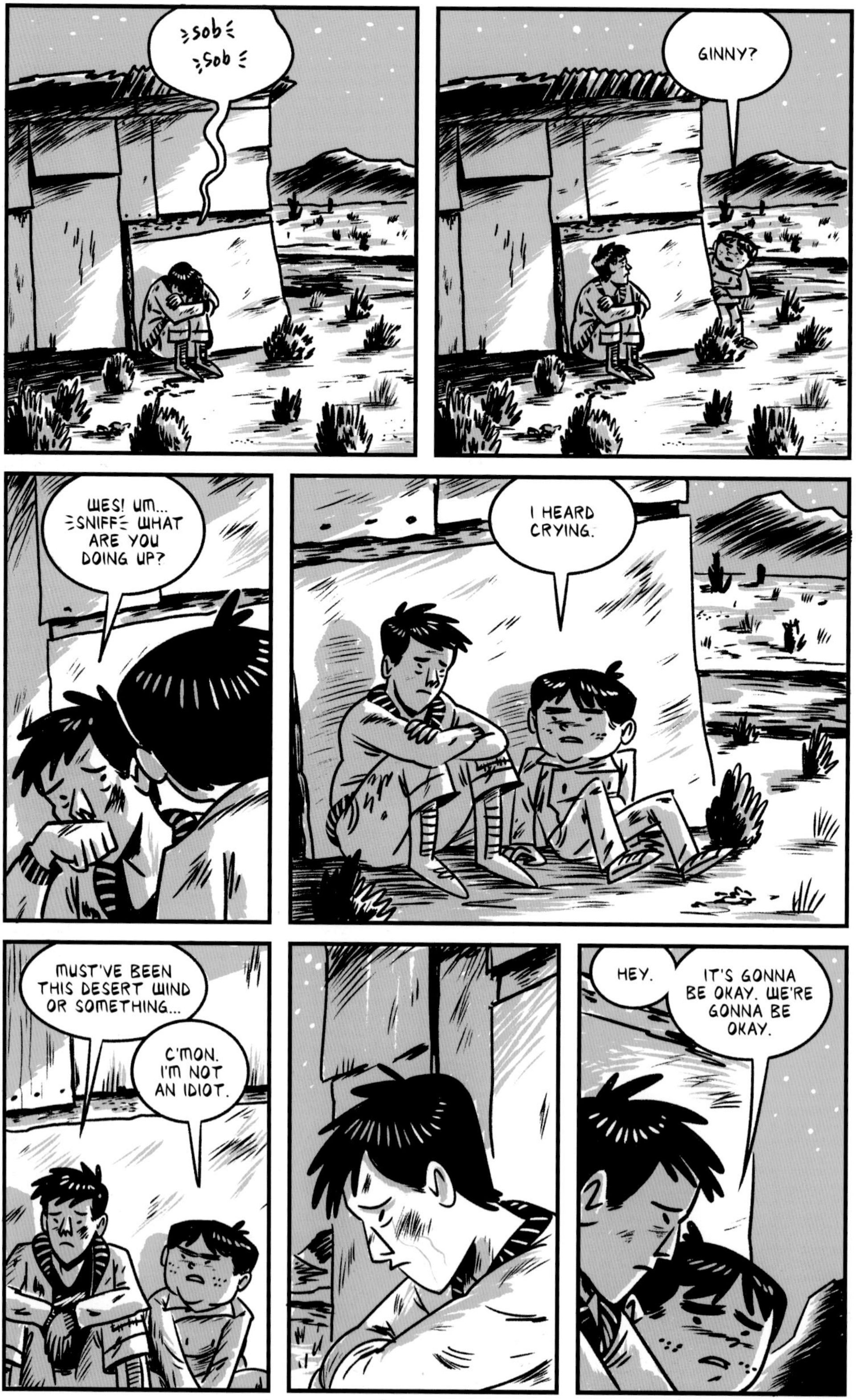
sob
sob
GINNY?
WES! UM... SNIFF WHAT ARE YOU DOING UP?
I HEARD CRYING.
MUST'VE BEEN THIS DESERT WIND OR SOMETHING...
C'MON. I'M NOT AN IDIOT.
HEY.
IT'S GONNA BE OKAY. WE'RE GONNA BE OKAY.

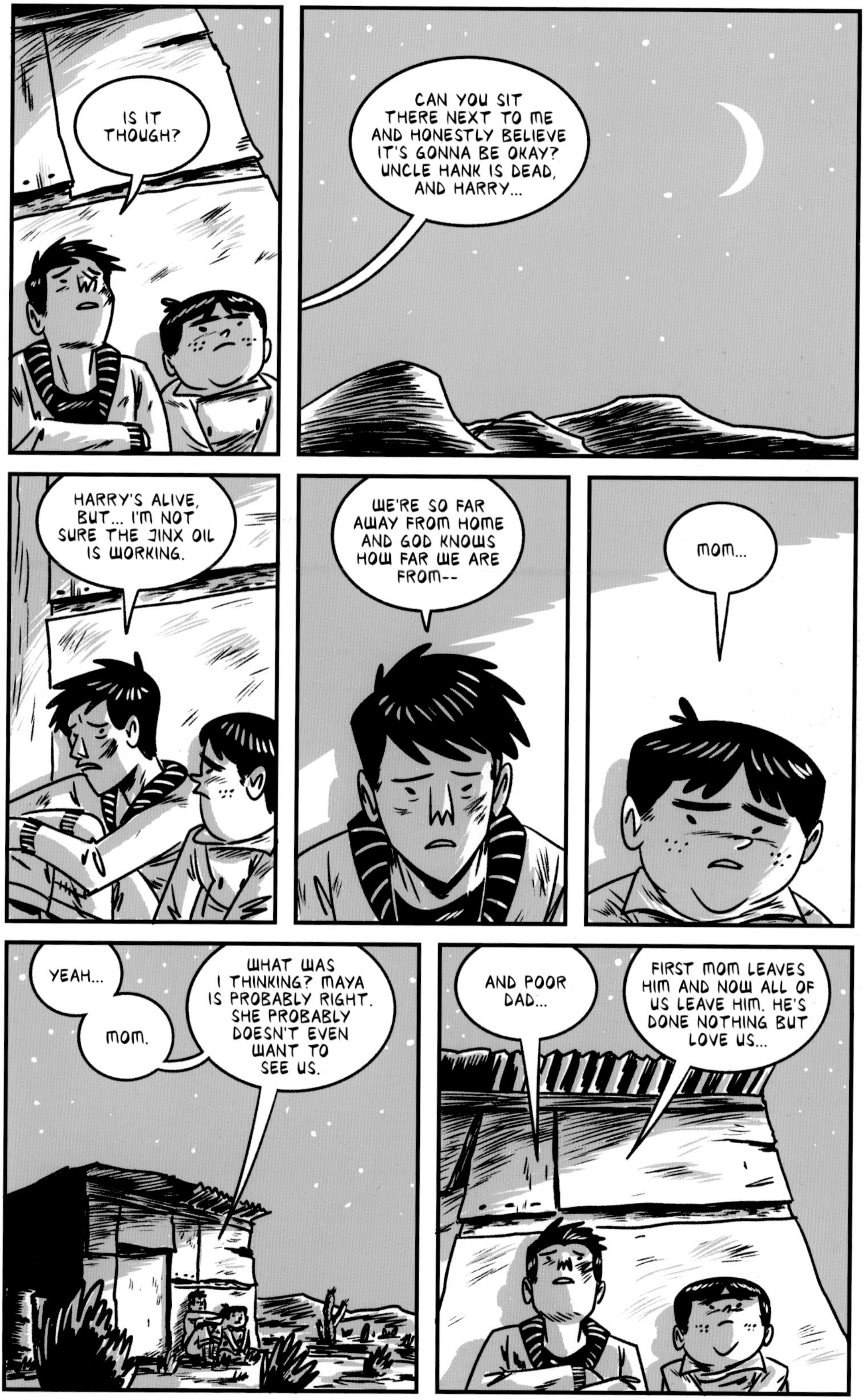
IS IT THOUGH?
CAN YOU SIT THERE NEXT TO ME AND HONESTLY BELIEVE IT'S GONNA BE OKAY? UNCLE HANK IS DEAD, AND HARRY...
HARRY'S ALIVE, BUT... I'M NOT SURE THE JINX OIL IS WORKING.
WE'RE SO FAR AWAY FROM HOME AND GOD KNOWS HOW FAR WE ARE FROM--
MOM...
YEAH...
MOM.
WHAT WAS I THINKING? MAYA IS PROBABLY RIGHT. SHE PROBABLY DOESN'T EVEN WANT TO SEE US.
AND POOR DAD...
FIRST MOM LEAVES HIM AND NOW ALL OF US LEAVE HIM. HE'S DONE NOTHING BUT LOVE US...

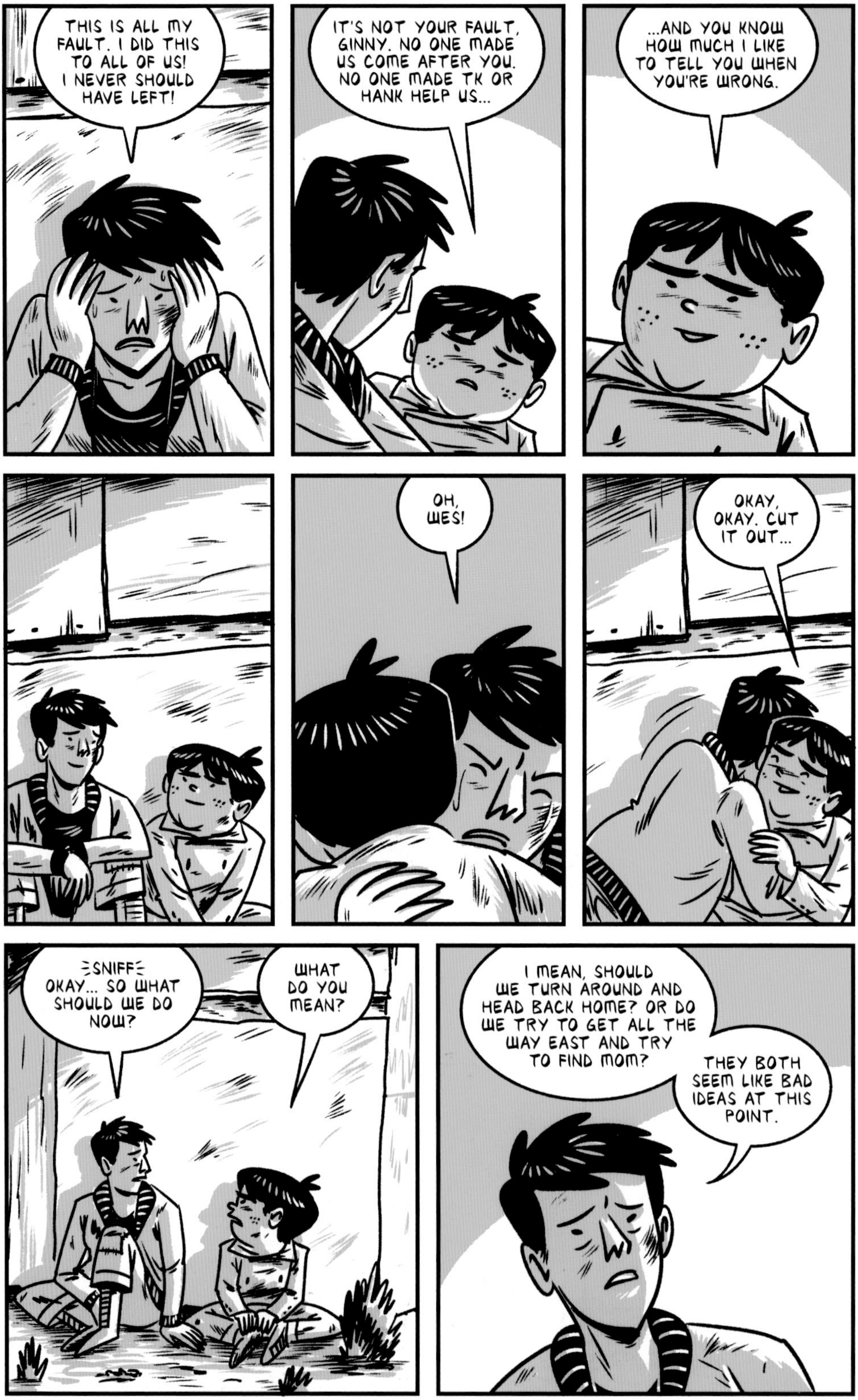
THIS IS ALL MY FAULT. I DID THIS TO ALL OF US! I NEVER SHOULD HAVE LEFT!
IT'S NOT YOUR FAULT, GINNY. NO ONE MADE US COME AFTER YOU. NO ONE MADE TK OR HANK HELP US...
...AND YOU KNOW HOW MUCH I LIKE TO TELL YOU WHEN YOU'RE WRONG.
OH, WES!
OKAY, OKAY. CUT IT OUT...
SNIFF
OKAY... SO WHAT SHOULD WE DO NOW?
WHAT DO YOU MEAN?
I MEAN, SHOULD WE TURN AROUND AND HEAD BACK HOME? OR DO WE TRY TO GET ALL THE WAY EAST AND TRY TO FIND MOM?
THEY BOTH SEEM LIKE BAD IDEAS AT THIS POINT.

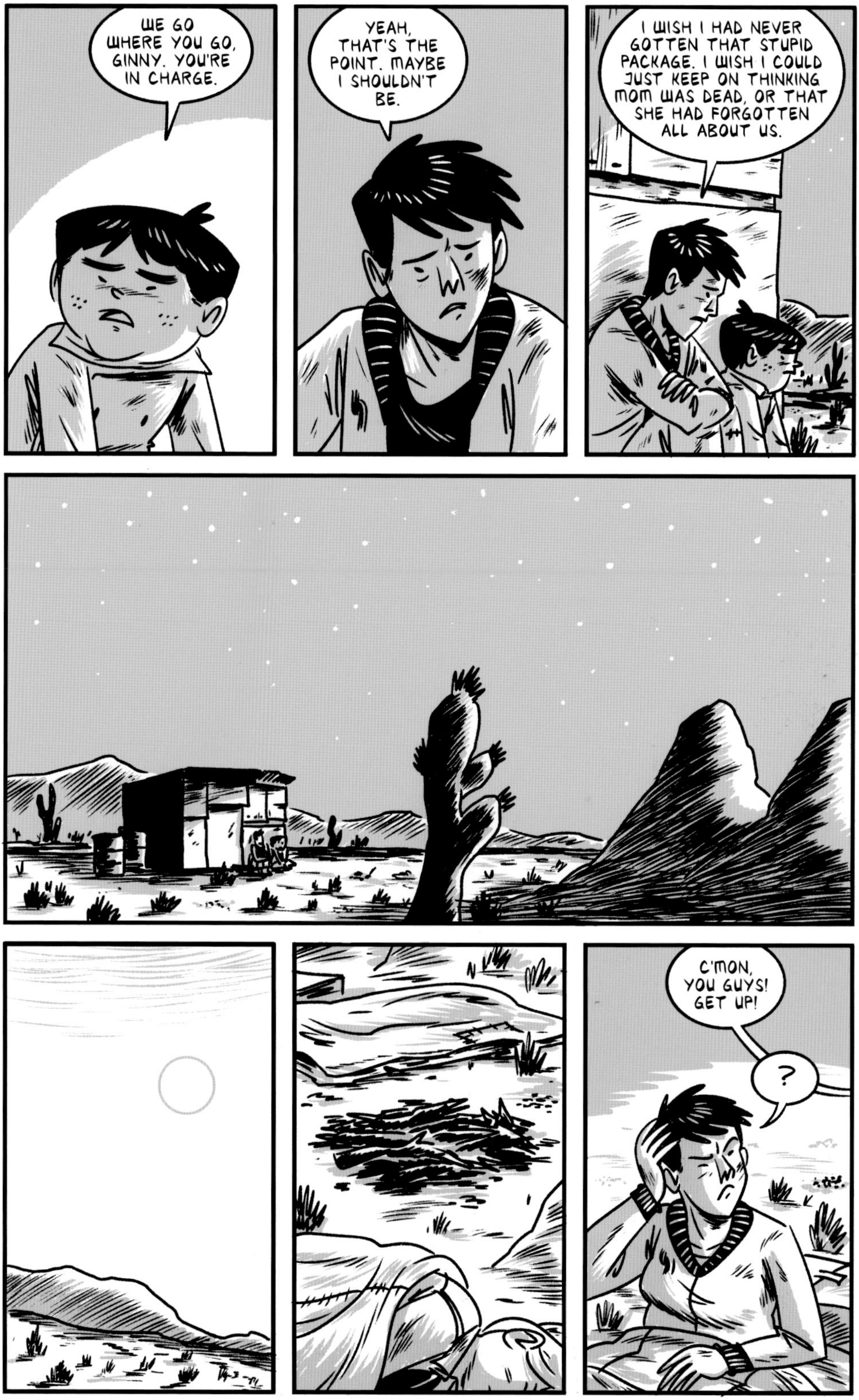
WE GO WHERE YOU GO, GINNY. YOU'RE IN CHARGE.
YEAH, THAT'S THE POINT. MAYBE I SHOULDN'T BE.
I WISH I HAD NEVER GOTTEN THAT STUPID PACKAGE. I WISH I COULD JUST KEEP ON THINKING MOM WAS DEAD, OR THAT SHE HAD FORGOTTEN ALL ABOUT US.
C'MON, YOU GUYS! GET UP!
?

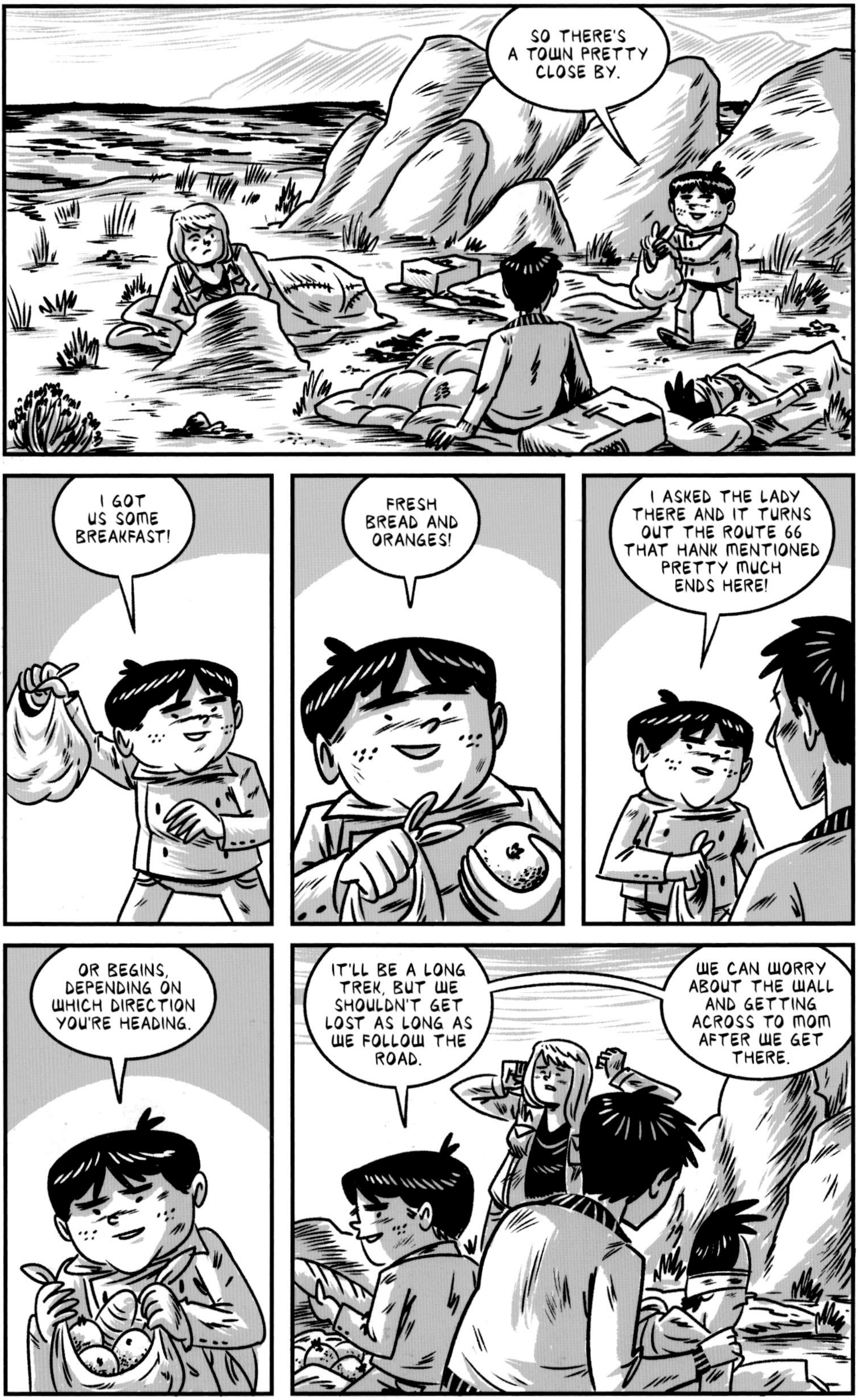
SO THERE'S A TOWN PRETTY CLOSE BY.
I GOT US SOME BREAKFAST!
FRESH BREAD AND ORANGES!
I ASKED THE LADY THERE AND IT TURNS OUT THE ROUTE 66 THAT HANK MENTIONED PRETTY MUCH ENDS HERE!
OR BEGINS, DEPENDING ON WHICH DIRECTION YOU'RE HEADING.
IT'LL BE A LONG TREK, BUT WE SHOULDN'T GET LOST AS LONG AS WE FOLLOW THE ROAD.
WE CAN WORRY ABOUT THE WALL AND GETTING ACROSS TO MOM AFTER WE GET THERE.

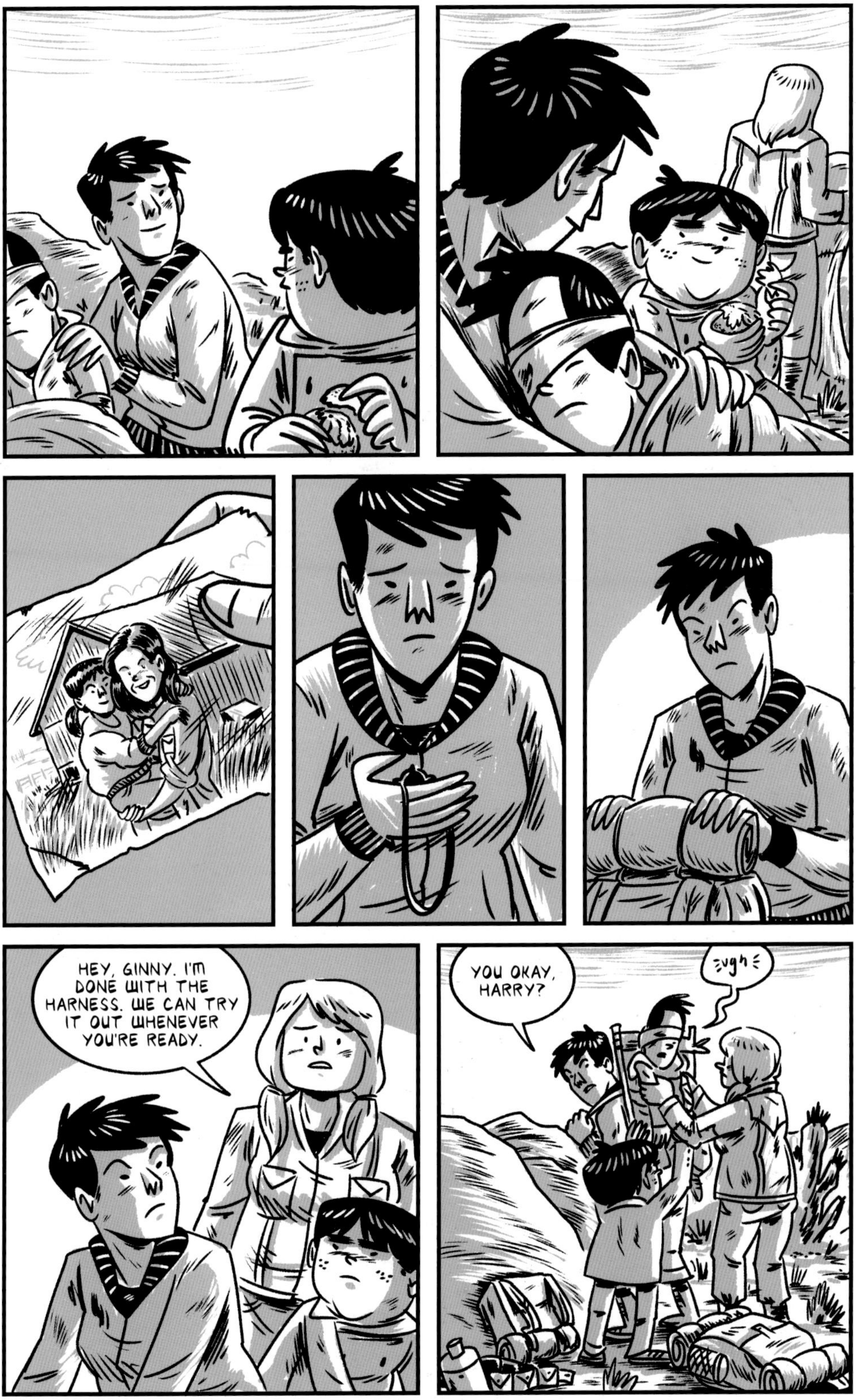
HEY, GINNY. I'M DONE WITH THE HARNESS. WE CAN TRY IT OUT WHENEVER YOU'RE READY.
YOU OKAY, HARRY?
ugh

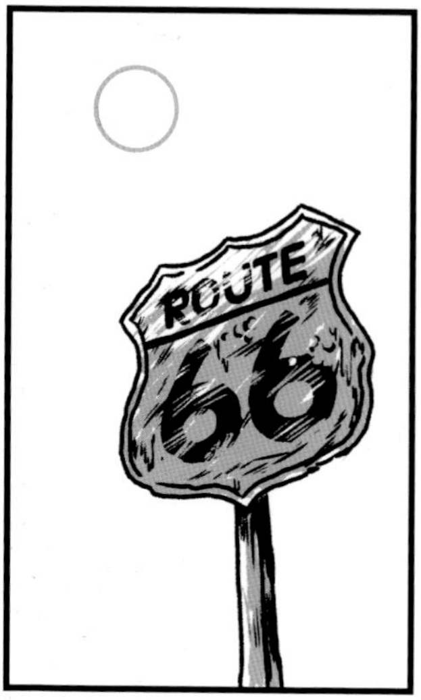
ROUTE
66

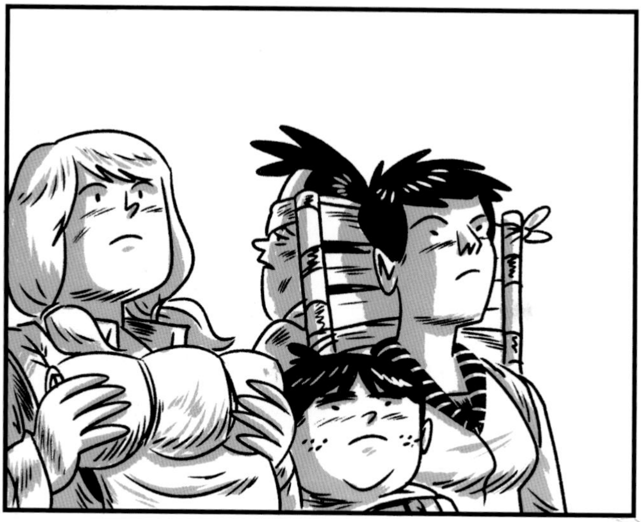

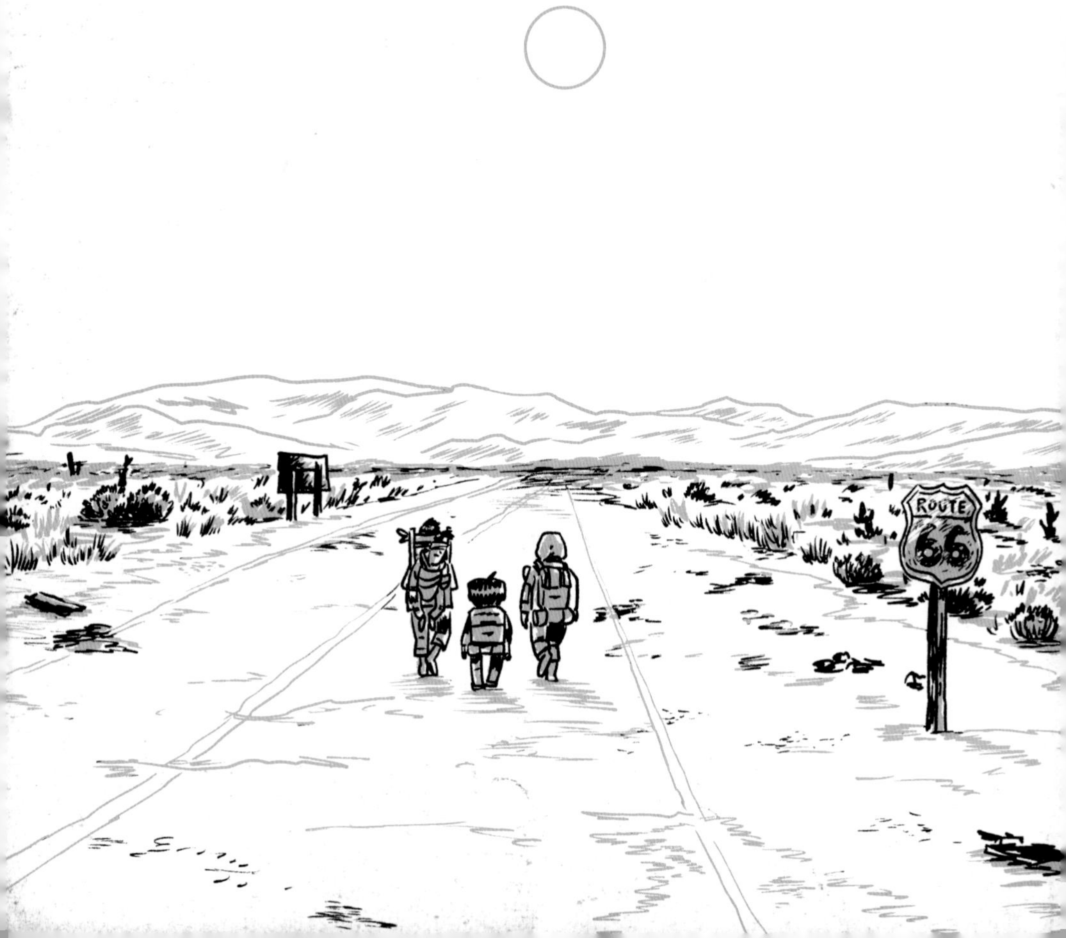
ROUTE
66

...TO BE CONTINUED

This book took a very long time to make and wouldn't be possible without so many amazing people.

Jen for her unwavering support and unconditional love.

Jeremiah and Justin for all of our adventures (and fighting) growing up.
No matter what, we always had each other.

Dad, Mom, and Uncle Phuc for always supporting me, even about
this comics thing.

Breena, Maria, Greg, MK, and Jason for being there from the very beginning
and giving me feedback on those early drafts. And for Aron, Lisa, Meg, Patrick,
Grayson, Nyssa, and Lucy who also support, encourage, and inspire me
with their work and friendship.

Clive and Seaerra for the laughs, the support, the friendship
and the workdays at Palio and the summer studio.

Xan for all your hard work behind the scenes helping me
get this book in shape, and for being excited for the book!

Vance for convincing me to go all digital. I miss inking with a brush,
but I can't imagine how much longer it would have taken me.

All of my students at PNCA who get me excited for comics every
time I see their work. I take that energy with me every page I draw.

The Blazers for having a, um, let's say lackluster 2019/2020 season. It was so
frustrating to watch games this season (pre-COVID-19 shutdown) that
I got so much work done, especially down the stretch.

trevorpearce and Hassan A. who did the models on Sketchup I used for Four
Dollars' tugboat and the Gogu runabout, respectively. I don't know you, but you
saved my life the last half of the book. I am also happy to never have to draw
another boat in the foreseeable future.

And of course Robin, my editor, for her patience, keen eye, and graciousness
throughout the whole thing. I hope you don't have to proof the digital version.

And Oni Press for giving this book a home at a time I wasn't sure
I would even make comics anymore.

xoxo

FIRST DRAWINGS

Here are some of the first ink drawings for the Crane siblings, Rooster, and the Crane house in Portland. The date on these says 2010, when I originally came up with the story. The idea started back then but didn't get much further than these drawings and a really rough pitch that got rejected. You can see how much they have changed and how much better I've gotten!

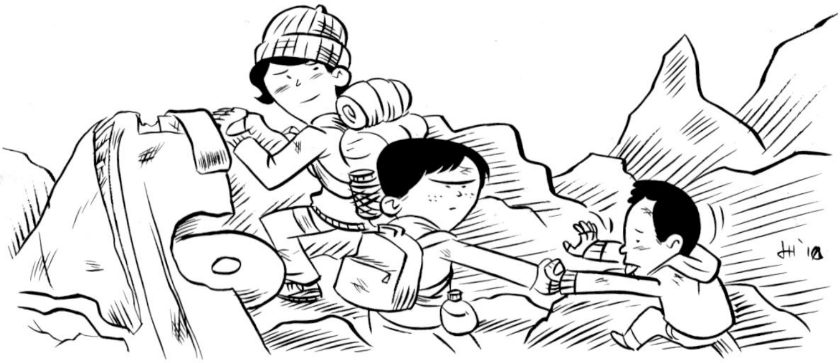

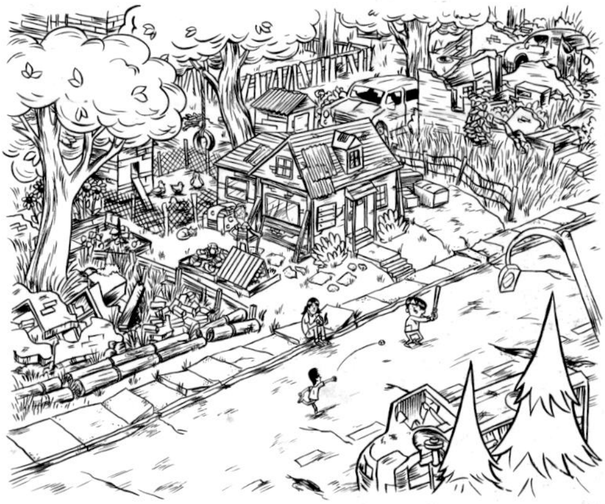

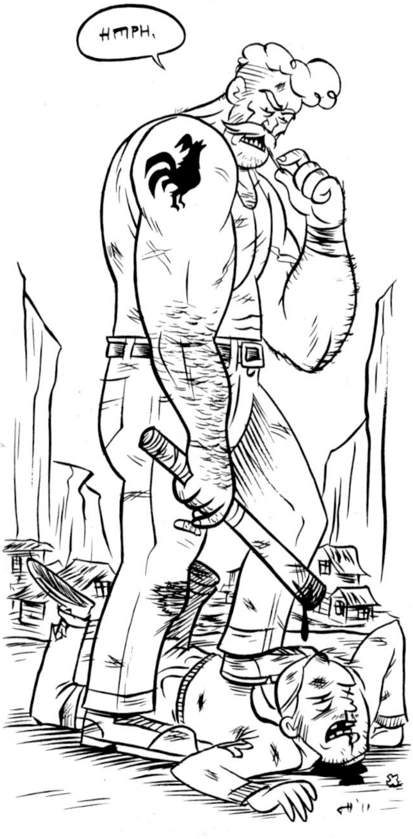
HMPH.

I was pretty discouraged by that rejection, but the editor was right in her feedback: It was underdeveloped, and the world-building wasn't quite there. Between that and some serious life changes getting in the way, I didn't work on the project for a couple of years. When I did pick it up again, I knew that although I still had a lot of the actual story to write, I'm a visual thinker, and I needed to see how things actually looked in comics form to help me really get a sense of the project.

I decided to take what would end up being chapter four and draw it all out. I picked this section because it had strong interactions between the characters, introduced a lot of the world-building, and had some excitement and action in the end.

This really helped. It gave me a much stronger vision of what I was doing and helped me finish plotting out the rest of the book. And when Oni had its open submissions, I had a complete chapter as a sample and a much stronger pitch ready to submit.

Of course, during the process of actually making the book, I would end up needing to redraw this chapter. I had completely switched my process to working digitally, and at that point, the pages were years old and I was a better artist now.

I basically just used the old pages as "pencils" and inked over them. There were a few cases where I decided to redraw the panels, mainly for compositional purposes.

Here are two panels that show how different some of them were.

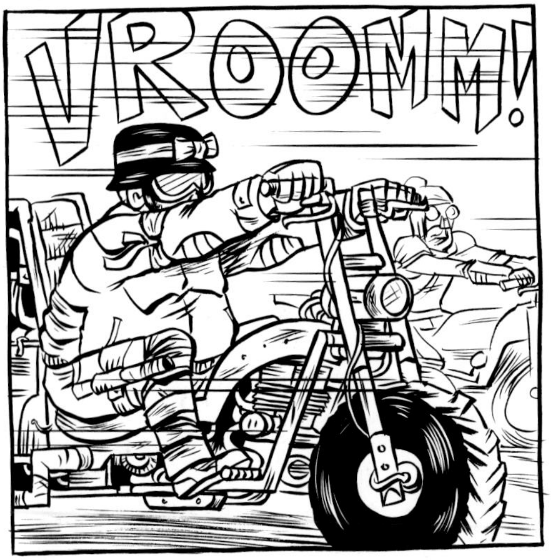
VROOMM!

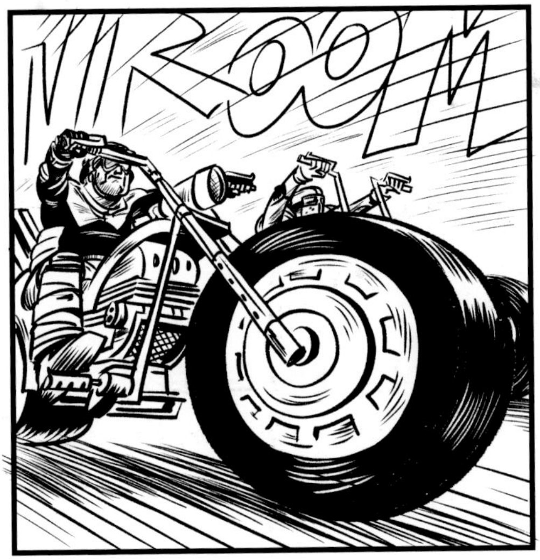
VROOOM

The following pages give a good side-by-side comparison and show how some of the changes were a lot more subtle.

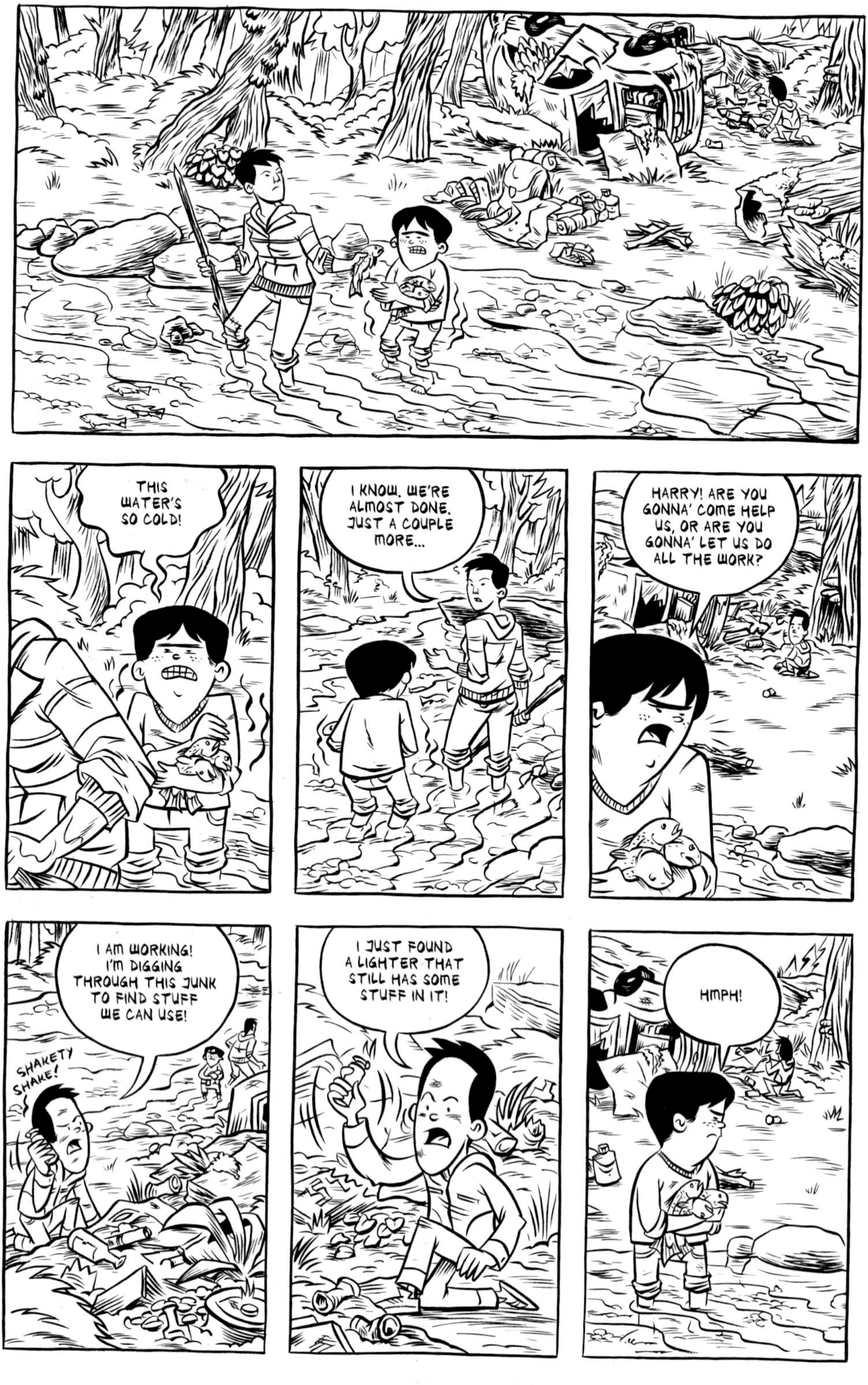
THIS WATER'S SO COLD!
I KNOW. WE'RE ALMOST DONE. JUST A COUPLE MORE...
HARRY! ARE YOU GONNA' COME HELP US, OR ARE YOU GONNA' LET US DO ALL THE WORK?
I AM WORKING! I'M DIGGING THROUGH THIS JUNK TO FIND STUFF WE CAN USE!
SHAKETY SHAKE!
I JUST FOUND A LIGHTER THAT STILL HAS SOME STUFF IN IT!
HMPH!

While I have been working on the book, I get asked a lot on why I chose to just do it in two-color instead of full color. I also get asked why I picked pink.

As far as pink, I wanted a mid-value color that was the opposite of what you see in most post-apocalyptic stories that are drab brown and grey.

In regard to the two-color process, first is pure practicality. I am color blind (it's certain oranges and greens that look like a brown to me), but also it takes much, much longer to do full color.

The other reason is because I think two-tone or a limited palette fits comics better. Comics exist and function in the in-between places. In comics, we're given some information, but the reader is required to participate in bringing it to life. They see characters and environments, and read dialogue, but it's the reader who sees two panels and creates the action in their head; they read the sound effects and word balloons and decide what things sound like. Two-color works in the same way. There is generally enough information there to help create things like form, shadows, and atmosphere, but the reader is still an active participant in filling out those details.

Also, in terms of getting the most bang for your buck from your tools, having black and just one spot color opens up a bunch of possibilities.

Since black will always stick out more, if I need to push something into the background or soften it, I can do what's called a color hold. This is when I fill the linework with that color. It really helps with things like atmospheric perspective in the example below.

Also, even just with two colors, I can get multiple values from that mixture. If I need a lighter value, I can use a hatching with the spot color.

Simply adding the spot color to linework creates a middle value.

And if I want a darker shadow, but slightly lighter than a full-out spot black, I can mix the black with the spot color equally.

I often remind my students over and over: Comics isn't a sprint. It's a long, long marathon. Anything you can do to shave off time to help you keep pushing forward is huge. This can be something like changing up your process completely to work digitally, or even utilizing a technique like this!

JONATHAN HILL is an award-winning cartoonist who lives in Portland, OR. His comics and illustrations have been featured in publications by Fantagraphics, Lion Forge, tor.com, Powell's City of Books, *The Believer* Magazine, and the Society of Illustrators. His first two books, *Americus* and *Wild Weather*, were created with writer MK Reed and published by First Second Books. Jonathan also teaches comics at the Pacific Northwest College of Art and serves on the board of directors at Literary Arts. *Odessa* is the first book he has written and drawn himself.

ALSO FROM ONI PRESS

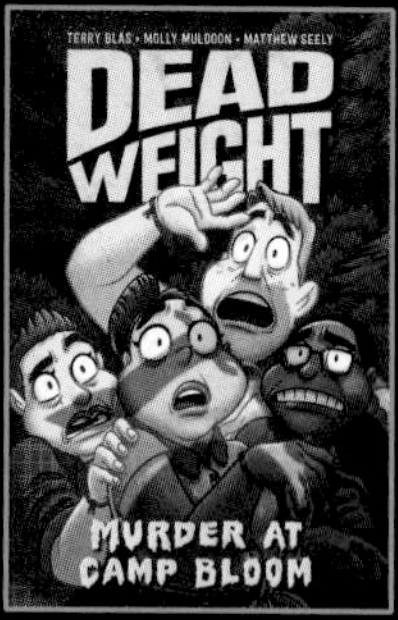
TERRY BLAS • MOLLY MULDOON • MATTHEW SEELY
DEAD WEIGHT
MURDER AT CAMP BLOOM

DEAD WEIGHT: MURDER AT CAMP BLOOM
By Terry Blas, Molly Muldoon, and Matthew Seely
Jessie, Noah, Tony, and Kate are at Camp Bloom for different reasons. But when one of their counselors is murdered, they band together to find the killer.

THE BLACK MAGE
By Daniel Barnes and D.J. Kirkland
Tom Token is the first Black Mage to be accepted to St. Ivory Academy, an all-white school. Amidst microaggressions and blatant racism, he discovers a sinister plot that puts him in grave danger.

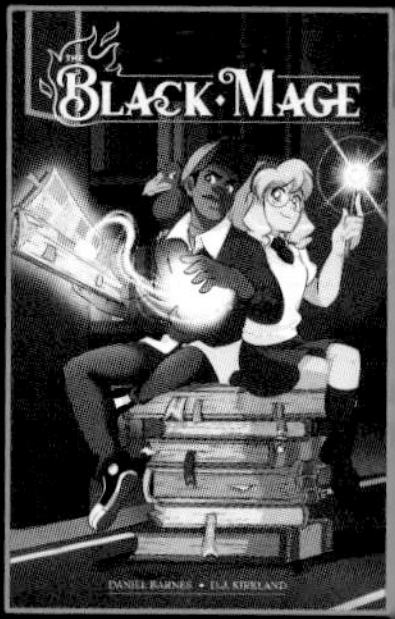
BLACK MAGE
DANIEL BARNES • D.J. KIRKLAND

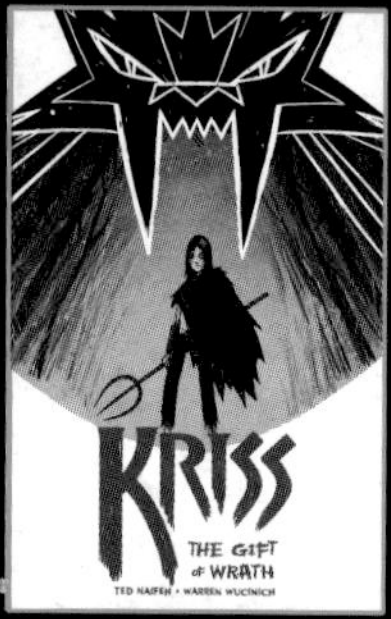
KRISS
THE GIFT of WRATH
TED NAIFEH • WARREN WUCINICH

KRISS: THE GIFT OF WRATH
By Ted Naifeh and Warren Wucinich
Kriss is a young boy trapped in a small village who knows he's destined for more. When he kills a sabercat that's been attacking the town, he gains a mighty—but uncontrollable—power.

MORNING IN AMERICA
By Magdalene Visaggio and Claudia Aguirre
The Sick Sisters may be delinquents, but they're also the only ones in their small Ohio town willing to look into a series of paranormal disappearances.

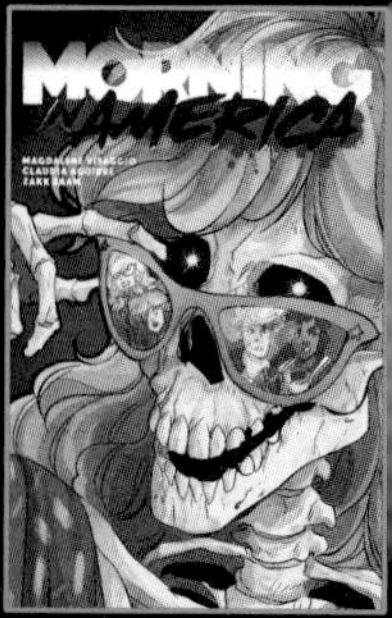
MORNING IN AMERICA

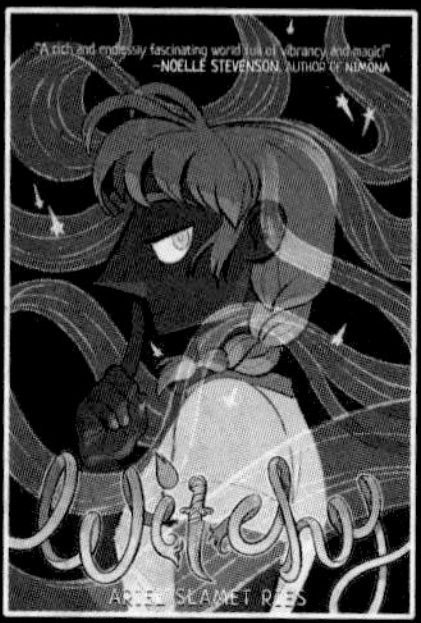
NOELLE STEVENSON, AUTHOR OF NIMONA
Witchy
ARIEL SLAMET RIES

WITCHY
By Ariel Slamet Ries
Ever since her father was killed for being too powerful, Nyneve has hidden her own magical abilities. When her powers are discovered, she has no choice but to go on the run.